THE MIND AND HEART OF THE NEGOTIATOR

PRENTICE HALL BUSINESS PUBLISHING
MANAGEMENT TITLES FOR 2001

Bowin/Harvey: Human Resource Management: An Experiential Approach 2/e
Caproni: The Practical Coach: Management Skills for Everyday Life 1/e
Carrell/Heavrin: Labor Relations and Collective Bargaining 6/e
Coulter: Strategic Management in Action 2/e
Coutler: Entrepreneurship in Action 1/e
Daniels/Radebaugh: International Business 9/e
David: Strategic Management: Concepts and Cases 8/e
David: Concepts in Strategic Management 8/e
David: Cases in Strategic Management 8/e
Dessler: Management: Leading People and Organizations in the 21st Century 2/e
DiBella: Learning Practices: Assessment and Action for Organizational Improvement (OD Series)
Ghemawat: Strategy and the Business Landscape: Core Concepts 1/e
Gomez-Mejia/Balkin/Cardy: Managing Human Resources 3/e
Greer: Strategic Human Resource Management 2/e
Harvey/Brown: Experiential Approach to Organization Development 6/e
Hersey/Blanchard/Johnson: Management of Organizational Behavior: Leading Human Resources 8/e
Howell/Costley: Understanding Behaviors for Effective Leadership 1/e
Hunger/Wheelen: Essentials of Strategic Managment 2/e
Hunsaker: Training in Managerial Skills 1/e
Jones: Organizational Theory 3/e
Mische: Strategic Renewal: Becoming a High-Performance Organization 1/e
Martocchio: Strategic Compensation 2/e
Narayanan: Managing Technology and Innovation for Competitive Advantage 1/e
Osland/Kolb/Rubin: The Organizational Behavior Reader 7/e
Osland/Kolb/Rubin: Organizational Behavior: An Experiential Approach 7/e
Robbins: Organizational Behavior 9/e
Robbins/DeCenzo: Fundamentals of Management 3/e
Sanyal: International Management 1/e
Sloane/Witney: Labor Relations 10/e
Thompson: The Mind and Heart of the Negotiator 2/e
Tompkins: Cases in Management and Organizational Behavior Vol. I 1/e
Wexley/Latham: Developing and Training Human Resources in Organizations 3/e

Other Books of Interest

Clawson: Level Three Leadership 1/e (1999)
French/Bell: Organizational Development 6/e (2000)
George/Jones: Essentials of Managing Organizational Behavior 1/e (2000)
George/Jones: Understanding and Managing Organizational Behavior 2/e (1999)
Greenberg: Managing Behaviors in Organizations 2/e (1999)
Greenberg/Baron: Behavior in Organizations 7/e (2000)
Nahavandi: Art and Science of Leadership 2/e (2000)
Pierce/Newstrom: The Manager's Bookshelf 5/e (2000)
Robbins: Essentials of Organizational Behavior 6/e (2000)
Smith: Women at Work 1/e (2000)
Thompson: Making the Team 1/e (2000)
Yukl: Leadership in Organizations 4/e (1998)

SECOND EDITION

THE MIND AND HEART
OF THE NEGOTIATOR

Leigh L. Thompson

Kellogg Graduate School of Management
Northwestern University

Upper Saddle River, New Jersey

Thompson, Leigh L.
  The mind and heart of the negotiator / Leigh L. Thompson—2nd ed.
    p. cm.
  Includes bibliographical references and indexes.
  ISBN 0-13-017964-7
    1. Negotiation in business.   I. Title

HD58.6.T478 2000
658.4'052—dc21   00-040666

Acquisitions Editor: Melissa Steffens
Assistant Editor: Jessica Sabloff
Editorial Assistant: Samantha Steel
Executive Marketing Manager: Michael D. Campbell
Media Project Manager: Michele Faranda
Permissions Coordinator: Suzanne Grappi
Director of Production: Michael Weinstein
Manager, Production: Gail Steier de Acevedo
Production Coordinator: Kelly Warsak
Manufacturing Buyer: Natacha St. Hill Moore
Associate Director, Manufacturing: Vincent Scelta
Cover Design: Jill Little
Cover Illustration: Robert Weeks
Full Service Composition: Carlisle Communications Ltd.

15 14 13 12 11
ISBN 0-13-017964-7

To the loves of my life:
Bob, Sam, Ray, and Anna

BRIEF CONTENTS

PART I   ESSENTIALS OF NEGOTIATION   1

Chapter 1   Negotiation: The Mind and the Heart   2

Chapter 2   Preparation: What to Do Before Negotiation   9

Chapter 3   Distributive Negotiation: Slicing the Pie   33

Chapter 4   Win-Win Negotiation: Expanding the Pie   61

PART II   ADVANCED NEGOTIATION SKILLS   83

Chapter 5   Developing a Negotiating Style   84

Chapter 6   Establishing Trust and Building a Relationship   109

Chapter 7   Power, Persuasion, and Ethics   137

Chapter 8   Creativity and Problem Solving in Negotiations   158

PART III   APPLICATIONS AND SPECIAL SCENARIOS   187

Chapter 9   Multiple Parties, Coalitions, and Teams   188

Chapter 10   Cross-Cultural Negotiation   220

Chapter 11   Tacit Negotiations and Social Dilemmas   246

Chapter 12   Negotiating via Information Technology   273

APPENDICES

Appendix 1   Are You a Rational Person? Check Yourself   295

Appendix 2   Nonverbal Communication and Lie Detection   317

Appendix 3   Third-Party Intervention   324

Appendix 4   Negotiating a Job Offer   329

CONTENTS

PREFACE TO THE NEW EDITION   xvii

PREFACE   xix

PART I   ESSENTIALS OF NEGOTIATION   1

CHAPTER 1   Negotiation: The Mind and the Heart   2

Negotiation as a Core Management Competency   2
Dynamic Nature of Business   3
Interdependence   3
Competition   4
Information Age   4
Diversity   4

Most People Are Ineffective Negotiators   4

The Major Sins of Negotiation   5

Why Are People Ineffective Negotiators?   5
Absence of Relevant and Diagnostic Feedback   5
Satisficing   6
Self-Reinforcement   6

Debunking Negotiation Myths   6
Myth 1: Good Negotiators Are Born   6
Myth 2: Experience Is a Great Teacher   7
Myth 3: Good Negotiators Take Risks   7
Myth 4: Good Negotiators Rely on Intuition   7

Learning Objectives   8

The Mind and Heart   8

CHAPTER 2   Preparation: What to Do Before Negotiation   9

Self-Assessment   10
What Do I Want?   10
What Is My Alternative to Reaching Agreement in This Situation?   11
Identify the Issues in the Negotiation   15
Identify the Alternatives for Each Issue   15
Identify Packages of Offers   15
Assess Your Risk Propensity   16
Dealing with Uncertainty   17
Endowment Effects   18
Am I Going to Live to Regret This?   19
Preference Reversals   19

Choosing versus Rejecting   20
Violations of the Sure Thing Principle   21
Do I Have an Appropriate Level of Confidence?   22

Sizing Up the Other Party   22
Who Are the Other Parties?   22
Are the Parties Monolithic?   23
Issue Mix   23
Others' Interests and Position   23
Other Negotiators' BATNAs   23

Situation Assessment   24
Is the Negotiation One-Shot, Long-Term, or Repetitive?   25
Do the Negotiations Involve Scarce Resources, Ideologies, or Both?   25
Is the Negotiation One of Necessity or Opportunity?   25
Is the Negotiation an Exchange or Dispute Situation?   26
Are There Linkage Effects?   27
Is Agreement Required?   27
Is It Legal to Negotiate?   27
Is Ratification Required?   28
Are There Time Constraints or Other Time-Related Costs?   28
Are Contracts Official or Unofficial?   29
Where Do the Negotiations Take Place?   29
Are Negotiations Public or Private?   29
Is Third-Party Intervention a Possibility?   30
Are There Conventions in Terms of the Process of Negotiation (Such as Who Makes the First Offer)?   30
Do Negotiations Involve More Than One Offer?   30
Do Negotiators Communicate Explicitly or Tacitly?   31
Is There a Power Differential between Parties?   31
Is Precedent Important?   31

Conclusion   31

CHAPTER 3   Distributive Negotiation: Slicing the Pie   33

The Bargaining Zone and the Negotiation Dance   34
Bargaining Surplus   36
Negotiator's Surplus   36

Pie-Slicing Strategies   37
Strategy 1: Know Your BATNA   38
Strategy 2: Research the Other Party's BATNA   38
Strategy 3: Set High Aspirations   39
Strategy 4: Make the First Offer   40
Strategy 5: Counteroffer Immediately   40
Strategy 6: Avoid Stating Ranges   41
Strategy 7: Make Bilateral (Not Unilateral) Concessions   41
Strategy 8: Use an Objective-Appearing Rationale to Support Your Offers   42
Strategy 9: Appeal to Norms of Fairness   42
Strategy 10: Do Not Fall for the "Even Split" Ploy   42

The Most Commonly Asked Questions   43
Should I Reveal My Reservation Point?   43
Should I Lie about My Reservation Price?   43

How Can I Tell Whether Someone Is Lying to Me?   44
Should I Try to Talk the Other Party out of Her Reservation Point?   44
Should I Attempt to Be Fair?   45
Should I Make a "Final Offer" or Commit to a Position?   45
How Do I Help the Other Party to Save Face?   45

The Power of Fairness   46
Principle 1: There Are Multiple Methods of Fair Division   46
Principle 2: Rules of Fairness Are Highly Context Dependent   46
Principle 3: People Are Concerned about the "Other Guy"   48
Principle 4: People Seek Equity in Their Relationships with Others   49
Principle 5: When People Sense Inequity, They Will Attempt to Restore Equity   50
Principle 6: People Need to Maintain Their Egos   51
Principle 7: People Care Not Only about the Size of Their Slice, but the Process Used to Get There   53
Principle 8: Judgments about What Is Fair Are Driven by the Nature of the Relationship We Have with the Other Party   54
Principle 9: Egocentrism Taints Judgments of Fairness   54
Principle 10: People Do Not Realize That They Are Self-Serving   57
Principle 11: Avoid Problems Through Wise Pie Slicing   58

Conclusion   60

CHAPTER 4   Win-Win Negotiation: Expanding the Pie   61

What Is Win-Win Negotiation Anyway?   62

Telltale Signs of Win-Win Potential   62
Does the Negotiation Contain More than a Single Issue?   63
Can Other Issues Be Brought In?   63
Can Side Deals Be Made?   63
Do Parties Have Different Preferences across Negotiation Issues?   63

A Pyramid Model   64

Most Common Pie-Expanding Errors   65
False Conflict   65
The Fixed-Pie Perception   66

Strategies That Do Not Really Work   67
Commitment to Reaching a Win-Win Deal   67
Compromise   67
Focusing on a Long-Term Relationship   67
Adopting a "Cooperative Orientation"   67
Taking Extra Time to Negotiate   67

Strategies That Work   68
Build Trust and Share Information   68
Ask Diagnostic Questions   68
Provide Information   69
Unbundle the Issues   69
Make Package Deals, Not Single-Issue Offers   69
Make Multiple Offers Simultaneously   70
Structure Contingency Contracts by Capitalizing on Differences   70
Presettlement Settlements (PreSS)   72
Search for Postsettlement Settlements   73

An Application of Integrative Strategies   73
  Preparation: Identifying and Prioritizing Issues   74
  During Negotiation: Search for Trade-Offs and Avoid Compromise   74
  Search for Level 2 Pie-Expanding Agreements   76
  Expand the Pie by Adding Issues   76
  Devise Contingency Contracts around Different Beliefs   77
  Postnegotiation Analysis   79

A Strategic Framework for Reaching Integrative Agreements   79
  Resource Assessment   80
  Assessment of Differences   80
  Offers and Trade-Offs   81
  Acceptance/Rejection Decision   81
  Prolonging Negotiation and Renegotiation   81

Do Not Forget about Claiming   82

Conclusion   82

PART II   ADVANCED NEGOTIATION SKILLS   83

CHAPTER 5   Developing a Negotiating Style   84

Tough Versus Soft Negotiators   84

Motivation-Approach-Emotion   85

Motivations   85
  Assessing Your Motivational Style   85
  Strategic Issues Concerning Motivational Style   89

Approach   91
  Assessing Your Approach   92
  Strategic Issues Concerning Approaches   94

Emotions   101
  Assessing Your Emotional Style   102
  Strategic Advice for Dealing with Emotions at the Table   106

Putting It All Together   108

CHAPTER 6   Establishing Trust and Building a Relationship   109

Why Care about Trust?   109

Relationships in Negotiation   110
  Negotiation in Personal Relationships   110
  Business Relationships   114
  Embedded Relationships   116
  Assessing the Quality of Relationships   117

Three Types of Trust Relationships   117
  Deterrence-Based Trust   118
  Knowledge-Based Trust   120
  Identification-Based Trust   120

Building Trust: Rational and Deliberate Mechanisms   121
  Transform A-Type Conflict into C-Type Conflict   122
  Agree on a Common Goal or Shared Vision   123
  Create a Place for Conflict and Get It out in the Open   123

Expand the Pie   *123*
Use Fairness Criteria That Everyone Can Buy Into   *124*
Capitalize on Network Connections   *124*
Find a Shared Problem or a Shared Enemy   *124*
Focus on the Future   *125*
Use a Fair Procedure   *125*
Negotiate Roles   *125*

Building Trust: Implicit Emotional Mechanisms   126
Similarity   *126*
Mere Exposure   *126*
Good Mood   *127*
Physical Presence   *127*
Reciprocity   *128*
Do Not Gloat   *128*
Schmoozing   *129*
Flattery   *129*
Mimicking   *129*
Self-Disclosure   *129*

Threats to Trust   130
Breaches of Trust   *130*
Miscommunication   *130*
Poor Pie Expansion   *130*
Dispositional Attributions   *130*
Egocentrism   *131*
Reputation   *131*
Focusing Too Much on Rules   *132*
Focusing on the "Bad Apple"   *132*
Social Comparison   *132*

Repairing Broken Trust   132
Step 1: Insist on a Personal Meeting Right Away   *133*
Step 2: Tell the Other Party That You Value the Relationship   *133*
Step 3: Apologize for Your Behavior   *133*
Step 4: Let Them Vent   *134*
Step 5: Do Not Get Defensive, No Matter How Wrong You Think They Are   *134*
Step 6: Ask for Clarifying Information   *134*
Step 7: Say That You Understand Their Perspective   *134*
Step 8: Let Them Tell You What They Need   *134*
Step 9: Paraphrase Your Understanding of What They Need   *135*
Step 10: Think about Ways to Prevent a Future Problem   *135*
Step 11: Do an Evaluation of the Situation at a Scheduled Date   *135*
Step 12: Plan a Future Together   *135*

Conclusion   136

CHAPTER 7   Power, Persuasion, and Ethics   137
Your BATNA Is Your Most Important Source of Power in Negotiation   138
Tapping into Your Power   138
Information   *139*
Status   *139*
Social Networks   *141*

Physical Appearance *141*
The Effects of Power on Those with Less Power *142*
The Effects of Power on Those Who Hold Power *142*

Persuasion Tactics 142
Two Routes to Persuasion *143*
Central Route Persuasion Tactics *143*
Peripheral Route Persuasion Tactics *146*

Ethics 151
Questionable Negotiation Strategies *152*
Under What Conditions Do People Engage in Deception? *154*
Strategies for Determining Ethical Behavior *155*

Conclusion 156

CHAPTER 8 Creativity and Problem Solving in Negotiations 158

Creativity in Negotiation 158
Test Your Own Creativity *159*

Creative Negotiation Agreements 162
Fractionating Problems into Solvable Parts *162*
Finding Differences: Issue Alignment and Realignment *162*
Expanding the Pie *163*
Bridging *163*
Cost Cutting *163*
Nonspecific Compensation *163*
Structuring Contingencies *164*

Threats to Effective Problem Solving and Creativity 167
The Inert Knowledge Problem *167*
Availability Heuristic *170*
Representativeness *170*
Anchoring and Adjustment *171*
Unwarranted Causation *171*
Belief Perseverance *172*
Illusory Correlation *172*
Just World *173*
Hindsight Bias *173*
Functional Fixedness *173*
Set Effect *174*
Selective Attention *174*
Overconfidence *174*
The Limits of Short-Term Memory *175*

Creative Negotiation Strategies 175
Incubation *175*
Rational Problem-Solving Model *176*
Fluency, Flexibility, and Originality *177*
Brainstorming *178*
Convergent versus Divergent Thinking *178*
Deductive Reasoning *179*
Inductive Reasoning *180*
Flow *181*

What Is Your Mental Model of Negotiation?   182
  Haggling   182
  Game-playing   182
  Relationship   182
  Problem Solving   183

Conclusion   183

PART III   APPLICATIONS AND SPECIAL SCENARIOS   187

CHAPTER 9   Multiple Parties, Coalitions, and Teams   188

Analyzing Multiparty Negotiations   188

Multiparty Negotiations   189
  Key Challenges of Multiparty Negotiations   190
  Key Strategies   196

Coalitions   198
  Key Challenges of Coalitions   198
  Strategies for Maximizing Coalitional Effectiveness   202

Principal-Agent Relationship   203
  Key Challenges   203
  Strategies for Effectively Working with Agents   205

Constituent Relationships   207
  Challenges for Constituent Relationships   207
  Strategies for Improving Constituent Relationships   209

Team Negotiation   210
  Challenges That Face Negotiating Teams   211
  Strategies for Improving Team Negotiations   212

Intergroup Negotiation   213
  Challenges of Intergroup Negotiation   213
  Strategies for Optimizing Intergroup Negotiations   215

Conclusion   218

CHAPTER 10 Cross-Cultural Negotiation   220

An Approach to Learning about Cultures   221
  Defining Culture   221
  Culture as an Iceberg   222

Cultural Values and Negotiation Norms   222
  Individualism versus Collectivism   223
  Egalitarianism versus Hierarchy   229
  Direct versus Indirect Communications   232

Key Challenges of Intercultural Negotiation   234
  Expanding the Pie   234
  Sacred Values and Taboo Trade-Offs   234
  Biased Punctuation of Conflict   237
  Intergroup Biases   237
  Stereotypes   238
  Affiliation Bias   238

Faulty Perceptions of Conciliation and Coercion   *239*
Naïve Realism   *239*

Predictors of Success in Intercultural Interactions   240

Advice for Cross-Cultural Negotiations   241
*Anticipate Differences in Strategy and Tactics that May Cause
    Misunderstandings*   *241*
*Analyze Cultural Differences to Identify Differences in Values That Expand
    the Pie*   *241*
*Recognize That the Other Party May Not Share Your View of What Constitutes
    Power*   *242*
Avoid Attribution Errors   *242*
Avoid Ethnocentrism   *242*
Find Out How to Show Respect in the Other Culture   *242*
Know Your Options for Change   *243*

Conclusion   245

CHAPTER 11 Tacit Negotiations and Social Dilemmas   246

Business as a Social Dilemma   247
Decentralization   *247*
Strategic Alliances   *248*
Specialization   *248*
Competition   *248*

Common Myths about Interdependent Decision Making   248
Myth 1: "It's a Game of Wits: I Can Outsmart Them"   *249*
Myth 2: "It's a Game of Strength: Show 'em You're Tough"   *249*
Myth 3: "It's a Game of Chance: Hope for the Best"   *249*

The Prisoner's Dilemma   249
Cooperation and Defection as Unilateral Choices   *250*
Rational Analysis   *250*
The Tournament of Champions   *253*

Social Dilemmas   256
The Tragedy of the Commons   *258*
Types of Social Dilemmas   *260*
How to Build Cooperation in Social Dilemmas   *260*

Escalation of Commitment   266
Avoiding the Escalation of Commitment in Negotiations   *269*

Conclusion   270

CHAPTER 12 Negotiating via Information Technology   271

Place-Time Model of Social Interaction   272
Face-to-Face Communication   *273*
Same Time, Different Place   *275*
Different Time, Same Place   *276*
Different Place, Different Time   *277*

Information Technology and Negotiation Behavior   280
Status and Power: The "Weak Get Strong" Effect   *280*
Social Networks   *281*

Risk Taking   *282*
Rapport and Social Norms   *283*
Paranoia   *284*
New Roles   *285*

Strategies for Enhancing Technology-Mediated Negotiations   286
Initial Face-to-Face Experience   *286*
One-Day Videoconference/Teleconference   *286*
Schmoozing   *287*

On-Line Commercial Negotiations   287
On-Line Auction Houses   *287*
Mediation Houses   *289*
Shopping Houses   *289*

Conclusion   291

APPENDIX 1 Are You a Rational Person? Check Yourself   **293**

APPENDIX 2 Nonverbal Communication and Lie Detection   **315**

APPENDIX 3 Third-Party Intervention   **322**

APPENDIX 4 Negotiating a Job Offer   **327**

REFERENCES   **337**

SUBJECT INDEX   **365**

AUTHOR INDEX   **373**

PREFACE TO THE NEW EDITION

When I wrote *The Mind and Heart of the Negotiator* in 1998, my intent was to introduce executives and managers to the lessons of social psychology as well as behavioral decision making for negotiation. Since the publication of the first version, I have attempted to improve upon not only the content of the book but its organization. My students and colleagues were delightfully to-the-point when suggesting changes that would improve the book. Therefore, I have made four major changes to the revised edition of *The Mind and Heart of the Negotiator:*

- **More case studies and real-life negotiations:** I have included many more examples and illustrations of negotiating in managerial and executive contexts. Each chapter opens with a case analysis (often from the business world, but I include other scenarios as well). Furthermore, many of the points in the chapters are supplemented with illustrations and examples drawn from actual negotiations, both contemporary and historical. I do not use these examples to prove a theory; rather, I use them to illustrate how many of the concepts in the book are borne out in real-world situations.

- **Skills-based approach:** I provide more practical take-away points for the manager and the executive. A good example is chapter 9, on groups and multiple parties. The previous version of this book provided a lens for examining multiple-party negotiations. This edition of the book provides practical advice for several different kinds of multiparty situations. Moreover, I include more practical advice in the chapters on pie slicing (distributive bargaining) and pie expanding (integrative negotiation).

- **New chapters and appendices:** By popular demand, I have included several new chapters in the book. There is a new chapter on negotiating style, which focuses on motivations, emotions, and disputing styles. There is also a new chapter on power and persuasion in negotiation, which focuses on rational as well as psychological influence tactics. I have also included a new chapter on creativity and problem solving, which brings in a lot of cutting-edge research from cognitive psychology in terms of how to think out-of-the-box. In addition to these three new chapters, I have expanded the sections on cross-cultural negotiation and information technology into their own chapters (in the previous version, these two chapters were combined). Similarly, I have developed two independent chapters focusing on preparation and distributive bargaining skills. I have also included four new appendices focusing on commonly asked questions about rationality, nonverbal behavior and deception, third-party mediation and arbitration, and how to negotiate a job offer.

- **New, updated research:** Perhaps most importantly, I have included the latest research on negotiator decision making and behavior, thus keeping the book up-to-date and true to its strong research focus and theory-driven approach.

I took the task of revising *The Mind and Heart of the Negotiator* very seriously. Every single paragraph in every single chapter went through a dramatic revision. I have benefited greatly from the advice, comments, and critiques given to me by my students and colleagues, and I hope that their advice keeps coming, so that I am able to improve upon the book even further.

PREFACE

Negotiation is a topic of great interest to executives, MBA students, undergraduates, consultants, lawyers, doctors, salespeople, social workers, realtors, engineers, nurses, administrators, and people in the public sector. I have taught negotiation skills to all of these groups. I am always struck by the commonality of concerns raised by participants. Many people want to know how to best leverage their power, reach "win-win" agreements, develop a comfortable negotiation style, and deal with multiple parties. There already are several wonderful books about negotiation in existence. Many of these books offer practical, prescriptive advice; many contain reviews of important negotiation studies. But there are few books that combine cutting-edge research with practical, prescriptive advice for negotiators. The purpose of this book is to provide executives and managers from all different kinds of industries with solid, research-based advice and practical tools.

This book has three unique features:

1. **Rigorous, cutting-edge research:** All of the material in this book is produced by leading scholars in the broad field of negotiation and represents hard science, in the strict sense of the phrase.
2. **Focus on skills:** The ultimate purpose of this book is to provide sound prescriptive advice for helping negotiators reach their negotiation goals. Thus, each chapter contains strategies and skills for improving negotiation effectiveness.
3. **The mind and the heart:** This book not only contains practical advice based upon rational models of economic behavior, but it also contains practical advice based upon psychological insights about human behavior. The book's title, *The Mind and Heart of the Negotiator,* reflects the dual focus of the book. It contains several sections in which managers and executives are invited to test their own rationality; it also contains several sections in which managers and executives explore insights about human behavior. Throughout this book, we maintain a balance of objective, rational analysis and insights about psychological behavior.

The Mind and Heart of the Negotiator separates fact from fiction and outlines—in a clear, step-by-step fashion—how young managers, as well as seasoned executives, can improve their ability to negotiate effectively. Each chapter opens with a case analysis (or two). The reader of this book will learn how to effectively prepare for negotiation, maximize his or her ability to expand the pie of resources in a negotiation (win-win negotiation), enhance his or her power in negotiation, sharpen his or her creative thinking about negotiation, assess and develop an appropriate negotiation style, effectively deal with multiple parties, navigate social dilemmas, learn strategies for negotiating across cultures, and learn how to negotiate via information technology.

The 12 chapters of this book are arranged into three major parts. Part I, "Essentials of Negotiation," contains four chapters that are essential for the improvement of a negotiator's ability to expand, and simultaneously slice, the pie of resources. Chapter 1 reviews the major myths about negotiation, the most common negotiator shortcomings, and the learning principles upon which this book is based. Chapter 2 teaches negotiators how to effectively prepare for a negotiation in terms of what information to assess about the other party and how to diagnose the situation they are in. Chapter 3 focuses on the distributive aspect of negotiation (which we call "slicing the pie") and coaches negotiators on how to leverage their power within a negotiation. Chapter 4 is arguably the most important chapter in this book, focusing on how to achieve integrative agreements (also known as win-win agreements). It contains useful and practical strategies for expanding the pie and maximizing joint gain.

Section II focuses on "Advanced Negotiation Skills." Chapter 5 teaches negotiators how to assess and develop their own negotiating style, outlining the major motives people bring to negotiation, the different emotional styles that negotiators adopt, and the different ways negotiators can approach dispute situations. This chapter has the dual function of serving as a "wake-up call" for negotiators and providing alternative strategies to add to their repertoire. Chapter 6 focuses on how to establish trust in a negotiating relationship. It reviews the major kinds of trust and types of negotiation relationships, focusing on the rational approaches to assessing and enhancing trust, as well as psychological approaches. Chapter 7 focuses on power and influence in a negotiation. It reviews the major bases of a negotiator's power and how to improve upon them, as well as how to deal with power ploys launched by the opponent. Chapter 8 deals with creativity in negotiation. It challenges readers to assess their own creative and problem-solving skills, and then, in a step-by-step fashion, outlines methods for increasing your creative abilities at the negotiation table.

Section III focuses on "Applications and Special Scenarios." Chapter 9 deals with groups and multiple parties at the bargaining table. It provides advice for navigating constituent interests, the formation of coalitions, and principal-agent relationships, among many others. Chapter 10 focuses on negotiation across cultures. It invites readers to assess their own cultural assumptions and provides them a method for assessing the cultural assumptions of other parties. It outlines the major shortcomings to effective cross-cultural negotiation and provides a step-by-step guide for improving the effectiveness of cross-cultural negotiation. Chapter 11 focuses on social dilemmas and situations in which negotiators have an incentive to compete against one another. The classic prisoner's dilemma game is analyzed, and its multiparty equivalent, the social dilemma, is treated as well, with applications to real-world industries. Finally, chapter 12 focuses on negotiating via information technology. We introduce a place-time model of social interaction and discuss the advantages, as well as the pitfalls, of negotiating in impoverished media.

We have also included four special appendices in this book. Appendix 1 invites negotiators to examine the rationality of their own behavior and thinking. Appendix 2 provides a short course on nonverbal skills and lie detection. Appendix 3 provides guidance for third-party intervention (namely, mediation and arbitration). Finally, appendix 4 provides tips for negotiating a job offer.

Each of the chapters includes three learning aids in addition to the regular text: (1) real-life examples from actual people and companies as chapter-opening cases; (2) sidebars (lively examples and notes of interest for the hungry reader); and (3) figures, tables, and boxes for summarizing key points and illustrating concepts.

The research and ideas in this book come from an invaluable set of scholars in the fields of social psychology, organizational behavior, sociology, negotiation, and cognitive psychology. During the past 13 years, my research, thinking, and writing has been enriched in very important ways by the following people: Wendi Adair, Linda Babcock, Max Bazerman, Terry Boles, Jeanne Brett, Susan Brodt, Karen Cates, Gary Fine, Craig Fox, Adam Galinsky, Dedre Gentner, Robert Gibbons, Kevin Gibson, James Gillespie, Rich Gonzalez, Deborah Gruenfeld, Reid Hastie, Peter Kim, Shirli Kopelman, Rod Kramer, Laura Kray, Terri Kurtzburg, John Levine, Allan Lind, George Loewenstein, Jeff Loewenstein, Deepak Malhotra, Beta Mannix, Vicki Medvec, Dave Messick, Terry Mitchell, Don Moore, Michael Morris, Keith Murnighan, Janice Nadler, Robin Pinkley, Ashleigh Rosette, Nancy Rothbard, Vanessa Seiden, Harris Sondak, Tom Tyler, Kathleen Valley, Leaf Van Boven, Kimberly Wade-Benzoni, Laurie Weingart, and Judith White. In *The Mind and Heart of the Negotiator,* I use the pronoun "we" because so much of my thinking has been influenced and shaped by this set of eminent scholars.

A number of people read the book in an earlier form and provided very helpful comments. In particular, I am deeply indebted to Jeanne Brett and Karen Cates of the Kellogg Graduate School of Management and John Darley of Princeton University for their insight and advice. The following outside reviewers wrote detailed comments that had the most impact on the revision: Laura Kray, University of Arizona; Edward Bergman, University of Pennsylvania; Douglas Benton, Cal State University; Ann Bartel, Columbia University; Roger Mayer, Baylor University; and Sheryl Ball, Virginia Tech.

The revision of this book would not have been possible without the dedication, organization, and editorial skills of Rachel Claff, who created the layout, organized hundreds of drafts, mastered the figures, and researched many case studies for this book.

I completed this book while I was at the Kellogg School of Management, a place whose spirit is motivating, energizing, and inspirational. I feel honored to live and work in the midst of so many great people, and I am indebted to Dean Don Jacobs, the Kellogg Teams and Groups Center, and the Dispute Resolution Research Center for their generous support of this book. I am particularly indebted to Jeanne Brett and Max Bazerman, who had the vision to establish the Dispute Resolution Research Center (DRRC) at Kellogg in 1985, and to the Hewlett Foundation, for their generous support of the DRRC.

Grants from the National Science Foundation's Decision Risk and Management Science program have made it possible for me to conduct several of the research studies that I discuss in this book. I am also grateful for a grant received by the Citigroup Research Council, which made possible many of the studies about learning and negotiation reviewed in this book.

This book is very much a team effort of the people I have mentioned here, whose talents are diverse, broad, and extraordinarily impressive. I am deeply indebted to my colleagues and my students, and I feel grateful that they have touched my life and this book.

3

PART I

ESSENTIALS OF NEGOTIATION

1
NEGOTIATION
The Mind and the Heart

In 1998, the National Basketball Association (NBA) owners initiated a 202-day lockout of players, resulting in a loss of about $1 billion for owners and about half a billion dollars in foregone salaries for basketball players. Fans were frustrated and disenchanted, and supporters and advertisers lost millions.

In 1999, the members of the World Trade Organization met in Seattle, Washington to lower trade barriers. The members of the organization could not even agree on an agenda and the meeting was an utter failure.

During 1999, Belinda Clark handled about 200 job offers for nursing assistants, research scientists, and a number of other employees. All but about 10 of these candidates took the initial offer without attempting to negotiate for something extra or more. Clark was delighted, but puzzled. The job applicants apparently did not realize that the offers Clark made were just starting points. She says, laughing, "I don't say anything if they don't." (Clark 1999, 88)

These examples suggest that negotiating is not easy. This is a problem, considering that people negotiate in their personal and business relationships, within organizations, between companies, across industries, and among nations. Furthermore, negotiations occur between two people and, in other cases—such as the World Trade Organization—hundreds of people. The variety of negotiation contexts presents special challenges for managers, who are required to demonstrate competencies in all of these contexts. This book is designed to improve managers' and executives' negotiation skills across a wide variety of situations.

The working definition of **negotiation** used in this book is "an interpersonal decision-making process by which two or more people agree how to allocate scarce resources." By this definition, it is difficult to imagine how people can get through a single day without negotiating.

NEGOTIATION AS A CORE MANAGEMENT COMPETENCY

Effective negotiation skills are increasingly important for executives, leaders, and managers in the business world. There are five key reasons for this.

DYNAMIC NATURE OF BUSINESS

Mobility and flexibility are the dictates of the new world of work. The dynamic, changing nature of business means that people must negotiate and renegotiate their existence in organizations throughout the duration of their careers. The advent of decentralized business structures and the absence of hierarchical decision making provide opportunities for managers, but they also pose some daunting challenges. For example, most people do not stay in the same job that they take upon graduating from college or receiving their MBA degree; furthermore, most people will not have the same job as their predecessor. These realities mean that people must continually create possibilities, integrate their interests with others, and recognize that there will be competition both within companies and between companies (see Sidebar 1–1). Managers must be in a near-constant mode of negotiating opportunities.

SIDEBAR 1–1. NEW BUSINESSES AND CAREERS

According to *Business Week* (Alderman, 1999), it is the "era of the employee," with the tightest labor market in 29 years. This means that employees are in a one-up position, and employers need to keep them happy. For example, Doug Ross, the owner of Evolution Film & Tape Inc., a television production company in North Hollywood, California, lets his employees create their own hours, dress as they please, and bring their children to work—all in order to stay competitive. Employees and companies are in positions to negotiate all kinds of things, such as opportunities for training, flex time, family leave, health insurance, and other benefits. Another example: The California-based Cheesecake Factory, Inc., pays salaries 20 percent above market rates. It also gives stock options to all its general managers, as well as new BMW 323s. This sounds expensive, but Cheesecake Factory says it has actually saved money, losing only two general managers in the last two years in an industry where a 38 percent turnover is the average (Conlin, Coy, Palmer, and Saveri 1999).

According to Linda Greene, associate vice-chancellor for academic affairs at the University of Wisconsin—Madison, "Many important events essential to professional success and professional satisfaction happen every day in the workplace and they are not always announced in advance" (Kalk 2000, 1E). In truth, negotiation comes into play when people participate in important meetings, get new assignments, head a team, participate in a reorganization process, and set priorities for their work unit (Kalk 2000). Ideally, negotiation should be second nature, but often, it is not.

INTERDEPENDENCE

The increasing interdependence of people within organizations, both laterally and hierarchically, implies that people need to know how to integrate their interests and work together across business units and functional areas. This not only occurs within companies, as people from different departments and units integrate their knowledge to create a product or service, but it also occurs between people from different companies, as is the case with strategic alliances. The increasing degree of specialization and expertise in the business world implies that people are more and more dependent on others to supply the components for a complete service or product. It is unwise to assume that others have similar incentive structures, so managers need to know how to promote their own interests while simultaneously creating joint value for their organizations. This requires negotiation.

COMPETITION

Business is increasingly competitive. In today's economy, a few large firms are emerging as dominant players in the biggest markets. These industry leaders often enjoy vast economies of scale and earn tremendous profits. The losers are often left with little in the way of a market, let alone a marketable product (Frank and Cook 1995). This means that companies must be experts in the vast fields of competition. Managers not only need to function as advocates for their products and services, but they must also recognize the competition that is inevitable between companies and, in some cases, between units within a given company. Understanding how to navigate this competitive environment is essential for successful negotiation.

INFORMATION AGE

The information age also provides special opportunities and challenges for the manager as negotiator. Computer technology, for example, extends a company's obligations and capacity to add value to its customers. This must be accomplished in a way that also benefits the company. Further, with ever-improving technology making it possible to communicate with people anywhere in the world, managers need to be able to negotiate at a moment's notice. Thus, the ability to determine relevant information from irrelevant information is critical for successful negotiation in the information-overload age.

DIVERSITY

Increasing diversity means that managers need to develop negotiation skills that can be successfully employed with people of different nationalities, backgrounds, and styles of communication. Thus, negotiators who have developed a bargaining style that works only within a narrow subset of the business world will suffer unless they can broaden their negotiation skills to effectively work with different people across functional units, industries, and cultures (Bazerman and Neale 1992). It is a challenge to develop a negotiation skill set generalizable enough to be used across different contexts, groups, and continents, but specialized enough to provide meaningful behavioral strategies in any given situation. This book provides the manager with such skills.

MOST PEOPLE ARE INEFFECTIVE NEGOTIATORS

Because negotiation is so important for personal and business success, it is rather surprising that most people do not negotiate very well—judging from their performance in realistic business negotiation simulations (for reviews, see Neale and Bazerman 1991; Thompson and Hrebec 1996; Thompson 1990a). For example, in a recent investigation of senior-level executives from major companies across the world, 95 percent reached suboptimal outcomes in a realistic business simulation; in practical terms, they "left money on the table." They are not alone. A voluminous body of evidence indicates that people consistently leave money on the table, walk away from profitable deals, and in some cases, settle for something worse than they could otherwise obtain by pursuing a different course of action.

THE MAJOR SINS OF NEGOTIATION

There are four major shortcomings in negotiation we have observed and documented in our research. They are:

1. **Leaving money on the table** (also known as "lose-lose" negotiation) occurs when negotiators fail to recognize and exploit win-win potential.
2. **Settling for too little** (also known as "the winner's curse") occurs when negotiators make too-large concessions, resulting in a too-small share of the bargaining pie.
3. **Walking away from the table** occurs when negotiators reject terms offered by the other party that are demonstrably better than any other option available to them. (Sometimes this is traceable to hubris or overweening pride; other times, it results from gross miscalculation.)
4. **Settling for terms that are worse than your alternative** (also known as the "agreement bias") occurs when negotiators feel obligated to reach agreement even when the settlement terms are not as good as their other alternatives.

This book teaches you how to avoid these errors, create value in negotiation, get your share of the bargaining pie, reach agreement when it is profitable to do so, and quickly recognize when agreement is not a viable option in a negotiation.

WHY ARE PEOPLE INEFFECTIVE NEGOTIATORS?

The dramatic instances of lose-lose outcomes, the winner's curse, walking away from the table, and the agreement bias raise the question of why people are not more effective at the bargaining table if negotiation is indeed critical for business success. The reason is not due to a lack of motivation or lack of intelligence on the part of negotiators. Many of the managers who fall victim to the major sins of negotiation do so for three primary causes: absence of feedback, satisficing, and self-reinforcement.

ABSENCE OF RELEVANT AND DIAGNOSTIC FEEDBACK

Most people have little opportunity to learn how to negotiate effectively. The problem is not lack of experience but a shortage of timely and accurate feedback. Even those people who have daily experiences in negotiation receive very little feedback on their negotiating effectiveness. The absence of feedback results in two human biases that further prevent negotiators from optimally benefiting from experience. The first problem is the **confirmation bias,** or the tendency for people to see what they want to see when appraising their own performance. The confirmation bias leads people to selectively seek information that confirms what they believe is true. Whereas the confirmation bias may seem perfectly harmless, it results in a myopic view of reality and can hinder learning. A second problem associated with the absence of relevant and diagnostic feedback is **egocentrism,** which is the tendency for people to view their experiences in a way that is flattering or fulfilling for themselves. This may increase a manager's self-esteem; however, in the long run, it does a disservice to managers by preventing them from learning effectively. For example, it was egocentrism and the corresponding inability to recognize her own shortcomings that lead to the removal of Jill Barad as chairperson/CEO of toy maker Mattel Inc. (Byrne and Grover 2000). According to analysts, Barad never assumed responsibility for earnings surprises or adverse announcements. Instead, she blamed her subordinates and sacked them.

SATISFICING

The second reason why people often fall short in negotiation is due to the human tendency to satisfice (Simon 1955). **Satisficing** is the opposite of *optimizing:* In a negotiation situation, as we will argue later in this book, it is important to optimize one's strategies by setting high aspirations and attempting to achieve as much as possible; in contrast, when people satisfice, they settle for something less than they could otherwise have. Over the long run, satisficing (or the acceptance of mediocrity) can do one's self and one's company a disservice because there is a variety of effective negotiation strategies and skills that can be cheaply employed to result in dramatic increases in profit (we will discuss these strategies in detail in the next three chapters).

SELF-REINFORCEMENT

The final reason why people perform poorly in negotiation is due to a principle known as **self-reinforcement,** which is the reluctance to try something new or change certain behaviors. It works like this: People are reluctant to change their behavior and experiment with new courses of action because of the risks associated with experimentation. In short, the fear of losing keeps people from experimenting with change. Negotiators instead rationalize their behavior in a self-perpetuating fashion. The fear of making mistakes may result in a manager's inability to improve his or her negotiation skills. In this book, we remove the risk of experimentation by providing several exercises and clear demonstrations of how changing one's behavior can lead to better results in negotiation.

DEBUNKING NEGOTIATION MYTHS

Before we start on our journey toward developing a more effective negotiation strategy, we need to dispel several faulty assumptions and myths about negotiation. These myths hamper people's ability to learn effective negotiation skills and, in some cases, reinforce poor negotiation skills. In the following section, we expose the four most prevalent myths about negotiation behavior.

MYTH 1: GOOD NEGOTIATORS ARE BORN

A pervasive belief is that good negotiation skills are something that people are born with, not something that can be readily learned. This is false because most excellent negotiators are self-made. In fact, there are very few naturally gifted negotiators. We tend to hear their stories, but we must remember that their stories are *selective,* meaning that it is always possible for someone to have a lucky day or a fortunate experience. This myth is often perpetuated by the tendency of people to judge negotiation skills by their car-dealership experiences. Whereas purchasing a car is certainly an important and common type of negotiation, it is not the best context by which to judge your negotiation skills. The most important negotiations are those that we engage in every day with our colleagues, supervisors, co-workers, and business associates. These relationships provide a much better index of one's effectiveness in negotiation. In short, effective negotiation requires practice and feedback. The problem is that most of us do not get an opportunity to develop effective negotiation skills in a disciplined fashion; rather, most of us learn by doing. As the second myth reveals, experience is helpful, but not sufficient.

MYTH 2: EXPERIENCE IS A GREAT TEACHER

We have all met that person at the cocktail party or on the airplane who boasts about his or her great negotiation feats and how he or she learned on the job (Bazerman and Neale 1992). It is only partly true that experience can improve negotiation skills; in fact, naïve experience is largely ineffective in improving negotiation skills (Thompson and DeHarpport 1994). There are three strikes against natural experience as an effective teacher. First, in the absence of feedback, it is nearly impossible to improve performance. For example, can you imagine trying to learn mathematics without ever doing homework or taking tests? Without diagnostic feedback, it is very difficult to learn from experience.

The second problem is that our memories tend to be selective, meaning that people tend to remember their successes and forget their failures or shortcomings. This is, of course, comforting to our ego, but it does not improve our ability to negotiate.

Finally, experience improves our confidence, but not necessarily our accuracy. People with more experience grow more and more confident, but the accuracy of their judgment and the effectiveness of their behavior does not increase in a commensurate fashion. Overconfidence can be dangerous because it may lead people to take unwise risks.

MYTH 3: GOOD NEGOTIATORS TAKE RISKS

A pervasive myth is that effective negotiation necessitates taking risks and gambles. In negotiation, this may mean saying things like "This is my final offer" or "Take it or leave it" or using threats and bluffs. This is what we call a "tough" style of negotiation. Tough negotiators are rarely effective; however, we tend to be impressed by the tough negotiator. In this book, we teach negotiators how to evaluate risk, how to determine the appropriate time to make a final offer and, more importantly, how to make excellent decisions in the face of the uncertainty of negotiation.

MYTH 4: GOOD NEGOTIATORS RELY ON INTUITION

An interesting exercise is to ask managers, and anyone else who negotiates, to describe their approach to negotiating. Many seasoned negotiators believe that their negotiation style involves a lot of "gut feeling," intuition, and "in-the-moment" responses. We believe that this type of intuition does not serve people well. Effective negotiation involves deliberate thought and preparation and is quite systematic. The goal of this book is to help managers effectively prepare for negotiation, become more self-aware of their own strengths and shortcomings, and develop strategies that are **proactive** (i.e., those that anticipate the reactions of their opponent) rather than **reactive** (i.e., those that are dependent upon the actions and reactions of their opponent). Thus, excellent negotiators do not rely on intuition; rather, they are deliberate planners.

LEARNING OBJECTIVES

This book promises three things: First (and most important), reading this book will *improve your ability to successfully negotiate.* You and your company will be richer, and you will experience fewer sleepless nights, because you will have a solid framework and excellent toolbox for successful negotiation. However, in making this promise, we must also issue a warning: Successful negotiation skills do not come through passive learning. Rather, you will need to actively challenge yourself. We can think of no better way of doing this than to supplement this book with classroom experiences in negotiation, where managers can test their negotiation skills, receive timely feedback, and refine their negotiation strategies on a repeated basis.

Second, we provide you with a *general strategy for successful negotiation.* This book explicitly does not support a contextual model of negotiation, which prescribes using different negotiation strategies with different types of people, situations, and industries. Rather, we believe that negotiation skills are transferable across situations. In saying this, we do not mean to imply that all negotiation situations are identical. This is patently false because negotiation situations differ dramatically across cultures and activities. However, there are key negotiation principles that are essential in all of these different contexts. The skills in this book are effective across a wide range of situations, ranging from complex, multiparty, multicultural deals to one-on-one personal exchanges.

Finally, this book offers an *enlightened model of negotiation.* Being a successful negotiator does not depend on your opponent's lack of familiarity with a book like this or a lack of training in negotiation. In fact, it would be ideal for you if your key clients and customers knew about these strategies. This approach follows what we call a *fraternal twin model,* which assumes that the other person you are negotiating with is every bit as motivated, intelligent, and prepared as you are. Thus, the negotiating strategies and techniques outlined in this book do not rely on "outsmarting" or tricking the other party; rather, they teach you to focus on simultaneously expanding the pie of resources and ensuring the resources are allocated in a manner that is favorable to you.

THE MIND AND HEART

Across all of the sections of this book, we focus on the *mind* of the negotiator as it involves the development of deliberate, rational, thoughtful strategies for negotiation. We also focus on the *heart* of the negotiator because it involves emotions, psychology, and the intuitive aspects of negotiation. This book strikes a balance between these two approaches to negotiation situations.

2

PREPARATION
What to Do Before Negotiation
☙

Unsure about her worth at the outset of a job search, Holly Peckham found a United States salary database on a Web site created by Marchall Consultants, a New York executive search firm. It contained a wealth of valuable information about salaries supplied by more than 16,000 communications professionals. Based upon her research, Peckham concluded that she should be making about $37,000 a year as an account executive at a PR agency serving high-tech clients. That was $9,000 more than she was earning as an assistant account executive at Schwartz Communications in Waltham, Massachusetts. Chen PR, another firm, offered Peckham $32,000 and a promotion. Peckham refused, citing her online research. "I told them the national average was between $36,000 and $38,000 and that I would be happy coming for between $34,000 and $36,000." She was then offered $34,000 and accepted. According to upper management at Chen, it was Peckham's research and experience that persuaded the firm to increase their salary offer. (Lublin 1998)

The most important aspect of negotiation occurs before negotiators are at the bargaining table. As the opening example in this chapter illustrates, preparation is the key to successful negotiation. Most people clearly realize that preparation is important, yet they do not prepare in an effective fashion. Faulty preparation is not due to lack of motivation or ineptitude; rather, it has its roots in negotiators' faulty perceptions about negotiation. Most negotiators view negotiation as a situation in which parties' interests are completely opposed. This faulty perception is known as the **fixed-pie perception** (Bazerman and Neale 1983; Thompson and Hastie 1990); most negotiators (about 80 percent of them) operate under this perception.

Negotiators who have fixed-pie perceptions usually take one of three roads when preparing for negotiation:

1. They resign themselves to capitulating to the other side (also known as *soft bargaining*).
2. They prepare themselves for an attack (also known as *hard bargaining*).
3. They *compromise* in an attempt to reach a midpoint between their opposing desires. (This is often regarded to be a win-win negotiation, but in fact, it is not.)

Depending on what the other party decides to do in the negotiation, fixed-pie perceptions can either lead to a battle of wills (e.g., if both parties are in attack mode), mutual compromise (i.e., if both parties are soft), or a combination of attack and capitulation. The common assumption among all three approaches is that concessions are necessary by one or both parties to reach an agreement. The fixed-pie perception is usually always wrong; thus, choosing between capitulation, attack, and compromise is not an effective approach to negotiation.

A more accurate model of negotiation is a *mixed-motive* decision-making enterprise. As a mixed-motive enterprise, negotiation involves both cooperation and competition. In this chapter, we review the essentials of preparation for negotiation, whether it be with a next-door neighbor, a corporate executive officer, or someone from a different culture. We argue that excellent preparation encompasses three general abilities:

1. self-assessment
2. assessment of the other party
3. assessment of the situation

Next, we systematically review each of these abilities and the skills they require. For each, we pose questions that a negotiator should ask him or herself when preparing for negotiation.

SELF-ASSESSMENT

The most important questions a negotiator needs to ask of him or herself at the outset of negotiation are "What do I want?" and "What are my alternatives?" By far, the first question is the most intuitive and the easier of the two to answer. Even so, many people do not think carefully about what they want before entering negotiations. The second question defines a negotiator's power in the situation and influences the ultimate outcome of the negotiation. We take up these questions in more detail.

WHAT DO I WANT?

In any negotiation situation, a negotiator needs to determine what constitutes an ideal situation for him or herself. This is known as a **target** or **aspiration.** Identifying a target or aspiration may sound straightforward enough, but three major problems often arise at this point:

1. The first problem is the case of the *underaspiring negotiator,* who sets his or her target and/or aspirations too low. The underaspiring negotiator opens the negotiation by requesting something that is immediately granted, and this results in a regrettable state of affairs known as the **winner's curse** (Akerlof 1970; Neale and Bazerman 1991). The winner's curse occurs when a negotiator makes an offer that is immediately accepted by the other party. The immediate acceptance of one's offer by an opponent signals that a negotiator did not ask for enough.
2. The second problem is the case of the *overaspiring* or *positional negotiator.* This type of negotiator is too "tough"; he or she sets the target point too high and refuses to make any concessions.

3. The third problem is what we call the *grass-is-greener negotiator*. These negotiators do not know what they really want—only that they want what the other party does not want to give them and do not want what the other party is willing to offer. This type of negotiation behavior is also known as **reactive devaluation** (Ross and Stillinger 1991). For example, in a survey of opinions regarding possible arms reductions by the United States and the Soviet Union, respondents were asked to evaluate the terms of a nuclear disarmament proposal, a proposal that was either allegedly taken by the United States, Soviet Union, or a neutral third party (Ross and Stillinger 1991). In all cases, the proposal was identical; however, reactions to it depended upon who allegedly initiated it. The terms were seen as unfavorable to the United States when the Soviets were the initiators, even though the same terms appeared moderately favorable when attributed to a neutral third party and quite favorable when attributed to the United States (see also Oskamp 1965).

WHAT IS MY ALTERNATIVE TO REACHING AGREEMENT IN THIS SITUATION?

A negotiator needs to determine his or her best alternative to a negotiated agreement. This is so important that it has been made into an acronym: **BATNA** (**B**est **A**lternative **t**o a **N**egotiated **A**greement; Fisher, Ury, and Patton 1991). A BATNA determines the point at which a negotiator is prepared to walk away from the negotiation table. In practice, this means that negotiators should be willing to accept any set of terms that is superior to their BATNA and reject outcomes that are worse than their BATNA. Surprising as it may seem, negotiators often fail on both counts.

A BATNA is not something that a negotiator wishes for; rather, it is determined by harsh reality and external factors. A common problem we have seen in our training of MBA students and executives is that negotiators are reluctant to recognize their real BATNAs, and they fall prey to wishful thinking and unrealistic optimism. The best means of preparation is to continually try to improve your BATNA. One strategy for doing this is to follow Bazerman and Neale's (1992) "falling in love" rule, which applies to most negotiation situations. According to this rule, negotiators should not fall in love with one house, one job, or one set of circumstances, but rather, try to identify two or three options of interest. By following this strategy, the negotiator has a readily available set of alternatives that represent viable options should their current alternative come at too high a price or be eliminated. The falling in love rule is difficult to follow because most people set their sights on one target job, house, or set of terms and exclude all others. Many negotiators are reluctant to recognize their BATNAs and get them confused with their aspiration point. Another problem associated with the failure to properly identify one's BATNA is that it can be influenced and manipulated by the other party during the course of negotiation.

Do not Let the Other Party Manipulate Your BATNA

A negotiator's BATNA should not change during the course of negotiation unless, for some reason, the objective situation has changed. Many savvy negotiators attempt to manipulate the other party's perception of their own BATNA. Negotiators are most likely to fall prey to this ploy when they have not adequately prepared for the negotiation and have conjured up a BATNA not based on objective information.

In a negotiation situation, the person who stands to gain most by changing our mind should be the least persuasive. Thus, it is important to develop a BATNA before commencing negotiations and to stick to it during the course of negotiations. It is helpful to write your BATNA in ink on a piece of paper and put it in your pocket before negotiating. If you feel tempted to settle for less than your BATNA, that may be a good time to pull out the paper, call a halt to the negotiation process, and go home and engage in an objective reassessment.

Determine Your Reservation Point

Once the negotiator has identified her BATNA, she is in an excellent position to determine her reservation point. The **reservation point** is determined not by what the negotiator wishes and hopes for, but rather, by what her BATNA represents. Consider the example of an MBA student negotiating her employment terms. Let's imagine that the MBA student has a $90,000 job offer from company A, with some stock options, moving expenses, and a signing bonus. The student is interested in getting an offer from company B. Thus, company A is her BATNA. The question the student should ask herself is, What does company B need to offer me so that I feel that it is identical to the offer made by company A? This represents her reservation point, which includes all things relevant to the job offer: not only salary, stock options, moving expenses, and signing bonus, but also quality of life and feelings about the city to which she will move, etc. A reservation point, then, is a *quantification* of a negotiator's BATNA.

Many negotiators fail to assess their reservation point when they prepare for negotiation. This is a fatal flaw that can lead to two unfortunate outcomes. In some instances, negotiators may agree to an outcome that is worse than their BATNA. In our example, the student could agree to a set of employment terms at company B that are actually worse for her than what company A is offering. A second problem is that negotiators may often reject an offer that is better than their BATNA: For example, the MBA student may reject a package from company B that is actually more attractive than the offer from company A. Whereas this may seem completely ludicrous from an objective standpoint, the incidence of agreeing to something worse than one's BATNA and rejecting an offer better than one's BATNA is quite high. To avoid both of these errors, we suggest that the negotiator follow the steps outlined in Box 2–1.

Be Aware of Focal Points

Negotiators who make the mistake of not developing a reservation point before they negotiate often focus on an arbitrary value that masquerades as a reservation price. Such arbitrary points are **focal points.** Focal points can be salient numbers, figures, or values that appear to be valid but have no basis in fact—your roommate's job offer, for example. A good example of the arbitrariness of focal points is provided by an investigation in which people made estimations about the number of African countries in the United Nations (Tversky and Kahneman 1974). In the investigation, people stood before a "wheel of fortune"; the wheel was spun and landed on a number. People were then asked to indicate whether there were more or fewer African countries in the United Nations than the number shown on the wheel and then estimate the total number. People who landed on a high number estimated many more than those who had,

BOX 2–1

DEVELOPING A RESERVATION POINT

Step 1: Brainstorm Your Alternatives
Imagine that you want to sell your house. You have already determined your target point—in this case, $275,000. That is the easy part. The real question is, What is the lowest offer you will accept for your home? This step involves thinking about what you will do in the event that you do not get an offer of $275,000 for your house. Perhaps you may reduce the list price by $10,000 (or more), perhaps you may stay in the house, or you may consider renting. You should consider as many alternatives as possible. The only restriction is that the alternatives must be feasible—that is, realistic. This involves research on your part.

Step 2: Evaluate Each Alternative In this step, you should order the various alternatives identified in step 1 in terms of their relative attractiveness, or value, to you. If an alternative has an uncertain outcome, such as reducing the list price, you should determine the probability that a buyer will make an offer at that price. For example, suppose that you reduce the list price to $265,000. You assess the probability of a buyer making an offer of $265,000 for your house to be 70 percent, based on recent home sale prices in the area. Your reservation price is based on research, not hope. The best, most valuable, alternative should be selected to represent your BATNA.

Step 3: Attempt to Improve Your BATNA Your bargaining position can be strengthened substantially to the extent that you have an attractive, viable BATNA. Unfortunately, this is the step that many negotiators fail to fully develop. To improve your BATNA in this case, you might contact a house rental company and develop your rental options, or you may make some improvements that have high return on investment (e.g., new paint). Of course, your most attractive BATNA is to have an offer in hand on your house.

Step 4: Determine Your Reservation Price Once you have determined your most attractive BATNA, it is now time to identify your reservation price—the least amount of money you would accept for your home at the present time. Once again, it is *not* effective to pull this number out of thin air. It *must* be based on fact.

For example: Suppose that you assess the probability of getting an offer on your house of $265,000 (or higher) to be 60 percent. Suppose that you assess the probability that you will get an offer of $250,000 or higher to be 95 percent. You think there is a 5 percent chance that you will not get an offer of $250,000 and will rent your house. You can use this information to assess your expected probabilities of selling your house:

Reduce the price of your home to $265,000
$$P_{sale} = 0.60\%$$

Reduce the price of your home to $250,000
$$P_{sale} = 0.35\%$$

Rent out the house
$$P_{rent} = 0.05\%$$

The probabilities represent the chances that you think your house will sell at a particular price or will have to be rented. Thus, you think that if the list price of your house is reduced to $265,000, it is 60 percent likely that you will receive an offer of that amount within six weeks. If you reduce the price of your home to $250,000, you are 95 percent certain that you will get an offer. (Note that we write this as 35 percent because it includes the 60 percent probability of receiving an offer of $265,000.) Finally, you think there is a 5 percent chance that you will not get an offer of $250,000 or more in the next six weeks and that you will have to rent your house—a value you assess to be worth only $100,000 to you at the present time.

Continued

> **BOX 2–1**
>
> ## DEVELOPING A RESERVATION POINT—
> ### *continued*
>
> Note that in our calculation, the probabilities always sum to exactly 100 percent, meaning that we have considered all possible events occurring. No alternative is left to chance. An overall value for each of these "risky" alternatives is assessed by multiplying the value of each option by its probability of occurrence:
>
> Value of reducing price to $265,000
>   = $265,000 × 0.6 = $159,000
>
> Value of reducing price to $250,000
>   = $250,000 × 0.35 = $87,500
>
> Value of renting the house
>   = 100,000 × 0.05 = $5,000
>
> As a final step, we add all of the values of the alternatives to arrive at an overall evaluation:
>
> 0.6 ($265,000) + 0.35 ($250,000) +
> 0.05 ($100,000) = $159,000 + $87,500
>   + $5,000 = $251,500
>
> This value is your reservation price. It means that you would never settle for anything less than $251,500 in the next six weeks.[1] It also means that if a buyer were to make you an offer right now of $251,000, you would seriously consider it because it is very close to your reservation price. Obviously, you want to get a lot more than $251,500, but you are prepared to go as low as this amount at the present time.
>
> The offers that you receive in the next six weeks can change your reservation point. Suppose a buyer offers to pay $260,000 for the house next week. This would be your reservation point by which to evaluate all subsequent offers.
>
> ---
>
> [1]After six weeks, you may reduce the price of your home to $250,000.
>
>

by chance, landed on a low number. It would seem absurd to base judgments on the wheel-of-fortune number, but people did.

Be Aware of Sunk Costs

Sunk costs are just what they sound like—money that you have invested in something that is, for all practical purposes, gone. Economic theory asserts that only future costs and benefits should affect decisions. However, the problem is that people have a hard time forgetting the past, and they often try to recoup sunk costs. This can lead to trouble. One type of sunk cost is the purchase price that home sellers paid for their house. Simply stated, at some point in the past, a person purchased her house for a certain price. That price, by economic standards, is a sunk cost and should, for all practical purposes, be irrelevant to the negotiation the seller has with a buyer today. However, most people are affected by the past. To examine this, Diekmann, Tenbrunsel, Shah, Schroth, and Bazerman (1996) conducted a simulation of sellers and buyers in real estate negotiations. In all cases, the Multiple Listing Service (MLS) sheet describing the house was identical, as was the current real estate market. However, negotiators were given different information about their previous purchase price. Buyers offered significantly higher amounts for a condominium with larger sunk costs, indicating that the seller's sunk costs influenced the buyer's behavior. Moreover, sellers' BATNAs were significantly lower when they had low, as opposed to high, sunk costs. Final settlements were significantly lower in the low (as opposed to high) sunk cost situations. When preparing for negotiations, negotiators need to be aware that sunk costs will not only influence their own behavior but the behavior of their opponents.

Do not Confuse Your Target Point with Your Reservation Point

Negotiators often make the mistake of using their target point as their reservation point. Thus, the negotiator has a clear sense of what he or she would like to achieve but has not thought about the least acceptable terms he or she could live with. This is a poor negotiation strategy and can result in one of two fatal flaws. The negotiator who lacks a well-formed reservation point runs the risk of agreeing to a settlement that is worse than what he or she could do by following another course of action. In other cases, the negotiator may walk away from potentially profitable deals. For example, many home sellers turn down early offers on their house that are superior to their reservation point, only to be forced to accept an offer of less value at some later point in time.

IDENTIFY THE ISSUES IN THE NEGOTIATION

Many negotiators make the mistake of identifying only a single issue to be negotiated in a situation. Usually, this is money (e.g., in the sale of a house, the selling price may seem like the central issue of negotiation; similarly, in a job negotiation, salary may emerge as the key issue). It is a grave mistake to focus on a single issue in a negotiation because, in reality, there are more issues at stake in most negotiation situations. By identifying other issues, negotiators can add value to negotiations. For example, in the purchase of a car, the payment terms, cash up-front, loan agreement, or warranty could all be negotiable issues. Negotiators should take time to brainstorm how a single-issue negotiation may be fractionated into multiple issues (Lax and Sebenius 1986). Unbundling negotiations into several issues goes against rationality because people have a tendency to simplify situations into single issues. However, negotiators should try to make single-issue negotiations more complex by adding in issues.

IDENTIFY THE ALTERNATIVES FOR EACH ISSUE

Once the negotiator has identified the issues to be negotiated, it is a good idea to identify several alternative courses of action within each issue. For example, in a negotiation for a new car, payment terms might be broken down into percentage paid up-front or percentage of interest on a loan; a loaner agreement might involve how many months or years the option is available to the purchaser, etc. By identifying issues and alternatives, negotiators create a type of matrix, organized such that the identified issues in the negotiation are located along the columns and the alternatives are located along the rows.

IDENTIFY PACKAGES OF OFFERS

Once a negotiator has identified the issues in a negotiation and identified alternatives within each issue, the next important step of preparation is to determine a variety of different, attractive packages. For example, an MBA student in a job interview might identify starting salary, signing bonus, and vacation days as key issues and identify several alternatives within these issues. The student might then take the step of identifying highly attractive packages that she could present as opening offers in the negotiation; for example, a starting salary of $90,000, three weeks of vacation per year, and a signing bonus of $10,000 might be psychologically equivalent to a starting salary of $100,000, 10 days of vacation per year, and a signing bonus of $12,000. Negotiators attempt to identify as many multiple-issue packages of offers as possible to present to the other party. This creates more degrees of freedom in negotiation. The most important aspect of identifying packages of offers is that the packages should all be of equivalent value or attractiveness to oneself. This requires that negotiators ask themselves some important questions about what they value and what is attractive to them. (There are a variety of ways of doing this; as a first step, it is wise to consult appendix 1, which helps prepare a negotiator to identify packages of equivalent value by testing the negotiator's rationality.)

We strongly discourage negotiators from stating a range (e.g., a salary range). This is not in any way equivalent to identifying packages of offers. By stating a range, the negotiator gives up important bargaining ground and moves too close to his or her BATNA. We call this a *premature concession*. By stating a range ("I would be interested in a salary between $90,000 and $100,000") a negotiator has already made a concession (implicitly agreeing to a salary of $90,000). Ideally, a negotiator should exhaust all possible deals before making a concession on any one of the issues he or she has identified. This can be best achieved by determining more than one way for a negotiator to satisfy his or her interests and aspirations. Another benefit of identifying packages of offers is that the negotiator does not give his or her opponent the impression that he or she is a *positional negotiator*. (A positional negotiator is a person who determines a set of terms that he would like to achieve in a negotiation, presents those terms, and refuses to budge on any dimension of any issue (Fisher, Ury, and Patton 1991).) By identifying multiple issues and multiple alternatives within each issue, a negotiator is in an excellent position to identify a variety of terms under which she can be equally happy.

ASSESS YOUR RISK PROPENSITY

Negotiation involves some risk, in the sense that there is uncertainty about the final outcome. Whereas the negotiator can and should be fairly sure that he or she can resort to her BATNA in the event that the present negotiation does not work out, most negotiation situations involve an element of risk. In this sense, a negotiator's BATNA acts as an important reference point from which other outcomes are evaluated. Outcomes and alternatives that fall short of one's BATNA are viewed as losses; outcomes that exceed a negotiator's reservation point or BATNA are viewed as gains. Ideally, negotiators should be risk-neutral, meaning that they should choose the course of action that maximizes their expected utility. However, we often see that negotiators are not risk-neutral, but rather, are risk-averse for gains and risk seeking for losses (Tversky and Kahneman, 1992). This is best demonstrated through an example. Suppose you are offered a choice between the following two options:

Option A: Receiving a cashier's check for $5,000
Option B: Playing a lottery-type game in which there is a 50 percent chance of winning a $10,000 cashier's check and a 50 percent chance of winning nothing

Under these circumstances, a great majority of negotiators choose option A, the sure thing. Note that the expected value of each choice is $5,000, which would mean that negotiators should be indifferent (or risk-neutral) between the two. However, the strong preference for option A over B reflects a fundamental principle of negotiator behavior: **risk aversion.**

Now, imagine yourself facing the following unenviable choice:

Option C: Paying $5,000 for an unexpected expense
Option D: Playing a game in which there is a 50 percent chance of paying
    nothing and a 50 percent chance of paying $10,000

Most people find it difficult to choose between options C and D because these choices are undesirable. However, when forced to make a decision, the majority of negotiators choose option D, even though the expected value of C and D is exactly the same—$5,000. Option D represents the "risky" alternative. The dominant choice of D over C reflects a fundamental principle of human psychology: risk-seeking behavior for losses.

At first, it might seem contradictory that people are both risk-averse and risk-seeking, but when we investigate how people frame their decisions, we see that a pattern emerges: People are generally risk-averse when gains are involved and are risk-seeking when losses are involved. A reference point defines what a person considers to be a gain or a loss. This can be a potential problem in negotiation because negotiators can be "framed." To see how this is true, consider the following example: Negotiators who are instructed to "minimize their losses" make fewer concessions, reach fewer agreements, and perceive the settlements to be less fair compared to those who are told to "maximize their gains" (Bazerman, Magliozzi, and Neale 1985; Neale and Northcraft 1986; Neale, Huber, and Northcraft 1987; for reviews, see Neale and Bazerman 1991). In short, the negotiators who are told to "minimize their losses" adopt more risky bargaining strategies (just as the majority of people choose option D over C in the earlier example), preferring to hold out for a better, but more risky, settlement. In contrast, those who are told to "maximize their gains" are more inclined to accept the sure thing (just as most people choose option A over B in the earlier example). Negotiators who view the glass as "half full" are more inclined to reach agreement, whereas negotiators who view the glass as "half empty" are more inclined to use threats and resort to their BATNAs. If one negotiator has a negative frame and the other has a positive frame, the negotiator with the negative frame reaps a greater share of the resources (Bottom and Studt 1993). Thus, a negotiator needs to be aware of the important psychological impact his or her reference point can have on his or her own behavior. Obviously, negotiators should carefully examine their reference points and be wary when their opponents attempt to manipulate their reference points.

DEALING WITH UNCERTAINTY

In many negotiation situations, settlement outcomes are determined without uncertainty at the time of settlement. For example, we know that we will drive home in a new car or earn a particular salary once the deal is negotiated. However, some negotiations contain an element of risk, even at the time of settlement. For example, consider buying a piece of real estate. Depending upon such things as the market, the land might be worth much more than what we pay, or much less. This situation is known as **contractual risk.**

The Mitsubishi Estate Company provided a dramatic example of the risk of erroneous estimates in negotiation (Bottom 1996). In October 1989, Mitsubishi agreed to pay the Rockefeller family trust $846 million in exchange for a controlling interest in the Rockefeller Group, Inc., which owns Rockefeller Center. Unfortunately, Mitsubishi, along with many others, failed to foresee the collapse of the New York real estate market, which dramatically lowered the value of the acquisition. In May 1995, Mitsubishi Estate Company was forced to seek bankruptcy protection primarily in an attempt to stem the $600 million in losses they had incurred on the investment (Pacelle 1995; Pacelle and Lipin 1995). Clearly, the Mitsubishi negotiators expected a much better payoff when they signed the original agreement to acquire the control of the property.

How does such contractual risk affect negotiator behavior? Under contractual risk, negotiators with negative frames (risk-seeking) are more likely to reach integrative agreement than those with positive frames (risk-averse). Why? The only route capable of attaining high aspirations entails some creative risk. Thus, if integrative negotiation outcomes involve "sure things," positive frames are more effective; however, if the integrative outcomes require negotiators to "roll the dice," negative frames are more effective.

ENDOWMENT EFFECTS

According to basic principles of rationality, the value or utility we associate with a certain object or outcome should not be influenced by irrelevant factors, such as who owns the object. Simply stated, the value of the object should be about the same, whether we are a buyer or a seller. (A note: Buyers and sellers might want to adopt different *bargaining positions* for the object, but their *private valuations* for the object should not differ as a consequence of who has possession of it.) However, negotiators' reference points may lead buyers and sellers to have different valuations for objects. Someone who possesses an object has a reference point that reflects his or her current endowment. When someone who owns an object considers selling it, he or she may view the situation as a loss. The difference between what sellers demand and what buyers are willing to pay is a manifestation of loss aversion, coupled with the rapid adaptation of the reference point. Therefore, we should expect that sellers will demand more for objects than buyers are willing to pay.

One example comes from a class of MBA students who were "endowed" with coffee mugs worth $6, as charged by the university bookstore (Kahneman, Knetsch, and Thaler 1990). The students who were not given a coffee mug were told that they had the opportunity to buy a mug from a student who owned one, if the student who owned the mug valued it less. The buyers' willingness to pay for the mug and the sellers' willingness to sell the mug were inferred from a series of choices (e.g., "receive $9.75" versus "receive mug," "receive $9.50 versus a mug," etc.). Basic rationality would predict that about half of the buyers will value the mug more than the seller and therefore trade will occur; similarly, about half of the sellers will value the mug more than the buyer and trade will not occur. The reference point effect, however, predicts that because of the loss-aversion behavior engendered by the seller's loss frame, trade will occur less than expected. Indeed, although 11 trades were expected, on average, only four took place. Sellers demanded in excess of $8 to part with their mugs; prospective buyers were only willing to pay list price (Kahneman, Knetsch, and Thaler 1990).

If sellers are risk-seeking by virtue of their endowment, how can it be that horses, cars, furniture, companies, and land are bought and sold every day? The endowment effect operates only when the seller regards him- or herself to be the owner of the object. If a seller expects to sell goods for a profit and views the goods as currency (for example, when MBA students are endowed with tokens rather than coffee mugs), the endowment effect does not occur.

AM I GOING TO LIVE TO REGRET THIS?

People evaluate reality by comparing it to its salient alternatives (Kahneman and Miller 1986). Sometimes we feel we made the "right" decision when we think about alternatives. Other times, we are filled with regret. What determines when we feel we did the right thing (e.g., took the right job, married the right person) or whether we feel regret? An important component in determining whether a person experiences regret is counterfactual thinking (Gilovich and Medvec 1994). **Counterfactual thinking,** or thinking about what might have been but did not occur, may be a reference point for the psychological evaluation of actual outcomes. In negotiation, immediate acceptance of a first offer by an opponent often means a better outcome for the proposing negotiator; however, the outcome is distinctly less satisfying (Galinsky, Seiden, Kim, and Medvec 1999). One of the benefits of having a first offer accepted is that it can positively affect preparation. Negotiators whose first offer is accepted by the opponent are more likely to prepare longer for a subsequent negotiation; it also makes negotiators reluctant to make the first offer again (Galinsky, Seiden, Kim, and Medvec 1999).

As an example, consider feelings of regret experienced by athletes in the Olympic games (Medvec, Madey, and Gilovich 1995). Although silver medalists should feel happier than bronze medalists because their performance is objectively superior, counterfactual reasoning might produce greater feelings of regret and disappointment in silver medalists than in bronze. Specifically, the bronze medalist's reference point is that of not placing at all, so winning a medal represents a gain. In contrast, the silver medalist views him- or herself as just missing the gold. With the gold medal as the referent, the silver medalist feels a loss. Indeed, videotapes of medalists' reactions (with the audio portion turned off) reveal that bronze medalists are perceived to be happier than silver medalists (Medvec, Madey, and Gilovich 1995). Further, silver medalists report experiencing greater feelings of regret than do bronze medalists.

PREFERENCE REVERSALS

Your business associate comes into your office filled with excitement. She explains that you have a great opportunity to invest in a new company. Two companies are for sale: company X and company Y. If profitable, company X could be worth $2 million. Your colleague estimates the chances to be 60 percent. Company Y could be worth $2.5 million, but the chances are only 40 percent. Which company should you invest in? Before reading further, pick which company you find to be the better investment.

A week later, your associate comes to you with another proposition. Again, the proposition involves two companies, but this time your associate wants you to put a dollar value on what you think they are worth. Company X has a 30 percent chance of success, and, if successful, will be worth $4 million. Company Y has a 20 percent chance of success, and, if successful, will be worth $5 million. What do you think is a fair price to pay for company X? Company Y?

When faced with decisions like these, people tend to be inconsistent. That is, in the first situation, they choose company X over company Y. However, in the second situation, they put a higher price tag on company Y than company X. In fact, your associates' second proposition is identical to the first proposition when all values/probabilities are divided/multiplied by 2.

Preference reversals are inconsistencies in choice. For example, people choose gambles that offer a greater chance to win over another gamble that offers a higher payoff but a lower chance to win but then assign a higher price (value) to the gamble offering the higher payoff than to the one with the greater chance to win (Slovic and Lichtenstein 1983). This pattern of preferences violates basic principles of decision theory and has been observed in several contexts, including professional gamblers in Las Vegas casinos (Lichtenstein and Slovic 1971). Why does intransitive choice happen?

The reason has to do with the aspects of the alternative that are salient to the decision maker. The prices of gambles are expressed in dollars, and, therefore, when evaluating the value of the gamble, people focus on the money they could win. In contrast, when gamblers choose between two gambles, the likelihood of winning is salient. In another example, people were presented with pairs of hypothetical students who had taken two courses. Their grades in one course and ranks in the other were shown: One student had a higher grade in one course, and the other student had a higher rank in the second. Some people were asked to predict which student would achieve a higher grade in a third course; others were asked to predict which student would receive a higher rank in a third course. The student with the higher grade was expected to perform better 56 percent of the time by the grade group and only 49 percent of the time by the rank group.

CHOOSING VERSUS REJECTING

Decision making is difficult because people do not often know how to trade off one attribute (e.g., salary) with another (e.g., quality of life) in a job choice. Decisions are often reached by focusing on considerations that justify the selection of one option over others (Simonson 1989; Tversky and Shafir 1992a, 1992b; Shafir and Tversky 1992; Shafir, Simonson, and Tversky 1993).

In one investigation, people were presented with pairs of options (Shafir and Tversky 1992). The option pairs were created so that one was an "enriched" option (included more positive and negative aspects) and the other was "impoverished" (included fewer positive and negative aspects). For example, one option pair concerned a child custody decision, wherein one parent had both positive and negative aspects (e.g., a very close relationship to the child but much work-related travel); the other parent had fewer positive and negative aspects (reasonable rapport with the child; average working hours). Some people were asked to indicate to which parent they would award custody; others were asked to which parent they would deny custody. According to decision theory, the two choices are objectively identical and therefore there should be no difference in decisions when people are asked to choose or reject one parent. Nevertheless, the "enriched" parent was the modal choice for being awarded *and* denied custody of the child. Why does this happen? The reason has to do with decision salience—the reasons for awarding and denying the "enriched" parent are more salient.

The implications for negotiation behavior are extremely serious. Remember the suggestion to prepare multiple-issue offers, in which a negotiator makes the opponent several offers (all of equal value). The opponent's response may be dramatically different if choosing rather than rejecting options. The message? Be cognizant of how you present choices to your opponent and how your opponent presents choices to you. Before making a commitment, ask yourself whether your choice would be the same if you were to either choose or reject an offer.

VIOLATIONS OF THE SURE THING PRINCIPLE

Imagine that you face a decision between going to graduate school X on the East Coast or graduate school Y on the West Coast. You must make your decision before you find out whether your start-up company has received funding from a venture capitalist. In the event you get the funding, the East Coast provides access to many more of your potential customers. In the event that funding does not come through, by going to the East Coast, you would be closer to your family, who could help you with finances. This sounds pretty straightforward so far: School X is your dominant choice no matter what the venture capitalist does. In other words, you have chosen school X regardless of whether you get funding. Making a decision between X and Y should not be hard—or should it?

When faced with uncertainty about some event occurring (such as whether your company will be funded), people are often reluctant to make decisions and will even pay money to delay decisions until the uncertain event is known. This is paradoxical because no matter what happens, people choose to do the same thing (Tversky and Shafir 1992b). Consider a situation in which a student has just taken a tough and exhausting qualifying examination (see Shafir 1994). The student has the option of buying a very attractive five-day Hawaiian vacation package. The results of the exam will not be available for a week, but the student must decide whether to buy the vacation package now. Alternatively, she can pay a nonrefundable fee to retain the right to buy the vacation package at the same price the day after the exam results are posted. When presented with these three choices, most respondents (61 percent) choose to pay a nonrefundable fee to delay the decision. Two other versions of the scenario are then presented to different groups of participants. In one version, the student passed the exam, and in the other version, the student failed. In both of these situations, respondents overwhelmingly preferred to go on the vacation. Thus, even though we decide to go on the vacation no matter what the results of the exam, we are willing to pay money to delay making this decision.

This behavior violates one of the basic axioms of rational theory of decision making under uncertainty: the **sure thing principle** (Savage 1954). According to the sure thing principle, if an alternative X is preferred to Y in the condition that some event, A, occurs, and if X is also preferred to Y in the condition that some event, A, does not occur, then X should be preferred to Y, even when it is not known whether A will occur or not.

Why would people pay a fee to a consultant or intermediary to delay the decision when they would make the same choice either way? Violations of the sure thing principle are rooted in the *reasons* people use to make their decisions. In the earlier example, people have different reasons for going to Hawaii for each possible event. If they pass the exam, the vacation is a celebration or reward; if they fail the exam, the vacation is an opportunity to recuperate. When the decision maker does not know whether he or she has passed the exam, he or she may lack a clear reason for going to Hawaii. In the presence of uncertainty, people may be reluctant to think through the implications of each outcome and, as a result, they violate the sure thing principle.

DO I HAVE AN APPROPRIATE LEVEL OF CONFIDENCE?

Consider a situation in which you are assessing the probability that a particular company will be successful. Some people might think the probability is quite good; others might think the probability is low; others might make middle-of-the-road assessments. For the negotiator, what matters most is making an assessment that is accurate. How accurate are people in judgments of probability? How do they make assessments of likelihood, especially when full, objective information is unavailable?

Judgments of likelihood for certain types of events are often more optimistic than is warranted. The *overconfidence effect* refers to unwarranted levels of confidence in people's judgment of their abilities and the occurrence of positive events and underestimates of the likelihood of negative events. For example, in negotiations involving third-party dispute resolution, negotiators on each side believe the neutral third party will adjudicate in their favor (Farber and Bazerman 1986, 1989; Farber 1981). Obviously, this cannot happen; the third party cannot adjudicate in favor of both parties. Similarly, in final-offer arbitration, wherein parties each submit their final bid to a third party who then makes a binding decision between the two proposals, negotiators consistently overestimate the probability that the neutral arbitrator will choose their own offer (Neale and Bazerman 1983; Bazerman and Neale 1982). Obviously, there is only a 50 percent chance of all final offers being accepted; nevertheless, both parties' estimates typically sum to a number greater than 100 percent. The message is to be aware of the overconfidence effect. When we find ourselves to be highly confident of a particular outcome occurring (whether it be our opponent caving in to us, a senior manager supporting our decision, etc.), it is important to examine why.

SIZING UP THE OTHER PARTY

Once the negotiator has gone through the preparation procedure for evaluating what he or she wants in a negotiation situation, it is time to think about the other party (or parties).

WHO ARE THE OTHER PARTIES?

It is always important to identify who the players are in a negotiation. A **party** is a person (or group of people with common interests) who acts in accord with his or her preferences. Parties are readily identified when they are physically present, but often, the most important parties are not present at the negotiation table. Such parties are known as the **hidden table** (Friedman 1992). When there are more parties involved in the negotiations, the situation becomes a team or multiparty negotiation, and the dynamics change considerably. There are a variety of issues that crop up as more parties enter the bargaining room. For example, with more than two parties, coalitions may develop, and teams of negotiators may form. Team and multiparty negotiations are so important that we devote an entire chapter to them in this book (chapter 9). Sometimes, it is obvious who the other parties are, and they have a legitimate place at the table. However, in other situations, the other parties may not be obvious at all, and their legitimacy at the table may be questionable. The negotiator should take the time to carefully ascertain who the parties are. Sometimes the most important and influential parties are not the ones who appear at the negotiation table; in part, their power comes from being away from the table.

ARE THE PARTIES MONOLITHIC?[1]

Being **monolithic** refers to whether parties on the same side of the table are in agreement with one another concerning their interests in the negotiation. Although it would make sense for parties on the same side to be of one voice, very often they are not. It is often the case that each party is composed of people who are on the same side but have differing values, beliefs, and preferences. For example, as twin vice-chairmen of Toys "R" Us, Michael Goldstein and Robert Nakasone presented a united front when negotiating for big initiatives. They made many important decisions jointly. However, their styles were not the same. Over time, their interests and styles clashed greatly, leading Robert Nakasone to ask Michael Goldstein to stop attending the all-important top-management Monday noontime meetings. Sometime later, Michael Goldstein asked Robert Nakasone to resign (Pereira and Lublin 1999).

ISSUE MIX

As we noted earlier, a negotiator takes the time to fractionate a single-issue negotiation into multiple issues. However, the other party may have a different set of issues that they have identified. This means that the two parties are, in a sense, talking "apples and oranges" once they come to the negotiation table.

OTHERS' INTERESTS AND POSITION

A negotiator should do as much research and homework as possible to determine what the other parties' interests are in the negotiation. For example, of the multiple issues identified, which issues are most important to the other party? What alternatives are most preferable to the other party?

OTHER NEGOTIATORS' BATNAS

This is probably the most important piece of information a negotiator can have in a negotiation. Unfortunately, unless you are negotiating with an extremely naïve negotiator, it is unlikely that your opponent will reveal her BATNA. However, a negotiator can and should do research about the other party's BATNA before negotiating. Most

---

[1]This question is raised by Raiffa (1982) in his seminal book *The Art and Science of Negotiation.*

negotiators severely underresearch their opponent's BATNA. For example, most people, when purchasing cars, have access to a wealth of information about dealers' costs; however, they do not access this information prior to negotiating with car salespersons (see Sidebar 2–1). This, of course, limits their ability to effectively negotiate. Along the same lines, many people do not adequately utilize real estate agents when purchasing houses. Real estate agents can provide a wealth of valuable information about the nature of the market and the history of a house that is for sale—all of which can be valuable when trying to determine an opponent's BATNA. The other party's aspiration point will be quite clear; however, the negotiator who determines only the other party's aspiration point and not her BATNA is in a severely disadvantageous negotiation position because her opponent's aspiration may act as an anchor in the negotiation process.

SIDEBAR 2–1. BY THE TIME YOU SEE CAR DEALERS, YOU SHOULD KNOW AS MUCH AS THEY DO

The wealth of information available for free on thousands of Web sites has nearly leveled the playing field for car buyers and sellers. Some would even say the buyer now has the advantage. "People now can walk into a dealership knowing more than what the dealer's salespeople often know," says Peter Steinlauf, president of Edmund Publications in Beverly Hills, California. Web sites like CarPoint and Edmunds provide all the tools a buyer needs to figure out what a car cost the dealer and how much you can expect for your trade-in. Not surprisingly, car manufacturer sites do not provide dealer cost information. Web sites like CarPoint explain hidden sources of dealer profit, such as "holdbacks"—a 2 to 3 percent kickback from manufacturers to dealer to help them finance their inventory, advertising fees, customer rebates, and dealer-incentive payments from carmakers. Larry Armstrong (1999) suggests having this information in hand when going to the dealer. It is important to know what kind of car you are interested in (check out car-enthusiast magazines' Web sites for this). According to Armstrong, buyers get what they want at the price they want. Bill Townsend, a 33-year-old Oracle marketing director who bought his red 1995 Mazda Miata from a Sunnyvale, California dealer referred by Autobytel.com, says "it was a huge savings of time and effort . . . but the real value was taking the haggling out of the process" (Armstrong, 1999, p. 120).

SITUATION ASSESSMENT

In addition to sizing up oneself and sizing up the other party in a negotiation, the negotiator is well advised to assess the negotiation situation. In some types of business interactions, there are norms that differ radically from other business situations. Assess the following *before* negotiating (see Raiffa 1982).[2]

---

[2]Many of the questions that follow are suggested by Raiffa (1982); we also expand his list.

IS THE NEGOTIATION ONE-SHOT, LONG-TERM, OR REPETITIVE?[3]

In a one-shot negotiation, a transaction occurs, and there are no future ramifications for the parties. Most negotiation situations are not one-shot situations, in which the parties involved come together only at one point in time to conduct business. Furthermore, even if the parties to negotiation change over time, there are often reputation effects that negotiators carry to the table. Because most people negotiate in the context of social networks, most negotiations are long-term in nature because reputation information is carried through social networks. Repetitive negotiations are situations in which negotiators must renegotiate terms on some regular basis (e.g., unions and their management). In long-term and repetitive negotiations, parties must consider how their relationship evolves and how trust is maintained over time. This topic is so important that we devote a special chapter to trust and relationships (chapter 6).

DO THE NEGOTIATIONS INVOLVE SCARCE RESOURCES, IDEOLOGIES, OR BOTH?

There are two major types of conflict: consensus conflict and scarce resource competition (Aubert 1963; Druckman and Zechmeister 1973: Kelley and Thibaut 1969; Thompson and Gonzalez 1997). **Consensus conflict** occurs when one person's opinions, ideas, or beliefs are incompatible with those of another, and the two seek to reach an agreement of opinion. For example, jurors' beliefs may differ about whether a defendant is innocent or guilty; two managers may disagree about whether someone has project-management skills; two people may argue over whether guns should be controlled. Consensus conflict is about ideology and fundamental beliefs, and as you might imagine, is difficult to resolve because it involves values and emotions. **Scarce resource competition** exists when people are in competition for limited resources. For example, when business partners are in conflict concerning how to divide responsibilities and profits, each may feel he or she deserves more than the other feels is appropriate. Many conflict situations involve not only scarce resources but ideologies. For example, the Israeli-Palestinian conflict involves the allocation of land (a scarce resource) but stems from fundamentally different ideologies.

IS THE NEGOTIATION ONE OF NECESSITY OR OPPORTUNITY?

In many cases, we must negotiate to meet our needs; in other situations, negotiations are more of a luxury or opportunity. As an example, consider a couple selling their house because they have been transferred to a different location. They must negotiate a contract on their house. Even if they have an attractive BATNA, they eventually must negotiate with someone to achieve their needs. In contrast, a person who is interested in enhancing her salary and benefits might seek out a negotiation to improve her employment situation. There is no pressing need to negotiate; rather, negotiation is sought out for opportunistic reasons. As another example, some people prefer to negotiate car prices; others do not. AutoNation USA differs from a typical dealership where

---

[3]Raiffa, H. (1982). *The Art and Science of Negotiation.* Cambridge, MA: Belknap.

negotiating on price is allowed. At AutoNation, all cars come with a prominent price tag attached, and there is no negotiation: Executives call it a "low" and "fair" price, but admit that a tough, persistent negotiator might find a cheaper price elsewhere (Nauman 1999).

Many people avoid negotiations of opportunity because they feel that they lack skills. For example, Mr. G. Klair, a customer service manager for Fry Electronics in Stanford, California, says, "you feel like a piece of meat when you walk into a dealership" (Eldridge 1998, L08). So when he bought his last two cars, he went to Stevens Creek Honda in San Jose, a no-haggle, one-price dealership. Mr. Klair admits that he could have found a better price on a Honda Accord at another dealer, but he does not care. He wants to buy his car like he buys his clothes and appliances—find it, and then pay what is on the price tag. Thus, many people find that negotiations of opportunity are uncomfortable and pass on them. However, this may, in the end, benefit the dealer and not the customer. The average new-car dealer earned $70 in net profit per new vehicle sold in 1997, according to the National Automobile Dealers Association. One-price dealers earned an average net profit of $250 per new vehicle sold, according to Mark Rikess, a dealer consultant specializing in one-price selling. Perhaps this is why William Lazarus likes to negotiate such opportunities: "I read *Money Magazine,* and I got a fax from *Consumer Reports* with the invoice price of the car. I had a good idea of what I was willing to pay" (Eldridge 1998, L08). (See Sidebar 2–2 for some consumer-oriented Web sites that can help car buyers.)

SIDEBAR 2–2. CONSUMER-ORIENTED WEB SITES TO HELP CAR BUYERS GET PREPARED

www.thecarconnection.com: Has some of the best up-to-date information and reviews, analyses, and columns from auto-industry experts.

www.theautochannel.com: This Web site has links to every automaker's Web site, daily automotive news, lease help, and chat rooms.

www.kbb.com: The Kelley Blue Book Web site can give you a good idea of what your trade-in is worth in your area.

www.edmunds.com: This Web site not only gives you the dealer's invoice, but the hold-back allowance, a profit that is built into the invoice cost that the manufacturer gives back to the deal, usually every quarter. It usually runs about 3 percent of the suggested retail price. The site also has rebates and incentive plans.

(Eldridge 1998)

IS THE NEGOTIATION AN EXCHANGE OR DISPUTE SITUATION?

Many negotiations are such that parties come together to attempt to exchange resources. In the classic example, a buyer sees greater value in a seller's goods than the seller wants for them, and an exchange takes place (money is paid for goods or services). In other situations, negotiations take place because a claim has been made by one party and has been rejected by the other party. This is known as a **dispute situa-**

tion (Ury, Brett, and Goldberg 1988). For example, a contractor may claim that a builder supplied faulty parts. The builder rejects this claim, and the two of them are in dispute. The difference between exchanges and disputes concerns the alternatives to mutual settlement. In an exchange situation, parties simply resort to their BATNAs; in a classic dispute situation, they often go to court, and a civil case ensues.

ARE THERE LINKAGE EFFECTS?[4]

Linkage effects refer to the fact that some negotiations affect other negotiations. Probably the most obvious example is in the case of law and setting precedent. Resolutions in one situation have implications for other situations. Often there will be direct linkages, such as when a multinational firm has operations in several countries, and a decision made in one country will carry over to other countries. Sometimes, there are indirect linkage effects, such as when a decision made at the negotiation table affects some interest group in a fashion that no one anticipates fully. For example, when the World Trade Organization met in Seattle during December 1999, hardly anyone predicted that the meetings would be called to a virtual halt by citizen protesters. Over 600 protestors who took to the streets to demonstrate against free trade were arrested. John J. Sweeney, the AFL-CIO's president, told the Clinton administration that no deal was better than a bad deal, which led to the failure to realize linkage effects and set up a study group within the trade organization to make recommendations on labor rights.

IS AGREEMENT REQUIRED?[5]

In many negotiation situations, reaching agreement is a matter of preference. For example, in a salary negotiation, a person might be willing to walk away from an offer from one company and either stay with their current company, start their own company, or delay negotiations indefinitely. However, in other situations, reaching agreement is not only the only course of action—it is required. For example, on August 17, 1981, when over 85 percent of the 17,500 air traffic controllers went on strike for better working conditions and improved wages, then-president Ronald Reagan forced the controllers to return back to work, or the government would assume that the striking controllers had quit. By the end of that week, over 5,000 Professional Air Traffic Controllers Organization (PATCO) members received dismissal notices from the FAA. Reagan stated that Congress had passed a law in 1947 forbidding strikes by government employees, including a nonstrike oath that each air controller must sign upon hiring.

IS IT LEGAL TO NEGOTIATE?

In the United States, it is illegal to negotiate the selling of human organs: In September 1999, the online auction house eBay had to retract a seller's posted auction for a human kidney (Harmon 1999). The bidding went up to $5.7 million before eBay called off the auction. However, in the Philippines, it is currently legal to sell kidneys, despite ongoing debate about the issue (see Sidebar 2–3).

---

[4]Raiffa (1982)
[5]Raiffa (1982)

> ## SIDEBAR 2–3. IS IT LEGAL TO NEGOTIATE?
> Consider the desperation that must have lead Romeo Roga, 36, of the Philippines to do what he did. Romeo's one-year-old son was sick with measles, and Roga needed cash to pay medical bills. He earned $1.25 a day carrying sacks of rice at the harbor—not enough to support his family of five children. Roga's stepfather told him he could earn $2,125 by selling his kidney. Said Roga, "I was forced to do it. It was a matter of survival" (Baguioro 1999, 50). The Roman Catholic Church denounces the business as unethical and exploitative. However, kidney patients like Jhoanne Reyes are willing to pay any price just to live. Doctors are seeking a middle ground, with the objective of preventing people from commercializing organ donation. Roga's kidney did not get him much. His son died, and the money has since run out. He tires easily with only one kidney. Says Roga, "At least I've helped someone" (Baguioro 1999, 50).

Sometimes, there are no specific laws about what can or cannot be negotiated; rather, there are strong cultural norms that are highly situation-specific. For example, most people in the United States do not negotiate the price of fruit at major grocery stores, but they do it freely in farmer's markets, such as the Pike Place Market in Seattle, Washington. But farmer's markets are not the only place to haggle. For example, Bill Meyer, 41-year-old father of six, rarely pays full price for anything: In grocery stores, he tries to get bargains on food that is going to spoil if it is not sold. In thrift stores, he gathers up a pile of stuff and offers a single price for it. At pizza parlors, he asks for pizzas that have not been picked up and gets them for $3 each (Trappen 1996). Most home electronic stores will negotiate, as well as stores that sell large, durable goods.

IS RATIFICATION REQUIRED?[6]

Ratification refers to whether a party to the negotiation table must have any contract approved of by some other body or group. For example, a corporate recruiter may need to have the salary and employment packages offered to recruits ratified by the company's human resources group or the CEO. In some circumstances, negotiators may tell the other side that ratification is required when it is not.

ARE THERE TIME CONSTRAINTS OR OTHER TIME-RELATED COSTS?[7]

Virtually all negotiations have some time-related costs. Although the negotiator who desperately needs an agreement, or for whom the passage of time is extremely costly, is likely to be at a disadvantage (Stuhlmacher, Gillespie, and Champagne 1998), more time pressure is not necessarily bad. It is important to distinguish time pressure that arises from a final deadline from time pressure that arises from time-related costs to one party or the other (Moore 2000). A final deadline impinges on all the parties to a negotiation if the passage of the final deadline means that all parties are left with an impasse.

Setting a final deadline on the negotiations can be helpful, especially if the passage of time is particularly costly to you (Moore 2000). This was exactly the strategy suc-

---

[6]Raiffa (1982)
[7]Raiffa (1982)

cessfully used to reach an agreement in the National Basketball Association strike of 1998 to 1999. The owners set a final deadline and threatened to walk out if they could not come to agreement with the players by January 5, 1999. The two sides came to agreement on January 4 on terms that dramatically favored the owners.

ARE CONTRACTS OFFICIAL OR UNOFFICIAL?

Many negotiation situations, such as the purchase of a house or a job offer, involve official contracts that legally obligate parties to follow through with stated promises. However, in several negotiation situations of equal or greater importance, negotiations are conducted through a handshake or other forms of informal agreements. There is considerable cultural variation in terms of what social symbols constitute agreement (handshakes versus taking tea together) and in terms of what situations are treated officially or unofficially. Considerable awkwardness can result when one party approaches the situation from a formal stance and the other treats it informally. Also, considerable ill will can result when implicit contracts are broken. (We take up the topic of broken trust in chapter 6.)

WHERE DO THE NEGOTIATIONS TAKE PLACE?

Common wisdom has it that it is to one's advantage to negotiate on one's own turf, as opposed to that of the other side. So important is this perception that great preparation and expense are undertaken to find neutral ground for important negotiations. For example, for the summit between ex-president Ronald Reagan and Soviet leader Mikhail Gorbachev, the site was carefully selected. The two met at the Chateau Fleur d'Eau in Geneva, Switzerland. Similarly, the multiparty Irish talks were stalled in 1991 when conflict broke out concerning where the next set of talks would be held. The Unionists, who agreed to talk directly to Irish government ministers about the future of Northern Ireland, were anxious to avoid any impression of going "cap in hand" to Dublin, and therefore wanted the talks held in London, the capital to which they were determined to remain connected. In contrast, the Social Democratic and Labor Party, which represented the majority of Catholic moderates in the province, preferred that the talks be held in Dublin, the capital to which they felt a strong allegiance (Lewthwaite 1991).

ARE NEGOTIATIONS PUBLIC OR PRIVATE?[8]

In many areas, the negotiation dance takes place under the public eye. In other negotiation situations, negotiations occur privately. For example, Kelman's (1991) work in resolving the Israeli-Palestinian negotiations occurred under strict privacy. As Kelman notes, privacy was instrumental for progress between parties:

> The discussions are completely private and confidential. There is no audience, no publicity, and no record, and one of the central ground rules specifies that statements made in the course of a workshop cannot be cited with attribution outside the workshop setting. These and other features of the workshop are designed to enable and encourage workshop participants to engage in a type of communication that is usually not available to parties involved in an intense conflict relationship. (p. 214)

---

[8]Raiffa (1982)

In contrast, one of the unique aspects of sports negotiations is that they take place in a fishbowl atmosphere, with fans and the media observing every move at the bargaining table (Staudohar, 1999). Staudohar notes the risk that this kind of attention can lead to a media circus, with owners and players projecting their opinions on issues and events:

> The dickering back and forth makes for entertaining theater, but is a hindrance to the rational settlement of differences. It is customary, therefore, for both owners and players to be advised by their leaders to hold their tongues. NBA owners were made subject to fines of $1 million by the league for popping off in the media.

IS THIRD-PARTY INVENTION A POSSIBILITY?[9]

In many negotiation situations, it is commonplace (and even expected) to have third-party intervention. Most commonly, third-party intervention takes the form of mediation or arbitration. However, in other areas, it is unheard of to have third-party intervention. The mere presence of third parties may serve to escalate negotiation situations, who egocentrically believe that third parties will favor their own position. In other situations, it is less common (and perhaps a sign of personal failure) to involve third parties. Third-party intervention is so important that we devote appendix 3 to it in this book.

ARE THERE CONVENTIONS IN TERMS OF THE PROCESS OF NEGOTIATION (SUCH AS WHO MAKES THE FIRST OFFER)?

In many negotiations, people have complete freedom of process. However, in other negotiations, there are strong conventions and norms in terms of how the process of negotiation unfolds. For example, when people buy or sell houses in the United States, the first offer is typically made by a prospective buyer, and all offers are formalized in writing. However, there are marked differences across the country, with some home negotiations being conducted via spoken word and some via official contract.

DO NEGOTIATIONS INVOLVE MORE THAN ONE OFFER?

In some situations, it is typical to go back and forth several times before a mutually agreeable deal is struck. In other situations, this is considered unacceptable. In the real-estate world, for example, buyers and sellers expect to negotiate. These same people, however, would not dream of negotiating in Nordstrom's.

As another example, many employers now expect that job candidates will attempt to negotiate what is initially offered to them, but for many, extending the haggling is not acceptable. Carl Kusmode, found of the Tiburon Group, an Internet recruiter in Chicago, said he withdrew an offer to a database administrator who kept upping his price. "It became insulting," Kusmode said (Clark 1999). Thus, a negotiation should go one or two rounds, not 10. Negotiation norms, however, vary from industry to industry. As an example, consider what happened to Jay Kaplan, real estate entrepreneur (Kaplan 1994). He had been traveling through the southeastern United States for eight consecutive days, he had met with five different owners trying to purchase apartment

---

[9]Raiffa (1982)

buildings and shopping centers. Each meeting was a marathon session, with offers and counteroffers, each lasting until dawn before an agreement was made. By the eighth day, with one meeting left, Kaplan was tired and decided to use a single-offer strategy. After asking for some aspirin and putting on his most exhausted face, Kaplan said to the other party: "You're asking \$4.3 million for your property. I want to buy it for \$3.7 million. Let's save ourselves the trouble for a long negotiation. I'm going to make you only one offer. It will be my best shot, and it will be a fair one. If you're a reasonable man, I'm sure you'll accept it" (Kaplan 1994, E6). The strategy backfired. Kaplan then offered the other party \$4.025 million, and the other party rejected it. They haggled for four hours until they agreed on \$4.275. The opponent later told Kaplan that there was no way he was going to accept the first offer made—no matter what it was.

DO NEGOTIATORS COMMUNICATE EXPLICITLY OR TACITLY?

In a typical buyer-seller negotiation or employment negotiation, negotiators communicate explicitly with one another. However, in other situations, communication is not explicit but tacit, and people communicate through their actions. This issue is so important that we devote an entire chapter to it (chapter 11 on social dilemmas).

IS THERE A POWER DIFFERENTIAL BETWEEN PARTIES?

Technically, negotiation occurs between people who are interdependent, meaning that the actions of one party affect those of the other party and vice versa. If one person has complete authority over another and is not affected by the actions of others, then negotiation cannot occur. However, it is often the case that low-power people can affect the outcomes of high-powered others. For example, a CEO has more power than a middle-level manager in the company, but the manager can undoubtedly affect the welfare of the company and the CEO. The presence or absence of a power differential between negotiating parties can strongly affect the nature of negotiations. This topic is so important that we devote an entire chapter to power and influence in this book (chapter 7).

IS PRECEDENT IMPORTANT?

In many negotiation situations, precedent is important, not only in anchoring negotiations on a particular point of reference but defining the range of alternatives. Often the major argument that negotiators must confront when attempting to negotiate for themselves is the other side's statement that he or she must follow precedent. In a sense, the negotiator fears that making a decision in one case will set him or her up for future negotiations. Of course, most precedents allow for quite a great deal of interpretation on the part of the precedent-follower and the person attempting to challenge the precedent. Often times, negotiators will invoke precedent as a way of cutting off negotiations.

CONCLUSION

Effective preparation places the negotiator at a strategic advantage at the bargaining table. We outlined three general areas of preparation: the self, the other party, and the context or situation. In terms of personal preparation, the negotiator who has

Table 2–1: Preparation worksheet for negotiations		
Self-Assessment	*Assessment of the Other Party*	*Assessment of the Situation*
• What do I want? (Set a target point) • What is my alternative to reaching agreement? (Identify your BATNA) • Determine your reservation point (see Box 2–1) • What focal points could influence me? • Have I ensured that my target point is not influenced by my reservation point? • What are the issues in the negotiation? • What are the alternatives for the issues in the negotiation? • Have I identified different packages of multiple-issue offers? • Have I assessed my risk propensity? • What is my level of confidence?	• Who are the other parties? • Are there parties who are likely to not be at the table? • Are the parties monolitic? • What issues are relevant to the other party? • What are the other party's interests? • What are the other party's alternatives for each issue? • What is the other party's position? • What is the other negotiator's BATNA?	• Is the negotiation one-shot, long-term, or repetitive? • Do the negotiations involve scarce resources, conflict of ideologies, or both? • Is the negotiation of necessity or opportunity? • Is the negotiation an exchange or dispute situation? • Are there linkage effects? • Is agreement required? • Is it legal to negotiate? • Is ratification required? • Are there time constraints or other time-related costs? • Are contracts official or unofficial? • Where do negotiations take place? • Are negotiations public or private? • Is third-party intervention a possibility? • Are there conventions in terms of the process of negotiation? • Do negotiations involve more than one offer by each party? • Do negotiators communicate explicitly or tacitly? • Is there a power differential among parties? • Is precedent important?

identified her BATNA and set a reservation price and a target point is in a much better position to achieve her objectives. The negotiator who has prepared for negotiation knows when to walk away and how much is reasonable to concede. The negotiator who has adequately researched his opponent's BATNA and interests is less likely to be tricked or confused by the other party. We outlined several issues concerning the negotiation situation that the negotiator should consider prior to commencing negotiations. For your convenience, a summary preparation form is presented in Table 2–1. We suggest the negotiator use it when preparing for negotiations. The next two chapters focus on pie-slicing and pie-expanding strategies in negotiations.

3

DISTRIBUTIVE NEGOTIATION

Slicing the Pie

❧

Lewis Kravitz, an Atlanta executive coach and former outplacement counselor, advises patience and knowing when not to speak in the heat of negotiations. In one instance, he was coaching a young man who had just been sacked by his team. The young man felt desperate and told Kravitz he was willing to take a $2,000 pay cut and accept $28,000 for his next job. Kravitz told the man to be quiet at the bargaining table and let the prospective employer make the first offer. At the man's next job interview, the employer offered him $32,000, stunning the overjoyed job seeker into momentary silence. The employer interpreted the silence as dissatisfaction and upped the offer to $34,000 on the spot. (Lancaster 1998)

The merger of America Online and Time Warner was not exactly a walk in the park. Two major companies—a front-runner in the New Economy and a leader of the Old Economy—were far apart on a lot of issues. The key to success was staying at the table, according to Kenneth Novack, America Online's chief negotiator on the deal: "We kept on dribbling the ball, even when it seemed that there was no air in it" (Lohr and Holson 2000, 20). Another problem: Steve Case's original offer of a 50-50 ownership deal was no longer practical for America Online, given the sharp stock rise. However, his initial offer acted as an anchor point and it was difficult to move away from this anchor. Steve Case's trick in moving away from this anchor was a combination of two things: (1) Re-anchoring Time Warner on a new split, 60-40, and (2) a very patient bargaining style. The result: A 55-45 percent split, making both sides feel like winners. (Lohr and Holson 2000)

In the first example, the young negotiator ended up with a larger slice of the bargaining pie than he ever imagined; however, he did not really know what he was doing. In the second example, the parties knew what they were doing. This chapter is about figuring out how to do as well as you can for yourself in negotiations while preserving the relationship with the other party.

You have analyzed the negotiation situation as best you can. You have thought about your target point and your BATNA in a realistic fashion, developed a reservation point, and have used all available information to assess your opponent's BATNA. Now the time has come for face-to-face negotiation. In this chapter, we will address the first of the two central goals of negotiation: slicing the pie. This chapter will discuss who should make the first offer, how you should respond to an offer made by the other party, the proper amount of concessions to make, and what to do if you are confronting an "old school" negotiator.

The entire process of making an opening offer and then ending up with a mutually agreeable settlement is known as the **negotiation dance** (Raiffa 1982). Unfortunately, most of us have never taken lessons in the negotiation dance or know what to do once we find ourselves on the dance floor. Should we lead? Should we follow? There are a few hard and fast rules of thumb, but there are many choices that the negotiator must make that are not so clear-cut. We wrestle with these in this chapter.

Whereas this chapter deals with slicing the pie, it is important to realize that most negotiations involve a win-win aspect (*expanding* the pie), which we discuss in detail in the next chapter. However, even in win-win negotiations, the pie of resources created by negotiators eventually has to be sliced, and it is pie slicing that we discuss first because it tends to be more straightforward and intuitive. First, we discuss the bargaining zone, then we discuss 10 ways to increase your slice of the pie. Finally, we take up the topic of fairness as it applies to slicing the pie.

THE BARGAINING ZONE AND THE NEGOTIATION DANCE

Typically, negotiators' target points do not positively overlap. For example, in most situations, the seller wants more for the product or service she is selling than the buyer is willing to pay her. However, it is often (but not always) the case that negotiators' reservation points *do* overlap, and reaching mutual settlement is profitable for both parties. However, the challenge of negotiation is to reach a settlement that is most favorable to oneself and does not give up too much of the bargaining zone. The **bargaining zone,** or **settlement zone,** represents the region between each party's reservation point. We may reliably predict that the final settlement of a negotiation will fall somewhere above the seller's reservation point and below the buyer's reservation point (Raiffa 1982). In our discussion of the bargaining zone, we use a buyer-seller example for simplicity. However, the same analysis applies to other negotiations that do not involve buyers and sellers.

There are some important principles that every negotiator should know when it comes to slicing the pie. First, it is important to realize that the bargaining zone can be either positive or negative (see Figs. 3–1A and 3–1B).

In a positive bargaining zone, negotiators' reservation points overlap. This means that mutual agreement is better than resorting to BATNAs. For example, consider the bargaining zone in Figure 3–1A. The seller's reservation point is $11; the buyer's reservation point is $14. The most the buyer is willing to pay is $3 greater than the very least the seller is willing to accept. The bargaining zone is between $11 and $14, or $3; if the negotiators reach agreement, the settlement will be somewhere between $11 and $14. If the parties fail to reach agreement in this situation, the outcome is an impasse and is **suboptimal,** because negotiators leave money on the table and are worse off not reaching agreement than reaching agreement.

In some cases, the bargaining zone may be nonexistent or even negative. However, the parties may not realize this, and they may spend fruitless hours trying to reach an agreement. This can be costly for negotiators, and during the time in which they are nego-

FIGURE 3–1A Positive Bargaining Zone

FIGURE 3–1B Negative Bargaining Zone

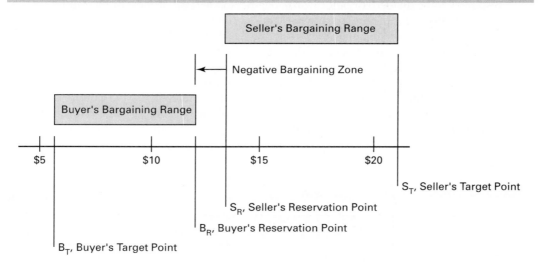

tiating, their opportunities may be worsening. For example, consider the bargaining zone in Figure 3–1B, in which the seller's reservation point is $14 and the buyer's reservation point is $12. The most the buyer is willing to pay is $2 less than the seller is willing to accept at a minimum. This is a **negative bargaining zone;** there is no positive overlap between the parties' reservation points. In this situation, negotiators should exercise their best alternatives to agreement. Because negotiations are costly to prolong, it is in both parties' interests to determine whether there is a positive bargaining zone. If there is not, the parties should not waste time negotiating; instead, they should pursue other alternatives.

BARGAINING SURPLUS

So far, we have made the point that mutual settlement is possible when parties' reservation points overlap and is impossible when parties' reservation points do not overlap. **Bargaining surplus** is the amount of overlap produced by parties' reservation points. It is a measure of the size of the bargaining zone (what we refer to in this chapter as "the pie"). The bargaining surplus is a measure of the value that a negotiated agreement offers to both parties over the alternative of not reaching settlement. Sometimes this is very large; other times it is very small. Skilled negotiators know how to reach agreements when the bargaining zone is small.

NEGOTIATOR'S SURPLUS

We have noted that negotiated outcomes will fall somewhere in the bargaining zone. But what determines *where* in this range the settlement will occur? Obviously, each party would like the settlement to be as close to the other party's reservation point as possible, thereby maximizing his or her slice of the pie. In our example in Figure 3–1A, the seller would prefer to sell close to $14; the buyer would prefer to buy close to $11. The best possible outcome for the negotiator is one that just meets the other party's reservation point, thereby inducing the other party to settle, but allows the focal negotiator to reap as much gain as possible. This provides the focal negotiator with the greatest possible share of the resources to be divided. In other words, one person gets all or most of the pie.

The positive difference between the settlement outcome and the negotiator's reservation point is the **negotiator's surplus** (see Fig. 3–2). Notice that the total surplus of the two negotiators adds up to the size of the bargaining zone. Negotiators want to maximize their surplus in negotiations; surplus represents resources in excess of what is possible for negotiators to attain in the absence of negotiated agreement.

The fact that negotiated settlements fall somewhere in the bargaining zone and that each negotiator tries to maximize his share of the bargaining surplus illustrates the **mixed-motive** nature of negotiation. That is, negotiators are motivated to cooperate

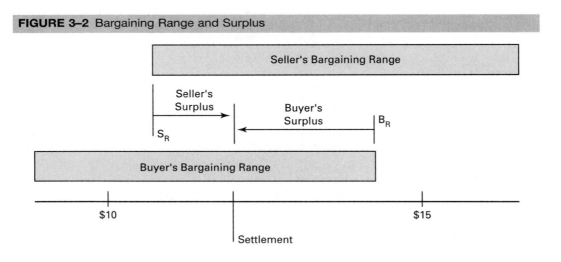

FIGURE 3–2 Bargaining Range and Surplus

with the other party to ensure that settlement is reached if there is a positive bargaining zone, but they are motivated to compete with one another to claim as much of the bargaining surplus as they can.

PIE-SLICING STRATEGIES

The most frequently asked question about negotiation is, "How can I achieve the most of the bargaining surplus for myself?" The simple answer to this question is to determine the other party's reservation point and offer him or her the option that represents this reservation point. For example, if we are a potential home buyer and we discern that the seller's reservation point is $251,000, that is an ideal offer to make, assuming it well exceeds our reservation point. However, this is easier said than done. How would we get this information? Most negotiators will never reveal their reservation point, but it may emerge unintentionally. Raiffa (1982) cautions negotiators not to reveal their reservation points and cites a humorous story wherein one party opens with a direct request for information about his opponent's reservation price: "Tell me the bare minimum you would accept from us, and I'll see if I can throw in something extra." The opponent, not to be taken in, quips, "Why don't you tell us the very maximum that you are willing to pay, and we'll see if we can shave off a bit?" (p. 40). This example illustrates the essence of negotiation: How do people make sure they reach agreement if the bargaining zone is positive but claim as much of the pie as possible?

There is another problem as well. Even if someone reveals his reservation point, there is no way to verify that he is telling the truth. When the other party tells us her reservation point, we are faced with the dilemma of determining whether the information is to be trusted. The negotiator is always at an information deficit because the other party's reservation point is usually not verifiable—it includes subjective factors—whereas a BATNA is based on objective factors and can therefore be verifiable.

Given that "private" information about reservation points is inherently unverifiable, there would seem to be little point to negotiation. After all, if you can never tell if the other person is telling the truth, then communication would seem fruitless. Even so, we know that people negotiate all the time in the absence of such information. When people negotiate, they are constantly making judgments about the other person's reservation point and interests.

There may be some conditions that allow negotiators to be more confident about the other party's reservation point. For example, if the person with whom we are negotiating shows us a signed letter from a competitor company containing a high salary offer, we can be fairly confident about the candidate's reservation point. Similarly, if a person says something that is not in her interest, we may have more reason to believe it. For example, if a seller tells us she does not have another buyer and is under pressure to sell, we might believe her because this statement is not in her interest. This leads to an important cautionary note: It is not necessarily in your best interest to misrepresent your reservation point because you risk the possibility of disagreement. For example, imagine that you are trying to sell your used CD player because you have been given another, nicer model as a gift. You would be willing to accept $100 for the used model (your reservation point, based upon a pawnbroker's offer), but you would ideally like to get $200 (your target point). You place an ad, and a potential buyer calls offering to pay $110. If you tell the caller that you have an offer of $120, you risk the possibility that the potential buyer will say "take it." It might be in your interest not to let potential buyers believe that your reservation price is $200 (see Farrell and Gibbons 1989).

There are two major problems with slicing the pie. First, negotiators should be willing to settle for outcomes that exceed their reservation point and reject offers that are worse than their reservation point. This seems infinitely rational; however, as noted earlier, people frequently settle for outcomes worse than their BATNA and often reject offers that are better than their BATNA. As a case in point, most strikes are eventually settled on terms that could have been reached earlier, without parties incurring the costs that the strike imposes (Keenan and Wilson 1993; Roth 1993). The key question is why this seemingly irrational behavior occurs. The problem can usually be traced to either cognitive or emotional biases. We will elaborate on some of these biases later in this chapter.

If negotiators follow the following 10 strategies, they can substantially increase the probability that they will obtain a favorable slice of the pie. Although there are no guarantees, the following strategies are the best advice that we can offer for enhancing one's ability to garner more resources for one's self.

STRATEGY 1: KNOW YOUR BATNA

It is truly surprising how many negotiators do not think about their BATNA prior to entering negotiation. It is equally surprising how many negotiators inadvertently reveal their BATNA during negotiation. Negotiators also lie about their BATNA during negotiation. We believe that all three of these behaviors should be avoided in negotiation. First, we strictly caution negotiators against entering into a negotiation without knowing exactly what their BATNA is. Second, we strongly prescribe that negotiators spend a considerable amount of time attempting to improve upon their BATNA before entering into a negotiation. Third, we caution that unless negotiators are willing to settle for terms that are identical to their BATNA, they should not reveal their BATNA during the course of negotiation, even in the friendliest of situations. Finally, we do not believe that negotiators should lie about their BATNA during negotiation. Lying is problematic for ethical reasons (which we will discuss in chapter 7) but also can pose problems in a straightforward, economic sense. For example, if you lie about your BATNA, you reduce the size of the bargaining zone. This means that negotiations in which there is a positive bargaining zone may end in impasse because your lie has falsely indicated a negative bargaining zone. It will be difficult for you to save face in such a situation, so we strongly advise against lying about your BATNA—and, at the same time, you should not reveal your BATNA to the other party. As will become evident, revealing information about one's BATNA or reservation point is not a pie-expanding strategy; it is a pie-slicing strategy, and as a pie-slicing strategy it has the effect of reducing a negotiator's power in a negotiation.

STRATEGY 2: RESEARCH THE OTHER PARTY'S BATNA

Whereas determining the other party's BATNA may be easier said than done, a dramatically high number of negotiators fail to research the opponent's BATNA. There are a variety of ways in which negotiators can garner information that may reveal something about the opponent's alternatives (especially with the Internet opening up new possibilities—a topic we discuss in chapter 12).

However, most negotiators fail to gather this information and put themselves in a less advantageous bargaining position. Negotiators might also want to refer to the lie-detection strategies discussed in appendix 2 as methods by which to determine the other party's BATNA.

But be careful when the other party discloses! When a negotiation opponent discloses her BATNA at the outset of the negotiation, negotiators actually make less demanding offers, disclose more truthful information, and settle for less profit than when the opponent does not disclose her BATNA (Paese and Gilin 2000). This points to the powerful effect that reciprocity has on our own behavior.

STRATEGY 3: SET HIGH ASPIRATIONS

Aspirations or target points determine the "final demands" made by negotiators, more so than do BATNAs (Thompson 1995a). Stated simply, negotiators who set high aspirations end up with more of the pie than those who set lower aspirations. For example, negotiators who have unattractive reservation points and high aspirations actually demand more from their opponents than do negotiators with attractive BATNAs and low aspirations. Thus, it pays to set your aspirations high during a negotiation. Setting specific, challenging, and difficult goals results in greater profit than does setting easy or nonspecific goals (Huber and Neale 1986, 1987; Neale, Northcraft, and Earley 1990; Thompson 1995a). In many cases, nonspecific or easy goals lead to compromise agreements, which (as we will argue in the next chapter) are suboptimal. High aspirations exert a self-regulating effect on negotiation behavior: Negotiators who are assigned easy goals tend to set harder new goals; however, in spite of adjustments, their new goals are significantly easier than the goals chosen by the difficult-goal negotiators. Thus, it is to a negotiator's advantage to set a high, somewhat difficult, aspiration point early in the negotiation.

When a negotiator focuses on her target point during negotiation, this increases the value of the eventual outcome she receives (Galinsky, Mussweiler, and Medvec 1999). Similarly, negotiators who focus on "ideals" rather than "oughts" do better in terms of slicing the pie (Galinsky and Mussweiler 2000). However, the negotiator does not *feel* as satisfied as the negotiator who focuses on his reservation point or BATNA. Thus, focusing on targets leads people to do very well in negotiations, but feel worse; focusing on reservation points leads people to do worse, but feel better. This demonstrates that gut feeling or intuition can be misleading. Is there any way that the successful but unhappy negotiator can feel better? If negotiators think about their BATNA after the negotiation, they feel psychologically better (Galinsky, Mussweiler, and Medvec 1999).

We strongly advise negotiators to avoid the **winner's curse,** in which your first offer is immediately accepted by the other side because it is too generous. This signals that you did not set your aspirations high enough. Furthermore, we caution negotiators to avoid a strategy known as **boulwarism.** Boulwarism is named after Lemuel Boulware, former CEO of General Electric, who believed in making one's first offer one's final offer. As you might expect, this strategy is not very effective, and it often engenders hostility from the other side.

Another piece of advice: Do not become psychologically "anchored" by your reservation point. Stated simply: Do not let your reservation point drive your aspiration point; the two should be separate. Many negotiators who have learned to assess their BATNA and set an appropriate reservation point fail to think about their aspiration, or target, point. Consequently, the reservation point acts as a psychological anchor for their aspiration point and, in most cases, people make insufficient adjustments—they do not set their target high enough. We discourage negotiators from using any kind of multiplier or function based on their reservation point to determine their target because there is no logical reason to do so.

STRATEGY 4: MAKE THE FIRST OFFER

Folklore dictates that negotiators should let the opponent make the first offer. In fact, negotiators are at a pie-slicing advantage if they *do* make the first offer (Galinsky and Mussweiler 2000). In short, first offers act as an anchor point (Galinsky and Mussweiler 2000). First offers correlate at least .85 with final outcomes, suggesting they are *very* important (Galinsky and Mussweiler 2000)! However, there are a number of factors to think about when making an opening offer. First and foremost, your opening offer should not give away any part of the bargaining zone; otherwise, you will be at a pie-slicing disadvantage. Second, many people worry that they will "insult" the other party if they open too high (if they are selling) or too low (if they are buying). However, the fear of insulting the other party and souring the negotiations is more apparent than real. Managers tell us that when they are faced with an extreme opening offer from the other party, they are not insulted; instead, they prepare to make concessions.

There are distinct advantages associated with making the first offer in a negotiation. The first offer that falls within the bargaining zone can serve as a powerful focal point in negotiation. Recall, in the previous chapter, the example of the "wheel of fortune" and people's estimates of African nations within the United Nations. That was a case of insufficient adjustment from an arbitrary anchor. Making the first offer protects negotiators from falling prey to a similar anchoring effect when they hear the opponent's offer. Ideally, a negotiator's first offer acts as an anchor for the opponent's counteroffer.

One more thing about making the first offer: If you have made an offer to an opponent, then you should expect to receive some sort of counteroffer or response. Once you put an offer on the table, be patient. It is time for your opponent to respond. In certain situations, patience and silence can be important negotiation tools. Do not interpret silence on the other person's part to be a rejection of your offer. Many negotiators, especially those with a more urgent sense of time, tend to make premature concessions before their opponent has even had a chance to respond to their initial offer. Always wait to hear a response before making a further concession.

STRATEGY 5: COUNTEROFFER IMMEDIATELY

If your opponent has made you an offer, then the ball is in your court. It is wise to make a counteroffer in a timely fashion. This does two things. First, it diminishes the prominence of the opponent's initial offer as an anchor point in the negotiation. Second, it signals a willingness to negotiate. It also helps to think about the opponent's BATNA when she makes you an offer (Galinsky and Mussweiler 2000). Above all, do not adjust your BATNA based upon your opponent's offer, and do not adjust your target. It is extremely important not to be "anchored" by the opponent's offer. The final outcome of a negotiation is often the midpoint between the first two offers on the table that are within the bargaining zone (Raiffa 1982). Thus, if your first offer is within the bargaining zone, you have already given up precious bargaining ground. An effective counteroffer moves the focus away from the other party's offer as a reference point.

STRATEGY 6: AVOID STATING RANGES

As noted in chapter 2, we do not advise stating ranges. For example, employers often ask prospective employees to state a range in salary negotiations. Do not fall victim to this bargaining ploy. By stating a range, you are giving up precious bargaining ground. Your opponent will consider the lower end of the range as your target and negotiate down from there. A far better strategy is to respond to your opponent's request for a range by giving him or her several offers that would all be equally satisfying to you. This is an important point, and one to which we will return in the next chapter.

STRATEGY 7: MAKE BILATERAL (NOT UNILATERAL) CONCESSIONS

Negotiators who make fewer and smaller concessions are more effective in terms of maximizing their slice of the pie, compared to those who make larger and more frequent concessions (Siegel and Fouraker 1960; Yukl 1974). First offers are "openers." It is rare (but not impossible) for a first offer to be accepted. Most negotiators expect to make concessions during negotiation. (One exception is the bargaining style known as boulwarism, which we discussed before.) What is the best way to make such concessions so as to maximize your share of the bargaining zone? Two things to consider when formulating counteroffers and concessions are the **pattern of concessions** and the **degree of concessions.**

Pattern of Concessions
It is almost a universal norm that concessions take place in a *quid pro quo* fashion, meaning that negotiators expect a back-and-forth exchange of concessions between parties. People expect that concessions will be responded to with concessions in kind. However, negotiators *should not* offer more than a single concession at a time to an opponent. Wait for a concession on the opponent's part before making further concessions. An exception to this would be a situation in which you feel that the opponent's offer is truly near her reservation point.

Degree of Concessions
Even though negotiators may exchange concessions in a back-and-forth method, this does not say anything about the degree of concessions made by each party. Thus, a second consideration when making concessions is to determine how much to concede. The usual measure of a concession is the amount reduced or added (depending upon whether one is a seller or buyer) from one's previous concession. It is unwise to make consistently greater concessions than one's opponent.

The **graduated reduction in tension (GRIT) model** (Osgood 1962) is a method whereby parties avoid escalating conflict and reach mutual settlement. The GRIT model, based upon the reciprocity principle, calls for one party to make a concession and to invite the other party to reciprocate by making a concession. The concession offered by the first party is significant, but not so much that the offering party is tremendously disadvantaged if the opponent fails to reciprocate.

Hilty and Carnevale (1993) examined the degree of concessions made by negotiators over different points in the negotiation process (e.g., early on versus later). They compared black hat/white hat (BH/WH) negotiators with white hat/black hat (WH/BH) negotiators. BH/WH negotiators began with a tough stance, made few early concessions, and later made larger concessions. WH/BH negotiators did the opposite: They began with generous concessions and then became tough and unyielding. The BH/WH concession strategy proved to be more effective than the WH/BH strategy in eliciting concessions from an opponent.

STRATEGY 8: USE AN OBJECTIVE-APPEARING RATIONALE TO SUPPORT YOUR OFFERS

The way in which an offer is presented dramatically affects the course of negotiations. Ideally, present a rationale that appears to be objective and invites the opponent to buy into your rationale. If your proposals are labeled as "fair," "even splits," or "compromises," they carry more impact. The next section of this chapter takes up the topic of fairness in detail.

STRATEGY 9: APPEAL TO NORMS OF FAIRNESS

Fairness is a "hot button" in negotiation because most negotiators view themselves as fair, or wanting to be fair. The ideal pie-slicing strategy is to determine which norms of fairness would be appropriate for the situation and then use these norms to argue for your own target point. As a negotiator, you should be aware that fairness is subjective and therefore egocentric, meaning that a variety of norms of fairness exist, and negotiators usually focus on norms of fairness that serve their own interests (Loewenstein, Thompson, and Bazerman 1989). Thus, negotiators should realize that fairness is an arbitrary concept that can be used as a bargaining strategy with an opponent; however, the negotiator should simultaneously be prepared to counterargue when an opponent presents a fairness argument that does not serve her own interests.

STRATEGY 10: DO NOT FALL FOR THE "EVEN SPLIT" PLOY

A common focal point in negotiation is the "even split." In many negotiation situations, negotiators' offers to not overlap, such as in car- and house-buying negotiations. Inevitably, one person has the bright idea of "splitting the difference." The concept of the even split has an appealing, almost altruistic flavor to it. To many of us, it seems unreasonable to refuse to compromise or meet the other person halfway. So what is the problem with even splits? The problem is that they are based on arbitrarily arrived-at values. Consider a car-buying situation. Suppose you initially offered $23,000 for the car, then $24,000, and then, finally, $24,500. Suppose the salesperson initially requested $25,200, then reduced it to $25,000, and then to $24,600. The salesperson then suggests that you split the difference at $24,550, arguing that an even split of the difference would be "fair." However, the pattern of offers up until that point were not "even" in any sense. You made concessions of $1,500; the salesperson made concessions of $600.

Further, even if the concessions were of equal magnitude, this is no guarantee that the middle value is a "fair" value. It behooves a negotiator to begin with a high starting value and make small concessions. Often, the person who suggests the even split is in an advantageous position. Before accepting or proposing an even split, make sure the anchors are favorable to you.

THE MOST COMMONLY ASKED QUESTIONS

SHOULD I REVEAL MY RESERVATION POINT?

Revealing your reservation point is generally not a good strategy unless your reservation point is very good and you suspect that the bargaining zone is very narrow. If you reveal your reservation price, be prepared for the other party to offer you your reservation price.

As we saw earlier, the most valuable piece of information you can have about your opponent is his or her reservation point. This allows you to make your opponent an offer that barely exceeds his or her reservation point and claim all of the bargaining surplus for yourself. However, your opponent is no dummy and is not likely to reveal his reservation point. By the same token, if you reveal your reservation point, there is little to stop your opponent from claiming all of the surplus for himself.

Some negotiators reveal their reservation point to demonstrate that they are bargaining in good faith and trust the other party. These negotiators rely on their opponent's good will and trust their opponent not to take undue advantage of this information. This is a flawed and ineffective strategy. Negotiation is not an issue of trust; it is an issue of strategy. The purpose of negotiation is to maximize your surplus, so why create a conflict of interest with the other party by "trusting" them with your reservation point?

In some cases, negotiators are seduced into revealing their reservation point when their opponent assumes that they do not have a good BATNA. Consider, for example, Lucille, the manager of a small advertising company that books events and shows. One of her hard-driving clients was trying to talk Lucille down from a quote for a children's show to be held at a major amphitheater. The client challenged Lucille by speculating that she did not have "any real overhead." Outraged, Lucille told the client in detail about where the advertising dollars were spent. After her harangue, the client agreed to pay just a fraction more than the overhead costs and "not a penny more." Negotiators, wanting to prove their worth, will offer their reservation price as a defensive tactic. Lucille was tricked by her opponent into revealing her BATNA.

SHOULD I LIE ABOUT MY RESERVATION PRICE?

If negotiators do well for themselves by not revealing their reservation point, perhaps they might do even better by lying, misrepresenting, or exaggerating their reservation point. This is not advisable as a negotiation strategy for several reasons.

First, lying about your reservation point reduces the size of the bargaining zone. This means that negotiations in which the negotiator would prefer to reach an agreement will sometimes end in impasse. Negotiators who lie about their reservation point often find it very difficult to attempt to save face. It has been said that the most common lie in negotiation is "This is my final offer." It is embarrassing to continue negotiating after making such a statement. Do not back yourself into a corner.

There is another problem with lying: It affects your reputation. It is a very small world, and people in the business community develop reputations that quickly spread via electronic mail, telephone, and word of mouth. It is desirable to avoid being labeled as a negotiator who is more bark than bite and who misrepresents himself at the negotiation table. Misrepresenting your reservation price is a poor substitute for preparation and developing strategy.

HOW CAN I TELL WHETHER SOMEONE IS LYING TO ME?

The answer to this question depends on what is being lied about. There are many things to lie about in negotiation. Some lies may be complete falsifications (such as falsifying an inspection report or pretending that another buyer will be calling at any moment with an offer); other lies may be exaggerations (exaggerating the appraisal value of a particular property, exaggerating the attractiveness of one's BATNA). It is more difficult for liars to successfully carry off hard lies (i.e., complete falsifications of information) than to carry off easy lies (exaggerations). Consequently, it is easier for negotiators to detect complete falsifications.

What should you do to maximize the chances of catching a lie in negotiation? It is generally not an effective lie-detection strategy to ask people whether they are lying. Usually, they will say no. So what can you do? There are three steps the negotiator should take to catch someone in a lie. First, the negotiator should *test for consistency* in the other party's statements. Detectives and lawyers ask several questions of people who they think might be lying. Their questions are designed so that inconsistencies will emerge if a person is lying. It is very difficult for even the best of liars to be perfectly consistent in all aspects of a lie.

Second, the negotiator should *enrich the mode of communication.* If negotiations have been proceeding by phone, written correspondence, or e-mail, the negotiator who wants to catch a lie should insist on a face-to-face interaction. It is much more difficult for liars to monitor themselves when the communication modality is multichanneled (as it is in face-to-face negotiations). Telltale signs of lying are often found in nonverbal "leakage," such as in the hands or body, rather than the face or words, which liars usually carefully monitor (Ekman 1984; for more on nonverbal cues and lying, see appendix 2).

Finally, the negotiator should ask to see *proof or evidence.* For example, if the person with whom we are negotiating claims that the transmission in the car is less than a year old, we should ask to see receipts and contact the shop that replaced the transmission.

SHOULD I TRY TO TALK THE OTHER PARTY OUT OF HER RESERVATION POINT?

Probably not. Assuming that the other party is reasonably intelligent, motivated, and informed (like you), she is not likely to fall prey to this readily transparent negotiation ploy. Such attempts may actually backfire, entrenching the party more steadfastly in her position. Furthermore, you want to avoid the other negotiator's attempts to turn the tables on you with similar influence tactics. You probably would not fall for it, so why should they?

Some negotiators are inclined to use scare tactics such as, "If you do not sell your house to us, there will not be another buyer . . .", or "You'll regret not buying this company from me in 10 years when *I am* a billionaire. . . ." Scare tactics are not likely to be effective. They are likely to backfire or engender ill will.

SHOULD I ATTEMPT TO BE FAIR?

A typical negotiation situation usually involves two parties who each believe they are making whole-hearted, good-faith efforts to be fair and reasonable. Unfortunately, each party's idea of "fair and reasonable" seems worlds apart, and conflict rages on. So what is going on? Is one person lying? Are both people lying? No. Usually, both people are honestly putting forth "fair" settlement terms. The problem is that "fairness" is a vague concept that can be interpreted in many different ways.

There are about as many definitions of fairness as there are negotiators. Compounding this problem is the fact that most negotiators' ideas about fairness are usually self-serving or egocentric (i.e., biased in their own favor). Two people who are committed to finding "higher ground" and a "fair" solution, but who have completely opposing viewpoints on how to do this, will experience conflict and have difficulty negotiating.

The right question in a negotiation situation is not *whether* to be fair, but *how* to be fair. Do you want to split resources evenly? Equitably? Or focus on people's needs? Be explicit and ask the other party to be explicit. If you find the other person making appeals to "fairness," recognize this as a bargaining ploy and ask the other party to clarify what he or she has in mind. It may be a surprise to realize that both of you desire a "fair" outcome but have very different ideas about how to achieve this.

SHOULD I MAKE A "FINAL OFFER" OR COMMIT TO A POSITION?

In general, taking such a stance is not an effective negotiation strategy. Making an irrevocable commitment such as a "final offer" really should be done only when you mean it and you feel comfortable walking away from the bargaining table. Of course, you should only walk away from the bargaining table if your BATNA is more attractive than what the opponent is offering you. Intimidating the other party by making a commitment is risky. First, it is difficult to make "binding" commitments that appear to be credible. More important, it is difficult to reverse or rescind such statements once they are made, at least without looking or feeling foolish.

HOW DO I HELP THE OTHER PARTY TO SAVE FACE?

The best way to help the other party save face is not to let on, in any way, that you think they have lost face. There are several steps you can take whenever the other person seems to be taking an irrevocable stance, such as labeling an offer as "final."

First, you may not want to recognize statements made by the other party in the heat of conflict. You might say "Let me consider your offer and get back to you," rather than "So if this is your final offer, I guess things are over." By not acknowledging the finality of their offer, you provide the other party with an "out" to later resume negotiations. During the 1985 Geneva Summit meeting, for example, a tense moment occurred when Gorbachev glumly declared (after hours of negotiating with Reagan): "It looks as if we've reached an impasse" (Thomas 1985, 22). Instead of acknowledging this comment,

Reagan quickly suggested that they take a break and proposed taking a walk outside. This proved to be a critical move in allowing Gorbachev to come back to the table. Said Gorbachev: "Fresh air may bring fresh ideas." Reagan replied, "Maybe we'll find the two go together" (Thomas 1985, 22).

In other situations, you may have to help the other party by finding a face-saving strategy. Often this can be achieved by relabeling some of the terms of the negotiation. An excellent example of face saving occurred in the General Motors–Canadian UAW strike talks. The Canadian union had insisted on a wage increase; GM wanted to institute a profit-sharing scheme but keep wages at a minimum. A solution was devised that allowed each party to believe that they had achieved their main objective.

THE POWER OF FAIRNESS

Fairness is such an important aspect of pie slicing in negotiations that we need to expand upon it. Fairness and concerns about pie slicing pervade aspects of social life from corporate policy to intimate social relations (Deutsch 1985). Next is an "everything you have always wanted to know about fairness" course for the negotiator who is concerned with pie slicing. We develop our course around 11 principles of fairness of which every negotiator should be aware.

PRINCIPLE 1: THERE ARE MULTIPLE METHODS OF FAIR DIVISION

Fairness comes in many forms and types. Most often, negotiators use one of three fairness principles when it comes to slicing the pie: equality, equity, and need (Deutsch 1985):

1. **Equality rule,** or blind justice, prescribes equal shares for all. Outcomes are distributed without regard to inputs, and everyone benefits (or suffers) equally. The education system and the legal system in the United States are examples of equality justice: Everyone receives equal entitlement. In a university, all students have equal entitlement to career placement services.
2. **Equity rule,** or proportionality of contributions principle, prescribes that distribution should be proportional to a person's contribution. The free market system in the United States is an example of the equity principle. In many universities, students bid for classes; those who bid more points have greater entitlement to a seat in the course. Equity is such an important fairness rule that we will discuss it in detail.
3. **Needs-based rule,** or welfare-based allocation, states that benefits should be proportional to need. The social welfare system in the United States is based on need. In many universities, financial aid is based on need.

PRINCIPLE 2: RULES OF FAIRNESS ARE HIGHLY CONTEXT DEPENDENT

Fairness rules are highly context dependent, and different rules are used to slice the pie depending on the situation (Schwinger 1980). For example, most of us believe that our court/penal justice system should be equality based: Everyone should have the right to an equal and fair trial regardless of income or need. In contrast, most of us believe that academic grades should be assigned on the basis of an equity-based rule: Students who contribute more should be rewarded with higher marks. Similarly, most people agree that disabled persons are entitled to parking spaces and easy access to buildings.

The goals involved in a negotiation situation often dictate which fairness rule is employed (Mikula 1980). For example, if our goal is to minimize waste, then a needs-based or social welfare policy may be most appropriate (Berkowitz 1972). If our goal is to maintain or enhance harmony and group solidarity, equality-based rules are most effective (Leventhal 1976). If our goal is to enhance productivity and performance, equity-based allocation is most effective (Deutsch 1953).

Similarly, a negotiator's relationship to the other party strongly influences the choice of fairness rules. When negotiators share similar attitudes and beliefs, when they are physically close to one another, or when it is likely that they will engage in future interaction, they prefer equality rule. When the allocation is public (others know what choices are made), equality is used; when allocation is private, equity is preferred. Friends tend to use equality, whereas nonfriends or acquaintances use equity (Austin 1980). Further, people in relationships with others do not consistently employ one rule of fairness but, rather, use different fairness rules for specific incidences that occur within relationships. For example, when people in relationships are asked to describe a recent incident from their own relationships illustrating a particular justice principle (equity, equality, or need), need-based fairness is related to incidents involving nurturing and personal development, whereas equity and equality-based fairness are related to situations involving the allocation of responsibilities (Steil and Makowski 1989). In general, equality-based pie-slicing strategies are associated with more positive feelings about the decision, the situation, and one's partner.

Fairness rules also depend upon whether people are dealing with rewards versus costs. Whereas equality is often used to allocate benefits, equity is more commonly used to allocate burdens (Sondak, Neale, and Pinkley 1995). For example, in one investigation, people were involved in a two-party negotiation concerning a joint project (Ohtsubo and Kameda 1998). In the benefit-sharing condition, negotiators were told that their joint project produced a total earning of 3,000 GL (a hypothetical monetary unit) and that their task was to reach an agreement about how to divide this amount with their partner. Participants were told that they had personally incurred a cost of 1,350 GL for this project and that their final profile would be determined by subtracting 1,350 from the negotiated agreement amount. In the cost-sharing condition, the situation was exactly the same, except participants were told that they had personally invested 1,650 GL. Thus, the bargaining situation was identical in both situations, with the exception of the personal investment. Obviously, an equal split of 3,000 would mean 1,500 apiece. This would result in a gain in the benefit condition and a loss in the cost condition. As it turned out, negotiators were more demanding and tougher when bargaining how to share costs than benefits. Furthermore, there were fewer equal-split decisions in the cost condition.

The selection of fairness rules is also influenced by extenuating circumstances: Consider, for example, a physically handicapped person who attains an advanced degree. A person who overcomes external constraints is more highly valued than a person who does not face constraints but contributes the same amount. When a situation is complex, involving multiple inputs in different dimensions, people are more likely to use the equality rule. Thus, groups often split dinner bills equally rather than compute each person's share. This can lead to a problem, however. Group members aware of the pervasive use of equality may actually spend more individually. No group member wants to pay for more than he or she gets; if people cannot control the consumption of others, they consume more. Of course, when everyone thinks this way, the costs escalate, leading to irrational group behavior—a topic we discuss in the chapter on social dilemmas (chapter 11).

The multiple orientations are a potential source of conflict and inconsistency, however (Deutsch 1985). For example, people who are allocating resources choose different rules of fairness than do people who are on the receiving end: Allocators often distribute resources equally, even if they have different preferences. In contrast, recipients who have been inequitably, but advantageously, treated, justify their shares—even when they would not have awarded themselves the resources they received (Diekmann, Samuels, Ross, and Bazerman 1997).

PRINCIPLE 3: PEOPLE ARE CONCERNED ABOUT THE "OTHER GUY"

At a major telecommunications company where salaries are strictly confidential, employees developed an elaborate system for comparing their own salary to that of others. This type of behavior reveals that people often care more about how their slice of the pie compares to other people than the size of the slice in an absolute sense (Adams 1965; Deutsch 1985; Homans 1961; Blau 1964; Walster, Berscheid, and Walster 1973; see Box 3–1 for an example of social comparison).

Who do people compare themselves to? Three social comparison targets may be distinguished: upward comparison, downward comparison, and comparison with similar others.

1. **Upward comparison** occurs when people compare themselves to someone who is better off, more accomplished, or higher in status. The young entrepreneur starting his own software company may compare himself to Bill Gates. Oftentimes, people compare themselves upward for inspiration and motivation.
2. **Downward comparison** occurs when people compare themselves to someone who is less fortunate, able, accomplished, or lower in status. For example, when a young manager's marketing campaign proves to be a complete flop, he may compare himself to a colleague whose decisions led to the loss of hundreds of thousands of dollars. Downward comparison often makes people feel better about their own state.
3. **Comparison with similar others** occurs when people choose someone of similar background, skill, and ability with whom to compare. For example, John compares himself with other first-year MBA students when he wants to assess his skills in finance. Comparison with similar others is useful when people desire to have accurate appraisals of their abilities.

What drives the choice of the comparison other? A number of goals and motives may drive social comparison, including:

1. **Self-improvement:** People compare themselves with others who can serve as models of success (Taylor and Lobel 1989). For example, a beginning

> **BOX 3–1**
>
> ## SELF-INTEREST VERSUS SOCIAL COMPARISON
>
> Imagine that you are being recruited for a position in firm A. Your colleague, Jay, of similar background and skill, is also being recruited by firm A. Firm A has made you and Jay the following salary offers:
>
> Your salary: $75,000
>
> Jay's salary: $95,000
>
> Your other option is to take a position at firm B, which has made you an offer. Firm B has also made your colleague, Ines, an offer:
>
> Your salary: $72,000
>
> Ines' salary: $72,000
>
> Which job offer do you take, firm A's or firm B's? If you follow the principles of rational judgment outlined in appendix 1, you will take firm A's offer—it pays more money. However, if you are like most people, you prefer firm B's offer—you do not like feeling you are being treated unfairly (Bazerman, Loewenstein, and White 1992).

chess player may compare him- or herself with a grand master. Upward comparison provides inspiration, insight, and challenge, but it can also lead to feelings of discouragement and incompetence.

2. **Self-enhancement:** The desire to maintain or enhance a positive view of oneself. This leads people to bias information in self-serving ways. Rather than seek truth, people seek comparisons that show them in a favorable light. People make downward comparisons with others who are less fortunate, less successful, and so forth (Wills 1981).

3. **Accurate self-evaluation:** The desire for truthful knowledge about oneself (even if the outcome is not favorable).

PRINCIPLE 4: PEOPLE SEEK EQUITY IN THEIR RELATIONSHIPS WITH OTHERS

When it comes to relationships and slicing the pie, people make judgments about what is fair based on what they are investing in the relationship and what they are getting out of it. Inputs are investments in a relationship that usually entails costs. For example, the person who manages the finances and pays the bills in a relationship incurs time and energy costs. An output is something that a person receives from a relationship. The person who does not pay the bills enjoys the benefits of a financial service. Outputs, or outcomes, may be positive or negative. In many cases, A's input is B's outcome, and B's input is A's outcome. For example, a company pays (input) an employee (outcome) who gives her time and expertise (input) to further the company's goals (outcome).

Equity exists in a relationship if each person's outcomes are proportional to his or her inputs. Equity, therefore, refers to equivalence of the outcome/input ratio of parties; inequity exists when the ratio of outcomes to inputs is unequal. Equity exists when the profits (rewards minus costs) of two actors are equal (Homans 1961). However, complications arise if two people have different views of what constitutes a legitimate investment, cost, or reward, and how they rank each one. For example, consider salaries paid to basketball players in the NBA. With star players taking the greatest slice of the salary pie (capped at a fixed amount), little is left over to pay the last three or four players on a 12-person team roster. The minimum salary of $272,500 might seem extraordinarily high to the average person, but in the context of the team—with an average salary of $2.6 million and a star salary of $30 million per year to the Chicago Bulls' Michael Jordan in 1997—it reflects a sizeable disparity (Staudohar 1999).

Equity exists when a person perceives equality between the ratio of his or her own outcomes (O) to inputs (I) and the ratio of the other person's outcomes to inputs, where a and b represent two people (Adams 1965):

$$\frac{Oa}{Ia} = \frac{Ob}{Ib}$$

However, this equity formula is less applicable to situations in which inputs and outcomes might be either positive or negative. The basic equity formula may be reconstructed as:

$$\frac{Oa - Ia}{|Ia|^{ka}} = \frac{Ob - Ib}{|Ib|^{kb}}$$

This formula proposes that equity prevails when the disparity between person a's outcomes and inputs and person b's outcomes and inputs are equivalently proportional to the absolute value of each of their inputs. The numerator is "profit," and the denominator adjusts for positive or negative signs of input. Each k takes on the value of either $+1$ or -1, depending on the valence of participants' inputs and gains (outcomes – inputs).

PRINCIPLE 5: WHEN PEOPLE SENSE INEQUITY, THEY WILL ATTEMPT TO RESTORE EQUITY

Suppose that you were hired by your firm last year with an annual salary of $85,000. You felt happy about your salary, until you learned that your colleague, whom you regard to be of equivalent skill and background, is paid $5,000 more per year than you. How do you deal with this inequity? When people find themselves participating in an inequitable relationship, they become distressed; the greater the perceived inequity, the more distressed people feel. This distress drives people to attempt to restore equity to the relationship.

People who believe they are underpaid feel dissatisfied and seek to restore equity (Walster, Berscheid, and Walster 1973). For example, underpaid workers lower their level of effort and productivity to restore equity (Greenberg 1988) and, in some cases, leave organizations characterized by inequity to join an organization where wages are more fairly distributed, even if they are less highly paid in absolute terms (Schmitt and Marwell 1972).

Consider Sarah, who believes she is underpaid in her organization. She came to this conclusion when she had a "telling" conversation with Jay, an employee in the same department at her level. Jay was hired one year after Sarah; he is considerably older and has more experience. Now that Sarah knows that Jay is paid substantially more than her, she is distressed by the apparent inequity. How can Sarah deal with this situation? There are six means by which people may eliminate the tension arising from inequity (Adams 1965):

1. Alter your inputs (Sarah can work less hard, take on fewer projects, take days off, etc.).
2. Alter your outcomes (Sarah can ask for a raise or bonus).
3. Cognitively distort your inputs or outcomes (Sarah can minimize the importance of her contributions and maximize the perceived value of her outcomes; e.g., by deciding that work satisfaction is more important than a high salary).
4. Leave the situation (Sarah can quit her job).
5. Cognitively distort either the inputs or the outcomes of your exchange partner (Sarah may view Jay as contributing more and earning less than he actually does).
6. Change the object of comparison (Sarah may stop comparing herself to Jay and start comparing herself to someone with a similar amount of experience).

The use of the first two strategies depends on whether the person has been over- or under-rewarded. Overrewarded individuals can increase their inputs or decrease their outcomes to restore equal ratios, whereas underrewarded people must decrease their inputs or increase their outcomes. For example, people work harder if they think they are overpaid. Conversely, people may cheat or steal if they are underpaid (Greenberg 1990).

Given the various methods of restoring equity, what determines which method will be used? People engage in a cost-benefit analysis and choose the method that maximizes positive outcomes. Usually, this minimizes the necessity of increasing any of one's own inputs that are difficult or costly to change and also minimizes the necessity of real changes or cognitive changes in inputs/outcomes that are central to self-concept. Simply put, it is easier to change how we think about something than our behaviors. Further, this type of change minimizes the necessity of leaving the situation or changing the object of social comparison once it has stabilized. Thus, we are not likely to ask for a salary cut if we think we are overpaid, but we are more inclined to regard the work we do as more demanding (see Sidebar 3–1 for an examination of factors that can lead to reactions to inequity).

The equity drive is so strong that people who are denied the opportunity to restore equity will derogate others, thereby restoring *psychological equity*. If distortion must occur, people focus on the other person's inputs or outcomes before distorting their own, especially if such distortion threatens their self-esteem. Leaving the situation and changing the object of comparison involve the highest costs, because they disrupt the status quo and violate justice beliefs.

PRINCIPLE 6: PEOPLE NEED TO MAINTAIN THEIR EGOS

Social comparison is an inevitable fact of life in organizations and relationships. Even if we do not desire to compare ourselves with others, we inevitably hear about someone's higher salary, larger office, special opportunities, and grander budget. Social situations are constant reminders of how others—strangers, acquaintances, and friends—compare with us in terms of fortune, fame, and happiness. How do we react

SIDEBAR 3–1. DISTRIBUTED VERSUS CONCENTRATED UNFAIRNESS

Within an organizational setting, many acts of unfair or unjust behavior may occur. For example, a person of color may be passed over for a promotion. A woman with managerial skills may be relegated to administrative and secretarial tasks. How do employees react to injustice in the organization? Consider two hypothetical companies: A and B. In each company, the overall incidence of unfair behavior is identical. In company A, the unfair incidences (i.e., percentage of total acts) are targeted toward a single individual—a black female; in company B, the unfair incidences are spread among three individuals—a black female, a Hispanic male, and an older, handicapped white male. The fact that the incidences are concentrated on a single individual or spread out over many organizational members should be irrelevant, if the overall incidence of unfairness in each organization is the same. In practice, however, this is not what happens.

In a simulated organization, each of three employees was victimized in one out of three interactions with a manager. In another company, one of the three employees was victimized in all three out of three interactions with a manager; the two other employees were treated fairly. Thus, in both companies, the incidence of unfairness was identical. However, groups' overall judgment of the unfairness of the manager was greater when the injustice was spread across members than when it was concentrated on one individual. Most disconcertingly, targets of discrimination were marginalized by other group members. Blaming-the-victim effects may be more rampant when individuals are the sole targets of discrimination—ironically, when they need the most support (Lind, Kray, and Thompson 1996).

to social comparisons? Are we happy for other people—do we bask in their glory when they achieve successes—or are we threatened and angry?

People behave in ways that maximize their self-evaluation and minimize their losses in self-evaluation (Tesser 1988). That is, people "regulate" their behaviors and cognitions to maintain positive self-regard. When does performance of another individual enhance our personal self-evaluation, and when does it threaten our self-worth?

Antecedent Conditions

When we compare ourselves to another, we consider the relevance of the comparison to our self-concept. People have beliefs and values that reflect their central dimensions of the self. Some dimensions are highly self-relevant; others are irrelevant. It all depends upon how a person defines him- or herself. For example, consider Tim, a new product manager in a large firm. Tim prides himself on being a financial wizard, able to work the numbers, play the market, and manage his money successfully. On the other hand, Tim is not an athlete; he does not care about sports nor play them.

Performance

A second critical ingredient is the quality of our own and the other person's performance on a particular dimension. For example, Tim probably has some idea of how well he is doing financially as compared to other product managers by looking at stock reports or asset portfolios.

Closeness

The final critical piece of the puzzle is the relationship between ourselves and the target person. The performance of other people can affect our self-evaluation, especially when we are psychologically close to them. We focus on situations in which people who are close to us perform better than we do. For example, Tim compares himself to Laura, who is a product manager for a different division of the firm.

The Comparison Effect

When we observe someone who is close to us performing extremely well in an area that we highly identify with, our self-evaluation is threatened. Such "upward" comparisons can lead to envy, frustration, anger, and even sabotage. Upon hearing that a member of one's cohort made some extremely timely investments in companies that have paid off multifold and is now a millionaire three times over, people probably feel threatened if they pride themselves on their financial wizardry. The fact that our colleague excels in an area that we pride ourselves on rubs salt in the wounds of the psyche. For example, if Tim learns that Laura did well in her performance review this year, he is likely to feel threatened and envious.

The Reflection Effect

When another person outperforms us on a behavior that is irrelevant to our self-definition, the better their performance and the closer our relationship, the more we gain in self-evaluation. We take pride in their success. Imagine, for example, that Tim heard that his best friend, Jean, won an international sailboat race. Because sports are irrelevant to Tim's self-definition, Tim is not threatened. Furthermore, because Tim feels a connection to Jean, Jean's success reflects positively on Tim's evaluation of himself.

Responses to Comparison Effects

Jan and Ida are top salespeople at a competitive advertising agency; each of them vie for the biggest account. This situation has the makings of an uncomfortable social comparison effect. What choices do Jan and Ida have to handle the inevitable feelings of threat, anger, and contempt? They may each reduce their degree of closeness to the other. For example, they may minimize their friendship and invest in others who are less threatening to their self-definition, or Jan may decide to leave the company to reduce the feelings of constant threat. Another alternative is to change one's self-definition. Ida may pursue another area of interest, a different hobby, or redirect her personal pursuits to change the direct comparison. Another alternative is to change performance by improving. In some cases, this may be easy to do: Ida may sign up for a special training course that gives her an advantage over Jan. In other cases, this may be less feasible, especially if people perceive themselves as having invested all they can in their chosen domain.

PRINCIPLE 7: PEOPLE CARE NOT ONLY ABOUT THE SIZE OF THEIR SLICE, BUT THE PROCESS USED TO GET THERE

In addition to their slice of the pie, people are concerned with the way resources are distributed (Thibaut and Walker 1975, 1978; Leventhal 1976, 1980). In addition to evaluating the fairness of outcomes, people evaluate the fairness of the procedures by which those outcomes are determined. People's evaluations of the fairness of procedures determine their satisfaction and willingness to comply with outcomes. For example, when managers educate employees (i.e., explain to them why change is occurring, such as in the case of a merger), this increases employee commitment to the change (Kotter and Schlesinger 1979). The process of explaining decision in a change context helps employees to adapt to the change because the lack of an explanation is often regarded by employees as unfair, generating resentment toward management and toward the decision (Daly and Geyer 1994). Indeed, Daly (1995) found that, in an investigation of 183 employees of seven private-sector organizations that had each just completed a relocation, perceived fairness was higher when justification was provided in the case of unfavorable change.

PRINCIPLE 8: JUDGMENTS ABOUT WHAT IS FAIR ARE DRIVEN BY THE NATURE OF THE RELATIONSHIP WE HAVE WITH THE OTHER PARTY

Consider the following situation: You and a college friend have developed a potentially revolutionary (and profitable) idea for a new kind of water ski (see Loewenstein, Thompson, and Bazerman 1989). You have spent about half a year in your dorm basement developing a prototype of the new invention. Your friend had the original idea; you developed the design and materials and assembled the prototype. The two of you talk to a patent lawyer about getting a patent, and the lawyer tells you that there is a pending patent on a similar product, but the company will offer you $3,000 for one of the innovative features of your design. You and your friend gladly accept. What division of the $3,000 between you and your friend would you find to be most satisfying?

People's preferences for several possible distributions of the money for themselves and the other person were assessed (Loewenstein, Thompson, and Bazerman 1989). People's utility functions were social rather than individual, meaning that individual satisfaction was strongly influenced by the payoffs received by the other as well as the payoffs received by the self (see Fig. 3–3). Social utility functions were tent-shaped. The most satisfying outcome was equal shares for the self and other ($1,500 apiece). Discrepancies between payoffs to the self versus the other led to lower satisfaction. However, social utility functions were lopsided in that advantageous inequity (self receives more than other) was preferable to disadvantageous inequity (other receives more than self). Further, the relationship people had with the other party mattered: In positive or neutral relationships, people preferred equality; in negative relationships, people preferred advantageous inequity (see Sidebar 3–2 for an examination of different types of profiles).

People will pass up outcomes that entail one person receiving more than others and settle for a settlement of lower joint value but equal-appearing shares (McClelland and Rohrbaugh 1978). This is especially true when resources are "lumpy" (i.e., hard to divide into pieces), such as an oriental rug (Messick 1993).

PRINCIPLE 9: EGOCENTRISM TAINTS JUDGMENTS OF FAIRNESS

What is fair to one person may not be fair in the eyes of another. For example, consider a group of three people who go out for dinner. One person orders a bottle of expensive red wine, an appetizer, and a pricey main course. Another abstains from drinking and orders two inexpensive side dishes. The third orders a moderately priced meal. Then the bill arrives. The wine drinker immediately suggests that the group split the bill into thirds, explaining that this is the simplest approach. The teetotaler winces and

FIGURE 3–3 Social Utility as a Function of Discrepancy between Our
Own and Others' Outcomes

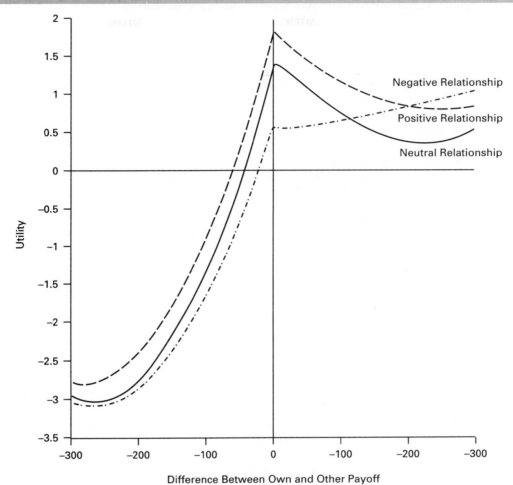

Difference Between Own and Other Payoff

Source: Loewenstein, G. F., L. Thompson, and M. H. Bazerman (1989). Social utility and decision making in inter-personal contexts. *Journal of Personality and Social Psychology, 57*(3), 426–441. Copyright © 1999 by the American Psychological Association. Reprinted with permission.

suggests that the group ask the waitress to bring three separate bills. The third group member argues that, because he is a graduate student, the two others should cover the bill, and he invites the two over to his house the next week for pizza. This example illustrates that in any situation, there are as many interpretations of fairness as there are parties involved. Two people may both truly want a fair settlement, but they may have very different and equally justifiable ideas about what is fair.

Why are people egocentric? People want or prefer more than what they regard as fair (basic hedonism). In short, our preferences are more primary, or immediate, than our social concerns. People are more in touch with their own preferences than with the concerns of others. We have immediate access to our preferences; fairness is a

> ## SIDEBAR 3–2. PROFILES OF PIE SLICERS
> Have you ever wondered whether most people are truly interested in other people or are only concerned about their own profit? To examine this question, MBA students were given several hypothetical scenarios, like the situation involving the ski invention, and asked what division of resources (and in some cases, costs) they preferred. Further, people made responses for different kinds of relationships: friendly ones, antagonistic ones, and neutral ones (Loewenstein, Thompson, and Bazerman 1989). Three types of people were identified:
> * **Loyalists** prefer to split resources equally, except in antagonistic relationships (27 percent).
> * **Saints** prefer to split resources equally no matter whether relationships are positive, neutral, or negative (24 percent).
> * **Ruthless competitors** prefer to have more resources than the other party, regardless of relationship (36 percent).

secondary judgment. For this reason, fairness judgments are likely to be tainted by preferences. Because preferences are primary and immediate, they often color a person's evaluation of fairness in a self-serving fashion. In a sense, our preferences act as a self-serving prime on our judgments of fairness.

Allocating more money to ourselves (see Box 3–2) is only one way that people show egocentric bias. Egocentric judgments of fairness also emerge in other ways. For example, people select fairness rules in a self-serving fashion: When people make minimal contributions, they often prefer equality rather than equity; however, when people's contributions are substantial, they opt for equity rather than equality (van Avermaet 1974). Even if people agree to use the same fairness rule, they think it is fair for them to get more than others in a similar situation because they think they would have contributed more (Messick and Rutte 1992).

Another way people can engage in egocentric evaluation is to selectively *weight* different aspects of the exchange situation in a way that favors themselves. Consider a situation in which participants are told how many hours they had worked on a task of assembling questionnaires as well as how many questionnaires they completed. The key dimensions are hours worked and productivity. Participants are then asked to indicate what they believe is fair payment for their work. Those who worked long hours but did not complete many questionnaires emphasize the importance of hours; in contrast, those who worked short hours but completed many questionnaires emphasize quantity completed. Thus, people emphasize the dimension that favors themselves (van Avermaet 1974).

Appeals to equality can also be self-serving (Messick 1993). At a superficial level, equality is trivially simple. Employing equality as a division rule in practice, however, is very complex because there are several dimensions on which equality may be established (see Harris and Joyce 1980). Furthermore, equality is not consistently applied. For example, when the outcome is evenly divisible by the number in the group, people will use equality more than when even division is not possible (Allison and Messick 1990).

BOX 3–2

EGOCENTRIC INTERPRETATIONS
OF FAIRNESS

You have worked for seven hours and have been paid $25. Another person has worked for 10 hours. It is piecemeal work. How much do you think the other person should get paid? If you are like most people, you believe the other person should get paid more for doing more work—about $30.29 on average. This is hardly a self-serving response. Now, let's turn this question on its head: The other person has worked for seven hours and has been paid $25. You have worked for 10 hours. What is a fair wage for you to be paid? The average response is $35.24 (Messick and Sentis 1979). The difference between $35.24 and $30.29 is about $5, which illustrates the phenomenon of egocentric bias: People pay themselves substantially more than they are willing to pay others for doing the same task.

SIDEBAR 3–3. FAIRNESS AND STRIKES

The likelihood and length of strikes may be directly predicted by the difference in perceived fair wages between management and union (Thompson and Loewenstein 1992). That is, if management and union have widely differing perceptions of what constitutes a fair settlement, a strike is more likely. Even more disconcertingly, providing each party (management and labor) with additional unbiased information concerning the dispute has the effect of exaggerating each party's perceptions of fair settlement outcomes and excluding parties in their positions. This is a good example of how more information is not always better in negotiations.

The major problem with egocentric judgment is that it makes negotiations more difficult to resolve (see Sidebar 3–3 for an example).

PRINCIPLE 10: PEOPLE DO NOT REALIZE THAT THEY ARE SELF-SERVING

The preceding examples suggest that people immediately seize upon any opportunity to favor themselves. However, in many situations, people would ultimately be better off by not having egocentric views. Consider arbitration situations: People's predictions of judges' behavior are biased in a manner that favors their own side. Efforts to de-bias litigants meet with virtually no success. Informing parties of the potential bias or providing them with information about the opponent's point of view does little to assuage biased perceptions of fairness, suggesting that egocentric biases are deeply ingrained (Babcock, Loewenstein, Issacharoff, and Camerer 1995).

People really do care about fairness but usually do not realize that they are behaving in a self-interested fashion. Egocentric judgments of responsibility and fairness are attributable to ways in which people process information. There are several cognitive mechanisms by which egocentric judgments could develop:

- **Selective encoding and storage.** Our own thoughts attract attention away from thinking about the contributions of others. We rehearse our own actions and fit them into our own cognitive schemas, which facilitates retention and subsequent retrieval. If encoding mechanisms lead to self-serving judgments of fairness, then a person who learns of the facts before knowing which side of a dispute he is on should not be egocentric. However, the egocentric effect still emerges even when the direction of self-interest occurs subsequent to the processing of information, suggesting that encoding is not the sole mechanism producing egocentric judgment.
- **Differential retrieval.** When making judgments of responsibility, people ask themselves, "How much did I contribute?" and they attempt to retrieve specific instances (Ross and Sicoly 1979). Because it is cognitively easier to retrieve instances involving oneself, there is a positive correlation between recall and responsibility attributions (Kahneman and Tversky 1982).
- **Informational disparity.** People are often not privy to the contributions made by others. This suggests that information, not goals, mediates the self-serving effect. Even when information is constant but goals are manipulated, however, the self-serving effects emerge (see Thompson and Loewenstein 1992), suggesting that information itself is not solely responsible for the egocentric effect (see Camerer and Loewenstein 1993).

Most situations are ambiguous enough that people can construe them in a fashion that favors their own interests. One unfortunate consequence is that people develop different perceptions of fairness even when they are presented with the same evidence. Consider a strike situation in which people are provided with background information on a hypothetical teachers' union and board of education. The background material is constructed so that some facts favor the teachers and other facts favor the board of education. On balance, the facts are equal. In one condition, both disputants are presented with extensive, identical background information concerning the dispute. In another condition, disputants are presented with abbreviated, much less extensive background information. Those who have extensive information are more likely to go on strikes that last longer and are more costly to both parties, compared to disputants who do not have extensive information, even though information is identical for both sides (Thompson and Loewenstein 1992). Information, even when shared among parties, creates ambiguity and provides fertile ground for unchecked self-interest to operate.

PRINCIPLE 11: AVOID PROBLEMS THROUGH WISE PIE SLICING

The distribution of resources (pie slicing) is an unavoidable and inevitable aspect of negotiation. What qualities should we live by when slicing the pie? Messick (1993) suggests the following: consistency, simplicity, effectiveness, and justifiability. To this list of qualities, we add consensus, generality, and satisfaction (Levine and Thompson 1996).

Consistency
One of the hallmarks of a good pie-slicing heuristic is consistency or invariance across settings, time, and respect to the enforcer of the procedure. For example, most of us would be outraged if those managers up for performance review did better if the meeting was scheduled in the morning versus the afternoon. This is a clear bias of the interviewer. Fairness procedures are often inconsistent because of heuristic decision making. Heuristic judgment processes are necessary when normative decision procedures are absent or when their application would be inefficient. Unfortunately, people are typically unaware of the powerful contextual factors that affect their judgments of fairness.

Simplicity
Pie-slicing procedures should be clearly understood by the individuals who employ them and those who are affected by them. Group members should be able to easily articulate the procedure used to allocate resources. This allows the procedure to be implemented with full understanding and the outcomes of the procedure to be evaluated against a clear criterion.

Effectiveness
Pie-slicing policies should produce a choice, meaning that the allocation procedure should yield a clear decision. If the procedure does not produce such a decision, then conflict may erupt among group members who try to identify and implement a decision post hoc.

Justifiability
Pie-slicing procedures should be justifiable to other parties. A fairness rule may be consistent, simple, and effective, but if it cannot be justified, it is not likely to be successful. For example, suppose that a manager of an airline company decides that raises will be based upon hair color: Blondes get big raises, brunettes do not. This policy is consistent, simple, and effective, but hardly justifiable.

Consensus
Group members should agree upon the method of allocation. Effective pie-slicing procedures are often internalized by group members, and norms act as strong guidelines for behavior and decision making in groups. Because social justice procedures often outlive current group members, new members are frequently indoctrinated with procedures that the group has found useful in the past (Bettenhausen and Murnighan 1985; Levine and Moreland 1994).

Generalizability
The pie-slicing procedure should be applicable to a wide variety of situations. Procedures and norms develop when intragroup conflict is expected, enduring, or recurrent, and effective policy therefore specifies outcome distribution across situations.

Satisfaction
The pie-slicing procedure should be satisfying to negotiators. This increases the likelihood they will follow through with their agreements.

CONCLUSION

When it comes to slicing the pie, the most valuable information is a negotiator's best alternative to reaching agreement (or BATNA). Nothing can substitute for the power of a strong BATNA. Negotiators can enhance their ability to garner a favorable slice of the pie by engaging in the following strategies: determining their BATNA prior to negotiations; attempting to improve upon their BATNA; researching the other party's BATNA; setting high aspirations; making the first offer; immediately reanchoring if the other party opens with an "outrageous" offer; resisting the urge to state a range; making bilateral, not unilateral, concessions; using objective-appearing rationales to support offers; and appealing to norms of fairness. We strongly advise that negotiators not reveal their reservation price (unless it is very attractive) and not lie about their BATNA. A negotiator who is well-versed in the psychology of fairness is at a pie-slicing advantage in negotiation.

4

WIN-WIN NEGOTIATION
Expanding the Pie

When managers and hourly workers of Bayou Steel in LaPlace, Louisiana, sat down to negotiate a new contract in January 1993, both sides thought a strike was improbable. "I'd never have dreamed it," said Ron Ferraro, president of United Steel Workers of America, Local 9121 (Schriefer 1995, p. 30). Bayou Steel managers went into labor talks hoping to build on the improved shop-floor relationship by using win-win negotiation. To help them with the win-win enterprise, Bayou Steel and Local 9121 enlisted the help of two facilitators from the Federal Mediation and Conciliation Services (FMCS). At first the negotiations went like clockwork, said Hank Vasquez, Bayou's president of human resources. "We identified our interests and concerns and 90 percent of the contract was done" (Schriefer 1995, p. 31). At the direction of the facilitators, the two sides started with easy issues to build momentum and trust for more difficult matters. Economic issues, such as base pay, overtime, vacation time, and incentives were put off until last. "We thought we had done all we could to manage worker expectations about pay raises," said Tom Postlewait, Bayou's vice president of plant operations (p. 32). However, angry union members believed that win-win was a subterfuge for taking advantage of the union members. Says Ferraro, "A lot of people think the company just suckered us in with this win-win stuff" (p. 32). When the parties started talking about the economic issues, they attempted to stick to win-win principles, but "it quickly changed to adversarial bargaining as the economic issues were placed on the table," said Willis Bartlett, one of the two FMCS commissioners (p. 32).

The United Steelworkers of America strike at Bayou Steel illustrates that "win-win" does not mean anything unless parties can actually apply it to real behavior. Even good-faith intentions can backfire if improperly acted upon. Most negotiations are not win-or-lose enterprises. Unfortunately, however, most people approach them as though they are. Win-win negotiation strategies are anything but intuitive, and many people who regard themselves to be win-win negotiators are often the people who leave money on the table. For example, in a recent simulation with business executives from major companies around the globe, every person indicated that they believed they reached a win-win deal; however, every executive had left money on the table. This came as quite a shock to these executives, but they gained an important insight: In our daily interactions with people, we often leave money on the table without even realizing it. We need to be hypervigilant concerning the creation and maximization of the pie of resources. This chapter provides managers with strategies for extracting all of the potential from negotiation situations.

WHAT IS WIN-WIN NEGOTIATION ANYWAY?

Many negotiators, upon reaching agreement, will proudly describe their negotiations as win-win. However, closer inspection usually reveals that money was squandered, resources wasted, and potential joint gain untapped. Clearly, negotiators' minds and hearts were in the right places, but they did not achieve what they really wanted—an integrative agreement that fully exploited parties' interests and all available options. Win-win negotiation is a nice idea that is too often poorly understood and poorly acted upon. Most people think that win-win negotiation means one or more of the following:

- **Compromise:** Win-win negotiation does not mean an even split or a compromise. There are several instances in which negotiators make compromises, yet leave money on the table.
- **Even split:** An even split of resources in no way ensures that an integrative agreement has been reached.
- **Feeling good:** Happiness, or feeling good, is no guarantee that money and resources have not been wasted; in fact, many "happy" negotiators needlessly waste resources unknowingly (Thompson, Valley, and Kramer 1995).
- **Building a relationship:** Even when people have a genuine interest in the other party, this does not mean that they are thinking creatively and crafting win-win deals. In fact, people who would seem to have the most interest in building a relationship with the other party (for example, husbands and wives, dating couples, and long-term partners) consistently fail to reach integrative agreements (Fry, Firestone, and Williams 1983; Thompson and DeHarpport 1998; Kurtzberg and Medvec 1999).

Win-win negotiation *really* means that all creative opportunities are exploited and no resources are left on the table. We call this **integrative negotiation.** There are hundreds of examples of money being left on the table in real-world negotiations; the problem is that people do not realize it. This is, of course, an example of the faulty feedback problem we discussed in chapter 1. This chapter provides strategies for reaching true win-win deals.

TELLTALE SIGNS OF WIN-WIN POTENTIAL

Integrative potential exists in just about every negotiation situation. However, people who negotiate for a living are decidedly more skeptical, especially when in the throes of negotiation: "Your research examples are cute, but they do not pertain to my real-life negotiation in buying my house or car, or negotiating my job. Those are really fixed-pie situations."

If win-win potential exists in most negotiation situations, how do we discover it? Most negotiations do not present themselves as win-win situations. Consequently, most people do not immediately see opportunities for reaching integrative agreements. It takes hard work to create integrative opportunities. The following questions are designed to determine the possibility for win-win negotiation. They are excellent questions for negotiators to ask when assessing the potential of a negotiation situation.

DOES THE NEGOTIATION CONTAIN MORE THAN A SINGLE ISSUE?

Most negotiation situations present themselves as single-issue negotiations. By defini-tion, single-issue negotiations are not win-win because whatever one party gains, the other party loses. However, even in the simplest of negotiations, it is possible to iden-tify more than one issue. The probability that negotiators will have identical prefer-ences across all of the issues is very small, and, as we will see, it is differences in pref-erences, beliefs, and capacities that may be profitably traded off to create joint gain (Lax and Sebenius 1986). For example, in the peace treaty talks between Syria and Israel, technical experts formed committees to identify several issues, including the extent of an Israeli withdrawal from the Golan Heights, water rights, security measures, and the timetable for implementing an agreement. Israel put the emphasis on security guarantees, and Syria placed greater weight on the withdrawal from the Golan Heights, thus allowing a more integrative agreement to emerge (Slavin 2000).

CAN OTHER ISSUES BE BROUGHT IN?

Another strategy is to bring other issues into the negotiation that were not previously considered. For example, in a four-day negotiation between San Marino, California, and the local firefighters' association, the key issue was salary. Firefighters wanted an increase. The negotiators began searching for several options to reach this goal by con-necting benefits to wages, allowing cost savings to be distributed to firefighters, and taking on additional duties (thereby increasing incomes). In addition, management spent a great deal of time providing the firefighters with information on cost-benefit analyses, operating costs, and other relevant budgetary information so that all parties could evaluate which options were the most practical and beneficial. This information sharing contributed not only to this negotiation but provided helpful information for future organizational discussions (Quinn, Bell, and Wells 1997).

CAN SIDE DEALS BE MADE?

In many situations, people are strictly cautioned not to make side deals or side pay-ments. In contrast, the ability to bring other people into negotiations to make side deals may increase the size of the bargaining pie. For example, consider the side deal that AT&T cooked up with Comcast Corporation in 1999. For a while, AT&T was in a vigorous battle with Comcast Corporation for the acquisition of MediaOne Group, Inc. A win-win side deal was created when AT&T provided Comcast with a number of its cable systems and about 2 million additional cable subscribers; in return, Comcast paid AT&T $9 billion, or about $4,500 per subscriber, for the additional customers. Most important for AT&T, Comcast withdrew their $48 billion bid for MediaOne. Thus, by offering a valuable side deal, AT&T was able to satisfy their competitor (Hofmann 1999).

DO PARTIES HAVE DIFFERENT PREFERENCES ACROSS NEGOTIATION ISSUES?

If parties have different strengths of preference across the negotiation issues, by defi-nition, this is a win-win negotiation (Froman and Cohen 1970). The key is to determine each party's preferences and devise a means of satisfying each party's most important interests while inducing them to make concessions on lower-priority issues.

A PYRAMID MODEL

True win-win or integrative negotiations leave no resources unutilized. We distinguish three "levels" of integrative, or win-win, agreements. The pyramid model presented in Figure 4–1 depicts the three levels of integrative agreements. Beginning at the base, each successive level subsumes the properties of the levels below it. Ideally, negotiators should always strive to reach level 3 integrative agreements. Higher levels are progressively more difficult for negotiators to achieve, but they are more beneficial to negotiators.

Level 1 integrative agreements are agreements that exceed parties' no-agreement possibilities, or reservation points. Reaching an agreement that exceeds parties' no-agreement possibilities creates value relative to their best alternative. Negotiators create value by reaching settlements that are better than their reservation points, or disagreement alternatives.

Level 2 integrative agreements are agreements that are better for both parties than are other feasible negotiated agreements. That is, negotiators create value with respect to one negotiated outcome by finding another outcome that all prefer.

The existence of such agreements, by definition, implies that the bargaining situation is not purely fixed-sum: Some agreements yield higher joint gain than do others. By definition, in purely fixed-sum situations, all outcomes sum to the same joint amount, and, therefore, no alternative agreement exists that improves one party's outcome while simultaneously improving or not reducing the outcome of the other party. If negotiators fail to reach agreement in a fixed-sum negotiation when the bargaining zone is positive, they have failed to reach a level 1 agreement. Unlike the pure fixed-sum case, integrativeness is much more difficult to assess in the more common mixed-motive case.

FIGURE 4–1 A Pyramid Model of Integrative Agreements

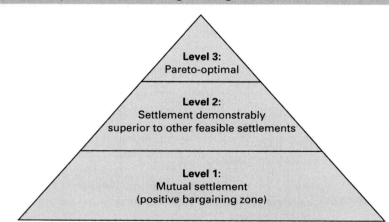

Level 3:
Pareto-optimal

Level 2:
Settlement demonstrably
superior to other feasible settlements

Level 1:
Mutual settlement
(positive bargaining zone)

Level 3 integrative agreements are those that are impossible to improve upon from the perspective of *both* parties. Technically speaking, level 3 integrative agreements are settlements that lie along the **pareto-optimal frontier** of agreement, meaning that no other feasible agreement exists that would improve one party's outcome while simultaneously not hurting the other party's outcome. This means that *any* agreement reached by negotiators in a purely fixed-sum situation is level 3—that is, there is no way to improve any negotiator's outcome without making the other party worse off. In reality, it is difficult to determine whether an agreement is level 3, but we will present some helpful techniques.

Reaching level 3 integrative agreements may sound easy enough, but observation of hundreds of executives' performance in business negotiation simulations reveals that less than 25 percent reach level 3 agreements, and of those, approximately 50 percent do so by chance.

MOST COMMON PIE-EXPANDING ERRORS

If reaching win-win negotiation agreements is the objective of most negotiators, what prevents them from doing so? There are two key problems negotiators encounter, which we describe next.

FALSE CONFLICT

False conflict, also known as **illusory conflict,** occurs when people believe that their interests are incompatible with the other party's interests when, in fact, they are not. For example, in the Cuban Missile Crisis, unbeknownst to the United States, Russia preferred to constrain the Cubans from provocative behavior and to minimize the contributions of the Chinese—an interest held by the United States (Walton and McKersie 1965). Similarly, in a labor strike at Dow Chemical Company, both union and management preferred the same wage increase; however, neither party realized this at the time of the strike (Balke, Hammond, and Meyer 1973).

In 1990, Thompson and Hastie uncovered a particularly insidious and widespread effect in negotiations: the **lose-lose effect.** They constructed a negotiation situation in which the parties involved had compatible interests on a subset of the negotiation issues. That is, both parties wanted the same outcome. At first, it seemed absurd to imagine any other outcome occurring other than the parties settling for what was obviously the best solution for themselves and the other person. However, a substantial number of negotiators not only failed to realize that the other person had interests that were completely compatible with their own, but they reached settlements that were less optimal for both parties than some other readily available outcome. A situation in which people fail to capitalize on compatible interests is a lose-lose agreement (Thompson and Hrebec 1996). In an analysis of 32 different negotiation studies across over 5,000 people, Thompson and Hrebec (1996) found that negotiators failed to realize compatible issues about 50 percent of the time and fell prey to the lose-lose effect about 20 percent of the time.

What should negotiators do to avoid lose-lose agreements? First, negotiators should be aware of the fixed-pie perception and not automatically assume that their interests are opposed to the other party. Second, negotiators should avoid making **premature**

concessions to the other party (i.e., making concessions on issues before they are even asked for). Finally, negotiators should develop an accurate understanding of the other party's interests—a skill we will explore soon.

THE FIXED-PIE PERCEPTION

The **fixed-pie perception** is the belief that the other party's interests are directly and completely opposed to one's own interests (Bazerman and Neale 1983; Thompson and Hastie 1990). Most untrained people have a fixed-pie understanding of negotiation. Most untrained negotiators view negotiation as a pie-slicing task: They assume that their interests are incompatible, that impasse is likely, and that issues are settled one by one rather than as packages (O'Connor and Adams 1996). For example, in one investigation, negotiators' perceptions of the other party's interests were assessed immediately before, during, and then following a negotiation (Thompson and Hastie 1990). Most negotiators perceived the other's interests to be completely opposed to their own. In fact, negotiators shared interests that could be profitably logrolled and completely compatible. In short, negotiators with fixed-pie perceptions literally throw money away.

How many negotiators squander resources as a result of the fixed-pie perception? Two-thirds of all (untrained) negotiators is a conservative judgment. In an investigation of the behavior of highly motivated MBA students engaged in a two-party negotiation exercise, 90 percent needlessly threw money away. Unfortunately, banishing the fixed-pie perception is very difficult. It is not enough to warn negotiators of its existence (Thompson 1991). Further, it is not enough for negotiators to have experience (Thompson 1990a, 1990b). It is not even enough for negotiators to receive feedback about their opponents' interests to eliminate the fixed-pie perception (Thompson and DeHarpport 1994). We will talk more about how to successfully challenge the fixed-pie perception when we examine biases and creativity (chapter 8).

Lack of time and effort do not explain lose-lose outcomes and the fixed-pie perception. The biggest detriment to the attainment of integrative agreements are the faulty assumptions we make about our opponent and the negotiation situation. One of the first realizations negotiators should make is that negotiation is not a purely competitive situation. Rather, most negotiation situations are mixed-motive in nature, meaning that parties' interests are imperfectly correlated with one another. Thus, the gains of one party do not represent equal sacrifices by the other. For example, consider a negotiation between two collaborators on a joint project: One is risk-averse and values cash up front more than riskier long-term payoffs; the other is more interested in long-term value than in current gains. The two may settle on a contract in which a large lump sum is paid to the risk-averse negotiator, and the other party reaps most of the (riskier) profits in the long term.

In fact, few conflicts are win-or-lose enterprises (Deutsch 1973). In most mixed-motive negotiations, parties realize at some level that they have two incentives vis-à-vis the other party: cooperation (so that they can reach an agreement and avoid resorting to their BATNAs) and competition (so that they can claim the largest slice of the pie). However, what this analysis misses is the incentive to *create* value, which is the key to win-win negotiation.

STRATEGIES THAT DO NOT REALLY WORK

We want to save negotiators time and heartache in their quest to expand the pie by outlining several strategies that, on a superficial level, might *seem* to be effective in expanding the pie and reaching win-win agreements, but in fact, do not really work.

COMMITMENT TO REACHING A WIN-WIN DEAL

Many negotiators head off to the negotiation table committed to reaching a win-win deal. They like the sound and intention of it; however, commitment to reaching a win-win deal does not guarantee that negotiators will reach a win-win deal. In fact, it may lull them into a false sense of security.

COMPROMISE

Negotiators often mistake win-win negotiations for equal-concession negotiations. Equal concessions, or "splitting the difference," does not really insure that a win-win negotiation has been reached. Concession making is a pie-slicing issue, not a pie-expanding strategy.

FOCUSING ON A LONG-TERM RELATIONSHIP

Oftentimes, negotiators believe that if they focus on the long-term nature of their relationship with the other party, this will ensure a win-win deal. This is a nice intention, but it does not guarantee that all the resources will be discovered and optimally exploited in the negotiation.

ADOPTING A "COOPERATIVE ORIENTATION"

It is nice when negotiators approach the negotiation table with benevolent attitudes and a cooperative orientation. However, negotiators' intentions to cooperate often keep them from focusing on the right information at the right time. For example, negotiators often attempt to cooperate by revealing their BATNA to the other party; revealing one's BATNA is a pie-slicing issue, not a pie-expanding issue. Negotiators often think cooperation means compromise, and compromises often mean lose-lose negotiation. For example, in 1996, MasterCard International wanted to figure out why the credit card company was losing money on some of its promotional deals. Subsequent analysis revealed that MasterCard was attempting to form good relationships with others (i.e., being cooperative), but they were giving away money and promotions and not asking for sufficient compensation in return (Kiser 1999). This is why Pruitt and Carnevale (1993) developed a dual-concern model of effective negotiation: high concern for the other party coupled with high concern for one's own interests.

TAKING EXTRA TIME TO NEGOTIATE

Negotiators often think that, with a little extra time, they can achieve all the joint gains possible in a negotiation. Extra time does not guarantee that negotiators will reach an integrative agreement (most negotiators wait until the last few moments of a negotiation to reach an agreement), and the quality of the negotiation does not improve with additional time. Furthermore, people tend to work to fill their time (McGrath, Kelly, and Machatka 1984). The same is true for negotiation. For example, we recently gave some people one hour, others two hours, and still others a week (via e-mail) to complete a two-party negotiation exercise. If time really makes a difference in terms of the quality of negotiated agreements, then the one-hour group should be expected to have inferior outcomes in terms of expanding the pie. However, this was not the case: There were no discernable differences between the three groups, suggesting that more time to negotiate does not improve the quality of negotiated agreements.

STRATEGIES THAT WORK

So much for the strategies that do not work. What does work when it comes to expanding the pie? Next, we identify nine strategies that can help you to expand the pie and create win-win negotiations (see also Bazerman and Neale 1982). We have ordered them in terms of the most obvious and intuitive strategies—the ones that your grandmother probably could have told you about—to the strategies that are extremely rare and much less intuitive. The first few strategies are ones that you can use when negotiating with someone who seems cooperative and trustworthy; the strategies that come later on this list are useful when dealing with "problem people" and/or extremely tough negotiators. We present them in rough order of the easiest to most advanced:

BUILD TRUST AND SHARE INFORMATION (Bazerman and Neale 1992)

If negotiators can build a trusting relationship and share information, this can greatly increase the probability that a win-win outcome will be reached. It is important to realize that the information that negotiators need to share is not information about their BATNAs, but rather, information about their *preferences* and *priorities* across the negotiation issues.

ASK DIAGNOSTIC QUESTIONS (Bazerman and Neale 1992)

A negotiator who asks the other party about his or her preferences is much more likely to reach integrative agreement than a negotiator who does not ask the other party about his or her priorities (Thompson 1991). The disappointing news, however, is that left to their own devices, negotiators do not seek information. For example, only about 7 percent of untrained negotiators seek information about the other party's preferences during negotiation, when it would be dramatically helpful to seek such information (Thompson 1991). Furthermore, diagnostic questions do not put negotiators on the defensive. In contrast, asking someone about her BATNA is likely to engender irritation. Ideally, it is important to understand how the negotiation ties to the company's business goals. For example, negotiating teams at one of Mexico's largest banks collaborated with financial analysts to determine the best way to work with clients who were not repaying their loans following the country's 1994 currency crisis. The analysts helped team members understand the bank's priorities and use them to come up with options for reaching agreements with debtors (Ertel 1999).

PROVIDE INFORMATION (Bazerman and Neale 1992)

In addition to seeking information about the other party, negotiators are wise to provide information about their own interests to the other party. This signals to the other party that you are willing to share information. Most important, by providing information about your interests (not your BATNA), you capitalize on the important psychological principle of reciprocity. That is, if you share information, the other party will often share as well. Negotiators who provide information to the other party about their priorities are more likely to reach integrative agreements than negotiators who do not provide this information (Thompson 1991). Further, the disclosing negotiator is not placed at a strategic disadvantage. The disclosing negotiator does not earn significantly more or less resources than his or her opponent.

It is a fallacy to believe that negotiators should never provide information to their opponent. Negotiations would not go anywhere if negotiators did not communicate their interests to the other party. Remember, you should negotiate as you would with your fraternal twin: If you do not provide information, neither will the other party. The important question, then, is not *whether* to reveal information, but *what* information to reveal.

Whereas many negotiators believe that they provide information during a negotiation, their opponent does not necessarily understand the information. This may be traceable to the illusion of transparency (Gilovich, Savitsky, and Medvec 1998). The **illusion of transparency** means that negotiators believe that they are revealing more than they actually are (i.e., they believe that others have access to information about them when in fact they do not). For example, in one investigation, negotiators judged whether an observer to the negotiation would be able to accurately discern their negotiation goals from their behavior (Vorauer and Claude 1998). Negotiators consistently overestimated the transparency of their objectives. Thus, people feel more like an "open book" with respect to their goals and interests in negotiation than they actually are.

UNBUNDLE THE ISSUES (Lax and Sebenius 1986)

Adding issues, unbundling issues, and creating new issues can transform a single-issue, fixed-pie negotiation into an integrative, multi-issue negotiation with win-win potential (Lax and Sebenius 1986). Integrative agreements require at least two issues and, in the case of negotiation *issues* (not parties), the more the merrier.

MAKE PACKAGE DEALS, NOT SINGLE-ISSUE OFFERS

Most negotiators make the mistake of negotiating each issue in a neat, agendalike fashion. This is a mistake for several reasons: First and foremost, negotiating each issue separately does not allow negotiators to make trade-offs between issues. To capitalize on different strengths of preference, negotiators need to compare and contrast issues and trade them off. Second, it may mean that impasse is more likely, especially if there is a narrow bargaining zone and trade-offs are necessary to reach a mutually profitable outcome. Finally, single-issue offers lure negotiators into compromise agreements, which, as we have seen, are usually not the best approach for win-win negotiations.

MAKE MULTIPLE OFFERS SIMULTANEOUSLY (Bazerman and Neale 1992)

In some cases, negotiators are disappointed and frustrated to find that their attempts to provide and seek information are not effective. This happens most commonly in the face of high distrust and less than amicable relations. Now what? Is all hope lost? Is there anything the negotiator can do? Fortunately, there is. The strategy of **multiple simultaneous offers** can be effective even with the most uncooperative of negotiators (Kelley and Schenitzki 1972; Kelley 1966). The strategy involves presenting the other party with at least two (and preferably more) proposals of *equal* value to oneself. The key of the multiple-offer strategy is threefold:

1. **Devise multiple-issue offers,** as opposed to single-issue offers (this gets away from sequential bargaining, which can lock people into lose-lose outcomes).
2. **Devise offers that are all of equal value to yourself** (thus, you have many ways to get what you want before making a concession).
3. **Make the offers all at the same time.** This last point is the hardest for most people to do because they negotiate like playing tennis: They make one offer and then wait for the other party to "return" a single offer; then they make a concession, and so on and so forth. In the multiple-offer strategy, a negotiator presents a "dessert tray" of offers to the other party and invites a reaction.

The multiple-offer strategy is based on the strategy of **inductive reasoning,** meaning that a negotiator can unilaterally deduce what the other party's true interests are and where the joint gains are. (We talk more about inductive, as well as deductive, reasoning, in chapter 8 on advanced negotiations and creativity.) By listening to the opponent's response, the negotiator learns about the other party's preferences. Thus, the negotiator acts as a "detective" by drawing conclusions based upon the opponents' responses to the multiple offers. The multiple-offer strategy has psychological benefits as well: When people perceive themselves as having more choices (as opposed to only one), they may be more likely to comply. The strategy can reveal valuable information about which issues are important to the other party.

STRUCTURE CONTINGENCY CONTRACTS BY CAPITALIZING ON DIFFERENCES

Negotiators not only have differences in interest and preference, but they view the world differently (Lax and Sebenius 1986). A book author may believe that the sales will be high; the publisher believes they will be more modest. Different interpretations of the facts may threaten already tenuous relations. Attempts to persuade the other person may be met with skepticism, hostility, and an escalating spiral of conflict. The surprising fact is that differences in beliefs—or expectations about uncertain events—pave the way toward integrative agreements. It is somewhat ironic that differences, rather than commonalities, can be more advantageous in negotiations (Lax and Sebenius 1986). The enlightened negotiator realizes that differences in beliefs, expectations, and tastes can create greater value than when both negotiators have identical preferences. The problem is that most people are uncomfortable when they sense differences and, instead of leveraging this opportunity, they either downplay their differences or ignore them.

There are many ways that negotiators can exploit differences to capitalize on integrative agreements (Lax and Sebenius 1986). Consider the following differences and the opportunities they create:

- Differences in the valuation of the negotiation issues
- Differences in expectations of uncertain events
- Differences in risk attitudes
- Differences in time preferences
- Differences in capabilities

Differences in Valuation

Negotiators have different strengths of preference for each issue. For example, in a negotiation for scarce office space, one person is more interested in a large office than a nice view; the other negotiator is more interested in a view than having extra space. They reach an agreement in which one person gets a large, windowless office and the other gets a small office with a great view. By trading off these issues, both were better off than by simply compromising on each issue. The strategy of trading off so as to capitalize on different strengths of preference is known as **logrolling** (Froman and Cohen 1970).

Differences in Expectations

Because negotiation often involves uncertainty, negotiators differ in their forecasts, or beliefs, about what will happen in the future. Consider the case of a woman and her brother who inherited a tool store from their father. The sister expected the profitability of the store to decline steadily; the brother expected the store to succeed. The sister wanted to sell the store; the brother wanted to keep it. A contingent contract was constructed: The brother agreed to buy his sister's share of the store over a period of time at a price based on her bleak assessment of its worth. The sister is guaranteed a certain return; the brother's return is based on how well the store does.

Consider another example. A city planner contracted with a building corporation to build and manage a condominium/retail center. The city's assessment of future sales was bleak, and so the city wanted to tax the units heavily. The corporation did not like the prospect of high taxes and believed that sales would be high in the coming year. A contingent contract was developed. The city promised the corporation a tax cap over 10 years as a function of yearly sales: Higher sales meant a lower tax cap; lower sales meant a higher tax cap. Each party was confident that his or her "best-case" scenario would come to pass.

Differences in Risk Attitudes

In other situations, negotiators agree on the probability of future events but feel differently about taking risks (Lax and Sebenius 1986). For example, two colleagues may undertake a collaborative project, such as writing a novel, for which they both agree that the probability of success is only moderate. The colleague with an established career can afford to be risk-seeking; the struggling young novelist may be risk-averse. The two may capitalize on their different risk-taking profiles with a contingent contract: The more risk-averse colleague receives the entire advance on the book; the risk-seeking colleague receives the majority of the risky profits after the publication of the novel.

Differences in Time Preferences

People may value the same event quite differently depending on *when* it occurs (Lax and Sebenius 1986). If one party is more impatient than the other, mechanisms for optimally sharing the consequences over time may be devised. Two partners in a joint venture might allocate the initial profits to the partner who has high costs for time, whereas the partner who can wait will achieve greater profits over a longer, delayed period.

Differences in Capabilities

People differ not only in their tastes, probability assessments, and risk preferences; they differ in their capabilities, endowments, and skills. Consider two managers who have different resources, capital, and support staff. One manager has strong quantitative, statistical skills and access to state-of-the-art computers; the other has strong marketing and design skills. Together, they may combine their differing skills and expertise in a mutually beneficial way, such as in the design of a new product concept. The development of successful research collaborations is fostered by differences in skills and preferences (Northcraft and Neale 1993).

Cautionary Note

Capitalizing on differences often entails **contingency contracts,** wherein negotiators make bets based upon different states of the world occurring. For contingency contracts to be effective, they should be able to be readily evaluated, leaving no room for ambiguity of interpretation. Conditions and measurement techniques should be spelled out in advance (Bazerman and Gillespie 1999). Further, a date or timeline should be mutually agreed upon. We go into more detail about contingency contracts in chapter 8 (creativity in negotiation).

PRESETTLEMENT SETTLEMENTS (PreSS)

Presettlement settlements (PreSS), engineered by Gillespie and Bazerman (1998), have three characteristics: They are *formal,* in that they encompass specific, binding obligations; *initial,* because they are intended to be replaced by a formal agreement; and *partial,* in that the parties do not address or resolve all outstanding issues. According to Gillespie and Bazerman (1998), presettlement settlements involve more than a simple handshake or "gentleman's agreement." Rather, a PreSS occurs in advance of the parties undertaking full-scale negotiations and are designed to be replaced by a long-term agreement. A PreSS resolves only a subset of the issues on which the parties disagree (i.e., partial). In some cases, instead of resolving any of the outstanding issues, a PreSS may simply establish a concrete framework for final negotiations.

Gillespie and Bazerman (1998) note that a famous example of PreSS is the 1993 Oslo accords between Israel and Palestine. The Oslo accords sought to establish an incremental process of negotiation and reciprocation that would lead to what both parties termed "final-status" talks. The parties agreed to wait to resolve the most difficult issues (e.g., borders, settlements, Jerusalem) until the final-status talks. As an initial step, the Israelis and Palestinians sought to resolve less difficult issues, thereby establishing a political dialogue and working toward formalized relations. For example, the Israelis agreed to release female prisoners, transfer disputed money, and withdraw from Hebron. The Palestinians agreed to revise their national charter, transfer suspected terrorists, and limit the size of the Palestinian police force. Gillespie and Bazerman (1998) noted that the PreSS framework has subsequently floundered due to heated rhetoric and escalating violence. (For another type of PreSS, see Box 4–1.)

> **BOX 4-1**
>
> ## NO-FIST (NORMAL OPERATIONS WITH A FINANCIAL STRIKE)
>
> Lax and Sebenius (1997) proposed a type of presettlement settlement (PreSS) in a letter to the editor of the *Wall Street Journal*. Lax and Sebenius noted that a planned strike by American Airlines pilots would result in the airline suffering revenue losses of more than $200 million per day. To avoid such a catastrophe, they recommended: "Once the [strike] deadline is imminent and negotiations are irretrievably stuck, the parties would agree to continue normal operations but to put some or all of their revenues and salaries into an escrow account controlled by a trusted outside party" (Lax and Sebenius 1997, A22). No matter how the escrow fund is eventually divided, both parties will be better off relative to a typical strike. NO-FIST produces a pareto-superior outcome for all concerned parties, including pilots, shareholders, customers, and nonpilot airline employees.
>
>

SEARCH FOR POSTSETTLEMENT SETTLEMENTS

A final strategy for expanding the pie is one in which negotiators reach an initial settlement that both agree to but spend additional time attempting to improve upon (each from their own perspective). In the **postsettlement settlement strategy,** negotiators agree to explore other options with the goal of finding another that both prefer more than the current one, or that one party prefers more and the other is indifferent to (Raiffa 1982). The current settlement becomes both parties' new BATNA. For any future agreement to replace the current one, both parties must be in agreement; otherwise, they revert to the initial agreement. It may seem counterintuitive, and perhaps downright counterproductive, to resume negotiations once an acceptable agreement has been reached, but the strategy of postsettlement settlements is remarkably effective in improving the quality of negotiated agreements (Bazerman, Russ, and Yakura 1987) and in moving an agreement from a level 1 agreement to a level 2 or 3 agreement.

The postsettlement settlement strategy allows both parties to reveal their preferences without fear of exploitation, because they can safely revert to their previous agreement. If better terms are found, parties can be more confident they have reached a level 2 or 3 settlement. If no better agreement is found, the parties may be more confident that the current agreement is level 3.

AN APPLICATION OF INTEGRATIVE STRATEGIES

The complexity and value of reaching integrative agreements is best understood through an example. Consider a classic buyer-seller negotiation. The buyer is the Windy City Theater (WCT), and the seller is POP Productions (POP). Imagine you are the general manager of the WCT. You would like to bring the musical *Oceania!* to the WCT for a week next April. *Oceania!* is represented and managed by POP, one of the largest producers of live entertainment in New York. You have a talk scheduled this

Table 4–1: WCT reservation and target points (columns 2 and 3); WCT's assessment of POP's reservation and target points (columns 4 and 5)

To-Be Negotiated Issue	WCT RP	WCT Target	POP RP*	POP Target*
Profit sharing (WCT/POP)	50-50	70-30	70-30	50-50
Salaries for cast and crew	$250,000/week	$175,000/week	$200,000/week	$275,000/week
Number of performances	9	11	11?	7
Lodging and board arrangements	WCT expense	POP expense	POP expense	WCT expense

*Note: WCT does not know POP's reservation or target points, but this is WCT's best estimate.

afternoon with the sales representative for POP. As general manager of WCT, you are committed to bringing quality live entertainment to the theater and structuring deals that are profitable for WCT. What steps should you take to maximize your profits?

PREPARATION: IDENTIFYING AND PRIORITIZING ISSUES

In preparation for your negotiation with POP, you make a list of the relevant issues to discuss:

1. Profit sharing of ticket revenues (typically, the theater and production company share ticket revenues, but the exact percentage is a matter of negotiation).
2. Salaries for the cast and crew (the theater pays a lump-sum salary to POP for the cast and crew, but the amount is negotiable).
3. The number of shows to be offered during the week (the typical number of shows is nine: five evening performances and four weekend matinees; however, the total number of shows could be reduced to seven or increased to add two weekday matinees—again, this is negotiable).
4. Lodging and meal costs for the cast and crew (lodging and board for the 100-member cast and crew for the week-run show can be expensive—who should pick up the tab? Again, this is a matter of negotiation).[1]

You spend the next week determining your reservation point and your best assessment of POP's reservation point. Specifically, you make the assessments listed in Table 4–1. Note that in this negotiation, WCT has a reservation point for *each* issue (as opposed to a general, summary reservation point).

DURING NEGOTIATION: SEARCH FOR TRADE-OFFS AND AVOID COMPROMISE

You make a strategic decision to let your opening offer represent what you believe to be POP's reservation point for each of the negotiation issues. You bring up these issues with POP and clearly state your preferences for each (see Table 4–2).

---

[1] This negotiation has been simplified to illustrate key points. Case available from the Dispute Resolution Research Center (DRRC), Kellogg Graduate School of Management, Northwestern University; e-mail: drrc@kellogg.nwu.edu.

Table 4–2:	WCT opening offer; POP's opening offer	
To-Be-Negotiated Issue	*Windy City Theater's Opening Offer*	*POP Production's Opening Offer*
Profit sharing (WCT/POP)	70-30	50-50
Salaries for cast and crew	$200,000/week	$250,000/week
Number of performances	11	7
Lodging and board arrangements	POP expense	WCT expense

Not surprisingly, POP rejects your opening proposal and counters by proposing a set of terms that represent your reservation point (Table 4–2, POP's opening offer). Obviously, POP did her homework! You use the flipchart in the meeting room to make a sketch of the proposals that looks like Table 4–2. A quick inspection of Table 4–2 reveals that your interests appear to be primarily opposed: POP wants 50 percent of net ticket revenues and bigger salaries than WCT wants to pay; POP wants to contract for fewer performances and desires complimentary lodging and board. You are feeling a little dismayed. This looks like a fixed-pie situation. POP then suggests that the two of you compromise by splitting the difference halfway on each of the issues. POP proposes the following:

Profit sharing:	60-40 (WCT/POP)
Cast and crew salaries:	$225,000/week
Performances:	9
Lodging:	WCT pays for hotel; POP pays for meals

You are pleased by POP's reasonable offer. It clearly punctures your reservation price for each issue, and so you seriously consider accepting it on the spot and concluding the negotiation. You call your financial advisor, who gives you an assessment of the expected value of these terms for you—about $236,000. You are unsure exactly how much the proposal is worth to POP, but it is an obvious improvement over your opening offer to her. You guesstimate that the proposal has a net value of $549,000 to POP (40 percent of $885,000 in ticket revenues = $354,000, plus $225,000 in salaries = $579,000 less $30,000 for food = $549,000. Graphically, this is point A plotted in Figure 4–2.) POP has her legal expert draw up the paperwork, and you are about to sign off. However, you decide to wait until morning.

That night, you call your financial advisor, who gives you more details about the projected profits figure. She explains that the added revenue from each additional show to the regularly scheduled nine performances would be $98,000 per performance. This means that if you add two matinee performances to the run of *Oceania!*, you could increase your profits by nearly $200,000! You speculate that lodging and food expenses for POP would be more expensive than adding additional performances because the cast and crew are already in town. You decide to propose a trade-off: You pay for the cast and crew's lodging and meals for the entire week (cost to you = $95,000); in exchange, POP adds two weekday matinee performances to the run. This would mean an increase in value to you of over $120,000 over the previous deal (or $356,000).

FIGURE 4–2 First Assessment of Profit to WCT and POP

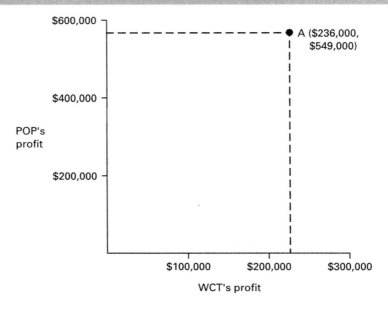

SEARCH FOR LEVEL 2 PIE-EXPANDING AGREEMENTS

The next morning, you propose the following offer (point B on Figure 4–3) to POP:

Profit sharing:	60-40 (WCT/POP)
Cast and crew salaries:	$225,000/week
Performances:	11
Lodging:	WCT pays for all hotel and meals (no charge to POP)

POP is clearly pleased. You estimate that POP's profits have increased by about $40,000—the savings she made on meals. In addition, it represents added value for you. This means that you have moved from a level 1 integrative agreement to a level 2 integrative agreement (see point B in Figure 4–3). POP's attorney prepares another contract for you to sign. However, you are still reluctant to sign a contract. You feel that the terms are acceptable but shudder at the thought that you nearly failed to realize the additional $120,000 in profit. You wonder: Is there more hidden value in this negotiation? You recall in your first meeting with POP that you also discussed another POP Productions Broadway show, *Bugles.* You discussed the possibility of bringing *Bugles* to WCT with your board of directors, who agreed that it would be considered profitable if cast and crew salaries were $100,000 or less. You decide to ask POP about her plans for *Bugles.*

EXPAND THE PIE BY ADDING ISSUES

When you mention *Bugles* to POP, her eyes light up, and she says that she has received a lot of feelers about *Bugles* but has not yet signed a contract with anyone for the week you are interested in. You ask POP point-blank about cast and crew salaries, and she

FIGURE 4–3 Second Assessment of Profit to WCT and POP

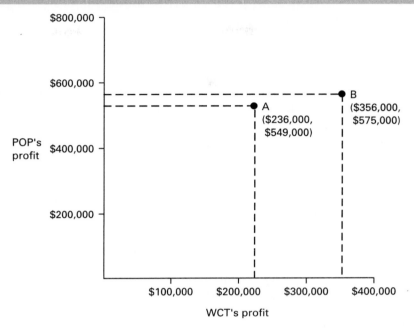

says POP is targeting $100,000 per week with a bottom line of $75,000. You offer POP $80,000 for *Bugles* at WCT. She accepts, and you have added another $20,000 of value to the deal for WCT! In addition, POP's profits have increased by at least $5,000 (see point C in Figure 4–4). POP phones her lawyer, and *Bugles* is written into the contract. Again, you delay closing the deal, suggesting that the two of you meet for coffee the next morning.

You go home to think about the deal. You are unsure how to add additional value without renegotiating the terms that you have already agreed to. You feel that it would be bargaining in bad faith to renegotiate the profit sharing of 60-40 WCT/POP. However, you remember POP saying she expected ticket sales for *Oceania!* to be about 85 to 90 percent of the house for the weeklong run of *Oceania!* In contrast, you are less optimistic about the show's likely success. In fact, your marketing manager projects sales of 75 percent of the house. Clearly, the two of you have very different beliefs about the success of the show. You wonder if POP would be willing to bet on it.

DEVISE CONTINGENCY CONTRACTS AROUND DIFFERENT BELIEFS

You open the meeting by telling POP you are more pessimistic about the show than she is. You explain that it is highly unlikely that ticket sales will be over 75 percent of the house based on your data, and you project $885,000 of net ticket sales. POP shakes her head in disagreement and claims that *Oceania!* will sell 85 percent of the house across all performances, which would mean net ticket revenues in excess of $1 million.

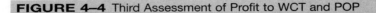

FIGURE 4–4 Third Assessment of Profit to WCT and POP

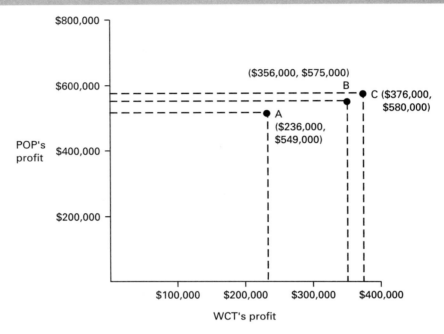

The two of you argue about this unproductively for nearly an hour. Finally, you realize there is no changing her mind, and you propose the following offer to POP:

- If ticket sales are less than $900,000, WCT takes 70 percent of the profits.
- If ticket sales are between $900,000 and $1 million, WCT takes 60 percent of the profits (original deal).
- If ticket sales are greater than $1 million, WCT takes 40 percent of the profits.

POP is very receptive and accepts the bet (point D in Figure 4–5). How valuable is this proposal to you? You are 80 percent sure that ticket sales will be under $900,000. You estimate there is a 10 percent chance that ticket sales will be between $900,000 and $1 million. You estimate there is a 10 percent chance that ticket sales will be greater than $1 million. You compute your expected value, using the expected utility principle:

$$0.8 \ (\$630,000) + 0.1(\$560,000) + 0.1(\$400,000) =$$
$$\$504,000 + \$56,000 + \$40,000 = \$600,000$$

Clearly, $600,000 is better than the original deal—the value of the deal to WCT has increased by $70,000 since your last meeting with POP. You estimate that POP's value increased by at least the same amount. Graphically, this is shown as point D in Figure 4–5. You now feel confident that you have negotiated a good deal for the WCT. Further, it is clear that the integrative negotiation process has had a positive impact on your relationship with POP.

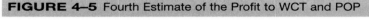

FIGURE 4–5 Fourth Estimate of the Profit to WCT and POP

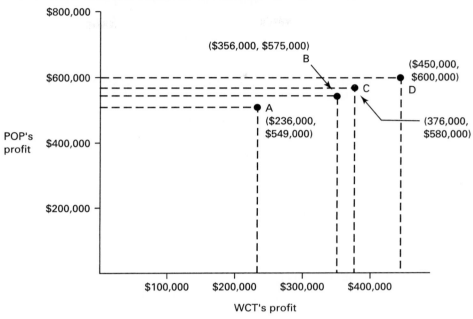

POSTNEGOTIATION ANALYSIS

As you fly home on the plane, you think back on the negotiations. The value of both parties' outcomes improved steadily. Figure 4–5 reflects the value (in thousands of dollars) of each successive proposal. Through a combination of logrolling, bridging interests, adding additional issues, and betting on different expectations, you successfully moved the negotiation from a level 1 integrative agreement to a level 3 integrative agreement.

A STRATEGIC FRAMEWORK FOR REACHING INTEGRATIVE AGREEMENTS

The discovery and creation of integrative agreements is much like problem solving. Problem solving requires creativity. Integrative agreements are devilishly obvious after the fact, but not before. Because negotiation is an ill-structured task, with few constraints and a myriad of possible "moves," a royal road for reaching integrative agreement does not exist. The closest we come to a generic "bag of tricks" is a decision-making model of integrative negotiation. The model is prescriptive; that is, it focuses on what negotiators *should* do to reach agreement, not what they *actually* do. The decision-making model of integrative negotiation is depicted in Figure 4–6. The model has five major components: resource assessment, assessment of differences, construction of offers and trade-offs, acceptance/rejection of decision, and renegotiation.

FIGURE 4–6 Decision-Making Model of Integrative Negotiation

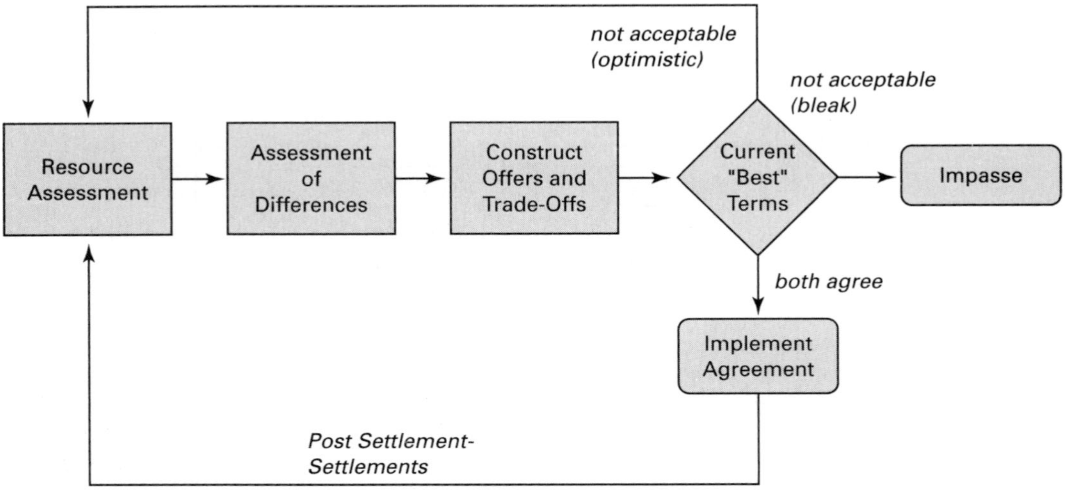

RESOURCE ASSESSMENT

Resource assessment involves the identification of the bargaining issues and alternatives. For example, consider an employment negotiation. The bargaining issues may be salary, vacation, and benefits. The feasible salary range may be $60,000 to $100,000, vacation time may be one to five weeks, and benefits may include stock options or a company car. In this stage, parties identify the issues that are of concern to them in the negotiation. A superset emerges from the combination of both parties' issues.

In our earlier example, WCT considered the profit sharing, salaries, and number of performances to be the central issues; POP considered crew and cast lodging as an important issue. The union of both parties' issue sets forms the **issue mix** of the negotiation. In addition to specifying the issue mix, parties also define and clarify the alternatives for each issue. For example, WCT may consider between nine and 11 performances; POP may consider between seven and nine. The ultimate set of options for each issue is a superset of both parties' alternatives.

Later stages of resource assessment move beyond the mere identification of issues and alternatives to two higher-order processes: the **unbundling** of issues and alternatives, and the addition of new issues and alternatives. Unbundling (Lax and Sebenius 1986) of issues is important in negotiations that center around a single issue. Because mutually beneficial trade-offs require a minimum of two issues, it is important to fractionate conflict into more than one issue. In other instances, it may be necessary to add new issues and alternatives. The process of adding issues and alternatives is facilitated by discussing parties' interests.

ASSESSMENT OF DIFFERENCES

Once the issue mix and set of alternatives are identified, negotiators should focus on assessing their differences in valuation, probability assessment, risk preferences, time constraints, and capabilities (Lax and Sebenius 1986).

Two concerns should guide the assessment of interdependencies. First, each party should focus on his or her most important issues. Second, parties should focus on issues that are of high value to one party and of low cost for the other party to provide. For example, in WCT's case, lodging is relatively low cost in comparison to the additional revenues from weekday matinees.

OFFERS AND TRADE-OFFS

In this phase, parties should consider several potential trade-offs among valuations, forecasts, risks, time preferences, and capabilities, and eliminate those dominated by other alternatives. There is no sense in making a trade-off unless what you are offering the other party is more valuable to her than what it costs you to provide.

ACCEPTANCE/REJECTION DECISION

At some point, negotiators may land on an outcome both find minimally acceptable: It exceeds both parties' reservation points and constitutes a level 1 integrative agreement. Parties may end negotiations with this agreement, as POP was inclined to do after the first meeting with WCT. But the identification of a minimally acceptable agreement does not necessarily mean that settlement is efficient. Like WCT, negotiators should continue to explore the possibilities, depending on their costs for time and their subjective assessments of the likelihood of reaching a superior solution. Negotiators' aspirations and goals may influence the search process in negotiation; negotiators who set specific, challenging goals are more likely to continue to search for integrative agreements than do those who do not set goals or who set easy goals (Huber and Neale 1986).

PROLONGING NEGOTIATION AND RENEGOTIATION

Two feedback loops emanate from the decision stage: the decision to prolong negotiations and the decision to renegotiate.

Negotiators should prolong negotiations when the best agreement on the bargaining table fails to meet both parties' reservation points. Negotiators should reassess the resources by unpacking the initial set of issues and breaking them down to smaller issues that may be traded off. In addition to unpacking issues, negotiators may add issues and alternatives to the bargaining mix. If parties have identified all the issues and alternatives, identified differences to trade off, and a mutually agreeable solution has not been found, then they should call a halt to the negotiation and pursue their BATNAs.

In some instances, parties may decide to renegotiate after a mutually agreeable settlement has been reached. It may seem counterintuitive or counterproductive to resume negotiations once an acceptable agreement has been reached, but the strategy of postsettlement settlements is remarkably effective in improving the quality of negotiated agreements (Bazerman, Russ, and Yakura 1987) and in moving an agreement from a level 1 agreement to a level 2 or 3 agreement.

The postsettlement settlement strategy allows both parties to reveal their preferences without fear of exploitation, because they can safely revert to their previous agreement. If better terms are found, parties can be more confident they have reached a level 2 or 3 settlement. If no better agreement is found, the parties may be more confident that the current agreement is level 3.

DO NOT FORGET ABOUT CLAIMING

Sometimes, when negotiators learn about integrative agreements and expanding the pie, they walk off into the sunset and forget about the distributive (pie-slicing) element of negotiation. It is *not* an effective negotiation strategy to just focus on expanding the pie; the negotiator must simultaneously focus on claiming resources. After all, if a negotiator just focused on expanding the pie, he or she would be no better off because the other party would reap all the added value.

Sometimes negotiators will regard this advice as callous and state that they "trust" that the other party will want to be "fair" in the negotiations. This is a nice thought but does not square with reality. Negotiation is not a game of trust—so why tempt your opponent? Negotiators can successfully build and maintain collaborative, mutually beneficial relationships if they both focus on claiming as well as expanding the pie.

We have witnessed three stages in the evolution of the integrative negotiator. The first stage is what we call the "old-fashioned" negotiator. This is the negotiator who comes from the old school of bargaining and believes that to successfully negotiate, one must adopt a tough, hard stance. The second stage in the evolution of the negotiator is what we call the "flower child" negotiator. This is the negotiator who gets "turned on" to win-win negotiations and is so busy expanding the pie that he or she forgets to claim resources for him- or herself. Thus, the "flower child" is at a disadvantage in terms of slicing the pie. The third stage is what we call the "enlightened" negotiator, who realizes that negotiation has a pie-expanding aspect but at the same time does not forget to claim resources. Thus, this negotiator protects her own interests while expanding the pie. If you follow all the strategies outlined in this chapter, you will be an enlightened negotiator.

CONCLUSION

Virtually all negotiators want to reach integrative (or win-win) agreements; however, virtually all negotiators fail to do so—meaning that money and resources are left on the table. What is more, people are usually not aware that their negotiation outcomes are inefficient. The key reasons for lose-lose outcomes are illusory conflict and the fixed-pie perception. The successful creation of win-win negotiation deals involves building trust and sharing information about priorities and preferences (not BATNAs!); asking diagnostic questions; providing your opponent information about your priorities and preferences (not your BATNA!); unbundling issues; making package deals (not single-issue offers); making multiple offers simultaneously; structuring contingency contracts that capitalize on differences in negotiators' beliefs, expectations, and attitudes; and using the pre- and postsettlement settlement strategy. In their attempts to expand the pie, negotiators should not forget about claiming resources.

PART II

ADVANCED NEGOTIATION SKILLS

5

DEVELOPING A NEGOTIATING STYLE

When U.S. trade representative Charlene Barshefsky goes to the bargaining table to work out trade deals, she dons her signature silk scarves and hammers away. Once, she went without sleep for 51 hours to pound out a trade agreement with Japan; speaking in perfect turns of phrase, she was able to grind down the other side. Her colleagues were so impressed that they nicknamed her "Stonewall." She has also been called "Dragon Lady": In a negotiation with China, she threatened to pack her bags and leave for the airport, cueing her negotiation partner, Gene Sperling, a White House aide, to stalk theatrically away from the table after her. Some have described Barshefsky as a "sharp instrument," a "woman warrior who is genuinely responsive to people" (Hua 1999, 42). Armed with the precise speech of a litigator, Barshefsky is enormously skilled in wresting concessions from trading partners. In one negotiation, she did not even need to utter a single word to disconcert her counterpart—when a Japanese finance master said that the U.S. delegation had to "take or leave" the offer that was on the table, Barshefsky just laughed out loud. Through years of expertise, Barshefsky has developed her own effective bargaining style. She certainly has had some failures, but these are outweighed by many important successes. (Hua 1999)

TOUGH VERSUS SOFT NEGOTIATORS

Negotiators often make the mistake of choosing between one of two completely different negotiation styles or approaches: being tough or being soft (Bazerman and Neale 1992). The tough negotiator is unflinching, makes high demands, concedes very little, holds out until the very end, and often rejects offers that are within the bargaining zone. In contrast, the soft negotiator typically offers too many and too-generous concessions, reveals his or her reservation point, and is so concerned that the other party feels good about the negotiation that he gives away too much of the bargaining pie to the other party. About 78 percent of MBA students describe their style as "cooperative"; 22 percent describe themselves as "aggressive" (Lewicki and Robinson 1998). Neither approach is particularly effective in simultaneously expanding and slicing the pie, and both approaches are likely to lead to outcomes that negotiators regret. The tough negotiator is likely to walk away from potentially profitable interactions and may gain a reputation for being stubborn. This may intimidate others, but it will not change the size of the bargaining zone. On the other hand, the soft negotiator agrees too readily and never reaps much of the bargaining surplus.

The good news is that being tough or soft is not the negotiator's only choice—if the negotiator can become more strategic in the selection and implementation of her negotiation style. This chapter is designed to help you create a comfortable and effective negotiating style that allows you to (1) expand the pie, (2) maximize your slice, and (3) feel good about the negotiation.

MOTIVATION-APPROACH-EMOTION

The rest of this chapter focuses on three key dimensions of bargaining style: motivation, approach, and emotion. Our view is that basic motivations, such as self-interest or competition, drive behavior in negotiations, and that a negotiator can approach a negotiation with a focus on interests, rights, or power. Finally, the negotiator's emotions (or lack thereof) is also a type of bargaining style.

We will review each dimension and profile negotiators that characterize each style. Your job is to do an honest self-assessment of what your current negotiation style is. Chances are—if you are like most people—you will see your style as a little bit of each dimension, dependent upon the situation. However, most people tend to adopt more of one style than others—simply put, most people have a dominant, or instinctive, style. Furthermore, the people with whom you negotiate tend to see you as being more like one style rather than a blend of all of them.

Your first response in a negotiation situation is often a good indicator of your instinctive style. Take an honest look at yourself negotiating (tape-record or videotape yourself if you have to). Then ask people who are not afraid to give you frank feedback how they view you, in terms of style. You will probably be surprised at their responses!

Next, we review the various styles and discuss the pros and cons of each. Once you know your style, you are not locked into it forever. You have choices, and this chapter provides strategies for thinking about these choices.

MOTIVATIONS

People have different orientations toward the process of negotiation: Some people are individualists, seeking only their own gain; others are cooperative, seeking to maximize joint interests; and others are competitive, seeking to maximize differences. (For a complete list of possibilities, see Fig. 5–1.) Figure 5–1 depicts eight distinct motivational orientations, ranging from altruism (high concern for others' interests) to aggression (desire to harm the other party) to masochism (desire to harm one's self) and individualism (desire to further one's own interests). Cooperation represents a midpoint between altruism and cooperation; martyrdom represents a midpoint between altruism and masochism; sadomasochism represents a midpoint between masochism and aggression; and competition represents a midpoint between aggression and individualism.

ASSESSING YOUR MOTIVATIONAL STYLE

Although Figure 5–1 depicts several motivational orientations (MOs), the following three are most common: individualism, competition, and cooperation. (See Table 5–1, specifically.)

FIGURE 5–1 Subset of Social Values

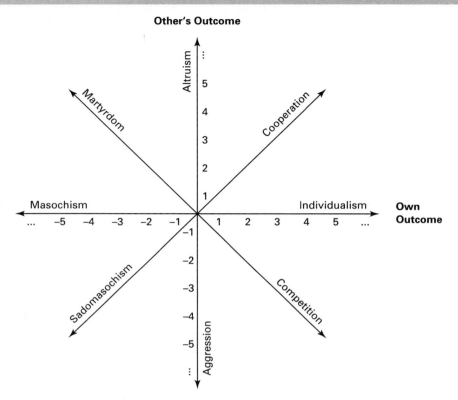

Source: McClintock, C. G. and E. van Avermaet (1982). Social values and rules of fairness: A theoretical perspective. In *Cooperation and Helping Behavior.* V. J. Derlega and J. Grezlak (eds.) New York: Academic Press, 43–71.

Table 5–1:   Motivational styles

| | MOTIVATIONAL STYLE | | |
	Individualistic	*Competitive*	*Cooperative*
Objective	Self-interest	Victory	Joint welfare
View of others	Self-interested	Competitive	Heterogeneous: some cooperators, some competitive; some individualistic
Situational factors that trigger this MO	Incentives to maximize own gain	Group competition When organizations make interpersonal comparisons salient	Social identity; superordinate goals

1. The **individualistic** negotiator prefers to maximize his or her own goals and has little or no concern for how much the other person is getting.
2. The **competitive** negotiator prefers to maximize the winning margin or "beat" the other side.
3. The **cooperative** negotiator prefers to maximize equality and minimize the difference between negotiators' outcomes.

Whether you tend to be an individualist, competitor, or cooperator is determined by hardwiring (e.g., your underlying personality) and by the situation (e.g., your relationship with the other party or the incentive system in place in your organization). Much of the time, negotiators' goals change depending upon the situation. For a quick assessment of your own motivational orientation, complete the nine questions in Box 5–1.

Your ability to understand how your goal is shaped by various external factors is a key step toward self-insight. Richard Shell (1999) has identified helpful strategies and tips designed for cooperative types and competitive types. According to Shell, if you are a cooperative negotiator, you need to become more assertive, confident, and prudent in negotiations to be more effective at pie expanding and pie slicing. He outlines seven tools for the overly cooperative negotiator:

1. **Avoid concentrating too much on your bottom line.** Instead, spend extra time preparing your goals and developing high aspirations.
2. **Develop your BATNA.** Know your options to negotiating.
3. **Get an agent and delegate the negotiation task.** It is not an admission of failure to appoint an agent, if you think she can act more assertively for you than you can yourself.
4. **Bargain on behalf of someone or something else, not yourself.** Sometimes people feel selfish when they negotiate; to get away from this limiting perception, think about other people, such as your family, your staff, even your "retired self," and negotiate on their behalf.
5. **Create an audience.** People negotiate more assertively when they have an audience. So, tell someone about your negotiation, make promises, and then report results.
6. **Say, "You will have to do better than that because . . . ," not "yes."** Cooperative people are programmed to say yes to almost anything. Rehearse not saying yes to everything that is proposed.
7. **Insist on commitments, not just agreements.** An agreement puts too much trust in the other party; instead, insist upon commitments and specific promises from the other party that have consequences if they are not followed.

Shell also outlines seven tools for competitive people. He cautions that competitive negotiators need to become more aware of others and legitimate their needs:

1. **Think about pie expansion, not just pie slicing.** Remember that you can increase your slice of the pie by creating a bigger pie.
2. **Ask more questions than you think you should.** It pays to really understand the other party's objectives and needs.
3. **Rely on standards.** Other people respond well to arguments based upon standards of fairness and objectivity.

<BOX 5–1>

MOTIVATIONAL STYLE ASSESSMENT

Each question presents three possible distributions of money (A, B, and C) to you and an opponent. Your task is to choose which of these distributions you most prefer. Indicate your true preference, not what you think you should choose. Be honest with yourself and circle only one alternative per question (Kuhlman and Marshello 1975).

	Payoff to you Payoff to other	A	B	C
1	You	$4,800	$5,400	$4,800
	Other party	$800	$2,800	$4,800
2	You	$5,600	$5,000	$5,000
	Other party	$3,000	$5,000	$1,000
3	You	$5,200	$5,200	$5,800
	Other party	$5,200	$1,200	$3,200
4	You	$5,000	$5,600	$4,900
	Other party	$1,000	$3,000	$4,900
5	You	$5,600	$5,000	$4,900
	Other party	$3,000	$5,000	$900
6	You	$5,000	$5,000	$5,700
	Other party	$5,000	$1,000	$3,000
7	You	$5,100	$5,600	$5,100
	Other party	$5,100	$3,000	$1,100
8	You	$5,500	$5,000	$5,000
	Other party	$3,000	$1,000	$5,000
9	You	$4,800	$4,900	$5,400
	Other party	$4,800	$1,000	$3,000

Compute your **cooperative** score by giving yourself one point for:
#1-c, #2-b, #3-a, #4-c, #5-b, #6-a, #7-a, #8-c, #9-a.

Compute your **competitive** score by giving yourself one point for:
#1-a, #2-c, #3-b, #4-a, #5-c, #6-b, #7-c, #8-b, #9-b.

Compute your **individualist** score by giving yourself one point for:
#1-b, #2-a, #3-c, #4-b, #5-a, #6-c, #7-b, #8-a, #9-c.

4. **Hire a relationship manager.** It is not a sign of failure to consult with someone concerning how to manage the "people side" of negotiations.
5. **Be scrupulously reliable.** Keep your word. Remember the egocentric bias: You see yourself as more honorable than others do, so you have got to go overboard.
6. **Do not haggle when you can negotiate.** Do not view the negotiation as a contest of wills on every little issue. Spend time thinking about all the

issues and the big picture. Remember that trade-offs mean that you will lose on some issues, in return for big gains on other issues.

7. **Always acknowledge the other party and protect her self-esteem.** Do not gloat about yourself. Remember that Dale Carnegie said that the word that other people most like to hear is their own name. So shower them with honest respect.

STRATEGIC ISSUES CONCERNING MOTIVATIONAL STYLE

Once you know your own (and the other party's) motivational style, how can you best use this information? There are a number of strategic issues when it comes to motivational style.

Do Not Lose Sight of Your Own Interests

In any negotiation situation, it is important not to lose sight of your own interests. Individualists do not need to worry about this, but cooperators and competitors do. Often, two cooperators end up with a lose-lose agreement because they fail to make their interests known to the other party (Thompson and DeHarpport 1998). Similarly, competitors are often so intent on "beating" the other side that they do not pay attention to their own interests. In a sense, they win the battle but lose the war. Thus, it is important that you maintain a high level of concern for your own interests as well as the other party's (Pruitt and Carnevale, 1993; de Dreu, Weingart, and Kwon 2000). As an example, suppose you are asked to chose between the following (based on Bazerman, Loewenstein, and White 1992):

Choice A: $500 for you and $500 for another person
Choice B: $600 for you and $800 for another person

An individualistic negotiator (interested in maximizing his or her own outcomes) chooses B, even though it means that the other person gets more money. In contrast, competitive negotiators (interested in maximizing the difference between their own and the other party's outcomes) choose A. Similarly, a cooperator chooses A as well. Most people evaluate choice A to be more desirable than choice B; however, when it actually comes down to making a choice, they choose B (Bazerman, Loewenstein, and White 1992). Thus, there is often a discrepancy between what people find "desirable" and what they actually do—in other words, people find it undesirable to earn less than their peers, but when it comes down to it, they seek to maximize their own outcomes.

Most People Are Concerned with the "Other Guy"

People are very concerned with the payoffs received by others. In one investigation, people were given several choices concerning the division of a pie between themselves and another person (e.g., $300 you/$300 other versus $500 you/$800 other, etc.; Loewenstein, Thompson, and Bazerman 1989). They were asked to indicate how satisfactory each division of the pie was. If people were purely individualistic, satisfaction would only be driven by the amount of money for oneself. In fact, people were highly concerned with how much the "other person" received, so much so that people often preferred to earn less money, if it meant that this would equate outcomes between themselves and another person. For example, many people preferred $300 self/$300 other over $500 self/$800 other. When faced with a choice between $300 self/$300 other versus $800 self/$500 other, people still tended to prefer equality, but not nearly as strongly as when the self was disadvantaged.

There are distinct differences between the pie-expanding and pie-slicing strategies used by cooperators versus those used by competitors. Cooperators not only increase the size of the pie, they also prefer an equitable division of the pie in comparison to individualists and competitors. Furthermore, cooperation is strongly related to reciprocity: Relative to individualists and competitors, cooperators are more likely to engage in the same level of cooperation as their opponent (Van Lange 1999).

Use the Principle of Reinforcement to Shape Behavior

Negotiators can use basic principles of reinforcement (and punishment) to shape the behavior of their opponents. Use of reinforcement and punishment can be subtle, and the other party may not even be aware that you are using it. As an example, in one situation, a lecturer stood in front of a class. Half of the class was instructed to look interested, nod their heads, and smile approvingly (positive reinforcement); the other half of the class was told to look bored and disinterested (punishment). After a short time, the instructor moved to the side of the class that was reinforcing his behavior. One of the best ways to encourage an opponent to engage in a behavior is to positively reinforce it when you see her using it. It is important to reinforce the behavior immediately after it occurs, rather than delaying it. Similarly, one of the fastest ways of extinguishing behavior you *do not* want your opponent to use is to simply not respond.

Recognize the Power of Reciprocity

Integrative (pie-expanding) and distributive (pie-slicing) behaviors tend to be reciprocated (Brett, Shapiro, and Lytle 1998; Donohue 1981; Putnam 1983). Similarly, there is a tendency for people to reciprocate the MO of the other party. If you want to discourage a competitive MO in your opponent, then you need to resist the urge to reciprocate it.

Anticipate Motivation Clashes at the Bargaining Table

It is unlikely that your partner will have the same negotiation motivation as you, at least initially. What happens when motivations collide at the table? Consider what happens when a person with a cooperative orientation negotiates with a competitive person. The cooperator begins the negotiation in a cooperative fashion, but when she realizes that she is facing a competitor, she changes her own style. People with a cooperative orientation behave competitively when paired with a competitive opponent, whereas competitive players do not change (Kelley and Stahelski 1970). In another study, when different types of players were faced with a prosocial (cooperative) opponent, prosocial and individualistic players were more likely to cooperate than were competitive players, but they would compete when the other party competed; competitive players competed regardless of the behavior of the other party (McClintock and Liebrand 1988).

Anticipate Convergence

A negotiator's goal orientation (individualistic, cooperative, or competitive) provides an initial strategic approach to negotiations. During negotiation, people's strategies often change in response to how they view the other party and the situation. In particular, when a cooperator meets a competitor, the cooperator is the one to change. Thus, there is a strong tendency toward convergence of styles at the bargaining table (Weingart and Brett 1998).

Convergence of outcomes, as well as bargaining styles, occurs in later stages of negotiation (Gulliver 1979). As deadlines approach, people exchange specific proposals and make concessions (Lim and Murnighan 1994; Stuhlmacher, Gillespie, and Champagne 1998).

Be Aware of Positive Effects of Cooperation

When both negotiators have a cooperative orientation, they can be more effective in terms of maximizing the pie (Olekalns and Smith 1999; 1998; Pruitt and Lewis 1975; Weingart, Bennett, and Brett 1993). For example, in a study of multiparty negotiations, cooperative groups (four parties) outperformed individualists in terms of pie expanding (Weingart, Bennett, and Brett 1993). Highly cooperative negotiators use more integrative strategies (such as information exchange), make more proposals for mutual coordination, and use fewer distributive tactics (Olekalns and Smith 1999).

The Relationship with the Other Party Affects Motivational Orientation

Consider the following choice (from Loewenstein, Thompson, and Bazerman 1989):

Choice A: $4,000 for yourself
Choice B: 50 percent chance at $3,000; 50 percent chance at $5,000

Which do you choose? We asked 111 MBA students, and most of them (73 percent) chose the sure thing: choice A. This is an example of the risk-aversion principle we discussed in chapter 2. We then asked a separate, but comparable, group of MBA students to choose between:

Choice C: $4,000 for yourself
$6,000 for another person
Choice D: Self: 50 percent chance at $3,000, 50 percent chance at $5,000
Other: 50 percent chance at $7,000, 50 percent chance at $5,000

A close look at all four choices (A, B, C, and D) reveals that the C choice is identical to the A choice (except for the payoff to the other person), and the D choice is identical to the B choice (except for the payoff to the other person). Thus, if people were perfectly rational and consistent, they would choose C over D (given that most choose A over B). However, this is not what actually happens. People's choices are driven, in large part, by their relationship with the other party. Negotiators who have a positive relationship with the other person prefer the sure thing (C; 56 percent) over the gamble (D); in contrast, those who had a negative relationship with the other person preferred to gamble on D (67 percent) over C. Apparently, the type of relationship we have with another person affects our motivational orientation.

APPROACH[1]

According to Ury, Brett, and Goldberg (1988), negotiators use one of three types of approaches when in the process of conflict or dispute resolution:

1. **Interests:** Negotiators who focus on interests attempt to learn about the other's underlying needs, desires, and concerns. Negotiators with an interests-based approach often attempt to reconcile differing interests among parties in a way that addresses parties' most pressing needs and concerns.

---

[1]Ideas in this section are based on Ury, Brett, and Goldberg's (1988) interests, rights, and power model in dispute situations. We use their model in a negotiation context.

2. **Rights:** Negotiators who focus on rights apply standards of fairness to an analysis of negotiation. Standards may include terms specified by contracts, legal rights, precedent, or expectations based upon norms.
3. **Power:** Negotiators who focus on power attempt to resolve disputes by analyzing status, rank, and other types of power, such as the ability to hold out.

As an example of the difference between interests, rights, and power-based approaches, consider this statement made by an employer: "I am afraid that I cannot meet your desired salary requirements, but I do hope that you will realize that working in our firm is a wonderful opportunity and join us." Before reading further, take a moment to consider how you would respond if an employer said this to you during a negotiation. Three different negotiators might respond to the opponent's statement thusly:

1. **Interest-based negotiator response:** "I am very interested in joining your company if my interests can be met. I would be interested in hearing more about what parts of the entire employment package you can negotiate. For example, I am interested in whether the salary level you have indicated is one that is nonnegotiable in every instance, or what circumstances and concerns influence salary levels. You did not mention other aspects of the offer, such as stock options, vacations, and flex time. Can we discuss those at this point?"
2. **Rights-based negotiator response:** "I am very interested in joining your company if we can come up with a fair employment package. I would like to point out that my salary requirements are in line with those of other people joining similar companies. I would think it would be a competitive advantage for your company to offer employment packages that are competitive with those being offered by other companies. I believe that my record and previous experience mean that a higher salary would be fair in this case."
3. **Power-based negotiator response:** "I am very interested in joining your company, but I must tell you that other companies are offering me more attractive deals at this point. I would like to invite you to reconsider the offer so that I do not have to resort to turning your offer down, given that I think that we make a good match for one another. I hope that you will be able to make a competitive offer."

For a more complete description of interests-, rights-, or power-based approaches, see Table 5–2.

During the process of negotiating or resolving disputes, the focus may shift from interests to rights to power and back again. For example, in one investigation (Lytle, Brett, and Shapiro 1999), negotiators' statements were tape-recorded during a negotiation. Each statement that negotiators made was coded in terms of whether it reflected an interests-, rights-, or power-based approach. Parties moved frequently among interests, rights, and power in the same negotiation (23/25 dyads), with more emphasis on rights and power in the first and third quarters than in the second and fourth.

ASSESSING YOUR APPROACH

Next, we present each approach in more detail. Which one characterizes you?

Table 5–2: Approaches to negotiation

	Approach		
	Interests	*Rights*	*Power*
Goal	Self-interest Dispute resolution Understanding others' concerns	Fairness Justice	Winning Respect
Temporal focus	Present (what needs and interests do we have right now?)	Past (what has been dictated by the past)	Future ("What steps can I take in future to overpower other?")
Distributive strategies (pie slicing)	Compromise	Often produces a "winner" and "loser"; thus, unequal distribution	Often produces a "winner" and "loser"; thus, unequal distribution
Integrative strategies (pie expansion)	Most likely to expand the pie via addressing parties' underlying needs	Difficult to expand the pie unless focus is on interests	Difficult to expand the pie unless focus is on interests
Implications for future negotiations and relationship	Greater understanding Satisfaction Stability of agreement	Possible court action	Resentment Possible retaliation Revenge

Interests

Interests are a person's needs, desires, concerns, fears—in general, the things a person cares about or wants. Interests underlie people's positions in negotiation (the tangible items they *say* they want). Reconciling interests in negotiation is not easy. It involves probing for deep-seated concerns, devising creative solutions, and looking for trade-offs. We discussed some negotiation strategies in chapters 3 and 4, such as fashioning trade-offs or logrolls among issues, searching for compatible issues, devising bridging solutions, and structuring contingency contracts. It is difficult to immediately address interests in a negotiation because people tend to adopt positional tendencies, and emotions can often conceal interests. Negotiators who use an interest-based approach frequently ask other parties about their needs and concerns and, in turn, disclose their own needs and concerns.

Rights

Another way to negotiate is to rely on some independent standard with perceived legitimacy or fairness to determine who is right in a situation. Some rights are formalized by law or contract. Others are socially accepted standards of behavior, such as reciprocity, precedent, equality, and seniority in an organization (e.g., "I want a higher salary because this would be consistent with the incentive structure in this organization"). Rights are rarely clear-cut. They often differ from situation to situation and sometimes, contradictory standards apply. For example, a productive employee may want a salary increase based upon extreme productivity, yet the organization may focus on seniority. Reaching an agreement on rights, where the outcome will determine who gets what, can often be exceedingly difficult—frequently leading negotiators to involve a third party to determine who is right. The prototypical rights procedure involves **adjudication,** in which disputants present evidence and arguments to a neutral third party who has the power to hand down a binding decision. Negotiators who use a rights-based approach frequently say things like, "I deserve this," or "This is fair."

Power

Power is the ability to coerce someone to do something he or she would not otherwise do. Exercising power typically means imposing costs on the other side or threatening to do so. Exercising power may manifest itself in acts of aggression, such as sabotage, physical attack, or withholding benefits derived from a relationship. A prime example of a power move occurred when Time Warner yanked ABC stations off its systems in 11 cities at the beginning of the May sweeps period in 2000, a critical time for setting ratings and ad rates. Television viewers instead saw the words, "DISNEY HAS TAKEN ABC AWAY FROM YOU" in block letters scrolling across the screen (Larson 2000; see Sidebar 5–1 for the complete story).

Within a relationship of mutual dependence (e.g., labor and management; employee and employer), the question of who is more powerful rests on who is more dependent. In turn, one's degree of dependency on the other party rests on how satisfactory the alternatives are for satisfying one's interests. The better the alternative, the less dependent one is.

Power procedures include behaviors that range from insults and ridicule to strikes, beatings, and warfare. All have in common the intent to coerce the other side to settle on terms more satisfactory to the wielder of power. There are two types of power-based approaches (Ury, Brett, and Goldberg 1988): *threats* (in which one or both parties makes a threat) and *contests* (in which parties take action to determine who will prevail). Determining who is more powerful without a decisive and potentially destructive power contest may be difficult because power is ultimately a matter of perception. Despite objective indicators of power (e.g., financial resources), parties' perceptions of their own and each other's power do not often coincide. Moreover, each side's perception of the other's power may fail to take into account the possibility that the other will invest greater resources in the contest than expected, out of fear that a change in the perceived distribution of power will affect the outcomes of future disputes. Many power contests involve threatening avoidance (e.g., divorce), actually engaging in it temporarily to impose costs on the other side (e.g., a strike or breaking off diplomatic relations), or ending the relationship altogether.

STRATEGIC ISSUES CONCERNING APPROACHES

The Principle of Reciprocity

Negotiators should anticipate that the style you use in negotiation will often be reciprocated by the other party (Lytle, Brett, and Shapiro 1999). Do you want this to happen? In one investigation, the reciprocal rates were interests (42 percent), followed by

SIDEBAR 5–1. POWER MOVES

At 12:01 on the morning of May 1, 2000, the T.V. screen went blue on Time Warner Cable's WABC-TV feed, and a scrolling message in block letters began: "DISNEY HAS TAKEN ABC AWAY FROM YOU." After four months of fruitless negotiations over the rights to retransmit ABC signals over cable, Time Warner yanked ABC stations off its systems in 11 cities, including Houston, Philadelphia, Raleigh, and New York, during a period critical for setting ratings and ad rates. The "alert" aired on WABC-TV Channel 7 in New York, whose cable subscribers in 3.5 million homes went without their local ABC station. Time Warner said it wanted to extend talks until the end of the year, but ABC only offered an extension through May 24—the end of the sweeps. Time Warner laid blame squarely on Disney, ABC's corporate parent. "Disney is trying to inappropriately use its ownership of ABC television stations to extract excessive and unreasonable terms for its cable TV channels— terms that would add hundreds of millions of dollars in cost for Time Warner and its cable customers," said Fred D. Ressler, senior vice president of programming for Time Warner Cable (Larson 2000). Disney wanted higher fees for the cable rights to ABC and broader distribution by Time Warner for Disney's own cable programming, especially ESPN. The Cable Act of 1992 entitles over-the-air networks to compensation from cable systems that carry network signals. The agreement between Disney's ABC and Time Warner Cable expired on December 31, 1999. ABC blamed the impasse on Time Warner: "This is a punitive act, but Time Warner is only punishing their own customers through their cable system," said Tom Kane, president and general manager of WABC (Larson 2000).

power (27 percent) and rights (22 percent; Lytle, Brett, and Shapiro 1999). Thus, before negotiation, you should evaluate the pros and cons of interests, rights, and power. In general, interests are less risky than rights and power, as we will see later.

Interests Are Effective for Pie Expansion

Focusing on interests can usually resolve the problem underlying the dispute more effectively than focusing on rights or power. A focus on interests can help uncover "hidden" problems and help identify which issues are of the greatest concern to each party. Our advice is to put the focus on interests early in the negotiations. This raises an obvious question: If interests are effective, why doesn't everyone use them? Ury, Brett, and Goldberg (1988) identify several reasons, including lack of skill, the tendency to reciprocate rights and power, and strong cultural or organizational norms.

How to Refocus Your Opponent on Interests (away from Rights and Power)

Suppose that you enter a negotiation with an interests-based approach, but your opponent is focusing steadily on rights or power. This is making you angry, and you find yourself starting to reciprocate power and rights out of sheer self-defense. Yet you also realize that this is creating a lose-lose situation. How do you break out of the spiral of reciprocity? Next, we identify two sets of strategies that you can use: personal strategies (that you, as a person, can use in a face-to-face situation) and structural strategies (steps that an organization can take to create norms that engender an interest-based culture; Ury, Brett, and Goldberg 1988).

Personal Strategies *Do not reciprocate!* Reciprocation is a form of reward and encouragement of behavior. If you want to extinguish a behavior, then resist the urge to reciprocate. Do not reciprocate rights and power (Fisher, Ury, and Patton 1991; Ury, Brett, and Goldberg 1988). By not reciprocating, you can refocus your opponent. For example, in one investigation, Lytle, Brett, and Shapiro (1999) noted that there were a total of 499 instances in which negotiators made rights and/or power statements. When the other negotiator reciprocated, the focal negotiator stayed with rights and power arguments 39 percent of the time; however, when the other did not reciprocate, the focal negotiator stayed with rights and power arguments only 22 percent of the time (and hence, was refocused 77 percent of the time).

Provide opportunities to meet. Often, rights- and power-based approaches emerge when parties are out of touch and feeling uncertain about the intentions of the other side. Getting parties together for informal discussions can move them toward interests.

Cooling-off periods. It is easy to muster a rights-based response or power display in the heat of conflict. After all, an interest-based approach requires deeper levels of cognitive processing and the ability to get past the more obvious rights and power issues that are more likely to surface. Thus, it often serves parties' long-run interests to build in some cooling-off periods so as to allow them to better assess their own needs and interests, independent of rights and power issues.

Persist in your interests-based discussion. Many times, negotiators will have difficulty in their initial attempts to turn a rights- or power-based argument into an interest-based discussion. It is important for negotiators not to abandon their interests-based approach, but rather, to persist in their attempt to understand the other party's true underlying needs. Stephen Covey (1999) suggests that parties to conflict should be forced to empathize with each other. He has a strict ground rule: "You can't make your point until you restate the other person's point to his or her satisfaction" (Covey 1999, 5). People are often so emotionally invested that they cannot listen. According to Covey, they pretend to listen. So he asks the other party, "Do you feel understood?" The other party always says, "No, he mimicked me, but he doesn't understand me." The negotiator gets to state her point only when she is able to satisfy the other party (for an example of this, see Sidebar 5–2).

Do not make unilateral concessions. Making unilateral concessions is *not* effective for refocusing negotiations. In one study, concession making was less effective in refocusing negotiations from rights and power (60 percent refocused) as were other noncontentious communications (77 percent refocused; Lytle, Brett, and Shapiro 1999). Why? A unilateral concession may be seen as a reward for contentious behavior; therefore, it may encourage the repetition of such behavior.

Combining communication. Reciprocation is instinctive, especially under stress (Lerner 1985). Thus, you may find that your opponent is making you very angry, and you need to "flex your muscles." One effective strategy is to reciprocate rights or power, but *combine* it with interests-based questions or proposals (Ury, Brett, and Goldberg 1988). As an example, consider this statement from a computer company embroiled in a bitter dispute with a printing company (Lytle, Brett, and Shapiro 1999):

> "You know, your reputation could be seriously compromised by suing us, as we could just as easily go to all the other printing companies and let them

SIDEBAR 5–2. RESOLVING DIFFERENCES

The following is a quote from Steven Covey, chairman of the Franklin Covey Company and author of *Seven Habits of Highly Effective People* and *Families and Principle-Centered Leadership:*

Once the president of a company came to me and said, "Will you be a third-party facilitator in a lawsuit we face? None of us trusts the other party."

And I said, "You don't need me. You can do it yourself. Just put everything up front, and then ask if they would be willing to search for a better solution." So he called the president of the other company and made the invitation. The other president said, "No, let the legal process handle it." He probably thought, "He's just playing softball now. Let's stick with hardball."

My friend then said, "Listen, I'll send you our material, and then let's meet. I won't bring my attorney. Bring your attorney if you like. You don't even have to say a word. We'll just have lunch. You have nothing to lose and possibly something to gain."

So they came together, and he basically said, "I'm going to see if I can make your case for you, since you're not going to speak." He tried to show genuine empathy, and he described the other party's position in depth, surprising the other president with his empathy. He then said, "Do I have an accurate understanding?"

At that point, the president spoke up and said, "That's about half accurate, but I need to correct some inaccuracies."

His attorney said, "Don't say another word." He then told his attorney to essentially shut up because he could feel the power of this communication.

My friend captured every major point of the other case, using a flip chart, and then made his points. They then started discussing possible alternatives that would meet their needs. Shortly after lunch, they had their disagreement resolved.

You can experience the magic of synergy that comes from sincere empathy if you seek a creative, win-win third alternative to two opposing positions (Covey 1999, 5–6).

know how you have cheated us . . . but this is not going to solve the problem. Right now, we don't have any money to pay you and, even if you sue us, you will not be able to collect. Why don't we try to find a way to discuss this problem that might give both of us a chance to get what we really want out of this situation?" (p. 44)

Sending the opponent this kind of "mixed message" (rights and interests) gives them a chance to choose what to reciprocate—interests, rights, or power. Indeed, the combination strategy works: In one investigation, conflict spirals were avoided 75 percent of the time when negotiators reciprocated rights or power and combined the reciprocation with a noncontentious statement (Lytle, Brett, and Shapiro 1999). In contrast, nonreciprocation alone resulted in a change of focus only slightly more frequently (77 percent).

Label the process.   If you recognize that your opponent is using a rights- or power-based approach after you have tried to focus on interests, it might be useful to point this out and label the strategy you see him using. Recognizing or labeling a tactic as ineffective can neutralize or refocus negotiations (Fisher, Ury, and Patton 1991). In one investigation, Lytle et al. (1999) found that although process-labeling statements were relatively infrequent responses to rights and power approaches, they were quite effective when used, refocusing negotiators 82 percent of the time. Consider, for example, how one party in this investigation used the labeling strategy to defuse her opponent's rights-based argument:

> "We can argue all afternoon as to whether the language in the contract pertains to application software. I think it does not; you think it does. We are never going to agree about that. Let's see if we can move on. What about . . .". (p. 45)

Walk the talk.   If you are talking the language of interests, it is also important to follow through with interests-based behaviors. Nothing is more infuriating than a negotiator who says she wants to focus on interests, but then initiates a rights- or power-based move.

Structural Strategies   The following structural strategies are ones suggested by Ury, Brett, and Goldberg (1988) in their book, *Getting Disputes Resolved* (p. 42). The authors suggest several methods whereby dispute resolution systems can be designed and used within organizations, some of which are described here in detail. Each of these strategies is designed to reduce the costs of handling disputes and to produce satisfying, durable resolutions.

Put the focus on interests.   The parties involved should attempt to negotiate, rather than escalate to adjudication; this can be achieved by establishing a known negotiation procedure. For example, Ury, Brett, and Goldberg (1988, 42–43) note that when International Harvestor introduced a new procedure for oral (rather than written) handling of grievances at the lowest possible level, the number of written grievances plummeted to almost zero. Some organizations stay focused on interests via use of a *multistep negotiation procedure,* in which a dispute that is not resolved at one level of the organizational hierarchy moves to progressively higher levels. Another strategy is the *wise counselor,* in which senior executives are selected to consider disputes. By creating *multiple points of entry,* negotiators can have several points of access for resolving disputes. In some instances, *mandatory negotiations* can provide a way for reluctant negotiators to come to the table. By providing *skills and training* in negotiation, people will be better prepared to negotiate in an interest-based fashion. Finally, by providing opportunities for *mediation,* in which a third party intervenes, negotiators can often focus on interests. According to Ury, Brett, and Goldberg (1988),

> A mediator can help parties move past a deadlock over positions by getting them to identify their underlying interests and develop creative solutions that satisfy those interests . . . mediation can serve as a safety net to keep a dispute from escalating to a rights procedure, such as litigation or to a power procedure, such as a strike. (p. 49)

Build in "loop-backs" to negotiation.   According to Ury, Brett, and Goldberg (1988), interests-based procedures will not always resolve disputes, yet a rights or power contest can be costly and risky. Excellent structural solutions provide procedures that encourage negotiators to turn back from contests to negotiation. These are what Ury, Brett, and Goldberg call "loop-back" procedures:

- **Looping back from rights.** Some loop-back procedures provide information about a negotiators' rights as well as the likely outcome of a rights contest. Consider *information procedures* in which databases are created that can be accessed by negotiators who want to research the validity and outcome of their claims. *Advisory arbitration* is a method whereby parties are provided with information that would likely result if arbitration were to be carried out or the dispute were to go to court. *Minitrials* are procedures where "lawyers" (high-level executives in the organization who have not been previously involved) represent each side and present evidence and arguments that are heard by a neutral judge or advisor. Minitrials put negotiation in the hands of people who are not emotionally involved in the dispute and who have the perspective to view it in the context of the organization's broad interests.

- **Looping back from a power conflict.** There are a variety of strategies to move parties away from power contests back to interests. *Crisis procedures,* or guidelines for emergency communication written in advance, can establish communication mechanisms between disputants. For example, in disputes between the United States and the Soviet Union, a hotline serves a crisis procedure purpose; in addition, U.S. and Soviet officials have established nuclear risk reduction centers, staffed 24 hours in Washington and Moscow, for emergency communications (Ury, Brett, and Goldberg 1988, 55). Finally, *intervention by third parties* can halt power contests.

Provide low-cost rights and power backups. Should interest-based negotiation fail, it is useful to have low-cost rights and power backup systems. *Conventional arbitration* is less costly than court or private adjudication. Ury, Brett, and Goldberg (1988) note that 95 percent of all collective bargaining contracts provide for arbitration of disputes. *Med-arb* is a hybrid model in which the mediator serves as an arbitrator, if mediation fails. With the threat of arbitration in the air, parties are often encouraged to reach a negotiated solution. In final-offer arbitration, the arbitrator does not have authority to compromise between parties' positions, but rather, must accept one of the final offers made. Thus, each party has an incentive to make her final offer appear the most reasonable in the eyes of the neutral third party.

Build in consultation beforehand and feedback afterwards. *Notification and consultation* between parties prior to taking action can prevent disputes that arise through sheer misunderstanding. They can also reduce the anger and hostility that often result when decisions are made unilaterally and abruptly. *Postdispute analysis and feedback* is a method whereby parties learn from their disputes to prevent similar problems in the future. Similarly, by establishing a *forum,* consultation and postdispute analysis can be institutionalized so as to establish a forum for discussion.

Provide skills and resources. Oftentimes, people find themselves embroiled in conflict and negotiation when they never expected it. To the extent that they do not have resources or skills to resolve disputes, this can often lead to rights- and power-based actions (i.e., suing or firings). However, when these same people have been given skills in interests-based negotiations, they can often create opportunity from conflict in a way that is beneficial for everyone concerned.

High Costs Associated with Power and Rights

Focusing on who is right or who is more powerful (as in a strike) usually leaves at least one person perceiving him- or herself as a loser. Even if you are the winner in these situations, the problem is that often, losers do not give up, but appeal instead to higher courts or plot revenge. Rights are less costly than power, generally—power costs more in resources consumed and opportunities lost. For example, strikes cost more than arbitration, and violence costs more than litigation. Costs are incurred not only in efforts invested, but from the destruction of each side's resources. Power contests often create new injuries and a desire for revenge. Interests are less costly than rights. In summary, focusing on interests, compared to rights and power, produces higher satisfaction with outcomes, better working relationships, and less recurrence; it may also mean lower transaction costs.

Know *When* to Use Rights and Power

Despite their general effectiveness, focusing on interests is not enough: Resolving all disputes by reconciling interests is neither possible nor desirable (Ury, Brett, and Goldberg 1988). The problem is that rights and power procedures are often used when they are not necessary; a procedure that should be the last resort too often becomes the first move. In terms of when to use rights and power, the following conditions are key (Ury, Brett, and Goldberg 1988):

- **When the other party refuses to come to the table despite significant efforts to encourage him to do so.** In this case, no negotiation is taking place, and little is lost by using rights and power.
- **When negotiations have broken down and parties are at an impasse.** A credible threat, especially if combined with an interests-based proposal, may restart negotiations. Often, parties cannot reach agreement on the basis of interests because their perceptions of who is right or more powerful are so different that they cannot establish a range in which to negotiate. In this case, a rights procedure may be needed to clarify the rights boundary within which a negotiated resolution can be sought.
- **When the other party needs to know you have power.** Sometimes, people need to wield power simply to demonstrate that they have it (Ury, Brett, and Goldberg 1988). However, the consequences of imposing one's will can be costly. Your threats must be backed up with actions to be credible. Furthermore, the weaker party may fail to fully comply with a resolution based on power, thus requiring the more powerful party to engage in expensive policing.
- **When interests are so opposed that agreement is not possible.** Sometimes, parties' interests are so disparate that agreement is not possible. For example, when fundamental values are at odds (e.g., abortion beliefs), resolution can only occur through a rights contest (a trial) or power contest (a demonstration or legislative battle).

- **When social change is necessary.** To create social impact, a rights battle may be necessary. For example, consider the case of *Brown* vs. *The Board of Education,* which laid important groundwork for the elimination of racial segregation.

Know *How* to Use Rights and Power

We have made the point that negotiators need to know *when* to use rights and power. However, simply being able to recognize when to use these strategies does not in any way mean that their deployment will be successful. Following are some key things the negotiator needs to take into consideration when using rights and power:

Credibility   Power-based approaches typically focus on the future (e.g., "If you do not do such-and-such, I will withdraw your funding."). To be effective, the other party must believe that you have the ability to carry out the threat. If you are not seen as credible, people will call your bluff. Ideally, it is desirable to convince the other party that you have power without actually having to exert it.

Understand Your Opponent   Rights and power are ultimately challenges to the opponents' long-term and highly valued interests. Thus, threats need to be carefully focused on the other party's high-priority interests. If they are not, there is little incentive for the other party to comply with your threat.

Do Not Burn Bridges   We have made the point that rights and power are risky. It is important that you leave a pathway back to interest-based discussion. Ury, Brett, and Goldberg (1988) call this the "loop back to interests." Threats are very expensive to carry out; thus, it is critical that you are able to turn off a threat. This allows the other party to save face and reopen negotiations. If you do not provide yourself with a loop back to interests, you force yourself to carry out the threat. Furthermore, after you use your threat, you lose your power and ability to influence. Lytle, Brett, and Shapiro (1999, 48) suggest that if you are going to use rights or power, you should use the following sequence: (1) state a specific, detailed demand and deadline; (2) state a specific, detailed, credible threat (which harms other side's interests); and (3) state a specific, detailed, positive consequence that will follow if the demand is met.

EMOTIONS[2]

If approach (interests, rights, and power) is the *packaging* of negotiators' goals, then emotions are the *delivery* of the package. For example, we can imagine a power-based argument or threat delivered in any of these three ways: calm, cool, and collected; positive and constructive; or negative and heated. Thompson, Medvec, Seiden, and Kopelman (2000) outlined three distinct emotional styles:

1. **Unemotional and rational** (i.e., the "poker face" approach)
2. **Positive** (i.e., the friendly and nice approach)
3. **Negative** (i.e., the "squeaky wheel" or "rant 'n' rave" approach)

---

[2]Ideas in this section have been strongly influenced by collaboration with Shirli Kopelman, Vicki Medvec, Deepak Malhotra, Ashleigh Rosette, and Vanessa Seiden.

Table 5–3:	Emotional styles		
	Rational	**Positive**	**Negative**
Focus	Conceal or repress emotion	Create positive emotion in other party Create rapport	Use irrational-appearing emotions to intimidate or control other party
Distributive strategies (pie slicing)	Citing norms of fair distribution	Compromise for the sake of the relationship	Threats Often tough bargaining
Integrative strategies (pie expansion)	Systematic analysis of interests	Positive emotion stimulates creative thinking	Negative emotion may inhibit integrative bargaining
Implications for future negotiations and relationship	Not likely to say or do anything regrettable, but also may come across as "distant"	Greater feelings of commitment to relationship partner	Pressure to carry out threats or lose credibility

Table 5–3 depicts these three emotional styles (rational, positive, and negative) and describes their implications for distributive bargaining, integrative bargaining, and the relationship among negotiations.

ASSESSING YOUR EMOTIONAL STYLE

One way to assess your emotional style is to take the test in Box 5–2. It is also a good idea to ask two or three colleagues who are not afraid to give you honest feedback to complete the test according to how they view your emotional style in negotiations.

The Rational Negotiator: Keeping a Poker Face

The rational negotiator neither feels nor expresses emotion. Indeed, a common piece of advice in negotiation is to "keep a poker face." This advice stems from a belief that showing emotion is a sign of weakness and that emotion makes a negotiator vulnerable to giving away too much of bargaining pie. The absence of emotions is consistent with principles of rationality. In his book *The Art and Science of Negotiation*, Raiffa (1982, 120) lists "self-control, especially of emotions and their visibility" as the thirteenth most-important characteristic of effective negotiators (out of 34 key characteristics). Similarly, Nierenberg (1968) claims that

> People in an emotional state do not want to think, and they are particularly susceptible to the power of suggestion from a clever opponent . . . [an] excitable person is putty in the hands of a calm, even-tempered negotiator."
> (p. 46)

Moreover, Fisher, Ury, and Patton, in *Getting to Yes* (1991), caution that emotions may quickly bring a negotiation to an impasse or end. Emotions can impair the effective decision making necessary for negotiation. According to Janis and Mann (1977), decision makers experiencing high levels of emotional stress often undergo incomplete

BOX 5–2

EMOTIONAL STYLE QUESTIONNAIRE

Read each statement, and indicate whether you think this is true or false for you in a negotiation situation. Force yourself to answer each one as generally true or false (i.e., do not respond with "I don't know").

1. In a negotiation situation, it is best to "keep a cool head."

2. I believe that in negotiations you can "catch more flies with honey."

3. It is important to me that I maintain control in a negotiation situation.

4. Establishing a positive sense of rapport with the other party is key to effective negotiation.

5. I am good at displaying emotions in negotiation to get what I want.

6. Emotions are the downfall of effective negotiation.

7. I definitely believe that the "squeaky wheel gets the grease" in many negotiation situations.

8. If you are nice in negotiations, you can get more than if you are cold or neutral.

9. In negotiation, you have to "fight fire with fire."

10. I honestly think better when I am in a good mood.

11. I would never want to let the other party know how I really felt in a negotiation.

12. I believe that in negotiations, you can "catch more flies with a flyswatter."

13. I have used emotion to manipulate others in negotiations.

14. I believe that good moods are definitely contagious.

15. It is very important to make a very positive first impression when negotiating.

16. The downfall of many negotiators is that they lose personal control in a negotiation.

17. It is best to keep a "poker face" in negotiation situations.

18. It is very important to get the other person to respect you when negotiating.

19. I definitely want to leave the negotiation with the other party feeling good.

20. If the other party gets emotional, you can use this to your advantage in a negotiation.

21. I believe that it is important to "get on the same wavelength" as the other party.

22. It is important to demonstrate "resolve" in a negotiation.

23. If I sensed that I was not under control, I would call a temporary halt to the negotiation.

24. I would not hesitate to make a threat in a negotiation situation if I felt the other party would believe it.

Scoring Yourself

Computing your "R" score: Look at items #1, #3, #6, #11, #16, #17, #20, #23. Give yourself 1 point for every "true" answer and subtract 1 point for every "false" answer. Then add your scores. This is your R score (rational).

Computing your "P" score: Look at items #2, #4, #8, #10, #14, #15, #19, #21. Give yourself 1 point for every "true" answer and subtract 1 point for every "false" answer. Then add your scores. This is your P score (positive).

Computing your "N" score: Look at items #5, #7, #9, #12, #13, #18, #22, #24. Give yourself 1 point for every "true" answer and subtract 1 point for every "false" answer. Then add your scores. This is your N score (negative).

search, appraisal, and contingency-planning thought processes. As a result, they make defective decisions.

It is important, however, to draw a distinction between *expressing* and *feeling* emotion. Even though a negotiator may *feel* emotion, he or she dares not express it, lest it lead to less-than-desirable outcomes. According to economists, the negotiator who expresses relief, satisfaction, and approval risks settling for a worse outcome than does the poker-faced negotiator. Raiffa (1982) strictly cautions negotiators from displaying emotion: "Don't gloat about how well you have done" (p. 130).

The Positive Negotiator: You Can Catch More Flies with Honey

A very different emotional style is the "positive emotion" approach. Instead of repressing emotion and using a poker face, this negotiator believes that, when it comes to negotiation, "you can catch more flies with honey." There are three critical steps involved in the positive-emotion process: (1) feeling positive emotion, (2) expressing it, and (3) engendering it in the opponent.

Former president Ronald Reagan was a skilled negotiator who capitalized on positive emotion at the bargaining table. For example, during the Geneva Summit negotiations with Gorbachev, Reagan endeared himself to the Soviet leader by making jokes. On one occasion, Reagan told a joke about an American who says that his country is the best because he can walk into the White House and tell the president he is doing a lousy job; a Russian responds that his country is better because he can go into the Kremlin and tell Gorbachev the same thing—that Reagan is doing a lousy job running the United States. Gorbachev laughed, and the parties successfully moved forward in negotiations (Hoffman 1985).

The obvious question is whether positive emotion is effective. Indeed, empirical investigations reveal that positive emotion enhances the quality of negotiated settlements, as compared to poker-faced negotiations (Kumar 1997; Kramer, Pommerenke, and Newton 1993). Why is this? There are two key reasons, one having to do with how people process information when they are in a good mood, and the other having to do with the effect a good mood creates in others.

Positive Emotions and Information Processing People process information differently when in a positive mood, as opposed to a negative or neutral mood (Isen 1987). A good mood promotes creative thinking (Isen, Daubman, and Nowicki 1987), which, in turn, leads to innovative problem solving (Carnevale and Isen 1986). For example, Carnevale and Isen (1986) conducted an experiment in which some negotiators watched a funny movie and were given a gift. These negotiators reached more integrative negotiations and generated more creative ideas than negotiators who did not watch the movie and were not given a gift (see also Barry and Oliver 1996; Forgas 1996; Allred, Mallozzi, Matsui, and Raia 1997). In general, positive-mood negotiators use more cooperative strategies, engage in more information exchange, generate more alternatives, and use fewer contentious tactics than negative or neutral-mood negotiators (Carnevale and Isen 1986).

Positive Emotions and Their Effect on the Opponent Emotion in negotiation is a self-fulfilling prophecy; that is, negotiators' own emotions can determine the emotions of the other party and the nature of the conflict resolution. For example, in one investigation, people in a job-contract negotiation achieved lower joint gains when they experienced high levels of anger and low levels of compassion toward each other than when they experienced positive emotion (Allred et al. 1997). Furthermore, angry negotiators were less willing to work with each other and more likely to overretaliate (Allred et al. 1997).

The Irrational Negotiator: Rant 'N' Rave

Quite a different negotiation approach is to demonstrate blatant, negative emotions, such as anger, rage, indignation, and impatience. The irrational negotiator uses wild displays of negative emotion to coerce the other party to meet stated demands. However, the irrational negotiator is, in reality, highly rational. Sometimes, the more out of control and crazy a negotiator appears to be, the more effective she can be in a negotiation. By appearing unstable and volatile, the irrational negotiator convinces the opponent that she would sooner walk away from the table without having reached an agreement than settle for anything less than she desires. Thus, irrational negotiators are effective to the extent that they can convince the other party that they will follow through with what seems to be an extreme course of action, perhaps because they have nothing to lose (i.e., they convince the other party that they would be willing to take great risks that would perhaps hurt both parties if they do not get what they want). Grave examples of such tactics can be found throughout history. For example, before the German annexation of Austria, Hitler met to negotiate with the Austrian Chancellor von Schuschnigg. At some point in this dark historical meeting, Hitler's emotional style became irrational:

> [He] became more strident, more shrill. Hitler ranted like a maniac, waved his hands with excitement. At times he must have seemed completely out of control. . . . Hitler may then have made his most extreme coercive threats seem credible. . . . [He threatened to take von Schuschnigg into custody, an act unheard of in the context of diplomacy.] He insisted that von Schuschnigg sign an agreement to accept every one of his demands, or he would immediately order a march into Austria. (Raven 1990, 515)

The irrational negotiator is manipulative and downright Machiavellian at times. A negotiator who is faced with an irate opponent may capitulate to the other party to end the interaction quickly (Frank 1988). This, of course, only reinforces the irrational-appearing behavior, making it more likely to be used in the future. The irrational negotiating style does not just mean displaying anger. Displays of helplessness, pouting, and hurt feelings can be used to manipulate others in negotiations as well. Negotiators who are really angry and feel little compassion for the other party achieve fewer joint gains than negotiators who have positive emotional regard for the other party (Allred, Mallozzi, Matsui, and Raia 1997). Angry, negative negotiators do not appear to be effective at pie slicing (for a review of the effects of anger and retaliation in negotiation, see Allred in press).

What are the specific psychological principles that make the irrational negotiator effective? Consider the following (Thompson, Medvec, Seiden, and Kopelman 2000):

The Door-in-the-Face Technique   When a person makes an outlandish initial request, they are more likely to secure agreement to a subsequent, smaller request. This "door-in-the-face technique" is based on principles of perceptual contrast: If we lift a heavy object, set it down, and then lift a light object, we perceive the light object to be much lighter than it actually is (Cialdini 1975; Cann, Sherman, and Elkes 1975). Skilled negotiators have been profiting from perceptual contrast for years (Cialdini 1993). Consider the savvy car salesperson who shows the potential buyer the most expensive models before showing him the model in which he is actually interested. Compared to the $40K price tag of the expensive model, the $20K price tag of the intended sale seems much more reasonable. Similarly, the irrational negotiator who calms down a bit following a wild display of emotion may get what she wants.

Negative Reinforcement Negative reinforcement, or escape behavior, explains the increased likelihood of behavior that eliminates or removes an aversive stimulus (Skinner 1938). For example, if a radio is playing obnoxious music, you will turn it off, thus eliminating the unpleasant sounds. In a similar vein, because most people find it unpleasant to be around someone who is openly hostile, negative, and a "loose cannon," they may be willing to give the person what she wants just to remove themselves from this aversive situation. Unfortunately, this acts as positive reinforcement for the opponent. If someone acts irrational and you give in, this increases the likelihood of their engaging in negative behavior in the future. Thus, irrational negotiators may capitalize on, and be reinforced for, their negative emotional behavior.

Self-Regulation Most people like to prolong positive moods and exposure to positive stimuli and minimize negative moods. In fact, people "self-regulate" by actively working to maintain a desired positive mood (Baumeister, Leith, Muraven, and Bratslavsky 1998). One way to do this is to avoid negative stimuli. Most people find it unpleasant to interact with an irrational negotiator and, in order not to ruin their day, capitulate to the other side.

Squeaky Wheel Principle The **squeaky wheel principle** (Singelis 1998) states that a negotiator should demonstrate an unwillingness to move away from a stated position by escalating the level of hostility and using threats. Some qualitative evidence shows that the squeaky wheel does in fact get "greased": Schelling (1960) describes the situation of two people (we will call them A and B) in a rowboat. A threatens B that if he does not row, A will tip the boat over. This will not be as powerful as when A rocks the boat fervently while yelling to B that if B wants him to stop, he must row the boat. Thus,

> Initiating steady pain, even if the threatener shares the pain, may make sense as a threat, especially if the threatener can initiate it irreversibly so that only the other's compliance can relieve the pain they both share. (Schelling 1960, 196)

STRATEGIC ADVICE FOR DEALING WITH EMOTIONS AT THE TABLE

Keeping a Cool Head Is Easier Said than Done

Often, our emotions are not under our control. The very act of trying to keep a poker face may backfire, especially if people try too hard to do so. For example, when people tell themselves not to conjure up certain thoughts, they find that it is virtually impossible to refrain from thinking these exact thoughts. Indeed, people who spend more time trying to repair their negative moods are the most likely to suffer from persistent emotional problems such as depression and anxiety (Wegner and Wenzlaff 1996). Thus, it may be difficult not to express emotions if you are feeling them.

Controlling Emotion May Interfere with the Process of Entrainment
Entrainment is the process whereby one person's internal feelings are felt and acted upon by another person, such as when one person in a positive mood "affects" the mood of the other person with whom he or she is interacting (Kelly 1988). When people negotiate, they each synchronize their behavior in accordance with the behavioral and emotional states of the other person. In a sense, people develop an interpersonal rhythm that reflects a shared emotional and behavioral state. Entrainment is a natural biological process that is conducive to social relationships and rapport building (Kelly 1988). A negotiator who is deliberately focused on repressing emotion may interfere with this process, and an awkward, strained relationship may develop. For example, a poker-faced negotiator could create a more stilted interaction if the other party starts to react to and reflect his or her emotional state.

Emotions Are Contagious
If one negotiator conveys positive emotion, the other negotiator is likely to "catch" this positive emotional state and convey positive emotion as well (Hatfield, Caccioppo, and Rapson 1992). However, the same is true for negative emotion.

Positive Emotions Promote Integrative Bargaining
Examinations of positive affect on creative ability (Isen et al. 1987; Baron 1990) suggests that when people are experiencing a positive mood, they are more creative, generate integrative information, and more flexible in conveying their thoughts (Isen, Niedenthal, and Cantor 1992; Isen et al. 1987). Why does positive emotion work? It is largely due to a combination of the self-fulfilling prophecy, information processing, and the fact that positive affect is associated with more creative and varied cognitions. For example, people who experience positive emotion see relationships among ideas and link together nontypical category exemplars (Isen et al. 1992; Forgas and Moylan 1996). This builds rapport, which, in turn, helps to avoid impasse (Thompson, Nadler, and Kim 1999; Moore, Kurtzberg, Thompson, and Morris 1999; Drolet and Morris 1995, 2000) and facilitates the negotiation process.

Negative Emotion Must Be Convincing to Be Effective
Schelling (1960) offers the example of two negotiators playing a game of "chicken" in their cars—a highly risky game. One person assumes an advantage if she rips the steering wheel out of her car and throws it out the window, as long as her opponent sees her doing this. The other party is then forced into moving out of the way; in other words, he is forced to concede if both are to survive the game. But not just any behavior will suffice in order to evoke such concessions from the other party (Frank 1988): "For a signal between adversaries to be credible, it must be costly (or, more generally, difficult) to fake" (p. 99). Frightened that the negotiation may end in an impasse, the other party may be pressured to concede to what would normally be considered outrageous demands. This type of negotiation strategy is best characterized by the expression "The squeaky wheel gets the grease," and can be highly effective.

The Timing of Emotion Matters
People tend to remember an experience in terms of how they felt at the end of it (Redelmeier and Kahneman 1996; Kahneman, Fredrickson, Schreiber, and Redelmeier 1993; Fredrickson and Kahneman 1993). Indeed, the endpoint of an interaction bears critical negotiation power. For example, studies show that when

opponents end the negotiation on a humorous note (i.e., "I will throw in my pet frog"), acceptance rates are higher than when they do not end on a positive note (O'Quin and Aronoff 1981). Although we want to leave the other party feeling good, we should not show our opponent that *we* feel good. Conveying elation or gloating at the end of a negotiation makes our opponent feel less successful and less satisfied with the negotiation (Thompson, Valley, and Kramer 1995).

PUTTING IT ALL TOGETHER

We have systematically considered three different stylistic issues in negotiation: motivational orientation (individualistic, cooperative, or competitive); approach (interests, rights, or power-based); and emotional style (rational/cool-headed; positive; or seemingly irrational). We have discussed the pros and cons of each stylistic issue. The key messages of this chapter are as follows:

- **Get in touch with your own style in an honest and straightforward way.** If you still think you are out of touch, then ask someone else to appraise you in an honest way, using the diagnostic tools presented in this chapter.
- **Know your limits and your strengths.** We have seen that it is not better to adopt one particular style because each has its own weaknesses and strengths. Knowing your own stylistic limits and strengths is important.
- **Understand your opponent better.** Most naïve negotiators just assume that their opponent has the same orientation that they do. However, with 27 different style combinations, this is not likely. We hope that the styles we have described in this chapter act as a type of "wake-up call" on diversity. With these styles in mind, you can better size up your opponent and perhaps change her style through the various techniques we have discussed.
- **Expand your repertoire.** We often find that people do not feel comfortable with their bargaining style or do not find it effective. This chapter gives negotiators options for expanding their repertoire, especially at critical points during negotiation.

6

ESTABLISHING TRUST AND
BUILDING A RELATIONSHIP

Superagent and attorney Leigh Steinberg negotiated quarterback Drew Bledsoe's multiyear contract with New England Patriots owner Bob Kraft. The two of them were sitting in a loud, crowded hotel lobby during the National Football League (NFL) Owners' Conference. As they led up to their bargaining positions, other people were interrupting them, thus making it difficult to talk or build a connection. In the midst of the interruptions and chaos, Kraft proposed $29 million over 7 years. Steinberg countered with $51 million. Insulted, angry, and shaking his head, Kraft got up and walked out. Steinberg had made a mistake, but instead of inflaming the situation, he gave it more time. Six months later, Steinberg asked Kraft to dinner at a quiet Italian restaurant. He let Kraft vent anger and frustration over Bledsoe's proposed salary. It came out that Kraft had interpreted the high counteroffer as a signal that Bledsoe wanted nothing to do with the team and instead wanted to be a free agent. Calmly, Steinberg assured Kraft that Bledsoe wanted to stay. He explained that in the hubbub of the lobby six months earlier, Steinberg had not been able to create the solid rapport that they had that evening and had not been able to establish an atmosphere of trust. That night, they settled on $42 million. Says Steinberg, "The key to successful negotiations is to develop relationships, not conquests." (Dworetzky 1998a, A6)

WHY CARE ABOUT TRUST?

People need to trust each other to build a relationship, and good relationships often mean better negotiations. For example, Bob Adams, production area leader for high-tech resin manufacturer AOC in Valparaiso, Indiana, once believed that getting a good deal meant getting the lowest price, whether he was purchasing raw materials or contracting for pest-control services in the plant. But after negotiation training, he learned that establishing a good relationship with suppliers is just as important. Adams says he discovered the value of the relationship in negotiation when the Southern Pacific and Union Pacific railroads merged in 1997, causing delivery problems around the country. "I could call my suppliers and they would be gracious enough to track orders. They also looked for alternative ways to get products to us" (Kiser 1999, 126). People often feel better about pie slicing and are in a better position to expand the pie when they have a good relationship and trust one another. Furthermore, when people trust each other, they can spend less time worrying about trust and more time negotiating in a creative fashion.

Distrust often involves costly detection and regulation mechanisms. At the extreme, imagine a manager installing video cameras in every office in a building and spending exorbitant money on special software to monitor employees' e-mail exchanges. This manager would not have the time to negotiate in an effective fashion. On the other hand, it is completely naïve to trust everyone in all negotiations. What is the best way to establish trust in relationships and maintain trust over significant periods of time? This is the topic of this chapter.

In this chapter, we consider the most common types of negotiating relationships: personal, business, and embedded relationships. We discuss trust issues in each of these relationships. We use our "mind-heart" distinction to present methods for engendering trust in relationships. Some strategies are deliberate, mindful, and rational. In contrast, some are more psychological and play upon people's nonconscious attitudes, behaviors, and emotions. We identify factors most likely to threaten trust in a relationship and, most important, how to repair trust that has been broken.

RELATIONSHIPS IN NEGOTIATION

Most people negotiate in their personal lives. For example, people negotiate with spouses, friends, and neighbors (see Valley, Neale, and Mannix 1995). People also negotiate on a repeated basis with others in their personal life who do not necessarily fall into the categories of "friends" or "family" (e.g., homeowners negotiating with contractors; parents negotiating with other parents concerning car-pool arrangements; parents negotiating with nannies concerning child care, and so on). In addition to negotiating in our personal lives, we also negotiate in our business lives, with colleagues, supervisors, and staff members. In some cases, our personal life is intermingled with our business life, in a relationship that we cannot easily classify as strictly personal or strictly business; rather, it is a little and a lot of both. We refer to this type of relationship as an "embedded" relationship (Uzzi 1997). We will expose the relevant implicit norms and rules that lurk under each of these three types of relationships and their implications for trust in negotiations. The behavior of people in relationships is guided by shared sets of rules (see Argyle and Henderson 1984; Clark and Mills 1979). Individuals in relationships seek to abide by the rules of relationships and not violate the expectations of others.

NEGOTIATION IN PERSONAL RELATIONSHIPS

Most people negotiate quite often, even in the most intimate of personal relationships. However, they are often uncomfortable negotiating (Kurtzberg and Medvec 1999):

Thou Shalt Not Sell a Car to Thy Neighbor
A motto followed by many people is "Business and friendship do not mix." People are extraordinarily uncomfortable negotiating with their friends (Kurtzberg and Medvec 1999). Even the word "negotiation" is a threat to many friendships; thus, people avoid it. The reason for this discomfort is traceable to the nature of most friendships, which are built on communal norms, as opposed to exchange norms (Clark 1978). **Communal norms** prescribe that we should take care of the people we love and are close to, respond to their needs, and not "keep track" of who has provided what in a relation-

ship. Personal relationships are communal in nature, and we respond to others out of a heartfelt need to take care of their interests; in return, we expect that they will look after our own interests. Negotiation does not seem to have a place in these personal relationships. In contrast, **exchange norms** prescribe that people keep track of who has given and received goods in a relationship, and that a mental accounting system governs this exchange of resources. According to Kurtzberg and Medvec (1999), "Friendship dictates that we should be concerned with fairness and the other person's welfare, while negotiations dictate that we should get a good deal for ourselves" (p. 356). These two dictates are in conflict with one another.

The truth is that we negotiate with our friends all the time (for example, making child care arrangements, or planning parties or vacations together). People just do not call these things "negotiations"; rather, they say they are "working things out," "making plans," "figuring things out," etc. Above all, in these interactions, people are careful not to exchange money—and sometimes go to great and strange lengths in order not to.

An examination of how friends negotiate reveals some interesting findings (for a review, see Valley, Neale, and Mannix 1995). Not surprisingly, friends are less competitive than are strangers when they negotiate; they exchange more information, make more concessions, and make fewer demands. However, they are often less likely to reach level 3 integrative agreements (Thompson and DeHarpport 1998)! Why is this? A dominant reason concerns what we call the **fear of conflict,** which stems from a belief that conflict is dysfunctional and should not occur between people. Conflict, for many people, signals that something is wrong in the relationship, so they try to avoid it. As we have seen in our discussion of integrative strategies in chapter 4, it is often important to focus on differences of interests and maintain high aspirations to reach effective negotiated outcomes. When people avoid conflict and quickly compromise, they are likely to leave money on the table. This chapter is designed to help people negotiate with their friends and family so that they do not commit one of the four major sins of negotiation: leaving money on the table, rejecting perfectly good deals, accepting something worse than their BATNA, and/or not getting enough of the pie.

Conflict Is Bad: The Mismanagement of Agreement

Organizational psychologist Jerry Harvey's (1974) story of the road to Abilene (see Box 6–1) epitomizes the notion that among family and friends, conflict is to be avoided at all costs, even if it means a lose-lose outcome for all involved. The need for friends to maintain the illusion of agreement means that important differences in preferences, interests, and beliefs are often downplayed or buried. Paradoxically, it is precisely these kind of differences that *should* surface in any negotiation, to enable negotiators in personal relationships to trade off and develop contingency contracts. Somehow, friends and families need a way of making their differences known, so as to capitalize on them in a win-win fashion.

Responding to Needs

When it comes to slicing the pie, personal negotiations generally follow a "needs-based" rule; in short, whoever is neediest is granted first dibs when it comes to doling out the resources. Most of the time, people do not object to this idea. However, significant problems arise when people have different ways of assessing need. Often, people are hurt and annoyed that their needs are not met or that their needs seem less significant when

> **BOX 6–1**

THE ABILENE PARADOX

The July afternoon in Coleman, Texas (population 5,607) was particularly hot—104 degrees as measured by the Walgreen's Rexall Ex-Lax temperature gauge. In addition, the wind was blowing fine-grained West Texas topsoil through the house. But the afternoon was still tolerable—even potentially enjoyable. There was a fan going on the back porch; there was cold lemonade; and finally, there was entertainment. Dominoes. Perfect for the conditions. The game required little more physical exertion than an occasional mumbled comment, "Shuffle 'em," and an unhurried movement of the arm to place the spots in the appropriate perspective on the table. All in all, it had the markings of an agreeable Sunday afternoon in Coleman—that is, it was until my father-in-law suddenly said, "Let's get in the car and go to Abilene and have dinner at the cafeteria."

I thought, "What, go to Abilene? Fifty-three miles? In this dust storm and heat? And in an un-air-conditioned 1958 Buick?"

But my wife chimed in with "Sounds like a great idea. I'd like to go. How about you, Jerry?" Since my own preferences were obviously out of step with the rest I replied, "Sounds good to me," and added, "I just hope your mother wants to go."

"Of course I want to go," said my mother-in-law. "I haven't been to Abilene in a long time."

So into the car and off to Abilene we went. My predictions were fulfilled. The heat was brutal. We were coated with a fine layer of dust that was cemented with perspiration by the time we arrived. The food at the cafeteria provided first-rate testimonial material for antacid commercials.

Some four hours and 106 miles later we returned to Coleman, hot and exhausted. We sat in front of the fan for a long time in silence. Then, both to be sociable and to break the silence, I said, "It was a great trip, wasn't it?"

No one spoke. Finally my mother-in-law said, with some irritation, "Well, to tell the truth, I really didn't enjoy it much and would rather have stayed here. I just went along because the three of you were so enthusiastic about going. I wouldn't have gone if you all hadn't pressured me into it."

I couldn't believe it. "What do you mean 'you all'?" I said. "Don't put me in the 'you all' group. I was delighted to be doing what we were doing. I didn't want to go. I only went to satisfy the rest of you. You're the culprits."

My wife looked shocked. "Don't call me a culprit. You and Daddy and Mama were the ones who wanted to go. I just went along to be sociable and to keep you happy. I would have had to be crazy to want to go out in heat like that."

Her father entered the conversation abruptly. "Hell!" he said.

He proceeded to expand on what was already absolutely clear. "Listen, I never wanted to go to Abilene. I just thought you might be bored. You visit so seldom I wanted to be sure you enjoyed it. I would have preferred to play another game of dominoes and eat the leftovers in the icebox."

After the outburst of recrimination we all sat back in silence. Here we were, four reasonably sensible people who, of our own volition, had just taken a 106-mile trip across a godforsaken desert in a furnace-like temperature through a cloud-like dust storm to eat unpalatable food at a hole-in-the-wall cafeteria in Abilene, when none of us had really wanted to go. In fact, to be more accurate, we'd done just the opposite of what we wanted to do. The whole situation simply didn't make sense. (Harvey 1974) compared to others'. This, of course, is traceable to egocentric perceptions of fairness (see chapter 3 on pie slicing); however, because of the fear of conflict, friends often do not express their needs. It is precisely because friends and families expect their needs to be perfectly understood by others that they often do not adequately express them. Thus begins an escalating cycle of hurt feelings compounded by anger.

After Need Comes Equality
In a recent investigation of how friends and strangers divide a pie of resources, friends tended to use an **equality rule** (thereby allocating equal shares to everyone involved), whereas strangers and business associates used an **equity rule**—otherwise known as a **merit-based rule**—where those who have contributed more are expected to receive more (Austin 1980). Unfortunately, equality norms may promote compromise agreements, thereby inhibiting the discovery of integrative trade-offs. However, norms of equality are not blindly applied by people in close relationships. For example, friends who differ in their ability and effort in a joint task will favor the less able, but more diligent, partner in the allocation of resources (Lamm and Kayser 1978). Similarly, people in communal relationships will meet the other's needs, with no expectation of remuneration (Clark and Mills 1979). Equity, in which outcomes are allocated proportional to inputs, is a hallmark feature of the business world. For example, most of us do not expect to earn the same exact salary as our colleagues; we earn salaries based upon various contributions and inputs to the specific business situation. However, equity does not seem to have a legitimate role in personal relationships.

Avoid Market Pricing
Market pricing is a method by which everything is reduced to a single value or utility metric that allows for the comparison of many qualitatively and quantitatively diverse factors (Fiske 1992). Market pricing allows people to negotiate by making references to ratios of this metric, such as percentage share in a business venture. Money is the prototypical medium of market pricing relationships. Capitalism is the ultimate expression of market pricing. Market pricing can be viewed from another angle as a social influence device. In a true market pricing relationship, people will do virtually anything if offered enough money because "everyone has his price." For most people in personal relationships, market pricing is a threat to their relationship. Communal sharing, in which people are insensitive to market pricing, is the predominant mode of relating to close others. Because negotiation ultimately requires some type of pricing, it is often uncomfortable for people in close relationships.

Types of Resources
According to theories of rational behavior, most people are utility maximizers, meaning that they seek to maximize their outcomes. Most of the time, this is understood to mean monetary wealth. However, in personal relationships, people have a difficult time simply discussing monetary issues, much less attempting to maximize outcomes. It is important to realize that the maximization of utility does not just mean money. Consider Figure 6–1, which identifies six types of resources that people may exchange: love, money, services, goods, status, and information (Foa and Foa 1975). Each of these six types of resources varies in terms of particularism (how much utility we derive depends on who is providing it) and concreteness (how tangible it is). Love and status are less concrete than services or goods, and love is more particular than money.

FIGURE 6–1 Resources That May Be Exchanged in a Relationship

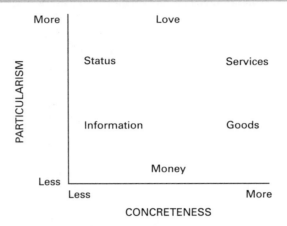

Source: Foa, U. and Foa, E. (1975). *Resource theory of social exchange.* Morristown, NJ: General Learning Press.

BUSINESS RELATIONSHIPS

Most people have little trouble with the idea of negotiating in the business world. In fact, most people regard negotiation in the business world to be of central importance and, consequently, a number of rituals and norms have developed around the practice of business negotiation. However, relationships and trust in the business world can be tricky. Business relationships have a host of complexities that we need to deal with to effectively expand the pie and slice it. Consider the following five issues:

We Choose Our Friends, but not Our Co-Workers

Basically, this means that we (usually) like our friends, but we do not necessarily like the people we do business with. Yet this does not excuse us from having to negotiate and deal with them. In fact, we must often deal with people whom we do not like and whom we may regard to be offensive. For example, a woman might find herself having to negotiate with a male who is a blatant sexist. It is often very difficult for people to separate their feelings about someone as a person from the business at hand.

Business Relationships Often Have Status and Rank Issues Associated with Them

Most friendships are not hierarchical—meaning that in friendships, people do not have different status and rank. In contrast, businesses are generally organized around rank and status—either explicitly (e.g., an organizational chart) or implicitly (e.g., salaries, number of supervisees, office space, etc.). Differences in power, as we shall see in chapter 7, set the stage for "hot" negotiations. Thus, negotiating in the business world is often considerably more challenging because negotiations about a given issue are embedded in a larger status negotiation among the actors in the organization. This, of course, can vary across cultures as well as organizations. As we will see in chapter 10, in some cultures, it is perfectly acceptable for members of different status and rank to meet each other at the bargaining table. However, in other cultures, people find this uncomfortable and insulting.

The Need for Swift Trust

The dynamic, changing nature of business interactions means that we need to build trust with people more rapidly, on basis of less information (often, with no past history) and, in many cases, with no expected meaningful future interaction. For example, a new temporary partnership involving the need for immediate trust was formed recently between auctioneer Sotheby's Holdings, Inc., and Rossi & Rossi, a London art dealer for an exhibition and sale of Tibetan art (Bensinger and Costello 1999). The partnership was well-timed, as long-neglected art and objects from Tibet and the Himalayas are of interest to both collectors and buyers. This exhibition marked the first time a major auction house partnered with an independent dealer to sell artwork publicly and far away from the auction block. Normally, the auction house does not own inventory; the new partnership, though, makes Sotheby's a dealer with its own inventory to protect and push. Sotheby's offered Rossi & Rossi the use of its gallery space and promoted the show with its sizeable marketing power in return for a share of the profits from the sale.

The partnership between Sotheby's and Rossi & Rossi is an example of **swift trust.** Swift trust is the mechanism that allows people to build trust quickly (Meyerson, Weick, and Kramer 1996). Many new business relationships require that strangers come together and produce a product, service, or carry out some task, and then immediately disband, perhaps never to see one another again. In contrast, our personal relationships are longer term; we have a past history with family and friends, and we expect to have future interactions with them. Business situations of the twenty-first century increasingly require swift trust, which is necessary among people who have a finite life span in a temporary system. The question is, How do we build trust when there is no past and it is likely that there will be no future? We deal with this issue later.

There Is No Such Thing as a One-Shot Business Situation

Taken alone, this statement contradicts the idea of swift trust. On the surface, it would seem that swift trust epitomizes the one-shot business situation, wherein people who do not know each other must somehow trust each other enough to do business and then terminate the relationship, never to see each other again. However, in the business world, through its web of networked relationships, it is impossible to not experience the consequences of our interactions with others. If these consequences percolate through our business networks, then the situation is technically not a one-shot interaction. Social networks mean that even though the particular people in a business interaction may never interact nor see one another again, their companies will interact again, and/or others in their social network will become apprised of the interaction, which will, in turn, affect the nature of future business interactions. Therefore, it is important to realize that the one-shot business situation may be a virtual impossibility.

Uncomfortable Business Relationships

Uncomfortable business relationships occur when a negotiation involves engaging in interactions that, in a personal context, would take on a different meaning, and thus, might be regarded as inappropriate. For example, consider two managers, a man and a woman, each married, who have late flights arriving in their destination city and very busy schedules, and nevertheless need to negotiate. They agree to meet at a bar, because it is the only location open that late at night. However, when they arrive at the bar, the waitstaff treats them as a couple. This is embarrassing for the business associates because their relationship is viewed in a different way by those outside the business context than by those on the "inside." This has implications for the negotiation; for example, if the waitstaff presents the check to the man, this can potentially create an uncomfortable power dynamic between them. (We will discuss this further in chapter 7.) Quite often, business opportunities are conducted in the context of social relationships (Uzzi 1997). For this reason, it is difficult to form close relationships across gender lines if they are built through social activities such as playing golf, going to the theater, or meeting for dinner, because these practices often have a different meaning between men and women than they do between persons of the same gender (Etzkowitz, Kemelgor, and Uzzi 1999).

EMBEDDED RELATIONSHIPS

Ka Cotter, executive vice president of The Staubach Co., was home recuperating from surgery when the doorbell rang. Marianne Staubach was coming by with dinner. Cotter has worked with CEO Roger Staubach for 17 years, and they are friends, having gone through the good, bad, and the ugly together. Their relationship is both business and friendship (Kunde 1997); in other words, it is an **embedded relationship.** The classic embedded relationship is the family business, wherein people who are related are doing business together.

The embedded relationship would seem to have several advantages, the most important of which is facilitating the nature of business exchange by initiating self-organizing governance arrangements that operate through expectations of trust and reciprocity, rather than expensive deterrence mechanisms (Uzzi 1999a). For example, in one empirical investigation, firms that embedded their bank exchanges in social attachments were more likely to have access to capital and received more favorable interest rates on loans (Uzzi 1999b).

Another example of an embedded relationship is that between Magic Johnson (former Los Angeles Lakers' star basketball player) and Jerry Buss (the Lakers' owner). They always socialized away from basketball and spent nearly every dinner together during home games. Formally, they were employer and employee: The employer would pay, and the employee would play. According to Magic Johnson, the two of them developed a relationship outside of the formal business because "he saw me as one of his kids" (Howard-Cooper 1996, 1). Says Johnson, "That's why I've never negotiated with him. . . . We never had a negotiation. He said, 'I want to give you this.' I said, 'OK.' He said, 'I want you to coach this team.' I said, 'OK.' It's been like that. It's no contract, you just say, 'OK.' That's how we have it" (Howard-Cooper 1996, 1). Buss calls Johnson his hero; Johnson calls Buss his surrogate father.

However, there are also pitfalls to an embedded relationship. We describe some of them next.

The Emotional Potential Is Higher

The emotional potential of embedded relationships is higher because there are more dimensions of the self-involved. When business and friendship combine, the emotional potential can often be overwhelming, and interpersonal conflict can result. For example, if someone has a poor exchange with a neighbor that leaves the friendship in question, this is quite disturbing, but the person can at least travel to work knowing that the situation is "contained." Similarly, a person may have a terrible day at work and still be able to go home that evening to take solace in friends and family. Somehow, the separation of work and friendship creates a "buffer zone" for the parties involved. However, when things go awry in an embedded relationship during the course of negotiation, all systems can potentially fail. Identity issues may be even more overwhelming for people who have low self-esteem (Brown 1993).

Internal Value Conflict

Personal relationships are driven by people's need for acceptance, love, and identity, whereas business relationships are generally guided by a need for achievement and utilitarian goals. In embedded relationships, people often experience more internal value conflict because competence and liking are at battle with one another. For example, we may find someone to be a delightful friend, a wonderful and empathic listener, and a good person to spend time with; however, this person may be incompetent at the business task at hand. Conversely, the person who is more competent may be annoying to us. The question is, Which of these factors do we respond to in the situation, competence or liking?

Myopia

We have seen that embedded relationships can often reduce the costs associated with surveillance. However, embedded relationships may create myopia if people are reluctant to move beyond their own networks. At the extreme, imagine a cliquish network in which people engage only in business matters with their friends. This may eventually result in a myopic view of reality, if people within the network are biased in their perceptions and not connected to others who may have more or better information. Valley and Thompson (1998) refer to these types of relationships as "sticky ties"—describing the resistance to change that emanates from ingrained habits of past social interaction. Further, mandating changes in social ties creates passive resistance or inertia, in that most people are reluctant to turn to new, untried partners for information, resources, and the variety of interactions that are required in organizations.

ASSESSING THE QUALITY OF RELATIONSHIPS

How can a negotiator go about assessing the quality of the relationship she has with someone? As a start, you can consider where your relationship stands on each of the dimensions listed in Table 6–1. If the majority of the dimensions of your relationship are listed on the right-hand side, this means than an effective relationship has developed.

THREE TYPES OF TRUST RELATIONSHIPS

Having reviewed the three types of relationships (personal, business, and embedded), we are ready to consider trust within relationships. Trust means different things to different people. Most of the time putting our trust in someone means that we could be exploited, and this would have great costs for us. Simply, if the other party is not trustworthy, we suffer. If on the other hand, the other party is trustworthy, both parties are better off. The problem with trust in relationships is that many situations involve some incentive for people to behave in an untrustworthy fashion so as to get ahead.

Next, we discuss three major types of trust: deterrence-based trust, knowledge-based trust, and identification-based trust (Shapiro, Sheppard, and Cheraskin 1992; Lewicki and Bunker 1996). The three types of trust we describe do not necessarily go hand-in-hand with the three types of relationships, although there are some natural correlations. We describe each of these now.

Table 6–1: Summary of dyadic dimensions along which relationships develop

From	To
Openness and Self Disclosure Limited to "safe," socially acceptable topics	Disclosure goes beyond safe areas to include personally sensitive, private, and controversial topics and aspects of self
Knowledge of Each Other Surface, "biographic" knowledge: Impressionistic in nature	Knowledge is multifaceted and extends to core aspects of personality, needs, and style
Predictability of Other's Reactions and Responses Limited to socially expected or role-related responses, and those based on first impressions or repeated surface encounters	Predictability of the other's reactions extends beyond stereotypical exchange and includes a knowledge of the contingencies affecting the other's reactions
Uniqueness of Interaction Exchanges are stereotypical, guided by prevailing social norms or role expectations	Exchanges are idiosyncratic to the two people, guided by norms that are unique to the relationship
Mulimodality of Communication Largely limited to verbal channels of communication and stereotypical or unintended nonverbal channels	Includes multiple modalities of communication, including nonverbal and verbal "shorthands" specific to the relationship or the individuals involved; less restrictiveness of nonverbal
Substitutability of Communication Little substitution among alternative modes of communication	Possession of and ability to use alternative modes of communication to convey the same message
Capacity for Conflict and Evaluation Limited capacity for conflict; use of conflict-avoidance techniques; reluctance to criticize	Readiness and ability to express conflict and make positive or negative evaluations
Spontaneity of Exchange Interactions tend to be formal or "comfortably informal" as prescribed by prevailing social norms	Greater informality and ease of interaction; movement across topical areas occurs readily and without hesitation or formality; communication flows and changes direction easily
Synchronization and Pacing Except for stereotyped modes of response, limited dyadic synchrony occurs	Speech and nonverbal responses become synchronized; flow of interaction is smooth; cues are quickly and accurately interpreted
Efficiency of Communication Communication of intended meanings sometimes requires extensive discussion; misunderstandings occur unless statements are qualified or elaborated	Intended meanings are transmitted and understood rapidly, accurately, and with sensitivity to nuance
Mutual Investment Little investment in the other except in areas of role-related or situation interdependencies	Extensive investment in other's well-being and efficacy

Source: Adapted from Galegher, J., Kraut, R. E., and Egido, C. 1990. *Intellectual teamwork: Social and technological foundations of cooperative work.* Mahwah, NJ: Lawrence Erlbaum & Associates.

DETERRENCE-BASED TRUST

Deterrence-based trust is based on consistency of behavior, meaning that people will follow through on what they promise that they are going to do. Behavioral consistency, or follow-through, is sustained by threats or promises of consequences that will result if consistency and promises are not maintained. The consequences most often used are punishments, sanctions, incentives, rewards, legal implications, and others. Deterrence-

SIDEBAR 6–1. DETERRENCE-BASED TRUST
Another striking example of deterrence-based trust is the negotiated agreement between explorer Christopher Columbus and King Ferdinand and Queen Isabella. Ferdinand and Isabella offered Columbus ships, men, and money to carry the faith and the Spanish flag to the West. However, Columbus refused to agree until his demands were met in writing. He insisted that he be knighted, made admiral of the Ocean Sea, and viceroy and governor general of all the lands that he would discover. He further demanded 10 percent of whatever would be acquired overseas. A handshake would not suffice. He insisted that the deal be set in writing, and so drafted a lengthy, detailed agreement between himself and the crown. This was an astonishingly bold move, considering that the king and queen held the power of life and death over him. The haggling went back and forth, and on April 17, 1492, the Pact of Santa Fe was agreed to by the rulers (Dworetzky 1998b).

based trust often involves contracts and various forms of bureaucracy and surveillance. Deterrence-based trust mechanisms are more common than you might think. More than 70,000 U.S. companies purchased surveillance software between 1990 and 1992, with a total expenditure of more than $500 million (Aiello 1993). There are other forms of deterrence. For example, in the Hawthorne plant in the 1940s, the established norm was that workers would not deviate from acceptable levels of production. Deviation from this norm would result in some people being labeled as overperformers (also known as "rate-busters") and some being labeled as underperformers (also known as "shirkers"). Whenever a worker was caught over- or underperforming, other plant workers would give them a sharp blow to the upper arm (called "binging"). (For another example, see Sidebar 6–1.)

There are two key problems with deterrence-based trust: First, it is expensive to develop and maintain these systems—they require development, oversight, maintenance, and monitoring—and second, there tends to be a backfiring effect. The backfiring is based upon psychological principles of **reactance;** in popular culture, this is also known as "reverse psychology." For example, it has been empirically demonstrated that the presence of signs reading "Do Not Write on These Walls under Any Circumstances" actually increases the incidence of people's violations of the vandalism norm (as compared to signs that say "Please Do Not Write on These Walls" or the complete absence of signs; Pennebaker and Sanders 1976). Similarly, people take longer to vacate a parking space when they know someone else is waiting for it (Ruback and Juieng 1997). People often have a negative reaction whenever they perceive that someone is controlling their behavior or limiting their freedom. When people think their behavior is under the control of extrinsic motivators, such as sanctions and rewards, intrinsic motivation is reduced (Enzle and Anderson 1993). Thus, surveillance may undermine people's motivation to engage in the very behaviors that such monitoring is intended to ensure. For example, Hochschild (1983) describes how fear of monitoring adversely impacted trust among flight attendants at Delta Airlines. Flight attendants came to fear and distrust their passengers because of a policy allowing passengers to write letters of complaint about in-flight service. The climate of distrust was further intensified when flight attendants became suspicious that undercover supervisors were posing as passengers. The system backfired. We will further discuss deterrence-based trust later.

KNOWLEDGE-BASED TRUST

Knowledge-based trust is grounded in behavioral predictability, and it occurs when a person has enough information about others to understand them and accurately predict their behavior. Whenever there is informational uncertainty or asymmetry in a relationship, there is opportunity for deceit, and one or both parties risk exploitation. Paradoxically, if there is no risk in an exchange situation, exploitation cannot occur, but high levels of trust will not develop (Thibaut and Kelley 1959). Thus, trust is a consequence or response to uncertainty (Kollock 1994; Granovetter 1973).

An intriguing example of the development of knowledge-based trust among negotiators concerns the sale of rubber and rice in Thailand (Siamwalla 1978; Popkin 1981). For various reasons, rubber is a product in which quality cannot be determined at the time of sale but only months later. Thus, when rubber is sold, the seller knows the quality of the rubber, but the buyer does not. This is a classic case of one-sided informational asymmetry. In contrast, in the rice market, the quality of rice can be readily determined at the time of sale (no informational uncertainty). It would seem that the rubber market, because of its informational asymmetries, would be characterized by exploitation on the part of sellers who would only sell cheap rubber at high prices, creating a market of lemons (Akerlof 1970). However, buyers and sellers in the rubber market have abandoned anonymous exchange for long-term exchange relationships between particular buyers and sellers. Within this exchange framework, growers establish reputations for trustworthiness, and rubber of high quality is sold.

Knowledge-based trust increases dependence and commitment among parties (Dwyer, Schurr, and Oh 1987; Kollock 1994). For example, suppliers who regularly negotiate with certain customers develop highly specialized products for their customers. Such product differentiation can create barriers to switching suppliers. In addition to economic dependence, people become emotionally committed to some relationships. For example, in markets characterized by information asymmetries, once negotiators develop a relationship with someone they find to be trustworthy, they remain committed to the relationship, even when it would be profitable to trade with others (Kollock 1994). When switching does occur, the party who is "left" feels indignant and violated. For example, the decision of major car manufacturers to switch to lower-cost suppliers has left their higher-cost long-time suppliers feeling betrayed. Similarly, people who expect to interact with others in the future are less likely to exploit them, even when given an opportunity (Marlowe, Gergen, and Doob 1966). When negotiators anticipate extended relationships, they are more likely to cooperate with customers, colleagues, and suppliers, but not with competitors (Sondak and Moore 1994). These relationships and the perception of low mobility among individuals promote development of integrative agreements across interactions, rather than only within given transactions (Mannix, Tinsley, and Bazerman 1995).

IDENTIFICATION-BASED TRUST

Identification-based trust is grounded in complete empathy with another person's desires and intentions. In identification-based trust systems, trust exists between peo-

Table 6–2:	Trust/relationship grid		
	Relationship		
Trust	**Personal Relationship**	**Business Relationship**	**Embedded Relationship**
Deterrence-based	Lack of trust Prenuptial agreements Surveillance	Theory X management Use of threats, punishments, sanctions Surveillance	Use of threats, punishments, sanctions
Knowledge-based	Sympathy for the other	Customer-driven focus Assessment of clients' needs	Understand and appreciate partners
Identification-based	True empathy for other Investment in other's welfare	Theory Y management Selection of employees who fit corporate culture and its values Restructuring to serve customer	Empathy Development of social identity

ple because each person understands, agrees with, empathizes with, and takes on the other's values because of the emotional connection between them; thus, they act for each other (Lewicki and Bunker 1996). Identification-based trust means that other people have adopted your own preferences.

In Table 6–2, we list the three types of relationships (personal, business, and embedded) and the three types of trust (deterrence-based, knowledge-based, and identification-based). We indicate the type and nature of interaction that may occur when different types of trust and different types of relationships intersect. Whereas it may seem that personal relationships would or should be completely grounded in knowledge-based or identification-based trust, this is not always the case. For example, a deterrence-based trust system is put in place when couples get prenuptial agreements, when husbands or wives pay private investigators to monitor the actions of their spouses, and when parents install video cameras to monitor childcare providers. In business relationships, the extreme form of theory X management has deterrence-based trust at the heart of its assumptions about human behavior. According to theory X management, workers are inherently lazy and need to be monitored within a punishment system so that they will perform their tasks. Theory Y and other enlightened forms of management assert that workers perform for the joy of working, and monitoring systems only decrease intrinsic interest.

BUILDING TRUST: RATIONAL AND DELIBERATE MECHANISMS

In the next part of this chapter, we take up the task of how to build trust when none may exist, how to identify the key threats to the development of trust in a relationship,

---

SIDEBAR 6–2. HOW MANAGERS SECURE COMMITMENT IN THE ABSENCE OF BINDING CONTRACTS

We recently conducted a survey to examine how businesspeople attempt to secure trust in relationships. We asked 52 MBA students to "imagine that you are involved in a negotiation situation where you need to get commitment (i.e., follow-through) from one or more of the people involved. The nature of the negotiation does not involve 'binding contracts.' How do you try to instill a sense of commitment in the absence of any binding contracts?" The responses varied dramatically:

- *Persuasion and consciousness-raising* (e.g., "I would reinforce the idea that this is the beginning of a long-term, multiple-contact relationship, and that it is in my counter-party's best interest to think about the repercussions of reneging on future negotiations"): 40 percent
- *Coercion and threat tactics* (e.g., humiliation, punishment, etc.): 37 percent
- *Nonverbal strategies* (e.g., handshakes, establishing rapport, ". . . look people in the eye, have them look at you, and say to you that they will do what you want them to do . . .", etc.): 29 percent
- *Verbal agreements:* 21 percent
- *Behavior modification* (e.g., tit for tat; social modeling): 19 percent
- *Rewards and benefits:* 13 percent
- *Public commitments* (e.g., ". . . by making the outcome public, the erring party would suffer public embarrassment and suffer loss of reputation . . ."): 13 percent
- *Alignment of incentives:* 13 percent
- *Collecting information about other's BATNA:* 12 percent
- *Written (nonbinding) agreements:* 6 percent
- *Creation of mutual enemy:* 4 percent
- *Creating escrow or collateral arrangements:* 2 percent

---

and how to repair trust once it is broken. In our discussions, we focus primarily on knowledge-based and identification-based trust. With a little bit of thinking, people can take some proactive steps to build trust in their relationships with others. Thinking about trust in a preemptive sense can save people much suffering and ward off potential problems. We outline 10 trust-building steps that have their roots in mindful, rational, deliberate behavior. (For an examination of how businesspersons attempt to secure trust, see Sidebar 6–2.)

TRANSFORM A-TYPE CONFLICT INTO C-TYPE CONFLICT

There are two basic types of conflict that can occur in relationships. **A-type conflict,** also known as **emotional conflict,** is personal, defensive, and resentful (Guetzkow and Gyr 1954). A-type conflict is often rooted in anger, personality clashes, ego, and tension. **C-type conflict,** also known as **cognitive conflict,** is largely depersonalized. It consists of argumentation about the merits of ideas, plans, and projects, independent of the identity of the people involved. C-type conflict is often effective in stimulating the creativity necessary for integrative agreement because it forces people to rethink problems and arrive at outcomes that everyone can live with. As a general principle, A-type conflict threatens relationships, whereas C-type conflict enhances relationships, provided that people are comfortable with it (see Jehn 1997).

AGREE ON A COMMON GOAL OR SHARED VISION

The importance of a common goal is summed up in a quote by Steve Jobs, who is associated with three high-profile Silicon Valley companies—Apple, NeXT, and Pixar: "It's okay to spend a lot of time arguing about which route to take to San Francisco when everyone wants to end up there, but a lot of time gets wasted in such arguments if one person wants to go to San Francisco and another secretly wants to go to San Diego" (Eisenhardt, Kahwajy, and Bourgeois 1997, 80). Shared goals do not imply homogeneous thinking, but they do require everyone to share a vision. Steve Jobs is not alone in his thinking. Colin Sewell-Rutter, a director of The Results Partnership, a consultancy that specializes in improving board-level communications, concludes that "The single most important source of problems within the boardroom is the lack of a shared vision, and shared corporate goals. . . . All the major difficulties ultimately stem from that" (Lynn 1997, 31).

The 1993 departure of Ernest Mario as chief executive of the pharmaceutical firm Glaxo (as it then was) illustrates how conflicts can also mask the fact that people never fundamentally agreed on what the company is about. Mario was thought to have been preparing a takeover of American rival Warner-Lambert, even though the then-chairman, Sir Paul Girolami, believed that the company should stick with its strategy of investing for organic growth. The result was a bitter conflict that culminated in Mario's departure with a $3 million payoff (it was only after Girolami retired that Glaxo made its first takeover in decades, when it bid for Wellcome).

CREATE A PLACE FOR CONFLICT AND GET IT OUT IN THE OPEN

Most people, even seasoned managers and executives, feel uncomfortable about conflict. It is much easier to capitalize on constructive conflict by creating a time and place for it to occur, rather than expecting it to naturally erupt. Furthermore, discussing the potential for conflict before it erupts is a lot more effective than trying to deal with it after the fact. As an example of how companies create a forum for conflict, see Box 6–2.

EXPAND THE PIE

Often, negotiations threaten the trust between people in a relationship because negotiators are dealing with a small bargaining zone. When negotiators are dealing with a small bargaining zone, they are more apt to make negative, dispositional attributions about the other party (Morris, Larrick, and Su 1999). What this means is that people do not say to themselves, "I bet we are having a hard time reaching agreement because the bargaining zone is small," but rather, "I bet we are having a hard time reaching agreement because the other party is being uncooperative and unpleasant." This, of course, can hinder the conflict resolution process and make reaching mutually beneficial agreements quite difficult. In a recent examination of this issue, members of two rival universities attempted to negotiate a deal in the presence of a very small bargaining zone (Nadler, Kurtzberg, Morris, and Thompson 1999). Participants were not

---

> **BOX 6–2**
>
> ## CREATING A FORUM FOR CONFLICT
>
> Bovis Construction Corporation, who has worked on the renovation of Los Angeles City Hall and the construction of a football stadium in Nashville, deals with conflict in an open fashion (Oldham 1998). Prior to each project, Bovis construction teams hold a planning session in which team members openly address potential conflicts. These planning sessions are conducted by company facilitators who encourage the project owner, architects, contractors, and other players to map out processes they plan to follow to get the job done. During the session, participants draft and sign a "win-win agreement," which includes a matrix that lays out what team members expect from one another. The first box in a matrix may detail the owner's responsibilities on the project, whereas the next box may look at the owner's expectations of the construction manager. Teams then use this matrix to review their progress on the project. Bovis managers agree that the process has not only decreased the adversity that is so prevalent on construction sites, but the firm has also saved millions of dollars and has completed projects on time.
>
>

told that the bargaining zone was small, and reaching agreement required highly creative, integrative bargaining strategies. A shocking number (50 percent) failed to reach agreement because they made negative attributions about the intentions of the other party. Those who did reach agreement indicated that they realized that the bargaining zone was small and expanded the pie to explore mutual gains.

USE FAIRNESS CRITERIA THAT EVERYONE CAN BUY INTO

Trust is often threatened when negotiators each have honest intentions to be fair, but have different ideas about what "fair" means. This can often lead to doubt, distrust, and suspicion. It is important for negotiators to discuss the fairness criteria they will use, particularly as it pertains to slicing the pie (see chapter 3). Often, negotiators can agree on a principle that can pave the way for a trusting relationship.

CAPITALIZE ON NETWORK CONNECTIONS

Negotiators who do not know each other may attempt to build a more trusting relationship by trying to find a common node in their social networks. Practically, what this means is that they engage in enough discussion to attempt to single out someone whom they both know. It has been said that there are only six degrees of separation between people (Burt 1999). Finding a common link in social networks signals not only similarity of interests, but it also creates accountability via common network relations.

FIND A SHARED PROBLEM OR A SHARED ENEMY

It is remarkable how the presence of a common enemy can unite people and build trust (Sherif, Harvey, White, Hood, and Sherif 1961). This happens for several reasons. First, it is often necessary for people to join forces to compete against a common enemy (for example, a shared goal of sorts was created during the Reagan-Gorbachev Summit talks). One evening, Reagan and Soviet leader Mikhail Gorbachev were drinking coffee after dinner on Lake Geneva. Secretary of State George P. Shultz turned to Georgi Kornienko, the Soviet first deputy foreign minister, and accused him of trying to stall summit negotiations on bilateral issues. "You, Mr. Minister, are responsible for this," Shultz declared. Then, turning to Gorbachev, the secretary of state added forcefully: "This man is not doing what you want him to do. He is not getting done what you want done." Reagan took advantage of the situation to create a common bond and looked at Gorbachev: "To hell with what they're doing. You and I will say, 'We will work together to make it come about.' " Reagan and Gorbachev then shook hands. That moment marked a critical turning point in the meeting (Hoffman 1985). A common goal, or common enemy, removes the perception that parties' interests are completely opposed and builds a new value that represents a higher-order principle that all parties find motivating.

FOCUS ON THE FUTURE

It is difficult for negotiators to agree on what happened in the past, but if they can forgive and forget and focus on their future together, this can go a long way toward building trust. For example, Sean M. Haley, warehousing operations manager for Sage Products Inc., an 800-employee medical-device manufacturer, considers negotiation of critical importance in managing the company's relationship with its distribution and transportation provider. Because his company gives all its freight to this third party, trust is essential. Once Haley identifies the appropriate contact for issues that arise, he negotiates a resolution of shipment problems. Haley has found that not assigning blame for occasional problems and focusing instead on what both parties must do in the future to ensure better customer service produces integrative outcomes (Turpin 1998).

USE A FAIR PROCEDURE

In addition to how much of the pie they get, people are very concerned with the process used to slice the pie. When people believe the process is just, they feel more comfortable with their outcomes (Lind and Tyler 1988). If negotiators can agree on a process for how they will undertake their negotiation, they can often build trust. However, we need to warn negotiators against the temptation to overly regulate their behavior (Naquin 1999; Sitkin and Roth 1993). If too many rules develop, they can often threaten a trusting relationship.

NEGOTIATE ROLES

If negotiators find themselves in a situation such as an uncomfortable business relationship (which we discussed earlier in this chapter), trust may be facilitated by talking about expectations early on in the negotiation. For example, a student working with a mentor may discuss the mentor-student relationship and the expectations contained therein; a summer intern may have a discussion with his or her direct supervisor concerning the expectations they have of one another's roles (see Kurtzberg and Medvec 1999).

BUILDING TRUST: IMPLICIT EMOTIONAL MECHANISMS

There are a variety of psychologically based ways of enhancing and building trust between people. These psychological mechanisms distinguish themselves from the rational, cognitive mechanisms discussed earlier in that people tend not to talk about these factors explicitly; rather, savvy negotiators know how to capitalize on them intuitively.

SIMILARITY

People who are similar to each other like one another (Griffin and Sparks 1990). The **similarity–attraction effect** occurs on the basis of very little, and sometimes downright trivial, information. For example, consider a situation in which people write down all of the ways in which they are similar to their opponent. A different group writes down all of the ways in which they are different or unique from their opponent. In fact, members of all groups are randomly composed. Those who perceive themselves to be similar to others are more concerned with equality, express more satisfaction with the outcome, and rate the entire experience to be more cooperative than do those who focus on their differences, even though they are in no objective sense more similar to others—they only think they are (Kramer, Pommerenke, and Newton 1993). The process of searching for similarities often has the effect of making people feel that they have more in common than would be expected by chance.

Another basis of similarity is group membership. Members of the same group perceive themselves to be more similar to one another than to members of different groups (out-groups). Negotiators treat members of out-groups differently than members of in-groups. Perceived similarity stirs up feelings of obligation to help similar others.

MERE EXPOSURE

The more we are exposed to something—a person, object, or idea—the more we come to like it. The mere exposure effect (Zajonc 1968) is extremely powerful and occurs below the level of our awareness. Advertisers know about the mere exposure effect. Why do you think that television ads are repeatedly shown to an audience? The more we are exposed to the ad, the more we come to like the product—up to a point. U.S. Senator George Mitchell developed a "quality time" strategy for helping to bridge relationships in the Northern Ireland peace process. In September 1999, he moved the talks between Ulster Unionist leader David Trimble and Sinn Fein president Gerry Adams to the London residence of U.S. Ambassador Phil Lader. Over meals, cocktails and informal get-togethers, Mitchell brought the men closer together (*Newsweek International,* 1999).

Savvy negotiators increase their effectiveness by making themselves familiar to the other party. Instead of having a single-shot negotiation, they suggest a preliminary meeting over drinks and follow with a few phone calls and unexpected gifts. By the time of the final negotiation, the target negotiator feels as though he or she is interacting with an old friend. (See Sidebar 6–3 for an example of how mere exposure increases liking.)

SIDEBAR 6–3. MERE EXPOSURE INCREASES LIKING

The effects of mere exposure on liking are demonstrated clearly in the classroom. In one investigation, student *A* attended 15 sessions of a course. For each session, she arrived before the class began, walked down the aisle, and sat at the front, where other students could see her. Student *B* did the same thing, but attended only 10 lectures. Student *C* came to class only five times. Student *D* never showed up. At the end of the term, the students in the class were shown slides of students *A, B, C,* and *D,* and were asked to indicate how "familiar" they found each one; how attractive they found each one, and how similar they believed each one was to them. The number of classes attended had a dramatic impact on attraction and similarity, but not familiarity (Moreland and Beach 1992).

GOOD MOOD

People in a good mood are more agreeable (Carnevale and Isen 1986; Forgas and Moylan 1996). Funny cartoons, unexpected little gifts, small strokes of fortune, and thinking positive thoughts all engender a good mood (see Isen and Baron 1991 for a review).

PHYSICAL PRESENCE

People form both personal and business relationships to others who are literally physically close to them. For example, even when students are seated alphabetically in a classroom, friendships are significantly more likely to form between those whose last names begin with the same or nearby letter (Segal 1974). This is what is called the **propinquity effect.** This may not seem important until you consider the fact that you may meet some of your closest colleagues, and perhaps even a future business partner, merely because of an instructor's seating chart! Similarly, those people given a corner seat or an office at the end of a corridor make fewer friends in the organization (Maisonneuve, Palmade, and Fourment 1952). If an instructor changes seat assignments once or twice during the semester, each student becomes acquainted with additional colleagues (Byrne 1961). To further see the power of the propinquity effect, consider the entering class of the Maryland State Police Training Academy (Segal 1974). Trainees were assigned to their classroom seats and to their dormitory rooms by the alphabetical order of their last names. Some time thereafter, trainees were asked to name their three best friends in the group; their choices followed the rules of alphabetization almost exactly. Larsons were friends with Lees, not with Abromowitzes or Xiernickes, even though they were separated by only a few yards (Byrne 1961; Kipnis 1957)!

As another example, consider friendship formation among couples in apartment buildings. In this particular case, residents had been assigned to their apartments at random as vacancies opened up, and nearly all of them were strangers when they moved in. When asked to name their three closest friends in the entire housing project, 65 percent named friends in the same building. Among those living in the same building, the propinquity effect was in play: 41 percent of next-door neighbors indicated they were close friends, compared to only 22 percent who lived two doors apart, and only 10 percent who lived on the opposite ends of the hall.

The propinquity effect has an impact on **functional distance:** Certain aspects of architectural design make it more likely that some people will come into contact with each other more often than with others, even though physically, the distances between them might be the same. For example, more friendships were made with people on the same floor than on another floor, presumably because having to climb stairs to go visiting required more effort than just walking down the hall.

RECIPROCITY

According to the **reciprocity principle,** we feel obligated to return in kind what others have offered or given to us. We referred to this powerful principle earlier as the law of the universe. This is not an overstatement, as all human societies subscribe to the rule permeating exchanges of all kinds (Gouldner 1960). Feelings of indebtedness are so powerful that if unresolved, they carry on into the future and are passed on to the next generation to repay. People feel upset and distressed if they have received a favor from another person and are prevented from returning it. Not surprisingly, people are aware of the powerful grip that reciprocity has on them. Often people will turn down favors and rewards from others because they do not want to be obligated.

So far we have said that reciprocity is powerful. There seems to be nothing inherently illogical or dangerous with reciprocity with regard to negotiation. Usually, reciprocity pertains more to the pattern of concessions than to the degree of concessions. This means that if someone does us a favor or makes a concession, we feel obligated to return the favor or concession. However, unless we are careful, we could be victimized by an opponent who preys on our feelings of indebtedness.

For example, suppose the opponent provides us with a favor, gift, or service that we never invited and perhaps even attempted to avoid. Our attempts to return it have been denied, and we are left with the unwanted gift. Even under these circumstances, the reciprocity rule may operate. Thus, we should beware of the unsolicited gift from our real estate agent, the courtesy token from our business associate, and the free lunch from the consulting firm. When faced with these situations, we should acknowledge the favor and then, if we still feel indebted, return the favor on a similar level.

DO NOT GLOAT

Negotiators should resist the urge to gloat or show signs of smugness following negotiation (see also Raiffa 1982). In a recent investigation, some negotiators gloated following their negotiation: ("I really feel good about the negotiation; I got everything I wanted."). Other negotiators made self-effacing remarks: "I really didn't do that well." Later, negotiators who overheard the other party gloat or make self-effacing remarks were given an opportunity to provide valuable stock options to these same parties. Those parties who gloated received significantly fewer stock options than those who made the self-effacing remarks (Thompson, Valley, and Kramer 1995).

SCHMOOZING

Small talk often seems to serve no obvious function. The exchange of pleasantries about the weather or our favorite basketball team seems to be purposeless, except for conforming to social etiquette. However, on a *preconscious* level, schmoozing has a dramatic impact on our liking and trust of others. For example, even a short exchange can lead people to develop considerably more trust in others than in the absence of interaction (Nadler, Kurtzberg, Morris, and Thompson 1999). According to Susan Pravda, co-managing partner of the Boston law office of Epstein, Becker, and Green, schmoozing is an important part of negotiations. She advises, "Don't walk in and start going through your list. If they have a baby picture on the desk, it doesn't hurt to say, 'oh, is that a new grandchild?' People like to talk about themselves. It can segue into what you're trying to achieve" (Lancaster 1998, B1). Peter J. Pestillo, executive vice president of corporate relations for Ford Motor and one of the auto industry's leading labor negotiators, is known for his golf dates with union negotiators. Says Pestillo, "If you know someone, you know something that might be more important to him than to you" (Lancaster 1998, B1).

FLATTERY

We like people who appreciate us and admire us. This means that we will tend to trust people more who like us. Many people believe that for flattery to be effective in engendering trust, it must be perceived as genuine. Surprisingly, even if people suspect that the flatterer has ulterior motives, this can still increase liking and trust under some conditions (Jones, Stires, Shaver, and Harris 1968).

MIMICKING

People involved in a face-to-face interaction tend to mirror one another in posture, facial expression, tone of voice, and mannerisms. This phenomenon, known as **social contagion,** is the basis for the development of rapport between people (Drolet, Larrick, and Morris 1998). On the surface, it might seem that mimicking others would be extremely annoying—almost like a form of mockery. However, the type of mimicry that is involved in everyday social encounters is quite subtle and definitely powerful. When two people are mimicking one another, their movements become almost like a choreographed dance. In this sense, people's behavior becomes synchronized. To the extent that our behaviors are synchronized with those of others, we feel more rapport, and this increases our trust in them. Whereas mimicry is crucial for smooth interaction between people, there is an important exception. Mimicry of positive facial expressions and emotions is conducive for pleasant social interaction, but in the case of negative expression and emotion, mimicking others is often not desirable. For example, well-adjusted couples are better at resisting *quid pro quo* behavior in angry exchanges, whereas unhappy couples seemed trapped in destructive tit-for-tat exchanges; anger is likely to spark an angry response (Gottman 1979).

SELF-DISCLOSURE

Self-disclosure means sharing information about oneself with another person. It is a way of building a relationship with another person by making oneself vulnerable, in that the self-disclosing negotiator is providing information that could potentially be exploited. Self-disclosure also explicitly invites the other person to reciprocate the disclosure, thereby increasing trust.

THREATS TO TRUST

Any number of things can threaten the trust that develops between people in a relationship. Here are nine things to be careful of:

BREACHES OF TRUST

One of the biggest threats to trust in a relationship is what is known as a **breach,** or **defection.** A breach occurs when one or both people violate the trust that has been built between them. For example, on November 14, 1998, the United States was set to attack Iraq for their refusal to let weapons inspectors investigate sites. According to the United States, Saddam Hussein had engaged in a direct breach of contract. This action made the United States extraordinarily angry. Joseph Cirinsione, an arms-control expert at the Carnegie Endowment, said: "The Iraquis have repeatedly lied. They've lied inside other lies" (Crossette and Erlanger 1998, A8). According to Samuel R. Berger, President Clinton's national security advisor, the United States had to strike Iraq swiftly and severely or lose all credibility.

MISCOMMUNICATION

In some cases, a real breach of trust does not occur between persons, but somehow, a miscommunication occurs that causes one or more parties to *interpret* it as such. Miscommunication is more likely when parties are not in regular contact, especially when they have little face-to-face contact.

POOR PIE EXPANSION

To the extent that negotiators are not skilled in using pie-expanding strategies (as we discussed in chapter 4 on integrative negotiation), trust between parties can be threatened. Therefore, it is imperative that negotiators be skilled in expanding the pie so as to increase and sustain trust between themselves and the other party.

DISPOSITIONAL ATTRIBUTIONS

Negotiators often make dispositional, as opposed to situational, attributions for the questionable behavior of the other party (Morris, Larrick, and Su 1999). This can be a threat to trust. A **dispositional attribution** is one that calls into question another person's character and intentions by citing them as the cause of a behavior or incident (e.g., arrogance, greed, etc.). In contrast, a situational attribution cites one or more situational factors as the cause of a behavior or incident (e.g., a traffic jam, the faulty mail-delivery system, etc.). When negotiators make dispositional attributions for their opponents' behaviors, this can threaten the trust between themselves and the other party, as it is much more difficult for people to respond to a dispositional attribution than a situational one. For example, Kramer and Wei (1999) examined how people interpret ambiguous and slightly negative social interactions (i.e., when a person you know does not acknowledge you when you walk past him). It turns out that the power or status differential is key in interpreting these situations. The high-power person who does not acknowledge a colleague usually reported having a busy day, or more often, not even being aware of the other person. In contrast, the low-power person was often extremely paranoid and upset, believing that the high-power person was attempting to ostracize or punish them. Thus, the low-power person makes a dispositional attribution for what is really a situational case.

EGOCENTRISM

Egocentrism, or the tendency to view one's own actions as good and worthy and the simultaneous tendency to view the behaviors of others in less favorable terms, can lead to breakdowns in trust. For example, most people tend to see themselves as being "wronged" more than they "wrong" others. In a recent investigation of ours, MBA students in a 10-week negotiation course were asked what percent of the time, on average, they deceived others. The average was 25 percent of the time—about one in every four negotiations. These students, however, said that they had been deceived during negotiations by other members of the class 35 percent of the time—about one in every three negotiations. This means that people are more likely to regard another's behavior as untrustworthy and their own behavior as trustworthy.

REPUTATION

If negotiators focus on negative reputation, rumor, or hearsay about another party, this can threaten the trust between them. Reputations are often more extreme and polarized than the person they represent; they can be summed up by four words: *judgmental, consistent, immediate,* and *inferential.* The reputations assigned to others tend to be highly evaluative, meaning that they are either "good" or "bad" (Osgood, Suci, and Tannenbaum 1957). Furthermore, the reputations we assign to others are highly internally consistent. Once we decide that someone is trustworthy, other qualities about this person are perceived as consistent with this favorable impression. This gives rise to the **halo effect,** which is the tendency to believe that people whom we trust and like are also intelligent and capable. In addition, as much as we do not like to believe that our judgments of others are influenced by their appearance, the halo effect can often be triggered on the mere basis of physical attractiveness. We like attractive people more than unattractive people; furthermore, we think attractive people are smarter and do better work (Dion, Berscheid, and Walster 1972; Landy and Sigall 1974).

Of course, the halo effect can work in the opposite direction: The **forked-tail effect** means that once we have formed a negative impression of someone, we tend to view everything else about them in a negative fashion. This is the reason why it is so difficult to recover from making a bad impression.

Our impressions of others are formed quickly and immediately, sometimes within the first few minutes of meeting someone. Furthermore, the judgments we make about people are often automatic (Bargh, Lombardi, and Higgins 1988). Finally, we form impressions of people on the bias of very limited information. If people in relationships rely on reputation alone, this may decrease trust.

FOCUSING TOO MUCH ON RULES

Negotiators who spend a lot of time discussing rules that will govern their interactions may experience a "boomerang effect" that will lead to the creation of more distrust between them (Naquin 1999; Sitkin and Roth 1993). Sitkin and Roth (1993) identify several mechanisms by which highly formalized management control systems lead to an escalating cycle of distrust, in that they undermine a sense of value of congruence, create hurt feelings, convey disrespect, and threaten people's sense of professional autonomy and confidence.

FOCUSING ON THE "BAD APPLE"

In all clique networks, there may be a person who has a reputation for being less trustworthy, tougher, or less easy to work with than other members of the clique. This person is what we call the "bad apple," and bad apples can stand out. The problem is that people's impression of the bad apple can spoil their impression of the entire bunch. For example, Naquin (1999) found that in negotiations between labor and management groups in a simulated interaction, negotiators were significantly less likely to trust the group as a whole than any individual in the group that they were dealing with. It seems that the "bad apple" in the group called the entire group's trustworthiness into question.

SOCIAL COMPARISON

Social comparison—or the need and desire of people to compare themselves to others in terms of competence, attractiveness, success, benefits, and many other qualities—inevitably leads to feelings of distrust. It is always possible to find some dimension on which we feel less equitably treated than others. Therefore, it is important for negotiators to realize that social comparison generally tends to be a losing proposition in terms of creating positive bonds between people.

REPAIRING BROKEN TRUST

There are three cases of broken trust between negotiators. In the first, which we call the *violator-and-victim case,* one party feels violated by the other party. The violator may or may not know that the victim feels wronged; thus, the revelation that trust has been broken may come as a surprise to the violator. A second case of broken trust is what we call the *dual-victim case,* in which each person feels wronged by the other. This can often be a more difficult situation to resolve because both parties feel uniquely violated, regard the other party to be completely at fault, and feel that an apology should be forthcoming. The third case of broken trust is what we call the *dual-violator case,* in which both people knowingly defected on one another simultaneously. For example, in studies of negotiators playing bargaining games like the prisoner's dilemma—where the parties can either make a cooperative or a competitive choice (see chapter 11 on social dilemmas)—both people simultaneously defect in a significant number of instances. The question raised is whether each person engaged in a violation of trust because they feared that the other party was going to break the trust as well, or whether they were motivated by greed.

STEPS TOWARD REPAIRING
BROKEN TRUST

Step 1: Insist on a personal meeting right away

Step 2: Tell the other party that you value the relationship

Step 3: Apologize for your behavior

Step 4: Let them vent

Step 5: Do not get defensive, no matter how wrong you think they are

Step 6: Ask for clarifying information

Step 7: Say that you understand their perspective

Step 8: Let them tell you what they need

Step 9: Paraphrase your understanding of what they need

Step 10: Think about ways to prevent a future problem

Step 11: Do an evaluation of the situation at a scheduled date

Step 12: Plan a future together

When trust has been broken in any of these three types of instances, it is often in both parties' interests to attempt to repair the trust because broken relationships are often very costly in terms of the emotions involved and the opportunities lost. However, it is possible to reestablish trust that has been broken (see Bottom, Gibson, Daniels, and Murnighan 2000). Next, we outline a process for repairing broken trust (see Box 6–3 for a quick summary). This process is ideally suited to the violator-and-victim case; it is possible to use in the other two cases with some minor adjustments.

STEP 1: INSIST ON A PERSONAL MEETING RIGHT AWAY

When trust has been violated, the victim will usually inform the violator that a perceived violation has occurred. This may either be done directly or through the "grapevine." The violator's first reaction is often one of surprise combined with denial, and he or she may feel a need to exonerate him or herself. The violator should insist on a personal, face-to-face meeting with the victim as quickly as possible. Indeed, verbal explanations are more effective than written explanations (Shapiro, Buttner, and Barry 1994).

STEP 2: TELL THE OTHER PARTY THAT YOU VALUE THE RELATIONSHIP

When a breach of trust has occurred, negotiators should affirm the other person. This means telling the other person that you value the relationship you have with him or her, and that you want to work things out.

STEP 3: APOLOGIZE FOR YOUR BEHAVIOR

Sincerity is very important. Violators should apologize for their behavior and accept responsibility for their actions. The expression of remorse following a wrongful act can mitigate punishment. The violator should apologize in a way that takes ownership for his or her actions or behavior, yet does not necessarily accept the victim's version of the violator's *intentions*. For example, a violator might tell a victim, "I am very sorry that I did not consult you before preparing the report." By saying this, the violator does not agree with the victim's accusation that the violator attempted to take more credit for the report; rather, the violator only identifies the action as being hurtful for the victim. Indeed, when companies acknowledge that they have committed acts that threaten their legitimacy (e.g., newspaper claims of illegal conduct), they are more successful in blunting criticism when they point to external, mitigating circumstances (e.g., company norms, budgetary problems, etc.; Elsbach 1994; Bies, Shapiro, and Cummings 1988).

STEP 4: LET THEM VENT

It is very important for victims to express their anger, rage, disappointment, and feelings of betrayal over the event. Merely talking about negative events can actually be part of the cure (Pennebaker, Hughes, and O'Heeron 1987). Research on procedural justice (Lind and Tyler 1988) indicates that if victims have a chance to express their disappointment, this is often an important step in the healing process.

STEP 5: DO NOT GET DEFENSIVE, NO MATTER HOW WRONG YOU THINK THEY ARE

Instinctively, violators will attempt to defend their own honor. However, it is very important not to behave defensively, no matter how misinformed or wrong you believe the other party to be. It is appropriate to tell the other person that you view the situation very differently and to point out that there are many ways of looking at the situation. Only after the victim has had an opportunity to vent and explain his perspective should the violator attempt to tell the victim, in very clear and simple terms, what his or her intentions were. For example, a violator might say, "My intention was to turn in the report and not bother too many people with unnecessary requests to edit it."

STEP 6: ASK FOR CLARIFYING INFORMATION

Violators should invite the victim to provide clarifying information in a nondefensive fashion. For example, a violator might say, "Am I wrong in thinking that you did not ask to be listed on the report?" or "Did you receive the draft copy that I sent the previous week?", etc.

STEP 7: SAY THAT YOU UNDERSTAND THEIR PERSPECTIVE

If a person feels that they are understood, the chances for rebuilding trust are greatly increased. It is very helpful if one party can truly empathize with the perceived victim (for example, "I can understand why you felt out-of-the-loop. I have felt that way before, too.").

STEP 8: LET THEM TELL YOU WHAT THEY NEED

Violators should not second-guess what the victims will need from them; on the other hand, victims need to tell violators what they need to feel better about the relationship.

A major stumbling block in the trust rebuilding process is that parties have different ideas about what is fair. The egocentric bias once again rears its ugly head with most harm doers perceiving themselves as more beneficent than the harmed. However, the mere fact of asking the harmed what she needs can go a long way toward rebuilding trust. For example, Bottom, Gibson, Daniels, and Murnighan (2000) found that in an empirical investigation of breaches of trust, harmdoers who asked "What can I do?" were more successful in rebuilding cooperation than those who did not ask or asked "What will it take?" According to Bottom et al. (2000), penance is critical to trust in mixed motive relationship. Aggravating a counterparty after a breech by making offers of penance that do not seem sincere may further antagonism. In contrast, volunteering to do penance, even in small amounts, is particularly effective. This step goes hand in hand with step 9.

STEP 9: PARAPHRASE YOUR UNDERSTANDING OF WHAT THEY NEED

Oftentimes, another misunderstanding can occur during the process of repairing broken trust, despite the best of intentions: Emotions are running high, and people may not be accurately perceiving the information exchanged between violator and victim. Therefore, the violator should paraphrase her understanding of what the victim says he needs, so that the victim can clarify or support what the violator is paraphrasing.

STEP 10: THINK ABOUT WAYS TO PREVENT A FUTURE PROBLEM

Do not just try to remedy the past; rather, think about a way to make sure that this problem, and any others like it, does not occur in the future. This may take some time, but it is well worth it.

STEP 11: DO AN EVALUATION OF THE SITUATION AT A SCHEDULED DATE

It is often wise to pull out your planners and decide upon a lunch or coffee meeting in a month or so to discuss how each party is feeling about the situation and occurrences since the breach of trust occurred. It is wise to schedule this date during the first meeting, because after this time, it may seem awkward to bring it up. This step ensures that parties will have a reason to meet and an opportunity to talk things through at a later date.

STEP 12: PLAN A FUTURE TOGETHER

Oftentimes, violators and victims tend to distance themselves from one another once a perceived violation has occurred. After all, the situation is uncomfortable, and people's instinct is to find a more comfortable situation. Therefore, it is very important for the violator and victim to plan a future together and build in some interdependence. This may mean collaborating on a future project or similar event. This future should be planned quickly, and parties should take steps to begin working with one another as soon as possible.

CONCLUSION

Establishing trust and building a relationship is key for effective negotiation. On an intuitive level, people realize this, yet many people do not know how to deal with the complexities involved in personal, business, and embedded relationships. We have seen that three types of trust—deterrence-based, knowledge-based, and identification-based—can exist in different types of relationships. We identified two routes by which to build trust in relationships: rational and deliberate mechanisms, and emotional mechanisms. In terms of rational strategies, negotiators can enhance trust in relationships by transforming A-type conflict into C-type conflict, agreeing on a common goal or shared vision, creating a place to air conflict, expanding the pie, using fairness criteria that everyone can buy into, capitalizing on network connections, finding a shared problem or shared enemy, focusing on the future (instead of the past), using a fair procedure, and negotiating roles. We noted that trust can also be enhanced through a variety of emotional mechanisms that operate below our level of conscious awareness, such as highlighting similarities, increasing exposure, creating a good mood, decreasing physical distance, reciprocity, refraining from gloating, schmoozing, flattery, mimicking, and self-disclosure. The biggest threats to trust are breaches of trust, miscommunication, poor pie expansion, dispositional and reputational attributions, focusing too much on rules, paying too much attention to the "bad apple," and social comparison. We outlined a 12-step procedure for repairing broken trust in a relationship.

7
POWER, PERSUASION, AND ETHICS

Madeleine Korbel Albright is the first female Secretary of State in U.S. history and the highest-ranking woman ever to serve in the executive branch of government. The tough-talking, wisecracking, former Georgetown University professor sought the job and accepted it eagerly, making no pretense of reluctance and offering no sham modesty about her stellar credentials (Lippman 2000). In her reign as Secretary of State, "Last Word" Albright has an impressive list of powerful accomplishments: she forged an alliance that finally faced down Serb aggression in the Balkans and held it together during the war, and she did this without a total rupture with Moscow. At the same time, she kept the Israeli-Palestinian peace negotiations from falling apart completely while Benjamin Netanyahu was prime minister so that Netanyahu's successor, Ehud Barak, could build on a foundation that was still intact. She nursed the relationship with China and opened the door to better relations with Iran. Her secret to power: "Interrupt!" At least this is the advice she gives to young women: "Don't wait for men to solicit your input" (Lippman 2000). And she walks the talk: In her course at Georgetown, she instituted a no-hand-raising rule because she believes that if students are told to raise their hands before speaking, women will do so, but men will not. Her successes with the variety of people she has to deal with reveal her remarkable persuasive skills and her bargaining power.

Power, in negotiation, is about getting a slice of the pie. However, power also has to do with creating new opportunities for joint gain. In this chapter, we advocate "enlightened power." The enlightened negotiator knows that he or she can get a bigger slice of the pie by creating a larger pie. The ultimately powerful negotiator knows how to expand the pie and how to offer the other party just enough over his BATNA so as to reach mutual settlement and keep the rest of the surplus for herself. It is certainly not always the case that negotiators attempt to get as much of the pie as they can; however, all negotiators need to know about the persuasion tactics available to them when it comes to slicing the pie. We outline two distinct types of influence strategies in this chapter that appeal to the mind and the heart, respectively. The "mindful" strategies are based upon principles of logic, information, and rationality. The "emotion-based" strategies play upon underlying human needs and motivations. Any and all of them are subject to ethical concerns—a topic that we visit at the end of the chapter.

Negotiators need to be aware that there are two ways that the power and persuasion strategies in this chapter can be read. One way is to read it as the *holder* of power: This chapter presents the negotiator with several options for increasing her power in a negotiation. However, the negotiator who reads this book must be aware that her *opponent* is reading this book; therefore, every strategy and tactic in this chapter could (and probably will) be used by the opponent in the future. Thus, it is important to remember the "fraternal twin" model that we introduced in chapter 1. At relevant points in this chapter, we will present "defense strategies" that negotiators can use to deal with a source of power or a persuasion tactic that she finds leveled against herself during the course of negotiation.

YOUR BATNA IS YOUR MOST IMPORTANT SOURCE OF POWER IN NEGOTIATION

If a negotiator has a great BATNA, negotiation is almost effortless. All she has to do is inform the other party about her alternatives and invite the other party to make an offer that is superior to her BATNA. Most of the time, however, people do not have a great BATNA—they have mediocre or lousy BATNAs. For this reason, we caution the negotiator to only reveal his BATNA if he is prepared for the other party to make an offer that is minimally superior to his BATNA, at best. It is imperative that negotiators attempt to cultivate and improve upon their BATNAs prior to negotiating. Negotiators who leverage their BATNAs will be the ones who reach settlement terms that are most favorable to themselves. Therefore, we strongly suggest that negotiators engage in the following strategies during the course of negotiations:

- **Keep your options open:** It is important to keep your options open even after you have come to the negotiation table with another party, because at any point prior to mutual settlement, negotiations could break down for a variety of predictable or unpredictable reasons. People have to fight against their instinctual need for closure and keep their options open in the event that negotiation does not work out.
- **Let the other party know that you have other options:** Your options will not be transparent to the other party unless you signal appropriately. Ethics may come into play at this point, because alluding to options that you do not actually have is misrepresentation. We do not advocate misrepresentation regarding your BATNA in negotiations. However, it is not misrepresentation to signal to the other party that you have alternative courses of action.
- **Assess the other party's BATNA:** You should use objective measures to evaluate your opponent's BATNA. Start early. Do not wait until you get to the negotiation table: The cues are harder to detect because most negotiators will not reveal their BATNAs. Spend some time before negotiation assessing current data (if you have it), previous years' data, current market trends—anything you can get. Also, use multiple sources. Your investment into researching the other party's BATNA is money and time well-spent.

TAPPING INTO YOUR POWER

BATNAs are not the only source of power in a negotiation. There are other important sources of power that negotiators need to be aware of before approaching the bargaining table.

INFORMATION

Information is a distinct advantage in negotiation. This is why we strongly advise negotiators to do as much homework as possible prior to negotiating (see chapter 2). Unfortunately, most negotiators do not know which information is most important to obtain for pie slicing. The most critical type of information is the other party's BATNA. In addition to information about the other party, negotiators need to be well-versed in their own position. In a negotiation situation, opponents will often attempt to talk the other party out of their position, or catch the other party off guard by asking questions they cannot answer. Thus, in addition to seeking information about the other party, it strongly behooves negotiators to have factual information at their fingertips that justifies their issues, interests, and position. A negotiator is wise to also have information that can help with integrative bargaining. To the extent that a negotiator can have information about the other party's interests and alternatives, this can also be effective in expanding the pie.

STATUS

Two types of status are relevant in most negotiation situations: primary status characteristics and secondary status characteristics. **Primary status characteristics** refer to marks and indicators of legitimate authority; for example, a person's rank within an organizational chart, the number of supervisees she has in her unit, and her various titles and degrees all denote primary status. Even when primary status is irrelevant in the context of a given negotiation, it can affect the process of negotiation. The impact of status on the conduct of bargaining can be quite enormous. For example, high-status individuals talk more, even when they do not necessarily know more. A high-status person will also generally control when he or she speaks in a conversation; furthermore, a low-status person will defer to the high-status person in terms of turn-taking in the conversation. These factors can affect pie slicing in a negotiation.

When primary status cues (such as rank and stature in an organization) are absent, or when people of equal status negotiate, people often pay attention to **secondary status characteristics,** which are cues and characteristics that have no legitimate bearing on the allocation of resources or on the norms of interaction, but nevertheless exert a powerful influence on behavior. Secondary status characteristics are also known as **pseudostatus characteristics** and include sex, age, ethnicity, status in other groups, and cultural background. The three most common secondary status characteristics are gender, age, and race. Quite simply put, men have more influence than women; older people have more influence than younger people; and white people have more influence than black people when it comes to interpersonal interaction (Mazur 1985). Typically, pseudostatus characteristics are highly visible. Pseudostatus characteristics, of course, have little to do with ability, but people act as if they do.

Status cues are noted very quickly, often within minutes after negotiators are seated at the bargaining table. Pseudostatus characteristics should not, in any normative or rational sense, exert an effect on the negotiation. However, they often do. Furthermore, even when a negotiator does not regard these pseudostatus cues to be significant (or even rejects them outright), if someone else at the bargaining table considers them significant, he or she can create a **self-fulfilling prophesy.** For an example of how the self-fulfilling prophesy works in another domain, consider the following: African-Americans who were asked to indicate their race prior to taking a scholastic aptitude test (SAT) performed significantly worse than African-Americans who were not asked to indicate their race beforehand (Steele and Aronson 1995). Presumably, African-American students, as well as the larger population, are well aware that one stereotype of African-Americans is that they are not as intellectually competent as their white peers. When an African-American person is made aware of the stereotype, and the fact that the activity in which they are engaging is relevant to that stereotype, presumably, he or she is vulnerable to fulfilling that stereotype. This is called **stereotype threat** (Steele 1997). At a cognitive level, stereotypical attributes such as lack of intelligence, laziness, and athleticism are connected to a person's behavioral repertoire, which is why the mere mention of a stereotype can lead to stereotypically consistent behaviors. Most important, people who seem most resistant to negative stereotyping (e.g., high-achieving, gifted African-Americans) fall prey to stereotype threat. This suggests that the self-fulfilling prophesy occurs because erroneous stereotypes are activated that hinder performance.

In a related study, Spencer, Steele, and Quinn (1999) examined the self-fulfilling prophesy effect among women in the domain of mathematics. A pervasive stereotype is that women are worse than men at solving difficult math problems (Benbow and Stanley 1980). According to Spencer et al. (1999), women only perform worse than men in situations in which they perceive themselves to be at risk of confirming the gender stereotype. Indeed, when women were told that no gender differences had been observed for a test they were about to take, no differences between men's and women's test scores were observed. However, when women were told that gender differences had been shown to exist, men outperformed women on the same tests.

Thus, in both of these examples, we find that traditionally disadvantaged persons (in this case, African-Americans and women) are vulnerable to fulfilling the negative stereotypes held about them, even when they do not regard these stereotypes to be true of themselves. A similar dynamic can happen in negotiations. For example, when a male who has traditional sex role values negotiates with a woman, his belief system may imperil the fair division of the bargaining pie (see Sidebar 7–1).

SIDEBAR 7–1. DETERMINANTS AND CONSEQUENCES OF SALARY NEGOTIATIONS BY MALE AND FEMALE MBA GRADUATES

When the salary-negotiating behaviors and starting salary outcomes of 205 MBA graduate students were investigated, there were no differences between men and women in terms of the proclivity to negotiate—meaning that women were just as likely as men to attempt to renegotiate the initial offers made to them by their employers. However, women did obtain lower monetary returns from negotiations (4.3 percent starting salary increment for men versus 2.7 percent for women). Over the course of a career, the accumulation of such differences may be substantial. One estimate is that the present value of women's cumulative pay shortfall would be over $29,000, in terms of a 30-year career (Gerhart and Rynes 1991).

SOCIAL NETWORKS

Whereas information power in a negotiation refers to the power associated with *what* you know, network power refers to the power associated with *who* you know. **Social capital** is the power that results from managers' access to other people within and outside of their organization. Social capital is a value that comes from who, when, and how to coordinate through various contacts within and beyond the organization. Whereas **human capital** refers to individual ability, social capital refers to opportunities created through social interactions. Managers with more social capital get higher returns on their human capital because they are positioned to identify and develop more rewarding opportunities (Burt 1992). Negotiators with high network power are those who act as **boundary spanners,** bridging functional gaps in organizations and units. In other words, they are the critical link between people who otherwise would not be in contact. As boundary spanners, they fill a unique spot within the organizational network by bringing together people, knowledge, and information that would not otherwise be brought together. A negotiator's position as a unique link in a network of relationships means that he or she can broker more opportunities than other members of the network who do not represent unique links within the organization and beyond. Furthermore, negotiators who are boundary spanners are in a position to make or break opportunities for other people. Negotiators who act as boundary spanners broker the flow of information between people and control information. Negotiators who bridge gaps are the people who know about, have a hand in, and exercise more control over rewarding opportunities. They have broader access to information because of their diverse contacts. This means that they are more often aware of new opportunities and have easier access to these opportunities than do their peers—even their peers of equivalent or greater human capital. For this reason, they are also more likely to be discussed as suitable candidates for inclusion in new opportunities and are more likely to be able to display their capabilities because they have more control over the substance of their work, defined by relationships with subordinates, superiors, and colleagues.

PHYSICAL APPEARANCE

It is a somewhat disturbing fact that physically attractive people are more effective in getting what they want than are less physically attractive people, independent of their actual skills. For example, the work produced by allegedly attractive people is more highly valued than that produced by less-attractive people. As a case in point, in one investigation, men evaluated an essay with a photo of the supposed author attached—either an attractive or an unattractive woman (as judged by an independent group of people). Even though the essays were identical in all instances, men's judgments of the essay were strongly affected by how attractive the woman in the picture was: The more attractive the person in the photo, the better the grade given (Landy and Sigall 1974). People think that attractive individuals are more talented, kind, honest, and intelligent (Eagly, Ashmore, Makhijani, and Longo 1991). As a consequence, attractive people are more persuasive in terms of changing attitudes (Chaiken 1979) and getting what they want (Benson, Karabenick, and Lerner 1976). Physical attractiveness has a favorable impact on sales effectiveness (Kivisilta, Honkaniemi, and Sundvi 1994; Reingen and Kernan 1993) and on income levels across a wide range of occupations (Hamermesh and Biddle 1994). By the way: Attractiveness is usually achieved through dress and grooming in most of these investigations.

The evaluation of an employment applicant can be affected by physical attractiveness as well (Dion 1972). Attractive people are evaluated more positively and are treated better than unattractive people. Attractive communicators and salespeople are more effective in changing other people's attitudes than unattractive ones (Kiesler and Kiesler 1969). This is the reason why sales campaigns often feature an attractive person attempting to sell a product or service. Attractive people are often presumed to have other positive qualities as well; for example, they are regarded to be more poised, interesting, sociable, independent, dominant, exciting, sexy, well-adjusted, socially skilled, and successful than unattractive persons (Dion and Dion 1987; Moore, Graziano, and Millar 1987). The underlying message: Be aware of how your judgment (and others') is affected by physical appearance.

THE EFFECTS OF POWER ON THOSE WITH LESS POWER

What are the psychological effects of those who have more power on those who have less power? In terms of perception and accuracy, those with less power are highly accurate in perceiving the behaviors and attitudes of those with higher power (Fiske and Dépret 1996). This makes a lot of sense, especially because those of lesser power are dependent upon those of higher power for important organizational rewards. If someone is in a position to control a variety of organizational benefits that could dramatically affect your well-being, you would probably closely scrutinize his behavior. However, this greater accuracy may come at a price. Those who are low in power may exhibit signs of paranoia, believing that they are being constantly scrutinized and evaluated by those who are higher in power (Kramer and Hanna 1988).

THE EFFECTS OF POWER ON THOSE WHO HOLD POWER

People who are high in power are often oblivious to people who have less power. (Gruenfeld, Keltner and Anderson 1998). Presumably, people who are high in power have little or no reason to pay attention to the goings-on of those who are less powerful than them. After all, the powerful are in control of the situation, and the actions of those who are not as powerful have little effect on the high-power person's well-being. Consequently, those who have more power tend to be less accurate about the situation. In terms of negotiation, people who are higher in power (whether it is a legitimate form of power or not) may be less vigilant and thorough in collecting information from those of lesser power. This may create a backfiring effect at the negotiation table. Those with more power also engage in less "self-monitoring" (Snyder 1974; Gruenfeld, Keltner, and Anderson 1998). For example, in one investigation, highly powerful people were secretly videotaped as they interacted with less powerful people. The interchange took place at a social gathering where refreshments were being served. Those who were higher in power tended to eat more and consume messier foods, which resulted in a messier appearance (Gruenfeld, Keltner, and Anderson 1998). Presumably, the more powerful people were less concerned with how they appeared to other people because they considered others' perceptions to be largely inconsequential. In contrast, those of lesser power engaged in a much higher level of monitoring their own behavior (i.e., ate less and were less messy in appearance).

PERSUASION TACTICS

You do not necessarily have to have power to be effective at persuasion. In this next section, we focus on the essentials of attitude change as it pertains to the negotiation table. Some negotiators are masters of attitude and behavior change. We will identify techniques that negotiators can use to induce attitude and behavior change in their opponents. However, we need to caution negotiators that power can be used against them as well.

There are two desires that are especially important in negotiation: the need to be liked and approved of, and the need to be rational and accurate. Savvy negotiators prey upon people's need to be approved of and respected by others and their need to believe that they are rational and logical. Next, we identify two primary routes to persuasion that tap into these two needs.

TWO ROUTES TO PERSUASION

There are two routes to persuasion (Chaiken, Wood, and Eagly 1996), roughly corresponding to our distinction between the mind and the heart of the negotiator. The first route is called the *central route* to persuasion. The central route is direct, mindful, and information-based. Here, such activities as evaluating the strength or rationality of an opponent's argument and deciding whether its content agrees or disagrees with a negotiator's current beliefs tend to occur. When an opponent's messages are processed via this central route, persuasion will occur, to the extent that the arguments presented by a negotiator are convincing and the facts marshaled on their behalf are strong ones. The central route is ideal when dealing with analytical people who tend to focus on information, facts, and data.

The other route is the *peripheral route* to persuasion. In contrast to the central route, very little cognitive or mindful work is performed when attempting to persuade someone via the peripheral route. Rather, persuasion, when it occurs, involves a seemingly automatic response to various cues. Typically, the cues relating to a person's prestige, credibility, or likability are the ones that will be successful when navigating the peripheral route. Persuasion is more likely to occur through the peripheral route when the negotiator is distracted or highly emotionally involved in the situation.

It is important for negotiators to be aware that the central and peripheral routes create two different "languages" by which to negotiate and persuade: The central route is rational, direct, cognitive, and information-based; the peripheral route is emotional and motivational. In the next sections, we deal with tactics that can be used via the central route and via the peripheral route. Again, we caution negotiators that all of these tactics can and probably will be used against them at some time in their negotiation career. Therefore, when describing each of these tactics, we indicate a defense strategy that a negotiator can use if he or she suspects that a particular tactic is being used against him or her. However, it is worthwhile to note that the best defensive system is awareness of these tactics and excellent preparation prior to entering into a negotiation.

CENTRAL ROUTE PERSUASION TACTICS

Central route persuasion tactics involve rational and deliberate strategies that can be used to organize the content and flow of information during a negotiation.

The Power of Agenda

In a negotiation, players explicitly or implicitly follow an agenda. Most commonly, negotiators discuss the issues in a one-by-one, "laundry list" fashion. Negotiations often concern who controls the agenda. For example, in the Middle East peace treaty talks between Syria and Israel, the hitch was what to discuss first. Tom Smerling, Washington director of the Israel Policy Forum, a group that supports an active U.S. role in Middle East peace talks, notes that virtually every international negotiation starts with a quarrel over the agenda (Slavin 2000).

As we indicated in chapter 4 on integrative negotiation, we strongly dissuade negotiators from considering issues one at a time. Rather, it is through the packaging of issues that integrative opportunities can be discovered. Nevertheless, the savvy negotiator may use the power of agenda not only to expand the pie, but to slice the pie in a manner favorable to him- or herself. The negotiator who lays out the issues in a way that reflects his or her own highest priorities may be more likely to achieve gains on his or her high-priority issues. **Defense:** It is a good idea to discuss what may seem to be an implicit or unspoken agenda (e.g., "I get the sense that you have an agenda of how you would like to cover the issues. I would like to hear your ideas and then tell you mine. Maybe we can come up with an agenda that makes sense for both of us, after hearing each other out.").

The Power of Alternatives

Negotiators who are able to generate alternatives within each of the issues may have a bargaining advantage because they tend to form alternatives that benefit themselves. Obviously, there are an infinite number of alternatives for any given bargaining situation; the savvy negotiator will specify alternatives that are most favorable to him or herself. **Defense:** You do not need to be too much on the defensive if your opponent is laying out the alternatives. This is helpful for you in trying to assess her needs and interests. Make sure that you have thought about your own alternatives and get those on the table.

The Power of Options

In our chapter on integrative bargaining (chapter 4), we strongly advocated that negotiators generate several options, all of equal value to themselves. The negotiator who takes control of generating options is at a power advantage in the negotiation. **Defense:** If you find your opponent suggesting several options, this is actually good news—it suggests that your opponent is not a positional negotiator. However, make sure that you do not offer unilateral concessions. The best way to avoid making unilateral concessions is to generate several options to present to the other party.

Attitudinal Structuring

If a negotiator suspects that an opponent has an uncertain or unspecified BATNA, he or she can influence the opponent's perception of his or her BATNA. Thus, a negotiator may manipulate his or her opponent into revealing his or her BATNA. **Defense:** The best strategy to use when an opponent attempts to manipulate your perception of your own BATNA is to have structured your BATNA well before entering into the negotiation. We have frequently witnessed instances in which a negotiator is manipulated into revealing his BATNA when an opponent makes the assumption that the negotiator's BATNA is weak. As an example, consider the following interchange between negotiators:

NEGOTIATOR A: You know, it is really a buyer's market out there. I would strongly suggest that you think about my offer [on your house] before you turn it down. There may not be any more buyers for a while.

NEGOTIATOR B: Actually, I have received a lot of interest on my house.

NEGOTIATOR A: In this market? That does not sound very likely to me. In fact, my sister is selling her house, and she has not had an offer yet.

NEGOTIATOR B: Actually, just last week, a buyer from out of state saw my house and said he would most likely make an offer of $230,000 this week. You can ask my agent about it, if you do not believe me.

NEGOTIATOR A: That is so interesting. Just last night my husband and I decided that we would most likely offer $231,000 for your house . . . imagine that!

From this interchange, we see that negotiator A was successful in getting negotiator B to reveal her BATNA by putting her on the defensive.

The Power of Contrast

Negotiators may often invent and present irrelevant alternatives for their opponent to consider. Often, the negotiator who proposes these irrelevant alternatives knows the other party will find them unacceptable, but psychologically, these alternatives can create a **contrast effect.** As an example of how the contrast effect works, consider the behavior of some real estate agents (see Cialdini 1993). Agents who want a prospective buyer to make an offer on a house may show the buyer several houses. They will arrange a house-shopping day such that they first show the prospective buyer some "doghouses" that may have been on the market for several months, are extremely unattractive, or are overpriced. The buyer may become somewhat depressed at the sight of these houses or at the high price tags they carry. At this point, the agent will show the buyer the houses that he or she really expects the buyer to consider. This creates a psychological contrast effect because the potential buyer will look upon these houses much more favorably than the more dilapidated, overpriced alternatives and will be more motivated to make an offer. In negotiation, contrast is often used when an opponent makes an extreme initial offer and then follows with an offer that appears more reasonable. Acceptance rates of the second offer are higher when it follows the initial extreme offer. **Defense:** The best defense against the contrast effect is a well-formed target point set prior to negotiation. For example, the prospective homebuyer should research the market enough to realize what value is available. In many negotiation situations, it is wise to counter a low offer made by the opponent with your target point. At all costs, negotiators need to avoid making premature concessions—concessions that they make before they have tried to get what they want.

Commitment and Consistency

The **consistency principle** is the fundamental need to be consistent in our beliefs, feelings, and behaviors, not only to others, but also to ourselves. To contradict ourselves, whether in thought or in deed, is a sign of irrationality. Thus, savvy negotiators will often attempt to get a verbal commitment from their opponent.

What are the implications of the consistency principle for the negotiator? If a negotiator agrees to something (i.e., particular set of terms, etc.), he or she is motivated to behave in a fashion consistent with his or her verbal commitment. A common bargaining ploy of salespeople is to ask customers about their intentions to buy (for example, "Are you ready to buy a car today at the right price?"). Most people would agree to this statement because it does not obligate them to buy a particular car. However, powerful psychological commitment processes begin to operate once we acknowledge ourselves to be a "buyer." **Defense:** Be careful what you agree to. If a car seller asks whether you are ready to buy a car, do not immediately say "Yes!" but rather, "That depends on how things go in terms of finding what I want and the terms I want."

Framing Effects: Capitalizing on the Half-Full or Half-Empty Glass

As we saw in chapter 2, people are risk-averse for gains and risk-seeking when it comes to losses. A **reference point** defines what a person considers to be the status quo from which gains and losses are evaluated. Savvy negotiators know that if they want to induce their opponent to maintain the status quo—that is, induce risk aversion or conservatism—they should present options as gains relative to a reference point. Similarly, if they want to induce change, they frame choices as losses. **Defense:** Determine your reference point prior to entering into a negotiation to avoid being "framed."

Fairness Heuristics: Capitalizing on Egocentric Bias

Fairness is a hot button in negotiation. To the extent that negotiators can characterize their offer as "fair," they increase the likelihood that it will be accepted by the other party. However, there are multiple indices and measures of fairness. **Defense:** Be aware of the many rules of fairness (e.g., equity, equality, and need). When an opponent puts forth a fairness ploy, the negotiator should be ready to present a counterargument that is favorable to and consistent with one's own perceptions of fairness (see chapter 3).

Time Pressure

Common intuition has it that the negotiator who is under the most time pressure is at a disadvantage in a negotiation. Whereas it is true that the negotiator who needs to come to an agreement more quickly (because his or her BATNA may deteriorate with time) is at a disadvantage, time limits may be an advantage for the negotiator (Moore 2000). **Defense:** Set a limit on how long you will negotiate. A final deadline limits the potential time-related costs. If you face a final deadline, whether or not you set it yourself, make sure that those with whom you are negotiating know about the time constraint this puts on them. If they want any deal at all, they will have to work to come up with an agreement before the deadline (Moore 2000).

PERIPHERAL ROUTE PERSUASION TACTICS

The strategies we describe next work through a fundamentally different mechanism—people's inherent need to be liked, approved of, and respected by others. The negotiator who uses the following strategies manipulates an opponent's sense of his or her own identity and, through these strategies, attempts to change the opponent's behavior. Martialling defense strategies are more difficult in the case of peripheral route persuasion tactics, because they often catch us off guard. A good defense is an awareness of common strategies.

Flattery

People like others who appreciate and admire them. People are more likely to trust others who like them, and respond more favorably when they are flattered. It would seem that the positive pie-slicing effects of flattery would be reversed if the flatterer is suspected of having ulterior motives; however, even if people suspect that the flatterer has another reason for flattering them, this can still increase liking and trust under some conditions (Jones, Stires, Shaver, and Harris 1968). The most strategic type of flattery, in terms of advancing one's own interest, is to flatter another person on a dimension that is important to him, but that he feels somewhat insecure about (Jones et al. 1968). John Wakeham, previous chief whip for Margaret Thatcher, says about Westminster politics: "I was absolutely fascinated by how Westminster actually works . . . the smoke-filled rooms, the nods and the winks. As a businessman, I found it more comprehensible than most politicians do. One thing I learnt as chief whip was the infinite capacity of human beings to absorb flattery" (Perkins 2000, 6).

Good Mood
Negotiators in a good mood are more agreeable (Carnevale and Isen 1986; Forgas and Moylan 1996). Funny cartoons, unexpected little gifts, small strokes of fortune, and thinking positive thoughts all engender a good mood (see Isen and Baron 1991 for a review). We know of a salesperson who has a smiling face on her business card. This serves two purposes: It engenders a good mood whenever people see her card, and, by the psychological process of association, it links positive feelings to the salesperson's name and company.

Similarity
The *liking principle* states that we are more agreeable with people whom we like. Liking for people is often based on superficial, arbitrary factors (e.g., someone wearing a sweatshirt emblazoned with our college's name or with a haircut similar to ours). Simply put, we like people whom we perceive to be similar to us. Negotiators are more likely to make concessions when negotiating with people they know and like. Savvy negotiators increase their effectiveness by making themselves similar to the other party. Many sales training programs urge trainees to "mirror and match" the customer's body posture, mood, and verbal style, because similarities along each of these dimensions actually lead to positive results (LaFrance 1985; Locke and Horowitz 1990; Woodside and Davenport 1974). Similarity in dress also has dramatic effects. For example, marchers in a political demonstration not only are more likely to sign the petition of a similarly dressed requester, but do so without bothering to read it first (Suedfeld, Bochner, and Matas 1971).

Delayed Liking
Should you show your liking for the other party immediately or wait awhile? In terms of gaining compliance from the other party, it is far more effective to *grow* to like the other party (Aronson and Linder 1965). The most effective type of liking—in terms of getting what you want from someone—is to not like the other person immediately. Rather, people who grow to like someone are more effective in getting what they want than if they show their liking for the other person immediately. For example, consider an investigation of evaluative feedback in which people were given one of four types of evaluations by a peer: completely positive, initially negative and then positive, relentlessly negative, and initially positive and then negative. The recipient of the evaluation feedback was then asked to indicate how much he or she liked the other party. Liking was highest for the other party who was initially negative and later became positive (Aronson and Linder 1965).

To Err Is Human
Negotiators are naturally suspicious of smooth-talking and attractive negotiators. Therefore, it is important to show your opponent that you are human and have your own foibles and faults. Showing the other person that you have flaws may endear them

to you. For example, in one investigation, people listened to someone who was highly competent (i.e., got 92 percent of very difficult exam questions correct). During a subsequent interview, it was revealed that this person was also very competent in other areas—an honor student, editor of the yearbook, and excellent at sports. In another situation, people heard the same person, but this time, he spilled coffee on himself during the interview. Even though the person had identical qualifications in both instances, when he made the human error (spilling coffee), he was liked much more than when he was "perfect." In fact, liking increased by 50 percent (Aronson, Willerman, and Floyd 1966)!

Priming and the Unconscious

People's judgments and behaviors are affected by **unconscious priming,** which refers to the impact that subtle cues and information in the environment have on our behavior (at a level below our conscious awareness). For example, in one investigation, people were presented with words on a computer screen that were associated with stereotypes about old age (e.g., "slow," "weak," "sickly," etc.). The words were flashed very quickly—in fact, people were not even aware that a word had been presented to them. Later on, when people were dismissed from the investigation, those who had seen the words related to old age walked more slowly down the hall, suggesting that the words that people were unconsciously exposed to triggered related behaviors (Bargh, Chen, and Burrows 1996).

As another example, consider the following hypothetical scenario: You and a business associate are formulating strategy for the next round of negotiations with an important client. The two of you are discussing your strategy at a local bar, where a big-screen TV is broadcasting a particularly vicious boxing match. You and your associate are not really watching the fight but hear the referee's calls and description of the action in the background. You notice that your associate talks about "packing a punch" and "hitting below the belt" and you wonder whether the social context is affecting your associate's judgment about negotiation. You suggest that the two of you walk down the street to the Honey Bear Cafe; the local music that night is a folk group called Brotherly Love. As the two of you are sipping coffee, your associate once again starts talking about the upcoming negotiations. You listen as he talks about "harmony" and "building a community" and wonder again whether features of your location are influencing your friend's judgment. This scenario illustrates how people are often manipulated by cues in the environment that act as primes. Sometimes these cues are random or naturally occurring products of the environment (such as in the bar); sometimes they may be "planted" (by a savvy negotiator). Obviously, it is important to understand how priming certain aspects of the situation may affect our own behavior.

Reciprocity

Madeleine Albright knows the powers of reciprocity. One of Albright's first public meeting with members of Congress was an appearance to testify before the House Appropriations Subcommittee, chaired by Republican Harold Rogers. Albright needed to be on good terms with Rogers because his subcommittee's jurisdiction included the State Department's operating budget. For the occasion, Albright carried with her a big box, gift-wrapped in red, white and blue ribbon. Inside was a book of photographs. Albright had learned that Rogers had lost all his papers and photographs in a fire at his home, a disaster that had erased many souvenirs of his career and compounded the grief caused by the recent death of his wife. Albright instructed embassies in countries he had visited to provide copies of photos taken on those occasions, and compiled them in an album which she bestowed on him right there in the committee hearing room (Lippman 2000).

According to the **norm of reciprocity,** people have a fundamental need to reciprocate. Negotiators will prey upon this need by doing favors for their opponent and capitalizing on their opponent's feelings of indebtedness. Your best defense against this tactic is to not accept favors, however small or trivial, unless a "thank you" will make you feel like there are no more IOU's.

According to the reciprocity principle, we feel obligated to return in kind what others have offered or given to us. We referred to this powerful principle earlier as the law of the universe. This is not an overstatement; all human societies subscribe to the rule permeating exchanges of all kinds (Gouldner 1960). Feelings of indebtedness are so powerful that if unresolved, they carry on into the future and are passed on to the next generation to repay (Gouldner 1960). People feel upset and distressed if they have received a favor from another person and are prevented from returning it. Not surprisingly, people are aware of the powerful grip that reciprocity has on them. Often people will turn down favors and rewards from others because they do not want to be obligated.

So far we have said that reciprocity is powerful. There seems to be nothing inherently illogical or dangerous with reciprocity with regard to negotiation. Usually, reciprocity pertains more to the pattern of concessions than to the degree of concessions. This means that if someone does us a favor or makes a concession, we feel obligated to return the favor or concession. However, unless we are careful, we could be victimized by an opponent who preys on our feelings of indebtedness.

For example, suppose the opponent provides us with a favor, gift, or service that we never invited and perhaps even attempted to avoid. Our attempts to return it have been denied, and we are left with the unwanted gift. Even under these circumstances, the reciprocity rule may operate. **Defense:** We should beware of the unsolicited gift from our real estate agent, the courtesy token from our business associate, and the free lunch from the consulting firm. When faced with these situations, we should acknowledge the favor and then, if we still feel indebted, return the favor on a similar level.

Reinforcement

Although people may not be aware of it, simple, nonverbal gestures such as nodding, smiling, and eye contact are forms of social reinforcement. When negotiators offer these reinforcements to their opponent when the opponent is saying things that the negotiator finds acceptable, but withholds reinforcement at other points during the negotiation, they may be successful in manipulating the behavior of his or her opponent. Consider, again, the interpersonal prowess of Madeleine Albright. Conservative Southern politicians like Republican Sonny Callahan generally have little in common with liberal Democrats like Albright—that is, until she turns on the charm via reinforcement. During a Chamber of Commerce dinner in Mobile, Alabama, Callahan presented Albright with a personally autographed copy of the book *Forrest Gump* by Winston Groom. Albright instinctively knew that she should reinforce the bond, and she told the crowd, "Well, taking a line out of this book, dealing with Sonny is a little bit like having a box of chocolates. You never know that you're going to get, but with Sonny you always know you've got a very sweet center" (Lippman 2000).

Social Proof

In the movie *When Harry Met Sally,* Sally (Meg Ryan) is having lunch with Harry (Billy Crystal) and demonstrating how women can fake sexual pleasure. An older woman at a nearby table sees Sally moaning in ecstasy and tells the waitress, "I'll have what she's having." The woman used the principle of social proof to guide her own behavior.

According to the **social proof principle,** we look to the behavior of others to determine what is desirable, appropriate, and correct. This is sensible in many respects; if we want to get along with others, it only makes sense to know what they expect. However, this fundamental psychological process can work against us in negotiations if we look toward others—especially our opponent—to determine an appropriate offer or settlement. For example, new-car dealers target the neighbors of recent customers. Bartenders often "seed" their tip jars, and church ushers "prime" collection baskets with coins. Social proof is why advertisers use the slogans "largest-selling" and "fastest-growing." One tactic, called the *list technique,* involves making a request after a target person has been shown a list of similar others who have already complied. For example, college students and homeowners donated money or blood to a charitable cause in much greater numbers when shown a list of others who had already done so (Reingen 1982). People do not realize the extent to which our behavior is influenced by those around us. Further, the more ambiguous the situation, the more likely we are to rely on situational cues and the behavior of others to tell us what to do.

Reactance Technique

Reactance technique (also known as "reverse psychology" or the "boomerang effect") refers to people's innate need to assert their individual freedom when others attempt to take it away (Brehm 1983). Negotiators can use an interesting form of reverse psychology to extract what they want and need from their opponent. (As a warning, we should point out that this technique can be extremely risky to use; we argue that negotiators practice with it before negotiating so as not to make fatal errors.)

One strategy for getting a "reaction" from your opponent is to paraphrase their position in a way that makes it sound more extreme than it actually is. For example, consider the following interchange that occurs after two hours of a negotiation in which each negotiator has stopped making concessions:

NEGOTIATOR A (*with deep sincerity and respect*): "So, what you seem to be saying is that you have put your best offer on the table. That is your final best offer; there are no other possibilities of any kind. Your offer is a line drawn in the sand."

NEGOTIATOR B (*looking slightly perplexed*): "Well, no, it is not entirely like that. I have tried to be clear about my company's position and feel committed to achieving our goals. And the final offer I made reflects my company's goals."

NEGOTIATOR A (*with resignation*): "I respect a person who makes a commitment, who draws a line in the sand and who will not move an inch from that position. Who has the resolve to stick to his guns, and the tenacity and firmness of an army and . . ."

NEGOTIATOR B (*interrupting negotiator A*): "Look, I am not drawing a line in the sand, or anything like that. I am a reasonable person, and I am willing to consider reasonable offers."

NEGOTIATOR A (*looking incredulous*): "You mean you have the power and the freedom to create more options? I was under the impression that you were tied to your position . . ."

NEGOTIATOR B (*somewhat defensively*): "Well, of course, I can do anything I want here—within reason. I can come up with other alternatives."
NEGOTIATOR A (*with interest*): "I am most interested in hearing about your ideas."

Foot-in-the-Door Technique

In the **foot-in-the-door technique,** a person is asked to agree to a small favor or statement (such as agreeing with a question like "Are you ready to buy a car today at the right price?" or signing a petition). Later, the same person is confronted with a larger request (e.g., buying a car or voting with a particular coalition in a departmental meeting). The probability that the person will agree to the larger request increases when that person previously agreed to the smaller request (Beaman, Cole, Preston, Glentz, and Steblay 1983). This strategy plays upon people's need to demonstrate consistent behavior.

Door-in-the-Face Technique

Another strategy for gaining compliance is called the **door-in-the-face technique** (or the **rejection-then-retreat tactic**), in which a negotiator starts off the negotiation by asking for a very large concession or favor from the other party—one that the opponent is almost certain to refuse (Cialdini 1975). When the refusal occurs, the negotiator makes a much smaller request, which is, of course, the option they wanted all along. We described this principle in chapter 3, which admonishes negotiators to state high aspirations. The high aspiration creates a contrast effect, in that the opponent views any request that is less extreme than the original to be more reasonable.

That's-Not-All Technique

Many negotiators engage in the **that's-not-all technique** (also known as **sweetening the deal**) by offering to add more to a negotiated package or deal. For example, car dealers often add options to the car in question as a "deal closer." Evidence suggests that the that's-not-all technique actually works: In a study involving a bake sale, when patrons asked about cupcake prices and were told that two cupcakes cost $0.75, 40 percent bought the cupcakes. However, when they were told that one cupcake cost $0.75 and another cupcake would be "thrown in" for free, 73 percent bought the cupcakes (Burger 1986).

ETHICS

The distributive aspect of negotiation may create incentives for people to violate ethical standards of interpersonal interaction. All of the tactics and strategies discussed in this chapter can be questioned in terms of whether they are ethically appropriate. There are some hard and fast rules concerning what is ethical in negotiation, but more often, there are many shades of gray. Ethics are a manifestation of cultural, contextual, and interpersonal norms that render certain strategies and behaviors unacceptable. According to Lewicki and Robinson (1998), negotiators evaluate tactics on a continuum of "ethically appropriate" to "ethically inappropriate" when deciding whether to use tactics. Between these two end points is a middle group or "gray area" in which tactics are viewed as marginally unethical, justifiable under some circumstances but not others, and highly contextual. Next, we address the question of what behaviors are regarded as unethical or questionable in negotiations, what factors give rise to them, and how to develop personal ethical standards.

QUESTIONABLE NEGOTIATION STRATEGIES

What follows is a compendium of negotiation tactics that are considered at least by some negotiators to be unethical (Lewicki 1983; Lewicki and Robinson 1998):

Misrepresentation of a Position to an Opponent

This occurs when a negotiator distorts his preferred settlement point. For example, a prospective employee negotiating a job contract may tell the employer that she cannot accept an offer of less than $100,000 per year, when in fact, she is willing to accept $85,000. Negotiators often believe that misrepresentation is necessary in order to create a rationale for the opponent to make concessions.

Bluffing

Bluffing occurs when a negotiator falsely states his intention to perform some act. Exaggeration of one's BATNA is a bluff. According to Lewicki (1983), a bluff can be a false promise or a false threat. A false promise (e.g., "if you do X, I will reward you") and a false threat (e.g., "if you do not do X, I will punish you") are false in the sense that the person stating the threat does not intend to or cannot follow through.

Falsification

Falsification is the stating of erroneous, incorrect information as though it were true. For example, a home seller who does not disclose known foundation problems in a house is guilty of falsification.

Deception

According to Lewicki (1983), deception occurs when a negotiator attempts to manipulate an opponent's logical and inferential processes, with the intent to lead the opponent to an incorrect conclusion or deduction. For example, negotiators may only present certain facts and not tell the opponent everything (the sin of omission). Withholding information or failing to providing information is often not regarded to be as reprehensible as falsification. After all, a negotiator could innocently claim that the opponent did not "ask the right questions" or that she did not think the information was relevant. For an example of the complexity of the sins of omission, consider the scenario in Box 7–1.

In some cases, negotiators may assemble a collection of information that lead the opponent to the wrong conclusion. For example, a negotiator may give every indication that she will vote in favor of a proposal, short of verbally stating so. When the vote comes and she does not support it, she may claim that she did not lie, yet her constituents will be outraged because they were led to believe otherwise.

Consider the following situation: Two people have been hired to act as a project team in a company. The two associates are given a large office to share, and they begin to arrange their workplace. There are two desks, and the only window can be enjoyed from one of the desks. A conversation between the two reveals that it is obvious that one wants the desk with the window view and is ready to make sacrifices on other joint resources to get this—like giving up the close parking space and the storage areas. Unbeknownst to him, the other colleague has a terrible fear of heights; the window overlooks a steep precipice outside, and frankly, she would prefer the other desk that is near an attractive tropical plant. She considers not mentioning her true preference, hoping that she can *appear* to make a sacrifice, and so extract more resources.

< **BOX 7–1** >

SINS OF OMISSION

A couple interested in purchasing a house had almost all aspects of a deal worked out. The realtor was aware that the couple would have strongly preferred to make an offer on House B, which had sold in the previous month to someone else and, therefore, had not been on the market when the couple was house shopping. The realtor showed the couple House A, and the couple made an offer on it, which was accepted. Prior to the closing on House A, House B came on the market again, due to a set of completely unforeseeable circumstances. The realtor was aware that House B was now on the market, but did not inform the couple prior to their closing on House A. It was only following the closing (and after a 7.5 percent commission was paid

to the realtor) that the realtor informed the couple that House B was now on the market and asked the couple whether they wanted to put their newly purchased House A on the market and purchase House B.

Did the agent engage in unethical behavior? In the eyes of the real estate agent, because House B was not officially listed, and because the couple did not inquire about whether House B was on the market, he did not engage in unethical behavior. In the eyes of the couple, it was unethical for the realtor not to inform them that their preferred house had become available when it did.

This strategy is known as **passive misrepresentation** because a negotiator does not mention her true preferences and allows the other party to arrive at an erroneous conclusion. Now, imagine that her colleague surprises her by asking her point-blank which desk she prefers—the one by the windows or the plant. Does she lie about her preferences? If so, this is an act of **active misrepresentation** if she deliberately misleads her opponent.

The strategic manipulation ploy is used about 28 percent of the time (O'Connor and Carnevale 1997). We do not advocate strategic misrepresentation of compatible issues as a bargaining ploy. It can backfire; you can be "caught" in a lie and can potentially engender ill will. Our advice is to be wary when expressing your preferences so that you do not become an unwitting victim of a strategic manipulation.

Selective Disclosure or Misrepresentation to Constituencies
This occurs when other people are involved in the negotiating relationship (see chapter 9 on multiparty negotiations). In such situations, negotiators may misrepresent the events that occur at the bargaining table to their constituencies, or they may misrepresent the constituents' desires to the opposing negotiator.

Traditional Competitive Bargaining
In an analysis of MBA students' perceptions of unethical behavior, traditional competitive bargaining behavior, such as hiding one's real bottom line, making very high or low opening offers, and gaining information by asking among one's contacts, was considered to be unethical (Lewicki and Robinson 1998). Indeed, self-rated "aggressive" negotiators are more accepting of such tactics than are self-rated "cooperative" negotiators (Lewicki and Robinson 1998).

SIDEBAR 7–2. RETRACTING AN OFFER

On November 5, 1999, the *New York Daily News* printed the wrong numbers in a Scratch 'N' Match lottery game. The *News,* citing game rules, said it would not honor "false winners," but it did announce that they would award the day's regular sum of $192,500 in prizes by holding a drawing the next month between all who sent in winning game cards. Not surprisingly, calls of anger and frustration flooded the hotline and telephone system, and people swarmed the lobby of the *News* building in New York. An elderly security guard in the building was punched and suffered a black eye, and irate game players threatened lawsuits (McFadden 1999).

Manipulation of Opponent's Network
This tactic involves an attempt to weaken an opponent's position by influencing her associates or constituency.

Reneging on Negotiated Agreements
In many important negotiations, deals are closed without formal contracts. For example, even in the purchase of houses and cars, there is often an understanding before official papers have been signed. Even after formal contracts are signed, there is often a period of recision, wherein either party can legally exit from the agreement. However, there can be considerable disagreement and ethical debate concerning whether parties have a right to renege on an agreement once an informal closing (such as a handshake) has occurred.

Retracting an Offer
There seems to be an unwritten rule that, once a negotiator puts an offer on the table, he or she should not retract it. This would be bargaining in bad faith. Even so, negotiators may need to retract offers because a mistake has been made: for example, a department store publishes winning lottery numbers, but there is a typo, and a large number of people believe themselves, mistakenly, to be winners (see Sidebar 7–2). However, what the offering negotiator may see as a mistake is often viewed by the recipient negotiator as bargaining in bad faith.

Nickel-and-Diming
Nickel-and-diming is a colloquialism that refers to the strategy of continually asking for "just one more thing" after a deal has presumably been closed. Most people are reluctant to make concessions when they fear that the other party will continue to prolong negotiations. Negotiators are more likely to make concessions if they feel that they will be successful in closing the deal. Thus, it is often an effective strategy to inform the other party of the terms you need to make the agreement final. Even better, prepare the official paperwork and indicate that you will "sign today" if your terms are met. The prospect of closing a deal is often enough of an enticement for negotiators to agree to the terms proposed by the other party.

UNDER WHAT CONDITIONS DO PEOPLE ENGAGE IN DECEPTION?

It is not clear how often or what factors trigger the use of deception in negotiation. To help shed light on this issue, we conducted a survey of MBA students enrolled in a

> ## SIDEBAR 7–3. CONDITIONS UNDER WHICH NEGOTIATORS SAY THEY WOULD ENGAGE IN DECEPTION (I.E., LYING) IN NEGOTIATIONS
>
> *Lie-for-a-lie:* When I suspect the other party is deceiving me (43 percent)
>
> *One shot:* In a one-shot situation, with no potential for a long-term relationship (38 percent)
>
> *Personal gain:* If there was a gain to be had (21 percent)
>
> *Not getting caught:* If I felt I could get away with it (19 percent)
>
> *Life or death:* If the situation was "life or death" (15 percent)
>
> *Low power:* If the other party had more power (i.e., to "level the playing field") (15 percent)
>
> *Protecting reputation:* When I would not have to worry about my reputation (13 percent)
>
> *Dislike:* If I did not like the other person (9 percent)
>
> *Fixed pie:* If the situation was purely distributive (4 percent)

negotiations class. We asked students to describe the conditions under which they personally would engage in deception (defined as lying) in negotiations. Somewhat surprisingly, most people were able to identify situations in which they would lie. Only two people out of 47 said that they would never deceive. Over 25 percent said that they would use "white lies" or exaggerations in nearly any negotiation. The most common reason for lying is when we think the other party is lying (see Sidebar 7–3).

STRATEGIES FOR DETERMINING ETHICAL BEHAVIOR

Ethics are often a problem in negotiations, not so much because people are inherently evil and make trade-offs between profit and ethics or fail to consider other people's interests and welfare, but rather, because of psychological tendencies that foster poor decision making (Messick and Bazerman 1996). This means that people often believe they are behaving ethically, but due to faulty information processing and other psychological shortcomings, problems result and negotiators cry foul. Some of the human biases that give rise to ethical problems in negotiation are the illusion of superiority, illusion of control, and overconfidence (see Messick and Bazerman 1996).

- **Illusion of superiority:** People tend to view themselves and their actions much more favorably than others view them (Taylor and Brown 1988). People tend to focus on their positive characteristics and downplay their shortcomings. In relative terms, people believe that they are more honest, ethical, capable, intelligent, courteous, insightful, and fair than others.
- **Illusion of control:** People tend to think that they have more control over events than they really do. For example, in games of chance, people often feel that they can control outcomes (Langer 1975). Obviously, this can lead to a type of gambler's fallacy in decision making. However, it can also give rise to ethical problems, such as when people make claims of quality control that cannot be met.
- **Overconfidence:** Most people are overconfident about their knowledge. For example, when people are asked factual questions and then asked to judge the probability that their answers are true, the probability judgments far exceed

the actual accuracy measures of the proportion of correct answers. On average, people claim to be 75 percent certain, when they are actually correct only 60 percent of the time (Fischhoff, Slovic, and Lichtenstein 1977).

Given that our judgments of ethical behavior will be biased, how can negotiators best calibrate their behaviors? Probably the most important thing that we can offer negotiators is a strategy for putting themselves in the shoes of the other party. After all, it does not matter whether *you* think your behavior was ethical—it is how your *opponent* feels that matters.

The Front-Page Test

The front-page test, or light-of-day test, poses the following ethical challenge to negotiators: Would you be completely comfortable if your actions and statements were printed in full on the front page of the local newspaper or were reported on the TV news? If not, then your behavior or strategies in question may be regarded as unethical.

The Golden Rule

The "golden rule" states, "Do unto others as you would have them do unto you." In this strategy, the negotiator asks him or herself "If the tables were turned, how would I feel if my opponent did this to me?" If the answer is "I wouldn't like it very much," then this means that the behavior in question may be regarded as unethical.

Getting Advice

It is wise to consult a third party—someone who takes an impartial view of the negotiation—to see how they regard your planned behavior. When consulting the third party, try to be as neutral as possible. To the extent that you can, describe the event or situation without indicating which role you are playing.

The Paraphrase Technique

Probably one of the most important strategies for avoiding ethical dilemmas in negotiation is to paraphrase your understanding of the situation for your opponent. This is often a good strategy to use at the close of each meeting in a protracted negotiation, so that there is understanding about where both parties stand and what perceptions each party holds.

The Single-Text Strategy

In the **single-text strategy,** each negotiator works off of a shared document—a strategy pioneered by Jimmy Carter in the Israel negotiations (Raiffa 1982). This technique literally puts negotiators on the same page. Susan Podziba of the Program on Negotiation at Harvard Law School uses the single-text strategy in her work on mediation. She challenges parties on both sides to design a consensus process in which everyone participates. People on both sides of a dispute develop a mission statement as well as ground rules that will govern their deliberations (e.g., What is an achievable goal? What is the deadline? What are the roles and responsibilities of the mediators?; Rosenfeld 2000).

CONCLUSION

We have discussed the use of power and persuasion at the bargaining table. A negotiator's BATNA is her most important source of power in negotiation. However, relying only on your BATNA as a source of power may mean that you get only the value of your BATNA in the present negotiation. Ideally, negotiators want to use their BATNA to leverage their position. To do this, negotiators must continually attempt to improve upon their BATNA and signal to the other party that they have alternatives. Status, independent of one's BATNA, is often a source of power in negotiation; however, people often rely on pseudostatus characteristics. Information is also an important source of power in negotiation; other sources of potential power are social networks and physical appearance. Negotiators should be well-versed in persuasion tactics that are aimed at the rational side of human behavior, including the power of agenda, the power of alternatives, the power of options, attitudinal structuring, the power of contrast, commitment and consistency, framing effects, egocentric biases, and time pressure. Negotiators also need to be aware of persuasion tactics aimed at the emotional side of human behavior, including flattery, creating a good mood, delayed (rather than immediate) liking, human clumsiness, priming, reciprocity, reinforcement, social proof, and reactance techniques. With all strategies, we caution negotiators to be on the defensive and to perform an "ethics check" on their own behavior.

8

CREATIVITY AND PROBLEM SOLVING IN NEGOTIATIONS

In 1991, two West Coast energy producers found a new way to help Columbia River salmon and improve Southern California's dirty air without spending a dime. Southern California Edison Co. and the Bonneville Power Administration entered into an agreement in 1991 that helped to protect young salmon in the Pacific Northwest. Under the agreement, Bonneville Power increased its release of water in the Columbia River during the summer, and Edison accepted the hydroelectric power that was generated. The flows helped young salmon swim through reservoirs more quickly, as large numbers of these fish get lost or eaten in slack water. In the fall and winter, Edison returned the power it borrowed from Bonneville. This meant that the company wouldn't need to run oil and coal-fired plants during the summer. This exchange of about 200 megawatts of power, enough for about 100,000 households, improved the downstream migration of young salmon in the river. It enhanced Southern California air quality by reducing the need to operate fossil fuel power plants during the smoggy summer months. Edison said that the arrangement cut the amount of pollution entering the Los Angeles basin by about 46 tons, the equivalent of taking about 5,000 cars off the highways. In this creative agreement, no money changed hands. (Koberstein 1991)

CREATIVITY IN NEGOTIATION

Usually, by the time managers return to the classroom for negotiation training, the cases and simulations presented to them have already been transformed into a neat, gamelike structure, complete with payoff charts. Managers are then challenged to come up with a mutually-agreeable solution. However, even under these "near perfect" learning conditions, people frequently leave money on the table.

Real-world negotiations are quite a bit more daunting than those that are used in managerial education. It is no wonder that the managers and executives that we talk to regard their own real-life negotiations to be more difficult than those encountered in the classroom. Real-world problems do not present themselves as structured games—rather, they come to us as messy situations that often *seem* to be truly fixed-sum in nature. However, it is a mistake to treat them as such.

The creative aspect of negotiation is too often ignored or downplayed by negotiators, who fixate on the competitive aspect of negotiation. This tendency is largely driven by the pervasive **fixed-pie perception,** or the belief that negotiation is a win or lose enterprise. Even negotiators who believe in win-win potential frequently misconstrue "expanding the pie" to mean compromising or feeling good, rather than a true joint gain process. Successful negotiation requires a great deal of creativity and problem solving, and the process of slicing the pie can be a lot easier when the pie has been enlarged via creative and insightful problem-solving strategies, such as in the case of Bonneville Power and Edison. This chapter is the "advanced course" in integrative bargaining—using problem solving and creativity to reach win-win outcomes.

This chapter provides the means by which negotiators can more skillfully transform their real negotiation situations into win-win enterprises. For starters, we invite negotiators to put their problem-solving skills and creativity to the test. Then we take up the topic of creativity in negotiation and what creative negotiation agreements look like. Next, we consider the biggest threats or killers of creative problem solving in negotiations. We conclude by offering an "exercise regimen" for keeping your creative mind sharp for a variety of managerial activities including, but not limited to, negotiation.

TEST YOUR OWN CREATIVITY

Box 8–1 contains 13 problems. Take 30 minutes right now to try to solve these problems. When in doubt, make your best guess, but make an honest attempt at solving each problem. As you go along, make a mental note of your thoughts about each problem as you try to solve it. Read the rest of the chapter before you look up the answers in Box 8–7 (at the end of this chapter). As you read the chapter, see whether any insights come to you and make a note of them.

BOX 8–1

CREATIVITY TEST

CARD DECISION[1]

Look at the following numbers/letters. Each number/letter represents a card. On each of the four cards, a letter appears on one side and a number on the other. Your task is to judge the validity of the following rule: "*If a card has a vowel on one side, then it has an even number on the other side.*" Your task is to turn over only those cards that have to be turned over for the correctness of the rule to be judged. What cards will you turn over? [*Circle those cards that you will turn over to test rule.*]

    E   K   4   7

PERSON IN A ROOM DECISION[2]

A person has been chosen at random from a set of 100 people, consisting of 30 engineers and 70 lawyers. What is the probability that the individual chosen at random from the group, Jack, is an engineer?

"Jack is a 45-year-old man. He is married and has four children. He is generally conservative, careful, and ambitious. He shows no interest in political and social issues and spends most of his free time on his many hobbies, which include home carpentry, sailing, and mathematical puzzles."

Jack is [*circle one*]:
an engineer   a lawyer

[1]Wason, P. C., & Johnson-Laird, P. N. (1972). *Psychology of reasoning: Structure and content.* Cambridge, MA: Harvard University Press.
[2]Kahneman, D., & Tversky, A. (1973). On the psychology of prediction. *Psychological Review, 80,* 237–251.

Continued

BOX 8–1

CREATIVITY TEST—*continued*

BETTING DECISION[3]

Which gamble would you rather play? [*Circle either A or B*].

    A: 1/3 chance to win $80,000

    B: 5/6 chance to win $30,000

Now, imagine that you have to choose one of the following gambles. Which one will you play? [*Circle either C or D*].

    C: 50% chance to win $10,000 & 50% chance to lose $10,000

    D: $0

WATER JUGS[4]

You have been given a set of jugs of various capacities and unlimited water supply. Your task is to measure out a specified quantity of water. You should assume that you have a tap and a sink so that you can fill jugs and empty them. The jugs start out empty. You are allowed only to fill the jugs, empty them, and pour water from one jug to another. As an example, consider problems #1 and #2:

Example Problem#	Capacity of Jug A	Capacity of Jug B	Capacity of Jug C	Quantity Desired
1	5 cups	40 cups	18 cups	28 cups
2	21 cups	127 cups	3 cups	100 cups

To solve problem #1, you would fill jug A and pour it into B, fill A again and pour it into B, and fill C and pour it into B. The solution to this problem is denoted by **2A + C.**

    To solve problem #2, you would first fill jug B with 127 cups, fill A from B so that 106 cups are left in B; fill C from B so that 103 cups are left in B; empty C and fill C again from B so that the goal of 100 cups in jug B is achieved. The solution to this problem can be denoted by **B-A-2C.**

Real Problems

Problem #	Capacity of Jug A	Capacity of Jug B	Capacity of Jug C	Desired Quantity	Solution
1	14	163	25	99	
2	18	43	10	5	
3	9	42	6	21	
4	20	59	4	31	
5	23	49	3	20	
6	15	39	3	18	
7	28	76	3	25	
8	18	48	4	22	
9	14	36	8	6	

[3]Tversky, A., & Kahneman, D. (1981). The framing of decisions and the psychology of choice. *Science, 211,* 453–458.
[4]Luchins, A. S. (1942). Mechanization in problem solving. *Psychological Monographs, 5*(46), whole no. 248.

BOX 8–1

CREATIVITY TEST—*continued*

STICK PROBLEMS[5]

You have six sticks, all of equal length. You need to arrange them to form four triangles that are equilateral and with each side one stick long. (You cannot break any sticks.) Indicate how you would do this.

LETTER SEQUENCE[6]

What is the next letter in the following sequence?

OTTFFSS___

GOLD CHAIN

Isaac is staying at a motel when he runs short of cash. Checking his finances, he discovers that in 23 days he will have plenty of money, but until then, he will be broke. The motel owner refuses to let Isaac stay without paying his bill each day, but because Isaac owns a heavy gold chain with 23 links, the owner allows Isaac to pay for each of the 23 days with one gold link. Then, when Isaac receives his money, the motel owner will return the chain. Isaac is very anxious to keep the chain as intact as possible, so he does not want to cut off any more of the links than absolutely necessary. The motel owner, however, insists on payment each day, and he will not accept advance payment. How many links must Isaac cut while still paying the owner one link for each successive day?

_____links

SUSAN AND MARTHA

Susan and Martha are discussing their children when Susan asks Martha for the ages of her three sons. Martha says, "The sum of their ages is 13 and the product of their ages is the same as your age." Susan replies, "I still do not know their ages." What must Susan's age be?

a. 24 b. 27 c. 63 d. 36 e. 48

NECKLACE[7]

A woman has four pieces of chain. Each piece is made of three links. She wants to join the pieces into a single closed ring of chain. To open a link costs 2 cents; to close a link costs 3 cents. All links are now closed. She has only 15 cents. How does she do it?

NINE DOT PROBLEM[8]

Consider the following nine dots. Draw four or fewer straight lines *without lifting your pencil from the paper* so that each of the nine dots has a line through it.

PIGPEN[9]

Nine pigs are kept in a square pen, as shown in the figure. Build two more square enclosures that would put each pig in a pen by itself.

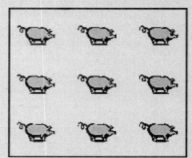

[5]Scheer, M. (1963). *Scientific American, 208,* 118–218.
[6]Letter sequence: Source unknown.
[7]Wickelgren, W. A. (1974). *How to solve problems.* San Francisco, CA: W. H. Freeman.
[8]Weisberg, R. W., and Alba, J. W. (1981). An examination of the alleged role of "fixation" in the solution of several insight problems. *Journal of Experimental Psychology: General, 110,* 169–192.
[9]Fixx, J. F. (1972). *More games for the super-intelligent.* New York: Warner Books.

Continued

BOX 8–1

CREATIVITY TEST—*continued*

WATERLILIES[10]

Water lilies on a certain lake double in an area every 24 hours. On the first day of summer, there is one water lily on the lake. On the sixtieth day, the lake is completely covered with water lilies. On what day is the lake half-covered?

BARTENDER PROBLEM[11]

A man walks into a bar and asks for a glass of water. The bartender points a shotgun at the man. The man says "Thank you," and walks out. What is going on in this situation?

[10]Sternberg, R. J., and Davidson, J. E. (1983). Insight in the gifted. *Educational Psychologist, 18,* 51–57.
[11]Dayton, T., Durso, F. T., and Shepard, J. D. (1990). A measure of the knowledge reorganization underlying insight. In R. W. Schraneveldt (Ed.), *Pathfinder associative networks: Studies in knowledge organization.* Norwood, NJ: Ablex.

CREATIVE NEGOTIATION AGREEMENTS

Creativity in negotiation often follows the pattern of the "Monday morning quarterback," meaning that in hindsight, it is easy to see creative opportunity in negotiations; however, it often eludes us in the moment. Next, we outline the hallmark characteristics of truly creative negotiations (see also Pruitt and Carnevale 1993).

FRACTIONATING PROBLEMS INTO SOLVABLE PARTS

Most negotiation situations present themselves to us as single-issue negotiations (that is, until some creative negotiator finds a way to break the problem into smaller parts and, in the process of doing so, prioritizes the issues and trades them off) (Lax and Sebenius 1986). The hallmark of a highly creative negotiated agreement is when negotiators can see integrative possibilities in a situation that appears to have only one single issue. Fractionating problems into solvable parts and creating multiple-issue negotiations from what appear to be single-issue negotiations is probably the most important aspect of creative negotiation (Lax and Sebenius 1986). We consistently find that people are very good at solving problems when the problems are presented directly to them; however, people are not very good at *defining* problems. Negotiation is mostly about defining a problem rather than solving it (i.e., searching for differences in such a way that trade-offs can be creative). Psychologists call this **problem representation,** as opposed to problem solving. This is not to say that problem solving is not an important skill. Rather, how a negotiator frames a problem can either set limits or create important opportunities in the problem-solving process.

FINDING DIFFERENCES: ISSUE ALIGNMENT AND REALIGNMENT

Before negotiators can find differences that can be traded off, they need to align the issues in such a way that permits the issues to be negotiated independently (and, ideally, traded off; Lax and Sebenius 1986). If the issues are linked, this creates a lot of constraints that limit negotiators' abilities to trade off issues. Ideally, negotiators should create issues that are **orthogonal** to one another, such that they can be traded off without having too many implications for other issues. Skilled negotiators know how to realign issues so as to find pockets of opportunity.

EXPANDING THE PIE

Expanding the pie is an important method by which to create integrative agreements. When negotiators effectively expand the pie, no one needs to make a concession. Rather, there is enough for all parties involved. At first glance, it may not seem that expanding the pie is a viable option in many negotiation situations. However, negotiators who labor under the fixed-pie perception may limit their options unnecessarily. Consider the case of the two truck companies in a dispute concerning which truck will be the first to reach a loading dock (from Pruitt and Carnevale 1993). Obviously, the first truck to reach the loading dock has the competitive advantage in several ways, not the least of which is the time investment involved in loading and unloading a shipment. The negotiation is successfully solved when the loading dock is expanded, allowing both trucks to unload at the same time.

BRIDGING

Oftentimes, it is not possible for negotiators to find a compromise solution, and expanding the pie does not work. Furthermore, perhaps neither party can get what they want in a trade-off that meets their interests. A **bridging** solution creates a new alternative that meets parties' underlying interests. Bridging alerts us to yet another reason to understand the other party's interests and to avoid positional bargaining. If negotiators understand the basic needs of their opponent, they are more likely to fashion bridging agreements. The opening example of the energy producers and the Pacific Northwest salmon is a bridging solution.

COST CUTTING

Sometimes, people are reluctant to negotiate because reaching any solution seems costly to them. Most people are risk-seeking when it comes to loss, meaning that they are extremely reluctant to make concessions, and may behave irrationally when they believe they will have to make concessions. Cost cutting is a way of making the other party feel whole by reducing their costs.

NONSPECIFIC COMPENSATION

In a nonspecific-compensation negotiated agreement, one negotiator receives what he or she wants, and the other is compensated (or paid) by some method that was initially outside the bounds of the negotiation. For example, Phil Jones, managing director of Real Time, the London-based interactive design studio, recalls an instance where he used nonspecific compensation in his negotiations. The problem was that his client, a Formula 1 motor-racing team, wanted to launch Internet Web sites but did not have the budget to pay him. However, in Phil Jones' eyes, the client was high profile and had creative, challenging projects that Real Time wanted to get involved with. Formula 1 came up with a nonspecific compensation offer to make the deal go through: tickets to some of the major Formula 1 meetings. It worked. Says Phil Jones: "The tickets are like gold dust . . . and can be used as a pat on the back for staff or as an opportunity to pamper existing clients or woo new ones" (Davies 1998, 128).

STRUCTURING CONTINGENCIES

Often, a major obstacle to reaching negotiated agreements concerns negotiators' beliefs about some future event or outcome (Lax and Sebenius 1986). Impasses often result from conflicting beliefs that are difficult to surmount, especially when each side is confident about the accuracy of his or her own prediction and consequently suspicious of the other side's forecasts. Often, compromise is not a viable solution, and each party may be reluctant to change his or her point of view. Fortunately, contingent contracts can provide a way out of the mire. With a **contingent contract,** differences of opinion among negotiators concerning future events do not have to be bridged; they become the core of the agreement (Bazerman and Gillespie 1999). According to Bazerman and Gillespie, companies can bet on the future rather than argue about it. In some areas of business, contingent contracts are commonplace. For example, CEOs regularly agree to tie their salary to a company's stock price, and, in the textbook publishing business, royalty rates to authors are often tied to sales.

However, in many business negotiations, contingency contracts are either ignored or rejected out of hand. There are several key reasons for this (Bazerman and Gillespie 1999): First, people are unaware of the possibility for contingent contracts. It often never occurs to people to bet on their differences when they are embroiled in conflict. Second, contingency contracts are often seen as a form of gambling, which is not good business. Third, there is often no systematic way of thinking about the formulation of such contracts, meaning that they *appear* to be a good idea, but how to formalize and act upon them remains an enigma. Fourth, many negotiators have a "getting to yes" bias, meaning that they focus on reaching common ground with the other party and are reluctant to accept differences of interest, even when this might create viable options for joint gain (Gibson, Thompson, and Bazerman 1994). In fact, most negotiators believe that differences of belief are a source of problems in a negotiation. The paradoxical view suggested by the contingency contract strategy states that differences are often constructive. With a contingency contract, negotiators can focus on their real mutual interests, not on their speculative disagreements (Bazerman and Gillespie 1999). When companies fail to find their way out of differences in beliefs, they often wind up in court, creating expensive delays, litigation costs, loss of control by both parties, and deteriorating BATNAs. (For an example of how negotiators failed to use contingency contracts and suffered costs, see Sidebar 8–1.)

Another wonderful feature of contingency contracts is that they provide a nearly perfect lie-detection device. In business negotiations, the fear of being deceived can be a major impediment to reaching agreements. Contingency contracts are a powerful method for uncovering deceit and neutralizing its consequences; they are particularly useful because they allow negotiators to test the opponent's veracity in a nonconfrontational manner, thereby allowing parties to save face. Contingency contracts also allow parties who are concerned about being cheated to safeguard themselves. This is precisely what Christopher Columbus was worried about when he negotiated an

SIDEBAR 8–1. FAILURE TO USE CONTINGENCY CONTRACTS

"Consider how a contingent contract might have changed the course of one of the century's most famous and most fruitless antitrust cases. In 1969, the U.S. Department of Justice [DOJ] filed a suit against IBM, alleging monopolistic behavior. More than a decade later, the case was still bogged down in litigation. Some 65 million pages of documents had been produced, and each side had spent millions of dollars in legal expenses. The DOJ finally dropped the case in 1982, when it had become clear that IBM's once-dominant share of the computer market was eroding rapidly.

During the case's thirteen futile years, IBM and the government had essentially been arguing over differences in their expectations about future events. IBM assumed that its market share would decrease in coming years as competition for the lucrative computer market increased. The government assumed that IBM, as a monopolist, would hold its large market share for the foreseeable future. Neither felt the other's view was valid, and so neither had a basis for compromise.

An efficient and rational way to settle this dispute would have been for IBM and the government to have negotiated a contingent contract—to have placed a wager on the future. They might have agreed, for example, that if by 1975 IBM still held at least 70 percent of the market—its share in 1969—it would pay a set fine and divest itself of certain businesses. If, however, its market share had dropped to 50 percent or lower, the government would not pursue antitrust actions. If its share fell somewhere between 50 percent and 70 percent, another type of contingency would take effect.

Constructing such a contingent contract would not have been easy. There were, after all, an infinite number of feasible permutations, and many details would have to have been hammered out. But it would have been far more rational—and far cheaper—to have the two sides' lawyers devote a few weeks to arguing over how to structure a contingent contract than it was for them to spend years filing motions, taking depositions, and reviewing documents."

Source: Bazerman and Gillespie 1999, 4–5.

agreement to the new world with Queen Isabella and King Ferdinand. Worried that he would risk life and opportunity and not gain anything, Christopher Columbus insisted that he be offered an opportunity to contribute one-eighth of the costs of future expeditions and be guaranteed one-eighth of all profits. Unfortunately, the crowns reneged on the deal upon his return, and Columbus had to go to court (Dworetzky 1998b).

By the same token, contingency contracts can build trust and good faith between negotiators, because incentives can be provided for each company to deliver exceptional performance. For example, Phil Jones, Real Time's managing director, was negotiating a deal with the Football Association (FA) for an e-commerce Web site dedicated to the U.K. bid for the 2006 World Cup. Real Time was responsible for the bid's logo and original Web site. "The FA have a limited budget to spend across a range of media, so I'm talking to them about perhaps receiving a percentage of what's sold from the new site. . . . That's really putting your money where your mouth is" (Davies 1998, 128). Therefore, contingency contracts provide a safety net, limiting each company's losses should an agreement unexpectedly go awry. (For a summary of the benefits of contingency contracts, see Box 8–2.)

> ⟨ **BOX 8–2** ⟩
>
> ## THE SIX BENEFITS OF CONTINGENT CONTRACTS
>
> 1. Contingent contracts allow negotiators to *build on their differences,* rather than arguing about them. Do not argue over the future. Bet on it.
>
> 2. Contingent contracts allow negotiators to *manage decision-making biases.* Although overconfidence and egocentrism can be barriers to effective agreements, contingent contracts use these biases to create a bet.
>
> 3. Contingent contracts allow negotiators to *solve problems of trust,* when one side has information that the other side lacks. The less informed party can create a contingency to protect themselves against the unknown information possessed by the other side.
>
> 4. Contingent contracts allow negotiators to *diagnose the honesty of the other side.*
>
> When one party makes a claim that the other party does not believe, a bet can be created to protect a negotiator against the lie.
>
> 5. Contingent contracts allow negotiators to *reduce risk through risk sharing.* The sharing of upside gains and losses not only can reduce risk, but it can also create goodwill by increasing the partnership between the parties.
>
> 6. Contingent contracts allow negotiators to *increase the incentive of the parties to perform* at or above contractually specified levels. Contingent contracts should be specifically considered when the motivation of one of the parties is in question.
>
> *Source:* Bazerman and Gillespie 1999.
>
>

Although we believe that contingency contracts can be valuable in many kinds of business negotiations, they are not always the right strategy to use. Bazerman and Gillespie (1999) suggest three key criteria for assessing the viability and usefulness of contingency contracts in negotiation:

1. Contingency contracts require *some degree of continued interaction between the parties.* Because the final terms of the contract will not be determined until sometime after the initial agreement is signed, there must be some amount of future interaction between parties, thereby allowing them to assess the terms of their agreement. Therefore, if the future seems highly uncertain, or if one of the parties is suspected of preparing to leave the situation permanently, contingency contracts may not be wise.

2. Parties need to think about the *enforceability* of the contingency contract. Under a contingency contract, one or more of the parties will probably not be correct about the outcome because the contract often functions as a bet. This creates a problem for the "loser" of the bet, who may be reluctant to reimburse the other party when things do not go his or her way. For this reason, the money in question might well be placed in escrow, thereby removing each party's temptation to defect.

3. Contingency contracts require a high degree of *clarity* and *measurability*. If an event is ambiguous, nonmeasurable, or of a subjective nature, overconfidence, egocentric bias, and a variety of other self-serving biases can make the objective appraisal of a contingency contract a matter of some opinion. Thus, we strongly suggest that parties agree up-front on clear, specific measures concerning how the contract will be evaluated. For this reason, it is often wise to consult a third party.

THREATS TO EFFECTIVE PROBLEM SOLVING AND CREATIVITY

There are a variety of human biases and shortcomings that threaten a person's ability to think creatively. People think along particular, well-worn lines and are often impervious to new ideas and insights. Next, we illuminate the most common threats to effective problem solving and creativity and make suggestions on how to avoid them. A key first step to preventing these biases is *awareness* of their existence.

THE INERT KNOWLEDGE PROBLEM

People's ability to solve problems in new contexts depends on the accessibility of their relevant knowledge. Simply stated, if a manager is confronted with new business challenges, he or she often consults his or her knowledge base for previous problems that have cropped up in an attempt to see which previous problem-solving strategies might be useful in solving the new problem. The **inert knowledge problem** is the inability to access relevant knowledge when we most need it (Whitehead 1929). Simply, the information necessary to solve a particular new problem is part of a manager's cognitive repertoire but is not accessible at the right time. This is not due to senility or amnesia, but rather, to the peculiar way that our long-term memories are constructed.

There is a striking dissociation between what is most *accessible* in our memories and what is most *useful* in human problem solving and reasoning. People often fail to recall what is ultimately most valuable for solving new problems (Forbus, Gentner, and Law 1995; Gentner, Rattermann, and Forbus 1993). For example, consider an example from Ross (1987). People studied examples containing principles of probability theory and then attempted to solve problems requiring the use of those principles. If the study and test stories were from the same context, people were more likely to be reminded of them than if the stories were from different contexts.

In another example, participants were given a story to read about a hawk giving feathers to a hunter (Gentner, Rattermann, and Forbus 1993). Participants were then given one of four stories resulting from the crossing of surface and structural similarity (i.e., a story with similar characters and plot, different characters but same plot, similar characters but different plot, or different characters and different plot). People were over four times more likely to recall this story when later shown a story with similar characters than when shown a story with different characters. The conclusion is that people often fail to recall what is ultimately most valuable for solving new problems (Forbus, Gentner, and Law 1995; Gentner, Rattermann, and Forbus 1993). Upon being informed of the correct approach to a negotiation, management students often express regret: "I knew that, I just did not think to use it."

BOX 8–3

THE TUMOR PROBLEM

Suppose you are a doctor faced with a patient who has a malignant tumor in his stomach. It is impossible to operate on the patient, but unless the tumor is destroyed, the patient will die. There is a kind of ray that can be used to destroy the tumor. If the rays reach the tumor all at once at a sufficiently high intensity, the tumor will be destroyed. Unfortunately, at this intensity, the healthy tissue that the rays pass through on the way to the tumor will also be destroyed. At lower intensities, the rays are harmless to healthy tissue, but they will not affect the tumor either. What type of procedure might be used to destroy the tumor with the rays and, at the same time, avoid destroying the healthy tissue (Gick and Holyoak 1980; adapted from Duncker 1945)?

Unfortunately, negotiators in the real world typically do not experience regret because they are not told when they have just made learning and application errors. Thus, the ability of managers to *transfer* knowledge from one context to another is highly limited. Transfer is the ability to apply a strategy or idea learned in one situation to solve a problem in a different, but relevant, situation. It is important to distinguish surface-level transfer from deep transfer. Surface-level transfer occurs when a person attempts to transfer a solution from one context to a superficially similar context. However, in most situations, it is desirable for people to apply solutions and strategies that have deep, meaningful similarities, rather than superficial ones. Unfortunately, this proves very difficult for most managers to do. In general, if two problems have similar surface (or superficial) features, managers are more likely to transfer knowledge from one problem situation to the other. Ideally, however, managers want to be able to transfer solutions to problems that have similar deep (or structural) features but that may have very different superficial features.

As a case in point, consider the "tumor problem" presented in Box 8–3. When presented with this problem, very few people successfully solve it; if it is preceded by the fortress problem in Box 8–4, the solution rate rises dramatically (Gick and Holyoak 1980). Even though a similar solution can be applied in both problems, because the surface information in each problem is quite different (one deals with a medical situation; the other, a political situation), people are often unable to access their knowledge about one of these problems to help them solve the other.

The same problem occurs in negotiation. Studies of MBA students, executives, and consultants acquiring negotiation skills reveal a dramatic inert knowledge problem (Loewenstein, Thompson, and Gentner 1999; Thompson, Loewenstein, and Gentner 2000; Gillespie, Thompson, Loewenstein, and Gentner 1999). Transfer rates are quite low when a key principle needs to be applied to different negotiation situations that involve different surface features. For example, when people are challenged with a negotiation situation involving a theater company that contains the potential for a contingency contract, they are often unable to employ the principle of contingency contracts even when they have received extensive training on this principle in a previous

---

BOX 8–4

THE FORTRESS STORY

A small country fell under the iron rule of a dictator. The dictator ruled the country from a strong fortress. The fortress was situated in the middle of the country, surrounded by farms and villages. Many roads radiated outward from the fortress like spokes on a wheel. A great general arose, who raised a large army at the border and vowed to capture the fortress and free the country of the dictator. The general knew that if his entire army could attack the fortress at once, it could be captured. His troops were poised at the head of one of the roads leading to the fortress, ready to attack. However, a spy brought the general a disturbing report. The ruthless dictator had planted mines on each of the roads. The mines were set so that small bodies of men could pass over them safely because the dictator needed to be able to move troops and workers to and from the fortress. However, any large force would detonate the mines. Not only would this blow up the road and render it impassable, but the dictator would destroy many villages in retaliation. A full-scale direct attack on the fortress therefore appeared impossible.

The general, however, was undaunted. He divided his army into small groups and dispatched each group to the head of a different road. When all was ready, he gave the signal, and each group charged down a different road. All of the small groups passed safely over the mines, and the army then attacked the fortress in full strength. In this way, the general was able to capture the fortress and overthrow the dictator (Gick and Holyoak 1980; adapted from Duncker 1945).

---

negotiation case involving a different context, such as a family-owned farm. The reason why is that we tend to use our previous knowledge only when it seems similar to a new problem. People do not appear to be able to recognize problems that may benefit from similar problem-solving principles and strategies.

The obvious question is, What can decrease the inert knowledge problem and increase people's ability to transfer knowledge they possess when faced with a situation that could potentially benefit from that knowledge? One answer appears to be quite simple and very powerful. It involves making an explicit comparison between two or more relevant cases (Gentner, Brem, Ferguson, and Wolff 1997). To the extent that people mentally compare cases or situations, they are able to create a problem-solving schema that is uncluttered by irrelevant surface information. Thus, problem-solving schemas created through this process of mental comparison are more portable and more likely to be called upon when negotiators are challenged with a novel problem. In the absence of comparison, it is not clear to negotiators which information about a situation is relevant or irrelevant. Furthermore, as helpful as making comparisons can be, recognizing *when* to make them is not always obvious. For example, in our training of MBA students and executives, we frequently presented negotiators with several training cases, usually on the same page. Very rarely did negotiators actively compare the cases printed on the same page, even though they contained a similar underlying principle. Thus, the key appears to be making comparisons among experiences, a strategy we elaborate upon later.

AVAILABILITY HEURISTIC

Which is more common: Words that start with the letter *K*—for example, *king*—or words with *K* as the third letter—for example, *awkward* (Kahneman and Tversky 1982)? In the English language, there are more than twice as many words with *K* as the third letter than there are words with *K* as the first letter. Despite this fact, the majority of people guess incorrectly, in that they assume that there are more words with *K* as the first letter. This is due to the **availability heuristic.** According to the availability heuristic, the more prevalent a group or category is judged to be, the easier it is for people to bring instances of this group or category to mind. This heuristic affects the quality of negotiators' judgments in that they may be biased by the ease with which information can be brought to mind. For example, in one investigation, people were presented with a list of 39 names of well-known people (Tversky and Kahneman 1973). Nineteen of these people were female; 20 were male. The women on the list happened to be more famous than the men. Afterwards, people were asked to judge how many women's names appeared on the list. People dramatically overestimated the number of female names, presumably because they were easier to recall—another illustration of the availability heuristic.

The availability heuristic is associated with the **false consensus effect** (Sherman, Presson, and Chassin 1984). The false consensus effect refers to the fact that most people think that others agree with them more than is actually warranted. For example, people who smoke estimate that 51 percent of others are smokers, but nonsmokers estimate that only 38 percent of people are smokers (Sherman, Presson, and Chassin 1984). Furthermore, people overestimate the proportion of people who agree with them about their attitudes concerning drugs, abortion, seatbelt use, politics, and even Ritz™ crackers (Nisbett, Krantz, Jepson, and Kunda 1995). When a negotiator falls victim to the availability heuristic, the likelihood of employing creative strategies (which are often less available) is severely undermined.

REPRESENTATIVENESS

Imagine that you have just met, for the first time, the person who is going to be your immediate supervisor. She is thin, wears glasses, is soft-spoken, and dresses conservatively. Later, you realize that you and your supervisor never discussed your hobbies and outside interests. Is your supervisor into reading books or sporting events? In answering such questions, people make judgments on the basis of a relatively simple rule: The more similar a person is to a group stereotype, the more likely he or she is to also belong to that group. Most people assume the supervisor is a book reader. Basically, the more a person *looks* like the stereotype of a group member, the more we are inclined to stereotype them as belonging to that group. The **representativeness** heuristic is based on stereotypes of people, which may often have a basis in reality, but are frequently outdated and wrong. Furthermore, reliance on stereotypical information can lead people to overlook other types of information that could potentially be very useful in negotiations. The most important type of information is related to base rates. **Base rates** are the frequency with which some event or pattern occurs in a general population. For example, consider a negotiator interested in purchasing a new car. One source of information concerning the new car is a popular consumer report. This report is based upon thousands and thousands of consumer data and research and therefore is highly reliable. However, in addition to consulting this source, people interested in purchasing a new car often consult their neighbors and friends.

Sometimes, a neighbor or friend may have had a personal experience with a car that is quite different than that reported in the consumer report magazine. Oftentimes, however, people who consult their neighbors and friends will discount perfectly valid information (i.e., the base rate information) and choose to rely upon a single, vivid data point. This is known as the **base rate fallacy.**

Faulty judgments of probability are associated with what is known as the **gambler's fallacy,** the tendency to treat chance events as though they have a built-in, evening-out mechanism. However, each event is independently determined. As an example, consider the following problem: Suppose you flip a coin and it comes up heads five times in a row. What do you think the next outcome will be? Most people feel that there is a greater-than-chance probability that the coin will come up tails. Actually, of course, the probability of a heads or tails outcome is always the same—50 percent—for each flip, regardless of the previous result. However, most people think that some sequences (such as heads, tails, heads, tails) are far more likely to occur than others (such as a string of heads or a string of tails; Tversky and Kahneman 1974).

ANCHORING AND ADJUSTMENT

Job candidates are often asked by recruiters what their salary range is. The job candidate, wanting to maximize his or her salary but at the same time not remove him- or herself from consideration because of unrealistic demands, faces a quandary. Similarly, the prospective home buyer struggles with what to make as an opening offer. What factors determine how we make such assessments of value?

According to Tversky and Kahneman (1974), people use a reference point as an anchor and then adjust that value up or down as deemed appropriate. For example, the prospective job recruit may have a roommate who just landed a job with a salary of $60,000. The candidate decides to use $60,000 as a starting point. There are two fundamental concerns with the **anchoring-and-adjustment process.** The first is that the anchors we use to make such judgments are often arbitrary (Tversky and Kahneman 1974). Oftentimes, anchors are selected on the basis of their temporal proximity, not their relevance to the judgment in question. The second is that we tend to make insufficient adjustments away from the anchor. That is, we are weighed down by the anchor. The message for the negotiator is clear: Carefully select anchors, and be wary if your opponent attempts to anchor you.

UNWARRANTED CAUSATION

Consider the following facts:

- Women living in the San Francisco area have a higher rate of breast cancer.
- Women of lower socioeconomic status are less likely to breast-feed their babies.
- People who marry at a later point in life are less likely to divorce.

Before reading further, attempt to explain each fact. When people are asked to do this, they frequently conclude the following:

- Living in San Francisco causes breast cancer.
- People of lower socioeconomic status are not given postnatal care.
- People become wiser as they grow older.

All of these are reasonable explanations, but they are all unwarranted based upon the information given. The tendency to infer a **causal relationship** between two events is unwarranted because we do not know the direction of causality (for example, it is possible that women with cancer are attracted to the Bay area). Further, a third variable could be the cause of the event (people who marry later may be richer or more educated). Maybe older, more professional women are attracted to the Bay area, and this group is statistically more susceptible to cancer. Maybe women of lower socioeconomic status are younger and less comfortable breast-feeding, more likely to be targeted by formula companies, or less likely to get maternity leave. The point is that there are a myriad of possible explanations.

BELIEF PERSEVERANCE

The perseverance effect is the tendency of people to continue to believe that something is true even when it is revealed to be false or has been disproved (Ross and Lepper 1980). For example, imagine that you have taken an aptitude test and have been told you scored poorly. Later, you learn the exam was misscored. Are you able to erase this experience? Not if you are like most college students, who continue to persevere in their beliefs (Ross and Lepper 1980). Why is this? Once a causal explanation is constructed, it is difficult to change it. If you or your negotiation opponent has an erroneous belief about the other, even when it is proven wrong, the belief may still prevail. The important implication is to carefully examine the beliefs you hold about your opponent and be cognizant of faulty beliefs they may have about you.

ILLUSORY CORRELATION

Illusory correlation is the tendency to see invalid correlations between events. For example, people often perceive relationships between distinct pieces of information as a mere consequence of their being presented at the same time (Hamilton and Gifford 1976). For example, in one investigation, people read diagnoses of mental patients (Chapman and Chapman 1967, 1969). Specifically, people were shown pictures allegedly drawn by these patients and then were given the patients' diagnoses to read. In actuality, there was no correlation at all between the types of pictures the patients allegedly drew and the nature of their diagnoses (paranoia, schizophrenia). Nevertheless, the people reviewing the evidence believed that they saw correlations—for example, between a diagnosis of paranoia and a drawing of a very large eye. Even when people are presented with contradictory or ambiguous evidence, they are extremely reluctant to revise their judgments. As another example, suppose you learn during the course of a negotiation with a business representative from country X that 60 percent of country X's male population is uneducated. Suppose that the same day you learn that 60 percent of crimes committed in that country are violent. Although there is no logical relation between the two statistics, most people assume that there is a correlation; that is, they assume that uneducated men from country X are responsible for violent crimes. In fact, there is no relationship between the two—it is illusory. Such correlations between separate facts are illusory because there is no objective basis for the relationships. Rather, our implicit theories are constructed so that we interpret relations between temporally proximate events.

JUST WORLD

Most of us believe that the world is a fair place: People get out of life what they deserve and deserve what happens to them (Lerner 1980). This leads to positive evaluations of others who have good things happen to them; for example, most people believe that "good" people are likely to win lotteries. Unwarranted negative impressions are produced when others suffer misfortune; for instance, we assume that bad people or ignorant people are victims of crimes (Saunders and Size 1986). **Blaming-the-victim attributions** are **defensive attributions** because they enable observers to deal with the perceived inequities in others' lives and maintain the belief that the world is just (Thornton 1992). In short, if we believe that bad things could easily happen to us (e.g., dying in an airplane crash or losing a limb), the world is scary and less predictable.

HINDSIGHT BIAS

The **hindsight bias** refers to a pervasive human tendency for people to be remarkably adept at inferring a process once the outcome is known but be unable to predict outcomes when only the processes and precipitating events are known (Fischhoff 1975). The hindsight bias, or the "I knew it all along" effect, makes integrative solutions to negotiation situations appear to be obvious when we see them in retrospect, although before they were discovered, the situation appeared to be fixed-sum.

We are frequently called upon to explain the causes of events, such as the demise of an organization or the success of a particular company. We often perceive events that have already occurred as inevitable. Stated another way, once we know the outcome of an event, we perceive the outcome to be an inevitable consequence of the factors leading to the outcome. This **creeping determinism** (Fischhoff 1975) accounts for the "Monday morning quarterback" or the "I knew it all along" phenomenon. That is, once someone knows the outcome, the events leading up to it seem obvious. The hindsight bias also accounts for why negotiators often think integrative agreements are obvious after the fact but fail to see them when encountering a novel negotiation.

FUNCTIONAL FIXEDNESS

Functional fixedness occurs when a problem solver bases a strategy on familiar methods (Adamson and Taylor 1954). The problem with functional fixedness is that previously learned problem-solving strategies hinder the development of effective strategies in new situations. The person fixates on one strategy and cannot readily switch to another method of solving a problem. That is, experience in one domain produces in-the-box thinking in another domain. Reliance on compromise as a negotiation strategy may produce functional fixedness.

The notion here is that past experience can limit problem solving. Consider the tumor problem presented in Box 8–3. The solution rate, when people are given the problem by itself, is 37 percent; however, when people are shown a diagram of an arrow going through a black dot and then given the problem, the solution rate drops to 9 percent (Duncker 1945). The diagram of the arrow going through the black dot depicted the function of the X-ray as a single line going through the human body; thus, it blocked people's ability to think of several rays focused on the tumor. Functional fixedness occurs when people have a mental block against using an object in a new way in order to solve a problem. In another example, people are challenged with the problem of how to mount a candle vertically on a nearby screen to function as a lamp. The only materials they are given are a box of matches, a box of candles, and a box of tacks. The creative solution is to mount the candle on top of the matchbox by melting the wax onto the box and sticking the candle to it, then tacking the box to the screen. This elegant solution is much harder to discover when the boxes are presented to people filled with tacks (i.e., the way the boxes are normally used), rather than emptied of their contents (Anderson 1995).

SET EFFECT

Closely related to the problem of functional fixedness is the **set effect,** in which prior experience can also have negative effects in new problem-solving situations. Also known as **negative transfer,** prior experience can limit a manager's ability to develop strategies that are of sufficient breadth and generality. Consider the water jug problem presented in Box 8–1. People who had the experience of working on all the water problems typically used a longer, costlier method to solve the problems. People without the experience of solving the problems almost always discovered the short, direct solution. Mechanized thought and set effects are the arthritis of managerial thinking and the wet blanket on the fires of creativity in negotiation.

SELECTIVE ATTENTION

In negotiations, we are bombarded with information—the opponents' physical appearance, his or her opening remarks, hearsay knowledge, nonverbal behavior, and so on. However, we perceive about 1 percent of all information in our stimulus field (Kaplan and Kaplan 1982). We perceive only a tiny fraction of what happens in the negotiation room. How do we know if we are paying attention to the right cues?

The basic function of our sensory information buffers is to parse and code stimulus information into recognizable symbols. Because external stimuli cannot get directly inside our heads, we cognitively represent stimuli as internal symbols and their interrelations as symbol structures. The sensory buffers—visual, auditory, and tactile—maintain the stimulus as an image or icon while its features are extracted. This activity occurs very rapidly and below our threshold of awareness. The features extracted from a given stimulus object comprise a coded description of the object. For example, our interaction with a colleague concerning a joint venture is an event that is real, but our minds are not video cameras that record everything; rather, we use a process known as **selective attention.**

OVERCONFIDENCE

Consider a situation in which you are assessing the probability that a particular company will be successful. Some people might think the probability is quite good; others might think the probability is low; others might make middle-of-the-road assessments. For the decision maker, what matters most is making an assessment that is accurate. How accurate are people in judgments of probability? How do they make assessments of likelihood, especially when full, objective information is unavailable?

Judgments of likelihood for certain types of events are often more optimistic than is warranted. The **overconfidence effect** refers to unwarranted levels of confidence in people's judgment of their abilities and the occurrence of positive events and under-estimates of the likelihood of negative events. For example, in negotiations involving third-party dispute resolution, negotiators on each side believe the neutral third party will adjudicate in their favor (Farber and Bazerman 1986, 1989; Farber 1981). Obviously, this cannot happen; the third party cannot adjudicate in favor of both parties. Similarly, in final-offer arbitration, wherein parties each submit their final bid to a third party who then makes a binding decision between the two proposals, negotiators consistently overestimate the probability that the neutral arbitrator will choose their own offer (Neale and Bazerman 1983; Bazerman and Neale 1982). Obviously, there is only a 50 percent chance of all final offers being accepted; nevertheless, typically, both parties' estimates sum to a number greater than 100 percent. The message is to beware of the overconfidence effect. When we find ourselves to be highly confident of a particular outcome occurring (whether it be our opponent caving in to us, a senior manager supporting our decision, etc.), it is important to examine why.

THE LIMITS OF SHORT-TERM MEMORY

Short-term memory is the part of our mind that holds the information currently in the focus of our attention and conscious processing. Unfortunately, short-term memory has severely limited capacity; only about five to nine symbols or coded items may be currently active. The "seven plus-or-minus two" rule extends to just about everything we try to remember (Miller 1956). Consider, for example, an interaction you might have with the president of a company concerning the details of a consulting project. The president tells you many facts about her company; you will recall, on average, five to nine pieces of information. Without deliberate rehearsal, the information in your short-term memory will disappear and be replaced with new information perceived by your sensory registers. Obviously, we perceive much more information than we ultimately store and remember.

CREATIVE NEGOTIATION STRATEGIES

The following strategies are designed to sharpen your creative mind. Thus, they are not specific to negotiation; rather, they are an exercise program for enhancing creativity. Because negotiation, like exercise, is an activity we need to engage in regularly, these strategies can be extraordinarily beneficial for increasing creativity in negotiation.

INCUBATION

Excellent problem solvers frequently report that after trying to solve a problem and getting nowhere, they put the problem aside for hours, days, and even weeks and, upon returning to it, can see the solution quickly. (For a real example of the incubation effect, see Sidebar 8–2.) The incubation phase is usually one step in a process of problem solving detailed here:

1. **Preparation.** During the preparation phase, the problem solver is busy gathering information and making preliminary attempts to arrive at a solution. The key here is to understand and define the problem. As we have noted, finding a good problem is the essence of effective negotiation.

> **SIDEBAR 8–2. INCUBATION EFFECTS**
> Numerous examples of incubation were reported by the famous French mathematician Poincaré (1929), including the following:
>
> > Then I turned my attention to the study of some arithmetical questions apparently without much success and without a suspicion of any connection with my preceding researches. Disgusted with my failure, I went to spend a few days at the seaside, and thought of something else. One morning, walking on the bluff, the idea came to me, with just the same characteristics of brevity, suddenness, and immediate certainty, that the arithmetic transformations of indeterminate ternary quadratic forms were identical with those of non-Euclidean geometry. (p. 388)

2. **Incubation.** When initial attempts to solve the problem have failed, problem solvers may put the problem aside to work on other activities or even to sleep. Although no one is sure why this helps, people often engage in implicit problem solving at a level below conscious awareness.
3. **Illumination.** During the illumination phase, the key to a solution often appears. This often happens when people are doing something completely unrelated to solving the problem.
4. **Verification.** In the verification phase, problem solvers need to check the solution to make sure it works. As an example, think about the necklace problem you were challenged with in Box 8–1, in which you are given four chains to make one necklace on a limited budget. Three groups of people worked on this problem (Silveira 1972). One group spent 30 minutes trying to solve it, with a solution rate of 55 percent. A different group spent 30 minutes trying to solve it but were interrupted during their solving period with a 30-minute break. In this group, 64 percent of participants solved the problem. A third group spent 30 minutes trying to solve the problem but were interrupted in their solving process by a four-hour break. Of this group, 85 percent solved the problem. Whereas we do not guarantee that difficult negotiation situations will always be met with illumination after putting the problem aside, it certainly cannot hurt to try.

RATIONAL PROBLEM-SOLVING MODEL

The rational problem-solving model, patterned after Pólya (1957, 1968), also describes four steps for solving a problem. However, unlike the incubation method, the rational problem-solving model is deliberate and incremental:

1. **Understand the problem.** In this step, the negotiator needs to ask him- or herself: *What is known? What is unknown? What are the data I am using? What are my assumptions?*
2. **Devising a plan.** During this step, the negotiator may ask him- or herself whether past experience is a profitable means of finding a solution method,

engaging in a search for similar problems, or perhaps restating the goal of the problem.

3. **Carrying out the plan.** In this step, the negotiator carries out the plan and, perhaps, tests it.

4. **Looking back.** In this step, the negotiator asks him- or herself whether he or she can obtain the result by using another method and looks at how it all fits together. In this step, it is important that the negotiator ask him- or herself what the key takeaway is.

FLUENCY, FLEXIBILITY, AND ORIGINALITY

What is creativity? What constitutes a creative idea? To be considered creative, an idea must be highly original and useful. The last part is the challenge—many people can come up with totally bizarre but useless ideas. The key is for these ideas to be valuable. One common way of evaluating creativity is via three indices: fluency, flexibility, and originality (Guilford 1959, 1967).

- **Fluency:** The ability to generate *many solutions* that all fit some requirement; a negotiator who is able to think of *several* solutions to a conflict (there is strength in numbers).
- **Flexibility:** The ability to change approaches to a problem, such as being able to solve a series of tasks that each require a different strategy; a negotiator who is able to generate many different *kinds* of solutions.
- **Originality:** The ability to generate unusual solutions, such as coming up with unique answers; a negotiator who is able to think of solutions that elude other people.

As a way of thinking about these three indices of creativity, do the following exercise: See how many possible uses you can think of for a cardboard box. (Give yourself about 10 minutes to do this.) Suppose that one person who completed this exercise, Geoff, generated two ideas: using the box as a cage for a hamster and as a kennel for a dog. Geoff would receive two points for fluency of ideas because these are two different ideas, but only one point for flexibility because the ideas are of the same category (i.e., a home for animals). Creative people generate more novel and unusual ways to use a cardboard box. Another person, Avi, generated these unusual ideas for a cardboard box: using it as a god, using it as a telephone (e.g., two boxes and some string), and trading it as currency. Avi would get a score of three points for fluency and three points for flexibility, because there are three separate categories of ideas for use, involving religion, communication, and economics. In addition, Avi's ideas are extremely original.

It is easy to see how flexibility in thought—that is, thinking about different categories of use—can influence originality. Thus, one simple key for enhancing creativity is to *diversify the use of categories.* By listing possible categories of use for a cardboard box (containers, shelter, building material, therapy, religion, politics, weaponry, communication, etc.), a person's score on these three dimensions could increase dramatically. Thus, a key strategy is to think in terms of *categories* of ideas—not just *number* of ideas. This can often help negotiators out of a narrow perspective on a conflict and open up new opportunities for creative solutions.

BRAINSTORMING

Alex Osborn, an advertising executive in the 1950s, wanted to increase the creativity of organizations. He believed that one of the main blocks to creativity was the premature evaluation of ideas. He was convinced that two heads were better than one when it came to generating ideas, but only if people could be trained to defer judgment of their own and others' ideas during the idea generation process. Therefore, Osborn developed the most widespread strategy used by organizations to encourage creative thought: brainstorming.

Brainstorming is a technique used by a large number of companies and organizations to unleash the creative group mind and avoid the negative impact of group dynamics on creativity. The goal of brainstorming is to maximize the *quantity* and *quality* of ideas. Osborn aptly noted that quantity is a good predictor of quality: A group is more likely to discover a really good idea if it has a lot of ideas to choose from. But there is even more to brainstorming than mere quantity. Osborn believed that the ideas generated by one person in a team could stimulate ideas in other people in a synergistic fashion.

Osborn believed that the collective product could be greater than the sum of the individual parts if certain conditions were met. Hence, he developed rules for brainstorming. Contrary to popular corporate lore that brainstorming sessions are wild and crazy free-for-alls where anything goes, brainstorming has defined rules (Osborn 1957, 1963). They are still widely used today, and several companies post the brainstorming guidelines and roles prominently in their meeting rooms (see Table 8–1). However, people do not often use them for negotiations.

CONVERGENT VERSUS DIVERGENT THINKING

There are two key skills involved in creative thinking: divergent thinking and convergent thinking (Guilford 1959, 1967). **Convergent thinking** is thinking that proceeds toward a single answer, such as the expected value of a 70 percent chance of earning $1,000 is obtained by multiplying $1,000 by 0.7 to reach $700. **Divergent thinking** moves outward from the problem in many possible directions and involves thinking without boundaries. It is related to the notion of flexibility of categories and originality of thought. Divergent thinking *is* out-of-the-box thinking.

Table 8–1: Rules for brainstorming

Expressiveness: Group members should express any idea that comes to mind, no matter how strange, weird, or fanciful. Group members are encouraged not to be constrained nor timid. They should freewheel whenever possible.

Nonevaluation: Do not criticize ideas. Group members should not evaluate any of the ideas in any way during the generation phase; all ideas should be considered valuable.

Quantity: Group members should generate as many ideas as possible. Groups should strive for quantity; the more ideas, the better. Quantity of ideas increases the probability of finding excellent solutions.

Building: Because all of the ideas belong to the group, members should try to modify and extend the ideas suggested by other members whenever possible.

Source: Adapted from Osborn, A. F. 1957. *Applied Imagination* (rev. ed.). New York: Scribner.

Many of the factors that make up creative problem solving seem most closely related to divergent thinking. However, ideas eventually need to be evaluated and acted upon. This is where convergent thinking comes in. In convergent thinking, a negotiator judges and evaluates the various ideas presented as to their feasibility, practicality, and overall merit.

People working independently excel at divergent thinking because there are no cognitive or social pressures to constrain their thought. In short, there are no conformity pressures. In contrast, people are much less proficient at divergent thinking. The key reasons have to do with conformity pressures. To avoid social censure, people assess the norms of the situation and conform to them. In contrast, groups excel compared to individuals when in comes to convergent thinking. Groups are better at judging the quality of ideas. This suggests that an effective design for promoting creativity in negotiation involves separating the generation of ideas—leaving this to individual team members—and then evaluating and discussing the ideas as a team. (However, divergent thinking is not always looked upon as favorable; see Sidebar 8–3.)

DEDUCTIVE REASONING

To be effective at negotiation, negotiators need to be good at deductive, as well as inductive, reasoning. First we take up the topic of **deductive reasoning,** or the process of drawing logical conclusions. For example, most people have some kind of training in solving logical syllogisms like the ones in Box 8–5. The difficulty in solving these syllogisms does not imply that managers are stupid; rather, it indicates that formal logic and individual (or psychological) processes are not necessarily the same. However, many people violate rules of logic on a regular basis. Some of the most common violations of the rules of logic are the following:

- **Agreement with a conclusion:** The desirability of the conclusion often drives people's appraisal of reality. This, of course, is a form of wishful thinking, as well as an egocentric bias. There is a strong tendency for people to judge the conclusions they agree with as valid, and the conclusions they disagree with as invalid.
- **Cognitive consistency:** People have a tendency to interpret information in a fashion that is consistent with information that they already know. The ten-

SIDEBAR 8–3. DIVERGENT THINKING

Divergent thinking (or creative thinking) is often not rewarded in schools and organizations. For example, Getzels and Jackson (1962) observed that teachers prefer students who have high IQs but are not high in creativity. High-IQ students and managers tend to gauge success by conventional standards (i.e., to behave as teachers expect them to and seek careers that conform to what others expect of them). In contrast, highly creative people use unconventional standards for determining success, and their career choices do not usually conform to expectations. Most educational training, including that of MBAs, favors logical or convergent thinking and does not nurture creative or divergent thinking.

BOX 8–5

SAMPLE SYLLOGISMS

Pick the conclusions that you can be sure of (Stratton 1983):

1. All S are M. All M are P. Therefore,

a. All S are P.

b. All S are not P.

c. Some S are P.

d. Some S are not P.

e. None of these conclusions is valid.

2. As technology advances and natural petroleum resources are depleted, the securing of petroleum from unconventional sources becomes more imperative. One such source is the Athabasca tar sands of northern Alberta, Canada. Because some tar sands are sources of refinable hydrocarbons, these deposits are worthy of commercial investigation. Some kerogen deposits are also sources of refinable hydrocarbons. Therefore:

a. All kerogen deposits are tar sands.

b. No kerogen deposits are tar sands.

c. Some kerogen deposits are tar sands.

d. Some kerogen deposits are not tar sands.

e. None of the above.

3. The delicate Glorias of Argentina, which open only in cool weather, are all Sassoids. Some of the equally delicate Fragilas, found only in damp areas, are not Glorias. What can you infer from these statements?

a. All Fragilas are Sassoids.

b. No Fragilas are Sassoids.

c. Some Fragilas are Sassoids.

d. Some Fragilas are not Sassoids.

e. None of the above.

If you think like most people, problem #1 is probably the easiest to solve (the answer is a). However, problems #2 and #3 generate much higher error rates (75 percent error rate for problem #2, with most errors due to picking answer c instead of e; 90 percent error rate for problem #3, mainly due to picking d instead of e).

---

dency for people to judge conclusions to be true, based upon whether the information agrees with what they already know to be true, illustrates the need for consistency in one's belief structure.

- **Confirmation bias:** People have a strong tendency to seek information that confirms what they already know. A good example of this is the card task presented in Box 8–1.

INDUCTIVE REASONING

Inductive reasoning is a form of hypothesis testing, or trial and error. In general, people are not very good at testing hypotheses, and they tend to use confirmatory methods. A good example is the card task in Box 8–1. Another example is the availability heuristic we discussed earlier, such that judgments of frequency tend to be biased by the ease with which information can be called to mind.

For example, people make inaccurate judgments when estimating probabilities. For example, consider the problem in Box 8–6 (Tversky and Kahneman 1974). When people are asked to answer this question, 22 percent select the first answer (i.e., the

---

< **BOX 8–6** >

THE HOSPITAL PROBLEM

A certain town is served by two hospitals (Tversky and Kahneman 1974). In the larger hospital, about 45 babies are born each day, and in the smaller hospital, about 15 babies are born each day. As you know, about 50 percent of all babies are boys. However, the exact percentage varies from day to day. Sometimes it may be higher than 50 percent, sometimes lower. For a period of one year, each hospital recorded the days in which more than 60 percent of the babies born were boys. Which hospital do you think recorded more such days?

1. The larger hospital
2. The smaller hospital
3. About the same (that is, within 5 percent of each other)

---

larger hospital), 22 percent select the second answer (i.e., the smaller hospital), and 56 percent select the third answer (i.e., both hospitals). They seem to make no compensation for large versus small sample sizes. They believe that an extreme event—for example, 60 percent of births being male—is just as likely in a large hospital as in a small one. In fact, it is actually far more likely for an extreme event to occur within a small sample because there are fewer cases to average. People often fail to take sample size into account when they make an inference.

In summary, managers do not form generalizations (reason inductively) in ways that statistics and logic suggest. When people make inferences about events based on their experience in the real world, they do not behave like statisticians. Rather, they seem to be heavily influenced by salient features that stand out in their memory, and they are swayed by extreme events even when the sample size is small.

FLOW

According to Csikszentmihalyi (1997), **autotelic experience,** or **flow,** is a particular kind of experience that is so engrossing and enjoyable that it becomes worth doing, even though it may have no consequences beyond its own context. Creative activities in life, such as music, sports, games, and so on, are typical sources for this kind of experience. Of course, people never do anything purely for its own sake—their motives are always a combination of intrinsic and extrinsic considerations. For example, filmmakers may make films for the joy of creating something artistic, but also because the film may make money or win an Academy Award™. Similarly, managers and executives create new products and ideas not only because they enjoy doing so, but because the products will make the company more profitable. However, if people are only motivated by extrinsic rewards, they are missing a key ingredient in terms of experience. In addition to the external rewards, they can also enjoy an activity, such as negotiation, for its own sake.

This kind of intense flow experience is not limited to creative endeavors. It is also found in the most mundane activities in the personal and business world, such as going to work every day, interacting with people, etc. An important condition for the flow experience is that a person feels that his or her abilities match the opportunities for action. If the challenges are too great for a person's skill, intense anxiety, or **choking,** can occur. However, if the person's skills outweigh the challenges of the experience, he or she may feel bored. The message is that *process* is more important than the *outcome* of the interaction. In a negotiation, this means that the process of working through differences, satisfying underlying needs, and creating value is more important than the content of the particular negotiation. To the extent that negotiation is viewed as unpleasant, uncomfortable, or a struggle, flow (and the creative process that can ensue from flow) is less likely to occur.

All of this raises an important question, which you are hopefully in a position to evaluate yourself: How do you regard the task of negotiation? Answering this question says a lot about how you try to resolve negotiation and your ultimate success in doing so. Because negotiation is a task that must be done on a repeated basis throughout the duration of one's life, especially in the business world, it is important for a negotiation to be an enjoyable process in and of itself, rather than a specific means to an end. We have identified four basic profiles that we call **mental models,** which describe how people tend to regard the task or process of negotiation. Because none of these describe a physical system but rather one of the most common and important forms of human interaction (negotiation), we refer to them as mental, rather than physical, models.

WHAT IS YOUR MENTAL MODEL OF NEGOTIATION?

There tend to be four distinct mental models of negotiation (Thompson and Loewenstein 2000). By far, the first three are the most common.

HAGGLING

Probably the most common mental model of negotiation is what we call the *haggling* model. The image this might conjure up is of two dogs fighting over one bone. Resolution in this model comes down to a struggle between two entities—people, companies, etc.—in which each is trying to obtain the biggest share of the pie. The haggling model is based upon a fixed-pie perception of negotiation.

GAME-PLAYING

The *game-playing* model of negotiation elevates negotiation from "fighting in the streets" to a refined game between two or more highly intelligent people. In game-playing, each person has his or her own interests in mind and, in many cases, a competitive interest—such that they attempt to beat the other party at the "game" of negotiation. This game is carried out, however, in an extremely civil and refined fashion. The ultimate version of the game-playing model is the chess game, in which people thoughtfully and strategically move pieces in an attempt to beat the other side.

RELATIONSHIP

A common mental model of negotiation is what we call the *relationship* model, which is often embraced by salespeople and companies that believe in treating their clients as partners. According to the relationship model, it is important to build rapport between people to nurture the long-term relationship that can develop, and in many cases, to make sacrifices in the name of creating long-term goodwill between parties.

PROBLEM SOLVING

The *problem-solving* model is a mental model of negotiation in which people consider negotiation to be the task of defining and solving a problem. The image this might conjure up is of two people sitting on the same side of the table, attempting to solve a crossword puzzle together. This model focuses on the collaborative or cooperative aspects of the task, and involves a great deal of creativity, reframing of the problem, and out-of-the-box thinking.

CONCLUSION

This chapter has illustrated some of the components of highly creative negotiation strategies. Creative negotiation agreements fractionate single-issue negotiations into those that involve multiple issues; align issues in ways that can be profitably traded off; search for ways to expand the pie; use bridging, cost-cutting, and nonspecific compensation; and structure contingency contracts. We have also highlighted some of the key mental blocks or (biases) that can stymie creative thought. In particular, the inert knowledge problem, availability bias, representativeness, anchoring and adjustment phenomenon, unwarranted causation, belief perseverance, illusory correlation, hindsight bias, functional fixedness, set effects, selective attention, and overconfidence tend to narrow the scope of possibilities. We have identified a number of strategies for enhancing creativity in negotiations, such as incubation, brainstorming, convergent and divergent thinking skills, and inductive and deductive reasoning. Most negotiators have mental models about negotiation that are inaccurate and limiting, such as the haggling model, gamesmanship, and relationships. We advocate a problem-solving mental model for thinking creatively about negotiations.

⟨ **BOX 8–7** ⟩

ANSWERS TO CREATIVITY TEST

CARD DECISION

Correct answer: E and 7

Averaging over a large number of experiments (Oaksford and Chater 1994), it has been found that 89 percent of people select E, which is a logically correct choice because an odd number on the other side would disconfirm the rule. However, 62 percent also choose to turn over the 4, which is not logically informative because neither a vowel nor a consonant on the other side would have falsified the rule. Only 25 percent elect to turn over the 7, which is a logically informative choice because a vowel behind the 7 would have falsified the rule. Only 16 percent elect to turn over K, which would not be an informative choice.

PERSON IN A ROOM DECISION

Correct answer: Jack is a lawyer.

This problem illustrates a classic base-rate problem. We are given information that the probability of any one person selected is equivalent to the stated base rates; the normatively appropriate solution is 30 percent, thus making it more likely that Jack is a lawyer. Yet, most people choose to ignore base rate information and assume that Jack is an engineer. An answer that goes against explicitly stated probability theory runs the risk of being one based on stereotypes. Groups may be more likely to defend the stereotype decision.

BETTING DECISION

Correct answer: A (for the first bet)

The normatively appropriate logic here is to use expected value theory, in which the expected value of a risky choice is determined by the value of the payoff multiplied by its probability. Using this technique, the expected value of bet A is $8 × 0.3333 = $2.66. The expected value of bet B is ($3 × 0.8333 = $2.5). Thus, bet A maximizes expected value. However, many people overweight high probabilities and end up choosing bet B. Groups tend to be riskier than individuals, so groups often choose riskier decisions, whether they are normatively appropriate or not. For the second bet, either answer is normatively correct because their expected values are the same.

WATER JUGS

Problem solvers can become biased by their experiences to prefer certain problem-solving operators in solving a problem. Such biasing of the problem solution is known as a set effect. Also known as the Einstellung effect, or mechanization of thought, this can paradoxically lead to worsened performance. The Einstellung effect involves remembering a particular sequence of operations, and it is memory for this sequence that is blinding managers to other possibilities. In this series of problems, all problems except 8 can be solved by using the B-2C-A method. For problems 1 through 5, this solution is the simplest, but for problems 7 and 9, the simpler solution of A + C also applies. Problem 8 cannot be solved by the B-2C-A method but can be solved by the simpler solution of A-C. Problems 6 and 10 are also solved more simply as A-C than B-2C-A.

Of the participants who received the whole setup of 10 problems, 83 percent used the B-2C-A method on problems 6 and 7, 64 percent failed to solve problem 8, and 79 percent used the B-2C-A method for problems 9 and 10. The performance of people who worked on all 10 problems was compared with the performance of people who saw only the last five problems. These people did not see the biasing B-2C-A problems. Fewer than 1 percent of these people used B-2C-A

> ## BOX 8–7

ANSWERS TO CREATIVITY TEST—
continued

solutions, and only 5 percent failed to solve problem 8. Thus, the first five problems can create a powerful bias for a particular solution. This bias hurt solution of problems 6 through 10.

STICK PROBLEM

> *Correct answer: Form a tetrahedron (kind of like a pyramid)*

Most people take the six sticks and form a square with an X in it. However, this solution is not acceptable because the triangles are not equilateral—each has a 90 degree angle. Another incorrect answer that is common is to form three of the sticks in a triangle and overlay them on another triangle upside down; this produces four triangles, but the sides of the triangle are not one stick in length. In order to solve the problem, the solver must think in three dimensions, making a pyramid with a triangle base. This is a general class of problem situations that often involve "insight"—a rearrangement of the parts in a certain way to solve a problem.

LETTER SEQUENCE

> *Correct answer: E*

The answer to this Eureka problem is E. The letters are the first seven letters of the first eight digits: one, two, three, four, five, six, seven, and eight.

GOLD CHAIN

> *Correct answer: 2*

The chain puzzle is a Eureka problem. Many groups answer 11 because that would involve cutting only every other link. The correct answer, however, is two. If the fourth and eleventh links are cut, all the values from 1 to 23 can be obtained by getting "change" back from the motel owner. Separate links (the fourth and the eleventh) are given on days 1

and 2, but on day 3, the three-link unit is given to the owner, who returns the separate links. These links are then used to pay on days 4 and 5, but on day 6, the six-link unit is used, and the owner returns the others as change. The process can be continued for 23 days.

SUSAN AND MARTHA

> *Correct answer: 36*

This is a disjunctive decision task. It is a Eureka problem, and the answer must be calculated. Only 14 combinations yield a total of 13 (e.g., 1, 1, 11; 1, 2, 10; 1, 3, 9, etc.), and only two of these have the identical product (1, 6, 6 and 2, 2, 9). If we assume that Susan knows her own age, she would still be confused only if she were 36.

NECKLACE

Initially, people tend to break a link on each chain, attach it to another chain, and then close it. The more elegant (and cheaper) solution is to break a single three-link piece and use its links to attach others. It costs 6 cents to open three links. The total connection cost is 9 cents, yielding a 15-cent necklace.

NINE DOT PROBLEM

> *Correct answer: See Panels 3 and 4*

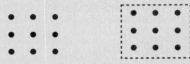

| Panel 1: | Panel 2: |
| The Nine-Dot Problem | Imposing an Imaginary Boundary |

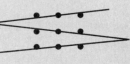

| Panel 3: | Panel 4: |
| An Expert Solution | A Creative Solution |

Continued

BOX 8–7

ANSWERS TO CREATIVITY TEST—
continued

Most people implicitly assume that the lines must be drawn within an imaginary boundary, as shown in the second panel of the diagram. One possible solution that is preferred by "experts" is given in the third panel of the diagram. The problem solver must go outside the self-imposed square boundary. Another creative solution uses lines that do not go through the center of the dots, as shown in the fourth panel of the diagram. This solution involves overcoming another self-imposed limit on the problem—namely, realizing that it is not necessary to draw the lines through the center of each dot. Thus, one major kind of conceptual block is the tendency to impose too many constraints on the problem (that is, to represent the problem in a way that limits the potential kinds of solutions). Overcoming the conceptual blocks is similar to overcoming functional fixedness or Einstellung; instead, look for alternative ways of representing the problem.

PIGPEN

Correct answer: See diagram

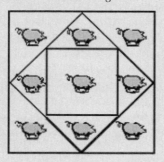

This is an "insight" problem. Most people assume that each pigpen must be square. The solution involves diamond-shaped pens.

WATERLILIES

Correct answer: Day 59

This is a pure "insight" problem. People initially approach the problem as one involving a linearly increasing quantity and simply divide the total time in half. However, because the lilies increase exponentially in area, this approach is incorrect, and another representation is called for. Such a change in representation can occur when the participant tries to imagine what happens as the pond fills up and he or she works backward from the last day, rather than carrying out a formal analysis of the problem.

BARTENDER PROBLEM

The man who walked into the bar had the hiccups. The bartender realized this and attempted to scare the daylights out of the man by pointing a gun at him. Some people are able to solve this problem immediately; others are not. This is a Eureka problem.

PART III

APPLICATIONS AND SPECIAL SCENARIOS

9
MULTIPLE PARTIES,
COALITIONS, AND TEAMS

❧

Once a month, Todd Schulke, an environmentalist, Hugh McKeen, a rancher, and Donal Weaver, a U.S. forest ranger, sit down at the same table and talk. There was a time, however, when all they did was glare at each other: In 1991, their village of Reserve, New Mexico, was the flash point for the antifederal government movement known as the Sagebrush Rebellion II. Over the past years, no less than 100 collaborative groups have formed nationwide, such as the Malpai Borderlands Group, the Quincy Library Group, and the Ponderosa Pines Partnership. Their members run the gamut from federal rangers, local officials, ranchers, minters, environmentalists, and developers. Their mission is to negotiate such seemingly incompatible things as logging and grazing and forest and wildlife preservation. Obviously, there are multiple parties at these bargaining tables who, previously, were at each other's throats. Now, however, they are making some slow, steady progress. Says forest ranger Weaver about his multiparty group: "We're developing a level of trust. When people sit face to face, they develop a mutual respect. People aren't as free to insult you and throw rotten tomatoes." (Florio 1997, A6)

Thus far, we have been in a two-party world of negotiation. In the opening example of this chapter, however, there are a complex assortment of players. Some are negotiators; some are agents; others are constituents. Often, negotiation situations are not purely one-on-one situations. There are often other people at the table and behind the scenes. To negotiate effectively in groups, negotiators need all of the skills we have described thus far, and then some. We will discuss the skills specific to multiparty negotiation in this chapter.

ANALYZING MULTIPARTY NEGOTIATIONS

Consider the multiparty negotiation described in Box 9–1. How might we analyze it? The negotiation involves a myriad of players, relationships, and issues (see Fig. 9–1). Negotiations within and between organizations are embedded in an intricate web of interdependent relationships and interests. Just as a complete understanding of human anatomy requires analyses at the levels of cell chemistry, tissues, organs, and organ systems, a complete understanding of negotiation within and between organizations requires analysis at several levels (Thompson and Fox 2000).

⟨ **BOX 9–1** ⟩

FILM GATE NEGOTIATION

Film Gate (FG), a new television production company, pitched a number of ideas for one-hour television specials to the three major networks. The executives at ABC liked one of the ideas and began negotiations with FG to develop the series. Because FG had never produced a network special, ABC insisted that FG co-produce the special with Tri-Color (TC), an experienced television production company. As it turns out, both FG and TC were represented by the same Hollywood agent (HA); in fact, TC was one of HA's largest and most established clients.

The FG negotiating team was composed of the president, chief financial officer, and head of production. Each member of the team found the prospect of working with TC modestly aversive, and after some discussion, the team was staunchly opposed to the plan. However, because there was no obvious alternative, they proceeded to negotiate. The key issues to be addressed were (1) credit for the program as listed in the titles, (2) monetary compensation, and (3) the option of follow-up programming with ABC. FG was most concerned with credit and the option of future programming so that they could establish a reputation within the industry.

However, FG felt pressure to please its major shareholder (SH) in the negotiations. SH was most concerned with the short-term profitability of FG and was unwilling to continue staking FG unless it would show a profit in the near future. FG decided therefore that money would be as important as credit in the negotiation with ABC and TC.

Working through HA, the three principals (ABC, FG, and TC) arrived at a deal that gave top billing and generous compensation to FG. However, HA later sent a memo to ABC stating that the production would be credited to "TC in association with FG," and that ABC's future options would be exercised, if at all, solely through TC. FG was infuriated by HA's apparent betrayal and found a new agent. Furthermore, FG threatened to sue HA; this threat proved ineffective because both FG and HA were convinced that a jury would side with them. Finally, FG explored the possibility with ABC of collaborating with Unicorn Productions (UP), another established production company. In light of this development, HA and TC relented, and the deal went through under the original terms (Thompson and Fox 2000).

We are grateful to Alan Fox for this example, which also appears in Thompson and Fox 2000.

In this chapter, we review six levels of analysis beyond one-on-one negotiation: (1) multiparty negotiations; (2) coalitions; (3) principal-agent relationships; (4) constituencies; (5) team negotiation; and (6) team-on-team negotiations or intergroup negotiations (see Fig. 9–2). For each level, we identify key challenges and then suggest practical advice and strategies for maximizing negotiation effectiveness.

MULTIPARTY NEGOTIATIONS

A **multiparty negotiation** is a group of three or more individuals, each representing their own interests, who attempt to resolve perceived differences of interest (Bazerman,

FIGURE 9–1 Film Gate Negotiation Structure

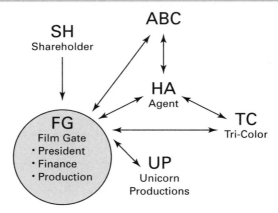

Mannix, and Thompson 1988; Kramer 1991). For example, a group of individuals who must collectively prepare and present a group project for a course grade is involved in a multiparty negotiation, as is a group of specialists in an architectural firm who must design a house for a client. The parties to a negotiation may be individuals, teams, or groups. The involvement of more than two principals at the negotiation table complicates the situation enormously: Social interactions become more complex, information-processing demands increase exponentially, and coalitions can form. In the dyadic case, parties cannot reach settlement without the consent of the opponent; however, in multiparty negotiations, parties can exclude individuals from an agreement.

In the example in Box 9–1, there are three principals involved in the multiparty negotiation: Film Gate, ABC, and Tri-Color. Unicorn Productions is a potential principal. A coalition may include Film Gate, ABC, and either Tri-Color or Unicorn Productions. Film Gate may pressure Tri-Color to concede on the terms of the agreement by threatening to collaborate with Unicorn Productions.

KEY CHALLENGES OF MULTIPARTY NEGOTIATIONS

There are several challenges at both the cognitive (mind) and the emotional (heart) level that crop up in multiparty negotiations. We present four key challenges of multiparty negotiations and follow with some practical advice.

Dealing with Coalitions

A key difference between two-party and group negotiations is the potential for two or more parties within a group to form a coalition to pool their resources and have a greater influence on outcomes (for a review, see Komorita and Parks 1995). A **coalition** is a (sub)group of two of more individuals who join together in using their resources to affect the outcome of a decision in a mixed-motive situation (see Murnighan 1978; Komorita and Parks 1995 for a review) involving at least three parties (Gamson 1964). For example, parties may seek to maximize control over other members, maximize their status in the group, maximize similarity of attitudes and

FIGURE 9–2 Levels of Analysis in Multiparty Negotiation

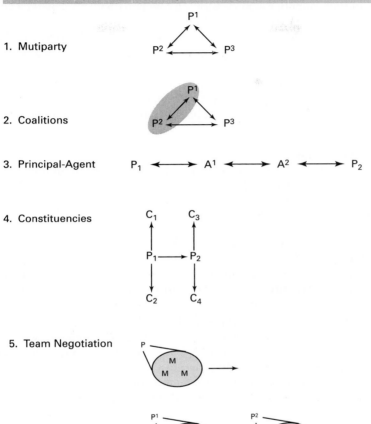

1. Mutiparty

2. Coalitions

3. Principal-Agent

4. Constituencies

5. Team Negotiation

6. Intergroup

P, principal C, constituency group; M, group member; A, agent

values, or minimize conflict among members. Coalition formation is one way that otherwise weak group members may marshal a greater share of resources. Coalitions involve both cooperation and competition: Members of coalitions cooperate with one another in competition against other coalitions, but compete against one another regarding the allocation of rewards the coalition obtains. Coalitions are so important that we have a special section to discuss them.

Formulating Trade-Offs
Integrative agreements are more difficult to fashion in multiparty negotiations because the trade-offs are more complex. In a multiparty negotiation, integrative trade-offs may be achieved either through circular or reciprocal logrolling (Palmer

and Thompson 1995). **Circular logrolling** involves trade-offs that require each group member to offer another member a concession on one issue while receiving a concession from yet another group member on a different issue. A circular trade-off is typified by the tradition of drawing names from a hat to give holiday gifts to people. People receive a gift from one person and give a gift to yet another person. Ideally, we give gifts that are more appreciated by the recipient than by the giver. In contrast, **reciprocal trade-offs** are fashioned between two members of a larger group. Reciprocal trade-offs are typified in the more traditional form of exchanging presents. Circular trade-offs are more risky than reciprocal trade-offs because they involve the cooperation of more than two group members.

Voting and Majority Rule

Groups often simplify the negotiation of multiple issues among multiple parties through voting and decision rules. However, if not used wisely, decision rules can thwart effective negotiation, both in terms of pie expansion and pie slicing. There are a number of problems associated with voting that we will now describe.

Problems with Voting and Majority Rule   **Voting** is the procedure of collecting individuals' preferences for alternatives on issues and selecting the most popular alternative as the group choice. The most common procedure used to aggregate preferences of team members is **majority rule.** However, majority rule presents several problems in the attainment of efficient negotiation settlements. Despite its democratic appeal, majority rule fails to recognize the strength of individual preferences. One person in a group may feel very strongly about an issue, but his or her vote counts the same as the vote of someone who does not have a strong opinion about the issue. Consequently, majority rule does not promote integrative trade-offs among issues. In fact, groups negotiating under unanimous rule reach more efficient outcomes than groups operating under majority rule (Thompson, Mannix, and Bazerman 1988; Mannix, Thompson, and Bazerman 1989).

Although unanimity rule is time consuming, it encourages group members to consider creative alternatives to expand the size of the pie and satisfy the interests of all group members. Because strength of preference is a key component in the fashioning of integrative agreements, majority rule hinders the development of mutually beneficial trade-offs. Voting in combination with other decision aids, such as agendas, may be especially detrimental to the attainment of efficient outcomes because it prevents logrolling (Thompson, Mannix, and Bazerman 1988; Mannix, Thompson, and Bazerman 1989).

There are other problems with voting. Group members may not agree upon a method for voting; for example, some members may insist upon unanimity, others may argue for a simple majority rule, and still others may advocate a weighted majority rule. Even if a voting method is agreed upon, it may not yield a choice. For example, a group may not find a majority if there is an even split in the group. Voting does not eliminate conflicts of interest, but instead, provides a way for group members to live with conflicts of interest; for this reason, majority rule decisions may not be stable. In this sense, voting hides disagreement within groups, which threatens long-term group and organizational effectiveness.

Voting Paradoxes   Consider a three-person (Raines, Warner, and Lassiter) product development team. The three are in conflict over which design to use—A, B, or C.

Table 9–1: Managers' preferences for product designs

Manager	Design A	Design B	Design C
Raines	1	2	3
Warner	2	3	1
Lassiter	3	1	2

The preference ordering is depicted in Table 9–1. Everyone is frustrated, and the group has argued for hours. As a way of resolving the conflict, Warner suggests voting between designs *A* and *B*. In that vote *A* wins, and *B* is tossed in the trash. Warner then proposes that the group vote between *A* and *C*. In that vote, *C* wins. Warner then declares that design *C* be implemented. Lassiter concludes that the group vote was fair and agrees to develop design *C*. However, Raines is perplexed and suggests taking another vote. Warner laughs and says, "We just took a vote and you lost—so just accept the outcome!" Raines glares at Warner and says, "Let's do the vote again, and I will agree to accept the outcome. However, this time I want us to vote between *B* and *C* first." Warner has no choice but to go along. In this vote *B* is the clear winner, and *C* is eliminated. Next, the vote is between *A* and *B*, and *A* beats *B*. Raines happily declares *A* the winner. Lassiter then jumps up and declares that the whole voting process was fraudulent, but cannot explain why.

Raines, Warner, and Lassiter are victims of the **condorcet paradox.** The condorcet paradox demonstrates that the winners of majority rule elections will change as a function of the *order* in which alternatives are proposed. Alternatives that are proposed later, as opposed to earlier, are more likely to survive sequential voting (May 1982). Thus, clever negotiators arrange to have their preferred alternatives entered at later stages of a sequential voting process.

The unstable voting outcomes of the product development team point to a larger concern, known as the **impossibility theorem** (Arrow 1963), which states that the derivation of group preference from individual preference is indeterminate. Simply put, there is no method of combining group members' preferences that guarantees that group preference has been maximized when groups have three or more members and there are three or more options. That is, even though each manager's preferences are transitive, the group-level preference is intransitive.

Strategic Voting   The problem of indeterminate group choice is further compounded by the temptation for members to **strategically misrepresent** their true preferences so that a preferred option is more likely to be favored by the group (Chechile 1984; Plott 1976; Ordeshook 1986; Plott and Levine 1978). For example, a group member may vote for his least-preferred option to ensure that the second choice option is killed. Raines could have voted strategically in the first election to ensure that his preferred strategy was not eliminated in the first round.

Consensus Decisions   Consensus agreements require the consent of all parties to the negotiation before an agreement is binding. However, consensus agreements do not imply unanimity. For an agreement to be unanimous, parties must agree inwardly as well as outwardly. Consensus agreements imply that parties agree *publicly* to a particular settlement, even though their *private* views about the situation may be in conflict.

Although consensus agreements are desirable, there are several problems with them. They are time consuming because they require the consent of all members, who are often not in agreement. Second, they often lead to compromise, in which parties identify a lowest common denominator acceptable to all. Compromise agreements are an extremely easy method of reaching agreement and are compelling because they appear to be fair, but they are usually inefficient because they fail to exploit potential pareto-improving trade-offs.

Communication Breakdowns

Most people take communication for granted in their interactions with multiple parties. In a perfect communication system, a sender transmits or sends a message that is accurately received by a recipient. There are at least three points of possible error: The sender may fail to send a message; the message may be sent, but is inaccurate or distorted; or, an accurate message is sent, but is distorted or not received by the recipient. In a multiparty environment, the complexity grows when several people are simultaneously sending and receiving messages.

Private Caucusing   When groups grow large, communication among all parties is difficult. One way of simplifying negotiations is for negotiators to communicate in smaller groups, thereby avoiding full-group communication. Group members often form private caucuses for strategic purposes. However, private caucusing may cause problems. Full-group communication is more time consuming but enhances equality of group members' outcomes, increases joint profitability, and minimizes perceptions of competition (Palmer and Thompson 1995). However, there is a caveat to the benefits of full communication. When the task structure requires group members to logroll in a reciprocal fashion (as opposed to a circular fashion), restricted communication leads to higher joint outcomes than full communication.

Biased Interpretation   People often hear what they want to hear when receiving messages, especially ambiguous ones. For example, when people are given neutral information about a product, they tend to interpret it in a way that is favorable toward their own position. Furthermore, they selectively pay attention to information in a report that favors their initial point of view and ignore or misinterpret information that contradicts their position.

Perspective-Taking Failures   People are remarkably poor at taking the perspective of others. For example, people who are privy to information and knowledge that they know others are not aware of nevertheless act as if others are aware of it, even though it would be impossible for the receiver to have this knowledge (Keysar 1998). This problem is known as the **curse of knowledge** (Camerer, Loewenstein, and Weber 1989). For example, in a simulation, traders who possessed privileged information that could have been used to their advantage behaved as if their trading partners also had access to the privileged information. Perspective-taking deficiencies also explain why some instructors who understand an idea perfectly are unable to teach students the same idea. They are unable to put themselves in their students' shoes to explain the idea in a way the students can understand.

Indirect Speech Acts   Each statement one person makes to another has an intended meaning that is couched in casual conversation. **Indirect speech acts** are the ways in which people ask others to do things—but in indirect ways. For example, consider the various ways of requesting that a person shut a door (see Table 9–2). Each

Table 9–2:	Different ways to make a request that require progressively more inferences and assumed common knowledge on the part of the receiver

1. Close the door.
2. Can you close the door?
3. Would you close the door?
4. It might help to close the door.
5. Would you mind awfully if I asked you to close the door?
6. Did you forget the door?
7. How about a little less breeze?
8. It's getting cold in here.
9. I really don't want the cats to get out of the house.

Sources: Adapted from Krauss, R. M. and Fussell, S. R. (1996). Social psychological models of interpersonal communication. In E. T. Higgins and A. W. Kruglanski (Eds.), *Social psychology: Handbook of basic principles* (pp. 655–701). New York: Guilford; Levinson, S. C. (1983). *Pragmatics* (p. 264). Cambridge, England: Cambridge University Press.

statement can serve as a request to perform that act although (except for "close the door") the sentence forms are not requests but assertions and questions. Thus, statements 2 through 9 are indirect speech acts; a listener's understanding of the intention behind a communicator's intention requires an extra cognitive step or two—and can often fail, especially in cases of stress.

Indirect speech acts are a function of the magnitude of the request being made (i.e., trivial requests, such as asking someone for the time of day, are easy to accommodate; asking someone if you can have a job is much more difficult to accommodate), the power the recipient has over the sender, and the social distance in the culture (Brown and Levinson 1987). Thus, as the magnitude of requests increases, the power distance increases, and as the social distance increases, requests made by negotiators will become more indirect. Of course, indirectness can be disastrous for effective communication.

Multiple Audience Problem   In some negotiation situations, negotiators need to communicate with another person in the presence of someone who should not understand the message. For example, consider a couple selling a house having a face-to-face discussion with a potential buyer. Ideally, the couple wants to communicate information to one another in a way that the spouse understands but the buyer does not—better yet, in such a way that the buyer is not even aware that a surreptitious communication is taking place. Fleming and Darley (1991) call this the **multiple audience problem.**

As it turns out, people are quite skilled at being able to communicate information to the intended recipient in a way that the other party is unaware of (Fleming and Darley 1991). People are able to "tune" their messages to specific audiences. For example, former president Ronald Reagan was gifted in his ability to send different messages to different audiences all within the same speech. Reagan's "evil empire" speech of March 8, 1983 to the National Association of Evangelicals (and, indirectly, the whole world) is a case in point. In the early sections of this speech, Reagan established identification with the evangelical audience through an ethos that exemplified their ideals, even using their technical vocabulary (e.g., "I believe in intercessionary prayer"). The section of his speech dealing with foreign policy was addressed to a complex array of audiences, foreign as well as domestic. The "evil empire" phrase had strong resonance not only with evangelicals, but with opponents of the Soviet Union everywhere, including elements within Poland and Czechoslovakia. For the benefit of his diplomatic audiences, however, Reagan carefully avoided specific references to evil actions of the Soviet Union, personally deleting from early drafts all references to chemical warfare in Afghanistan. And the speech's attack on the nuclear freeze movement of that time was balanced with a call for "an honest freeze," a term that created "presence" for his proposal for "extensive prior negotiations on the systems and numbers to be limited and on the measures to ensure effective verification and compliance" (Myers 1999, 65). To his audience in the international and diplomatic and arms control communities, including those within the Soviet Union, such praising alluded to extratextual facts that gave this part of the message a pragmatic connotation (Myers 1999).

KEY STRATEGIES

Given that multiparty negotiations are complex and present special challenges, what strategies and practices should negotiators put into place to enhance their ability to expand the pie and slice it in a multiparty context? Consider the following 10 strategies.

Manage the Information

People experience "information overload" when dealing with multiple parties and multiple issues. It is nearly impossible to keep track of the issues, alternatives, and preferences of each party without some kind of information management device. We strongly suggest that people form a grid or matrix that lists each party (along the rows) and each issue along the columns, and then keep track of each person's preferences for each issue. To the extent that this information can be publicly created and displayed, it can greatly enhance the ability of the group to find true win-win agreements.

Systematize Proposal Making

Our observations of multiparty negotiations suggest that negotiating groups severely mismanage their time. Groups tend to not make proposals and explore options and alternatives in a systematic fashion. This can lead to a major problem we label **tunnel vision,** which is the tendency for people in group negotiations to underestimate the number of feasible options available. For example, in one of our investigations, we asked people who had just completed a multiparty negotiation how many feasible agreements they thought were possible (the negotiation contained five issues and four to five alternatives within each issue). On average, people estimated that there were approximately four feasible outcomes for the group (the highest estimate was 12). In fact, there were 55! This illustrates the tunnel vision (and ensuing desperation) that can overtake a group if they fail to systematize their proposal making. We strongly encourage members to make several multi-issue proposals and to keep a record of which proposals have been considered.

Use Brainstorming Wisely!

We also encourage groups to use brainstorming wisely. Most groups suggest fewer and lower-quality ideas than do individuals thinking independently (Diehl and Stroebe 1987). We suggest instructing parties to group negotiation to engage in **brainwriting** prior to meeting face to face (Paulus 1998). Brainwriting, or solitary writing, is a strategy whereby group members independently write down ideas for resolving negotiations independently and then, later, when the group meets, they share those ideas.

Brainwriting capitalizes on the fact that individuals are better at generating ideas but groups are superior in terms of evaluating ideas.

Develop and Assign Process Roles

Multiparty negotiations need, at the very least, a time keeper, a process manager, and a recorder of information. We encourage groups to assign these roles to group members, then consider what additional process roles will be helpful prior to negotiating and assign these roles to other parties in the group. These roles can be rotated, so as not to give any particular member an advantage or disadvantage.

Stay at the Table

It is unwise for group members to break away from the table when all parties need to reach agreement (Palmer and Thompson 1995). When groups break away from the table, coalitions are more likely to form, which can be detrimental for the group as a whole (Mannix 1993).

Strive for Equal Participation

The problem of "uneven" participation, wherein one or two people do all the talking, is a big problem in group activities—negotiation being no exception. As the group grows larger, the "uneven participation" problem is more of an issue.

Allow for Some Points of Agreement, Even if Only on Process

Sometimes, group negotiations can get bogged down because it takes longer for parties to reach agreements—even on a single issue. Failure to reach agreement on negotiation issues can make group members feel that they are not making progress and that negotiations are stalemated. Further, it can create a combative atmosphere. A good strategy at this point is not to reach agreement just for the sake of reaching settlement, but instead, to agree on the process of reaching settlement. For example, a group member may suggest something like the following:

> I know that we have been working for over two hours and have not been able to agree on a single issue. We could take this as a sign of failure or ill will, but I do not think that would be wise. I suggest that we take 10 minutes as a group to list all of the settlements that we have considered and then independently rank them in terms of their favorability. This may give us some sense of where and how to look for possible agreements.

Avoid the "Equal Shares" Bias

There is often a tendency in group negotiations to divide things equally amongst the parties involved (see also chapter 3, on pie slicing). This is problematic for several reasons. First and foremost, as we have seen in chapter 3, there is no fair method of allocation. There are multiple criteria of fairness that all can be justified as "fair" in some sense, and none are necessarily superior to others. Second, there is a strong pressure in many groups to behave in an egalitarian fashion, but privately, people are not inclined to be egalitarian.

Avoid the Agreement Bias

We caution negotiators against the agreement bias, which we described in the previous chapter. Specifically, this occurs when negotiators focus on reaching common ground with the other party and are reluctant to accept differences of interest, even when this might create viable options for joint gain.

Another word of warning: In some negotiation situations, people are paid to break deals and stall agreement. That is, some parties at the table may not desire to reach settlement, but rather, have an incentive to forestall reaching settlement. For example, Crowne Plaza Hotel owner Steve Cohn went to incredible lengths to kill a deal that would bring a new Marriott Hotel to the Phoenix, Arizona, area. Cohn said that the Marriott hotel would kill his business and launched an attack to stop the negotiations. First he funded a petition drive to put the issue on the ballot. Council members, faced with the delay and uncertain outcome of a referendum vote, killed the Marriott deal. City officials quickly completed a second deal with an emergency clause, which prevented a public vote. In response, Cohn sued to block the hotels and then announced a petition drive for a ballot initiative requiring a public vote on the hotel deals. Cohn knows that Marriott will not wait the time needed to settle a lawsuit. Phoenix mayor Skip Rimsza said, "The delay continues to raise the cost and Cohn controls the delay" (Kossan 1999, B1).

Avoid Agendas

Groups often use agendas to organize the discussion of negotiation issues. This is true in complex discussions that involve several issues. By determining the order in which negotiation issues will be raised, discussed, and voted on, agendas are essential for efficient decision making. Agendas lead to less integrative agreements, however, than when issues are discussed simultaneously; they hinder the simultaneous discussion of issues (Mannix, Thompson, and Bazerman 1989; Thompson, Mannix, and Bazerman 1988).

COALITIONS

Coalitions face three sets of challenges: (1) the formation of the coalition, (2) coalition maintenance, and (3) the distribution of resources among coalition members. Next, we take up these challenges and provide strategies for maximizing coalition effectiveness.

KEY CHALLENGES OF COALITIONS

Optimal Coalition Size

What is the ideal size for a winning coalition? Ideally, coalitions should contain the minimum number of people sufficient to achieve a desired goal. Coalitions are difficult to maintain because members are tempted by other members to join other coalitions, and agreements are not enforceable (Mannix and Loewenstein 1993).

Trust and Temptation in Coalitions

Coalitional integrity is a function of the costs and rewards of coalitional membership; when coalitions are no longer rewarding, people will leave them. Nevertheless, there is a strong pull for members of coalitions to remain intact even when it is not rational to do so (Bottom, Eavey, and Miller 1996). According to the **status quo bias,** even when a new coalition structure that offers greater gain is possible, members are influenced by a norm of **coalitional integrity,** such that they stick with their current coalition (Bottom, Eavey, and Miller 1996). The implication is that negotiators should form coalitions early so as to not be left without coalitional partners.

Dividing the Pie

The distribution of resources among members of coalitions is complex because a normative method of fair allocation does not exist (Raiffa 1982). To illustrate this, consider

Table 9–3: Maximum funding caps as a function of parties in consortium

Organizations in Consortium	Cap for R&D Funding
Lindholm alone	0
Tepe alone	0
Clauson alone	0
Lindholm and Tepe	$220,000
Lindholm and Clauson	$190,000
Tepe and Clauson	$150,000
Lindholm, Tepe, and Clauson	$240,000

the following example. Lindholm, Tepe, and Clauson are three small firms producing specialized products, equipment, and research for the rehabilitation medicine community.[1] This area has become a critical, high-growth industry, and each firm is exploring ways to expand and improve its technologies through innovations in the research and development (R&D) divisions. Each firm has recently applied for R&D funding from the National Rehabilitation Medicine Research Council (NRMR).

The NRMR is a government agency dedicated to funding research in rehabilitation medicine and treatment. The NRMR is willing to provide funds for the proposed research, but because the firms' requests are so similar, they will fund only a **consortium** of two or three firms. The NRMR will not grant funding to Lindholm, Tepe, or Clauson alone.

The largest of the three firms is Lindholm, followed by Tepe, and then Clauson. The NRMR took a variety of factors into consideration when they caps on funding, as shown in Table 9–3.

The NRMR has strictly stipulated that for a consortium of firms to receive funding, the parties in the consortium (either two or three firms) must be in complete agreement concerning the allocation of resources among firms.

If you are Lindholm, what consortium would you consider to be the best for you? Obviously, you want to be in on some consortium, with either Tepe or Clauson or both, to avoid being left out in the cold. But what is the best division of resources within each of those consortiums? Suppose that you approach Tepe about a two-way venture, and Tepe proposes that she receive half of the $220,000 or $110,000 for herself. You argue that because you are bigger, and bring more synergy to the agreement, you should earn more. You demand $200,000 for yourself, leaving $20,000 for Tepe. At this point, Tepe threatens to leave you and approach Clauson. Tepe argues that she and Clauson can command $150,000 as a consortium without you, and each can receive $75,000. At this point, you argue that you can outbid her offer to Clauson with $80,000 and keep $110,000 for yourself. Just as Tepe is threatening to overbid you for Clauson, Clauson steps in and tells Tepe that she would want at least $100,000 of the $150,000 pie that she and Tepe could command. Tepe is frustrated, but relents.

You get nervous in your role as Lindholm. You certainly do not want to be left out. You could attempt to get Clauson or Tepe in a consortium. But, then, a thought occurs

---

[1]This example is based on the case *Federated Science Fund,* written by Elizabeth Mannix, available through the Dispute Resolution Research Center, Kellogg Graduate School of Management, Northwestern University; e-mail drrc@kellogg.nwu.edu.

to you: Maybe all three of you can be in a consortium. After all, all three firms command the greatest amount of funding ($240,000). But how should the $240,000 be divided between the three of you? You are the biggest firm, so you propose that you keep half of the $240,000 (or $120,000), that Tepe get $80,000, and that Clauson get $40,000. This strikes you as fair. At this point, Clauson gets upset and tells you that she and Tepe can go it alone and get $150,000. She thinks that your share is unfair and should be reduced to something less than $90,000. You then remind Clauson that you and Tepe can get $190,000 together, of which you certainly deserve at least half, which is better than the $90,000 offer. Then the three of you are at it again in a vicious circle of coalition formation and demolition.

The negotiation between Lindholm, Tepe, and Clauson illustrates the unstable nature of coalitions. In this example, the left-out party is always able to approach one of the two parties in the coalition and offer him or her a better deal, which can then be beaten by the remaining party, ad infinitum. Furthermore, splitting the pie three ways seems to offer no obvious solution. So, what should the three parties do? Is there a solution? Or are the parties destined to go around in circles forever?

Getting Out of the Vicious Circle   As a way out of the vicious circle, let's conceptualize the problem as a system of simultaneous equations to solve. Namely,

$$
\begin{aligned}
L + T &= \$220,000 \\
L + C &= \$190,000 \\
T + C &= \$150,000 \\
L + T + C &= \$240,000 \\
L + T + C &= (\$220,000 + \$190,000 + \$150,000)/2 \\
&= \$560,000/2 \\
&= \$280,000 \text{ total funds needed}
\end{aligned}
$$

However, it is impossible to solve all simultaneous equations. We are $40,000 short of satisfying each party's minimum needs. What should we do? Consider the following three solutions: the core solution, the Shapley solution, and a hybrid model (Raiffa 1982).

The core solution.   The core solution is a set of alternatives that are undominated (McKelvey and Ordeshook 1980). An alternative is in the core if no coalition has both the power and desire to overthrow it.

The first step in computing the core solution is to determine what would be each party's share if there were no shortage of funds. Thus, we solve for L, T, and C shares as follows:

$$
\begin{aligned}
(L + T) - (L + C) &= \$220,000 - \$190,000 \\
&= (T - C) = \$30,000 \\
(L + T) - (T + C) &= \$220,000 - \$150,000 \\
&= (L - C) = \$70,000 \\
(T + C) + (T - C) &= \$150,000 + \$30,000 \\
2T &= \$180,000 \\
T &= \$90,000 \\
L + T &= \$220,000 \\
L + \$90,000 &= \$220,000 \\
L &= \$220,000 - \$90,000
\end{aligned}
$$

$$L = \$130,000$$
$$L + C = \$190,000$$
$$\$130,000 + C = \$190,000$$
$$C = \$190,000 - \$130,000$$
$$C = \$60,000$$
check:
$$L = \$130,000$$
$$T = \$90,000$$
$$C = \$60,000$$
$$\text{Total} = \$280,000$$

Thus, if we had a total of $280,000, we could solve each equation. But, the harsh reality is that we do not. So, the second step is to get the total down to $240,000 by deducting $40,000 from somewhere. In the absence of any particular argument as to why one party's share should be cut, we deduct an equal amount, $13,333, from each party's share. In the final step, we compute the "core" shares as follows:

Lindholm:	$116,670
Tepe:	$76,670
Clauson:	$46,670

As Lindholm, you are delighted. Tepe agrees, but Clauson is not happy. She thinks that $46,670 is too little. She hires an outside consultant to evaluate the situation. The consultant proposes a different method, called the Shapley model.

The Shapley model. Consider a coalition formation in which one player starts out alone and then is joined by a second and third player. The Shapley model determines the overall payoff a player can expect on the basis of his or her **pivotal power,** or the ability to change a losing coalition into a winning coalition. The consultant considers all possible permutations of players joining coalitions one at a time. The marginal value added to each coalition's outcome is attributed to the pivotal player. The Shapley value is the mean of a player's added value (see Table 9–4). When all players bring equal resources, the Shapley value is the total amount of resources divided by the total number of people. This, of course, is the "equal division" principle, as well as the "equity principle."

When Clauson's consultant presents this report, Clauson is delighted—her share has increased by almost $20,000. Lindholm is nonplussed because her share has

Table 9—4: Analysis of pivotal power in Shapley model

Order of Joining	Lindholm Added Value	Tepe Added Value	Clauson Added Value
LTC	0	$220,000	$ 20,000
LCT	0	50,000	190,000
TLC	$220,000	0	20,000
TCL	90,000	0	150,000
CLT	190,000	50,000	0
CTL	90,000	150,000	0
Shapley (average)[2]	**98,333**	**78,333**	**63,333**

[2]These figures are rounded slightly.

decreased. Tepe is tired of all the bickering and proposes that they settle for something in between the two proposed solutions.

Raiffa's hybrid model.   We have presented two models to solve for shares in coalition situations. The medium-power player's share in both models is identical, but the high- and low-power player's shares fluctuate quite dramatically. It is possible that an egocentric argument could ensue between Lindholm and Clauson as to which model to employ. One solution is a hybrid model in which the mean of the Shapley and core values is computed (Raiffa 1982). This model yields the following shares:

Lindholm:	$107,500
Tepe:	$77,500
Clauson:	$55,000

Tips for Low-Power Players   We presented three different models of fair solutions. Each is compelling and defensible because each makes explicit the logic underlying the division of resources. It is easy to be a high-power player in coalition situations. However, the real trick is to know how to be an effective low-power player. Weakness can be power if you can recognize and disrupt unstable coalitions.

Power is intimately involved in the formation of coalitions and the allocation of resources among coalition members. Power imbalance among coalition members can be detrimental for the group. Compared to egalitarian power relationships, unbalanced power relationships produce more coalitions defecting from the larger group (Mannix 1993), fewer integrative agreements (Mannix 1993; McAlister, Bazerman, and Fader 1986), greater likelihood of bargaining impasse (Mannix 1993), and more competitive behavior (McClintock, Messick, Kuhlman, and Campos 1973). Power imbalance makes power issues salient to group members, whose primary concern is to protect their own interests. What is best for the coalition is often not what is best for the organization.

Is there an optimal way for multiple parties to allocate resources so that group members are not tempted to form coalitions that may hinder group welfare? Usually not. Whereas there are several defensible ways to allocate resources among coalition members, there is no single best way (for an extensive treatment, see Raiffa 1982).

STRATEGIES FOR MAXIMIZING COALITIONAL EFFECTIVENESS

Make Your Contacts Early

Because of the commitment process, people tend to feel obligated to others with whom they have made explicit or implicit agreements. For this reason, it is important to make contact with key parties early in the process of multiparty negotiation before they become psychologically committed to others.

Seek Verbal Commitments

One of the most effective strategies for enhancing coalitional effectiveness is to obtain verbal commitments from people with whom you want to develop trust and follow-through. Most people feel obligated to follow through with promises they make to others, even when verbal commitments are not legally binding in any sense (Cialdini 1993).

Allocate Resources among Coalitional Members Fairly

If one or more members of the coalition regard the proposed allocation of resources to be unfair, the coalition will be less stable and they will be likely to renege. To the extent to which coalitional members feel that the distribution of the coalition pie is fair, they are more likely to resist persuasion from others to break away from the coalition.

PRINCIPAL-AGENT RELATIONSHIP

An agent acts on the behalf of a principal party. An agent has a stake in the outcome (e.g., a real estate agent earns a commission on the sale of a house). In Figure 9-1, the Hollywood agent is an intermediary between Film Gate and ABC, and also between Tri-Color and ABC.

There are many advantages to using agents to represent one's interests. Agents provide substantive knowledge (e.g., a tax attorney), expertise in the negotiation process (e.g., a real estate agent), or special influence (e.g., a Washington lobbyist; Rubin and Sander 1988). Moreover, they provide emotional detachment (e.g., a divorce attorney) and tactical flexibility. However, there are costs to agency. Because they are usually compensated for their services, agents diminish the resources to be divided among the principals. Second, ineffective agents complicate the negotiation dynamic and thereby inhibit settlement. Most problematic, the agent's interests may be at odds with those of the principals (for an overview of principal-agent issues in economics, see Jensen and Meckling 1976).

For example, consider a typical home sale involving two principals and two agents. Is it wise for a home buyer to tell her agent her BATNA (how much she is willing to spend for a particular house)? Similarly, should a seller tell his agent the least amount of money he would accept for his home? Agents for home buyers desire higher selling prices because their fees are based on selling price. For this reason, it may not be in a buyer's interest to reveal his or her reservation price (i.e., the maximum he or she is willing to pay) to the agent. In fact, actual home sale prices point to a distinct disadvantage for parties with agents: Selling prices are lowest when the agent knows only the seller's reservation price and highest when the agent knows only the buyer's reservation price (Valley, White, Neale, and Bazerman 1992). Agents increase the likelihood of impasse (Bazerman, Neale, Valley, Zajac, and Kim 1992). Agents may be maximally effective only when their interests are aligned with those of the principal.

KEY CHALLENGES

Conflicting Incentives

Most agent-principal relationships have an incompatible incentive structure; the agent's interests are not perfectly aligned with those of the principal. Consider the conflict of interest that the Hollywood agent experiences by simultaneously representing two production companies in the negotiations with ABC. The longer-standing and more lucrative relationship with Tri-Color leads the agent to place the interests of that company ahead of the interests of Film Gate. Incentive compatibility is the only way to assure the agent serves your interests. For this reason, we warn principals to never reveal their BATNAs to their agents under any condition. Agents will routinely ask principals about their BATNA. Resist the urge to confide in your agent, no matter how nice of a person he or she seems to be. Your agent does not need to know your BATNA to effectively negotiate for you. It is unwise to trust someone to effectively represent your interests when their incentives are not aligned with yours. Ultimately, an agent's job is to broker a deal or to reach an agreement. Agents have an incentive to make transactions happen; for example, in home buying, a buyer's agent is really an employee of the selling company. The agent's preference is the higher price because he or she gets a commission. Furthermore, an agent may give biased information to get an agreement from their constituency.

Shrinking Bargaining Zone

Agents shrink the bargaining zone. Thus, adding agents into the picture means that more parties are dividing a fixed bargaining surplus. If the bargaining zone is small, this may mean that an impasse will occur. For an example of this, see Table 9–5.

Communication Distortion

Because it is often the agent doing the negotiating (rather than the principal), there is more opportunity for communication distortion to occur. There are infinite possibilities of how to send any one message. **Message tuning** refers to how senders tailor messages for specific recipients. People who send messages (e.g., "I have no fuel"; "I did not receive the attached file") will edit their messages in a way that they think best suits the recipient. For example, people give longer and more elaborate street directions and instructions to people whom they presume to be nonnatives or unfamiliar with a city (Krauss and Fussell 1991). Also, senders capitalize on the knowledge that they believe the recipient to already hold (e.g., "Turn right when you see that big tree that the city pruned last week"). For this reason, negotiators may send shorter, less complete messages to one another because they believe that they can capitalize on an existing shared knowledge base. However, negotiators often overestimate the commonality of information they share with others. Consequently, the messages they send become less clear (e.g., in the previous example, the other person may not know the location of the tree that was pruned by the city last week).

Message senders have a bias to present information that they believe will be favorably received by the recipient and will, therefore, distort messages (Higgins 1999). For example, when people present a message to an audience whom they believe is either for or against a particular topic, they err in the direction of adopting the audience's

---

Table 9–5: Buying a house: negotiation analysis

Consider the size of a bargaining zone for a house in which the seller's BATNA is $410,000, and the buyer's BATNA is $430,000, depending upon the size of the agents' commissions.

Commission	Seller RP* (adjusted from $410,000 1−c)	Bargaining Zone (Buyer RP [$430,000]− Seller RP)	Buyer Maximum Surplus	Seller Maximum Surplus	Agents' Surplus Range
0% (for sale by owner)	$410,000	20,000	$20,000	$20,000	$0
2%	$414,286	15,714	$15,714	$15,400	$4,286–$4,600
4%	$418,750	11,250	$11,250	$10,800	$8,750–$9,200
5%	$421,053	8,947	$8,947	$8,500	$11,503–$11,500
6%	$423,404	6,596	$6,596	$6,200	$13,404–$13,800

*Note: RP = Reservation Price.

point of view. It is as if they know that the messenger who brings unwelcome news is endangered—so one way of dealing with this is to modify the news. Unfortunately, message distortion can play havoc for effective teamwork.

Loss of Control

Because an agent is negotiating in your stead, you are giving up control over the process of negotiation and, ultimately, the outcome.

Agreement at Any Cost

Because agents have an incentive to reach agreement, they may fall prey to the "getting to yes" bias in which agreement becomes more important than the contents of the deal (Gibson, Thompson, and Bazerman 1994). Simply stated, the desire to reach agreement quickly and efficiently may lead agents to withhold information from principals that might impede a deal.

STRATEGIES FOR EFFECTIVELY WORKING WITH AGENTS

In working with an agent, it is to a negotiator's advantage to keep the following in mind:

Shop Around

Do not assume that the first agent you meet is uniquely qualified to represent you. Ask the agent what strategies and skills she has that will enable her to successfully represent your interests. Ask the agent about what she expects from you. Ask the agent about the nature of your relationship and what obligations, if any, you have to one another. For example, many real estate agents have easy-exit clauses that allow principals to remove agents without difficulty; in the absence of this clause, a principal might be committed to an agent for a lengthy period of time. For example, Darcy Bouzeous is one of the few women in the world who negotiates talent contracts for sports stars and media personalities. Says Bouzeous, "I'm not one of those people who represents somebody and then sees them three years later. I talk to my people often. As a matter of fact, I do not believe in having a retention agreement. If they do not like what I've done, I do not think they have to be stuck with me" (Bednarski 1990, 35). Ask your agent about her negotiation training and strategies. (For a list of questions to ask real-estate agents, see Table 9–6.)

Know Your BATNA before Meeting with Your Agent

Do your homework before meeting with your agent. Know your own BATNA. Prepare questions to ask your agent that will allow you to test the soundness of your BATNA,

Table 9–6:	Questions that potential home buyers should ask real-estate agents

1. Can you represent me as a buyer's agent?
2. How will you find me homes?
3. How can you leverage my down payment, interest rate, and monthly payment?
4. What different points will you be able to negotiate on my behalf?
5. How long have you been selling real estate—full time?
6. What can I expect in terms of communication?
7. Does your contract have an "easy exit" clause in it?
8. Will you cut your commission?

Source: Ron Holdridge, Re/Max Metro Realty, Seattle, Washington.

but do not give away your BATNA. For example, a home seller might say, "I would like to find out from you what average sales prices are for this type of home."

Communicate Your Interests to Your Agent without Giving Away Your BATNA

One of the most challenging tasks for a negotiator is to communicate her interests, priorities, and preferences, but not reveal her BATNA. You can help your agent to help you most effectively by listing, in order of priority, your key interests and what you perceive to be the alternatives within each of those areas of interest. Anticipate that your agent will, in so many words, ask you about your BATNA. When this question comes up (and it will!), focus the conversation onto your priorities (e.g., "I am not sure how helpful it is to tell you the most money I am willing to pay for the house you showed me today. However, I do want to emphasize that I am really interested in a home within this school district area, and a double garage. In fact, I would be willing to pay more for those features than a master suite and an updated kitchen").

Capitalize on the Agent's Expertise

Good agents will have a wealth of expertise in their particular area. Ask them about what they perceive to be their key strategies for targeting opportunities for you and closing deals.

Tap into Your Agent's Sources of Information

Agents, by virtue of their professional affiliations and networks, have access to a lot of information. However, you should not expect that passivity on your part will lead your agent to provide you with information. Rather, you need to ask your agent to provide key information for you. If your agent is unwilling or unable to do this, interview another agent and see whether he or she can provide the information.

Discuss Ratification

By nature of the principal-agent relationship, an agent's authority is limited with respect to making certain concessions or types of agreements (i.e., your agent cannot lower or increase your offer without explicit direction from you). Thus, agents may be able to resist making too many and too deep concessions that you might impulsively make in the heat of negotiation. In this sense, your agent provides a buffer zone between yourself and the other party.

Use Your Agent to Help Save Face

Sometimes, negotiators make what they regard to be perfectly reasonable proposals that have the effect of insulting the other party. When this happens (and if your opponent is an emotional type), negotiations may start on a losing course. In an agent-mediated negotiation, you can attempt to salvage damaged egos and relationships by blaming your agent.

Use Your Agent to Buffer Emotions

In keeping with this point about saving face, agents can be an effective emotional buffer between parties who may either dislike one another or are irrational types (see chapter 5 on bargaining styles). An effective agent will put a positive "spin" on the communications by each party and effectively "tune into" their principal's needs.

CONSTITUENT RELATIONSHIPS

When a negotiating party is embedded within an organization, several peripheral players may have an indirect stake in the outcome and influence the negotiation process. A **constituent** is ostensibly on the "same side" as a principal, but exerts an independent influence on the outcome through the principal. We distinguish three types of constituencies: superiors, who have authority over principals; subordinates, who are under the authority of principles; and constituencies, the party whom the principal represents—that is, for whom the principle is responsible and to whom the principal is accountable (collateral parties are represented by C in Fig. 9–2). In our example, Film Gate has a collateral relationship with its major shareholder, who acts in some ways as a superior

Collateral relationships refer to negotiations within organizations in which the negotiator is linked to other organizational actors, such as superiors, subordinates, or constituents. In our example, Film Gate is accountable to the major shareholder, who is ostensibly on their side, but has interests of his own. The shareholder's strong interest in short-term profitability leads Film Gate to weight the issue of financial compensation more heavily than it otherwise would in the negotiation.

Consider the organizational actor who is accountable to a constituency. There are two extremes of the organizational actor who represents a constituency: (1) the organizational puppet and (2) the organizational autocrat. The **organizational puppet** is elected to serve the interests of the larger constituency and negotiates on behalf of his or her constituents. The organizational puppet does not have decision control but depends upon approval of the constituency. The puppet's hands are tied. In contrast, the **organizational autocrat** has complete decision control. The negotiator does not seek the approval of his or her constituency before enacting an agreement. Negotiators should determine in advance whether or not their opponent has the power to ratify agreements. Is the opponent a puppet or an autocrat?

CHALLENGES FOR CONSTITUENT RELATIONSHIPS

Accountability

Negotiators at the bargaining table comprise the primary relationship in negotiation. The relationship that parties share with their constituents is the **second table** (Ancona, Friedman, and Kolb 1991). Constituents do not have to be physically present at the negotiation table for their presence to be strongly felt (Pruitt and Carnevale 1993; Tetlock 1985; Kramer, Pommerenke, and Newton 1993). Negotiators who are accountable to their constituents make higher demands and are less willing to compromise in negotiation than those not accountable to constituents (Ben-Yoav and Pruitt 1984; Carnevale, Pruitt, and Britton 1979; O'Connor 1994).

The second table has a paradoxical effect on the primary table: Representatives of constituents are not often given power to enact agreements; that is, the representative is not monolithic (Raiffa 1982). Whereas this would seem to reduce his or her power at the bargaining table, the opposite can be true. The negotiator whose "hands are tied" is often more effective than is the negotiator who has the power to ratify agreements. Anyone who has ever negotiated a deal on a new car has probably experienced the "my hands are tied" or "let me take it to the boss" ploy, in which the salesperson induces the customer to commit to a price that requires approval before a deal is finalized.

Accountability to collateral actors is an inevitable aspect of organizational life (Tetlock 1985, 1992). There are at least two motivational processes that are triggered by accountability: decision-making vigilance and evaluation apprehension.

Decision-Making Vigilance   Decision makers who are accountable for their actions consider relevant information and alternatives more carefully (Tetlock 1985, 1992). Accountability increases thoughtful, deliberate processing of information and decreases automatic, heuristic processing (see also Chaiken 1980; Fiske and Neuberg 1990). Accountability would seem to uniformly improve the quality of decisions made by negotiators and increase the likelihood of integrative agreements.

However, decision accountability may not always promote more thorough and unbiased processing of information if organizational actors are partisan to a particular view (Thompson 1995b). Imagine a situation in which an observer watches a videotape of people negotiating. Some observers are told to take an objective and impartial view of the situation; other observers are instructed to take the perspective of one of the parties. Further, some observers are told that they will be accountable for their actions and behaviors (e.g., they must justify their decisions to others who will question them), whereas others are not accountable. After watching the tape, observers indicate what they think each negotiator wanted. Accountable partisans fall prey to the fixed-pie assumption because they are motivated to reach a particular conclusion. However, nonpartisan observers are willing to reach whatever conclusion the data will allow, and their judgments are therefore driven by the evidence, not their desires.

Evaluation Apprehension and Face Saving   Negotiators who are accountable for their behaviors are concerned with how they are viewed by others. When people are concerned what others will think, they use face-saving strategies and make their actions appear more favorable to relevant others. Negotiators who want to save face will be more aggressive and uncompromising so that they will not be viewed as suckers or pushovers. Negotiators who are accountable to constituents are more likely to maintain a tough bargaining stance, make fewer concessions, and hold out for more favorable agreements compared to those who are not accountable (see Carnevale and Pruitt 1992). (For an interesting intervention in accountability and face saving, see Sidebar 9–1.)

SIDEBAR 9–1. WOMEN LEADERS FROM ISRAEL AND PALESTINE CONVENE FOR PEACE

Ten years ago, Sumaya Farhat-Naser lived in fear that her children would be gunned down on their way home from school in their Israeli-occupied neighborhood in the West Bank. Today, the Palestinian mother works alongside Israeli women for peace. Farhat-Naser was one of 100 delegates for "Women Waging Peace," a conference for women peacemakers held during December 1999. Women from conflict zones including Azerbaijan, Armenia, Columbia, Northern Ireland, Pakistan, South Africa and Sudan attended the conference to discuss how women could help end long-standing regional and religious conflicts perpetuated largely by men (Noonan 1999).

However, an interesting twist happens when teams are accountable for their actions at the bargaining table. A **diffusion of responsibility** occurs across members of the team (O'Connor 1997). Teams respond differently than solo negotiators to accountability pressure.

Conflicts of Interest

Negotiators often face a conflict between their goals and those of their constituency. For the manager interested in effective dispute resolution, it is not only important to understand the relationships negotiators share *across* the bargaining table, it is important to understand the hidden table of constituent relationships (see Kolb 1983). Consider a negotiation involving teams of two people who are either personally acquainted or strangers to one another. Each team reports to a manager. Some teams report to a "profit-oriented" manager who instructs the team to "serve the interests of the group at all costs." Some teams report to a "people-oriented" manager who instructs the team to maximize interests while maintaining harmonious intergroup relations. Teams who report to the "profit" supervisor claim a greater share of the resources than do teams who report to the "people" supervisor and teams not accountable to a manager (Peterson and Thompson 1997). When team members are acquainted, there are no differences in relative profitability. Why? Negotiators are better able to maximize profit when the goal is clear and they do not share a previous relationship.

STRATEGIES FOR IMPROVING CONSTITUENT RELATIONSHIPS

Understand Your Constituents

Representatives need to understand their constituents' real needs and interests, not just their positions. It make take awhile for constituents to express their real underlying needs, especially if face-saving concerns and pressure from the other side have moved them into staking out a position. In many cases, representatives act too early—before they understand their constituency's real needs—so as to demonstrate their competence. Representatives should not assume that constituents will immediately express their real interests.

Do Not Expect Homogeneity of Constituent Views

Constituencies are often composed of individuals and subgroups with different needs and interests. On some level, they realize that they can achieve more through collective action and representation, but be aware of heterogeneity of views within the constituency. For example, consider the negotiations between David Trimble and Gerry Adams of the Unionist and Republican parties in Ireland. Both leaders were personally anxious to make progress during March 1999; however, their freedom of movement was severely limited due to constituency pressures. Trimble leads a sharply divided union, which is structurally fragmented into several parties and often confused in its aims (McKittrick 1999).

Educate Your Constituents on Your Role and Your Limitations

Constituents, like other people, suffer from egocentric bias, meaning that they view the world from their own perspective in a self-serving fashion. From their point of view, they often see your role as one of educating the other side about the reality of the situation. They may often believe your task is easier than it really is. It is important to clearly define your role to your constituents early on in the process. This is an excellent time to set realistic expectations. It is important that you do not characterize yourself as an "evangelist" for their "crusade." Share with your constituents all possible outcomes, not just the favorable ones that they think will occur.

Help Your Constituents Do Horizon Thinking
Horizon thinking involves making projections about future outcomes. People have a difficult time thinking about future events (Gilbert and Wilson 2000), tend to under- or overestimate the duration of future emotional states (Gilbert, Pinel, Wilson, Blumberg, and Wheatley 1998), and fail to account for positive or negative circumstances that could arise (Loewenstein and Schkade 1999; Schkade and Kahneman 1998; Wilson, Wheatley, Meyers, Gilbert, and Axsom 1998). You can help your constituents develop a sound BATNA and realistic aspirations by helping them to engage in horizon thinking.

TEAM NEGOTIATION

Consider the following situations:

- a husband and wife negotiating with a salesperson on the price of a new car
- a group of disgruntled employees who approach management about wages and working conditions
- a large software company approaching a small software company concerning a joint venture.

In all of these examples, people join together on one side of the bargaining table as a team. Presumably, in each of these cases, one member could do all the negotiating for the team, but teams believe that they will be more effective if they are both at the bargaining table. Unlike solo negotiators, members of negotiating teams may play different roles for strategic reasons, such as "good cop-bad cop" (Brodt and Tuchinsky 2000). Are teams effective at exploiting integrative potential at the bargaining table? To answer the question of whether two heads are better than one, Thompson, Peterson, and Brodt (1996) compared three types of negotiation configurations—team vs. team, team vs. solo, and solo vs. solo negotiations. The presence of at least one team at the bargaining table dramatically increased the incidence of integrative agreement (see also Morgan and Tindale 2000). Why are teams so effective? Negotiators exchange much more information about their interests and priorities when at least one team is at the bargaining table than when two individuals negotiate (Thompson et al. 1996; Rand and Carnevale 1994; O'Connor 1994). Information exchange leads to greater judgment accuracy about parties' interests (Thompson et al. 1996; Rand and Carnevale 1994; O'Connor 1994), which promotes integrative agreement (Thompson 1991). The **team effect** is quite robust: It is not even necessary that members of teams privately caucus with one another to be effective (Thompson et al. 1996).

The presence of a team at the bargaining table increases the integrativeness of joint agreements (Rand and Carnevale 1994; O'Connor 1994), but what about the distributive component? Do teams outperform their solo counterparts? Not necessarily. Nevertheless, both teams and solo players *believe* that teams have an advantage—a **team efficacy effect** (O'Connor 1994; Rand and Carnevale 1994, Thompson et al. 1996). Even in situations in which teams reap greater shares of profit than their solo counterparts, solos are still better off negotiating with a team than with another solo player.

The solo negotiator earns less than the team, but the amount of jointly available resources is greater in the team-solo negotiation than in the solo-solo negotiation.

An intragroup analysis examines the benefits and shortcomings of teamwork. In the opening example, Film Gate is represented by a negotiating team of three individuals. Although these individuals must make decisions together, they each have disparate interests. What do we need to know to be effective team players?

CHALLENGES THAT FACE NEGOTIATING TEAMS

Picking your Teammates

We cannot tell you who to select for your negotiating team, but we can help you figure out what to look for. Consider the following three skills as criteria for choosing and evaluating teammates:

1. **Negotiation expertise:** People with good negotiation skills may be worth their weight in gold if, for example, they are able to devise an integrative solution to a complex conflict situation. A negotiation expert can streamline preparation, make sure that the team avoids the four major sins of negotiation, avoid destructive conflict strategies, and instigate a creative, problem-solving process.
2. **Technical expertise:** It helps to have someone with technical expertise in the domain of interest. For example, when house buying, it is wonderful to have someone who is skilled in architecture, plumbing, electricity, and so on. Furthermore, by tapping into technical expertise of our teammates, we can better prioritize our own interests.
3. **Interpersonal skills:** It often helps to have people with good interpersonal skills on a negotiating team, even if they are not specifically trained in negotiation. Negotiation involves many interpersonal skills, such as the ability to establish rapport, communicate effectively, and redirect a power- or rights-based argument to one focusing on interests (Ury, Brett, and Goldberg 1988).

How Many on the Team?

There is no magic number. Two or three heads can be better than one, but at some point, conformity pressures increase with group size, peaking at around five and then leveling off (Latané 1981). As teams grow in size, coordination problems increase.

Communication on the Team

Communication, or **information pooling,** is facilitated if members are acquaintances or share a relationship. For example, when the clues for solving a murder mystery game are distributed among group members, groups of friends are more likely to pool their diverse information than are groups of strangers (Gruenfeld, Mannix, Williams, and Neale 1996).

Team Cohesion

Cohesion is the strength of positive relations in a team (Evans and Dion 1991), the sum of pressures acting to keep individuals in a group (Back 1951), and the result of all forces acting on members to remain in a group (Festinger 1950). Cohesive groups perform better than less cohesive groups (Evans and Dion 1991). There are three sources of cohesion: (1) attraction to the group or resistance to leaving the group; (2) morale and motivation; and (3) coordination of efforts.

There are different kinds of bonds that keep teams together. **Common-identity groups** are composed of members who are attracted to the group; the individual members may come and go. For example, Joe is a member of a gay students' organization. He has several friends in the group, but the basis of his attraction to the group is its mission and purpose. **Common-bond groups** are composed of members who are attracted to particular members in the group (Prentice, Miller, and Lightdale 1994). Anne belongs to a bowling league. She has known some of the other players for over 20 years. If they were to move away, Anne would want to move as well since the basis of her attraction is the particular people in the group.

Information Processing

Often organizational members negotiate as a team or a group because no single person has the requisite knowledge and expertise required to negotiate effectively. Thus, knowledge is distributed among team members. How effective are teams at utilizing knowledge that is distributed among members?

The issue of how teams decide who is responsible for storing and retaining information is crucial to the effectiveness of the team. There are trade-offs involved in the storage of information. It is more efficient for each team member to be responsible for a particular piece of information so that each member is not overwhelmed by too much data. However, as the redundancy of storage is minimized, so are the chances of successfully retrieving the desired information. Furthermore, groups are less likely to consider and discuss information that is shared only by a subset of its members. They suffer from the **common information bias** (Stasser 1992; Gigone and Hastie 1993).

It cannot and should not be assumed that members of a group are privy to the same facts and information. People rely on others for information. In fact, members of product development teams rely on informal social exchanges more than technical reports for information. Teams of individuals can be more efficient by dividing the labor. However, distributed cognition is risky because if a team loses one of its members, information may be lost to the entire group. Thus, groups face a dilemma: divide responsibility, which increases their dependence upon each individual member; or share information, which is clumsy and redundant.

STRATEGIES FOR IMPROVING TEAM NEGOTIATIONS

Prepare Together

Preparing for a negotiation as a team is much more effective than if all members prepare separately. Preparing together creates a transactive memory system, in which group members understand the information that others have and how and when to access it. For example, in one investigation, groups were given instructions on how to assemble a transistor radio. Some groups trained together; in other groups, individuals trained individually (or with a different group). When it came to actual performance, groups who had trained together outperformed those who had trained individually or with different groups (Moreland, Argote, and Krishnan 1996).

Plan Scheduled Breaks

Make sure that you schedule breaks into your negotiation, so as to allow team members to meet privately. However, a word of caution: Many teams spend too much time in private caucus and not enough time at the table. This is ultimately not effective for negotiation.

Role-Play with Each Other

An effective preparation strategy is for teams to practice role-playing with one another. This can help team members develop a shared strategy and test the adequacy of their approach.

Assess Accountability

It is important to assess the extent to which team members are accountable to others outside of the team. For example, when teams are accountable to a supervisor, they are more effective than when they negotiate strictly on their own behalf (Peterson and Thompson 1997).

INTERGROUP NEGOTIATION

Individuals who represent different social groups often negotiate with members of other groups (see Deutsch 1973; Sherif 1936; Klar, Bar-Tal, and Kruglanski 1988). For example, members of a student council and university administrators, union and management negotiators, and groups of students from rival universities are all examples of intergroup negotiators.

CHALLENGES OF INTERGROUP NEGOTIATIONS

Stereotyping

In **intergroup negotiations,** parties identify with their organization and often hold negative impressions about members of the other organizations (Kramer 1991; for reviews, see Stroebe, Kruglanski, Bar-Tal, and Hewstone 1988; Worchel and Austin 1986). For example, Tri-Color is considered by Film Gate to be rather traditional, whereas actors within Tri-Color consider their company to be pragmatic and reliable. Meanwhile, Film Gate is considered by Tri-Color to be quixotic and naïve about the industry; actors within Film Gate consider the company to be daring and innovative. These disparate and possibly exaggerated perceptions influence both companies' willingness to collaborate.

Changing Identities

People identify with many different social groups (Kramer 1991). For example, a student might consider a relevant group to be the other students in his or her study group, the class as a whole, marketing majors in general, or the entire student body. At any given time, one group might be more or less salient to the student: At a football game, students might identify most strongly with the entire student body; in a dining hall, students might identify most strongly with a particular dorm or floor.

Imagine that you are in an organization in which marketing and finance are distinct subgroups located on different floors of a building. Contrast that to a situation in which marketing and finance are not separate functional units, but instead, part of the same product team. What happens in the case in which a marketing manager negotiates with a financial manager? Negotiations among individuals representing different social groups are less mutually beneficial than negotiations among individuals who perceive themselves as belonging to a larger social organization—one that encompasses all those present at the bargaining table (Kramer 1991). When people define their social identity at the level of the organization, they are more likely to make more organizationally beneficial choices than when social identity is defined at an individual or subgroup level. For example, when group members are instructed to consider features they have in common with another group, behavior toward out-groups is much more generous than when they consider features that are distinct (Kramer and Brewer 1984).

In-Group Bias

Group distinctions and social boundaries may be created on the basis of completely arbitrary distinctions (Tajfel 1970). For example, Thompson (1993) divided participants into two groups on the basis of an arbitrary procedure (random draws from a box). Then, individuals negotiated with either a member of their "own group" or the "other group." Even though the information concerning the negotiation situation was identical in both respects, negotiations with members of out-groups were anticipated to be more contentious than negotiations with members of in-groups; further, the mere anticipation of negotiation with an out-group member led to increased **in-group bias,** or positive evaluations of one's own group relative to the out-group.

When we anticipate negotiations with out-group members, we are more likely to engage in **downward social comparison** (Wills 1981). We evaluate the competitor to be less attractive on a number of organizationally relevant dimensions (such as intelligence, competence, and trustworthiness) than members of our group. However, after successful negotiation with out-groups, intergroup relations improve, and downward social comparison virtually disappears (Thompson 1993). Negotiation with out-group members is threatening to organizational actors, but to the extent that integrative agreements are feasible, negotiation has remarkable potential for improving intergroup relations. Although our initial expectations may be quite pessimistic, interactions with members of opposing groups often have a beneficial impact on intergroup relations if several key conditions are met, such as mutual dependence goal attainment (see Aronson and Bridgeman 1979).

People of high status, those of low status who have few alternatives, and members of groups who have an opportunity to improve their group are most likely to identify with their group. Members of groups with lower perceived status display more in-group bias than members of groups with higher perceived status (Ellemers, Van Rijswijk, Roefs, and Simons 1997). However, high-status group members show more in-group bias on group status-related dimensions, whereas low-status group members consider the in-group superior on alternative dimensions (Ellemers and Van Rijswijk 1997).

Extremism

Groups in conflict often misperceive each other's beliefs. Parties in conflict do not have an accurate understanding of the views of the other party and exaggerate the position of the other side in a way that promotes the perception of conflict (Ross and Ward 1996; Robinson, Keltner, Ward, and Ross 1994). Each side views the other as holding more extreme and opposing views than is really the case. Consider the 1986 Howard Beach incident, involving the death of a young African-American man who was struck by a passing car as he attempted to escape from a group of white pursuers in the Howard Beach neighborhood of New York City. This ultimately led to the trial and conviction of some (but not all) of the young man's pursuers. Many details of the case were ambiguous and controversial, leading each party to take exaggerated perceptions of the views of the other parties, thereby exacerbating the perception of differences in opinion.

Why is this? According to the **naïve realism** principle (Ross and Ward 1996), people expect others to hold views of the world similar to their own. When conflict erupts, people are initially inclined to sway the other party with evidence. When this fails to bridge interests, people regard dissenters as extremists who are out of touch with reality.

STRATEGIES FOR OPTIMIZING INTERGROUP NEGOTIATIONS

Separate Conflict of Interest from Symbolic Conflict

Conflict between groups does not always arise from competition over scarce resources. Many conflicts between groups do not have their roots in resource scarcity, but rather, in fundamental differences in values (Bobo 1983). Consider for example, the strong protests made against busing by people whose lives are not affected by it (Sears and Allen 1984). Presumably, people who do not have children or grandchildren are not affected by busing. However, they tend to have strong feelings about it. Busing does not represent an economic issue to them, but rather, a symbolic issue. It is important to understand which issues are symbolic and which are economic.

Search for Common Identity

To the extent groups in conflict can share a common identity, conflict and competition can decrease dramatically (Kramer and Brewer 1986). Kramer notes that people in organizations can identify at different levels within their organization (e.g., person, group, department, unit, organization as a whole, etc.). For example, in one investigation, groups were told to focus on their group identities. Other groups who were involved in an objectively identical conflict were told to focus on the collective organization. Cooperation was greatly increased when groups focused on the collective, rather than their group identities.

Avoid the Out-Group Homogeneity Bias

Suppose that three white managers watch a videotape of a discussion among members of a mixed-race group, composed of three African-American men and three Caucasian men. After watching the videotape, the managers are presented with the actual text of the conversation and asked to indicate who said what. They are very good at remembering whether an African-American or Caucasian person made a particular comment, but their accuracy in terms of differentiating which African-American male said what is abysmal (Linville, Fischer, and Salovey 1989). Thus, within-race (or within-group) errors are more prevalent than between-race errors, because people categorize members of outgroups not as individuals, but simply as "black Americans." Thus, it is important for people to treat members of outgroups as individuals.

Contact

The "mere contact" strategy is based on the principle that greater contact among members of diverse groups increases cooperation among group members. Unfortunately, contact in and of itself does not lead to better intergroup relations, and in some cases may even exacerbate negative relations among groups. For example, contact between African Americans and Caucasians in desegregated schools does not reduce racial prejudice (Gerard 1983; Schofield 1986); there is little relationship between interdepartmental contact and conflict in organizations (Brown, Condor, Mathew, Wade, and

Williams 1986); and college students studying in foreign countries become increasingly negative toward their host countries the longer they remain in them (Stroebe, Lenkert, and Jonas 1988).

Several conditions need to be in place before contact can have its desired effects of reducing prejudice.

- **Social and institutional support:** For contact to work, there should be a framework of social and institutional support. That is, people in positions of authority should be unambiguous in their endorsement of the goals of the integration policies. This fosters the development of a new social climate in which more tolerant norms can emerge.

- **Acquaintance potential:** A second condition for successful contact is that it be of sufficient frequency, duration, and closeness to permit the development of meaningful relationships between members of the groups concerned. Infrequent, short, and casual interaction will do little to foster more favorable attitudes and may even make them worse (Brewer and Brown 1998). This type of close interaction will lead to the discovery of similarities and disconfirm negative stereotypes.

- **Equal status:** The third condition necessary for contact to be successful is that participants have equal status. Many stereotypes of out-groups comprise beliefs about the inferior ability of out-group members to perform various tasks. If the contact situation involves an unequal-status relationship between men and women, for example, with women in the subordinate role (e.g., taking notes, acting as secretaries), stereotypes are likely to be reinforced rather than weakened (Bradford and Cohen 1984). If, however, the group members work on equal footing, prejudiced beliefs become hard to sustain in the face of repeated experience of task competence by the out-group member.

- **Shared goal:** When members of different groups depend on each other for the achievement of a jointly desired objective, they have instrumental reasons to develop better relationships. The importance of an overriding, clear, shared group goal is a key determinant of intergroup relations. Sometimes a common enemy is a catalyst for bonding among diverse people and groups. For example, by "waging a war against cancer," members of different medical groups and laboratories can work together.

- **Cross-group friendships:** Sometimes it is not necessary for groups to have real contact with one another to improve intergroup relations. If group members know that another member of their own group has a friendship or relationship with a member of the out-group, or a cross-group friendship, in-group members have less negative attitudes toward the out-group (Wright, Aron, McLaughlin-Volpe, and Ropp 1997). It is not necessary that all members of a group have cross-group friendships; merely knowing that one member of the group does can go a long way toward reducing negative out-group attitudes.

Many of these strategies are preventative in their approach warding off unhealthy, destructive, type A competition between groups. What steps can a manager take to deal with conflict after it has erupted?

The GRIT Strategy

The **GRIT model,** or **G**raduated and **R**eciprocal **I**nitiative in **T**ension Reduction, is a model of conflict reduction for warring groups. Originally developed as a program for international disarmament negotiations, it can be used to deescalate intergroup problems on a smaller, domestic scale as well (Osgood 1979). The goals of this strategy are to increase communication and reciprocity between groups while reducing mistrust, thereby allowing for deescalation of hostility and creation of a greater array of possible outcomes. The model prescribes a series of steps that call for specific communication between groups in the hope of establishing the "rules of the game." Other stages are designed to increase trust between the two groups as the consistency in each group's responses demonstrates credibility and honesty. Some steps are necessary only in extremely intense conflict situations in which the breakdown of intergroup relations implies a danger for the group members.

Mikhail Gorbachev's decisions in the period from 1986 to 1989 closely resemble the GRIT model (Barron, Kerr, and Miller 1992). Gorbachev made a number of unilateral concessions that resulted in serious deescalation of world tensions in this period. On two occasions, the Soviets stalled resumption of atmospheric nuclear testing despite their inability to extend the prior treaty with the Reagan administration. They then agreed twice to summit meetings despite the Reagan administration's refusal to discuss the Star Wars defense system. They then agreed to the Intermediate and Strategic Range Nuclear Missile (INF) Treaty (exceeding the United States' requests for verification) with continued refusal by the United States to bargain about Star Wars. Next came agreements on the Berlin Wall and the unification of Germany. Eventually, even the staunchly anti-Communist/anti-Soviet Reagan-Bush regime had to take notice. This led to a period of mellowing tensions between these two superpowers (see Table 9–7).

Although the GRIT model may seem overly elaborate and therefore inapplicable to most organizational conflicts, the model clarifies the difficulties inherent in establishing mutual trust between parties that have been involved in prolonged conflict. Although some of the stages are not applicable to all conflicts, the importance of clearly announcing intentions, making promised concessions, and matching reciprocation are relevant to all but the most transitory conflicts.

Table 9–7:   GRIT strategy

1. Announce your general intentions to deescalate tensions and your specific intention to make an initial concession.
2. Execute the initial concession unilaterally, completely, and, of course, publicly. Provide as much verification as possible.
3. Invite reciprocity from the out-group. Expect the out-group to react to these steps with mistrust and skepticism. To overcome this, continued concessions should be made.
4. Match any reciprocal concessions made by the out-group and invite more.
5. Diversify the nature of your concessions.
6. Maintain your ability to retaliate if the out-group escalates tension. Any such retaliation should be carefully calibrated to match the intensity of the out-group's transgression.

Source: Barron, R. S., Kerr, N. L., and Miller, N. (1992). *Group process, group decision, group action* (p. 151). Pacific Grove, CA: Brooks/Cole.

CONCLUSION

Multiparty negotiations require all of the pie-slicing and pie-expanding skills of two-party negotiations, and then some. We have seen that the key challenges of multiparty negotiations are the development and management of coalitions, the complexity of information management, voting rules, and communication breakdowns. We discussed several different levels of analysis involved in multiparty negotiations and key strategies to finesse each situation, including coalition management, principal-agent relationships, team negotiation, intergroup negotiation, and dealing with constituencies. Having explored a few features of the Film Gate negotiation at each level of analysis, it is clear that all levels are necessary to fully understand and capitalize on the dynamics of multiparty negotiations. For example, had we restricted our analysis merely to the level of the interaction between the principles, we would have failed to detect the conflict of interests of the Hollywood agent and would have failed to appreciate the role of group polarization and outgroup stereotyping in Film Gate's reluctance to work with Tri-Color. Table 9–8 summarizes the six levels of analysis, the key challenges facing the negotiator at each level, and the best strategies to surmount these challenges.

Table 9–8: Summary of challenges and strategies for each level of multiparty analysis

Level of Analysis	Challenges	Strategies
Multiparty negotiation	Coalition formation Difficulty formulating trade-offs Voting paradoxes • Strategic voting Majority rule suppresses strength of preference Communication breakdowns • Private caucusing • Biased interpretation • Perspective taking failures • Indirect speech acts • Multiple audience problem	Information management Systematize proposal making Use brainstorming wisely Develop and assign process roles Stay at the table Strive for equal participation Avoid the "equal shares" bias Avoid the "agreement bias" Avoid agendas
Coalitions	Optimal coalition size? Trust and temptation Dividing the pie	Core solution Shapley model Raiffa's (1982) hybrid model Make contacts early Seek verbal commitments Allocate resources fairly
Principal-agent relationships	Conflicting incentives Shrinking bargaining zone Communication distortion Loss of control Agreement at any cost	Shop around Know your BATNA before meeting your agent Communicate interests, but do not reveal your BATNA Capitalize on agent's expertise Tap into agent's sources of information Discuss ratification Use agent for saving face Use agent to buffer emotions
Principal-constituency relationships	Accountability • Evaluation apprehension • Face saving Conflict of interest	Understand constituents' interest Do not expect homogeneity within constituencies Educate constituents on your role and limitations Help constituents do horizon thinking
Team negotiation	Choosing team mates How many on the team? Communication within the team Team cohesion Information processing	Prepare as a team (not separately) Plan scheduled breaks (to regroup) Role-play with each other Determine accountability
Intergroup negotiation	Stereotyping Changing identities In-group bias Extremism	Separate conflict of interest from symbolic conflict Search for common identity Avoid outgroup homogeneity bias Contact GRIT strategy

10

CROSS-CULTURAL
NEGOTIATION

Jayant J., representing an Indian software company, waited impatiently for a local manufacturer in Sao Paulo, Brazil to clinch a business deal. After waiting almost one-and-a-half hours, it took all his effort to welcome the relaxed Brazilian, who barged into the lounge without even an apology and started the conversation with a joke. The Brazilian's habit of communicating by standing very close and touching Jayant frequently made Jayant, a stickler for etiquette, very uncomfortable and irritated. At the close of the deal, the Brazilian's reply for a firm commitment, "si Deus quizer" ("if God wishes"), was the final straw for Jayant, who thought the Brazilian was being vague. The meeting was a failure and they never met again. (Mishra and Sinha 1999).

A Japanese manager wanted to study a multimillion-dollar business proposal before he gave his American counterpart an answer. "Give me five minutes," he said. The American smiled back and waited. A few seconds later, the American's mouth twitched. Then he fidgeted a bit more. A whole 18 seconds later, the American interrupted the silence, startling the Japanese businessman, who was much more accustomed to the silence. (Iwata 1995).

Negotiations across cultures are commonplace and, in many cases, a requirement for effective management in multinational and international companies. As the opening examples indicate, they do not always go smoothly. Most managers cannot expect to negotiate only with people of their own country or culture throughout their career. In fact, North Americans are a minority—about 7 percent of the world's population. To get a better sense of the world's composition, imagine that there are only 100 people in the world. If this were the case, there would be 55 Asians, 21 Europeans, 9 Africans, 8 South Americans, and 7 North Americans (Triandis 1994).

As the opening example illustrates, cross-cultural negotiations are anything but easy. Even under near-ideal circumstances, negotiators from the same culture leave money on the table. When people from *different* cultures get together to negotiate, they may leave even more money on the table (Brett in press). Failure to expand the pie has a number of undesirable ripple effects, including (but not limited to) parties feeling exploited in the negotiation, the souring of a potentially rewarding relationship, and the destruction of potential global relationships.

Often, value is left on the table because people are not prepared for the challenges of cross-cultural negotiation. This chapter provides a business plan for effective cross-cultural negotiation. We begin by defining culture; then, we identify the key dimensions by which culture affects judgment, motivation, and behavior at the bargaining table. Next, we identify the biggest barriers to effective intercultural negotiation and provide strategies for effective cross-cultural negotiation.

AN APPROACH TO LEARNING ABOUT CULTURES

We need to make one thing perfectly clear up front: This chapter does not provide a list of how to negotiate with people of different cultures. Thus, we do not offer different advice on a country-by-country basis. We do not do this for two reasons. First, it would be contrary to the book's focus, which is to provide generalizable negotiation skills that work across contexts. In addition, we do not want to promote cultural stereotypes. By making a generic list of characteristics for cultures, we magnify the stereotypes, which is neither practical nor informative. Most people prefer to be considered as unique individuals, yet we are often too quick to lump people from different countries together as being "all the same."

A more useful approach is to develop a framework for thinking about culture. There are several advantages to doing this. First, there is a great deal of diversity among people in any culture. A cultural framework is sensitive to heterogeneity within cultural groups. Second, most cultures are different today than they were 10 years ago—stereotypes in place today will be outdated tomorrow. We need a dynamic framework that allows us to learn how cultures change and grow. This chapter provides a means by which to expose our own cultural beliefs and those of others, how to avoid mistakes, and how to profit from intercultural negotiations.

DEFINING CULTURE

Many people conceive of culture strictly in terms of geography; however, culture does not just pertain to nations and countries. Rather, culture is the unique character of a social group; the values and norms shared by its members set it apart from other social groups (Lytle, Brett, and Shapiro 1999). Culture concerns economic, social, political, and religious institutions. It also concerns the unique products produced by these groups—art, architecture, music, theatre, and literature (Brett, in press). Cultural institutions preserve and promote a culture's ideologies. Culture influences mental models of how things work, behavior, and cause-and-effect relationships. To broaden our thinking about culture, consider that there are possible cultural differences contained in all of the following:

- families
- social groups and departments in an organization
- organizations
- industries
- states
- regions
- countries
- societies (e.g., foraging, horticultural, pastoral, agrarian, industrial, service, information)

- continents
- hemispheres

Nations, occupational groups, social classes, genders, races, tribes, corporations, clubs, and social movements may become the bases of specific subcultures. When thinking about culture and diversity, avoid the temptation to think of it as a single dimension (e.g., country of origin); culture is a complex whole, and it is best to use as many criteria to discern one culture from another.

CULTURE AS AN ICEBERG

We use Schneider's (1997) model of culture as an iceberg (see also Brett, in press, for extensive treatment). Typically, about one-ninth of an iceberg is visible; the rest is submerged. As Figure 10–1 indicates, the top (visible) part of the cultural iceberg is the behaviors, artifacts, and institutions that characterize a culture. This includes things such as traditions, customs, habits, and the like. These obvious behaviors and artifacts are an expression of deeper-held values, beliefs, and norms. Driving these values and norms are fundamental assumptions about the world and humanity, at the cultural iceberg's "base." The artifacts and customs that characterize a culture are not arbitrary; rather, they are manifestations about fundamental values and beliefs about the world. Thus, to change such expressions and customs would be to challenge centuries-old beliefs and values.

CULTURAL VALUES AND NEGOTIATION NORMS

Cultures can differ in many dramatic ways. Next, we identify three dimensions of culture, following Brett (in press; see Table 10–1):

- individualism vs. collectivism
- egalitarianism vs. hierarchy
- direct vs. indirect communication

FIGURE 10–1 Culture as an Iceberg

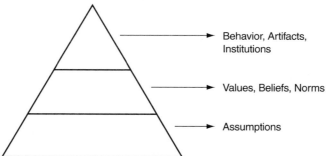

Source: Schneider, S. C. (1997). *Managing across cultures.* Upper Saddle River, NJ: Prentice Hall.

Table 10–1: Dimensions of culture

Cultural Dimension

Goal: **Individual versus collective orientation**	*Individualists/Competitors:* Key goal is to maximize own gain (and perhaps the difference between oneself and others); source of identity is the self; people regard themselves as free agents and independent actors.	*Collectivists/Cooperators:* Key goal is to maximize the welfare of the group or collective; source of identity is the group; individuals regard themselves as group members; focus is on social interaction.
Influence: **Egalitarianism versus hierarchy**	*Egalitarians:* Do not perceive many social obligations; often regard BATNA to be major source of bargaining power.	*Hierarchists:* Regard social order to be important in determining conflict management strategies; subordinates are expected to defer to superiors; superiors are expected to look out for subordinates.
Communication: **Direct versus indirect**	*Direct Communicators:* Engage in explicit, direct information exchange; ask direct questions; are not affected by situational constraints; face-saving issues likely to arise.	*Indirect Communicators:* Engage in tacit information exchange such as storytelling, inferencemaking; situational norms.

Source: Brett, J. M. (in press). *Negotiating globally: How to negotiate deals, resolve disputes, and make decisions across cultural boundaries.* Manuscript in preparation. San Francisco, CA: Jossey-Bass.

These three dimensions refer to motivation, influence, and information, respectively (Brett in press). Specifically, as we will discuss, *individualism-collectivism* refers to the basic human motive concerning preservation of the self versus the collective. The dimension of *egalitarianism-hierarchy* refers to the means by which people influence others, either laterally or hierarchically. Finally, *direct-indirect communication* refers to the manner in which people exchange information and messages.

INDIVIDUALISM VERSUS COLLECTIVISM

A key way in which many cultures differ is in terms of individualism and collectivism (Triandis 1994; Hofstede 1980; Schwartz 1994). Next, we will describe individualistic and collectivist cultural values and then identify negotiation strategy issues.

Individualism

In chapter 5 on bargaining style, we outlined three motivational orientations: individualistic, competitive, and cooperative. Individualism, as a cultural style, epitomizes the individualistic motivational orientation.[1] In individualistic cultures, the pursuit of happiness and regard for personal welfare are paramount. People in individualistic cultures give

---

[1] For simplicity, we include competitive style with individual style.

priority to their personal goals, even when these goals conflict with those of their family, work group, or country. Individual happiness and expression are valued more than collective and group needs. Consequently, individual accomplishments are rewarded by economic and social institutions. Furthermore, legal institutions in individualist cultures are designed to protect individual rights. One implication of individualism concerns the use of distributive tactics. People who are more self-interested are motivated to use more tactics that increase their bargaining power. Indeed, U.S. MBA students are more tolerant of certain kinds of ethically questionable tactics than are non-U.S. MBA students (Lewicki and Robinson 1998). Specifically, U.S. MBA students are more accepting of competitive bargaining tactics and bluffing, which raises the possibility that U.S. negotiators may be perceived as less ethical by their international counterparts (see Lewicki and Robinson 1998). On the other hand, U.S. negotiators are significantly less accepting of misrepresentation to an opponent's network. The norm in the United States of not spreading stories, particularly to the network of friends, is well entrenched.

Collectivism

Collectivist cultures are rooted in social groups, and individuals are viewed as members of groups. People in collectivist cultures give priority to in-group goals. The dominant motive is concern for, and belonging to, the group. People of collectivist cultures view their workgroups and organizations as fundamental parts of themselves. Collectivists are concerned about how the results of their actions affect members of their in-group; they share resources with in-group members, feel interdependent with in-group members, and feel involved in the lives of in-group members (Hui and Triandis 1986; Billings 1989). Not surprisingly, collectivist cultures are more concerned with maintaining harmony in interpersonal relationships with the in-group than are individualistic cultures. For example, collectivists prefer to negotiate rather than go to court (Leung 1988). Social norms and institutions promote the interdependence of individuals through emphasis on social obligations, and the sacrifice of personal needs for the greater good. Legal institutions place the greater good of the collective above the rights of the individual, and political and economic institutions reward classes of people as opposed to individuals (Brett in press). Whereas individualists want to save face and are concerned with their personal outcomes, collectivists are concerned with others' outcomes as well. The tendency of North Americans to engage in self-enhancement, an individualistic trait, is more than skin-deep. In one investigation of Canadians (individualists) and Japanese (collectivists), behaviors were covertly measured (Heine, Takata, and Lehman 2000). Canadians were reluctant to conclude that they had performed worse than their average classmate (self-enhancement); in contrast, Japanese were hesitant to conclude that they had performed better—in short, they self-criticized.

Implications for Negotiation

There are a variety of implications for the conduct of negotiation regarding individualism-collectivism. We will outline seven of them:

- social networks
- cooperation
- in-group favoritism
- social loafing versus social striving
- endowment
- dispositionalism versus situationalism
- preferences for dispute resolution

Table 10–2: Dominant norms of business relations

Culture	Dominant Attitude	Business Relationships
North American: *Market norms*	Economic individualism	Short-lived Low-multiplexity
Chinese: *Familial norms*	Filial loyalty Economic collectivism	Directed upward to powerful
German: *Legal-bureaucratic norms*	Economic collectivism	Bounded by formal rules Low affectivity
Spanish: *Affiliative norms*	Self-expressive collectivism	Long-lived High affectivity

Source: Morris, M. W., Podolny, J. M., and Ariel, S. (1999). *Missing relations: Incorporating relational constructs into models of culture.* Paper presented at 1998 SESP conference, Lexington, Kentucky.

Social Networks   Cultures differ dramatically in terms of their social networks (Morris, Podolny, and Ariel 1999). Specifically, members of different cultures differ in terms of the density of their work friendships (i.e., how many friendships they share at work), the overlap of instrumental and socioemotional ties (i.e., whether the people they seek out for information are also the ones whom they seek out for comfort and emotional support), the closeness of the tie, the longevity of the tie, and whether the network relationships are upward, lateral, or downward-directed. In one study, U.S. and Hong Kong students negotiated with someone whom they believed to be a friend or a stranger from their own culture. As expected based upon their collectivist orientation, the Hong Kong students changed their behavior more when interacting with a friend than did the U.S. students (Chan et al. 1994).

Morris, Podolny, and Ariel (1999) examined four cultures—North American, Chinese, German, and Spanish—and proposed that each culture developed social networks within the organization according to a different set of norms (see Table 10–2). North American business relationships are characterized by a market orientation, in which people form relationships according to the market standard of whether it is profitable. Practically, this means that North Americans form ties without the prior basis of friendship, paying attention only to instrumentality. Chinese business relationships are characterized by a familial orientation, in which employees make sacrifices for the welfare of the organization. Sharing resources within the in-group, loyalty, and deference to superiors characterize network relationships. German business relationships are characterized by legal-bureaucratic orientation, formal categories, and rules. Finally, Spanish business relationships are characterized by affiliative orientations, such as sociability and friendliness. A controlled cross-national comparison of network relationships in Citibank supported these network norms (Morris, Podolny, and Ariel 1999).

Cooperation   People from collectivist cultural traditions engage in more cooperative behavior in mixed-motive interactions than do people from individualistic cultures (Cox, Lobel, and McLeod 1991). Greater cooperation in the face of uncertainty and the potential for exploitation imply that people from collectivist cultures place greater emphasis on the needs and goals of their group and are more likely to be willing to sacrifice personal interests for the attainment of group goals. Awareness of different cultural norms can be a powerful bargaining strategy. For example, consider the negotiations that took place in Kyoto in 1997 to reach a pact on global warming. For more than a week, the negotiators at the Kyoto climate-change conference had been haggling over the terms of a treaty that would go a long way toward dealing productively with global warming. In the last hours of the negotiation, all of the world's industrialized nations had agreed to firm targets for reducing six different greenhouse gases. All but Japan, that is. The Japanese had been assigned the most modest goal: cut emission 6 percent below 1990 levels by the year 2012, compared with 7 percent for the United States and 8 percent for the 15 nations of the European Union. But the Japanese would not budge. Five percent was their limit. So the U.S. delegation called Washington to report the impasse, and at 2 A.M., an exhausted Vice President Al Gore got on the phone with Japanese Prime Minister Ryutaro Hashimoto. Gore's cross-cultural skills were sharp: He first praised Hashimoto for Japan's leadership in playing host to the conference (focusing on hierarchical cultural norms) and then he pointed out how bad it would look for the host country to derail the agreement over a measly percentage point (focusing on collective well-being). It worked (Lemonick 1997).

In-Group Favoritism   In-group favoritism is the strong tendency to favor the members of one's own group more than those in other groups, even when there is no logical basis for doing so. The in-group bias is so powerful that even when groups are formed on the basis of an arbitrary procedure, such as by drawing lots or random assignment, people tend to evaluate their group members more positively and reward them with more resources than members of the out-group (Tajfel 1982). As might be expected, members of collectivist cultures display more in-group favoritism than members of individualistic cultures. For example, when group boundaries are made salient, this creates more competitive behavior among members of collectivist cultures than members of individualistic cultures (Espinoza and Garza 1985). Moreover, members of collectivistic cultures become more competitive when they perceive their group to be in the minority (Espinoza and Garza 1985). Whereas in-group favoritism often has positive effects for members of in-groups, it can be deleterious for members of out groups and for intergroup relations (see chapter 9 for more on intergroup negotiation).

Social Loafing versus Social Striving   **Social loafing** is the tendency for people to work less hard and contribute less effort and resources in a group context than when working alone. For example, people clap less loudly, work less hard, and contribute less when working in a group, as opposed to working alone (Kerr 1983). Social loafing should occur less in collectivist cultures than individualist cultures, presumably because individualist cultures do not reward group effort, but collectivist cultures do. In a study of social loafing among management trainees in the United States and the People's Republic of China, Americans students loafed (individual performance declined in a group setting), but Chinese students did not (Earley 1989). In fact, among Japanese participants, the opposite pattern occurred in the group: Social striving—collectivist concerns for the welfare of the group—increased individual's motivation and performance (Shirakashi 1985; Yamaguchi, Okamoto, and Oka 1985).

Endowment   Collectivism has implications for the ownership of resources. The endowment effect is the tendency for people to place more value on something that is currently in their possession than something that they do not own, independent of the value of the good itself. In chapter 2, we noted that students who are given a coffee mug or a ballpoint pen demand a higher price to sell it than are students who are asked to make an offer to buy the coffee mug or ballpoint pen (Kahneman, Knetsch, and Thaler 1990). Individualist cultures show a strong endowment effect; however, members of collectivist cultures do not (Carnevale and Radhakrishnan 1994). Rather, people from collectivist cultures show a group endowment effect—they value a good or resource more in contexts where they believe others can share it (Carnevale and Radhakrishnan 1994, experiment 2).

Dispositionalism versus Situationalism **Dispositionalism** is the tendency to ascribe the cause of a person's behavior to his or her character or underlying personality. **Situationalism** is the tendency to ascribe the cause of a person's behavior to factors and forces that are outside of a person's control. For example, suppose that you are in the midst of a high-stakes negotiation, and you place an urgent call to your negotiation partner. Your partner does not return your call, yet you know she is in town because you have contacted her secretary. What is causing your partner's behavior? It is possible that your partner is irresponsible (dispositionalism); similarly, it is possible that your partner never got your message (situationalism). Depending upon what you think the true cause is, your behavior toward your partner is going to be very different—anger versus forgiveness, perhaps (Rosette, Brett, Barsness, and Lytle 2000).

People from individualistic cultures view causality differently than do members of collectivist cultures. Dispositionalism is more widespread in individualistic than in collectivist cultures. To see how deep-seated these cultural differences are, look at Figure 10–2, panels A & B.

In Figure 10–2, panels A and B, the blue fish swims on a trajectory that deviates from that of others (indicated by darkest arrows). When asked to describe what was going on in videotapes of swimming fish whose movements were similar to those illustrated in Figure 10–2, members of individualistic cultures (Americans) perceived more influence of internal factors (dispositionalism), whereas members of collectivist cultures (Chinese) perceived more external influence (situationalism) on the blue fish's motions (Morris and Peng 1994). Specifically, Chinese people were more likely to view the fish as wanting to achieve harmony, whereas Americans were more likely to view the blue fish as striking out on his own. Similarly, an investigation of stories in American and Chinese newspapers reveals that English-language newspapers are more dispositional and Chinese-language newspapers are more situational when explaining the same crime stories (Morris and Peng 1994). Specifically, when newspaper articles about "rogue trader" scandals were analyzed, U.S. papers made more mention of the individual trader involved, whereas Japanese papers referred more to the organization (Menon, Morris, Chiu, and Hong 1999). Similarly, when a team member behaves in a maladjusted way, U.S. participants are more likely to focus on the member's traits, whereas the Hong Kong participants focus on situational factors. Dispositionalism also affects biases: people from individualistic cultures, such as the United States, are more likely to fall prey to the fixed-pie bias than are people from collectivistic cultures, such as Greece (Gelfand and Christakopoulou 1999).

Preferences for Dispute Resolution Morris, Leung, and Sethi (1999) note that there are four types of dispute resolution procedures that members of different

FIGURE 10–2 Dispositionalism versus Situationalism

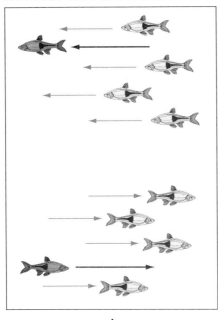
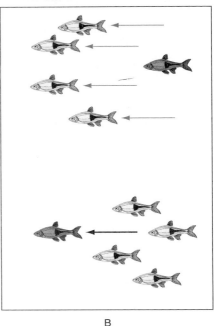

A   B

Diagrams showing trajectories of fish. The blue fishes have the darkest arrows in these diagrams. In A, the group joins the individual (top), and the individual joins the group (bottom); in B, the group leaves the individual (top), and the individual leaves the group (bottom).

Source: Adapted from Morris, M. W., and Peng, K. (1994). Culture and cause: American and Chinese attributions for social and physical events. *Journal of Personality and Social Psychology, 67*(6), 949–971.

cultures can use to resolve disputes: bargaining, mediation, adversarial adjudication, and inquisitorial adjudication. In *bargaining,* or negotiation, two disputants retain full control over the discussion process and settlement outcome. In *mediation,* disputants retain control over the final decision, but there is a third party who guides the process. In *adversarial adjudication,* a judge makes a binding settlement decision, but disputants retain control of the process. Finally, in *inquisitorial adjudication,* disputants yield control over both the process and the final decision to a third party. Collectivist cultures like China differ from individualistic cultures like the United States in terms of preferences for dispute resolution (Morris, Leung, and Sethi 1999; Leung 1987). Specifically, members of collectivist cultures prefer more informational procedures (like bargaining) whereas American prefer more formal procedures. Furthermore, cultural differences in attributional tendencies (i.e., collectivists viewing behavior as a function of situation; individualists viewing behavior as a function of disposition) create even more of a gap between preferences. Specifically, when negotiators encounter a disagreeable person across the bargaining table, individualists attribute that person's behavior to underlying disposition and desire more formal dispute resolution procedures; in contrast, collectivists are more likely to ascribe behavior to situational factors and prefer informal procedures (Morris, Leung, and Sethi 1999).

EGALITARIANISM VERSUS HIERARCHY

A key factor that influences behavior across cultures is the means by which people influence others and the basis of power in relationships. Some cultures have relatively permeable status boundaries and are egalitarian. Other cultures have relatively fixed status boundaries, and influence is determined by existing hierarchical relationships. We describe these in greater detail now.

Egalitarian Power Relationships

In egalitarian power relationships, everyone expects to be treated equally. Egalitarian power relationships do not mean that everyone is of equal status, but rather, status differences are easily permeated. Social boundaries that exist within organizations are permeable, and superior social status may be short-lived. Egalitarian cultures empower members to resolve conflict themselves. Furthermore, the base of power in negotiations may differ; in egalitarian cultures, one's BATNA and information are key sources of power (and status and rank are irrelevant). This is not necessarily true of hierarchical cultures.

Hierarchical Power Relationships

In some cultures, there is great deference to status; status implies social power and is not easily permeated or changed. Social inferiors are expected to defer to social superiors who, in return for privilege, are obligated to look out for the needs of social inferiors (Leung 1987). Conflict threatens the stability of a hierarchical society; it implies either that social inferiors have not met expectation or that social superiors have not met the needs of social inferiors (Brett in press). The norm in hierarchical cultures is not to challenge high-status members; thus, conflict is less frequent between members of different social ranks than in egalitarian cultures (Brett in press). Furthermore, conflict between members of the same social rank in hierarchical cultures is more likely to be handled by deference to a superior than by direct confrontation between social equals (Leung 1987). In cultures, just like organizations, hierarchy reduces conflict by providing norms for interaction. The key source of power in negotiation is status, rather than one's BATNA (although there are high correlations).

To examine which countries were collectivist and which were hierarchical, Hofstede (1980) analyzed the responses that IBM employees gave to a values questionnaire. The respondents were diverse in nationality, occupation within IBM, age, and sex. Figure 10–3 presents a grid of where different countries fall in terms of individualism and power distance. Power distance reflects the tendency to see a large distance between those in the upper part of a social structure and those in the lower part of that structure.

It is clear from Figure 10–3 that individualism and power distance are highly correlated: Countries high in collectivism are also high in power distance. The most collectivist high-power countries are Venezuela, several other Latin American countries, the Philippines, and Yugoslavia. The most individualistic, low-power-distance countries were English-speaking Scandinavia, Austria, and Israel.

Implications for Negotiation

Choosing Your Representative   Cultural differences in power sources and power displays can be dramatic and unsettling because power is the basis for pie slicing. One of the first issues that negotiators must consider prior to intercultural negotiations is who will do the negotiating. In egalitarian cultures, power is usually determined by one's

FIGURE 10–3 Position of Countries on Power Distance and Individualism

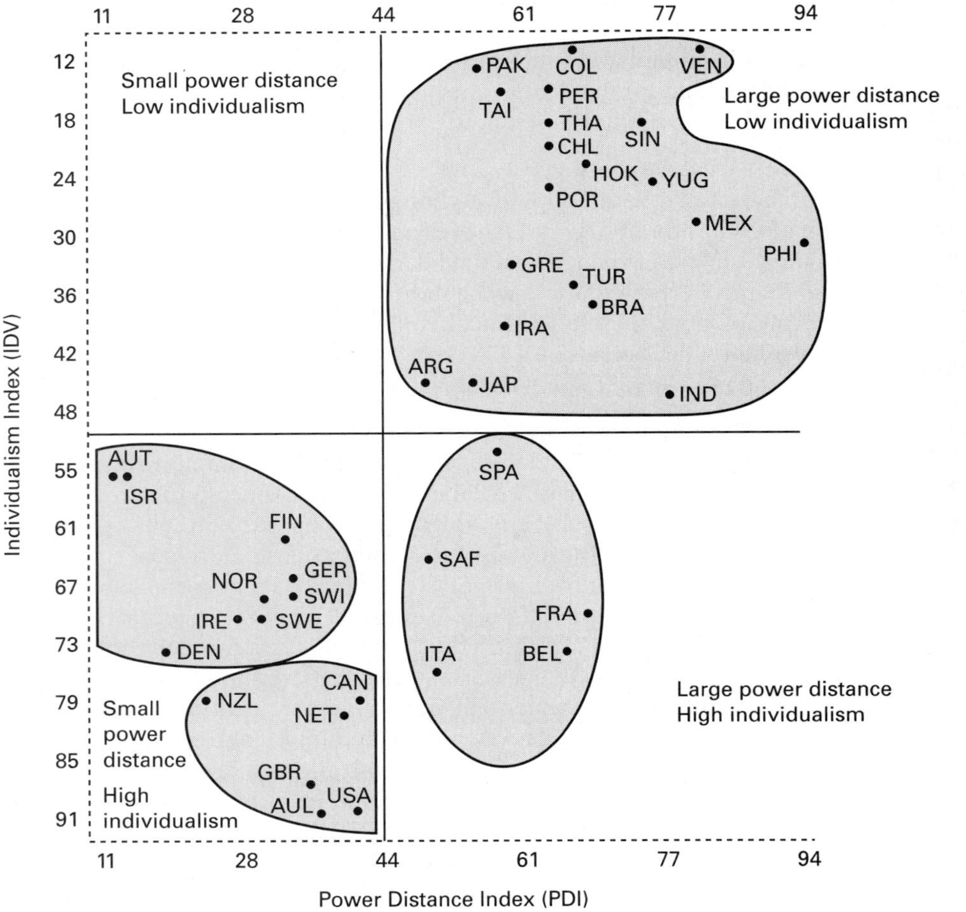

Source: Hofstede, G. (1980). *Culture's consequences: International differences in work-related values.* Beverly Hills: Sage. 223. Reprinted by permission of Sage Publications, Inc.

BATNA and thus, when different-status persons find themselves at the bargaining table, this is not unusual. In contrast, in hierarchical cultures, power is associated with one's position and rank, and it is insulting to send a lower-rank employee to meet with a CEO. For example, in China, relationships follow people, not organizations. The ideal negotiator is an "old friend of China" with whom the Chinese have had positive experiences or owe favors (Pachtman 1998).

Understand the Network of Relationships In cultures that have hierarchical power relationships, negotiations often require several levels of approval, all the way up to the top. For example, in one failed negotiation, the central government of China voided McDonalds' long-standing agreement with the Beijing city government because leases of over 10 years require central government approval (Pachtman 1998).

BOX 10–1

RELATIONSHIP VERSUS INTERESTS-BASED APPROACHES

Tinsley (1996) asked Chinese students in Hong Kong and American students to indicate how they would respond to a conflict scenario. The two cultural groups had very different approaches that reflected their cultural orientation. Specifically, the Hong Kong students preferred to use relational bargaining (asking a superior for a resolution; consulting with third parties for advice; discussion what the social group feels is the right way to resolve the issue), and the American students preferred an individual interests approach (offering information about their interests; asking the other person to explain his or her interests; making the other party to make a proposal to resolve things).

Further, in an investigation of actual behaviors, U.S. negotiators showed stronger norms for discussing interests and synthesizing multiple concerns as compared to Hong Kong negotiators who espoused concerns for the collective and authority (Tinsley & Brett 1997). U.S. negotiators resolved more issues and had outcomes that were more integrative than the Chinese. Hong Kong negotiators's outcomes were more likely to involve upper management.

In the centralized Chinese authority structure, negotiators seldom have the authority to approve the final deal. One by-product of this is that Chinese negotiators will attempt to secure a deal that is clearly weighted in their favor, so that it will be easier to persuade the higher authorities that the Chinese "won" the negotiation.

Face Concerns   Saving and giving face are important in hierarchical cultures. Negotiators need to know how to give face to others. This raises the esteem of the negotiator in the eyes of their superiors and will in turn help them give face to their stakeholders. For example, flattery is a common form of Chinese face saving (Pachtman 1998). Pachtman cautions:

> Be aware of the effect flattery has on you; the proper response is not "thank you," but a denial and an even bigger compliment in return. Apologies are another powerful way to give face, but can obligate the apologizer; be prepared with a token concession in case the Chinese decide to "cash in" on your apology. (p. 25)

The Conduct of Negotiation   A Western view of negotiation holds that each party is expected to voice their own interests, and a back-and-forth exchange will occur. An Eastern view of negotiation is quite different. For example, negotiation among Japanese persons is similar to that of father and son, according to Adler (1991). The status relationship is explicit and important. The son (seller) carefully explains his situation and asks for as much as possible because he will have no chance to bicker once the father (buyer) decides. The son (seller) accepts the decision because it would hurt the relationship to argue and because he trusts the father (buyer) to care for his needs. (See Box 10–1 for cultural differences between Hong Kong and U.S. MBA students.)

DIRECT VERSUS INDIRECT COMMUNICATIONS

Cultures have very different ways of communicating the same message. Direct versus indirect information sharing is a cultural dimension that refers to the amount of information contained in an explicit message versus implicit contextual cues (Hall 1976). For example, different cultures have different norms about information-sharing strategies in negotiation (Hall 1976). Broadly speaking, in some cultures the norms favor direct communication, whereas in other cultures, people communicate in an indirect, discreet fashion. The indirect-direct communication dimension has a direct implication for how much people should rely on contextual cues (Hall and Hall 1990; Cohen 1991).

Direct Communication

In a direct-communication culture, like the United States, messages are transmitted explicitly and directly, and communications are action-oriented and solution-minded (Ting-Toomey 1985). In direct-communication cultures, people step right up and tell you to your face what you did wrong, favoring direct confrontation and discussing problems freely. In a direct-communication culture, the meaning is contained in the message; information is provided explicitly, without nuance (Brett in press). Furthermore, information is *context-free,* meaning that where and under what conditions the information is provided is pretty much irrelevant. In negotiations, this means parties will often ask direct questions about interests and alternatives.

Indirect Communication

In some cultures, people avoid direct confrontation when there is conflict. This is not to say they do not address conflict; rather, it is done indirectly. The meaning of communication is inferred rather than directly interpreted; the context of the message stimulates preexisting knowledge that is then used to gain understanding (Brett in press). In negotiations, asking direct questions is not normative; rather, making a lot of proposals is a matter of indirect communication (Adair et al. 1998). The pattern of proposals allows inferences to be made about what is important to each party and where points of concession might be. In contrast to direct cultures, indirect cultures (like Japan) transmit messages indirectly and implicitly, and communication is elusive (Ting-Toomey 1985). For example, Japanese negotiators are less likely to say no and more likely to remain silent than U.S. negotiators when confronted with an option that is not favorable (Graham and Sano 1984; March 1990). (For a classification of direct- and indirect-communication cultures, see Table 10–3.)

The key point concerning direct versus indirect communication is that culture affects how negotiators share information. Negotiators from direct cultures prefer sharing information directly, asking questions, and getting—in return for giving—answers. In contrast, negotiators from indirect cultures prefer sharing information indirectly, telling stories in an attempt to influence their opponents, and gleaning information from proposals (Adair et al. 1998). Cultural norms and values have implications for the reciprocity principle in negotiation. For example, Adair (1999a) investigated intracultural and intercultural negotiation between the United States and Japan. Negotiators reciprocated culturally normative behaviors. Specifically, U.S. negotiators were more likely to reciprocate direct information exchange; in contrast, Japanese negotiators were more likely to reciprocate indirect information exchange.

Table 10–3: Direct and indirect communication cultures

Direct Communication Cultures	*Indirect Communication Cultures*
Germany	Japan
United States	Russia
Switzerland	France
Scandinavian cultures	Arabs
	Mediterranean peoples
	In general, cultures in which people have extensive information networks among family, friends, colleagues, and clients, and who are involved in close, personal relationships

Source: Brett, J. M. (in press). *Negotiating globally: How to negotiate deals, resolve disputes, and make decisions across cultural boundaries.* San Francisco, CA: Jossey-Bass.

Implications for Negotiation

Getting information out on the table is critical for expanding the pie; relying on context alone to convey information necessary to craft integrative agreements is not enough (Adair et al., 1998). Adair et al. (1998) investigated negotiation strategies in six cultures: France, Russia, Japan, Hong Kong, Brazil, and the United States. Cultures that used direct (as opposed to indirect) information-sharing strategies or a combination of direct and indirect strategies reached the most integrative, pie-expanding agreements. Furthermore, exchanging information about preferences and priorities was insufficient. For example, in the same study of intracultural negotiations involving the United States, Japan, Brazil, France, Russia, and Hong Kong, negotiators from Russia and Hong Kong generated the lowest joint gains, or integrative agreements (Adair et al. 1998). Russia and Hong Kong are indirect-communication countries. However, Japanese negotiators had high joint gains, even though they are an indirect-communication culture as well. Why? The difference is that Japanese negotiators engaged in more direct information exchange (i.e., asking questions) than the negotiators from Russia or Hong Kong. Thus, making comparisons and contrasts to identify trade-offs and direct reactions appears to be essential (Adair et al. 1998).

One of the implications of indirect communication is that relationships often come before the mechanics of deal making. In direct cultures, the process of deal making comes first; in other cultures, the relationship comes first and provides a context for making deals. As a case in point, Vinita Kennedy, director of consulting services for the Lacek Group, a Minneapolis marketing firm, learned that lesson when she took an assignment in Tokyo in 1997. One of Kennedy's jobs was to help All Nippon Airways create a rewards program with local hotel chains. "You need to develop a relationship with people before you can get your business done," she says (Kiser 1999, 117). Consequently, decisions are not made as quickly as they are in the United States. "Everyone has to go back and talk to their whole department and get full buy-in before they can move to the next step," she says (p. 117). And if a Japanese customer does not like the terms of the deal, he will not come out and say so. "It's rare that a Japanese person will tell you 'no' ", she says. "You need to read between the lines" (p. 117).

KEY CHALLENGES OF INTERCULTURAL NEGOTIATION

What are the key challenges facing negotiators when negotiating across cultures? We identify eight common intercultural challenges now.

EXPANDING THE PIE

Negotiators have more difficulty expanding the pie when negotiating across cultures than within a culture. In a landmark study of five countries (Japan, Hong Kong, Germany, Israel, and the United States), Brett (in press) examined intracultural (within the same culture) negotiations versus intercultural (across cultures) negotiations, and found that negotiations between Japan and the United States resulted in a smaller expansion of the pie than did intracultural negotiations (Japan-Japan and U.S.-U.S. negotiations). In another study, Brett and Okumura (1998) examined joint gains in intra- and intercultural negotiations between Japanese and U.S. negotiators and found that joint gains were significantly lower in intercultural negotiations, as opposed to intracultural negotiations. The key reason appeared to be the degree to which parties understood the priorities of the opponents and the opportunity for exploiting compatible issues. In cross-cultural negotiations, negotiators' bargaining styles did not match, meaning that they had less understanding of the opponent's priorities and consequently did not create as much value. Each culture expected the other culture to adopt its own style of negotiating—for example, North Americans expected others to talk directly, whereas people from indirect cultures expected to use other, implicit forms of communication, such as heuristic trial and error. U.S. negotiators exchange information directly and avoid using influence strategies when negotiating intra- and interculturally. In contrast, Japanese negotiators exchange information indirectly and use influence when negotiating intraculturally, but adapt their behaviors when negotiating interculturally (Adair, Okumura, and Brett 1999; Adair 1999b).

SACRED VALUES AND TABOO TRADE-OFFS

Sacred values, or protected values, are the beliefs, customs, and assumptions that form the basis of a group or culture's belief system (Tetlock, Peterson, and Lerner 1996; Baron and Spranca 1997). Sacred values are, by definition, those values and beliefs that people regard to be so fundamental that they are not discussible nor debatable. Sacred values resist trade-offs with other values, particularly economic values. Most people are concerned about their participation in transactions of sacred values, rather than just the consequences that result. For example, most people would not think of negotiating a child's life or selling one's soul (if it were possible). Most people experience anger at the thought of making trade-offs with sacred values and engage in denial of the need for trade-offs through wishful thinking. (For an example of how to assess sacred or protected values, see Box 10–2). "Yes" or "Not Sure" answers imply that the value is secular (tradeable); "No" answers imply the value is sacred.

Sacred values are the opposite of secular values, which are issues and resources that can be traded and exchanged. Within a culture, there is near-universal ascription to sacred values, with some notable exceptions. However, between cultures, there can be extreme conflict when one culture regards an issue to be sacred and another treats

> ### BOX 10–2
>
> ## SACRED VALUES
>
> *Instructions: Following is a list of actions that some people oppose. Some of these are happening right now, and others are not. Suppose that those in favor of each were willing to pay a great deal of money to see the action carried out. Please answer these questions with a "Yes," "No," or "Not Sure," answer according to whether or not you would accept money to perform these actions. (adapted from Baron and Spranea 1997)*
>
> ### ACTIONS:
>
> 1. Destruction of natural forests by human activity, resulting in the extinction of plant and animal species forever.
> 2. Raising the IQ of normal children by giving them (completely safe) drugs.
> 3. Using genetic engineering to make people more intelligent.
> 4. Performing abortions of normal fetuses in the early stages of pregnancy.
> 5. Performing abortions of normal fetuses in the second trimester of pregnancy.
> 6. Fishing in a way that leads to the painful death of dolphins.
> 7. Forcing women to be sterilized because they are retarded.
> 8. Forcing women to have abortions when they have had too many children, for the purposes of population control.
> 9. Putting people in jail for expressing nonviolent political views.
> 10. Letting people sell their organs (for example, a kidney or an eye) for whatever price they can command.
> 11. Refusing to treat someone who needs a kidney transplant because he or she cannot afford it.
> 12. Letting a doctor assist in the suicide of a consenting terminally ill patient.
> 13. Letting a family sell their daughter in a bride auction (that is, the daughter becomes the bride of the highest bidder).
> 14. Punishing people for expressing nonviolent political opinions.
>
>

it as secular. Taboo trade-offs occur when sacred values are proposed for exchange or trade (Tetlock, Peterson, and Lerner 1996).

Most people are horrified and shocked when parents offer to sell their children, citizens sell their right to a jury trial, and immigrants buy voting privileges. However, consider O. Henry's famous story *The Gift of the Magi,* in which a woman sells her hair to buy her husband a watch fob for Christmas. This is a tender and acceptable trade-off. Consider the "oldest profession," in which people buy and sell sexual pleasure. Clearly, there is a very thin line between acceptable and taboo trade-offs. On a purely rational level, these exchanges simply reflect the powerful **trade-off** principle we discussed in chapter 4 on integrative bargaining.

The trade-off principle is ideal for handling scarce resource conflicts that contain issues that are fungible. Principles of rationality (see appendix 1) assume that people are able to compare resources and make apple and orange comparisons among resources and trade them in a way that maximizes their outcomes. Rational bargaining theory assumes that everything is comparable and has a price (see appendix 1). However, the notion of trading becomes unconscionable in some conflict situations (Tetlock, Peterson, and Lerner 1996). People sometimes refuse to place a monetary value on a good or even think of trading it. To even suggest a trade is cause for moral outrage and soured negotiations. Attaching a monetary value to a bottle of wine, a house, or the services of a gardener can be a cognitively demanding task but raises no questions about the morality of the individual who proposes the sale or trade. In contrast, attaching monetary value to human life, familial obligations, national honor, and the ecosystem seriously undermine one's social identity or standing in the eyes of others (Schlenker 1980). In a dispute concerning the construction of a dam that would remove native Indians from their ancestral land, a Yavapia teenager said, "The land is our mother. You don't sell your mother" (from Espeland 1994).

Proposals to exchange sacred values (e.g., body organs) for secular ones (for example, money, time, or convenience) constitute taboo trade-offs. Given the inherently sacred values that operate in many countries, the familiar notions of trading and logrolling, so important to interests-based negotiation, are likely to be considered unacceptable and reprehensible to members of different cultures.

Sacred and secular issues are culturally defined (Tetlock et al. 1996); there are no absolutes. Sociocultural norms affect the sacredness of certain positions, such as smoking, which is now generally considered baneful but in the recent past was completely acceptable. The sanctity of issues is also influenced by the labels and names used to define conflicts. For example, in 1994, all three members of Alaska's congressional delegation began referring to the part of the Arctic National Wildlife Refuge (ANWR) that would be subject to oil exploration as the "Arctic Oil Reserve." The group believed that this term was more accurate because that part of the refuge was not officially classified as either wilderness or refuge. Environmentalists, on the other hand, objected to this term and did not even like the use of the acronym ANWR because they worried that unless the words *wildlife refuge* were clearly stated, the public would not understand the value of the land.

Truly sacred values cannot exist because we make value trade-offs every day, meaning that everyone "has their price." The implication is that with sufficient compensation, people are willing to trade off a "sacred" value. The critical issue is not how much it takes to compensate someone for a sacred issue but, instead, what factors allow trade-offs to occur on sacred issues.

The term *sacred* describes people's preferences on issues on which they view themselves as uncompromising. It immediately becomes obvious, however, that labeling an issue as sacred may be a negotiation ploy, rather than a reflection of heartfelt value. By anointing certain issues as sacred, and removing them from bargaining consideration, a negotiator increases the likelihood of a favorable settlement. The strategy is similar to the irrevocable commitment strategy (Schelling 1960). We refer to issues that are not really sacred, but positioned as such, as **pseudosacred**.[2] Thus, for example, if the Yavapia Indians would trade one acre of land for a hospital, new school, or money, then the land is not truly sacred but pseudosacred.

---

[2] We are indebted to Max Bazerman for this term.

BIASED PUNCTUATION OF CONFLICT

The **biased punctuation of conflict** occurs when people interpret interactions with their adversaries in self-serving and other-derogating terms (Kahn and Kramer 1990). An actor, *A*, perceives the history of conflict with another actor, *B*, as a sequence of *B-A*, *B-A, B-A* in which the initial hostile or aggressive move was made by *B*, causing *A* to engage in defensive and legitimate retaliatory actions. Actor *B* punctuates the same history of interaction as *A-B, A-B, A-B,* however, reversing the roles of aggressor and defender. The biased punctuation of conflict is a frequent cause of warfare. Consider the long sad history of international conflict between the Arabs and Israelis. Each country chooses different historical moments of origin in order to justify its own claims to land, and thus casts the other country in the role of the invader.

Negotiation behaviors are a continuous stream of cause-and-effect relationships where each person's actions influence the actions of others (Jones and Gerard 1967). To an outside observer, their interaction is an uninterrupted sequence of interchanges. However, people who are actively engaged in conflict do not always see things this way. Instead, they organize their interactions into a series of discrete causal chunks (Swann, Pelham, and Roberts 1987), a process known as **causal chunking** or **punctuation** (Whorf 1956). Causal chunks influence the extent to which people are aware of their influence on others, as well as their impressions of others. There are two kinds of chunking patterns: self-causal and other-causal. People form self-causal chunks (for example: "My action causes my partner's action") when they possess an offensive set, and other-causal chunks when they possess a defensive set.

Disagreement about how to punctuate a sequence of events and a conflict relationship is at the root of many cross-cultural disputes. When each country representative is queried, they explain their frustrations and actions as defenses against the acts of the other country. As a result, conflict escalates unnecessarily.

INTERGROUP BIASES

We noted in chapter 9 that most people display an in-group bias by evaluating members of their own group more favorably than members of out-groups and reward members of their own group more resources than members of out-groups, even when allocations of resources do not affect their own welfare (Doise 1978). There is a nearly universal tendency to rate one's own group as superior to other groups, even on the basis of little or no information. For example, even when members of groups do not know one another and never interact, people show in-group favoritism (Brewer 1979; Tajfel 1982; Tajfel and Turner 1986). However, conflict between groups and intergroup bias does not always arise from competition over scarce resources. Much intergroup bias stems from fundamental differences in cultural values. Symbolic conflict can occur between cultural groups due to clashes of values and fundamental beliefs.

One unfortunate by-product of in-group favoritism is the tendency to view people from different cultures as more alike than they really are. Thus, the phrase "they all look alike" means that within-race and within-culture errors are more prevalent than between-race or between-cultural errors, because people categorize members of other cultures not as individuals, but as part of a group. As an example, consider the long-standing conflict between pro-choice and pro-life activists on the abortion issue (see Sidebar 10–1).

SIDEBAR 10–1. STEREOTYPING THE OTHER PARTY

As an example of how members of groups tend to stereotype the other party, consider the conversation that occurred between Naomi Wolf, author of the best-seller *The Beauty Myth,* and Frederica Mathewes-Green, a syndicated religion columnist and author of a book called *Right Choices.* Try to figure out which woman made which of the following comments during a discussion in 1996:

> Where the pro-life movement has made its mistake is to focus only on the baby, and not the woman . . . You can boil 25 years of the pro-life rhetoric down to three words: "It's a baby."

> There's a whole industry to promote bonding with the wanted fetus, yet unwanted fetuses are treated as though they are unwanted lumps of batter.

The criticism of the pro-life movement's "it's a baby" focus came from Mathewes-Green, one of the movement's own. The criticism of the pro-choice movement's "unwanted lumps of batter" rhetoric came from Wolf, a staunch abortion-rights supporter.

When Wolf and Mathewes-Green met to talk, Wolf said that it was the first time that she had ever "knowingly been in the presence of a pro-lifer" (Shirk 1996, 11B). To her surprise, the other side was willing to have a conversation. And Mathewes-Green acknowledged that the pro-life movement had invited being stereotyped by "focusing only on the baby and not the woman" (Shirk 1996, 11B).

STEREOTYPES

Stereotypes of cultural groups are common. However, they often do not have a basis in reality. The problem is that if people act as if stereotypes are true, they are likely to create a self-fulfilling prophecy, whereby the stereotypes affect behavior. For example, in a negotiation study, Americans described their Japanese counterparts as being "poker-faced" or as displaying no facial expressions. However, in the laboratory, a camera that was focused on each person's face during an intercultural negotiation recorded all facial expressions and revealed no differences in the number of facial expressions (smiles and frowns) between the Americans and Japanese. What's going on? Americans are not able to "read" Japanese expressions, and they wrongly describe them as "expressionless" (Graham 1993).

AFFILIATION BIAS

The **affiliation bias** occurs when people evaluate a person's actions on the basis of his or her affiliations rather than on the merits of the behavior itself. For example, when football fans watch a game, they believe the other side commits more infractions than does their own team (Hastorf and Cantril 1954). Consider the following actions that a country could take: establishing a rocket base close to the borders of a country with whom it has strained relations; testing a new assault weapon; or establishing trade relations with a powerful country. People's perceptions of the acceptability of these actions differ dramatically as a function of the perceived agent. For example, during the time of the Cold War, U.S. citizens regarded the above actions to be much more beneficial when the United States was the one responsible than when the then-U.S.S.R. engaged in the same actions (Oskamp 1965). People perceive the same objective behavior as either sinister or benign, merely as a consequence of the agent's affiliation.

FAULTY PERCEPTIONS OF CONCILIATION AND COERCION

During World War II, the American journalist Edward R. Murrow broadcasted nightly from London, reporting on the psychological and physical consequences of the Nazi bombing of British cities (Rothbart and Hallmark 1988). Contrary to Nazi intent, the bombing did not move the British toward surrender. It had quite the opposite effect, strengthening rather than diminishing British resolve to resist German domination. Shortly after the United States entered World War II, the Americans joined the British in launching costly bombing raids over Germany. In part, the intent was to decrease the German people's will to resist. Later research reported by the Office of Strategic Services that compared lightly and heavily bombed areas found only minimal differences in civilians' will to resist.

Several other conflicts follow the same psychological pattern, such as Pearl Harbor, South Africa, and North Vietnam. Each of these instances point to important differences in countries' perceptions of what will be effective in motivating an enemy and what will be effective in motivating themselves or their allies. Coercion is viewed as more effective with our enemies than with ourselves, whereas conciliation is viewed as more effective with ourselves than with our enemies. The unfortunate consequence, of course, is that this perception encourages aggressive rather than constructive action.

There are three key reasons why this occurs (Rothbart and Hallmark 1988). A preference for punitive strategies with one's enemies may reflect a desire to inflict injury or pain, as well as a desire to influence behavior in a desired direction. The relative preference for punishment is based on an incompatible desire to both injure and modify the behavior of the enemy. Alternatively, people may be inclined to use more coercive strategies with an opponent because the appearance of toughness conveys information about their motives and intentions, which, in the long run, may bring about the desired result. Finally, the mere creation of mutually exclusive, exhaustive social categories (e.g., "them" and "us") leads to different assumptions about members of such groups: More favorable attributes are assigned to in-group than to out-group members (Brewer 1979; Tajfel 1970). Social categorization processes may be particularly powerful in cross-cultural disputes because of stereotypes.

NAÏVE REALISM

There is a heated debate among English teachers concerning which books should be on the required reading list for American high school students. The Western Canon Debate features traditionalists, who prefer to have classics on the reading list, and revisionists, who believe that the reading list should be more racially, ethnically, and sexually diversified. In a recent analysis, traditionalists and revisionists were interviewed about their own and the other party's preferred books (Robinson and Keltner 1996). Most strikingly, each party exaggerated the views of the other side in a way that made their differences bigger rather than smaller. Traditionalists viewed revisionists to be much more extreme than they really were; revisionists viewed traditionalists to be much more conservative. In fact, the groups agreed on seven out of the 15 books on the reading list! Nevertheless, each group greatly exaggerated the difference between their own and the other's belief systems in a way that exacerbated the conflict. Further, people perceived the other side to be more uniform in their views, whereas they perceived their own views to be more varied and heterogeneous (Linville, Fischer, and Salovey 1989). This faulty perception, of course, leads to beliefs such as "They're all alike." Ideological conflict is often exacerbated unnecessarily as partisans construe the other person's values to be more extremist and unbending than they really are.

For example, in 1995, Republican Congressman George Gekas of Pennsylvania was accused by the opposing partisan party of espousing antienvironmental attitudes. The angered Gekas mocked the accusation: "Mr. Speaker and members of the House, I hate clean air. I don't want to breathe clean air. I want the dirtiest air possible for me and my household and my constituents. That's what the supporters of this motion want people to believe about our position on these riders. Now, you know that's absolutely untenable" (National Public Radio, November 3, 1995).

The **fundamental attribution error** occurs when people explain the causes of the behavior of others in terms of their underlying dispositions and discount the role of situational factors (Ross 1977). Many environmental disputes involve a group that is believed to be interested in the economic development of the environment and an opposing group that represents the interests of the ecosystem. According to the fundamental attribution error, when each group is asked to name the cause of the dispute, each will attribute the negative aspects of conflict to the dispositions of the other party. Specifically, developers regard environmentalists to be fanatic lunatics; environmentalists regard developers to be sinister and greedy.

PREDICTORS OF SUCCESS IN INTERCULTURAL INTERACTIONS

Your pharmaceutical company wants to expand its international base. You are charged with the task of selecting a few managers to participate in a special global initiatives assignment in various countries. You know that failure rates as high as 70 percent can be avoided (Copeland and Griggs 1985). These costs include not only the lost salary of an executive, the cost of transporting the family, and the cost of setting up an office abroad, but also include damage to your organization, lost sales, on-the-job mistakes, and loss of goodwill. Unfortunately, ready-made personality measures are not good predictors of success abroad. The following have some value in predicting success (Triandis 1994; Martin 1989):

- Conceptual complexity: People who are conceptually complex (think in terms of shades of gray, rather than black and white) show less social distance to different others (Gardiner 1972).
- People who use broad categories adjust to new environments better than do narrow categorizers (Detweiler 1980).
- Empathy.
- Sociability.

- Critical acceptance of stereotypes.
- Openness to different points of view.
- Interest in host culture.
- Task orientation.
- Cultural flexibility (the ability to substitute activities in the host culture for own culture valued activities).
- Social orientation (the ability to establish new intercultural relationships).
- Willingness to communicate (e.g., use the host language without fear of making mistakes).
- Patience (suspend judgment).
- Intercultural sensitivity.
- Tolerance for differences among people.
- Sense of humor.
- Skills in collaborative conflict resolution.

ADVICE FOR CROSS-CULTURAL NEGOTIATIONS

Brett (in press) has researched and proposed several strategies that can improve cross-cultural effectiveness. These include the following.

ANTICIPATE DIFFERENCES IN STRATEGY AND TACTICS THAT MAY CAUSE MISUNDERSTANDINGS

Negotiators from different cultures differ in terms of three major dimensions that affect their negotiation behavior and style: individualism-collectivism, hierarchy-egalitarianism, and direct-indirect communications. The negotiator who is able to anticipate differences in terms of these three dimensions is going to be at a pie-expanding and pie-slicing advantage in intercultural negotiations. Further, when encountering differences, the negotiator who is aware of cultural differences will not make negative attributions about her opponent, but instead, view discomfort as a natural consequence of different cultural styles.

ANALYZE CULTURAL DIFFERENCES TO IDENTIFY DIFFERENCES IN VALUES THAT EXPAND THE PIE

We noted in chapter 4 (integrative negotiation) and chapter 8 (creativity in negotiation) that it is differences, rather than similarities, between negotiators that can open up windows for expanding the pie and creating joint gain. Presumably, there are more degrees of difference between members of different cultures than members of the same culture. This means that the amount of integrative, or win-win, potential is higher in intercultural negotiations, as opposed to intracultural negotiations. The culturally enlightened negotiator will search for differences in beliefs, values, risk profiles, expectations, and abilities that can be used to leverage opportunities for joint gain, such as through the creation of value-added trade-offs (logrolling) and the construction of contingency contracts.

RECOGNIZE THAT THE OTHER PARTY MAY NOT SHARE YOUR VIEW OF WHAT CONSTITUTES POWER

The other party's estimate of his or her power may be based on factors that you think are irrelevant to the negotiation. This means that negotiators from egalitarian cultures should be prepared to present information about their company and products, even when they think such information should have no bearing on the outcome. In failing to make a presentation comparable to the one made by the negotiator from the hierarchical culture, negotiators from egalitarian cultures risk appearing weak. By the same token, negotiators from hierarchical cultures should be aware that power-based persuasion, although normative in deal-making negotiations in their own cultures, is not normative in egalitarian cultures. Furthermore, in egalitarian cultures, power-based persuasion is likely to be reciprocated directly with power-based persuasion and may lead to impasse (Brett and Okumura 1998). One American businessperson suffered due to a lack of understanding about cultural behavioral styles. After long, hard bargaining, a U.S. firm had landed a large contract with a Japanese firm. At the signing ceremony, however, the Japanese executive began reading the contract intently. His scrutiny seemed endless. The American panicked and offered to take $100 off of each item. What the U.S. executive did not know was that the Japanese president was merely demonstrating authority, not backing out (*Chicago Sun Times,* February 10, 1986).

AVOID ATTRIBUTION ERRORS

An attribution error is the tendency to ascribe someone's behavior or the occurrence of an event to the wrong cause. For example, people often attribute behaviors of others to their underlying personality (e.g., a smile from another person is often attributed to a "good" disposition; similarly, a frown is presumed to be a manifestation of a grouchy personality; Ross 1977). However, the behavior of others is more often a reflection of particular features of the situation, rather than enduring personality traits. Negotiators who are interculturally naïve are more likely to fall prey to the **fundamental attribution error**—the tendency to view people's behavior as a manifestation of their personality (Ross 1977) than are people who are interculturally sensitive, who are more likely to view behavior as a manifestation of cultural and situational norms.

AVOID ETHNOCENTRISM

Ethnocentrism is the tendency for people to view members of their own culture, as well as its artifacts and institutions, more favorably than members of different cultures (Sumner 1906). Ethnocentrism, or the universal strong liking of one's own group and the simultaneous negative evaluation of out-groups, generates a set of universal reciprocal stereotypes in which each culture sees itself as good and the other culture as bad, even when both groups engage in the same behaviors. Whereas the behavior may be similar, the interpretation is not: "We are loyal; they are clannish; we are brave and willing to defend our rights; they are hostile and arrogant."

FIND OUT HOW TO SHOW RESPECT IN THE OTHER CULTURE

One of the most important preparatory steps a negotiator can take when commencing intercultural negotiation is to find out how to show respect in the other culture. It is a

SIDEBAR 10–2. FAILING TO SHOW RESPECT IN ANOTHER CULTURE CAN LEAD TO CONFLICT

In 1992, the Walt Disney Company undertook a $5 billion EuroDisney theme park project in Paris. It began with great visions of a united workforce wearing Disney dress and adopting American grooming. Behavioral codes banned alcohol in the park, and meetings were conducted in English. The French perceived all of this as an unnecessary cultural imposition. They retaliated with insults, storming out of training meetings and initiating lawsuits. The French press joined in by launching an anti-Disney campaign, and French railroad workers regularly initiated strikes from the Paris-EuroDisney train for months. The annual employee turnover hit a crippling 25 percent, pushing up labor costs by 40 percent. Disney paid a heavy price before making amends (Mishra and Sinha 1999).

fallacy to assume that the other culture will have the same customs as one's own culture and that ignorance of customs will be forgiven. For an example of a failure to show respect in another culture, see Sidebar 10–2.

KNOW YOUR OPTIONS FOR CHANGE

Succeeding in international business requires that people gain international competence as well as business competence (Matsumoto 1996). You have done your homework, researched your negotiation opponent's culture, and have a good idea of what to expect during the meeting and which customs are important. You have also uncovered an unsettling fact: In your client's culture, women are regarded as property and second-class citizens. They are not supposed to be opinionated or hold jobs with decision-making importance. Imagine that you are a man, and your key business associate is a woman, trained at an Ivy League university, well-versed in cultural issues and your client's strategic situation. For you both to sit at the bargaining table would be an insult to your client. Your supervisor is pressing you to open the door to this client's company. What do you do?

This is an unenviable situation. It is difficult to imagine leaving our colleague behind; you need her skills and, moreover, you do not want to break up your partnership. Yet, bringing her involves an inevitable culture clash. Further, shutting the door on this client shuts the door on the entire country. You have thoughts about enlightening your client, but wonder whether a five-minute lesson from you can overcome centuries of discrimination sewn into the fabric of a country.

There is no best answer to this dilemma. However, the manager who identifies this situation early on is in a better situation to positively address it than is the manager who naïvely steps off the plane with the issue unresolved.

Sometimes, options for change are driven by skill sets—or lack thereof. Most Americans are monolingual, compared to other cultures. Furthermore, members of other cultures know that Americans are monolingual, and so, adapt accordingly. For example, Lindsley (1999) observed interactions between North Americans and Mexicans and observed that Mexican bilingual managers immediately switched to

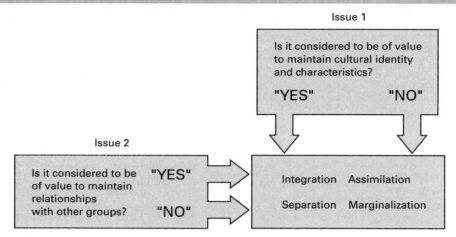

FIGURE 10–4 Acculturation Framework

Source: Berry, J. W. (1980). Acculturation as varieties of adaptation. In A. Padilla (ed.), *Acculturation: Theory, models, and some new findings.* Boulder, CO: Westview. Reprinted with permission.

English when interacting with North Americans; however, North American linguistic accommodation was a rare occurrence.

Before reading further, think about what courses of action you might take. Berry (1980) described four ways for two cultures to relate to each other (see Fig. 10–4). The first issue is whether the individual (or group) finds it valuable to maintain distinct cultural identity and characteristics. The second issue is whether the individual (or group) desires to maintain relationships with other (cultural) groups.

- **Integration** is a type of acculturation whereby each group maintains its own culture and also maintains contact with the other culture. Thus, you bring your client to the meetings, and clearly uphold your firm's egalitarian attitudes, yet also make it clear that you have a strong desire to build relationships with the other group.
- **Assimilation** occurs when a group or person does not maintain its culture but does maintain contact with the other culture. You leave your associate at home and try to follow the mores of the other party's culture.
- **Separation** occurs when a group or individual maintains its culture but does not maintain contact with the other culture. You bring your associate to the meetings and remain oblivious to the other group's culture, or, you tell your supervisor you do not want this assignment.
- **Marginalization** occurs when neither maintenance of the group's own culture nor contact with the other culture is attempted. You leave your associate at home and do not attempt to understand the cultural values of the other firm. Marginalization is the most unfavorable condition (Berry, Poortinga, Segall, and Dasen 1992).

CONCLUSION

Negotiating across cultures is a necessity for success in the business world because globalization is a major objective of most companies. Unfortunately, cross-cultural negotiations frequently result in less effective pie expansion than do intracultural negotiations. Part of the problem is a lack of understanding cultural differences. We used Brett's (in press) tripartite model of culture and identified individualism-collectivism, egalitarianism-hierarchy, and direct-indirect communication as key dimensions of cultural differences. Key challenges of intercultural negotiation are expanding the pie, dealing with sacred values and taboo trade-offs, biased punctuation of conflict, intergroup biases, the affiliation bias, faulty perceptions of conciliation and coercion, and naïve realism. We suggested that negotiators learn to analyze cultural differences to identify differences in values that could expand the pie, recognize different conceptions of power, avoid attribution errors, avoid ethnocentrism, find out how to show respect in other cultures, and assess options for change, including, integration, assimilation, separation, and marginalization.

11

TACIT NEGOTIATIONS AND SOCIAL DILEMMAS

༄

Several members of a well-respected, decentralized research and development (R&D) department in an organization needed laboratory space. The department decided that each organizational member should develop and maintain his or her own laboratory space so as to allow for specialization and reduce bureaucratic control and overhead. Each year, members made a laboratory facilities request that was considered by a committee. The committee was charged with the task of allocating research space on a yearly basis. External funding was the primary criterion that determined allocations: The greater one's external funding, the more laboratory resources were granted.

The committee began to encounter a problem as the organization grew in personnel, but not in physical facilities. Every year, each member requested his or her previous allocation and augmented this with an additional request for more resources. Each year, the committee struggled to meet basic needs, and turned down all new requests. Precedent became the key factor in determining allocations.

As the organization acquired more and more organizational members, each with their own idiosyncratic laboratory needs, the physical facilities of the organization were at a maximum. This had several undesirable consequences: First, organizational members who did not require laboratory space continued to request it, fearing they would not have space in the future when and if they needed it. Second, and most seriously, the space shortage drastically curtailed the recruitment of new organizational members. Whereas the department realized that attracting new members was ultimately necessary for the survival and development of the organization as a whole, old-timers were reluctant and often outright opposed to recruiting new members, especially those who had extensive laboratory needs.

When the department approached the larger organization about the dilemma, they were politely told to solve the problem internally, and recommended that members share space. The organizational members were strongly opposed to this suggestion. Morale and cooperation in the department declined steadily. After several lean hiring seasons, the organization's reputation and overall productivity suffered seriously. When asked to explain the ultimate demise of the R&D group, individual members pointed to the unbridled greed of others in the department.

Has anything like this ever happened to you? It seems preposterous that intelligent and well-meaning people could engage in behaviors that seem so self-destructive. The R&D group is not unique. Similar examples of competitive behavior leading to huge financial losses occurred in the cola advertising wars and the airline wars of the 1980s and the telephone long-distance rate wars of the 1990s. Other examples include population control, free trade, the budget deficit, cartels, and unionization. And they occur quite frequently within companies as well—as the opening example of this chapter suggests.

So far, we have focused on negotiation situations in which people seek to reach mutual agreement in terms of a binding contract. We call these **explicit negotiations.** In contrast, there are many negotiations that occur within and between organizations that are conducted implicitly, without contracts and explicit agreements. We call these **tacit negotiations** (Schelling 1960). In tacit negotiations, negotiators are interdependent with respect to outcomes, but they make independent decisions. Unlike traditional negotiations, parties do not need to meet and talk for an outcome to be reached. Rather, their fate is determined by the actions that they take and the actions taken by others. People can either behave in a cooperative and trusting fashion (e.g., an employee makes a modest request for company resources) or in a competitive and distrusting fashion (e.g., an employee "pads" a request or perhaps shirks teamwork in favor of advancing his or her own career). Another example: A company engages in a negative advertising campaign. The company's main competitor then starts to advertise negatively. As a result, both companies suffer.

In organizational and group life, our welfare depends upon the actions of others. The situation that results when people engage in behaviors that maximize self-interest but lead to collective disaster, such as a bidding war or what happened in the R&D department, is a **social dilemma.** In this chapter, we discuss two kinds of social dilemmas: two-person dilemmas and multiperson dilemmas. The two-person dilemma is the **prisoner's dilemma;** the multiperson dilemma is a social dilemma. They are dilemmas because the choices available to negotiators are risky. Some choices risk exploitation; others risk antagonizing others. We will also discuss how dilemmas may be effectively handled.

BUSINESS AS A SOCIAL DILEMMA

At least four challenges of the future suggest that people will have to learn how to engage in effective tacit negotiation and intelligently navigate social dilemmas, both inside their own companies as well as with other companies.

DECENTRALIZATION

Many companies are moving away from top-down, hierarchical management systems to decentralized management systems, where managers are empowered to make decisions, broker deals, and capitalize on opportunities. However, because of decentralization of business units, there is often conflict of interest—meaning that the parties involved have their own interests in mind, which are not necessarily aligned with those of others. In these situations, managers face a choice between acting in ways that further their own interests or in ways that further the interests of the other party (perhaps with some expense to their own interests).

STRATEGIC ALLIANCES

In many industries and across industries, companies are forming strategic alliances. Alliances are crucial for companies who are in battle for market shares. Increasing competitive pressures make it imperative that companies develop new strengths and deliver products and services quickly and at a lower cost. Strategic alliances allow companies to develop products and rapidly expand their markets while managing risk and costs through resource sharing. However, the majority of alliances are unsuccessful (Segil 1999). Fifty-five percent of alliances and 78 percent of mergers and acquisitions fall apart within three years and only 23 percent recover the costs. Key factors in the development of strategic alliances include the management of competition. Whereas some companies refuse to consider alliances with competitors, others find ways to transform the relationship into profitable partnerships (Segil 1999).

SPECIALIZATION

To the extent that business units and companies are highly specialized, this means that their dependence on others increases. For example, General Motors has several plants that specialize in only one area of manufacturing (e.g., brakes, etc.). However, to assemble a complete automobile, it is necessary for each of the plants to cooperate with one another. If employees at one plant go on strike, they can create havoc in other plants and halt the production of automobiles. The members of each plant have an incentive to further their own interests (e.g., increasing their wages), but often, this comes at the expense of other plants and the company as a whole.

COMPETITION

Competitors routinely face social dilemmas. Some industries seem particularly vicious, such as telephone companies. Other industries have attempted to find points of cooperation that can align their competitive goals. For example, in 1998, two national dairy companies using separate advertising campaigns agreed to create a single marketing plan to increase milk sales in the United States. Dairy Management, Inc., which used "Got Milk?" campaign, and the National Fluid Milk Processor Promotion Board, which used a popular collection of advertisements in which celebrities wear milk mustaches, coordinated campaigns to increase total fluid milk sales by 4 percent by the year 2000 (Elliott 1998).

COMMON MYTHS ABOUT INTERDEPENDENT DECISION MAKING

In approaching social dilemmas and tacit negotiation, people are often guilty of mythological thinking. We expose the three leading myths that impair decision making before presenting what we believe is an effective decision-making strategy.

MYTH 1: "IT'S A GAME OF WITS: I CAN OUTSMART THEM"

Many people believe that they can stay one move ahead of the "other guy." However, effective decision making in noncooperative situations is not about outsmarting people. It is unrealistic to believe we can consistently outwit others—an egocentric illusion. A better and more realistic goal is to understand the incentive structure in the situation and take the perspective of the other party. In the fraternal twin model, we need to imagine that the person we are dealing with is every bit as intelligent and motivated as we are—it is pretty hard to outwit ourselves!

MYTH 2: "IT'S A GAME OF STRENGTH: SHOW 'EM YOU'RE TOUGH"

This negotiator goes into battle fighting fire with fire. The problem is that this behavior can unnecessarily escalate conflict situations, especially if people have a false sense of uniqueness.

MYTH 3: "IT'S A GAME OF CHANCE: HOPE FOR THE BEST"

This negotiator believes that outcomes are not predictable and depend on ever-changing aspects of the situation: personality, mood, time of day, and so on. This person erroneously believes that either it takes a long time to figure out a good strategy or it is just downright impossible.

In this chapter, we suggest that tacit negotiation and dilemmas are neither games of wits, strength, or chance, but decision opportunities. We will use principles of logic and psychology to optimally deal with these situations.

THE PRISONER'S DILEMMA

Thelma and Louise are common criminals who have just been arrested on suspicion of burglary. There is enough evidence to convict each suspect of a minor breaking-and-entering crime, but insufficient evidence to convict the suspects on a more serious felony charge of burglary and assault. The district attorney immediately separates Thelma and Louise after their arrest. Each suspect is approached separately and presented with two options: confess to the serious burglary charge or remain silent (not confess). The consequences of each course of action depend on what the other decides to do. The catch is that Thelma and Louise must make their choices independently. They cannot communicate with each other in any way prior to making an independent, irrevocable decision. The decision situation that each suspect faces is illustrated in Figure 11–1, which indicates that Thelma and Louise will go to prison between 0 and 15 years, depending upon what the other partner chooses. Obviously, this is an important decision. Imagine that you are an advisor to Thelma. Your concern is not morality or ethics; you are simply trying to get her a shorter sentence. What do you advise her to do?

Ideally, it is desirable for both suspects to not confess, thereby minimizing the prison sentence to one year for each (cell A). This option is risky, however. If one confesses, then the suspect who does not confess goes to prison for the maximum sentence of 15 years—an extremely undesirable outcome (cell B or C). In fact, the most desirable situation from the standpoint of each suspect would be to confess and have the

FIGURE 11–1 Consequences of Thelma and Louise's Behaviors

Thelma

	Do not confess (remain silent)	Confess
Do not confess (remain silent)	A T = 1 yr L = 1 yr	B T = 0 yrs L = 15 yrs
Confess	C T = 15 yrs L = 0 yrs	D T = 10 yrs L = 10 yrs

Louise

Note: Entries represent prison term length. T = Thelma's term length; L = Louise's term length.

other person not confess. This would mean that the confessing suspect would be released, and his or her partner would go to prison for the maximum sentence of 15 years. Given these contingencies, what should Thelma do? Before reading further, stop and think about what you think is her best course of action.

The answer is not easy, which is why the situation is a dilemma. It will soon be demonstrated that when each person pursues the course of action that is most rational from her point of view, the result is mutual disaster. That is, both Thelma and Louise go to prison for 10 years (cell D). The paradox of the prisoner's dilemma is that the pursuit of individual self-interest leads to collective disaster. There is a conflict between individual and collective well-being that derives from rational analysis. It is easy for Thelma and Louise (as well as for the R&D department members) to *see* that each could do better by cooperating, but it is not easy to know *how* to implement this behavior. The players can get there only with coordinated effort.

COOPERATION AND DEFECTION AS UNILATERAL CHOICES

We will use the prisoner's dilemma situation depicted in Figure 11–1 to analyze players' decision making. We will refer to the choices that players make in this game as **cooperation** and **defection,** depending upon whether they remain silent or confess. The language of cooperation and defection allows the prisoner's dilemma game structure to be meaningfully extended to other situations that do not involve criminals, but nevertheless have the same underlying structure, such as whether an airline company should bid for a smaller company, whether a cola company should engage in negative advertising, or whether a department member should demand lab space.

RATIONAL ANALYSIS

We will use the logic of game theory to provide a rational analysis of this situation. In our analysis, we will consider three different cases: (1) one-shot, nonrepeated play situations (as in the case of Thelma and Louise); (2) the case in which the decision is repeated for a finite number of terms (such as might occur in a yearly election for a position on a five-year task force); and (3) the case in which the decision is repeated for a potentially infinite number of trials or the end is unknown (such as might occur in financial companies, airlines, hotels, and soap manufacturers).

Case 1: One-Shot Decision

As we noted in appendix 1, game theoretic analysis relies on the principle of dominance detection. That is, the easiest and first principle we should try to invoke is to detect whether one strategy—confession or remaining silent—is dominant. A dominant strategy results in a better outcome for player 1 no matter what player 2 does.

To illustrate the dominance principle, suppose that you are Thelma and your partner in crime is Louise. First, consider what happens if Louise remains silent (does not confess). Thus, we are focusing on the first row in Figure 11–1. If you remain silent, this puts you in cell A: You both get one year. This outcome is not too bad, but maybe you could do better. Suppose that you decide to confess. This puts you in cell B: You get 0 years, and Louise gets 15 years. Certainly no prison sentence is much better than a one-year sentence, so confession seems like the optimal choice for you to make, given that Louise does not confess.

Now, what happens if Louise confesses? In this situation, we are focusing on row 2. If you remain silent, this puts you in cell C: You get 15 years, and Louise gets 0 years. This is not very good for you. Now, suppose that you confess; this puts you in cell D: You both get 10 years. Neither outcome is splendid, but 10 years is certainly better than 15 years. Given that Louise confesses, what do you want to do? The choice amounts to whether you want to go to prison for 15 years or 10 years. Again, confession is the optimal choice for you.

We have just illustrated the principle of **dominance detection:** No matter what Louise does (remains silent or confesses), it is better for Thelma to confess. Confession is a dominant strategy; under all possible states of the world, players in this game should choose to confess. We know that Louise is smart and has looked at the situation and its contingencies in the same way as Thelma and has reached the same conclusion. In this sense, mutual defection is an **equilibrium outcome,** meaning that no player can unilaterally (single-handedly) improve her outcome by making a different choice.

Thus, both Thelma and Louise are led through rational analysis to confess, and they collectively end up in cell D, where they both go to prison for a long period of time. This seems both unfortunate and avoidable. Certainly, both suspects would prefer to be in cell A than in cell D. Is there some way to escape the tragic outcomes produced by the prisoner's dilemma? Are we doomed to collective disaster in such situations?

It would seem that players might extricate themselves from the dilemma if they could communicate, but we have already noted that communication is outside of the bounds of the noncooperative game. Further, because the game structure is noncooperative, any deals that players might make with one another are nonbinding. For example, antitrust legislation prohibits companies from price fixing, which means that any communication that occurs between companies regarding price fixing is unenforceable, not to mention punishable by law.

What other mechanism might allow parties in such situations to avoid the disastrous outcome produced by mutual defection? One possibility is to have both parties make those decisions over **multiple trials.** That is, suppose that the parties did not make a single choice but instead made a choice, received feedback about the other player's choice, experienced the consequences, and then made another choice. Perhaps repeated interaction with the other person would provide a mechanism for parties to coordinate their actions. If the game is to be played more than once, players might reason that by cooperating on the first round, cooperation may be elicited in subsequent periods. We consider that situation next.

Case 2: Repeated Interaction over a Fixed Number of Trials

Instead of making a single choice and living with the consequence, suppose that Thelma and Louise were to play the game in Figure 11–1 a total of 10 times. It might seem strange to think about criminals doing this, so it may be useful to think about two political candidates deciding whether or not to engage in negative campaigning (hereafter referred to as campaigning). There are term limits in their state—they can run and hold office for a maximum of five years. There is an election every year. During each election period, each candidate makes an independent choice (to campaign or not), then learns of the other's choice (to campaign or not) and experiences the resultant outcome. After the election, the candidates consider the same alternatives once again and make an independent choice; this continues for five separate elections.

We will use the concept of dominance as applied above to analyze this situation, but we need another tool that tells us how to analyze the repeated nature of the game. **Backward induction** is the mechanism by which a person decides what to do in a repeated game situation, by looking backward from the last stage of the game.

We begin by examining what players should do in election 5 (the last election). If the candidates are making their choices in the last election, the game is identical to that analyzed in the one-shot case from earlier. Thus, the logic of dominant strategies applies, and we are left with the conclusion that each candidate will choose to campaign. Now, given that we know that each candidate will campaign in the last election, what will they do in the fourth election?

From a candidate's standpoint, the only reason to cooperate (or to not campaign) is to influence the behavior of the other party in the subsequent election. That is, a player might signal a willingness to cooperate by making a cooperative choice in the period before. We have already determined that it is a foregone conclusion that both candidates will defect (choose to campaign) in the last election, so it is futile to choose the cooperative (no campaigning) strategy in the fourth election. So, what about the third election? Given that candidates will not cooperate in the last election, nor in the second-to-last election, there is little point to cooperating in the third-to-last election for the same reason that cooperation was deemed to be ineffective in the second-to-last election. As it turns out, this logic can be applied to every election in such a backward fashion. Moreover, this is true in any situation with a finite number of elections. This leaves us with the conclusion that defection remains the dominant strategy even in the repeated trial case. [1]

---

[1]Formally, if the prisoner's dilemma is repeated finitely, all Nash equilibria of the resulting sequential games have the property that the noncooperative outcome, which is pareto-inferior, occurs in each period, no matter how large the number of periods.

This is surely disappointing news. It suggests that cooperation is not possible even in long-term relationships. This runs counter to intuition, observation, and logic, however. We must consider another case, arguably more realistic of the situations we want to study in most circumstances, in which repeated interaction continues for an infinite or indefinite amount of time.

Case 3: Repeated Interaction for an Infinite or Indefinite Amount of Time

In the case in which parties interact with one another for an infinite or indefinite period of time, the logic of backward induction breaks down. There is no identifiable end point from which to reason backward. We are left with forward-thinking logic.

If we anticipate playing a prisoner's dilemma game with another person for an infinitely long or uncertain length of time, we reason that we might influence their behavior with our own behavior. That is, we may signal a desire to cooperate on a mutual basis by making a cooperative choice in an early trial. Similarly, we can reward and punish their behavior through our actions.

Under such conditions, the game theoretic analysis indicates that cooperation in the first period is the optimal choice (Kreps, Milgrom, Roberts, and Wilson 1982). Should our strategy be to cooperate no matter what? No! If a person adopted cooperation as a general strategy, this would surely lead to exploitation. So, what strategy would be optimal to adopt? Before reading further, stop and indicate what is a good strategy.

THE TOURNAMENT OF CHAMPIONS

In 1981, Robert Axelrod, a leading game theorist, posed this very question to readers in an article in *Science* magazine. Axelrod spelled out the contingencies of the prisoner's dilemma game and invited members of the scientific community to submit a strategy to play in a prisoner's dilemma tournament. To play in the tournament, a person had to submit a strategy (a plan that would tell a decision maker what to do in every trial under all possible conditions) in the form of a computer program written in FORTRAN code. Axelrod explained that each strategy would play all other strategies across 200 trials of a prisoner's dilemma game. He further explained that the strategies would be evaluated in terms of the maximization of gains across all opponents they faced. Hundreds of strategies were submitted by eminent scholars from around the world.

The Winner Is a Loser

The winner of the tournament was the simplest strategy submitted. The FORTRAN code was only four lines long. The strategy was called **tit-for-tat** and was submitted by Anatol Rapoport. Tit-for-tat accumulated the greatest number of points across all trials with all of its opponents. The basic principle for tit-for-tat is simple. Tit-for-tat always cooperates on the first trial, and on subsequent trials, it does whatever its opponent did on the previous trial. For example, suppose that tit-for-tat played against someone who cooperated on the first trial, defected on the second trial, and then cooperated on the third trial. Tit-for-tat would cooperate on the first trial and the second trial, defect on the third trial, and cooperate on the fourth trial.

Tit-for-tat never beat any of the strategies it played against. Because it cooperates on the first trial, it can never do better than its opponent. The most tit-for-tat can do is earn as much as its opponent. If it never wins (i.e., beats its opponent), how can tit-for-tat be so successful in maximizing its overall gains? The answer is that it induces cooperation from its opponents. How does it do this? Several characteristics make tit-for-tat an especially effective strategy for inducing cooperation.

Psychological Analysis of Why Tit-for-tat Is Effective

Not Envious   One reason why tit-for-tat is effective is that it is not an envious strategy. That is, it does not care that it can never beat the opponent. Tit-for-tat can never earn more than any strategy it plays against. Rather, the tit-for-tat strategy is designed to maximize its own gain in the long run.

Nice   Tit-for-tat always begins the interaction by cooperating. Furthermore, it is never the first to defect. Thus, tit-for-tat is a nice strategy. This is an important feature because it is difficult for people to recover from initial defections. Competitive, aggressive behavior often sours a relationship. Moreover, aggression often begets aggression. The tit-for-tat strategy neatly avoids the costly mutual escalation trap that can lead to the demise of both parties.

Tough   Although tit-for-tat is a nice strategy, it is not a pushover. A strategy of solid cooperation would be easily exploitable by an opponent. Tit-for-tat can be provoked— it will defect if the opponent invites competition. Tit-for-tat reciprocates defection. This is an important feature of its strategy. By reciprocating defection, tit-for-tat conveys the message that it cannot be taken advantage of. Indeed, tit-for-tat players effectively move competitive players away from them, thus minimizing noncooperative interaction (Van Lange and Visser 1999).

Forgiving   We have noted that tit-for-tat is tough in that it reciprocates defection. It is also a forgiving strategy in the sense that it reciprocates cooperation. This is another important feature of the tit-for-tat strategy. It is often difficult for people in conflict to recover from defection and end an escalating spiral of aggression. Tit-for-tat's eye-for-an-eye strategy ensures that its responses to aggression from the other side will never be more than it receives.

Not Clever   Ironically, one reason why tit-for-tat is so effective is that it is not very clever. It is an extremely simple strategy, and other people can quickly figure out what to expect from a player who follows it. This predictability has important psychological properties. When people are uncertain or unclear about what to expect, they are more likely to engage in defensive behavior. When uncertainty is high, people often assume the worst about another person. Predictability increases interpersonal attraction.

In summary, tit-for-tat is an extremely stable strategy. Negotiators who follow it often induce their opponents to adopt the tit-for-tat strategy. However, very few of the executives who play prisoner's dilemma games actually follow tit-for-tat. For example, in our analysis of over 600 executives playing the prisoner's dilemma game, the defection rate is nearly 40 percent, and average profits are only one-tenth of the possible maximum! But tit-for-tat is not uniquely stable; there are other strategies that are stable as well. For example, solid defection is a stable strategy. Two players who defect on every trial have little reason to do anything else. The message is that once someone has defected, it is very difficult to renew cooperation.

Recovering from Defection

Suppose that you are the manager of a large HMO. The health care industry is highly competitive, with different companies vying to capture market share by touting low deductibles and so on. You have analyzed the situation with your competitors to be a noncooperative game. You have thought about how your competitor must view the situation, and you have decided to take a cooperative approach and *not* engage in negative advertising. Later that week, you learn that your opponent has taken out a full-page ad in *The Wall Street Journal* that denigrates your HMO by publicizing questionable statistics about your mortality rates, quotes from angry patients, and charges about physicians. You counter with some negative TV spots. You are spending a lot of money and are angry. Can you stop this escalating spiral of defection? Probably so, if you consider the following strategies.

Make Situational Attributions   We often blame the incidence of escalating, mutually destructive conflict on others' ill will and evil intentions. We fail to realize that we might have done the same thing as our competitor had we been in his or her shoes. Why? We punctuate events differently than do our opponents. We see our behavior as a defensive *response* to the other. In contrast, we view the other as engaging in unprovoked acts of aggression. The solution is to see the other side's behavior as a response to our own actions. In the preceding situation, your competitor's negative ad campaign may be a payback for your campaign a year ago.

Tiny Steps   Trust is not rebuilt in a day. We rebuild trust incrementally by taking tiny steps. For example, the GRIT (graduated reduction in tension relations) strategy calls for conflicting parties to offer small concessions (Osgood 1979). This reduces the risk for the party making the concession.

Getting Even and Catching Up   As we saw in the chapter 3 on distributive negotiation (pie slicing), people are hyperconcerned with fairness. The perception of inequity is a major threat to the continuance of relationships. One way of rebuilding trust is to let the other party "get even" and catch up. The resurrection of a damaged relationship may depend on repentance on the part of the injurer and forgiveness on the part of the injured (Bottom, Gibson, Daniels, and Murnighan 1996). Even more surprising is that it is the thought that counts: Small amends are as effective as large amends in generating future cooperation.

Make Your Decisions at the Same Time   Imagine that you are playing a prisoner's dilemma game like that described in the Thelma and Louise case. You are told about the contingencies and payoffs in the game and then asked to make a choice. The twist in the situation is that you are either told that your opponent: (1) has already made her choice earlier that day, (2) will make her choice later that day, or (3) will make her choice at the same time as you. In all cases, you will *not* know the other person's choice before making your own. When faced with this situation, people are more likely to cooperate when their opponent's decision is temporally contiguous with their own decision—that is, when the opponent makes her decision at the same time (Morris, Sim, and Girrotto 1995). Temporal contiguity fosters a causal illusion: the idea that our behavior at a given time can influence the behavior of others. This logical impossibility is not permissible in the time-delayed decisions.

In the prisoner's dilemma game, people make choices simultaneously; therefore, one's choice cannot influence the choice that the other person makes on a given trial—only in subsequent trials. That is, when Thelma makes her decision to confess or not, this does not influence Louise, unless she is telepathic. However, people *act as if* their behavior influences the behavior of others, even though it logically cannot.

In an intriguing analysis of this perception, Douglas Hofstadter wrote a letter, published in *Scientific American,* to 20 friends (see Box 11–1). Hofstadter raised the question of whether one person's action in this situation can be taken as an indication of what all people will do. He concluded that if players are indeed rational, they will either all choose to defect or all choose to cooperate. Given that all players are going to submit the same answer, which choice would be more logical? It would seem that cooperation is best (each player gets $57 when all cooperate and only $19 when they all defect). At this point, the logic seems like magical thinking: A person's choice at a given time influences the behavior of others at the same time. Another example: People explain that they have decided to vote in an election so that others will, too. Of course, it is impossible that one person's voting behavior could affect others in a *given* election, but people act as if it does. Hofstadter argues that decision makers wrestling with such choices must give others credit for seeing the logic that oneself has seen. Thus, we need to believe that others are rational (like ourselves) and that they believe that everyone is rational. Hofstadter calls this rationality **superrationality.** For this reason, choosing to defect undermines the very reasons for choosing it. In Hofstadter's game, 14 people defected, and six cooperated. The defectors received $43; the cooperators received $15. Robert Axelrod was one of the participants who defected, remarking that in a one-shot game, there was no reason to cooperate.

SOCIAL DILEMMAS

Sometimes, managers find themselves involved in a prisoner's dilemma that contains several people (e.g., in the opening example of the research group). In these types of situations, negotiators find themselves choosing between cooperative strategies and self-interested strategies. The multiperson prisoner's dilemma is known as a social dilemma. (See Sidebars 11–1 and 11–2 for other types of social dilemma—volunteer dilemmas and ultimatum dilemmas.) In general, people tend to behave more competitively (in a self-interested fashion) in social dilemmas as compared to prisoner's dilemmas. Why is this?

First, the prisoner's dilemma involves two parties; the social dilemma involves several people. This *size difference* is important. People tend to behave more competitively in groups than in two-person situations (Insko et al. 1994). Second, the *costs of defection are spread out,* rather than concentrated upon one person. Simply stated, when one person makes a self-interested choice and others choose to cooperate, everyone but the defector absorbs some (but not all) of the cost. Thus, the defecting person can say to him- or herself that everyone is suffering a little bit, rather than a lot. This may lead to people being more inclined to look out for themselves.

Third, social dilemmas are *riskier* than prisoner's dilemmas. In the two-person dilemma, there is a certain minimal payoff to parties that can be anticipated in advance. However, this is not true in a social dilemma. The worst-case scenario is when

> ### BOX 11–1
>
> ## LETTER FROM DOUGLAS HOFSTADTER TO 20 FRIENDS IN *SCIENTIFIC AMERICAN*
>
> Dear _____ :
>
> I am sending this letter by special delivery to 20 of you (namely, various friends of mine around the country). I am proposing to all of you a one-round Prisoner's Dilemma game, the payoffs to be monetary (provided by *Scientific American*). It is very simple. Here is how it goes.
>
> Each of you is to give me a single letter: *C* or *D*, standing for "cooperate" or "defect." This will be used as your move in a Prisoner's Dilemma with *each* of the 19 other players.
>
> Thus, if everyone sends in *C*, everyone will get $57, whereas if everyone sends in *D*, everyone will get $19. You can't lose! And, of course, anyone who sends in *D* will get at least as much as everyone else. If, for example, 11 people send in *C* and nine send in *D*, then the 11 *C*-ers will get $3 a piece from each of the other *C*-ers (making $30) and will get nothing from the *D*-ers. Therefore, *C*-ers will get $30 each. The *D*-ers in contrast, will pick up $5 a piece from each of the *C*-ers (making $55) and will get $1 from each of the other *D*-ers (making $8), for a grand total of $63. No matter what the distribution is, *D*-ers always do better than *C*-ers. Of course, the more *C*-ers there are, the better *everyone* will do!
>
> By the way, I should make it clear that in making your choice you should not aim to be the *winner* but simply to get as much *money* for yourself as possible. Thus, you should be happier to get $30 (say, as a result of saying *C*
>
> along with 10 others, even though the nine *D*-sayers get more than you) than to get $19 (by saying *D* along with everyone else, so that nobody "beat" you.) Furthermore, you are not supposed to think that at some later time you will meet with and be able to share the goods with your coparticipants. You are not aiming at maximizing the total number of dollars *Scientific American* shells out, only at maximizing the number of dollars that come to *you!*
>
> Of course, your hope is to be the *unique* defector, thereby really cleaning up: with 19 *C*-ers, you will get $95 and they will each get 18 times $3, namely $54. But why am I doing the multiplication or any of this figuring for you? You are very bright. So are the others. All about equally bright, I would say. Therefore, all you need to do is tell me your choice. I want all answers by telephone (call collect, please) *the day you receive this letter.*
>
> It is to be understood (it *almost* goes without saying, but not quite) that you are not to try to consult with others who you guess have been asked to participate. In fact, please consult with no one at all. The purpose is to see what people will do on their own, in isolation. Finally, I would appreciate a short statement to go along with your choice, telling me *why* you made this particular one.
>
> Yours,
>
> Doug H.
>
> *Source:* Hofstadter, D. (1983). Metamagical thinking. *Scientific American 248:* 14–28.

the negotiator chooses to cooperate and everyone else defects. The costs of this are very great. Greater risk and more uncertainty leads people to behave in a more self-interested, competitive fashion.

Fourth, social dilemmas *provide anonymity* that prisoner's dilemmas do not. When someone defects in a two-party situation, it is obvious who did it. Anonymity is impossible. In short, people feel less accountable for their actions, and the resulting outcomes

> ### SIDEBAR 11–1. VOLUNTEER DILEMMA
> The **volunteer dilemma** is a situation in which at least one person in a group must sacrifice his or her own interests to better the group. An example is a group of friends who want to go out for an evening of drinking and celebration. The problem is that all cannot drink if one person must safely drive everyone home. A "designated" driver is a volunteer for the group. Most organized entities would not function if no one volunteered. The act of volunteering strengthens groups ties (Murnighan, Kim, and Metzger 1993).

in social dilemmas, because they can "hide among the group." When people feel less accountable, they are more inclined to behave in a self-interested, competitive fashion.

Finally, people in social dilemmas *have less control* over the situation. In a classic, two-party prisoner's dilemma, people can directly shape and modify the behavior of the other person. Specifically, by choosing defection, one person may punish the other; by choosing cooperation, he or she can reward the other. This is the logic and beauty of the tit-for-tat strategy. However, in a social dilemma, if someone defects, one person cannot necessarily punish the other on the next round because others will also be affected and, as we have seen, the costs of defection are spread out. Thus, there is a loss of control. Furthermore, because of the anonymity problem, we may not even know whom to punish.

THE TRAGEDY OF THE COMMONS

Imagine that you are a farmer. You own several cows and share a grazing pasture known as a "commons" with other farmers. There are 100 farmers who share the pasture. Each farmer is allowed to have one cow graze. Because the commons is not policed, it is tempting for you to add one more cow without fear of detection. By adding another cow, you can double your utility, and no one will really suffer. If everyone does this, however, the commons will be overrun and the grazing area depleted. The cumulative result will be disastrous. What should you do in this situation if you want to keep your family alive?

The analysis of the "tragedy of the commons" (from Hardin 1968) may be applied to many real-world problems, such as pollution, use of natural resources, and overpopulation. In these situations, people are tempted to maximize their own gain, reasoning that their pollution, failure to vote, and Styrofoam cups in the landfill will not have a measurable impact on others. However, if everyone engages in this behavior, the collective outcome is disastrous: Air will be unbreathable, there will not be enough votes in an election, and landfills will be overrun. Thus, in the social dilemma, the rational pursuit of self-interest produces collective disaster.

In the social dilemma situation, each person makes behavioral choices similar to those in the prisoner's dilemma: to benefit oneself or the group. As in the prisoner's dilemma, the choices are referred to as cooperation and defection. The defecting choice always results in better personal outcomes, at least in the immediate future, but universal defection results in poorer outcomes for everyone than does universal cooperation.

A hallmark characteristic of social dilemmas is that the rational pursuit of self-interest is detrimental to collective welfare. This has very serious and potentially dis-

SIDEBAR 11–2. ULTIMATUM DILEMMA

In an ultimatum bargaining situation, one person makes a final offer—an ultimatum—to another person. If the other person accepts the offer, then the first player receives the demand that he or she made, and the other player agrees to accept what was offered to him or her. If the offer is refused, then no settlement is reached—an impasse occurs—and negotiators receive their respective reservation points.

How should we negotiate in ultimatum situations? What kind of a final offer should we make to another person? When the tables are turned, on what basis should we accept or refuse a final offer someone makes to us?

Suppose someone with a $100 bill in hand comes to you and the person sitting on the bus beside you. This person explains that the $100 is yours to share with the other person if you can propose a split that the other person will agree to. The only hitch is that the division you propose is a once-and-for-all-decision: You cannot discuss it with the other person, and you have to propose a take-it-or-leave-it split. If the other person accepts your proposal, the $100 will be allocated accordingly. If the other person rejects your proposal, no one gets any money, and you do not have the opportunity to propose another offer. Faced with this situation, what should you do? (Before reading further, indicate what you would do and why.)

It is useful for us to solve this problem using the principles of decision theory and then see if the solution squares with our intuition. Once again, we use the concept of backward induction, working backward from the last period of the game. The last decision in this game is an ultimatum. In this game, player 2 (the person beside you on the bus) must decide whether to accept the proposal offered by you or reject the offer and receive nothing. From a rational standpoint, player 2 should accept any positive offer you make to him or her because, after all, something (even 1 cent) is better than nothing.

Now we can examine the next-to-last decision in the game and ask what proposal player 1 (you) should make. Because you know that player 2 should accept any positive offer greater than $0, the game theoretic solution is for you to offer $0.01 to player 2 and demand $99.99 for yourself. This is a **subgame perfect equilibrium** (Selten 1975) because it is rational within each period of the game. Said in a different way, even if the game had additional periods to be played in the future, your offer of $99.99 (to you) and $0.01 to the other person would still be rational at this point.

Contrary to game theoretic predictions, most people do not do this. That is, most player 1s propose amounts substantially greater than $0.01 for player 2, often around the midpoint, or $50. Further, player 2s often reject offers that are not 50-50 splits (Pillutla and Murnighan 1995). Thus, some player 2s choose to have $0 rather than $1, or $2—or even $49. Player 1s act nonrationally and so do player 2s. This seems completely counter to one's interests, or but, as we saw in chapter 2, people are often more concerned with how their outcomes compare to others than with the absolute value of their outcomes (see Loewenstein, Thompson, and Bazerman 1989; Messick and Sentis 1979).

astrous implications. (In this sense, social dilemmas contradict the principle of hedonism and laissez-faire economics.) That is, unless some limits are placed on the pursuit of personal goals, the entire society may suffer.

TYPES OF SOCIAL DILEMMAS

There are two major forms of the social dilemma: **resource conservation dilemmas** (also known as **collective traps**) and **public goods dilemmas** (also known as **collective fences;** see Messick and Brewer 1983). In the resource conservation dilemma, individuals take or harvest resources from a common pool (like the farmers in the commons). Examples of the detrimental effects of individual interest include pollution, budget fudging, harvesting (of fossil fuels), burning of fossil fuels, water shortages, and negative advertising (see Sidebar 11–3 and actual ads). The defecting choice occurs when people consume too much. The result of overconsumption is collective disaster. For groups to sustain themselves, the rate of consumption cannot exceed the rate of replenishment of resources.

In public goods dilemmas, people contribute or give resources to a common pool or community. Examples include donating to public radio and television, paying taxes, voting, doing committee work, and joining unions. The defecting choice is to not contribute. Those who fail to contribute are known as defectors or free riders. Those who pay while others free ride are affectionately known as suckers.

HOW TO BUILD COOPERATION IN SOCIAL DILEMMAS

Most groups in organizations could be characterized as social dilemma situations (Kramer 1991; Mannix 1993). Members are left to their own devices to decide how much to take or contribute for common benefit. Consider an organization in which members are allowed to monitor their use of supplies and equipment, such as computer manuals, Xerox paper, stamps, and envelopes. Each member may be tempted to overuse or hoard resources, thereby contributing to a rapid depletion of supply.

Many individual characteristics of people have been studied, such as gender, race, Machiavellianism, status, age, and so on (for a review, see Rubin and Brown 1975). There are few, if any, reliable individual differences that predict behavior in a prisoner's dilemma game. In fact, people cooperate more than rational analysis would predict. Many investigations use a single trial or fixed number of trials in which the rational strategy is solid defection. When the game is infinite or the number of trials is indefinite, however, people cooperate less than they should. What steps can the manager take to build greater cooperation and trust among organization members? We outline eleven strategies, organized in terms of the most effective (and expensive) to those that are less expensive.

Aligning Incentives

Monetary incentives for cooperation, privatization of resources, and a monitoring system increase the incidence of cooperation. For example, by putting in "high-vehicle occupancy" lanes on major highways, single drivers are more motivated to carpool. However, realignment of incentives can be time-consuming and expensive.

Monitoring Behavior

When we monitor people's behavior, they often conform to group norms. The same beneficial effects also occur when people monitor their own behavior. For example, when people meter their water consumption during a water shortage, they use less water (Van Vugt and Samuelson 1999). Moreover, people who metered expressed greater concern with the collective costs of overconsumption during a drought.

Reducing the Costs of Cooperation/Rewarding Cooperation

Often defectors are reluctant to cooperate because the costs of cooperation seem exorbitantly high. For example, people often defect by not paying their parking tickets because the price is high and they have several tickets. In some cases, city officials have allowed for amnesty delays for delinquent parking tickets, whereby people can cooperate at a cost less than they expected. Cities have adopted similar policies to induce people to return borrowed library books.

Cooperation can also be induced through reward and recognition in organizations. Recognition awards, such as gold stars, employee-of-the-month awards, and the like, are designed to induce cooperation, rather than defection, in a variety of organizational social dilemmas.

Minimizing Temptations to Defect

In some instances, cooperation can be induced by increasing the risk associated with defection. For example, some people do not pay their state or federal income tax in the United States. This is illegal and if a defector is caught, he or she can be convicted of a crime. The threat of spending years in jail often lessens the temptation of defection. However, most tacit negotiations in organizations are not policed in this fashion and therefore, defection is more tempting for would-be defectors.

Psychological Contracts and the Power of Commitment

People are more likely to cooperate when they promise to cooperate. Although any such promises are nonbinding and are therefore "cheap talk," people nevertheless act as if they are binding. Why is this? According to the **norm of commitment,** people feel psychologically committed to follow through with their word (Cialdini 1993). The norm of commitment is so powerful that people often do things that are completely at odds with their preferences or that are highly inconvenient. For example, once people agree to let a salesperson demonstrate a product in their home, they are more likely to buy it. Homeowners are more likely to consent to have a large (over 10 feet tall), obtrusive sign in their front yard that says "Drive Carefully" when they agree to a small request made the week before (Freedman and Fraser 1966).

SIDEBAR 11–3. COMPARATIVE ADVERTISING

Since the 1970s, there has been a trend toward "comparative advertising" in which companies compare their product with competitors' products and point out the advantages of their own product and the disadvantages of the competitors' products. Hardly any industry has managed to avoid comparative advertising. Advertisers have battled over milk quality, fish oil, beer taste, electric shavers, cola, coffee, magazines, cars, telephone service, banking, credit cards, and peanut butter. The ads attack the products and services of other companies. What is the effect of the attack ad? For the consumer, attack ads keep prices down and quality high. However, it can also lead to consumer resentment toward the industry. The effect is much more serious for the advertisers, who can effectively run each other out of business. (See examples of comparative advertising on subsequent pages.)

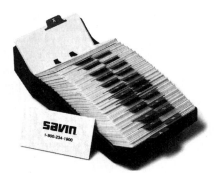

Sidebar 11–3. Example of negative (competitive) advertising.

Courtesy of The Savin Corporation, Stanford, Connecticut.

Business Class Legroom	
Delta BusinessElite	**36.5"**
Continental	31"
British Airways	24"
Lufthansa	23"
American Airlines	22"

Business Class Recline	
Delta BusinessElite	**160°**
Continental	152°
British Airways	140°
Lufthansa	135°
American Airlines	132°

Nonstop European Destinations	
Delta BusinessElite	**23**
Continental	17
American Airlines	12
British Airways	3
Lufthansa	3

Nonstop destinations from the U.S.

Concierge Service At Every Gateway	
Delta BusinessElite	**Yes**
Continental	No
British Airways	No
Lufthansa	No
American Airlines	No

Looks great on paper.
Feels even better in person.

Presenting Delta BusinessElite.™

There are a lot of reasons to fly Delta's new BusinessElite,

but don't take our word for it. Experience it for yourself.

With more personal space than other leading airlines' business

classes, and our convenient BusinessElite Concierge service at all

32 intercontinental destinations, we think you'll agree. BusinessElite

to Europe, Japan, India and Brazil simply outclasses business class.

BUSINESS *elite*

▲ **Delta Air Lines**

For reservations, visit us at www.bizelite.com or call Delta Air Lines at 1-800-241-4141. Or see your Travel Agent today.

Personal space is defined as the sum of legroom and recline. Legroom based on measurements taken from the foremost point of the bottom seat cushion to the back of the seat in front of it using non-bulkhead seats on a widebody aircraft of Continental (DC10-30), British Airways (747-200), Lufthansa (A340-300) and American Airlines (767-300). ©1999 Delta Air Lines, Inc.

Sidebar 11–3. Example of explicit comparative advertising.
Courtesy of Delta Airlines, Atlanta, Georgia.

Communication

A key determinant of cooperation is **communication** (Messick and Brewer 1983; Liebrand, Messick, and Wilke 1992; Komorita and Parks 1994; Sally 1995). If people are allowed to communicate with the members of the group prior to making their choices, the incidence and level of cooperation increase dramatically (Sally 1995). Why is this?

When people communicate with one another in social dilemma situations, they elicit commitments of cooperation from one another. Verbal commitments in such situations indicate the willingness of others to cooperate. In this sense, they reduce the uncertainty that people have about others in such situations and provide a measure of reassurance to decision makers. Commitments also shape subsequent behavior. People are extremely reluctant to break their word, even when their words are nonbinding. If people are prevented from making verbal commitments, they will attempt to make nonverbal ones. For example, some students who engaged in a prisoner's dilemma situation rubbed their tattoos prior to making an independent decision as a sign of commitment!

Building Social Identity

The other reason why communication is effective in engendering cooperation is that it allows group members to develop a social or group identity: Communication allows people to get to know one another and feel more attracted to their group. People derive a sense of identity from their relationships to social groups (Tajfel 1979). When our identity is traced to the relationships we have with others in groups, we seek to further the interests of these groups. This leads to more cooperative, or group-welfare, choices in social dilemmas.

Social identity is often built through relationships. For example, as a consequence of population growth, the politics of water distribution, and five years of drought, California had widespread shortages of water in 1991. Residents of many areas were encouraged to voluntarily conserve water and were subjected to regulations imposed by the Public Utilities Commission. A telephone survey of hundreds of residents of the San Francisco area revealed that people were more willing to support authorities when they had strong relational bonds to the authorities (Tyler and Degoey 1995). The effectiveness of authorities in eliciting cooperation in water-shortage dilemmas is linked to the social bonds that they share with community members.

Publicizing Commitment

In November 1995, USAir announced that it was putting its company up for sale (for a full treatment, see Diekmann, Tenbrunsel, and Bazerman 1998). Financial analysts speculated that the sale of USAir would lead to a bidding war between the major airlines, because whichever airline acquired USAir would have a market advantage. None of the airlines wanted to be in the position of not acquiring USAir and seeing another airline buy the company.

Following the announcement of the sale of USAir, a strange series of events followed that was not forecast by financial analysts: No one bid for USAir. Analysts did not realize that the major airlines had learned an important principle through their experience in the 1980s with the frequent flyer and triple mile programs, which were designed to be competitive strategies to capture market share. However, the approach

BOX 11–2

LETTER TO THE EMPLOYEES OF AMERICAN AIRLINES FROM ROBERT CRANDALL, CHAIRMAN

We continue to believe, as we always have, that the best way for American to increase its size and reach is by internal growth—not by consolidation. So we will not be the first to make a bid for USAir. On the other hand, if United seeks to acquire USAir, we will be prepared to respond with a bid, or by other means as necessary, to protect American's competitive position.

Source: S. Ziemba, *Chicago Tribune,* November 10, 1995.

backfired in the airline industry when all of the major airlines developed frequent flyer programs, and a price war began, which resulted in the loss of millions of dollars among airlines.

Robert Crandall, the chairman of American Airlines, was effective in averting a costly escalation war for USAir. How did he do this? Before reading further, stop and indicate what you would do if this was your company.

Robert Crandall wrote and published an open letter to the employees of American Airlines that appeared in the *Chicago Tribune* (see Box 11–2). The letter clearly indicated that American Airlines was interested in avoiding a costly bidding war with United Airlines for USAir. The letter clearly stated the *intentions* of American not to make an opening bid for USAir. The letter further indicated that American would bid competitively if United initiated bidding for USAir.

The letter effectively signaled the intentions of American Airlines in a way that made bidding behavior seem too costly. Although the letter was addressed to the employees of American Airlines, it is obvious that the real targets of this message were the other airlines.

Personalizing Others

People often behave as if they were interacting with an entity or organization rather than a person. For example, an embittered customer claims that the airline refused her a refund when in fact it was a representative of the airline who did not issue a refund. To the extent that others can be personalized, people are more motivated to cooperate than if they believe they are dealing with a dehumanized bureaucracy. Even more important is that people see you as a cooperator: People cooperate more when others have cooperated in a previous situation (Pillutla and Chen 1999).

Redefining the Game

According to rational analysis, only the payoffs of the game should influence one's strategy. However, our behavior in social dilemmas is influenced by our perceptions about what kinds of behavior are appropriate and expected in a given context. In an intriguing examination of this idea, people engaged in a prisoner's dilemma task. The game was not described to participants as a "prisoner's dilemma," though. In one condition, the game was called the "Wall Street game," and in another condition, the game was called the "community game" (Ross and Samuels 1993). Otherwise, the game, the payoffs, and the choices were identical. Whereas rational analysis predicts that defection is the optimal strategy no matter what the name, in fact, the incidence of cooperation was three times as high in the community game than in the Wall Street game, indicating that people are sensitive to situational cues as trivial as the name of the game. Indeed, people behave more competitively in social dilemmas involving economic decisions compared to those involving noneconomic decisions (Pillutla and Chen 1999).

Impression Management

Still another reason why people cooperate is that they want to believe that they are nice people. For example, one person attributed his decision to make a cooperative choice in the 20-person prisoner's dilemma game to the fact that he did not want the readers of *Scientific American* to think that he was a defector (Hofstadter 1983). This is a type of impression management (Goffman 1959).

Impression management raises the question of whether people's behavior is different when it is anonymous than when it is public. The answer appears to be yes. However, it is not always the case that public behavior is more cooperative than private behavior. For example, negotiators who are accountable to a constituency often bargain harder and are more competitive than when they are accountable for their behavior (see Carnevale, Pruitt, and Seilheimmer 1981).

ESCALATION OF COMMITMENT

Suppose you make a small investment in a start-up Internet company that seems to have great potential. After the first quarter, you learn that the company suffered an operating loss. You cannot recover your investment; your goal is to maximize your long-term wealth. Should you continue to invest in the company? Consider two possible ways to look at this situation: if you consider the performance of the company during the first quarter to be a loss, and if you view continued investment as a choice between:

1. losing the small amount of money you have already invested, or
2. taking additional risk by investing more money in the company, which could turn around and make a large profit or plummet even further.

The reference point effect described in chapter 2 would predict that most negotiators would continue to invest in the company because they have already adopted a "loss frame" based upon their initial investment. Suppose that you recognize that the Internet company did not perform well in the first period and consider your initial investment to be a sunk cost—that is, water under the bridge. In short, you adapt your reference point. Now, ask yourself whether it would be wiser to:

1. not invest in the company at this point (a sure outcome of $0), or
2. take a gamble and invest more money in a company that has not shown good performance in the recent past.

Under these circumstances, most people choose not to invest in the company because they would rather have a sure thing than a loss. A negotiator's psychological reference point also influences the tendency to fall into the escalation trap. Recall that negotiators are risk-seeking when it comes to losses and risk-averse for gains. When negotiators see themselves as trying to recover from a losing position, chances are they will engage in greater risk than if they see themselves as starting with a clean slate. Like the gambler in Las Vegas, negotiators who are hoping to hold out longer than their opponent (such as in a strike or in making a final offer) have fallen into the escalation trap. Most decision makers and negotiators do not readjust their reference point. Rather, they fail to adapt their reference point and continue to make risky decisions, which often prove unprofitable.

The **escalation of commitment** refers to the unfortunate tendency of negotiators to persist with a losing course of action, even in the face of clear evidence that their behaviors are not working and the negotiation situation is quickly deteriorating. There are two types of escalation dilemmas: personal and interpersonal. In both cases, the dilemma is revealed when a person would do something different if they had not already been involved in the situation.

Personal escalation dilemmas involve only one person, and the dilemma concerns whether to continue with what appears to be a losing course of action or to cut one's losses. Continuing to gamble after losing a lot of money, pouring money into a car or house that continues to break down or deteriorate, and waiting in long lines that are not moving are examples of personal escalation dilemmas. To stop is to in some sense admit failure and accept a sure loss. Continuing to invest holds the possibility of recouping losses. Consider, for example, the case of John R. Silber, previous president of Boston University, who decided to invest in Seragen, a biotechnology company with a promising cancer drug. After investing $1.7 million over six years, the value of the company in 1998 was $43,000 (Barboza 1998).

Interpersonal escalation dilemmas involve two or more people, often in a competitive relationship, such as negotiation. Union strikes are often escalation dilemmas, and so is war. Consider the situation faced by Lyndon Johnson during the early stage of the Vietnam War. Johnson received the following memo from George Ball, then under-secretary of state:

> The decision you face now is crucial. Once large numbers of U.S. troops are committed to direct combat, they will begin to take heavy casualties in a war they are ill-equipped to fight in a noncooperative if not downright hostile countryside. Once we suffer large casualties, we will have started a well-nigh irreversible process. Our involvement will be so great that we cannot—without national humiliation—stop short of achieving our complete objectives. Of the two possibilities I think humiliation will be more likely than the achievement of our objectives—even after we have paid terrible costs.
> (Sheehan et al. 1971, 450)

In escalation dilemmas, negotiators commit further resources to what appears to unbiased observers to be a failing course of action. In most cases, people fall into escalation traps because initially, the situation does not appear to be a losing enterprise. The situation becomes an escalation dilemma when the persons involved in the decision

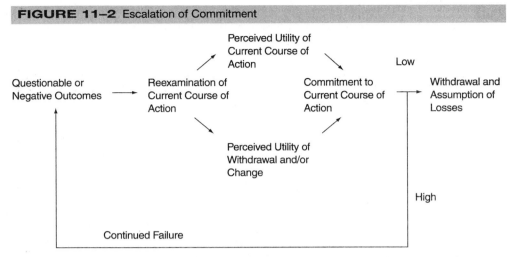

FIGURE 11–2 Escalation of Commitment

Source: Adapted from Ross, J., and Staw, B. M. (1993). Organizational escalation and exit: Lessons from the Shoreham Nuclear Power Plant. *Academy of Management Journal,* August, 701–732.

would make a different decision if they had not been involved up until that point, or when other objective persons would not choose that course of action. Often, in escalation situations, a decision is made to commit further resources to "turn the situation around," such as in the case of gambling (personal dilemma) or making a final offer (interpersonal dilemma). This process may repeat and escalate several times as additional resources are invested. The bigger the investment and the more severe the possible loss, the more prone people are to try to turn things around.

The escalation of commitment process is illustrated in Figure 11–2 (Ross and Staw 1993). In the first stage of the escalation of commitment, a person is confronted with questionable or negative outcomes (e.g., a rejection of one's offer by a negotiation opponent, decrease in market share, poor performance evaluation, a malfunction, or hostile behavior from a competitor). This external event prompts a reexamination of the negotiator's current course of action, in which the utility of continuing is weighted against the utility of withdrawing or changing course. This decision determines the negotiator's commitment to his or her current course of action. If this commitment is low, the negotiator may make a concession, engage in integrative negotiations (rather than distributive negotiations), or possibly revert to his or her BATNA. If this commitment is high, however, the negotiator will continue commitment and continue to cycle through the decision stages.

When negotiators receive indication that the outcomes of a negotiation may be negative, they should ask themselves: *What are the personal rewards for me in this situation?* In many cases, the *process* of the negotiation itself, rather than the *outcome* of the negotiation, becomes the reason for commencing or continuing negotiations. This leads to a self-perpetuating reinforcement trap, wherein the rewards for continuing are not aligned with the actual objectives of the negotiator. Ironically, people who have high, rather than low, self-esteem are more likely to become victimized by psychological forces—people with high self-esteem have much more invested in their ego and its maintenance than do those with low self-esteem (Taylor and Brown 1988). Sometimes face-saving concerns lead negotiators to escalate commitment. That is, some negotiators worry that they will look silly or stupid if they back down from an initial position. Ego protection often becomes a higher priority than the success of the negotiation.

AVOIDING THE ESCALATION OF COMMITMENT IN NEGOTIATIONS

Most negotiators do not realize that they are in an escalation dilemma until it is too late. Complicating matters is the fact that, in most escalation dilemmas, a negotiator (like a gambler) might have some early "wins" or good signs that reinforce their initial position. How can a negotiator best get out of an escalation dilemma?

Unfortunately, there is no magical, overnight cure. The best advice is to adopt a policy of risk management: be aware of the risks involved in the situation; learn how to best manage these risks; and set limits, effectively capping losses at a tolerable level. It is also important to find ways to get information and feedback about the negotiation from a different perspective.

Set Limits
Ideally, a negotiator should walk into the negotiation with a clearly defined BATNA. At no point should a negotiator make or accept an offer that is worse than his or her BATNA.

Avoid Tunnel Vision
A negotiator should get several perspectives on the situation. Ask people who are not personally involved in the negotiation for their appraisal. Be careful not to bias their evaluation with your own views, hopes, expectations, or other details, such as the cost of extricating yourself from the situation, because that will only predispose them toward your point of view. This is not what you want—you want an honest, critical assessment.

Recognize Sunk Costs
Probably the most powerful way to escape escalation of commitment is to simply recognize and accept sunk costs. Sunk costs are basically water under the bridge: money (or other commitments) previously spent that cannot be recovered. It is often helpful for negotiators to consider removal of the project, product, or program. In this way, the situation is redefined as one in which a decision will be made immediately about whether to invest or not; that is, if you were making the initial decision today, would you make the investment currently under consideration (as a continuing investment), or would you choose another course of action? If the decision is not one that you would choose anew, you might want to start thinking about how to terminate the project and move on to the next one.

Diversify Responsibility and Authority
In some cases, it is necessary to remove or replace the original negotiators from deliberations precisely because they are biased. One way to do this is with an external review or appointing someone who does not have a personal stake in the situation.

Redefine the Situation
Often, it helps to view the situation not as the "same old problem" but as a new problem to be dealt with. Furthermore, it often helps to change the decision criteria. For

example, consider how Johns-Manville, the asbestos manufacturer, handled catastrophe. As a manager at Manville for more than 30 years, Bill Sells witnessed colossal examples of self-deception. Manville managers at every level were unwilling to acknowledge the evidence available in the 1940s about the hazards of asbestos, and their capacity for denial held steady through the following decades, despite mounting evidence of old and new hazards:

> The company developed a classic case of bunker mentality: refusing to accept facts; assuming that customers and employees were aware of the hazards and used asbestos at their own risk; denying the need for and the very possibility of change at a company that had successfully hidden its head in the sand for 100 years. Manville funded little medical research, made little effort to communicate what it already knew, and took little or no proactive responsibility for the damage asbestos might do . . . with tragic consequences for workers' health and decidedly negative effects on maintenance costs, productivity, and profit. Once when he raised objections, Sells was told by his boss, 'Bill, you're not loyal,' to which he replied, 'No, no, you've got it wrong. I'm the one who *is* loyal.' (Teal 1996, 38)

In 1968, Sells successfully redefined the situation. He viewed it as one of business integrity, launching a $500,000 program to replace and rebuild nearly all the safety equipment at a troubled asbestos facility in Illinois. It was too late to save asbestos or its victims, but he put into practice important changes, such as funding arm's-length studies, immediate total disclosure, and the elimination of pro-company "spin" on any study results (Teal 1996).

CONCLUSION

Most people are involved in tacit negotiations, wherein they communicate through action and behavior. Prisoner's dilemmas and social dilemmas are characterized by the absence of contracts and enforcement mechanisms. Most people face choices between acting in a self-interested fashion or in a cooperative fashion that makes the negotiator vulnerable to exploitation. Optimal pie-expanding and pie-slicing strategies in the two-person prisoner's dilemma can be achieved via the tit-for-tat strategy, but tit-for-tat works only when a negotiator has a long-term perspective. However, many tacit negotiations within and between organizations involve more than two players and are social dilemmas. The best way to ensure cooperation from parties is to align incentives, remove temptations to defect, seek verbal commitments, communicate with involved parties, build social identity, publicize commitments, personalize others, redefine the situation, and help manage impressions. Escalation dilemmas occur when people invest in what is (by any objective standards) a losing course of action. People can deescalate via setting limits, getting several perspectives, recognizing sunk costs, and diversifying responsibility.

12

NEGOTIATING VIA INFORMATION TECHNOLOGY

LaRae Maruyama, controller for the U.S. Olympic Committee, sifted through about 300 Colorado Springs real-estate listings and looked at 60 houses over five months before she found what she wanted. Her search might have taken even longer, were it not for the Internet. Except for actual closing, home buyers and sellers can go through every stage of a home search without ever leaving their desks. According to the National Association of Realtors, some 23 percent of buyers now use the Internet as a search tool, up from only 2 percent in 1995. Most Web sites allow buyers to create a profile of the home they want, from location and price to the number of bathrooms (Hoffman 1999; see Sidebar 12–1 for Web sites related to home buying).

Yet, in the era where virtual offices, teleconferencing, and fax machines proliferate, something is missing that many business people need to close a deal—the human touch (Seaberry 2000). According to the Travel Industry Association, business travel continues to increase, despite the abundance of high-tech gadgets used to assist communication. Business travel has risen 14 percent since 1994, and the Association forecasts it will continue increasing by 3 percent a year. Modern technology has not killed the business trip for a very old-fashioned reason: People need to negotiate face-to-face. According to many, technology encourages travel. In other words, e-mail and videoconference eventually lead to a face-to-face meeting, or grow more business that means face-to-face deal making.

SIDEBAR 12–1. BUY, SELL, BORROW ON THE WEB (FROM HOFFMAN 1999)

Site/URL	Description
Cyberhomes www.cyberhomes.com	Claims to update listings daily
E-Loan www.e-loan.com	Compare and apply for mortgages from 70 lenders
Homeadvisor homeadvisor.msn.com	Good general information about real estate
Homebid.com www.homebid.com	On-line auction site
Homes.com www.homes.com	300,000 listings nationally
Iown.com www.iown.com	Mortgage broker with links to 25 lenders
Mortgage.com www.mortgage.com	Apply and get approval for home loans on-line
Owners.com: www.owners.com	For sellers who want to do it themselves
Realtor.com: www.realtor.com	Nearly 1.4 million listings throughout the United States

In an age of virtual negotiations, people put their trust in information technology to transcend time and place and make communication easier and faster. This chapter examines the impact of information technology on negotiation. We begin by describing a simple model of social interaction called the place-time model. This model will give us a framework through which we can evaluate the various forms of information technology and how they apply to negotiation. The model focuses on negotiators who either negotiate in the same or different physical location and at the same or different time. For each of these cases, we describe what to expect and ways to deal with the limitations of that communication mode. We follow this discussion with a section on how information technology affects negotiation behavior. We then describe strategies to help negotiators expand and divide the pie effectively.

PLACE-TIME MODEL OF SOCIAL INTERACTION

For any negotiation there are, broadly speaking, four possibilities, depicted in the place–time model in Table 12–1 (see also Johansen 1988; Englebart 1989). The **place-time model** is based on the options that negotiators have when doing business across different locations and times. As might be suspected, negotiation behavior unfolds differently in face-to-face situations than in electronic forums.

Richness is the potential information-carrying capacity of the communication medium (Drolet and Morris 2000). Communication media may be ordered on a continuum of richness, with face-to-face communication being at the relatively "rich" end, and formal, written messages, such as memos and business correspondence, being at the relatively "lean" or modality-restricted end (Daft and Lengel 1984; Daft, Lengel, and Trevino 1987; see Figure 12–1).

Face-to-face communication conveys the richest information because it allows for the simultaneous observation of multiple cues, including body language, facial expression, and tone of voice, providing people with a greater awareness of context. In contrast, formal numerical documentation conveys the least-rich information, providing few clues about the context. In addition, geographical propinquity and time constraints affect negotiations.

Let's consider each of the four types of communications in the place-time model in more detail.

Table 12–1:	Place-time model of interaction	
	Same Place	*Different Place*
Same Time	Face to face	Telephone Videoconference
Different Time	Single text editing Shift work	E-mail Voice mail

FACE-TO-FACE COMMUNICATION

Face-to-face negotiation is the clear preference of most negotiators and rightly so. Face-to-face contact is crucial in the initiation of relationships and collaborations, and people are more cooperative when interacting face-to-face than via other forms of communication. Personal, face-to-face contact is the lubricant of the business engine. Without it, things do not move very well, and relationships between people are often strained and contentious (see Sidebar 12–2 for an example).

FIGURE 12-1 Psychological Distancing Model

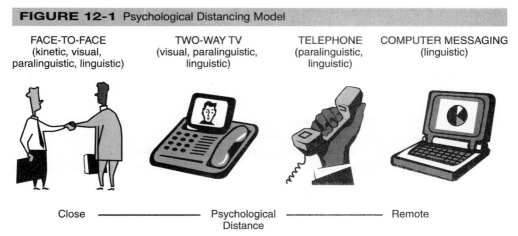

| FACE-TO-FACE (kinetic, visual, paralinguistic, linguistic) | TWO-WAY TV (visual, paralinguistic, linguistic) | TELEPHONE (paralinguistic, linguistic) | COMPUTER MESSAGING (linguistic) |

Close ———————— Psychological ———————— Remote
Distance

Source: Adapted from Wellens, A. R. (1989). Effects of telecommunication media upon information sharing and team performance: Some theoretical and empirical findings. *IEEE AES Magazine,* September, p. 14.

SIDEBAR 12–2. THE IMPORTANCE OF FACE-TO-FACE COMMUNICATION

A group of top managers at a progressive Silicon Valley company hated their weekly meetings, but enjoyed e-mail because it is quick, direct, and to the point. They thought meetings were "gassy, bloated, and a waste of time." So they decided to cancel their regular meetings and meet only when confronted with problems just too tough to handle over the network. Three months later, the same people resumed their regularly scheduled face-to-face meetings. They discovered that they had created a "morale-busting, network-generated nightmare." When the managers did get together, the meetings were unpleasant and unproductive. Precisely because they could use e-mail to reach consensus on easy issues, arguing the thorny issues face-to-face turned their "big problem" meetings into combat zones. E-mail interaction had eliminated the opportunity for casual agreement and social niceties that make meetings enjoyable. Even the e-mail communication became most hostile as participants maneuvered themselves in anticipation of the big-problem meeting (Schrage 1995).

Face-to-face negotiations are particularly important when negotiators meet for the first time. This is when norms of interaction are established and when misunderstandings should be resolved. Negotiators are more cooperative when interacting face-to-face rather than over the telephone (Drolet and Morris 1995). Face-to-face communication (as opposed to using the telephone or more restricting forms) fosters the development of interpersonal synchrony and rapport, and thus leads to more trusting, cooperative behavior (Drolet and Morris 1995). Face-to-face meetings are ideal for wrestling with complex negotiations. Valley, Moag, and Bazerman (1998) report that "Any mode of communication during bargaining increases the efficiency of outcomes over economic predictions" (p. 212). According to Valley et al. (1998), who investigated face-to-face versus writing-only and telephone negotiations, found that face-to-face negotiations resulted in more integrative (win-win) outcomes and more balanced distributions of surplus (even pie slicing) than writing-only or telephone negotiations. Further, writing-only negotiations had a higher incidence of impasse, and telephone negotiations increased the likelihood of losing buyers and highly profitable sellers.

In most companies, the incidence and frequency of face-to-face communication is nearly perfectly predicted by how closely people are located to one another: Employees who work in the same office or on the same floor communicate much more frequently than those located on different floors or in different buildings. The incidence of communication literally comes down to feet—a few paces can have a huge impact. For example, communication frequency between R&D researchers drops off logarithmically after only 5 to 10 meters of distance between offices (Allen 1977). Workers in adjacent offices communicate twice as often as those in offices on the same floor, including via e-mail and telephone transmissions (Galegher, Kraut, and Egido 1990).

Just what do people get out of face-to-face contact that makes it so important for smooth negotiations? First, face-to-face communication is easier and therefore more likely to occur than are other forms of communication. Simply stated, most people need a reason to walk up the stairs or to make a phone call. We underestimate how many negotiations occur from chance encounters—which virtually never happen in any mode but face-to-face because of perceived effort. Negotiations of opportunity are very important for long-term business success.

Second, although it is seldom consciously realized, people primarily rely on nonverbal signals to help them conduct social interactions. One estimate is that 93 percent of the meaning of messages is contained in the nonverbal part of communication, such as voice intonation (Meherabian 1971; see also appendix 2 on nonverbal communication). Perhaps this is why business executives will endure the inconvenience of travel across thousands of miles and several time zones so that they can negotiate face to face.

The emphasis on the human factor is not just old-fashioned business superstition. Important behavioral, cognitive, and emotional processes are set into motion when people meet face to face. However, unless people are specially trained, they do not know what exactly it is about face-to-face interaction that facilitates negotiation—they just know that negotiations are smoother and friendlier. Face-to-face negotiation allows people to develop rapport—the feeling of being "in sync" or "on the same wavelength" with another person—and rapport is a powerful determinant of whether they develop trust. Nonverbal (body orientation, gesture, eye contact, head nodding) and paraverbal (speech fluency, use of "uh-huhs" etc.) behaviors are key to building rapport. When the person we are negotiating with sits at a greater distance, has an indirect body orientation, backward lean, crossed arms, and avoids eye contact, we feel less rapport than when the same person sits with a forward lean and an open body posture and maintains steady eye contact.

However, we do not always have the luxury of meeting face to face. People often turn to the telephone, but even then, people do not always reach their party. Some estimates suggest that up to 70 percent of initial telephone attempts fail to reach the intended party (Philip and Young 1987).

SAME TIME, DIFFERENT PLACE

The same-time, different-place mode, in which people negotiate in real time but are not physically in the same place, is often the alternative to face-to-face negotiations. The most common means is via telephone (telephone-tag is different time, different place); videoconferencing is another example.

In telephone conversations, people lack facial cues; in videoconferencing, they lack real-time social cues, such as pauses, mutual gaze, and another person's nonverbal response to what is being said (looking away, rolling their eyes, or shaking or nodding their head).

When technology tries to replace the dynamics of face-to-face interaction, it often falls short. As a case in point, consider an engineering work group, located in two offices 1,000 kilometers apart, that experimented with an omnipresent video wall and cameras in all offices to link the sites together (Abel 1990). Generally, the engineers interacted across the distance as one cohesive group, but there were some disturbing incidents. Video links were not very effective in generating new relationships or in resolving divisive differences, and miscommunication was treated as rudeness. Members of a design team were unable to listen to each other's ideas until they met face-to-face for three days, where they reached consensus.

Next, we identify four key challenges to same-time, different-place negotiations:

Loss of Informal Communication

Probably the most limiting aspect of same-time, different-place negotiations is the inability to chat informally in the hall or inside offices. The impromptu and casual conversations that negotiators have in a restroom, by a water cooler, or walking back from lunch are often where the most difficult problems are solved and the most important interpersonal issues are addressed. Often, stalemated negotiations get resolved outside of the official bargaining forum. Beyond a very short distance, people miss out on spontaneous exchanges that occur outside of formal meetings. Many companies clearly realize that the informal communication that occurs in their organizations is what is most important and most critical, and they are doing something about it. A technique called "the talk show" is being used by several companies—IDEO, IBM, and Home Depot—to create forums for real, casual conversation. Informal talk is so important to Xerox PARC that they go to great lengths to support casual conversation. Take, for example, the company's use of whiteboards. A highly sophisticated version, known as the "zombie board," uses a camera that not only records whatever scribbling goes on the board but also scans, prints, and even pans across the room to a second whiteboard. A lower-tech version, found in nearly every public space in PARC, has no recording camera, but it is huge—running from floor to ceiling. Because of the board's size, researchers can talk and scribble for a longer period of time before they have to erase, and colleagues who pass by can see the evolution of the conversation, without having to ask to have everything repeated (Roberts 1999).

Lost Opportunity

Negotiations do not just occur when people are in disagreement and haggling over scarce resources. In fact, many negotiations are negotiations of opportunity—kind of like entrepreneurial joint ventures. Negotiations of opportunity, because they are not planned, usually occur during informal, chance encounters.

Separation of Feedback

Another negative impact of physical separation is the absence of feedback: Greater distance tends to block the corrective feedback loops provided in face-to-face negotiations. One manager contrasted how employees who worked in his home office negotiated with him, compared to employees 15 kilometers away (Armstrong and Cole 1995). Engineers in the home office would drop by and catch him in the hall or at lunch: "I heard you were planning to change project X," they would say. "Let me tell you why that would be stupid." The manager would listen to their points, clarify some details, and all would part better informed. In contrast, employees at the remote site would greet his weekly visit with formally prepared objections, which took much longer to discuss and were rarely resolved as completely as the more informal hallway discussions. In short, negotiators interacting remotely do not get the coincidental chances to detect and correct problems on a casual basis.

Negotiation Timing

Conflicts are expressed, recognized, and addressed more quickly if negotiators work in close proximity. A manager can spot a problem and "nip it in the bud" if he or she works near his or her employees. When people are physically separated, the issues are more likely to go unresolved; this contributes to an escalating cycle of destructive negotiation behavior.

Although there are many disadvantages for distance when it comes to negotiation, it is not always a liability for negotiators. The formality of a scheduled phone meeting can compel each party to better prepare for the negotiation and to address the issues more efficiently. Also, it can create a "buffer zone" between parties, meaning that it might be a good thing if one party does not see the other rolling his or her eyes.

DIFFERENT TIME, SAME PLACE

In the different-time, same-place mode, negotiators interact asynchronously, but have access to the same physical document or space. An example might be shift workers who pick up the task left for them by the previous shift; another example would be two collaborators working on the same electronic document. After one colleague finishes, she gives the text to her partner, who further edits and develops it. Although people seldom realize it, they negotiate quite frequently in an asynchronous fashion. Take the example of a distributed team of software engineers located in Bangalore, Palo Alto, and London, working on the development of a piece of software. Their "24-hour laboratory" makes active use of global time differences. At the end of the working day, the Bangalore group downloads its work to the London team, which contributes its bit; this is in turn picked up by the Palo Alto team (Haour 1998).

DIFFERENT PLACE, DIFFERENT TIME

In the different-place, different-time model, negotiators communicate asynchronously in different places. Kiser (1999) notes that just as the telephone became an important medium for working out deals, the Internet is rapidly becoming the medium of choice for many "technobargainers." The most common example is electronic mail (e-mail): Jerry, who is in Seattle, sends a message to Sally, who is in Japan. With e-mail, parties do not have to be available simultaneously for negotiation to occur. Asynchronous, distributed communication seems to be growing at a faster rate than other forms of communication, such as the telephone. For example, the telephone has been around for 120 years, but less than half of the people on the planet have ever made a phone call. In contrast, the Internet is only about 30 years old, and as of the close of the year 2000, there will be anywhere between 200 million to 1 billion Internet users in the world. E-mail messages currently outnumber letters sent by the U.S. postal service.

Five considerations are important in e-mail:

Substance

The *substantive* component is the content of the message. However, content by itself can be ambiguous and misinterpreted unless there is some other clue in the message about how to interpret the content. Consider, for example, the following statement in an e-mail message: "You are so right all the time." We do not know whether this person is displaying extreme deference, sarcasm, or appreciation.

Affect

The *affective* aspect of an e-mail message allows us to interpret the content. People communicate affect in words (e.g., "I am so angry"), but also in symbols or emoticons. Tables 12–2 illustrates the most common emotional expressions in e-mail exchange.

It takes some time to become interpersonally skilled on e-mail. Many a novice has made an unwitting mistake only to be rebuffed and flamed. For example, one colleague we know is not a touch typist; he looks at the keyboard rather than the screen when typing. Unbeknownst to him at the time, the "caps lock" key was depressed during a long message. Not wanting to retype the message, he sent it in uppercase. His recipient responded, "Why are you shouting at me—don't you know that is impolite?"

Procedure

The *procedural* aspect of an e-mail message is the way in which communicators deal with and overcome the place/time constraints. The procedural aspect focuses on how people communicate about how they communicate (e.g., "I only read e-mail once every three days, so do not expect a quick reply"; "I would like to forward this to my committee, if you do not mind"). We know of a manager who became irate when she did not get a response for a week after sending an e-mail message to a government agency; only later did she realize that the recipient's gateway was blocked for security reasons during the Gulf War. In a different instance, a colleague was horrified to find that his e-mail message to a friend had been forwarded to 300 people. In yet another instance, a manager was disturbed to learn on a site visit with her distant collaborator that the collaborator had not deleted the messages that he had received from her in the past three years. The manager insisted that the messages be deleted in front of her eyes.

Table 12–2:	Emotions in e-mail communication used to express emotion
Emotion	**Definition**
:)	The basic smiley. This smiley is used to inflect a sarcastic joking statement since we can't hear voice infection over e-mail.
;-)	Winky smiley. User just made a flirtatious and/or sarcastic remark. More of a "don't hit me for what I just said" smiley.
:-(	Frowning smiley. User did not like the last statement or is upset or depressed about something.
:-T	Indifferent smiley. Better than a :-(but not quite as good as a :-).
:->	User just made a really biting sarcastic remark. Worse than a ;-).
>:->	User just made a really devilish remark.
>;->	Winky and devil combined. A very lewd remark was just made.
|-)	hee hee
|-D	ho ho
:-o	oops
:-P	nyahhh!

Relations

The *relational* aspect of an e-mail message is the way in which communicators attempt to humanize interaction. The relational aspect addresses the relationship between the communicators. The relational aspect is often revealed in greetings (e.g., "hey buddy"; "hi magnet man"). Some of these are personalized; others are not, such as when communicators have a standard sign-off or quote at the end of their message (e.g., "Seize the day"). Relational messages build common ground (e.g., "What did you think of that Bulls game?"). Very simple statements can go a long way toward humanizing electronic interaction (e.g., "It's late, and I am eating dinner now").

Some communicators never deal with the relational aspect; they focus on content and procedure and supply enough affective markers to have their messages understood. For tips on conducting successful email negotiations, see Box 12–1.

Permanent Record

Electronic communication can be a powerful form of social control, both at an organizational and individual level. Virtually no one would disagree that computers keep a perfect record of communications: Even though messages that are composed and sent disappear from the screen, they are stored intact in several computer systems, accessible to virtually anyone intent on finding the information, even after they have been deleted. Yet, people act as if messages are ephemeral (Sproull and Keisler 1991). For example, in his congressional hearing, Oliver North was extremely careful in his spoken interviews (presumably aware that the camera was on him indelibly recording every utterance); however, he was obviously much more lax in his computer mail (Sproull and Keisler 1991).

On the other hand, people are sometimes aware of the written record created when using electronic forms of communication, and consequently adjust both the content and the tone of their messages accordingly. People may hesitate to frankly express their views in the way they would via face-to-face communication, where they can have more confidence in the private nature of their conversation. As a

KEYS TO SUCCESSFUL E-MAIL NEGOTIATION

Given that you are involved in a negotiation that must proceed via information technology, how can you best achieve your goals? The following prescriptions are important (Thompson 2000):

Make your messages concise and clear. Most people overestimate the ability of other people to make sense out of what they mean (Keysar 1994). People have a hard enough time deciphering our messages in face-to-face interactions; accuracy decreases dramatically in e-mail exchanges. Many people assume that longer means clearer. It does not. People have a short attention span and often dislike long e-mail messages, or perhaps even stop reading them if they began to fall off of the screen. Most people are capable of only retaining seven, plus-or-minus two, ideas in their head at any one time. As a general rule of thumb, most e-mail messages should fit on a single screen. **Screen loading,** or the tendency to write very long messages, can lead to annoyance on the part of the recipient, especially if he or she is busy. Negotiations are more productive when the parties exchange a greater number of shorter e-mails, rather than fewer, but longer e-mails. Increasing the rate of e-mail exchange prevents misunderstanding because misperceptions can be quickly rectified. This also builds reciprocity in exchange.

Responding to e-mail. The asynchronous nature of e-mail provides people with the dubious luxury of not having to immediately receive or respond to e-mail messages. However, the sender of e-mail messages often expects a timely response. Not responding to e-mail may be perceived as rejection and disinterest. Further, newer forms of software allow senders to ascertain whether the recipient has read their e-mail. Failure to provide a timely response to e-mail is akin to giving the "silent treatment" to someone. Suspicion and hostility increase as the communication between parties diminishes.

Meta-communication. **Meta-communication** is communication about communication. This boils down to people talking about how they should communicate. This is of critical importance in electronic interaction because the norms of turn taking and conversation are not clear. In any electronic communication, it is important to let team members know how often you check your e-mail, whether you or someone else reads and responds to your e-mail, and whether you forward your e-mail to others.

Light-of-day test. The golden rule of e-mail is the **light-of-day test**—is what you are saying in the e-mail suitable to be read by your mother, supervisor, or jury? Could it appear on the front page of the newspaper? If not, it is probably not a good idea to send it.

Watch your temper. **Flaming** refers to the insults, criticisms, and character assassinations that people hurl over e-mail. Flaming remarks make fun of grammar, are patronizing (e.g., "I would recommend that you more closely read my first transmission prior to responding"), and include labeling and accusations (e.g., "That is completely ridiculous"; "Your idea is ludicrous"), character attacks, backhanded compliments ("I am glad to see that you have come around to my point of view"), and blunt statements (e.g., "Why don't we stop treating each other as fools and start talking seriously?"). Flaming and other negative interpersonal behaviors often stem from feelings of isolation (Keisler, Zubrow, Moses, and Gellar 1985). In contrast, face-to-face groups have mechanisms and norms, such as conformity pressure, that largely prevent flaming (Rhoades and O'Connor 1996).

People react to each other with less politeness, empathy, or inhibition if they cannot sense the other's social presence (Short, Williams, and Christie 1976). Negotiators are much more likely to issue threats when communicating via information technology.

Continued

<BOX 12–1>

KEYS TO SUCCESSFUL E-MAIL NEGOTIATION—*continued*

There is more uncertainty, doubt, and ambiguity in electronic mail exchanges. This stems from the asynchronous nature of communication. As a consequence, people become frustrated and seek to control the exchange by issuing threats (e.g., "I am not going to read my e-mail again"; "if I do not hear from you by 5 P.M., I will assume that the specifications are acceptable"). Along these lines, do not chastise or deliver negative feedback via e-mail; face-to-face (or telephone) communication is more appropriate.

result, electronic communication may inhibit open exchange of ideas and viewpoints, because people fear that their message will fall into the wrong hands or that their message will be used in the future in a way that was not intended. Lawyers are trained to be sensitive to the potential impact of memorializing communication in writing, and law firms that use e-mail often try to limit potential harmful consequences by attaching a disclaimer to the bottom of every message (whether business or personal) sent from the firm's network. An example of one firm's standard email disclaimer is as follows:

> This message originates from the law firm of X, Y, and Z. It contains information which may be confidential or privileged and is intended for the individual or entity named above. It is prohibited for anyone else to disclose, copy, distribute, or use the contents of this message. All personal messages express views solely of the sender, which are not to be attributed to X, Y, and Z, and may not be copied or distributed without this disclaimer.

INFORMATION TECHNOLOGY AND NEGOTIATION BEHAVIOR

Information technology has extremely powerful effect on social behavior (Keisler and Sproull 1992). Many people are surprised at how they find themselves behaving when communicating via e-mail. To be successful, negotiators must not only know how to negotiate via technology but also understand the social dynamics that it produces.

STATUS AND POWER: THE "WEAK GET STRONG" EFFECT

In face-to-face interactions, people do not contribute to conversation equally. Walk into any classroom, lunch discussion, or business meeting, and it will be immediately obvious that one person in a two-party group does most of the talking, and a handful of people do more than 75 percent of the talking in a larger group. One person or one clique usually dominates the discussion. In face-to-face interactions, participation is not equal, even when performance depends on contributions. Most social interaction follows the form of that depicted in Figure 12–1.

Who dominates the discussion? Almost without exception, status predicts domination. Higher-status people talk more, even if they are not experts on the subject. Not surprisingly, managers speak more than subordinates, and men speak more than women. If there is no inherent organizational status system, negotiators rely on superficial symbols of status, such as gender, age, and race. Situational factors also affect perceived status. The person who sits at the head of the table talks more than those on the sides, even if seating arrangement is arbitrary (Strodtbeck and Hook 1961). Appearance can affect status: Those in business suits talk more than others. Dynamic cues can define status, such as nodding in approval, touching (high-status people touch those of lower status but not vice versa), hesitating, and frowning.

What happens when negotiators interact via technology, such as electronic mail? The traditional status cues are missing, and the dynamic cues are distinctly less impactive. This has a dramatic effect on negotiation behavior: Power and status differences are weakened. People who are in traditionally weak positions in face-to-face negotiations become more powerful when communicating via information technology because status cues are harder to read (Sproull and Keisler 1991).

When people receive e-mail from others, we do not know the sender's status or, for that matter, where the person works or if they are at a company. Electronic communication lacks many of the status markers common in face-to-face interaction. People who would normally not approach others in person are much more likely to initiate e-mail exchange. Traditional, static cues like position and title are not as obvious on e-mail. It is often impossible to tell whether you are communicating with a president or clerk on e-mail because traditional e-mail simply lists the person's name, not title. Addresses are often shortened and may be difficult to comprehend. Even when they can be deciphered, e-mail addresses identify the organization, but not the subunit, job title, social importance, or level in the organization of the sender. Dynamic status cues, such as dress, mannerisms, age, and gender, are also missing in e-mail. In this sense, e-mail acts as an equalizer because it is difficult for high-status people to dominate discussion.

The absence of these cues leads people to respond more openly and less hesitatingly than in face-to-face interaction. People are less likely to conform to social norms and other people when interacting via electronic communication.

Overall, the amount of participation will be less in electronic versus face-to-face communication, but the contributions of members will be more equal (for a review, see McGrath and Hollingshead 1994). For example, when groups of executives meet face to face, men are five times more likely than women to make the first decision proposal. When those same groups meet via computer, women make the first proposal as often as men do (McGuire, Keisler, and Siegel 1987). Furthermore, the time to complete a task is longer on e-mail than in face-to-face interaction, probably because people talk much faster than they write.

SOCIAL NETWORKS

In traditional organizations, social networks are determined by who talks to whom; in the new organization, social networks are determined by who communicates with whom via technology. Peripheral people who communicate electronically become better integrated into their organization (Eveland and Bikson 1988). Computerized interaction increases the resources of low-network people.

The nature of social networks that shape negotiation behavior change dramatically when information technology enters the picture as a form of communication. E-mail networks, or connection between people who communicate via electronic e-mail, increase the information resources of low-network people. When people need assistance (e.g., information or resources), they often turn to their immediate social network. When such help is not available, they use weak ties, such as relationships with acquaintances or strangers, to seek help that is unavailable from friends or colleagues. However, there is a problem: In the absence of personal relationships or the expectation of direct reciprocity, help from weak ties might not be forthcoming or could be of low quality.

Some companies, particularly global companies and those in the fields of information technology and communications, need to rely on e-mail and employees within the company forming connections with each other on the basis of no physical contact. The incentives for taking the time to assist someone who is dealing with a problem and is located in a different part of the world are pretty minuscule.

Tandem Corporation is a global computer manufacturer that has a highly geographically dispersed organization (Sproull and Keisler 1991). Managers in the Tandem Corporation need technical advice to solve problems, but they cannot always get useful advice from their local colleagues. Simply stated, the local social networks are often not sufficient to solve problems. What can be done?

One possibility is to catalogue or store information in some easily accessible database. In a technical company, this would mean published reports and scientific manuals. However, engineers and managers do not like to consult technical reports to obtain needed information; most of the information they use to solve their problems is obtained through face-to-face discussions. People in organizations usually prefer to exchange help through strong collegial ties, which develop through physical proximity, similarity, and familiarity.

An investigation of Tandem's e-mail revealed some startling and encouraging findings (Sproull and Keisler 1991): Managers who put out a request for technical assistance received an average of 7.8 replies per request. All of the replies were serious, and respondents spent 9 minutes per reply. The replies solved the problem 50 percent of the time. Information providers gave useful advice and solved the problems of information seekers, despite their lack of a personal connection with the person requesting information.

Is it sending or receiving messages that expands one's social network and ultimate organizational commitment? The amount of e-mail a person sends (but not receives) predicts commitment (Sproull and Keisler 1991). Thus, e-mail can provide an alternate route to letting people have a voice if they are low contributors in face-to-face meetings.

RISK TAKING

Consider the following choices:

1. $20,000 return over two years
2. 50 percent chance of $40,000 return; 50 percent chance of nothing

Obviously, option 1 is the "safe" (riskless) choice; option 2 is the risky choice. However, these two options are mathematically identical, meaning that in an objective sense, people should not favor one option over the other (see also appendix 1). When posed with these choices, most people are risk-averse, meaning that they select the option that has the sure payoff as opposed to holding out for the chance to win big (or, equally as likely, not win at all). Consider what happens when the following choice is proposed:

1. Sure loss of $20,000 over two years
2. 50 percent chance of losing $40,000; 50 percent of losing nothing

Most managers are risk-seeking and choose option 2. Why? According to the **framing effect** (chapter 2; Kahneman and Tversky 1979), people are risk-averse for gains and risk-seeking for losses. This can lead to self-contradictory, quirky behavior. By manipulating the reference point, a person's fiscal policy choices can change.

Groups tend to make riskier decisions than do individuals given the same choice. Thus, risk-seeking is greatly exaggerated in groups who meet face-to-face. Paradoxically, groups who make decisions via electronic communication are risk-seeking for both gains and losses (McGuire, Keisler, and Siegel 1987). Furthermore, executives are just as confident of their decisions whether they are made through electronic communication or face-to-face communication. For example, in comparisons of people negotiating face to face, by e-mail, or by a combination of both (Shell 1999), people who use only e-mail reach more impasses. According to Shell, "people tend to escalate disagreement when they focus on the issues and position without the benefit of the contextual, personal information that comes across when we speak or go face to face with our counterpart" (p. 106).

RAPPORT AND SOCIAL NORMS

As we saw in chapter 6, building trust and rapport is critical for negotiation success. Rapport would seem more difficult to establish with impoverished mediums of communication (Drolet and Morris 2000). For example, Drolet and Morris (2000) tested the hypothesis that visual access between negotiators fosters rapport and thus facilitates cooperation and pie expansion. They instructed some negotiators to stand face to face or side by side (unable to see each other) in a simulated strike negotiation. Face-to-face negotiators were more likely to coordinate on a settlement early in the strike, resulting in higher joint gains. Further, rapport was higher between face-to-face negotiators than between side-by-side negotiators. In a different investigation (Drolet and Morris 2000), comparisons were made between face-to-face, videoconference, and audio-only negotiation interactions. Face-to-face negotiators felt a greater amount of rapport than did negotiators in the videoconference and audio-only conditions. Further, independent observers judged face-to-face negotiators to be more "in sync" with each other. Face-to-face negotiators had more trust in each other and were more successful at coordinating their decisions.

When social context cues are missing or weak, people feel distant from others and somewhat anonymous. They are less concerned about making a good appearance, and humor tends to fall apart or to be misinterpreted. Additionally, the expression of negative emotion is no longer minimized because factors that keep people from expressing negative emotion are not in place when they communicate via information technology. Simply, in the absence of social norms that prescribe the expression of positive emotion, people are more likely to express negative emotion. When people communicate via e-mail, they are more likely to negatively confront others. Conventional behavior, such as politeness rituals and acknowledgment of others' views decrease; rude, impulsive behavior, such as flaming, increases. In fact, people are eight times more likely to "flame" (denigrate each others' character, intelligence, and grammar) in electronic discussion than in face-to-face discussion (Dubrovsky, Keisler, and Sethna 1991). One MBA student lost a job when he sent his supervisor an e-mail message that was perceived as insensitive. The student was using e-mail to renegotiate his job responsibilities and proceeded to outline what he saw as problems within the organization and the people who were running it. Shortly thereafter, he was called into a meeting with the senior staff, and everyone was holding a copy of his e-mail (Kiser 1999).

When interacting via e-mail, people tend to respond more openly, yet they are less likely to conform to social norms and traditional politeness rituals. They focus more on the content of the task and less on the etiquette of the situation. For example, bad news is conveyed to superiors with less delay on e-mail than in face-to-face encounters (Sproull and Keisler 1991). People are more rude on e-mail than in face-to-face interactions. Not surprisingly, conflicts are sharper and escalate more quickly.

PARANOIA

On the TV show *Saturday Night Live,* Pat (Julia Sweeney) was a character whose sex was unknown. Pat had an androgynous name, wore baggy clothes, and did not display any stereotypical male or female characteristics or preferences. Most people found it maddening to interact with Pat without knowing his or her gender. Gender ambiguity also happens when interacting via technology. It is generally impolite to ask someone whether he or she is a man or woman. Therefore, we are left feeling uncertain. Uncertainty, consequently, increases paranoia. Paranoid people are more likely to assume the worst about another person or situation (Kramer 1995).

When technological change creates new social situations, traditional expectations and norms lose their power. People invent new ways of behaving. Today's electronic technology is impoverished in social cues and shared experience. People "talk" to other people, but they do so alone (Sproull and Keisler 1991). As a result, their messages are likely to display less social awareness. The advantage is that social posturing and sycophancy decline. The disadvantage is that politeness and concern for others decline. Two characteristics of computer-based communication, the plain text and perceived ephemerality of messages, make it relatively easy for a person to forget or ignore his or her audience and consequently send messages that ignore social boundaries, disclose the self, and are too blunt (Sproull and Keisler 1991).

Consider the following exchange:

NEGOTIATOR A: "If I do not get your answer by tomorrow, then I assume that you agree with my proposal."

NEGOTIATOR B: "From my perspective, I do not see any rationale, or any incentive to transfer this revolutionary technology to your division."

NEGOTIATOR A: "I do not have to remind you how pushing the issue up the corporate ladder can prejudice both our careers."

NEGOTIATOR B: "Your offer is ridiculous."

NEGOTIATOR A: "It is my final offer."

Did this exchange occur in a meeting room or via the Internet? Most people correctly note that this exchange occurred on the Internet. The phenomenon of flaming suggests that through electronic mail, actions and decisions (not just messages) might become more extreme and impulsive (Sproull and Keisler 1991).

NEW ROLES

With the development of any technology, there are first- and second-level effects (Sproull and Keisler 1991). First-level effects are those associated with efficiency. They are the direct, intended effects. Second-level effects are those that are not intended, predicted, or anticipated. They have to do with how the social system is affected by technology. Indirect effects are caused by behavior that technology makes feasible and how people use options. Indirect effects lead to the development of new social roles. For example, the development of the computer led to the development of the hacker, user consultant, and management of information specialist (MIS; Sproull and Keisler 1991).

A good example is the telephone (from Sproull and Keisler 1991). The first-level effect of the telephone was that of an efficient replacement for the telegraph. It was originally sold as a tool for business. In 1878, the Pittsburgh telephone directory had 12 pages of entries, which were all for businesses and businessmen. Telegraph companies offering telephones for lease at $50/year advertised: "The telephone has ceased to be a novelty and has become a recognized instrument for business purposes." A selling point for the business manager was that "no skill whatsoever" was required in the use of the instrument. The Bell Telephone Company partners decided to prepare for the distant possibility that people would use the telephone for social purposes as well. By the 1920s, Bell System was emphasizing the social character of the telephone with claims such as "Friends who are linked by telephone have good times," and "Friendship's path often follows the trail of the telephone wire." Today, the telephone is the backbone of virtually all social and organizational life. People once wondered if the telephone would increase the authority of the boss inside the firm by allowing him or her to call subordinates at any hour of the day. Instead, the telephone gave employees a chance to call their supervisors and each other. The telephone democratized more workplaces than it bureaucratized and networked more organizations than it created fiefdoms.

The full possibilities of new technologies are hard to foresee. The inventors and early adopters emphasize the planned uses and underestimate the second-level effects. For example, the first internet, known as ARPANET, was developed in the 1960s so that academicians could communicate their research ideas and data (usually large reports). It was only after the Gulf War and the 1992 presidential election that the "information superhighway," the World Wide Web, and the Internet became common forms of communication for laypersons and businesses.

The unanticipated consequences of technology often have less to do with efficiency effects and more to do with changing social arrangements of interpersonal interactions, such as ideas about what is important and procedures/norms guiding behavior. Second-level effects often emerge somewhat slowly as people renegotiate changed patterns of behavior and thinking. Second-level effects are not caused by technology operating autonomously on a passive organization or a society. Instead, they are constructed by people as their design and use of technology interacts with, shapes, and is shaped by the technological, social, and policy environment. Second-level and unanticipated effects are not always positive and innovative. Place dependence can develop, wherein a group becomes dependent on technology to function, but they do not realize it. If the system is changed or altered, group productivity declines.

STRATEGIES FOR ENHANCING TECHNOLOGY-MEDIATED NEGOTIATIONS

Often, negotiators do not have the luxury of face-to-face meetings for the duration of their negotiations. Under such circumstances, what strategies can be taken to enhance successful pie expansion and pie slicing? Consider the following:

INITIAL FACE-TO-FACE EXPERIENCE

Oftentimes, people can develop rapport on the basis of a short face-to-face meeting. This can reduce uncertainty and build trust. Face-to-face contact humanizes people and creates expectation for negotiators to use in their subsequent long-distance work together. For example, Christopher H. Browne, managing director of Tweedy Browne Company, a New York–based investment-management firm, is a self-professed "e-mail junkie." When he presented the University of Pennsylvania with a gift of $10 million, it was his suggestion that they hammer out the details about payment and purpose of the gift on-line. However, he was careful to make this suggestion after an initial face-to-face meeting about the gift with university officials. Four days and several e-messages later, the deal was completed. Both Browne and university officials said that the process could have taken weeks, had they relied on telephone calls and faxes. University officials said that they were going to make a personal trip to New York to thank Browne: "Even though this [the deal] was done in cyberspace, we don't want to lose sight of the fact that there are real people involved" (Carlson 2000, 2).

ONE-DAY VIDEOCONFERENCE/TELECONFERENCE

If an initial, face-to-face meeting is out of the question, an alternative may be to at least get everyone on-line so that people can attach a name to a face. Depending upon the size of the team and locations of different members, this alternative may be more feasible than a face-to-face meeting. For example, in one investigation, negotiators who had never met one another were instructed to have a short phone call prior to commencing e-mail–only negotiations (Morris, Nadler, Kurtzberg and Thompson 2000). Another group did not have an initial phone call with their opponent. The sole purpose of the phone call was to get to know the other person. The simple act of chatting and exchanging personal information built rapport and overcame some of the communication difficulties associated with the impoverished medium of e-mail. Negotiators who engaged in the initial phone conversation found that their attitudes toward their opponents changed; negotiators who had chatted with their opponent felt less competitive and more cooperative before the negotiation began, compared with negotiators who had not chatted with their opponent. In the end, negotiators who had made personal contact with their opponent felt more confident that future interaction with the same person would go smoothly. A relationship of trust was thus developed through the rapport-building phone call prior to the negotiation. Not surprisingly, negotiators who had had an initial phone call were less likely to reach impasse, and achieved higher joint gains compared to those who did not have the initial phone call. The simple act of making an effort to establish a personal relationship through telephone contact before engaging in e-mail negotiations can have dramatic positive consequences.

SCHMOOZING

Schmoozing (as described in chapter 6) is our name for superficial contact between people that has the psychological effect of having established a relationship with someone. There are a variety of non-face-to-face schmoozing strategies, such as exchanging pictures or biographical information or engaging in a simple get-acquainted e-mail exchange (Moore, Kurtzberg, Thompson, and Morris 1999). The effectiveness of electronic schmoozing has been put to the test, and the results are dramatic: Schmoozing increases liking and rapport and results in more profitable business deals than when people simply "get down to business" (Moore, Kurtzberg, Thompson, and Morris 1999). Perhaps the most attractive aspect of schmoozing is that it is relatively low-cost and efficient. Merely exchanging a few short e-mails describing yourself can lead to better business relations. However, you should not expect people to naturally schmooze—at least at the outset of a business relationship. Team members working remotely have a tendency to get down to business. As a start toward schmoozing, tell the other person something about yourself that does not necessarily relate to the business at hand (e.g., "I really enjoy sea kayaking"); also, provide a context for your own work space (e.g., "It is very late in the day, and there are 20 people at my door, so I do not have time to write a long message"). Furthermore, ask questions that show you are interested in the other party as a person; this is an excellent way to search for points of similarity. Finally, provide the link for the next e-mail or exchange (e.g., "I will look forward to hearing your reactions on the preliminary report, and I will also send you the tapes you requested").

ON-LINE COMMERCIAL NEGOTIATIONS

A variety of on-line services have developed pertaining to negotiations, ranging from auction houses to mediation services. Next, we will selectively review some of these emerging technologies and their implications for negotiation.

ON-LINE AUCTION HOUSES

eBay (www.ebay.com) is a personal trading community in which people can buy and sell almost anything. eBay is like a giant flea market, where the auction categories include automobiles, antiques, books, movies, music, coins and stamps, collectibles, computers, dolls and figures, jewelry and gemstones, photo and electronics, pottery and glass, sports memorabilia, toys, and miscellaneous items. There are over 2,000 categories of items, and more than 2.5 million auctions take place each day. To start bidding, people must

SIDEBAR 12–3. AUCTIONING: IT'S ALL IN A NAME

"It was one of the hottest sellers at Sotheby's recent Americana sale: A 250-year-old armoire hailed in the catalogue as 'from the collection of Mr. and Mrs. Russel S. Hayden.' So were the Haydens jet-setting socialites? High-profile philanthropists? Try retired civil servants from Massapequa, New York" (Costello 2000, W12). According to John Nye, the furniture specialist at Sotheby's who organized the sale, they are just regular people. However, the armoire sold for over $48K—eight times as much as was expected. What's going on?

In an age of faceless anonymity, people want some identity associated with what they buy. According to Kathleen Guzman, the name effect operates on eBay as well, because people "no longer want anonymous things, they want something to brag about, like their BMWs" (Costello 2000, W12).

register. Bidding and browsing are free of charge; sellers are charged a small fee. In addition, there is a reputation mechanism built-in, wherein buyers and sellers can post information about their experiences.

One of the major advantages of eBay (and other auction houses) is that it reaches the global marketplace. For example, Sharon Balkowitsch used to sell antiques from a stall in Bismarck, North Dakota. There were few buyers in her hometown of 54,000, and prices were low. She started putting her wares up for auction on eBay in 1998, and suddenly she was rich: An Art Deco ashtray she bought for $20 was bid up quickly and sold for $290. A vase she got for $5 went to a buyer for $585. Checks have been pouring in from Iceland, Egypt, and China. Says Sharon: "The top month I ever had in the stall I sold 15 items. Now I can sell 15 items in an hour" (Cohen 1999, 74).

Another advantage of eBay is the reputation factor involved. When Pierre Omidyar, founder of eBay, first began his company, he found himself thrust into a new and unwanted role: grievance officer. Buyers and sellers with complaints about each other were e-mailing him personally and asking him to step in. Omidyar urged them to work things out amicably between themselves. But if eBayers really had to gripe, he decided, they should do it publicly on the site: "I wanted to reinforce the notion that if you're going to bring a complaint about someone, do it out in the open. You can't come running to Daddy" (Cohen 1999, 75). This was the genesis of the Feedback Forum. And it's working, with fewer than 27 complaints of fraud per 1 million auctions (Anders 1999). Further, he had another idea: People could build reputations by being nice. Overwhelmingly, feedback posted on eBay is positive (Cohen 1999).

Web auctions are like the world's biggest yard sale—a place where millions of buyers and sellers meet in a kind of virtual swap or where companies with excess inventory can reach eager customers. However, "an auction is not a negotiation between buyer and seller, it's a competition among buyers," says Jay Waler, founder and vice chairman of Priceline.com (Mieskowski 1998, 289). Some sellers are finding that attaching identities to items increases their value (see Sidebar 12–3).

MEDIATION HOUSES

Cybersettle (www.cybersettle.com) is an on-line, computer-assisted method for settling insurance claims. Conceived and designed by two lawyers, Cybersettle empowers disputants to negotiate settlements on line. Offers and demands made by each party are confidential, and when a settlement occurs, only the settlement amount is revealed. When settlement does not occur, parties can pursue traditional methods of litigation without bias, given that the offers and demands are never revealed.

A claim becomes available for settlement through Cybersettle when a sponsor (for example, an insurance company) initiates the claim on the Cybersettle system. The claimants (or their attorneys) are immediately notified that their claim is available for settlement on-line. There are three key steps in the Cybersettle process: (1) A sponsor initiates a case on the Cybersettle system and submits first-, second-, and third-round settlement offers. The offers expire once a predetermined period of time has elapsed. (2) Cybersettle sends an alert to the involved claimants or their attorneys informing them that the case is on-line and available for settlement. (3) The claimant submits three rounds of settlement demands. For each round, Cybersettle compares the demand to the corresponding offer. If the offer and the demand are within an agreed-upon formula (typically 30 percent or $5,000), the case immediately settles for the median amount. If a settlement is reached, Cybersettle notifies both parties and issues a written confirmation. If no settlement is reached in the process, both parties are notified and are free to continue with traditional litigation methods. (To see how the Cybersettle formula works in practice, look at Box 12–2.)

SHOPPING HOUSES

Priceline.com (www.priceline.com) is an on-line personal shopping service in which people indicate how much they will pay for airline tickets, hotel rooms, new cars and trucks, home financing, etc. Priceline.com then "shops" for these items for the customer. The customer names her own price, and if Priceline.com can find what the customer wants for that price, the customer's credit card is charged. Is it a good deal? The reviews are mixed (see www.bestfares.com/newsdesk/stories98/n9967.htm).

Some Web sites, such as hagglezone.com and makeusanoffer.com, are Web retailers targeted at the segment of the population that prefers haggling versus fixed-price negotiation. A buyer begins by choosing a product category and, ultimately, a specific product. Once the product is chosen, the buyer can choose one of three animated figures, who serve as the buyer's negotiation partners: Monte, Dot Com, or Stubby, each of whom supposedly has a different personality and negotiation style. (For a description of a typical experience, see Sidebar 12–4.)

BOX 12–2

EXAMPLES FROM AN ON-LINE MEDIATION HOUSE

Below are examples from the Web site Cybersettle.com (from www.cybersettle.com/how/step_03.htm):

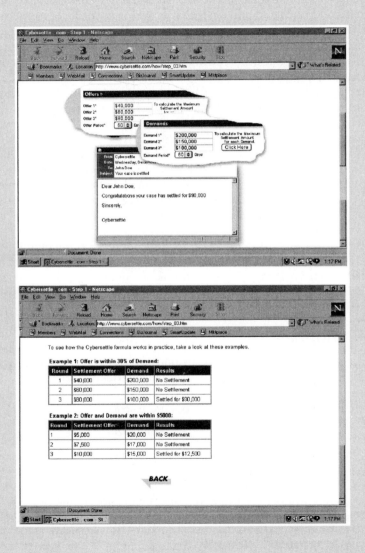

SIDEBAR 12–4. A TYPICAL EXPERIENCE ON HAGGLEZONE.COM

Once negotiations begin, Stubby (user's choice) recognizes whether you are a new user and welcomes you. He invites you to make the first offer at $310, based upon a $325 list price. You anchor low, at $250, and Stubby comes back with $300. You push him and offer $251, recognizing that one of the rules of the site is that your offers must always go up. Stubby comes back with $291, and a tip sheet informs you that "too many moves will get you booted." You decide to test this, and offer $252. Stubby is getting uncomfortable and lets you know that your bid increments are getting frustrating. You decide to push again and offer $253. Stubby gets angry. He does not offer a counterbid and instead ridicules you. You are $30 apart, and you push again and offer $255. Surprisingly, he accepts and acknowledges how he "gave in" to your "strong bargaining."

The seller's agents are preprogrammed with sophisticated decision-making algorithms that account for supply and demand, returns, fulfillment charges, and the relative experience of the buyer. Thus, these cartoons are "perfect" agents in the sense that they never tire and make silly mistakes, and will do exactly what they are programmed to do (Hobson 1999).

CONCLUSION

We used the place-time model of social interaction to examine how the medium of communication affects negotiation. We noted in particular how more often people are negotiating in impoverished communication environments and how such environments affect status and power relationships, social networks, risk-taking propensity, rapport and norm-following, and paranoia. We examined how new technologies are also leading to fundamental changes in the way disputes are resolved.

APPENDIX 1

ARE YOU A RATIONAL PERSON?
Check Yourself

Many negotiators consistently violate key principles of rationality. That leaves them open to being exploited or making poor decisions about negotiation. The purpose of this appendix is to introduce the key principles of rational behavior and to check your own rationality. First, we present the key principles of *individual rationality,* which focuses on how people make independent decisions. Then we present and discuss *game theoretic rationality,* which focuses on how people make interdependent decisions.

WHY IS IT IMPORTANT TO BE RATIONAL?

Let's first consider why it is important for a negotiator to be rational. Perhaps if we behave irrationally, we might confuse our opponent and reap greater surplus for ourselves; or, we might simply be better off following intuition rather than logic. Rational models of negotiation behavior offer a number of important advantages for the negotiator:

- **Pie expansion and pie slicing.** Models of rational behavior are based upon the principle of maximization such that the course of action followed guarantees that the negotiator will maximize his or her interests (whether that is monetary gain, career advancement, prestige, etc.). In short, there is no better way to maximize one's interests than by following the prescriptions of a rational model.
- **Stop kidding yourself.** The rational models that we present in this appendix make clear and definitive statements regarding the superiority of some decisions over others. Thus, they do not allow you to justify or rationalize your behavior. The truth may hurt sometimes, but it is a great learning experience.
- **Measure of perfection.** Rational models provide a measure of perfection or optimality. If rational models did not exist, we would have no way of evaluating how well people perform in negotiation nor what they should strive to do. We would not be able to offer any advice to negotiators because we would not have any consensus about what a "good" outcome is. Rational models provide an ideal.
- **Diagnosis.** Rational models serve a useful diagnostic purpose because they often reveal where negotiators make mistakes. Because rational models are built on a well-constructed theory of decision making, they offer insight about the mind of the negotiator.

FIGURE A1–1

Source: Drawing by Ged Melling. *The Economist,* December 24, 1994–January 6, 1995. Used with permission.

- **Dealing with irrational people.** As we have seen, it is not an effective bargaining strategy to attempt to outsmart or trick your opponent. We have further seen that people often follow the norm of reciprocity—even for negative and ineffective behaviors. A negotiator who is well-versed in rational behavior can often deal more effectively with irrational people.
- **Being consistent.** Another advantage of rational models is that they can help us be consistent. Consistency is important for several reasons. Inconsistency in our behavior can inhibit learning. Furthermore, it can send our opponent ambiguous messages. When people are confused or uncertain, they are more defensive, and trust diminishes.
- **Making decisions.** Rational models provide a straightforward method for thinking about decisions and a way of choosing among options, which, if followed correctly, will produce the "best" outcome for the chooser, maximizing his or her own preferences (as we will see in this appendix).

As the cartoon (Fig. A1–1) suggests, people's behavior is not always rational. Even so, principles and assumptions derived from rational models are still a fundamental part of our "mix" for understanding human behavior.

INDIVIDUAL DECISION MAKING

Negotiation is ultimately about making decisions. If we cannot make good decisions on our own, joint decision making will be even more difficult. Let's examine individual rationality. Sometimes our decisions are trivial, such as whether to have chocolate cake or cherry pie for dessert. Other times, our decisions are of great consequence, such as when we choose a career or a spouse. Our decisions about how to spend the weekend may seem fundamentally different from deciding what to do with our entire life, but there are generalities that cut across domains. Rational decision-making models provide the tools necessary for analyzing trivial decisions as well as those of monumental importance. There are three main types of decisions: riskless choice, decision making under uncertainty, and risky choice.

RISKLESS CHOICE

Riskless choice, or decision making under certainty, involves choosing between two or more readily available options. For example, a choice between two apartments is a riskless choice, as is choosing among 31 flavors of ice cream or selecting a book to read. Often, we do not consider these to be decisions because they are so simple and easy. However, at other times, we struggle when choosing among jobs or careers, and we find ourselves in a state of indecision.

Imagine that you have been accepted into the MBA program at your top two choices: university X and university Y. This enviable situation is an **approach-approach conflict,** meaning that in some sense, you cannot lose—both options are attractive; you need only to decide which alternative is best for you. You have to make your final choice by next week. On your coffee table is a large stack of brochures, descriptions, and information about the schools. How should you begin to analyze the situation?

To analyze this decision situation, we will employ a method known as **multiattribute utility technique** (or **MAUT,** see Baron 1988, for an overview). According to MAUT, there are five main tasks to do: (1) identify the alternatives, (2) identify dimensions or attributes of the alternatives, (3) evaluate the utility associated with each dimension, (4) weight or prioritize each dimension in terms of importance, and (5) make a final choice.

Identification of Alternatives

The first step is usually quite straightforward. The decision maker simply identifies the relevant alternatives. For example, you would identify the schools to which you had been accepted. In other situations, the alternatives may not be as obvious. For example, in many situations, the identification of alternatives often requires complex problem solving. In the case that you did not get any acceptance letters, you must brainstorm about what to do with your life.

Identification of Attributes

The second step is more complex and involves identifying the key attributes associated with the alternatives. The attributes are the features of the alternatives that make them appealing or unappealing. For example, when choosing among schools, relevant attributes might include the cost of tuition, reputation of the program, course requirements, placement options, weather, cultural aspects, family, and faculty. There is no limit to the number of attributes that you may identify as relevant to your decision.

Utility

The next step is to evaluate the relative utility or value of each alternative for each attribute. For example, you might use a 1 to 5 scale to rate how each school fares on each of the identified attributes. You might evaluate the reputation of university X very highly (+5) but the weather as very unattractive (+1); you might evaluate university Y's reputation to be moderately high (+3) but the weather to be fabulous (+5). MAUT assumes preferential independence of attributes (i.e., the value of one attribute is independent of the value of others).

Weight

In addition to determining the evaluation of each attribute, the decision maker also evaluates how important that attribute is to him or her. The importance of each attribute is referred to as weight in the decision process. Again, we can use a simple numbering system, with 1 representing relatively unimportant attributes and 5 representing very important attributes. For example, you might consider the reputation of the school to be very important (+5) but the cultural attributes of the city to be insignificant (+1).

Making a Decision

The final step in the MAUT procedure is to compute a single, overall evaluation of each alternative. To do this, first multiply the utility evaluation of each attribute by its corresponding weight, and then sum the weighted scores across each attribute. Finally, select the option that has the highest overall score. An example of this procedure is illustrated in Table A1–1.

We can see from the hypothetical example in Table A1–1 that university X is a better choice for the student compared to university Y. However, it is a close decision. If the importance of any of the attributes were to change (e.g., tuition cost, reputation, climate, or culture), then the overall decision could change. Similarly, if the evaluation of any attributes changes, then the final choice may change. Decision theory can tell us how to *choose*, but it cannot tell us how to weigh the attributes that go into making choices.

According to the **dominance principle,** one alternative *dominates* another if it is strictly better on at least one dimension and at least as good on all others. For example, imagine if university Y had been evaluated as a 5 in terms of tuition cost, a 5 in ranking, a 4 in climate, and a 4 in culture; and university X had been evaluated as a 1, 5, 4, and 3, respectively. In this case, we can quickly see that university Y is just as good as university X on two dimensions (reputation and climate) and better on the two remaining dimensions (tuition cost and culture). Thus, university Y dominates university X. Identifying a dominant alternative greatly simplifies decision making: If one alternative dominates the other, we should select the dominating option.

Table A1–1:	Multi-attribute decision making	
Attribute (weight)	University Y (evaluation)	University X (evaluation)
Tuition cost (4)	Inexpensive (5)	Expensive (1)
Reputation (5)	Medium (3)	High (5)
Climate (3)	Lousy (1)	Great (5)
Culture (1)	Good (4)	Lacking (1)

Utility of University $(Y) = (4*5) + (5*3) + (3*1) + (1*4) = 42$
Utility of University $(X) = (4*1) + (5*5) + (3*5) + (1*1) = 45$

The example seems simple enough. In many situations, however, we are faced with considering many more alternatives, each having different dimensions. It may not be easy for us to spot a dominant alternative when we see one. What should we do in this case? The first step is to eliminate from consideration all options dominated by others, and choose among only the nondominated alternatives that remain.

The dominance principle as a method of choice seems quite compelling, but it applies only to situations in which one alternative is clearly superior to others. It does not help us with the agonizing task of choosing among options that involve trade-offs among highly valued aspects. We now turn to situations that defy MAUT and dominance detection.

DECISION MAKING UNDER UNCERTAINTY

Sometimes we must make decisions when the alternatives are uncertain or unknown. These situations are known as decision making under uncertainty or decision making in ignorance (Yates 1990). In such situations, the decision maker has no idea about the likelihood of events. Consider, for example, a decision to plan a social event outdoors or indoors. If the weather is sunny and warm, it would be better to hold the event outdoors; if it is rainy and cold, it is better to plan the event indoors. The plans must be made a month in advance, but the weather cannot be predicted a month in advance. The distinction between risk and uncertainty hinges upon whether probabilities are known exactly (e.g., as in games of chance) or whether they must be judged by the decision maker with some degree of imprecision (e.g., almost everything else). Hence, "ignorance" might be viewed merely as an extreme degree of uncertainty where the decision maker has no clue (e.g., probability that the closing price of Dai Ichi stock tomorrow on the Tokyo stock exchange is above 1,600 yen).

RISKY CHOICE

In decision making under uncertainty, the likelihood of events is unknown; in risky-choice situations, the probabilities are known. Most theories of decision making are based on an assessment of the probability that some event will take place. Because the outcomes of risky choice situations are not fully known, outcomes are often referred to as "prospects."

Negotiation is a risky choice situation because parties cannot be completely certain about the occurrence of a particular event. For instance, a negotiator cannot be certain that mutual settlement will be reached because negotiations could break off as each party opts for his or her BATNA. To understand risky-choice decision making in negotiations, we need to understand expected utility theory.

Expected Utility Theory
Expected Utility Theory (EU) has a long history, dating back to the sixteenth century when French noblemen commissioned their court mathematicians to help them gamble. Modern utility theory is expressed in the form of gambles, probabilities, and payoffs. Why do we need to know about gambling to be effective negotiators? Virtually all negotiations involve choices, and many choices involve uncertainty, which makes them gambles. Before we can negotiate effectively, we need to be clear about our own preferences. Utility theory helps us do that.

EU is a theory of choices made by an individual actor (von Neumann and Morgenstern 1947). It prescribes a theory of "rational behavior." Behavior is rational if a person acts in a way that maximizes his or her decision utility or the anticipated satisfaction from a particular outcome. The maximization of utility is often equated with the maximization of monetary gain. But there are many nonmonetary kinds of satisfaction. Obviously, people care about things other than money. For example, weather, culture, quality of life, and personal esteem are all factors that bear on a job decision, in addition to salary.

EU is based on revealed preferences. People's preferences or utilities are not directly observable but must be inferred from their choices and willful behavior. To understand what a person really wants and values, we have to see what choices she makes. Actions speak louder than words. In this sense, utility maximization is a tautological statement: A person's choices reflect her utilities; therefore, all behaviors may be represented by the maximization of this hypothetical utility scale.

EU is based on a set of axioms about preferences among gambles. The basic result of the theory is summarized by a theorem stating that if a person's preferences satisfy the specified axioms, then her behavior maximizes her expected utility. Before we can talk about what rational behavior is, we need to understand what a utility function is.

Utility Function

A **utility function** is the quantification of a person's preferences with respect to certain objects such as jobs, potential mates, and ice cream flavors. Utility functions assign numbers to objects and gambles that have objects as their prizes (e.g., flip a coin and win a trip to Hawaii or free groceries). For example, a manager's choice to stay at her current company could be assigned an overall value, say a 7 on a 10-point scale. Her option to take the new job might be assigned a value of either 10 or 2, depending on how things work out for her at the new job. One's current job is the sure thing; the second job, because of its uncertainty, is a gamble. How should we rationally make a decision between the two?

We first need to examine our utility function. The following seven axioms guarantee the existence of a utility function. The axioms are formulated in terms of preference-or-indifference relations defined over a set of outcomes (see also Coombs, Dawes, and Tversky 1970). As will become clear, the following axioms provide the foundation for individual decision making as well as negotiation, or joint decision making.

Comparability   A key assumption of EU is that everything is comparable. That is, given any two objects, a person must prefer one to the other or be indifferent to both; no two objects are incomparable. For example, a person may compare a dime and a nickel or a cheeseburger and a dime. We might compare a job offer in the Midwest to a job on the West Coast. Utility theory implies a single, underlying dimension of "satisfaction" associated with everything. However, we can all recall instances wherein we refused to make comparisons. This often happens in the case of social or emotional issues, like marriage and children. However, according to utility theory, we need to be able to compare everything to be truly rational. Many people are uncomfortable with this idea, just as people can be in conflict about what is or is not negotiable.

Closure   The closure property states that if x and y are available alternatives, then so are all the gambles of the form (x, p, y) that can be formed with x and y as outcomes.

In this formulation, x and y refer to available alternatives; p refers to the probability that x will occur. Therefore (x, p, y) states that x will occur with probability p, otherwise y will occur. The converse must also be true: $(x, p, y) = (y, 1 - p, x)$, or y will occur with probability $(1 - p)$, otherwise x will occur.

As an example, imagine that you assess the probability of receiving a raise from your current employer to be about 30 percent. The closure property states that the situation expressed as a 30 percent chance of receiving a raise (otherwise, no raise) is identical to the statement that you have a 70 percent chance of not receiving a raise (otherwise, receiving a raise).

So far, utility theory may seem to be so obvious and simple as to be absurd to spell out in any detail. However, we will soon see how people violate basic "common sense" all the time, and hence, behave irrationally.

Transitivity   Transitivity means that if we prefer x to y and y to z, then we should prefer x to z. Similarly, if we are indifferent between x and y and y and z, then we will be indifferent between x and z.

Suppose your employer offers you one of three options: a transfer to Seattle, a transfer to Pittsburgh, or a raise of $5,000. You prefer a raise of $5,000 over a move to Pittsburgh, and you prefer to move to Seattle more than a $5,000 raise. The **transitivity property** states that you should therefore prefer a move to Seattle over a move to Pittsburgh. If your preferences were not transitive, you would always want to move somewhere else. Further, a third party could become rich by continuously "selling" your preferred options to you.

Reducibility   The **reducibility axiom** refers to a person's attitude toward a compound lottery, in which the prizes may be tickets to other lotteries. According to the reducibility axiom, a person's attitude toward a compound lottery depends only on the ultimate prizes and the chance of getting them as determined by the laws of probability; the actual gambling mechanism is irrelevant, $(x, pq, y) = [(x, p, y), q, y)]$.

Suppose that the dean of admissions at your first-choice university tells you that you have a 25 percent chance of getting accepted to the MBA program. How do you feel about the situation? Now, suppose the dean tells you that there is a 50 percent chance that you will not get accepted and a 50 percent chance that you will face a lottery-type admission procedure, wherein half the applicants will get accepted and half will not. Which situation do you prefer to be in? According to the reducibility axiom, both situations are identical. Your chances of getting admitted into graduate school are the same in each case: exactly 25 percent. The difference between the two situations is that one involves a **compound gamble** and the other does not.

Compound gambles differ from simple ones in that their outcomes are themselves gambles rather than pure outcomes. Furthermore, probabilities are the same in both gambles. If people have an aversion or attraction to gambling, however, these may not seem the same. This axiom has important implications for negotiation; the format by which alternatives are presented to negotiators—in other words, in terms of gambles or compound gambles—strongly affects our behavior.

Substitutability   The **substitutability axiom** states that gambles that have prizes about which people are indifferent are interchangeable. For example, suppose one prize is substituted for another in a lottery but the lottery is left otherwise unchanged.

If you are indifferent between the old and the new prizes, you should be indifferent between the lotteries. If you prefer one prize to the other, you will prefer the lottery that offers the preferred prize.

As an illustration, imagine you work in the finance division of a company, and your supervisor asks you how you feel about transferring to either the marketing or sales division in your company. You respond that you are indifferent between the two. Then your supervisor presents you with a choice: Either you can be transferred to the sales division, or you can move to a finance position in an out-of-state parent branch of the company. After wrestling with the decision, you decide that you prefer to move out of state rather than transfer to the sales division. A few days later, your supervisor surprises you by asking whether you prefer to be transferred to marketing or to be transferred out of the state. According to the substitutability axiom, you should prefer to transfer because, as you previously indicated, you are indifferent to marketing and sales; they are substitutable choices.

Betweenness   The **betweenness axiom** asserts that if x is preferred to y, then x must be preferred to any probability mixture of x and y, which in turn must be preferred to y. This principle is certainly not objectionable for monetary outcomes. For example, most of us would rather have a dime than a nickel and would rather have a probability of either a dime or a nickel than the nickel itself. But consider nonmonetary outcomes, such as skydiving, Russian roulette, and bungee jumping. To an outside observer, people who skydive apparently prefer a probability mixture of living and dying over either one of them alone; otherwise, one can easily either stay alive or kill oneself without ever skydiving. People who like to risk their lives appear to contradict the betweenness axiom. A more careful analysis reveals, however, that this situation, strange as it may be, is not incompatible with the betweenness axiom. The actual outcomes involved in skydiving are (1) staying alive after skydiving, (2) staying alive without skydiving, or (3) dying while skydiving. In choosing to skydive, therefore, a person prefers a probability mix of (1) and (3) over (2). This analysis reveals that "experience" has a utility.

Continuity or Solvability   Suppose that of three objects, A, B, and C, you prefer A to B and B to C. Now, consider a lottery in which there is a probability, p, of getting A and a probability of $1 - p$ of getting C. If $p = 0$, the lottery is equivalent to C; if $p = 1$, the lottery is equivalent to A. In the first case, you prefer B to the lottery; in the second case, you prefer the lottery to B. According to the **continuity axiom,** there is a value, p, between 0 and 1 for which you are indifferent between B and the lottery. Sounds reasonable enough.

Now consider the following example from von Neumann and Morgenstern (1947) involving three outcomes: receiving a dime, receiving a nickel, and being shot at dawn. Certainly, most of us prefer a dime to a nickel and a nickel to being shot. The continuity axiom, however, states that there is a point of inversion at which some probability mixture involving receiving a dime and being shot at dawn is equivalent to receiving a nickel. This derivation seems particularly disdainful for most people because no price is equal to risking one's life. However, the counterintuitive nature of this example stems from an inability to understand very small probabilities. In the abstract, people believe they would never choose to risk their life but, in reality, people do so all the time. For example, we cross the street to buy some product for a nickel less, although by doing so we risk getting hit by a car and being killed.

In summary, whenever these axioms hold, a utility function exists that (1) preserves a person's preferences among options and gambles and (2) satisfies the expectation principle: The utility of a gamble equals the expected utility of its outcomes. This utility scale is uniquely determined except for an origin and a unit of measurement.

Expected Value Principle

Imagine that you have a rare opportunity to invest in a highly innovative start-up company. The company has developed a new technology that allows cars to run without gasoline. The cars are fuel efficient, environmentally clean, and less expensive to maintain than regular gasoline-fueled cars. On the other hand, the technology is new and unproven. Further, the company does not have the resources to compete with the major automakers. Nevertheless, if this technology is successful, an investment in the company at this point will have a 30-fold return. Suppose you just inherited $5,000 from your aunt. You could invest the money in the company and possibly earn $150,000—a risky choice. Or you could keep the money and pass up the investment opportunity. You assess the probability of success to be about 20 percent. (A minimum investment of $5,000 is required.) What do you do?

The dominance principle does not offer a solution to this decision situation because there are no clearly dominant alternatives. But the situation contains the necessary elements to use the **expected-value principle,** which applies when a decision maker must choose among two or more prospects, as in the previous example. The "expectation" or "expected value" of a prospect is the sum of the objective values of the outcomes multiplied by the probability of their occurrence.

To see how the expected-value principle works, let's evaluate the expected value of this risky choice. An expected value requires us to compute an overall value for the decision alternatives. This can be done by multiplying the value of the alternative by its probability. For example, suppose you are offered a choice between earning a $50,000 salary or a salary based on profit sharing, such that there is a 20 percent chance your salary would be $20,000; a 20 percent chance of $35,000; a 20 percent chance of $50,000; a 20 percent chance of $75,000; and a 20 percent chance of $100,000. Which salary structure should you take? The overall value of the profit-sharing salary may be computed as follows:

$$\text{Overall value of profit-sharing salary} = 0.20(\$20,000) + 0.2(\$35,000) +$$
$$0.2(\$50,000) + 0.2(\$75,000) + 0.2(\$100,000) = \$4,000 + \$7,000 +$$
$$\$10,000 + \$15,000 + \$20,000 = \$56,000$$

If we compare the flat salary of $50,000 to the profit-sharing salary's expected value ($56,000), it is easy to see that the profit-sharing salary has a higher expected value.

Now, what about our investment option? For a variety of reasons, you believe there is a 20 percent chance that the investment could result in a return of $150,000, which mathematically is $0.2 \times \$150,000 = \$30,000$ or $30,000 − $5,000 (initial investment) = $25,000. There is an 80 percent chance that the investment could result in a complete loss of your money, which mathematically is $0.8 \times -\$5,000 = -\$4,000$. We can now compute the expected value of the risky choice by summing these values, or $25,000 − $4,000 = $21,000. Thus, the expected value of this gamble is $21,000.

The expected value of the certain option, not investing the money, may be computed the same way. In this case, it is certain (100 percent probability) that you can keep the money if you do not invest; therefore, the calculation is $5,000 × 1 = $5,000. The expected-value principle dictates that the decision maker should select the prospect with the greatest expected value. In this case, the risky option (with an expected value = $21,000) has the greater expected value than the sure option (expected value = $5,000).

A related principle applies to evaluation decisions, or situations where decision makers must state, and be willing to act upon, the subjective worth of a given alternative. Suppose you could choose to "sell" your opportunity to invest to another person. What would you consider to be a fair price to do so? According to the expected-value evaluation principle, the evaluation of a prospect should be equal to its expected value. That is, the "fair price" for such a gamble would be $21,000. Similarly, the opposite holds: Suppose that your next-door neighbor held the opportunity but was willing to sell the option to you. According to the expected-value principle, people would pay up to $21,000 for the opportunity to gamble.

The expected-value principle is intuitively appealing, but should we use it to make decisions? To answer this question, it is helpful to examine the rationale for using expected value as a prescription. Let's consider the short-term and long-term consequences (Yates 1990). Imagine that you will inherit $5,000 every year for the next 50 years. Each year, you must decide whether to invest the inheritance in the start-up (the risky choice) or keep the money (the sure choice). The expected value of a prospect is its long-run average value. This principle is derived from a fundamental principle: **the law of large numbers** (Feller 1968; Woodroofe 1975). The law of large numbers states that the mean return will get closer and closer to its expected value the more times a gamble is repeated. Thus, we can be fairly sure that after 50 years of investing your money, the average return would be about $21,000. Some years you would lose, others you would make money, but on average, your return would be $21,000. When you look at the gamble this way, it seems reasonable to invest.

Now imagine that the investment decision is a once-in-a-lifetime opportunity. In this case, the law of large numbers does not apply to expected-value decision principle. You will either make $150,000, make nothing, or keep $5,000. There is no in-between. Under such circumstances, there are often very good reasons to reject the guidance of the expected value principle (Yates 1990). For example, suppose that you need a new car. If the gamble is successful, buying a car is no problem. But if the gamble is unsuccessful, you will have no money at all. Therefore, you may decide that buying a used car at or under $5,000 is a more sensible choice.

Risk Attitudes   The expected-value concept is the basis for a standard way of labeling risk-taking behavior. For example, in the previous situation you could either take the investment gamble or receive $21,000 from selling the opportunity to someone else. In this case, the "value" of the sure thing (i.e., receiving $21,000) is identical to the expected value of the gamble. Therefore, the "objective worths" of the alternatives are identical. What would you rather do? Your choice reveals your **risk attitude.** If you are indifferent to the two choices and are content to decide on the basis of a coin flip, you are **risk-neutral** or **risk-indifferent.** If you prefer the sure thing, then your behavior may be described as **risk-averse.** If you choose to gamble, your behavior is classified as **risk-seeking.**

Although there are some individual differences in people's risk attitudes, individuals do not tend to exhibit consistent risk-seeking or risk-averse behavior (Slovic 1962, 1964). Rather, risk attitudes are highly context dependent. The fourfold pattern of risk attitudes predicts that people will be risk-averse for moderate to high probability gains and low-probability losses, and risk seeking for low-probability gains and moderate- to high-probability losses (Tversky and Kahneman 1992; Tversky and Fox 1995).

Expected Utility Principle

How much money would you be willing to pay to play a game with the following two rules: (1) An unbiased coin is tossed until it lands on heads. (2) The player of the game is paid \$2 if heads appears on the opening toss, \$4 if heads first appear on the second toss, \$8 on the third toss, \$16 on the fourth toss, and so on. Before reading further, indicate how much you would be willing to pay to play the game.

To make a decision based upon rational analysis, let's calculate the expected value of the game by multiplying the payoff for each possible outcome by the probability of its occurring. Although the probability of the first head appearing on toss n becomes progressively smaller as n increases, the probability never becomes zero. In this case, note that the probability of heads for the first time on any given toss is $(1/2)^n$, and the payoff in each case is ($\$2^n$); hence, each term of the infinite series has an expected value of \$1. The implication is that the value of the game is infinite (Lee 1971)! Even though the value of this game is infinite, most people are seldom willing to pay more than a few dollars to play it. Most people believe that the expected-value principle in this case produces an absurd conclusion. The observed reluctance to pay to play the game, despite its objective attractiveness, is known as the **St. Petersburg paradox** (Bernoulli 1738/1954).

How can we explain such an enigma? We might argue that expected value is an undefined quantity when the variance of outcomes is infinite. Because, in practice, the person or organization offering the game could not guarantee a payoff greater than its total assets, the game was unimaginable, except in truncated and therefore finite form (Shapley 1977). So what do we do when offered such a choice? We have decided that to regard it as "priceless" or even to pay hundreds of thousands of dollars would be absurd. So, how should managers reason about such situations?

Diminishing Marginal Utility   The reactions people have to the St. Petersburg game are consistent with the proposition that people decide among prospects not according to their expected objective values, but rather according to their expected subjective values. That is, the psychological value of money does not increase proportionally as the objective amount increases. To be sure, virtually all of us like more money than less money, but we do not necessarily like \$20 twice as much as \$10. And the difference in our happiness when our \$20,000 salary is raised to \$50,000 is not the same as when our \$600,000 salary is raised to \$630,000. Bernoulli proposed a logarithmic function relating the utility of money, u, to the amount of money, x. This function is **concave,** meaning that the utility of money decreases marginally. Constant additions to monetary amounts result in less and less increased utility. The principle of **diminishing marginal utility** is related to a fundamental principle of psychophysics, wherein good things satiate and bad things escalate. The first bite of a pizza is the best; as we get full, each bite brings less and less utility.

FIGURE A1–2 Utility as a Function of Value

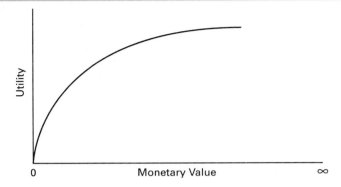

The principle of diminishing marginal utility is simple, yet profound. It is known as "everyman's utility function" (Bernoulli 1738/1954). According to Bernoulli, a fair price for a gamble should not be determined by its expected (monetary) value, but rather by its expected utility (see Fig. A1–2). Thus, the logarithmic utility function in Figure A1–2 yields a finite price for the gamble.

According to EU, each of the possible outcomes of a prospect has a utility (subjective value) that is represented numerically. The more appealing an outcome is, the higher its utility. The expected utility of a prospect is the sum of the utilities of the potential outcomes, each weighted by its probability. According to EU, when choosing among two or more prospects, people should select the option with the highest expected utility. Further, in evaluation situations, risky prospects should have an expected utility equal to the corresponding "sure choice" alternative.

Expected utility (EU) principles have essentially the same form as expected value (EV) principles. The difference is that expectations are computed using objective (dollar) values in EV models as opposed to subjective values (utility) in EU models.

Risk Taking   A person's utility function for various prospects reveals something about his or her risk-taking tendencies. If a utility function is concave, a decision maker will always choose a sure thing over a prospect whose expected value is identical to that sure thing. The decision maker's behavior is risk-averse (Fig. A1–3A). The risk-averse decision maker would prefer a sure $5 over a 50-50 chance of winning $10 or nothing—even though the expected value of the gamble [0.5 ($10) + 0.5 ($0) = $5] is equal to that of the sure thing. If a person's utility function is convex, he or she will choose the risky option (Fig. A1–3B). If the utility function is linear, his or her decisions will be risk-neutral and, of course, identical to that predicted by expected value maximization (Fig. A1–3C).

If most managers' utility for gains are concave (i.e., risk-averse), then why would people ever choose to gamble? Bets that offer small probabilities of winning large sums of money (e.g., lotteries, roulette wheels) ought to be especially unattractive, given that the concave utility function that drives the worth of the large prize is considerably lower than the value warranting a very small probability of obtaining the prize.

FIGURE A1–3 Risk Attitudes

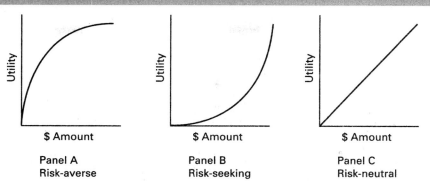

| Panel A | Panel B | Panel C |
| Risk-averse | Risk-seeking | Risk-neutral |

Imagine that, as a manager, one of your subordinates comes to you with the following prospects based upon the consequences of a particular marketing strategy:

Strategy A: 80 percent probability of earning $40,000 or nothing
Strategy B: Earn $30,000 for sure

Which do you choose? Only a small minority of managers (20 percent) choose strategy A over strategy B. Meanwhile, suppose that another associate on a different project presents you with the following two plans:

Strategy C: 20 percent probability of earning $40,000 or nothing
Strategy D: 25 percent probability of earning $30,000 or nothing

Faced with this choice, a clear majority (65 percent) choose strategy C over strategy D (the smaller, more likely prize) (adapted from Kahneman and Tversky 1979).

However, in this example, the manager's choice behavior violates EU, which requires consistency between the A versus B choice and the C versus D choice. In Figure A1–4B, C versus D should be treated the same as a two-stage lottery because the theory considers final states of wealth rather than incremental changes (Fig. A1–4A). In the first stage, there is a 25 percent chance of surviving to a second stage offering A versus B. When the ratio of the value of the two lottery prizes is fixed, the preference between respective options should be completely determined by the ratio of the probability of winning the prizes.

In the A versus B and C versus D choices, the ratio is the same: (0.8/1) = (0.20/0.25). However, managers' preferences usually reverse. According to the **certainty effect,** people have a tendency to overweight certain outcomes relative to outcomes that are merely probable. The reduction in probability from certainty (1) to a degree of uncertainty (0.8) produces a more pronounced loss in attractiveness than a corresponding reduction from one level of uncertainty (0.2) to another (0.25). Managers do not think rationally about probabilities. Those close to 1 are often (mistakenly) considered sure things. On the flip side is the possibility effect: the tendency to overweight outcomes that are possible relative to outcomes that are impossible.

Decision Weights
Decision makers transform probabilities into psychological decision weights. The decision weights are then applied to the subjective values. Prospect theory proposes a

FIGURE A1–4 Allais Paradox Decision Tree

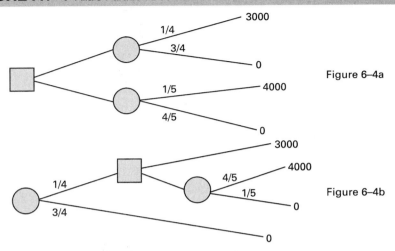

Figure 6–4a

Figure 6–4b

Source: Adapted from Kahneman, D. and A. Tversky (1979). Prospect theory: An analysis of decision under risk. *Econometrica 47,* 263–291. Copyright © by The Econometric Society.

FIGURE A1–5 A Weighting Function for Decision Under Risk

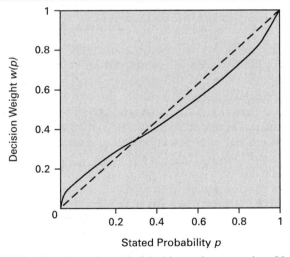

Source: Fox, C. R. (1998) A belief-based model of decision under uncertainty. *Management Science, 44,* 879–896. Copyright © by The Econometric Society.

relationship between the probabilities' potential outcomes and the weights those probabilities have in the decision process.

Figure A1–5 illustrates the probability weighting function proposed by cumulative prospect theory. It is an inverted-S function that is concave near 0 and convex near 1. There are several noteworthy features of the probability-weighting function.

Extremity Effect People tend to overweight low probabilities and underweight high probabilities.

Crossover Point The **crossover probability** is the point at which objective probabilities and subjective weights coincide. Prospect theory (Kahneman and Tversky 1979) does not pinpoint where the crossover occurs, but it is definitely lower than 50 percent.

Subadditivity Adding two probabilities, p_1 and p_2, should yield a probability $p_3 = p_1 + p_2$. For example, suppose you are an investor considering three stocks, A, B, and C. You assess the probability that stock A will close two points higher today than yesterday to be 20 percent, and you assess the probability that stock B will close two points higher today than yesterday to be 15 percent. The stocks are two different companies in two different industries and are completely independent. Now consider the price of stock C, which you believe has a 35 percent probability of closing two points higher today. The likelihood of a two-point increase in either stock A or B should be identical to the likelihood of a two-point increase in stock C. The probability-weighting relationship, however, does not exhibit additivity. That is, for small probabilities, weights are subadditive, as we see from the extreme flatness at the lower end of the curve. This means that most decision makers consider the likely increase of either stocks A or B to be less likely than an increase in stock C.

Subcertainty Except for guaranteed or impossible events, weights for complementary events do not sum to 1. One implication of the **subcertainty** feature of the probability-weight relationship is that for all probabilities, p, with $0 < p < 1$, $\pi(p) + \pi(1 - p) < 1$.

Regressiveness According to the **regressiveness principle,** extreme values of some quantity do not deviate very much from the average value of that quantity. The relative flatness of the probability-weighting curve is a special type of regressiveness suggesting that people's decisions are not as responsive to changes in uncertainty as are the associated probabilities. Another aspect is that nonextreme high probabilities are underweighted, and low ones are overweighted.

The subjective value associated with a prospect depends on the decision weights and the subjective values of potential outcomes. Prospect theory (Kahneman and Tversky 1979) makes specific claims about the form of the relationship between various amounts of an outcome and their subjective values. Figure A1–6 illustrates the generic prospect theory value function.

There are three noteworthy characteristics about the value function. The first pertains to the decision maker's **reference point.** There is a focal amount of the pertinent outcome at which smaller amounts are considered losses and larger amounts gains. That focal amount is the negotiator's reference point. People are sensitive to *changes in wealth*.

A second feature is that the shape of the function changes markedly at the reference point. For gains, the value function is concave, exhibiting diminishing marginal value. As the starting point for increases in gains becomes larger, the significance of a constant increase lessens. A complementary phenomenon occurs in the domain of losses: Constant changes in the negative direction away from the reference point also

FIGURE A1–6 A Hypothetical Value Function

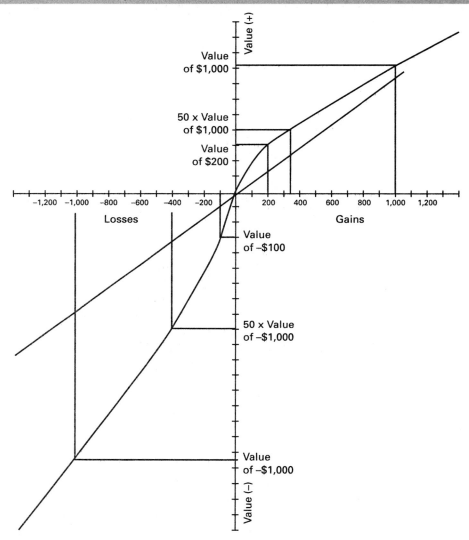

Source: Kahneman, D. and A. Tversky (1979). Prospect theory: An analysis of decision under risk. *Econometrica, 47,* 263–291. Copyright © by The Econometric Society.

assume diminishing significance the farther from the reference point the starting point happens to be.

Finally, the value function is noticeably steeper for losses than for gains. Stated another way, gains and losses of identical magnitude have different significance for people; losses are considered more important. We are much more disappointed about losing $75 than we are happy about making $75.

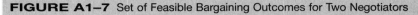

FIGURE A1–7 Set of Feasible Bargaining Outcomes for Two Negotiators

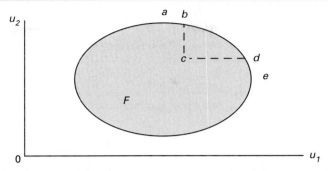

Source: Adapted from Harsanyi, J. C. (1990). Bargaining. In J. Eatwell, M. Milgate, and P. Newman, (eds.) *The new palgrave: A dictionary of economics.* New York: Norton: 54–67.

Combination Rules

How do decision weights and outcome values combine to determine the subjective value of a prospect? The amounts that are effective for the decision maker are not the *actual* sums that would be awarded or taken away, but are instead the *differences* between those sums and the decision maker's reference point.

SUMMING UP: INDIVIDUAL DECISION MAKING

Decisions may sometimes be faulty or irrational if probabilities are not carefully considered. A negotiator's assessment of probabilities affects how he or she negotiates. Clever negotiators are aware of how their *own* decisions may be biased, as well as how the decisions of others may be manipulated to their own advantage. Now that we know about how individuals make decisions, we are ready to explore multiparty, or interdependent, decision making.

GAME THEORETIC RATIONALITY

Each outcome in a negotiation situation may be identified in terms of its utility for each party. In Figure A1–7, for example, party 1's utility function is represented as u_1; party 2's utility function is represented as u_2. Remember that utility payoffs represent the **satisfaction** parties derive from particular commodities or outcomes, not the actual monetary outcomes or payoffs themselves. A bargaining situation like that in Figure A1–7 has a feasible set of utility outcomes, or *F,* defined as the set of all its possible utility outcomes for party 1 and party 2 and by its conflict point, *c,* where $c = (c_1, c_2)$. *c* represents the point at which both parties would prefer not to reach agreement—the reservation points of both parties.

There are two key issues concerning rationality at the negotiation table, one pertaining to pie slicing and one pertaining to pie expansion: (1) People should not agree to a utility payoff smaller than their reservation point; and (2) negotiators should not agree on an outcome if another outcome exists that is pareto-superior (i.e., one that is more preferable to one party and does not decrease utility for the other party) (e.g., level 3 integrative agreements in chapter 4).

For example, in Figure A1–7, the area F is the feasible set of alternative outcomes expressed in terms of each negotiator's utility function. The triangular area bcd is the set of all points satisfying the individual rationality requirement. The upper-right boundary $abde$ of F is the set of all points that satisfy the joint rationality requirement. The intersection of the area bcd and of the boundary line $abde$ is the arc bd: It is the set of all points satisfying both rationality requirements. As we can see, b is the least favorable outcome party 1 will accept; d is the least favorable outcome party 2 will accept.

The individual rationality and joint rationality assumptions do not tell us how negotiators should divide the pie. Rather, they tell us only that negotiators should make the pie as big as possible before dividing it. How much of the pie should you have?

NASH BARGAINING THEORY

Nash's (1950, 1953) bargaining theory specifies how negotiators should divide the pie, which involves "a determination of the amount of satisfaction each individual should expect to get from the situation or, rather, a determination of how much it should be worth to each of these individuals to have this opportunity to bargain" (p. 155). Nash's theory makes a *specific* point prediction of the outcome of negotiation, the **Nash solution,** which specifies the outcome of a negotiation if negotiators behave rationally.

Nash's theory makes several important assumptions: Negotiators are rational; that is, they act to maximize their utility. The only significant differences between negotiators are those included in the mathematical description of the game. Further, negotiators have full knowledge of the tastes and preferences of each other.

Nash's theory builds on the axioms named in EU by specifying additional axioms. By specifying enough properties, we exclude all possible settlements in a negotiation, except one. Nash postulates that the agreement point, u, of a negotiation, known as the Nash solution, will satisfy the following five axioms: uniqueness, pareto-optimality, symmetry, independence of equivalent utility representations, and independence of irrelevant alternatives.

Uniqueness
The **uniqueness axiom** states that there is a unique solution to each bargaining situation. Simply stated, one and only one best solution exists for a given bargaining situation or game. In Figure A1–8, the unique solution is denoted as u.

Pareto-Optimality
The bargaining process should not yield any outcome that both people find less desirable than some other feasible outcome. The pareto-optimality (or efficiency) axiom is simply the joint rationality assumption made by von Neumann and Morgenstern (1947) and the level 3 integrative agreement discussed in chapter 4. The **pareto-efficient frontier** is the set of outcomes corresponding to the entire set of agreements that leaves no portion of the total amount of resources unallocated. A given option, x, is a member of the pareto frontier if, and only if, no option y exists such that y is preferred to x by at least one party and is at least as good as x for the other party.

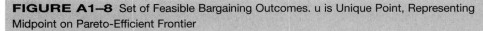

FIGURE A1–8 Set of Feasible Bargaining Outcomes. u is Unique Point, Representing Midpoint on Pareto-Efficient Frontier

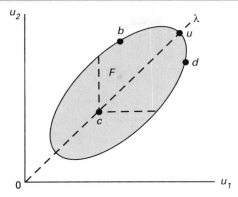

Source: Adapted from Harsanyi, J. C. (1990). Bargaining. In J. Eatwell, M. Milgate, and P. Newman, (eds.) *The new palgrave: A dictionary of economics.* New York: Norton: 54–67.

Consider Figure A1–8: Both people prefer settlement point u (u_1, u_2), which eliminates c (c_1, c_2) from the frontier. Therefore, settlement points that lie on the interior of the arc *bd* are pareto-inefficient. Options that are not on the pareto frontier are dominated; settlements that are dominated clearly violate the utility principle of maximization. The resolution of any negotiation should be an option from the pareto-efficient set because any other option unnecessarily requires more concession on the part of one or both negotiators.

Another way of thinking about the importance of pareto-optimality is to imagine that in *every* negotiation, whether it be for a car, a job, a house, a merger, etc., there is a table with hundreds, thousands, and in some cases, millions of dollars sitting on it. It is yours to keep, provided that you and the other party (e.g., a car dealer, employer, seller, business associate, etc.) agree how to divide it. Obviously, you want to get as much money as you can—this is the distributive aspect of negotiation. Imagine, for a moment, that you and the other negotiator settle upon a division of the money that both of you find acceptable. However, imagine that you leave half or one-third or some amount of money on the table. A fire starts in the building, and the money burns. This is equivalent to failing to reach a pareto-optimal agreement. Most of us would never imagine ever allowing such an unfortunate event to happen. However, in many negotiation situations, people do just that—they leave money to burn.

Symmetry

In a symmetric bargaining situation, the two players have exactly the same strategic possibilities and bargaining power. Therefore, neither player has any reason to accept an agreement that yields a lower payoff than that of the opponent.

Another way of thinking about symmetry is to imagine interchanging the two players. This should not change the outcome. In Figure A1–8, this means that u_1 will be equal to u_2. The feasible set of outcomes must be symmetrical with respect to a hypothetical 45-degree line, λ, which begins at the origin 0 and passes through the point c, thereby implying that $c_1 = c_2$. If we extend this line out to the farthest feasible point, *u,* that is the *Nash point,* wherein parties' utilities are symmetric.

The symmetry principle is often considered to be the fundamental postulate of bargaining theory (Harsanyi 1962). When parties' utilities are known, the solution to the game is straightforward (Nash 1950). As we have noted, however, players' utilities are usually not known. This uncertainty reduces the usefulness of the symmetry principle. That is, symmetry cannot be achieved if a negotiator has only half of the information (Schelling 1960).

The pareto-optimality and symmetry axioms uniquely define the agreement points of a symmetrical game. The remaining two axioms extend the theory to asymmetrical games in which the bargaining power is asymmetric.

Independence of Equivalent Utility Representations

Many utility functions can represent the same preference. Utility functions are behaviorally equivalent if one can be obtained from the other by an order-preserving linear transformation—for example, by shifting the zero point of the utility scale or by changing the utility unit. A distinguishing feature of the Nash solution outcome is that it is independent of the exchange rate between two players' utility scales; it is invariant with respect to any fixed weights we might attach to their respective utilities.

The solution to the bargaining game is not sensitive to positive linear transformations of parties' payoffs because utility is defined on an interval scale. Interval scales such as temperature preserve units of measurement but have an arbitrary origin (i.e., zero point) and unit of measurement. The utility scales for player 1 and player 2 in Figure A1–8 have an arbitrary origin and unit of measurement.

For example, suppose that you and a friend are negotiating to divide 100 poker chips. The poker chips are worth $1 each if redeemed by you and worth $1 each if redeemed by your friend. The question is: How should the two of you divide the poker chips? The Nash solution predicts that the two of you should divide all of the chips and not leave any on the table (pareto-optimality principle). Further, the Nash solution predicts that you should receive 50 chips, and your friend should receive 50 chips (symmetry principle). So far, the Nash solution probably sounds fine. Now, suppose that the situation is slightly changed. Imagine that the chips are worth $1 each if redeemed by you, but they are worth $5 each if redeemed by your friend. (The rules of the game do not permit any kind of side payments or renegotiation of redemption values.) Now, how should the chips be divided? All we have done is transform your friend's utilities using an order-preserving linear transformation (multiply all her values by 5) while keeping your utilities the same. The Nash solution states that you should still divide the chips 50-50 because your friend's utilities have not changed; rather, they are represented by a different, but nevertheless equivalent, linear transformation.

Some people have a hard time with this axiom. After all, if you and your friend are really "symmetric," one of you should not come out richer in the deal. But consider the arguments that could be made for one of you receiving a greater share of the chips. One of you could have a seriously ill parent and need the money for an operation; one of you might be independently wealthy and not need the money; or one of you could be a foolish spendthrift and not deserve the money. Moreover, there could be a disagreement: One of you regards yourself to be thoughtful and prudent but is regarded as silly and imprudent by the other person. All of these arguments are outside the realm of Nash's theory because they are **indeterminate.** Dividing resources to achieve *monetary* equality is as arbitrary as flipping a coin.

But wait a minute. In negotiation, doesn't everything really boil down to dollars? No. In Nash's theory, each person's utility function may be normalized on a 0 to 1 scale so that his or her "best outcome" = 1 and "worst outcome" = 0. Therefore, because the choices of origin and scale for each person's utility function are unrelated to one another, actual numerical levels have no standing in theory, and no comparisons of numerical levels can affect the outcome.

This axiom has serious implications. By permitting the transformation of one player's utilities without any transformation of the other player's, it destroys the possibility that the outcome should depend on interpersonal utility comparisons. Stated simply, it is meaningless for people to compare their utility with another. The same logic applies for comparing salaries, the size of offices, or anything else.

However, people do engage in interpersonal comparisons of utility (chapter 3). The important point is that interpersonal comparisons and arguments based on "fairness" are inherently subjective. There is no rational method for fair division.

Independence of Irrelevant Alternatives

The **independence of irrelevant alternatives** axiom states that the best outcome in a feasible set of outcomes will also be the best outcome in any smaller subset of feasible outcomes that still contains that outcome. For example, a subset of a bargaining game may be obtained by excluding some of the irrelevant alternatives from the original game, without excluding the original agreement point itself. The exclusion of irrelevant alternatives does not change the settlement.

Consider Figure A1–8: The Nash solution is point *u*. Imagine that the settlement options in the half-ellipse below the 45-degree line are eliminated. According to the independence of irrelevant alternatives axiom, this should not affect the settlement outcome, which should still be *u*.

This axiom allows a point prediction to be made in asymmetric games by allowing them to be enlarged to be symmetric. For example, imagine that the game parties play is an asymmetric one like that just described (that is, the half-ellipse below the 45-degree line is eliminated). Such a bargaining problem would be asymmetric, perhaps with player 2 having an advantage. According to Nash, it is useful to expand the asymmetric game to be one that is symmetric—for example, by including the points in the lower half of the ellipse that mirrors the half-ellipse above the 45-degree line. Once these points are included, the game is symmetric, and the Nash solution may be identified. Of course, the settlement outcome yielded by the new, expanded game must also be present in the original game.

The independence of irrelevant alternatives axiom is motivated by the way negotiation unfolds (Harsanyi 1990). Through a process of voluntary mutual concessions, the set of possible outcomes under consideration gradually decreases to just those around the eventual agreement point. This axiom asserts that the winnowing process does not change the agreement point.

In summary, Nash's theorem states that there is a unique solution that possesses these properties. Nash's solution selects the unique point that maximizes the geometric average (i.e., the product) of the gains available to people as measured against their reservation points. For this reason, the Nash solution is also known as the Nash product.

If all possible outcomes are plotted on a graph whose rectangular coordinates measure the utilities that the two players derive from them, as in Figures A1–7 and A1–8, the solution is a unique point on the upper-right boundary of the region. The point is unique because, if there were two, the two could be joined by a straight line representing available alternative outcomes achievable by mixing, with various odds, the probabilities of the original two outcomes, and the points on the line connecting them would yield higher products of the two players' utilities. In other words, the region is presumed convex by reason of the possibility of probability mixtures, and the convex region has a single maximum-utility-product point, or Nash point.

APPENDIX 2

❦

NONVERBAL COMMUNICATION AND LIE DETECTION

The purpose of this appendix is to help you: (1) be a better *reader* of nonverbal communication and (2) be a better *sender* of nonverbal communication.

WHAT ARE WE LOOKING FOR IN NONVERBAL COMMUNICATION?

What exactly do we mean by nonverbal communication? Nonverbal communication is anything that is "not words." Specifically, this includes:

- **Vocal cues or paralinguistic cues.** Paralinguistic cues include pauses, intonation, and fluency. Vocal cues, such as tone and inflection, are nonverbal; they include volume, pace, and pitch.
- **Facial expressions.** Smiling, frowning, or expressing surprise. "Facial expressions are books without covers" (DePaulo and Friedman 1998).
- **Eye contact.** Often, a high level of held gazing can be interpreted as sign of liking or friendliness. However, in other cultures, the norms may differ: Prolonged eye contact in some cultures is a sign of dominance or aggression (Ellsworth and Carlsmith 1973).
- **Interpersonal spacing.** The distance between people when they talk or communicate.
- **Posture.**
- **Body movements.** When people are experiencing greater arousal, or nervousness, they tend to make more movements.
- **Gesture.** There are three basic kinds of gestures: (1) *emblems* (which symbolize certain messages, such as the American thumbs-up for "OK," and the finger-on-the-lips for "quiet"); (2) *illustrators* (which embellish a verbal message, such as the widening of hands and arms when talking about something that was large; and (3) *adaptors,* which include things like touching one's nose or twitching in such a way that does not embellish or illustrate a particular point.
- **Touching.** Touching another person (in an appropriate way) often leads to positive reactions.

Nonverbal communication is informative because it is relatively irrepressible in that people cannot control it. What nonverbal signals do negotiators look for, and what do they reveal? To address this question, we conducted a survey of 50 MBA students who had recently completed a multiparty negotiation. The majority of students relied on

---

BOX A2–1

NONVERBAL BEHAVIORS

What nonverbal behaviors mean you should not trust someone?
- fidgeting
- excessive smiling; sheepish smiles
- overly serious tone; lack of emotion
- averting eyes; lack of eye contact
- being too quiet

What nonverbal behaviors mean you can trust someone?
- direct speech
- open gestures and behavior
- smiling
- pointing

Note: These are behaviors that are *perceived* to be linked to trust; they are not actually indicative of trust.

---

three nonverbal cues as a window into other party's true feelings and intentions: (1) eye contact (people who are lying avoid looking the other party straight in the eyes); (2) closed body posture ("When he leans toward me while he talks, I tend to trust him more.);" and (3) nervousness, twitching, and fidgeting (if people play with their shoestrings, tap their pen, bite their lip, or indicate any other nervous tension, it usually signals anxiety and nervousness). Other indicators mentioned, although much less frequently included, are lack of gestures (too much stillness), emotional outbursts, and autonomic responses, such as sweating and blushing.

What particular nonverbal behaviors do negotiators notice that lead them to distrust someone? (See Box A2–1 for a list of such behaviors.)

Next, we consider three aspects of nonverbal communication of interest to anyone in the corporate world: (1) gender differences, in terms of ability and accuracy, (2) nonverbal abilities of powerful and dominant people, and (3) nonverbal abilities of charismatic people (DePaulo and Friedman 1998). Obviously, power and charisma have implications for success at the bargaining table.

ARE WOMEN MORE "NONVERBALLY GIFTED" THAN MEN?

Popular culture has it that women are more nonverbally sensitive than are men. Scientific evidence indicates that, in many ways, women are more skilled in terms of **nonverbal expression** (DePaulo and Friedman 1998; Hall 1984). In general, women are more open, expressive, approachable, and actively involved in social interaction than are men. Their faces are more readable than men's, and they smile and gaze at other people and approach them more closely than do men. Women are also gazed at more, and approached more closely than are men (Hall 1984). During interactions, women seem more focused on the other person, and they also elicit more warmth and less anxiety from others (Abramowitz, Abramowitz, and Weitz 1976). It is worth pointing out, however, that the sexes are held to different standards of appropriate expressivity; women are typically considered more expressive, and men are viewed as more composed (Hall 1987). Women anticipate greater costs and fewer rewards than men if they fail to express positive emotion in response to someone else's good news (Stoppard and Gun-Gruchy 1993).

Nonverbal expressiveness is linked with social power. Greater expressivity is required by those of lower social status and power (Henley 1977); women traditionally have lower social status than men. Indeed, in studies of visual dominance (measured as the ratio of time a person spends looking at his or her partner while speaking relative to the time spent looking while listening), women are often less dominant. As a general rule, high-power people are more visually dominant than low-power people (Dovidio and Ellyson 1982). When women have uncertain support in a leadership position, men express more visual dominance than women (Brown, Dovidio, and Ellyson 1990). When people show more visual dominance, they are perceived as more powerful. Furthermore, when women and men are assigned to different power roles, low-power people (regardless of gender) are better able to read their partner's cues (Snodgrass 1985, 1992).

In terms of **nonverbal reception,** women are no better than men at recognizing covert messages, such as discrepant or deceptive communication (which we will discuss later). However, when people are being truthful, women are more accurate than men; however, when people are being deceptive (i.e., when the negotiator is pretending to like someone), women are less accurate than men (DePaulo, Epstein, and Wyer 1993; Rosenthal and DePaulo 1979a, 1979b).

In short, women are better at detecting feelings, but are not necessarily better at detecting deception. Why is this? Anyone who is inferior in status is more sensitive to states of mind of their superiors. For example, when women and men are assigned to be supervisors or subordinates in organizational simulations, there are no differences in emotional sensitivity between genders: Subordinates, regardless of gender, are more sensitive than their superiors.

DOMINANCE

Human beings often assert dominance and power through nonverbal cues. Dominant people sit higher, stand taller, talk louder, and have more space and more resources than nondominant people. Dominant people are more likely to invade others' space (e.g., putting their feet up on their own or someone else's desk), make more expansive gestures, walk in front of others, sit in front of others or sit at the head of a table, interrupt more often, control time, and stare the other party down more, but tend to look away more often when the other party is speaking (DePaulo and Friedman 1998).

High social power is reliably indicated by patterns of looking while speaking and listening. People with less power look more when listening than when speaking. In contrast, more powerful people look about the same amount when listening as when speaking (Exline, Ellyson, and Long 1975).

When men and women have equal knowledge, power, and expertise (or when men have more), men behave *visually* as though they really are more powerful. However, when women have the advantage, they "look" like powerful people more often than men (Dovidio, Brown et al. 1988; Dovidio, Ellyson et al. 1988).

PERSONAL CHARISMA

Charisma is a social skill having to do with verbal and nonverbal expressiveness. People vary strikingly in the intensity, expansiveness, animation, and dynamism of their nonverbal (and verbal) behaviors (Friedman et al. 1980; Halberstadt 1991; Manstead

1991). Differences in expressiveness are linked directly to affection, empathy, influence, and professional success, as well as to interpersonal experiences, such as the regulation of one's own emotional experiences and physical and mental health.

Expressiveness, or "spontaneous sending," is the ease with which people's feelings can be read from their nonverbal expressive behaviors when they are not trying to deliberately communicate their feelings to others (Buck 1984; Notarius and Levenson 1979). Expressiveness instantly makes a difference in setting the tone of social interactions. Even commonplace interpersonal behaviors, such as walking into a room and initiating a conversation (Friedman, Riggio, and Casella 1988) or greeting someone who is approaching (DiMatteo, Friedman, and Taranta 1979) suggest this social skill is immediately influential. Why? Expressive people make better first impressions and, even over time, they are better liked than unexpressive people (Cunningham 1986). Expressive people are considered to be more attractive than unexpressive people (DePaulo et al. 1992). Furthermore, expressive people capture people's attention (Sullins 1989) and then "turn on" the expressive behavior of other people (Buck 1989). Expressive people are good actors, feigning convincing expressions of feelings that they are not actually experiencing (Buck 1975). It follows that they are also good liars (DePaulo et al. 1992).

The most interpersonally successful communicators are nonverbally sensitive, nonverbally expressive, nonverbally self-controlled, and motivated to perform for their "audiences" (DePaulo and Friedman 1998). In social interactions, expressive people can "set the tone and frame the field" (DePaulo and Friedman 1998, 14).

DETECTING DECEPTION

Nonverbal sensitivity (in terms of accuracy) is a plus in negotiation, as it is in most social interaction. For instance, doctors who are good at reading body language have more satisfied patients (DiMatteo, Hays, and Prince 1986). Students who are nonverbally sensitive learn more than less sensitive students (Bernieri 1991). However, nonverbal sensitivity is difficult to achieve. As a skill, it is not correlated with intelligence, and it is very "channel-specific": Skill at understanding facial expression and body movements is measurably different from skill at understanding tone of voice (DePaulo and Rosenthal 1979). The good news is that nonverbal sensitivity improves with age (Buck 1984; Zuckerman, Blanck, DePaulo, and Rosenthal 1982).

Reading and sending nonverbal messages in negotiation is one thing; detecting deception (and pulling off deception) is another. Obviously, it is to a negotiator's advantage to be able to detect deception at the negotiation table. In fact, there is a strong belief that relying on nonverbal cues may be our only hope of detecting deception. People believe that either liars cannot control their nonverbal behaviors and therefore these behaviors will "leak out" and betray the liar's true feelings; or, liars simply will not think to attempt to control all of their nonverbal cues (Ekman and Friesen 1969).

Unfortunately, there are no perfect nonverbal indicators of deception. In fact, most people cannot tell from demeanor when others are lying (Ekman, O'Sullivan, and Frank 1999). In fact, accuracy rates are close to chance levels (see DePaulo 1994, DePaulo, Lassiter, and Stone 1982; Zuckerman, Koestner, and Driver 1981). People who have been professionally trained (e.g., law enforcement groups) can be more accurate (Ekman et al. 1999). For example, law-enforcement officers and clinical psychologists are very accurate in judging videotapes of people who are lying or telling the truth (Ekman, O'Sullivan and Frank 1999).

What follows is our best advice for the accurate detection of deception.

DO NOT RELY ON A PERSON'S FACE

Most people look at a person's face when they want to detect deception, but this is not very effective. Perceivers are able to detect deception at greater-than-chance levels from every individual channel or combination of channels with the exception of one— the face (Zuckerman, DePaulo, and Rosenthal 1981). In fact, people are better off when they cannot see another's face. Facial expressions are misleading at worst and, at best, are of qualified use as cues to deceit.

TONE OF VOICE

Paying attention to tone of voice is a better indicator of deception than is facial expression (DePaulo, Lassiter, and Stone 1982). There is useful information in the voice that people do not often look for or detect. People's pitch is higher when they are lying than when they are telling the truth; they speak more slowly and with less fluency and engage in more sentence repairs (Ekman 1992).

MICROEXPRESSIONS

Deception can be detected in the face if you are specially trained to look for microexpressions (or if you have a videotape that you can play back to look for microexpressions). **Microexpressions** are expressions that people show on their face for about one-tenth of a second. These expressions reveal how a person is truly feeling, but because of social pressure and self-presentation, they are quickly wiped away by the person feeling them. As an example, consider an investigation in which the facial expressions of men and women participants were secretly observed while they were interacting with male and female assistants specially trained to act as leaders during a group discussion (Butler and Geis 1990). The results were clear: Female leaders received more negative nonverbal cues (microexpressions) from other members of the group than did male leaders. Moreover, male leaders also received more positive nonverbal cues per minute than did female leaders. Disturbingly, these findings emerged even though participants strongly denied any bias against females.

INTERCHANNEL DISCREPANCIES

To detect deception, look for inconsistencies among these channels, such as tone of voice, body movements, gestures, etc. As a general rule, watch the body, not the face, and look for clusters of clues. *Illustrators* are another type of body movement that can provide clues about deception (Ekman 1992). Illustrators depict speech as it is spoken. It is the hands that usually illustrate speech—giving emphasis to a word or phrase, tracing the flow of thought in the air, drawing a picture in space, or showing an action can repeat or amplify what is being said. Eyebrow and upper eyelid movements can also provide emphasis illustrators, as can the entire body or upper torso. Illustrators are used to help explain ideas that are difficult to put into words. For example, people are more likely to illustrate when asked to define the word *zigzag* than the word *chair*. Illustrators increase with involvement with what is being said; people illustrate less than usual when they are uninvolved, bored, disinterested, or deeply saddened. Illustrators are often confused with emblems, but it is important to distinguish them because these two kinds of body movements may change in opposite ways when people lie: Emblematic slips may increase, whereas illustrators will usually decrease. People who feign concern or enthusiasm can be betrayed by the failure to accompany their speech with increased illustrators, and illustrators decrease when a person does not know exactly what to say. For example, if a liar has not adequately worked out his lie in advance, he will have to be cautious and carefully consider each word before it is spoken.

EYE CONTACT

People who are lying blink more often, have dilated pupils, and have lower eye contact than truth-tellers. However, blinking rates and dilation of pupils are almost impossible to detect with the naked eye. Although eye contact is the number-one cue used by MBA students to detect deceit, it is not reliable; often, it is irrelevant, primarily because it is something that people can control too readily.

BE AWARE OF EGOCENTRIC BIASES

Negotiators tend to regard themselves as truthful and honest and their opponents as dishonest, indicating an egocentric bias. For example, in our investigation, MBA students thought they deceived others in a 10-week negotiation course 25 percent of the time, whereas they thought that they had been deceived by others 35 percent of the time.

THE GREATER THE MOTIVATION, THE EASIER IT IS TO DETECT A LIAR

When people are more motivated, they are more emotional (DePaulo and Kirkendol 1989). It is hard to conceal these feelings. An exception might be people who have great practice at lying and few qualms about the appropriateness of stretching the truth in a selling context, such as experienced salespersons (DePaulo and DePaulo 1989).

DECEPTION AND SECRECY CAN CREATE A LIFE OF ITS OWN

People who are told to keep a secret can become preoccupied with the secret (Wegner 1994). The secret becomes more accessible in their memory and absorbs their consciousness (as judged by word association and reaction times). Why? Keeping a secret takes mental control. Often, secrecy is linked to obsession and attraction (Wegner, Lane, and Dimitri 1994). For example, in a card-playing game, some pairs were told to engage in "nonverbal communication" with their feet to try to influence the game. They were told to either keep it a secret from the other couple or let it be known. After the game, those players who engaged in more nonverbal, secret communication reported more attraction to the other party than those who did not engage in the secretive behavior (Wegner, Shortt, Blake, and Page 1990).

THE POWER OF TRIANGULATION

One of the best methods of lie detection is **triangulation,** which is a method by which a person uses several methods to diagnose a certain situation. For example, if a person wants to accurately assess the time of day, relying on only one clock can be risky. A better method is to use two or three clocks or different timepieces. Similarly, if a person wants to "catch" a liar, a good strategy is to examine nonverbal cues, verbal cues, and perhaps outside evidence as well.

THIRD-PARTY INTERVENTION

Sometimes, despite the best of intentions, the negotiation process breaks down, and parties reach an impasse. In such instances, parties either threaten legal action or perhaps seek third-party intervention. Sometimes, on the way to court, parties try third-party intervention. Third-party intervention can be an excellent means of reaching settlement when BATNAs are terrible and the costs of disagreement are high.

In some instances, parties find it wise to make mediation-arbitration contingencies if they are unable to reach agreement, thereby promising in advance to avoid legal action. For example, as the first wave of Y2K-inspired lawsuits began to emerge, a group of the largest companies vowed not to let the litigation grow into a torrent. A dozen multinational corporations, including General Mills, McDonalds's Corp., Philip Morris, and Bank of America, signed a commitment to use mediation, not litigation, for Y2K disputes with supply-chain partners and vendors (McKendrick 1999).

Next, we review the roles of third parties, key challenges facing third parties, and strategies for enhancing the effectiveness of third-party intervention.

THIRD-PARTY ROLES

There are a number of ways in which a third party may intervene in a dispute (see Rubin, Pruitt, and Kim 1994 for a more complete discussion).

OUTCOME VERSUS PROCESS CONTROL

Most commonly, third-party intervention takes the form of mediation or arbitration. In mediation, the third party has process (but not outcome) control. The mediator aids disputants in resolving the dispute but does not have the power to impose a settlement. In arbitration, third parties have process and outcome control. Principals present their case or final offer to a third party, who has the power to impose a solution. Arbitration may be passive or inquisitive, and the arbiter can have full discretion to impose any kind of settlement or have constraints such as the requirement to choose one side's final offer. There are two major types of arbitration: traditional and final offer. In traditional arbitration, each side submits a proposed settlement to the arbitrator, who is at liberty to come up with settlement terms that both sides must agree to. Oftentimes, the final settlement may be a midpoint between the settlement terms submitted by either party. For example, on Cybersettle.com, the on-line out-of-court settlement service, the algorithm immediately imposes a final settlement outcome that is midway between the last two offers submitted by either party. Thus, each side has an incentive to shape the arbitrator's final judgment by submitting an offer that is self-serving. To counteract this tendency, final-offer arbitration was developed (Farber 1981). In final-offer arbitration, each party submits a final offer, and the arbitrator must choose among the settlement terms submitted. Thus, there is an incentive for parties to propose fair settlement terms so as to maximize the chance of their own terms being selected.

FORMAL VERSUS INFORMAL

The roles of many, perhaps most, third parties are defined on the basis of some formal understanding among the disputants, or on the basis of legal precedents or licensing and certification procedures. Third-party roles are effective to the extent that they are acknowledged by the disputants as implying a legitimate right to be in the business of resolving conflicts. Formal roles include professional mediation, arbitration, or ombudsperson. However, there are a variety of informal third-party roles, such as a friend who intervenes in a marriage dispute.

INVITED VERSUS UNINVITED

Most commonly, a third party intervenes at the request of one or both of the principals. For example, a divorcing couple may seek the services of a divorce mediator. Such invited roles are effective for two reasons: First, the invitation to intervene suggests that at least one of the parties is motivated to address the dispute in question. Second, the invitation makes the third party appropriate, acceptable, and desirable, thereby increasing clout and legitimacy. Uninvited roles may include that of a customer in an airport witnessing a conflict between a flight agent and a passenger.

INTERPERSONAL VERSUS INTERGROUP

Third parties typically intervene in disputes between individuals. In more complex situations, third-party intervention can occur in disputes between groups or nations.

CONTENT VERSUS PROCESS ORIENTATION

Some third-party roles focus primarily on the content of a dispute, such as the issues or substance under consideration. Others focus more on the process of decision making and on the way in which decisions are taking place. Arbitrators (and to a lesser extent, mediators) are typically content-oriented. In contrast, marriage counselors are more process-focused.

CHALLENGES FACING THIRD PARTIES

There are a number of challenges that face the third party. We will now outline some of the more important challenges (see Bazerman and Neale 1992).

INCREASING THE LIKELIHOOD THAT PARTIES REACH AN AGREEMENT IF A POSITIVE BARGAINING ZONE EXISTS

Effective third-party intervention not only assesses whether a positive bargaining zone exists, but it helps parties reach agreement if it does. If settlement is not likely, it is to both parties' advantage to realize this quickly and resort to their BATNAs.

PROMOTING A PARETO-EFFICIENT OUTCOME

It is not enough for third parties to help negotiators reach agreement. Ideally, third parties should strive for pareto-optimal win-win agreements. Obviously, this will not happen if the third party is not properly trained in integrative bargaining strategies or places a higher premium on reaching agreement over reaching a win-win agreement. Third parties should not let the desperation of the negotiators narrow their own view of the possibilities for integrative agreement.

PROMOTING OUTCOMES THAT ARE PERCEIVED AS FAIR IN THE EYES OF DISPUTANTS

When people feel that a deal is fair, they are more likely to agree to it, less likely to renege on it, and more likely to come to the table in the future. For example, take Martin Scheinman, who makes his living as a labor arbitrator. Union leaders who do not trust one another trust Scheinman. Appointed to a second presidential mediation board after the original one could not settle the LIRR dispute, Scheinman engineered a settlement with one union when all seemed hopeless. One of his keys is proposing settlements that seem fair in the eyes of disputing parties, and one of the ways that he appeals to this sense of fairness is by making parties look good (Fessenden 1987).

IMPROVING THE RELATIONSHIP BETWEEN PARTIES

Ideally, effective third-party intervention should increase the level of trust and rapport between parties.

EMPOWERING PARTIES IN THE NEGOTIATION PROCESS

It has been said that a good counselor is a person who works herself out of a job. The same can be said of mediators. An excellent mediator not only helps parties reach integrative settlements, but improves the ability of parties to reach settlements on their own. Ideally, the ability of negotiators to effectively resolve conflict and reach effective outcomes should be enhanced via the influence of a third party.

DEBIASING NEGOTIATORS

Biased perceptions run rampant among negotiators, even in the best of circumstances. When conflict has escalated and parties are emotional, biased perceptions further escalate. Third parties should attempt, whenever possible, to debias negotiations. Unfortunately, there is not just one bias lurking in the jungle of conflict, but rather, several:

Exaggeration of Conflict Bias

There is a pervasive bias to exaggerate differences between oneself and the opposite party (in negotiation) and even in third parties (in mediation; Morris 1995). For example, when students from rival universities watch the same videotape of a football game, they perceive their own team as committing fewer infractions than those attributed to their team by the opposing side (Hastorf and Cantril 1954). The problem is that people generally underestimate the extent to which their beliefs are shaped by subjective construal rather than by direct perception of objective reality (Griffin and Ross 1991).

Examination of partisans of both sides of contemporary social conflict (e.g., liberal versus conservative groups, pro-life versus pro-choice groups) reveal that partisans overestimate the extremity and consistency of the view of the other side (Robinson, Keltner, Ward, and Ross 1994). For example, Robinson and Keltner (1996) interviewed English professors throughout California who either represented traditionalist or revisionist views of literature. They were required to list the books that they would teach in an introductory literature class and to list the books that they believed professors on the other side of the revisionist/traditionalist conflict would choose. Each party dramatically overestimated the extent of conflict; in fact, both groups agreed on seven out of the 15 books on the reading list.

Hostile Media Bias

Sometimes, parties on both sides of a conflict will view an even-handed media report to be partial to the other side. For example, news accounts of the 1982 Beirut Massacre were judged by partisans on both sides of the Arab-Israel conflict to be partial to the other side (Vallone, Ross, and Lepper 1985). Similarly, in another investigation, negotiators role-played an organizational mediation. Both sides to the conflict perceived the mediator to be partial to the opponent. Even when a mediator is partial to a particular side, that party often fails to realize this and assumes the mediator is biased against him.

Overconfidence Bias

In general, disputants overestimate the extent to which their beliefs are shared by a third party. For example, when negotiators are asked to estimate their likelihood of prevailing in final-offer arbitration, they are overconfident that the third party will favor their proposal (Bazerman and Neale 1982; Neale and Bazerman 1983). The evidence for bias in judgment is the finding that parties on both sides of the dispute estimate a greater than 50 percent chance of prevailing. Obviously, they cannot both be right.

The hostile media bias and the overconfidence bias seem to be contradictory. That is, it just cannot be that people feel that the mediator is simultaneously taking the view of the other side yet also more likely to agree with their own position. The apparent inconsistency stems from the nature of the judgment made by negotiators (Morris and Su 1995). In a direct test of this question, Morris and Su examined negotiators' perceptions of mediator behavior in a realistic simulation of a conflict in an organization. It was revealed that each negotiator simultaneously displayed an egocentric (overconfidence) bias, evaluating his or her own behaviors as more successful than that of the counterparts'. However, when asked about the amount and content of the mediators attention to disputants, they saw themselves as coming up short: Each party perceived that the mediator spent more time talking and listening to their opponent, allowing more faulty arguments from the opponent and showing less resistance to the opponent's persuasion attempts. Also, each side perceived the mediator as less receptive to their concerns and less active in exploring their interests than those of the opponent.

MAINTAINING NEUTRALITY

There is no guarantee that third parties are neutral (Gibson, Thompson, and Bazerman 1994). In fact, third parties evince many of the biases that plague principals, such as framing effects (Carnevale 1995). Even a neutral mediator may be mistakenly viewed as partial to one's adversary (Morris and Su 1995). Also, third parties may have a bias to broker an agreement at any cost, which may be disadvantageous to the principals— if there is no positive bargaining zone. Finally, the threat of third-party intervention may inhibit settlement if principals believe that an arbitrator is inclined to impose a compromise settlement. For this reason, final-offer arbitration may be more effective than traditional arbitration (Farber 1981; see also Chelius and Dworkin 1980; cited in Raiffa 1982, table 4).

Managers are often called on to resolve disputes in organizations (Tornow and Pinto 1976). In contrast to traditional arbitrators and mediators, managers may have a direct stake in the outcome and an ongoing relationship with the disputants. In addition, managers are more likely to have technical expertise and background knowledge about the dispute. Although several intervention techniques are available to managers, they often choose techniques that maximize their own control over the outcome (Sheppard 1984; Karambayya and Brett 1989).

STRATEGIES FOR ENHANCING EFFECTIVENESS OF THIRD-PARTY INTERVENTION

What steps can negotiators take in order to maximize the effectiveness of third-party intervention or, ideally, avoid it altogether? There is no magical prescription, but we strongly advocate the following:

TEST YOUR OWN POSITION

A good scientists will set up an experiment in which there are "blinds." For example, in testing the effectiveness of a particular drug, some patients might be given the drug and the other group a placebo or sugar pill. The experimenter further blinds herself to which group was given what and assesses the outcome. The same should be true for your own negotiation position. For example, if you find yourself in a terrible struggle with a merchant or neighbor, describe the situation in such a way to the third party such that she does not know what role you are playing in the struggle (i.e., she is "blind," just as the experimenter is blind). Then ask the third party for her honest opinion.

ROLE-PLAY A THIRD PARTY IN YOUR OWN DISPUTE

Describe the negotiation situation you are in to some colleagues who might be willing to play the roles involved. Then take on the role of a third party in the situation. Try to come up with a solution to which both parties feel comfortable agreeing.

APPENDIX 4

❦

NEGOTIATING A JOB OFFER

When negotiating a job, you need all of the essential skills covered in Part I of the book (chapters 1, 2, 3, and 4). In addition, you should be comfortable with your own bargaining style (and know its limits; see chapter 5). You should be well versed in building trust and rapport (chapter 6) and know the ins and outs of power (chapter 7) and how to kindle creativity (chapter 8). This appendix is designed to provide you with even more skills for this all-important negotiation that will reoccur throughout your life. We have organized the appendix into three phases: Preparation, in-vivo process, and postoffer.

PREPARATION

What follows is a preparation worksheet for an MBA student who is preparing for salary negotiations with potential employers. This is an extremely important negotiation because it will affect one's livelihood and welfare for years to come. A misassumption at this point can have dramatic effects on one's personal and professional well-being.

STEP 1: FIGURE OUT WHAT YOU REALLY WANT

This sounds easy enough, but for a 28-year-old, this means an ability to project forward in time and to be concerned with things like retirement and benefits. Karen Cates of the Kellogg School (1997) recommends working through a checklist of needs and wants (see Box A4–1). Cates further suggests a practical, step-by-step approach to compensation and benefits (see Table A4–1).

STEP 2: DO YOUR HOMEWORK

This means really researching the company and the industry. Fortunately, the Internet is dramatically changing the ability of people to get information quickly and easily, especially when it comes to salaries. Several Web sites offer salary surveys, job listings with specified pay levels, and even customized compensation analyses. For example, JobSmart, run by a regional public library agency in San Mateo, California, offers links to 150 free salary surveys on the Web that draw about 4,000 visitors each day. Exec-U-Net, a for-profit job search network, divulges free information about the salary, bonus, and stock options offered for about 650 upper-management positions, entirely updated every two weeks. However, for many jobs, cyberspace pay information represents only a starting point. In other words, these Web sites can only tell you if you are in the ballpark and can stop you from underbidding yourself (see Sidebar A4–1).

BOX A4–1

CHECKLIST OF NEEDS AND WANTS (CATES, 1997)

Necessary Living Expenses	*Additional Living Expenses*
Housing (including utilities) Auto Computer/telecom Child care Insurance (auto, home, life, professional) Personal (food, medical, clothing, household) Student loan debt service Taxes (income, property, etc.)	Recreation and entertainment (vacations, events, activities, books, etc.) Services (professional and household) Continuing education Children's expenses (lessons, schooling) Gifts, charity

Table A4–1: Compensation and benefits (Cates, 1997)

Compensation	*Retirement*	*Paid Leave*	*Protection*
Salary Bonus Other variable pay Stock/equity interest	Pension/401K Guaranteed pay plans (supplemental unemployment) Savings plans	Vacation, sick, and personal days Training time Holidays and special travel considerations	Insurance (life, disability, health, other) Care plans (child, elder) Wellness programs

STEP 3: DETERMINE YOUR BATNA AND YOUR ASPIRATION

A negotiator always has a BATNA. Some students who are beginning to negotiate with firms will agitatedly claim that they do not have a BATNA because they do not have any job offers in hand. What they are saying is that they do not have what they consider to be an *attractive* BATNA, but they inevitably have a plan for what they will do if they do not get a job offer. Perhaps they will travel to Europe; perhaps they will do freelance or volunteer work, take a research assistantship at a university, or search for a nonprofessional job while they continue their career search. All of these are possible BATNAs; they should be thought about and the best one focused upon and evaluated carefully.

Our BATNAs are never as attractive as we would like them to be. The rare times when we have two or more fabulous job offers in hand, two bids on our house, and lucrative investment opportunities, we can afford to push for a lot more in negotiations. Obviously, you are in a much better position to successfully negotiate an attractive compensation package if your BATNA is attractive.

It is important to think about how we might improve upon our BATNA. Most negotiators do not spend adequate time attempting to improve their current situation. As a result, they approach negotiations feeling more desperate than they need to be.

Improving your BATNA is often difficult because it seems to be at odds with what you are trying to negotiate. Consider Tom, a second-year student who, in May, does not

SIDEBAR A4–1. HOW THE INTERNET CAN HELP YOU OBTAIN A BETTER SALARY

Executive recruiter Korn/Ferry International unexpectedly got a firsthand lesson in salary information on cyberspace when they created an electronic job-search venture called Futurestep with *The Wall Street Journal.* To compile an internal database of possible applicants for midlevel managerial vacancies, Futurestep offers people a free analysis of their salary and bonus potential, among other things. Unexpectedly, several Korn/Ferry recruiters signed up for Futurestep and found that they were underpaid. For example, Peter Reed, a 28-year-old recruiter in Korn/Ferry's Chicago office, says that he found out he was 18 percent below prevailing rates. Reed says that Futurestep analysis will be part of his action plan when it comes to review time. The result: Korn/Ferry increased his base salary 10 percent (Lublin 1998).

have a job lined up. Tom has an interview scheduled on Friday of next week with a telecommunications company. Feeling somewhat desperate, Tom discussed his upcoming interview with a friend, Lisa, who is practiced in negotiation. Lisa suggested that Tom attempt to line up a position as a research assistant in the marketing department of the business school. At first Tom resisted: "Why should I do that? Shouldn't I do that if I strike out at the company?" Lisa then explained, "No, that is precisely the point; you will have a better interview (and subsequent negotiation) if you have alternative options." It took about three days of Tom's time to talk with two professors who were interested in hiring a research intern to work on a marketing project at a local company. They were delighted to have Tom's expertise and offered him a job that he was able to use as a BATNA in his negotiations with the telecommunications company, which eventually did offer him a position.

STEP 4: RESEARCH THE EMPLOYER'S BATNA

Developing your BATNA is only half of the work that needs to be done before the negotiation. The next step is to determine the other party's BATNA, which requires tapping into multiple sources of information. Consider Sal, who recently received an offer from a small progressive software firm that had been in operation for only two years. She was reasonably happy with the offer but wondered what would happen if she attempted to negotiate some of the terms, specifically the salary.

As a first step, Sal visited the career placement center and got all the printed information she could about the firm, which was not much because the company was so new. Next, Sal contacted some of the employees she had met while on her interview at the firm and suggested that they have a casual lunch. At the lunch, Sal was careful not to grill them for information but made inquiries into where the company was going and what problems there were to solve. This meeting revealed some important information about the firm's current situation. Sal then went to the World Wide Web and did a search on the company, which revealed a lot of information about the company's current prospects. The Web sites turned up the names of some individuals who, although not employed by the company, seemed to have an insider view. Sal contacted these people through the

Internet. Finally, Sal had a friend contact the personnel department of the company. The friend explained he was considering going to business school someday and wanted to find out about the company and its salary structure (all of this was true).

Through her search process, Sal was able to better determine the following important information about the company: the wage structure of the company, where the company falls in the distribution of players in its industry, its standard package, insurance, which elements were variable (e.g., bonus, vacation), recent staff problems and needs, and what candidate qualities were considered most important.

STEP 5: DETERMINE THE ISSUE MIX

You have made your best assessment of the employer's BATNA. The negotiation is fast approaching. Now what? The next step is to determine the issues that are important to you in this negotiation. Do not make the mistake of letting the employer define the issues for you. Be ready to talk about your concerns and priorities.

After you have determined which issues are important from your perspective, go back through your list and attempt to create an even more detailed list, breaking down each of the issues into smaller and smaller subsets. For example, Andrew, in his negotiations with a Chicago firm, initially listed salary, signing bonus, vacation, and moving expenses as his key issues. On a second pass through his list, Andrew listed base salary, fringe benefits, commissions, vacation duration, paid vacation, and flextime opportunities as issues to discuss with the employer. Breaking up the issues into smaller and smaller subsets does two things. First, it allows the negotiator to be much more specific about what is important (e.g., the paid aspect of a vacation or the number of days allowed off). Second, it provides much greater opportunity for creative agreements.

In addition to focusing on the issues and concerns of importance to you, anticipate the other party's perspective. Again, information and research can help here.

STEP 6: PREPARE SEVERAL SCENARIOS

Most likely, the negotiations will not go at all as planned. Rather than being caught off guard, prepare your response to several different scenarios, including the following:

- The employer agrees immediately to your counteroffer.
- The employer makes a low-ball offer (in your eyes) and flatly states, "This is our final offer."
- The employer makes one small concession.
- The employer asks you to make a reasonable offer.

IN VIVO: DURING THE NEGOTIATION ITSELF

You have done your preparation. Now it is time for the actual negotiation.

THINK ABOUT THE BEST WAY TO POSITION AND PRESENT YOUR OPENING OFFER

Remember to couch your offer in terms of a clear rationale. Use objective standards. Focus and select those standards that are favorable to you, and be prepared to indicate why standards unfavorable to you are inappropriate.

Consider Marie, who landed a job offer in a consulting firm. Marie is rather young for a senior management position and was offered a starting salary that was on the low side for senior management personnel. Marie did not have a particularly strong BATNA. In her next meeting with the employer, Marie carefully pointed out that she was indeed younger than most of the other senior management but that this was a great advantage for the company because she was young and energetic and on the up-slope of what was sure to be a long and productive career. In short, Marie sold herself as having more to offer; rather than as having a lot of experience. The strategy worked.

ASSUME THAT THEIR OFFER IS NEGOTIABLE

A survey conducted by the Society for Human Resource Management found that eight out of 10 recruiters were willing to negotiate pay and benefits with job applicants, but only one-third of the job applicants surveyed said they felt comfortable negotiating (Clark 1999). Most job applicants do not push employers at the negotiating table. The failure to negotiate a first offer from an employer can cost workers a lot of money. "A 22-year-old who secures a $2,000 increase in annual salary at his or her first job will, because of the compounding effects of years of raises to follow, most likely generate roughly $150,000 in extra income over the course of a 40-year career" (Clark 1999). The effect is even more dramatic for an MBA student negotiating a job offer of a $90,000. What's more, if you do not negotiate for what you want in that brief window between your receipt of a job offer and your acceptance of it, you may never get it. You are never more powerful than when you are responding to "their offer" because it is the one time that the employer may want you more than you want him (Clark 1999). What are some things to ask for in your negotiation? (For a list of possibilities, see Sidebar A4–2.) Do not ask, "Can we negotiate this offer you have made?" because a negative response can put you in a weak position. Rather, assume that the offer is negotiable and begin by articulating your needs and interests. Cates (1997) advises saying the following: "I have some questions about the insurance coverage that I would like to talk about if we can," or "I have some concerns about your moving allowance, and I need to talk to you about it."

IMMEDIATELY REANCHOR THEM BY REVIEWING YOUR NEEDS AND YOUR RATIONALE

Indicate your interest in working for their company, and tell them how your needs (and wants) can be met in a variety of ways. Many candidates have reached impasse because employers have falsely assumed that the candidates did not want the job when they did. Thus, keep reiterating your heartfelt interest in their company. Cates (1997) advises to "get your requests on the table and keep them there." According to Cates, salary negotiations are really about candidates helping recruiters to solve their problems. In other words, let the employer know what they can do to make their offer more appealing. This even comes to sharing your own prioritization and MAUT analysis of the issues.

DO NOT REVEAL YOUR BATNA UNLESS YOU WANT TO RECEIVE IT

Negotiators have a million ways of asking people about their BATNAs. Asking a potential job recruit about his or her current salary and wage package is one of them.

SIDEBAR A4–2. THINGS TO ASK FOR WHEN NEGOTIATING AN OFFER (CLARK 1999)

Some things to ask for when negotiating an offer (other than a higher salary, which is always worth asking for):

- free parking
- season passes (ski lift, opera, whatever your fancy)
- money to move your hobbies (horses, motorcycles) to the new location
- right to hire an assistant
- right to take three-hour lunches (as long as the work gets done)
- right to take off of work if the wind is blowing at a certain speed (if your hobby is windsurfing)
- car
- signing bonus (or bonus for achieving certain milestones)
- severance pay
- stock options or profit sharing
- accelerated performance review (if you are confident that you need only six months to prove you deserve a raise)
- clothing allowance (typical only in the fashion and entertainment industries)
- computer, cell phone, laptop or other home-office equipment (especially common at technology companies, but spreading quickly)
- flexible scheduling (does not cost real cash)
- memberships: dues for professional associations and athletic clubs
- telecommuting: ask for this ahead of time, since most companies still handle this worker by worker
- tuition reimbursement and coverage of books, fees, non-core courses
- vacation: extra days and scheduling

Remember that this is your business, not the recruiter's. If you are currently employed, redirect the discussion by indicating what it is going to take to move you (e.g., a more exciting job and a wage package commensurate with the job). If you are not employed, respond by explaining what it will take to hire you. Again, ward off direct attacks about previous wages by explaining that whether or not you will accept a position depends on the nature of the job offer and wage package.

You should be prepared to take the initiative in the conversation, especially for less-structured interviews further along in the process of negotiation. It is often helpful to practice by role-playing.

If the employer attempts to get you to talk about why you are leaving a former job or why you are interested in leaving, avoid falling into the trap of trashing a former employer, even if you did have a miserable experience. It is a small world, and there could be a relationship involved that you do not immediately see. Even more important, the employer will probably get the wrong impression about you (e.g., regard you as a troublemaker or as overly critical).

If you have not yet been offered the job but sense that the employer wants to find out what you desire in a job offer, avoid talking about salary or specific terms until you have a job offer. You are in a much weaker position to negotiate before you have a job offer than after you are offered a position. If you have been told that "things will work out" or that "a job offer is coming," express appreciation and inquire when you will receive formal notice. After that, schedule a meeting to talk about the terms.

While you are negotiating, you should assume that everything is negotiable. If you are told that some aspect of the job is "not negotiable," ask questions, such as whether everyone (new hires and veterans) receives the same treatment.

REHEARSE AND PRACTICE

It is important to plan for negotiation. According to Michael Chaffers, a senior consultant with CMI, a negotiation group in Cambridge, Massachusetts, "A pitch for a raise is no different than making a presentation on any subject: It helps to practice beforehand and even do some role playing. Tell an empty chair what you plan to say to your boss (though you might want to make sure no one's around to see you). If you can find a willing participant, have them play the boss, while acting cantankerous and giving you flack" (Anonymous 1999, 96).

POST-OFFER: YOU HAVE THE OFFER, NOW WHAT?

DO NOT IMMEDIATELY AGREE TO THE OFFER

Do not start negotiating until you have a firm job offer and a salary figure from the employer. Do not prolong things, however; this only frustrates the employer. Instead, give the employer positive reinforcement. Cates (1997) suggests something like, "This looks great. I need to go over everything one last time before we make this official. I will call you at [a specific time]."

GET THE OFFER IN WRITING

If the employer says that it is not standard to make written offers, be sure to consult with others who would know this (e.g., the company's human resources division). At the very least, inform them that you will type up what your understanding is and put it in a letter or memo to them. It is a good idea to keep notes for yourself regarding the points agreed to during each meeting. Further, you can offer to type up your notes and send them to the employer for clarification.

BE ENTHUSIASTIC AND GRACIOUS

Someone has just made you an offer. Thank them and show your appreciation, but do not accept immediately. Say, instead, "Let me go home and think about it." Make an appointment to return the following day and state your negotiating position in person.

ASSESS THEIR POWER TO NEGOTIATE WITH YOU

Before you begin negotiating or contemplating a counteroffer, determine who in the company has the ability to negotiate. Generally, those persons higher up in the organization are the ones who negotiate and the ones who care most about hiring good people. You should be well-versed about the advantages and disadvantages of negotiating with an intermediary, such as a human resources manager (see chapter 9 on multiple parties). If you sense that things are not going well in the negotiation, try to bring someone else into the loop. However, do this in a gracious way, so as not to antagonize the person with whom you are dealing.

TELL THEM EXACTLY WHAT NEEDS TO BE DONE FOR YOU TO AGREE

A very powerful negotiating strategy is to let the employer know exactly what it will take for you to agree. This is an effective technique because the employer can put aside any fears about the negotiation dragging on forever and being nickel-and-dimed to death. When you make your demands, though, ground them in logic and clear rationale. Requesting something too far out of whack may lose you the job. Ross Gibson, vice president for human resources at American Superconductor in Boston, says he judges applicants by the way they negotiate—and withdraws offers from those who come across as immature or greedy (Clark 1999).

DO NOT NEGOTIATE IF YOU ARE NOT OR COULD NOT BE INTERESTED

Suppose that you are the lucky person sitting on four job offers, all from consulting firms (A, B, C, and D). You have done enough research, cost-benefit analysis, and soul-searching to determine that, in your mind, firms A and B are superior in all ways to firms C and D. The question is: Should you let firms C and D off the hook, or string them along so as to potentially improve your power position when negotiating with firms A and B? Our advice is to politely inform firms C and D that you will not be accepting their offers at this time. You still have a wonderful BATNA, and this saves everyone a lot of time.

EXPLODING OFFERS

Exploding offers are ones that have a "time bomb" element to them (e.g., "Our offer is only good for the next week"). The question is how to deal with exploding offers. Consider the case of Carla, who has no less than six interviews scheduled, including one interview at company A. Company A interviews Carla and makes her an exploding offer, with a deadline of the following week. Carla's interviews extend into the next four weeks. What should she do? This is obviously a gambling decision (see appendix 1 on risky decision making). In our experience, firms usually do not rescind exploding offers once they have made them (unless it is for family, medical, and emergency reasons, as a matter of courtesy). Generally, we advise that job candidates who receive an exploding offer above their BATNA seriously consider the offer. It certainly cannot hurt to inform your other companies that you have an exploding offer and move up the time of the interview, if at all possible.

DO NOT TRY TO CREATE A BIDDING WAR

Bidding wars regularly occur on Wall Street, in professional athletics, and in the business world. We do not advise, however, that job candidates attempt to create bidding wars between companies. Rather, we advise that job candidates signal to potential employers that they have attractive BATNAs, that they do not want to start a bidding war, and that they tell their top-rated company what it would take to get them to work at the company.

KNOW WHEN TO STOP PUSHING

According to Cates (1997), it is important to know when to stop negotiating. Cates suggests that negotiators stop when they see one or more of the following signals.

- The other side is not responsive.
- Reciprocal concessions are becoming miniscule.
- After some back and forth, they say "enough!"

USE A RATIONAL STRATEGY FOR CHOOSING AMONG JOB OFFERS

If you find yourself in the lucky position of having multiple offers, you are then faced with a choice. First, you should recognize this enviable position as an approach-approach conflict. How should you weigh the choices? The simplest way is to use MAUT by constructing a grid listing the choices along a row (e.g., firm A, firm B) and the relevant attributes along a column underneath (e.g., salary, fringe benefits, travel, vacation, bonus, etc.). Then, fill in the grid with the details of the offer and how they "stack up" compared to the others (on a 1 to 5 or 1 to 10 scale in your mind). Next, you can simply add the columns to find a quick "winner." A more sophisticated version of this strategy is to multiply each grid value by how important it is before adding columns (with importance defined on a 1 to 5 scale). For example, for most people, salary is highly important (maybe a 5), whereas moving expenses are less important (maybe a 1 or 2). This gives a more fine-grained assessment (see appendix 1 for a step-by-step approach to the MAUT).

REFERENCES

᠙

Abel, M. J. (1990). Experiences in an exploratory distributed organization. In J. Galegher, R. E. Kraut, and C. Egido (Eds.), *Intellectual teamwork: Social and technological foundations of cooperative work* (pp. 489–510). Hillsdale, NJ: Lawrence Erlbaum.

Abramowitz, C. V., Abramowitz, S. I., and Weitz, L. J. (1976). Are men therapists soft on empathy? Two studies in feminine understanding. *Journal of Clinical Psychology, 32*(2), 434–437.

Adair, W. (1999a). Exploring the norm of reciprocity in the global market: U.S. and Japanese intra- and intercultural negotiations. Working paper, J. L. Kellogg Graduate School of Management, Northwestern University, Evanston, IL.

Adair, W. (1999b). U. S. and Japanese mental models for negotiation. Working paper, J. L. Kellogg Graduate School of Management, Northwestern University, Evanston, IL.

Adair, W., Brett, J. M., Lempereur, A., Shikhirev, P., Tinsley, C., and Lytle, A. (1998). Culture and negotiation strategy. Working paper, J. L. Kellogg Graduate School of Management, Northwestern University, Evanston, IL.

Adair, W., Okumura, T., and Brett, J. M. (1999). Negotiation behavior when cultures collide: The U. S. and Japan. Working paper, J. L. Kellogg Graduate School of Management, Northwestern University, Evanston, IL.

Adams, S. (1965). Inequity in social exchange. In L. Berkowitz (Ed.), *Advances in experimental social psychology* (Vol. 2). New York: Academic Press.

Adamson, R. E., and Taylor, D. W. (1954). Functional fixedness as related to elapsed time and situation. *Journal of Experimental Psychology, 47,* 122–216.

Adler, N. J. (1991). *International dimensions of organizational behavior.* Boston: PWK-Kent.

Aiello, J. R. (1993). Computer-based monitoring: Electronic surveillance and its effects. *Journal of Abnormal Social Psychology, 23,* 499–507.

Akerlof, G. (1970). The market for lemons: Quality uncertainty and the market mechanism. *Quarterly Journal of Economics, 84,* 488–500.

Alderman, L. (December 6, 1999). What comes next. *Business Week,* p. 30.

Allen, T. J. (1977). *Managing the flow of technology: Technology transfer and the dissemination of technological information within the R&D organization.* Cambridge, MA: MIT Press.

Allison, S. T., and Messick, D. M. (1990). Social decision heuristics in the use of shared resources. *Journal of Behavioral Decision Making, 3*(3), 195–204.

Allred, K. G. (1999). Anger and retaliation: Toward an understanding of impassioned conflict in organizations. In R. J. Bies, R. J. Lewicki, and B. H. Sheppard (Eds.), *Research on negotiations in organizations* (vol. 7, pp. 27–38). Greenwich, CT: JAI Press.

Allred, K. G., Mallozzi, J. S., Matsui, F., and Raia, C. P. (1997). The influence of anger and compassion on negotiation performance. *Organizational Behavior and Human Decision Processes, 70*(3), 175–187.

Altman, I., and Taylor, D. A. (1973). *Social penetration: The development of interpersonal relationships.* New York: Holt, Rinehart & Winston.

Ancona, D. G., Friedman, R. A., and Kolb, D. M. (1991). The group and what happens on the way to "yes." *Negotiation Journal, 2,* 155–173.

Anders, G. (January 15, 1999). How eBay will battle sham bids, mislabeling. *The Wall Street Journal,* p. B1.

Anderson, J. R. (1995). *Cognitive psychology and its implications* (4th ed.). New York: Freeman.

Anonymous. (1999). Tips from a negotiation coach. *Machine Design, 71*(3), 96.

Argyle, M., and Henderson, M. (1984). The rules of relationships. In S. Duck and D. Perlman (Eds.), *Understanding personal relationships: An interdisciplinary approach.* Beverly Hills, CA: Sage.

Armstrong, D. J., and Cole, P. (1995). Managing distances and differences in geographically distributed work groups. In S. E. Jackson and M. N. Ruderman (Eds.), *Diversity in work teams: Research paradigms for a changing workplace* (pp. 187–215). Washington, DC: American Psychological Association.

Armstrong, L. (1999). Kicking tires on the Web. *Business Week, 3626,* 120.

Aronson, E., and Bridgeman, D. (1979). Jigsaw groups and the desegregated classroom: In pursuit of common goals. *Personality and Social Psychology Bulletin, 5,* 438–446.

Aronson, E., and Linder, D. (1965). Gain and loss of esteem as determinants of interpersonal attractiveness. *Journal of Experimental Social Psychology, 1*(2), 156–171.

Aronson, E., Willerman, B., and Floyd, J. (1966). The effect of a pratfall on increasing interpersonal attractiveness. *Psychonomic Science, 4,* 227–228.

Arrow, K. J. (1963). *Social choice and individual values.* New Haven, CT: Yale University Press.

Aubert, V. (1963). Competition and dissensus: Two types of conflict and conflict resolution. *Conflict Resolution, 7,* 26–42.

Austin, W. (1980). Friendship and fairness: Effects of type of relationship and task performance on choice of distribution rules. *Personality and Social Psychology Bulletin, 6,* 402–408.

Babcock, L., Loewenstein, G., Issacharoff, S., and Camerer, C. (1995). Biased judgments of fairness in bargaining. *The American Economic Review, 85*(5), 1337–1343.

Back, K. W. (1951). Influence through social communication. *Journal of Abnormal Social Psychology, 46,* 9–23.

Baguioro, L. (November 1, 1999). Kidneys for sale. *Newsweek,* p. 50.

Balke, W. M., Hammond, K. R., and Meyer, G. D. (1973). An alternate approach to labor-management relations. *Administrative Science Quarterly, 18*(3), 311–327.

Barboza, D. (September 20, 1998). Loving a stock, not wisely, but too well. *The New York Times,* Section 3, p. 1.

Bargh, J. A., Chen, M., and Burrows, L. (1996). Automaticity of social behavior: Direct effects of trait construct and stereotype activation on action. *Journal of Personality and Social Psychology, 71*(2), 230–244.

Bargh, J. A., Lombardi, W. J., and Higgins, E. T. (1988). Automaticity of chronically accessible constructs in person-situation effects on person perception: It's just a matter of time. *Journal of Personality and Social Psychology, 55*(4), 599–605.

Baron, J. (1988). Decision analysis and utility measurement. *Thinking and deciding* (pp. 330–351). Boston: Cambridge University Press.

Baron, J., and Spranca, M. (1997). Protected values. *Organization Behavior and Human Decision Processes, 70*(1), 1–16.

Baron, R. A. (1990). Environmentally induced positive affect: Its impact on self-efficacy, task performance, negotiation, and conflict. *Journal of Applied Social Psychology, 20*(5), 368–384.

Barron, R. S., Kerr, N. L., and Miller, N. (1992). *Group process, group decision, group action.* Pacific Grove, CA: Brooks/Cole.

Barry, B., and R. L. Oliver (1996). Affect in dyadic negotiation: A model and propositions. *Organization Behavior and Human Decision Processes, 67*(2), 127–144.

Baumeister, R. F., Leith, K. P., Muraven, M., and Bratslavsky, E. (1998). Self-regulation as a key to success in life. In D. Pushkar and W. M. Bukowski (Eds.), *Improving competence across the lifespan: Building interventions based on theory and research* (pp. 117–132). New York: Plenum Press.

Bazerman, M. H., and Gillespie, J. J. (1999). Betting on the future: The virtues of contingent contracts. *Harvard Business Review, 77*(4), 155–160.

Bazerman, M. H., Loewenstein, G, and White, S. (1992). Reversals of preference in allocating decisions: Judging an alternative versus choosing among alternatives. *Administrative Science Quarterly, 37,* 220–240.

Bazerman, M. H., Magliozzi, T., and Neale, M. A. (1985). Integrative bargaining in a competitive market. *Organizational Behavior and Human Decision Processes, 35*(3), 294–313.

Bazerman, M. H., Mannix, E., and Thompson, L. (1988). Groups as mixed-motive negotiations. In E. J. Lawler and B. Markovsky (Eds.), *Advances in group processes: Theory and research* (Vol. 5). Greenwich, CT: JAI Press.

Bazerman, M. H., and Neale, M. A. (1982). Improving negotiation effectiveness under final offer arbitration: The role of selection and training. *Journal of Applied Psychology, 67*(5), 543–548.

Bazerman, M. H., and Neale, M. A. (1983). Heuristics in negotiation: Limitations to effective dispute resolution. In M. Bazerman and R. Lewicki (Eds.), *Negotiating in organizations* (pp. 51–67). Beverly Hills, CA: Sage.

Bazerman, M. H., and Neale, M. A. (1992). *Negotiating rationally.* New York: Free Press.

Bazerman, M. H., Neale, M. A., Valley, K., Zajac, E., and Kim, P. (1992). The effect of agents and mediators on negotiation outcomes. *Organizational Behavior and Human Decision Processes, 53,* 55–73.

Bazerman, M. H., Russ, L. E., and Yakura, E. (1987). Post-settlement settlements in dyadic negotiations: The need for renegotiation in complex environments. *Negotiation Journal, 3,* 283–297.

Beaman, A. L., Cole, N., Preston, M., Glentz, B., and Steblay, N. M. (1983). Fifteen years of the foot-in-the-door research: A meta-analysis. *Personality and Social Psychology Bulletin, 9,* 181–186.

Bednarski, P. J. (October 22, 1990). When stars need pacts, she's hired. *Chicago Sun-Times,* p. 35.

Benbow, C. P., and Stanley, J. C. (1980). Sex differences in mathematical ability: Fact or artifact? *Science, 210*(4475), 1262–1264.

Bensinger, K., and Costello, D. (March 19, 1999). Art and money. *Wall Street Journal,* p. W16.

Benson, P. L., Karabenick, S. A., and Lerner, R. M. (1976). Pretty pleases: The effects of physical attractiveness, race, and sex on receiving help. *Journal of Experimental Social Psychology, 12*(5), 409–415.

Ben-Yoav, O., and Pruitt, D. G. (1984). Accountability to constituents: A two-edged sword. *Organization Behavior and Human Processes, 34,* 282–295.

Berkowitz, L. (1972). Social norms, feelings and other factors affecting helping behavior and altruism. In L. Berkowitz (Ed.), *Advances in experimental social psychology* (Vol. 6, pp. 63–108). New York: Academic Press.

Bernieri, F. J. (1991). Interpersonal sensitivity in teaching interactions. *Personality and Social Psychology Bulletin, 17*(1), 98–103.

Bernouilli, D. (L. Sommer, trans.) (1954). Exposition of a new theory on the measurement of risk. (Original work published in 1738.) *Econometrica, 22,* 23–36.

Berry, J. W. (1980). Acculturation as varieties of adaptation. In A. Padilla (Ed.), *Acculturation: Theory, models, and some new findings.* Boulder, CO: Westview.

Berry, J. W., Poortinga, Y. H., Segall, M. H., and Dasen, P. R. (1992). *Cross-cultural psychology: Research and applications.* New York: Cambridge University Press.

Bettenhausen, K., and Murnighan, J. K. (1985). The emergence of norms in competitive decision-making groups. *Administrative Science Quarterly, 30,* 350–372.

Bies, R. J., Shapiro, D. L., and Cummings, L. L. (1988). Causal accounts and managing organizational conflict: Is it enough to say it's not my fault? *Communication Research, 15*(4), 381–399.

Billings, D. K. (1989). Individualism and group orientation. In D. M. Keats, D. Munroe, and L. Mann (Eds.), *Heterogeneity in cross-cultural psychology* (pp. 22–103). Lisse, The Netherlands: Swets and Zeitlinger.

Blau, P. M. (1964). *Exchange and power in social life.* New York: Wiley.

Bobo, L. (1983). Whites' opposition to busing: Symbolic racism or realistic group conflict? *Journal of Personality and Social Psychology, 45*(6), 1196–1210.

Bottom, W. P. (1996). Negotiating risks: Sources of uncertainty and the impact of reference points on concession-making and settlements. Unpublished manuscript, Washington University, St. Louis.

Bottom, W. P., Eavey, C. L., and Miller, G. J. (1996). Getting to the core: Coalitional integrity as a constraint on the power of agenda setters. *Journal of Conflict Resolution, 40*(2), 298–319.

Bottom, W. P., Gibson, K., Daniels, S., and Murnighan, J. K. (1996). Rebuilding relationships: Defection, repentance, forgiveness and reconciliation. Working paper, Washington University, St. Louis.

Bottom, W. P., Gibson, K., Daniels, S., and Murnighan, J. K. (2000). Resurrecting cooperation: The effects of explanations, penance, and relationships. Working paper, Washington University, St. Louis.

Bottom, W. P., and Studt, A. (1993). Framing effects and the distributive aspect of integrative bargaining. *Organizational Behavior and Human Decision Processes, 56*(3), 459–474.

Bradford, D. L., and Cohen, A. R. (1984). *Managing for excellence.* New York: John Wiley and Sons.

Brehm, S. S. (1983). Psychological reactance and social differentiation. *Bulletin de Psychologie, 37*(11–14), 471–474.

Brett, J. M. (in press). *Negotiating globally: How to negotiate deals, resolve disputes, and make decisions across cultural boundaries.* San Francisco, CA: Jossey-Bass.

Brett, J. M., and Okumura, T. (1998). Inter- and intracultural negotiation: U.S. and Japanese negotiators. *Academy of Management Journal, 41*(5), 495–510.

Brett, J. M., Shapiro, D. L., and Lytle, A. (1998). Breaking the bonds of reciprocity in negotiations. *Academy of Management Journal, 41*(4), 410–424.

Brewer, M. (1979). In-group bias in the minimal intergroup situation: A cognitive-motivational analysis. *Psychological Bulletin, 86,* 307–324.

Brewer, M. B., and Brown, R. J. (1998). Intergroup relations. In D. T. Gilbert, S. T. Fiske, and G. Lindzey (Eds.), *The handbook of social psychology* (4th ed., vol. 2, pp. 554–594). New York: McGraw-Hill.

Brodt, S. E., and Tuchinsky, M. (2000). Working together but in opposition: An examination of the "good cop/bad cop" negotiating team tactic. *Organizational Behavior and Human Decision Processes, 81*(2), 155–177.

Brown, C. E., Dovidio, J. F., and Ellyson, S. L. (1990). Reducing sex differences in visual displays of dominance: Knowledge is power. *Personality and Social Psychology Bulletin, 16*(2), 358–368.

Brown, J. D. (1993). Motivational conflict and the self: The double-bind of the low self-esteem. In R. Baumeister (Ed.), *Self-esteem: The puzzle of low self-regard* (pp. 117–130). New York: Plenum.

Brown, P., and Levinson, S. (1987). *Politeness: Some universals in language use.* Cambridge, England: Cambridge University Press.

Brown, R. J., Condor, F., Mathew, A., Wade, G., and Williams, J. A. (1986). Explaining intergroup differentiation in an industrial organization. *Journal of Occupational Psychology, 59,* 273–286.

Buck, R. (1975). Nonverbal communication of affect in children. *Journal of Personality and Social Psychology, 31*(4), 644–653.

Buck, R. (1984). On the definition of emotion: Functional and structural considerations. *Cahiers de Psychologie Cognitive, 4*(1), 44–47.

Buck, R. (1989). Subjective, expressive, and peripheral bodily components of emotion. In H. Wagner and A. Manstead (Eds.), *Handbook of social psychophysiology* (pp. 199–221). Chichester, England: John Wiley and Sons.

Burger, J. M. (1986). Increasing compliance by improving the deal: The that's-not-all technique. *Journal of Personality and Social Psychology, 51,* 277–283.

Burt, R. S. (1992). *The social structure of competition.* Cambridge, MA: Harvard University Press.

Burt, R. S. (1999). Entrepreneurs, distrust, and third parties: A strategic look at the dark side of dense networks. In L. L. Thompson, J. M. Levine, and D. M. Messick (Eds.), *Shared cognition in organizations: The management of knowledge* (pp. 213–244). Mahwah, NJ: Lawrence Erlbaum.

Butler, D., and Geis, F. L. (1990). Nonverbal affect responses to male and female leaders: Implications for leadership evaluations. *Journal of Personality and Social Psychology, 58*(1), 48–59.

Byrne, D. (1961). Interpersonal attraction and attitude similarity. *Journal of Abnormal and Social Psychology, 62,* 713–715.

Byrne, J. A., and Grover, R. (February 21, 2000). Mattel's lack-of-action figures. *Business Week,* p. 50.

Camerer, C., and Loewenstein, G. (1993). In B. A. Mellers and J. Baron (Eds.), *Psychological perspectives on justice* (pp. 155–181). Boston: Cambridge University Press.

Camerer, C. F., Loewenstein, G., and Weber, M. (1989). The curse of knowledge in economic settings: An experimental analysis. *Journal of Political Economy, 97,* 1232–1254.

Cann, A., Sherman, S. J., and Elkes, R. (1975). Effects of initial request size and timing of a second request on compliance: The foot in the door and the door in the face. *Journal of Personality and Social Psychology, 32*(5), 774–782.

Carlson, S. (February 9, 2000). Penn officials use e-mail to negotiate a $10-million gift. *The Chronicle of Higher Education,* 1–2.

Carnevale, P. J. (1995). Property, culture, and negotiation. In R. M. Kramer and D. M. Messick (Eds.), *Negotiation as a social process: New trends in theory and research* (pp. 309–323). Thousand Oaks, CA: Sage.

Carnevale, P. J., and Isen, A. (1986). The influence of positive affect and visual access on the discovery of integrative solutions in bilateral negotiations. *Organizational Behavior and Human Decision Processes, 37,* 1–13.

Carnevale, P. J., and Pruitt, D. G. (1992). Negotiation and mediation. *Annual Review of Psychology, 43,* 531–582.

Carnevale, P. J., Pruitt, D. G., and Britton, S. (1979). Looking tough: The negotiator under constituent surveillance. *Personality and Social Psychology Bulletin, 5,* 118–121.

Carnevale, P. J., Pruitt, D. G., and Seilheimmer, S. (1981). Looking and competing: Accountability and visual access in integrative bargaining. *Journal of Personality and Social Psychology, 40,* 111–120.

Carnevale, P. J., and Radhakrishnan, S. (1994). Group endowment and the theory of collectivism. Unpublished manuscript, Department of Psychology, University of Illinois at Urbana–Champaign.

Cates, K. (1997). Tips for negotiating a job offer. Unpublished manuscript, J. L. Kellogg Graduate School of Management, Northwestern University, Evanston, IL.

Chaiken, S. (1979). Communicator physical attractiveness and persuasion. *Journal of Personality and Social Psychology, 37*(8), 1387–1397.

Chaiken, S. (1980). Heuristic versus systematic information processing and the use of source versus message cues in persuasion. *Journal of Personality and Social Psychology, 39*(5), 752–766.

Chaiken, S., Wood, W., and Eagly, A. H. (1996). Principles of persuasion. In Higgins, E. T., and Kruglanski, A. W. (Eds.), *Social psychology: Handbook of basic principles* (pp. 702–742). New York: Guilford Press.

Chan, D. K. S., Triandis, H. C., Carnevale, P. J., Tam, A., and Bond, M. H. (1994). Comparing negotiation across cultures: Effects of collectivism, relationship between negotiators, and concession pattern on negotiation behavior. Unpublished manuscript, Department of Psychology, University of Illinois at Urbana–Champaign.

Chapman, L. J., and Chapman, J. P. (1967). Genesis of popular but erroneous diagnostic observations. *Journal of Abnormal Psychology, 72,* 193–204.

Chapman, L. J., and Chapman, J. P. (1969). Illusory correlation as an obstacle to the use of valid psychodiagnostic signs. *Journal of Abnormal Psychology, 74*(3), 271–280.

Chicago Sun Times (February 10, 1986). Cultural differences can make or break a deal. Financial Section, p. 60.

Chechile, R. (1984). Logical foundations for a fair and rational method of voting. In W. Swapp (Ed.), *Group decision making.* Beverly Hills: Sage.

Chelius, J. R., and Dworkin, J. B. (1980). The economic analysis of final-offer arbitration as a conflict resolution device. *Journal of Conflict Resolution, 24,* 293–310.

Cialdini, R. B. (1975). Reciprocal concessions procedure for inducing compliance: The door-in-the-face technique. *Journal of Personality and Social Psychology, 31*(2), 206–215.

Cialdini, R. B. (1993). *Influence: Science and practice.* New York: HarperCollins.

Clark, K. (November 1, 1999). Gimme, gimme, gimme: Job seekers don't realize they can ask for more—lots more. *U.S. News and World Report,* pp. 88–92.

Clark, M. S. (1978). Reactions to a request for a benefit in communal and exchange relationships. *Dissertation Abstracts International, 38,*(10–B), 5089–5090.

Clark, M., and Mills, J. (1979). Interpersonal attraction in exchange and communal relationships. *Journal of Personality and Social Psychology, 37,* 12–24.

Cohen, A. (December 27, 1999). The eBay revolution: How the online auctioneer triggered a revolution of its own. *Time,* pp. 74–77.

Cohen, R. (1991). *Negotiating across cultures: Communication obstacles in international diplomacy.* Washington, DC: United States Institute of Peace Press.

Conlin, M., Coy, P., Palmer, A. T., and Saveri, G. (December 6, 1999). The wild new workforce. *Business Week,* p. 38.

Coombs, C. H., Dawes, R. M., and Tversky, A. (1970). *Mathematical psychology: An elementary introduction.* Englewood Cliffs, NJ: Prentice Hall.

Copeland, L., and Griggs, L. (1985). *Going international.* New York: Random House.

Costello, D. (March 24, 2000). Next up for bid: Some stuff owned by a guy named Joe. *The Wall Street Journal Europe,* p. 31.

Covey, S. R. (1999). Resolving differences. *Executive Excellence, 16*(4), 5–6.

Cox, T. H., Lobel, S. A., and McLeod, P. L. (1991). Effects of ethnic group cultural differences in cooperative and competitive behavior on a group task. *Academy of Management Journal, 34*(4), 827–847.

Crossette, B., and Erlanger, S. (November 17, 1998). Allies see bombing of Iraq as inevitable. *New York Times,* pp. A1, A8.

Csikszentmihalyi, M. (1997). *Finding flow: The psychology of engagement with everyday life.* New York: Basicbooks.

Cunningham, M. R. (1986). Measuring the physical in physical attractiveness: Quasi-experiments on the sociobiology of female facial beauty. *Journal of Personality and Social Psychology, 50,* 925–935.

Daft, R. L., and Lengel, R. H. (1984). Information richness: A new approach to managerial behavior and organization design. *Research in Organization Behavior, 6,* 191–223.

Daft, R. L., Lengel, R. H., and Trevino, L. K. (1987). Message equivocality, media selection, and manager performance: Implications for information systems. *MIS Quarterly, 11*(3), 355–366.

Daly, J. P. (1995). Explaining changes to employees: The influence of justifications and change outcomes on employees' fairness judgments. *Journal of Applied Behavioral Science, 31*(4), pp. 415–428.

Daly, J. P., and Geyer, P. D. (1994). The role of fairness in implementing large-scale change: Employee evaluations of process and outcome in seven facility relocations. *Journal of Organizational Behavior, 15,* 623–638.

Davies, J. (November 1998). The art of negotiation. *Management Today,* pp. 126–128.

de Dreu, C. K. W., Weingart, L. R., and Kwon, S. (2000). Influence of social motives on integrative negotiation: A meta-analytic review and test of two theories. *Journal of Personality and Social Psychology, 78*(5), 889–905.

DePaulo, B. M. (1994). Spotting lies: Can humans learn to do better? *Current Directions in Psychological Science, 3*(3), 83–86.

DePaulo, B. M., Blank, A. L., Swaim, G. W., and Hairfield, J. G. (1992). Expressiveness and expressive control. *Personality and Social Psychology Bulletin, 18*(3), 276–285.

DePaulo, B. M., Epstein, J. A., and Wyer, M. M. (1993). Sex differences in lying: How women and men deal with the dilemma of deceit. In M. Lewis and C. Saarni (Eds.), *Lying and deception in everyday life* (pp. 126–147). New York: Guilford Press.

DePaulo, B. M., and Friedman, H. S. (1998). Nonverbal communication. In D. T. Gilbert, S. T. Fiske, and G. Lindzey (Eds.), *The handbook of social psychology* (4th ed.). New York: McGraw-Hill.

DePaulo, B. M., and Kirkendol, S. E. (1989). The motivational impairment effect in the communication of deception. In J. C. Yuille (Ed.), *Credibility assessment* (pp. 51–70). Dordrecht, The Netherlands: Kluwer.

DePaulo, B. M., Lassiter, G. D., and Stone, J. I. (1982). Attentional determinants of success at detecting deception and truth. *Personality and Social Psychology Bulletin, 8*(2), 273–279.

DePaulo, B. M., and Rosenthal, R. (1979). Telling lies. *Journal of Personality and Social Psychology, 37*(10), 1713–1722.

DePaulo, P. J., and DePaulo, B. M. (1989). Can deception by salespersons and customers be detected through nonverbal behavioral cues? *Journal of Applied Social Psychology, 19*(18, Pt. 2), 1552–1577.

Detweiler, R. (1980). The categorization of the actions of people from another culture: A conceptual analysis and behavioral outcome. *International Journal of Intercultural Relations, 4,* 275–293.

Deutsch, M. (1953). The effects of cooperation and competition upon group processes. In D. Cartwright and A. Zander (Eds.), *Group dynamics* (pp. 319–353). Evanston, IL: Row, Peterson.

Deutsch, M. (1973). *The resolution of conflict.* New Haven, CT: Yale University Press.

Deutsch, M. (1985). *Distributive justice: A social-psychological perspective.* New Haven, CT: Yale University Press.

Diehl, M., and Stroebe, W. (1987). Productivity loss in brainstorming groups: Toward the solution of a riddle. *Journal of Personality and Social Psychology, 61,* 392–403.

Diekmann, K. A., Samuels, S. M., Ross, L., and Bazerman, M. H. (1997). Self-interest and fairness in problems of resource allocation. *Journal of Personality and Social Psychology, 72*(5), 1061–1074.

Diekmann, K., Tenbrunsel, A., and Bazerman, M. H. (1998). Escalation and negotiation: Two central themes in the work of Jeffrey Z. Rubin. In D. Kolb and M. Aaron (Eds.), *Essays in memory of Jeffrey Z. Rubin.* Cambridge, MA: Program on Negotiation.

Diekmann, K. A., Tenbrunsel, A. E., Shah, P. P., Schroth, H. A., and Bazerman, M. H. (1996). The descriptive and prescriptive use of previous purchase price in negotiations. *Organizational Behavior and Human Decision Processes, 66*(2), 179–191.

DiMatteo, M. R., Friedman, H. S., and Taranta, A. (1979). Sensitivity to bodily nonverbal communication as a factor in practitioner-patient rapport. *Journal of Nonverbal Behavior, 4*(1), 18–26.

DiMatteo, M. R., Hays, R. D., and Prince, L. M. (1986). Relationship of physicians' nonverbal communication skill to patient satisfaction, appointment noncompliance, and physician workload. *Health Psychology, 5*(6), 581–594.

Dion, K. L. (1972). Physical attractiveness and evaluations of children's transgressions. *Journal of Personality and Social Psychology, 24*(2), 207–213.

Dion, K. L., and Dion, K. K. (1987). Belief in a just world and physical attractiveness stereotyping. *Journal of Personality and Social Psychology, 52*(4), 775–780.

Dion, K., Berscheid, E., and Walster, E. (1972). What is beautiful is good. *Journal of Personality and Social Psychology, 24*(3), 285–290.

Doise, W. (1978). *Groups and individuals: Explanations in social psychology.* Cambridge: Cambridge University Press.

Donohue, W. A. (1981). Analyzing negotiation tactics: Development of a negotiation interact system. *Human Communication Research, 7*(3), 273–287.

Dovidio, J. F., Brown, C. E., Heltman, K., Ellyson, S. L., et al. (1988). Power displays between women and men in discussions of gender-linked tasks: A multichannel study. *Journal of Personality and Social Psychology, 55*(4), 580–587.

Dovidio, J. F., and Ellyson, S. L. (1982). Decoding visual dominance: Attributions of power based on relative percentages of looking while speaking and looking while listening. *Social Psychology Quarterly, 45*(2), 106–113.

Dovidio, J. F., Ellyson, S. L., Keating, C. F., Heltman, K., et al. (1988). The relationship of social power to visual displays of dominance between men and women. *Journal of Personality and Social Psychology, 54*(2), 233–242.

Drolet, A., Larrick, R., and Morris, M. W. (1998). Thinking of others: How perspective-taking changes negotiators' aspirations and fairness perceptions as a function of negotiator relationships. *Basic and Applied Social Psychology, 20*(1), 23–31.

Drolet, A. L., and Morris, M. W. (1995). Communication media and interpersonal trust in conflicts: The role of rapport and synchrony of nonverbal behavior. Unpublished manuscript, Stanford University, Palo Alto, CA.

Drolet, A. L., and Morris, M. W. (2000). Rapport in conflict resolution: Accounting for how nonverbal exchange fosters cooperation on mutually beneficial settlements to mixed-motive conflicts. *Journal of Experimental Social Psychology, 36,* 26–50.

Druckman, D., and Zechmeister, K. (1973). Conflict of interest and value dissensus: Propositions on the sociology of conflict. *Human Relations, 26,* 449–466.

Dubrovsky, V. J., Keisler, S., and Sethna, B. N. (1991). The equalization phenomenon: Status effects in computer-mediated and face-to-face decision-making groups. *Human-Computer Interaction, 6*(2), 119–146.

Duncker, K. (1945). On problem solving. *Psychological Monographs, 58,* 270.

Dworetzky, T. (September 22, 1998a). Sports superagent Leigh Steinberg. *Investors' Business Daily,* p. A6.

Dworetzky, T. (December 11, 1998b). Explorer Christopher Columbus: How the West's greatest discoverer negotiated his trips' financing. *Investor's Business Daily,* p. 1BD.

Dwyer, F. R., Schurr, P. H., and Oh, S. (April 1987). Developing buyer-seller relationships. *Journal of Marketing, 51,* 11–27.

Eagly, A. H., Ashmore, R. D., Makhijani, M. G., and Longo, L. C. (1991). What is beautiful is good, but . . . : A meta-analytic review of research on the physical attractiveness stereotype. *Psychological Bulletin, 110*(1), 109–128.

Earley, P. C. (1989). Social loafing and collectivism: A comparison of the United States and the People's Republic of China. *Administrative Science Quarterly, 34,* 565–581.

Eisenhardt, K. M., Kahwajy, J. L., and Bourgeois, L. J., III. (1997). How management teams can have a good fight. *Harvard Business Review, 75*(4), 77–85.

Ekman, P. (1984). The nature and function of the expression of emotion. In K. Scherer and P. Ekman (Eds.), *Approaches to emotion.* Hillsdale, NJ: Erlbaum.

Ekman, P., and Friesen, W. V. (1969). Nonverbal leakage and clues to deception. *Psychiatry, 32*(1), 88–106.

Ekman, P., O'Sullivan, M. O., and Frank, M. G. (1999). A few can catch a liar. *Psychological Science, 10*(3), 263–266.

Ekman, P. M. (1992). *Telling lies: Clues to deceit in the marketplace, politics, and marriage.* New York: W. W. Norton.

Eldridge, E. (March 29, 1998). Dealers turn to one-price sales. *Denver Post,* p. L-08.

Ellemers, N., and Van Rijswijk, W. (1997). Identity needs versus social opportunities: The use of group level and individual level identity management strategies as a function of relative group size, status, and in-group identification. *Social Psychology Quarterly, 60*(1), 52–65.

Ellemers, N., Van Rijswijk, W., Roefs, M., and Simons, C. (1997). Bias in intergroup perceptions: Balancing group identity with social reality. *Personality and Social Psychology Bulletin, 23*(2), 186–198.

Elliott, S. (February 6, 1998). Milk promoters agree to cooperate. *New York Times,* p. D17.

Ellsworth, P. C., and Carlsmith, J. M. (1973). Eye contact and gaze aversion in aggressive encounters. *Journal of Personality and Social Psychology, 33,* 117–122.

Elsbach, K. D. (1994). Managing organizational legitimacy in the California cattle industry: The construction and effectiveness of verbal accounts. *Administrative Science Quarterly, 39*(1), 57–88.

Englebart, D. (November 1989). Bootstrapping organizations into the 21st century. Paper presented at a seminar at the Software Engineering Institute, Pittsburgh.

Enzle, M. E., and Anderson, S. C. (1993). Surveillant intentions and intrinsic motivation. *Journal of Personality and Social Psychology, 64,* 257–266.

Ertel, D. (May 1999). Turning negotiation into a corporate capability. *Harvard Business Review, 77*(3), 55–70.

Espeland, W. (1994). Legally mediated identity: The national environmental policy act and the bureaucratic construction of interests. *Law and Society Review, 28*(5), 1149–1179.

Espinoza, J. A., and Garza, R. T. (1985). Social group salience and interethnic cooperation. *Journal of Experimental Social Psychology, 21,* 380–392.

Etzkowitz, H., Kemelgor, C., and Uzzi, B. (1999). *Social capital and career dynamics in hard science: Gender, networks, and advancement.* New York: Cambridge University Press.

Evans, C. R., and Dion, K. L. (1991). Group cohesion and performance: A meta-analysis. *Small Group Research, 22,* 175–186.

Eveland, J. D., and Bikson, T. K. (1988). Work group structures and computer support: A field experiment. *Transactions on Office Information Systems, 6*(4), 354–379.

Exline, R. V., Ellyson, S. L., and Long, B. (1975). Visual behavior as an aspect of power role relationships. In P. Pliner, L. Krames, and T. Alloway (Eds.), *Advances in the study of communication and affect* (*Vol. 2: Nonverbal communication of aggression;* pp. 21–52). New York: Plenum.

Farber, H. S. (1981). Splitting the difference in interest arbitration. *Industrial and Labor Relations Review, 35,* 70–77.

Farber, H. S., and Bazerman, M. H. (1986). The general basis of arbitrator behavior: An empirical analysis of conventional and final offer arbitration. *Econometrica, 54,* 1503–1528.

Farber, H. S., and Bazerman, M. H. (1989). Divergent expectations as a cause of disagreement in bargaining: Evidence from a comparison of arbitration schemes. *Quarterly Journal of Economics, 104,* 99–120.

Farrell, J., and Gibbons, R. (1989). Cheap talk can matter in bargaining. *Journal of Economic Theory, 48,* 221–237.

Feller, W. (1968). *An introduction to probability theory and its applications* (Vol. 1, 3rd ed.). New York: Wiley.

Fessenden, F. (February 2, 1987). A man who gets them talking. *Newsday,* p. 6.

Festinger, L. (1950). Informal social communication. *Psychological Review, 57,* 271–282.

Fischhoff, B. (1975). Hindsight does not equal foresight: The effect of outcome knowledge on judgment under uncertainty. *Journal of Experimental Psychology: Human Perception and Performance, 1,* 288–299.

Fischhoff, B., Slovic, P., and Lichtenstein, S. (1977). Knowing with certainty: The appropriateness of extreme confidence. *Journal of Experimental Psychology: Human Perception and Performance, 3*(4), 552–564.

Fisher, R., Ury, W., and Patton, B. (1991). *Getting to yes* (2nd ed.). New York: Penguin.

Fiske, A. P. (1992). The four elementary forms of sociality: Framework for a unified theory of social relations. *Psychological Review, 99*(4), 689–723.

Fiske, S. T., and Deprét, E. (1996). Control, interdependence, and power: Understanding social cognition in its social context. In W. Stroebe and M. Hewstone (Eds.), *European Review of Social Psychology, 7,* 31–61.

Fiske, S. T., and Neuberg, S. L. (1990). A continuum of impression formation, from category-based to individuating processes: Influences of information and motivation on attention and interpretation. In M. P. Zanna (Ed.), *Advances in experimental social psychology* (Vol. 23, pp. 1–74). New York: Academic Press.

Fleming, J. H., and Darley, J. M. (1991). Mixed messages: The multiple audience problem and strategic communication. *Social Cognition, 9*(1), 25–46.

Florio, G. (October 19, 1997). Battle over Western land ends up in committee. *The Seattle Times,* p. A6.

Foa, U., and Foa, E. (1975). *Resource theory of social exchange.* Morristown, NJ: General Learning Press.

Forbus, K. D., Gentner, D., and Law, K. (1995). MAC/FAC: A model of similarity-based retrieval. *Cognitive Science, 19*(2), 141–205.

Forgas, J. P. (1996). The role of emotion scripts and transient moods in relationships: Structural and functional perspectives. In G. J. O. Fletcher and J. Fitness (Eds.), *Knowledge structures in close relationships: A social psychological approach* (pp. 275–296). Mahwah, NJ: Lawrence Erlbaum.

Forgas, J. P., and Moylan, S. J. (1996). On feeling good and getting your way: Mood effects on expected and actual negotiation strategies and outcomes. Unpublished manuscript, University of New South Wales.

Frank, R. H. (1988). *Passions within reason: The strategic role of the emotions.* New York: Norton.

Frank, R. H., and Cook, P. J. (1995). *The winner-take-all society.* New York: Penguin.

Fredrickson, B. L., and Kahneman, D. (1993). Duration neglect in retrospective evaluations of affective episodes. *Journal of Personality and Social Psychology, 65*(1), 45–55.

Freedman, J. L., and Fraser, S. C. (1966). Compliance without pressure: The foot-in-the-door technique. *Journal of Personality and Social Psychology, 4,* 195–203.

Friedman, H. S., Prince, L. M., Riggio, R. E., and DiMatteo, M. R. (1980). Understanding and assessing nonverbal expressiveness: The Affective Communication Test. *Journal of Personality and Social Psychology, 39*(2), 333–351.

Friedman, H. S., Riggio, R. E., and Casella, D. F. (1988). Nonverbal skill, personal charisma, and initial attraction. *Personality and Social Psychology Bulletin, 14*(1), 203–211.

Friedman, R. (1992). The culture of mediation: Private understandings in the context of public conflict. In D. Kolb and J. Bartunek (Eds.), *Hidden conflict: Uncovering behind-the-scenes disputes* (pp. 143–164). Beverly Hills, CA: Sage.

Froman, L. A., and Cohen, M. D. (1970). Compromise and logroll: Comparing the efficiency of two bargaining processes. *Behavioral Science, 30,* 180–183.

Fry, W. R., Firestone, I. J., and Williams, D. L. (1983). Negotiation process and outcome of stranger dyads and dating couples: Do lovers lose? *Basic and Applied Social Psychology, 4,* 1–16.

Galegher, J., Kraut, R. E., and Egido, C., eds. (1990). *Intellectual teamwork: Social and technological foundations of cooperative work.* Hillsdale, NJ: Erlbaum.

Galinsky, A., and Mussweiler, T. (2000). Promoting good outcomes: Effects of regulatory focus on negotiation outcomes. Working paper, Northwestern University, Evanston, IL.

Galinsky, A. D., Seiden, V., Kim, P. H., and Medvec, V. H. (1999). The dissatisfaction of having your first offer accepted: The role of counterfactual thinking in negotiations. Working paper, Northwestern University, Evanston, IL.

Galinsky, A. D., Mussweiler, T., and Medvec, V. H. (1999). Disconnecting subjective and objective utility: The role of negotiator focus. Working paper, Northwestern University, Evanston, IL.

Gamson, W. (1964). Experimental studies in coalition formation. In L. Berkowitz (Ed.), *Advances in experimental social psychology* (Vol. 1). New York: Academic Press.

Gardiner, G. S. (1972). *Aggression.* Morristown, NJ: General Learning Corp.

Gelfand, M. J., and Christakopolou, S. (1999). Culture and negotiator cognition: Judgment accuracy and negotiation processes in individualistic and collectivistic cultures. *Organizational Behavior and Human Decision Processes, 79*(3), 248–269.

Gentner, D., Brem, S., Ferguson, R., and Wolff, P. (1997). Analogy and creativity in the works of Johannes Kepler. In T. B. Ward, S. M. Smith, et al. (Eds.), *Creative thought: An investigation of conceptual structures and processes* (pp. 403–459). Washington, DC: American Psychological Association.

Gentner, D., Rattermann, M. J., and Forbus, K. D. (1993). The roles of similarity in transfer: Separating retrievability from inferential soundness. *Cognitive Psychology, 25*(4), 524–575.

Gerard, H. (1983). School desegregation: The social science role. *American Psychologist, 38,* 869–878.

Gerhart, B., and Rynes, S. (1991). Determinants and consequences of salary negotiations by male and female MBA graduates. *Journal of Applied Psychology, 76*(2), 256–262.

Getzels, J. W., and Jackson, P. W. (1962). *Creativity and intelligence: Explorations with gifted students.* New York: Wiley.

Gibson, K., Thompson, L., and Bazerman, M. H. (1994). Biases and rationality in the mediation process. In L. Heath, F. Bryant, and J. Edwards (Eds.), *Application of heuristics and biases to social issues* (Vol. 3). New York: Plenum.

Gick, M. L., and Holyoak, K. J. (1980). Analogical problem solving. *Cognitive Psychology, 12,* 306–355.

Gigone, D., and Hastie, R. (1993). The common knowledge effect: Information sharing and group judgment. *Journal of Personality and Social Psychology, 65,* 959–974.

Gilbert, D. T., Pinel, E. C., Wilson, T. D., Blumberg, S. J., and Wheatley, T. P. (1998). Immune neglect: A source of durability bias in affective forecasting. *Journal of Personality and Social Psychology, 75*(3), 617–638.

Gilbert, D. T., and Wilson, T. D. (2000). Miswanting: Some problems in the forecasting of future affective states. In J. P. Forgas (Ed.), *Feeling and thinking: The role of affect in social cognition. Studies in emotion and social interaction, second series* (pp. 178–197). New York: Cambridge University Press.

Gillespie, J. J., and Bazerman, M. H. (April 1998). Pre-settlement Settlement (PreSS): A simple technique for initiating complex negotiations. *Negotiation Journal,* 149–159.

Gillespie, J. J., Thompson, L., Loewenstein, J., and Gentner, D. (October 1999). Lessons from analogical reasoning in the teaching of negotiation. *Negotiation Journal,* pp. 363–371.

Gilovich, T., and Medvec, V. H. (1994). The temporal pattern to the experience of regret. *Journal of Personality and Social Psychology, 67*(3), 357–365.

Gilovich, T., Savitsky, K., and Medvec, V. H. (1998). The illusion of transparency: Biased assessments of others' ability to read one's emotional states. *Journal of Personality and Social Psychology, 75*(2), 332–346.

Goffman, E. (1959). *The presentation of self in everyday life.* Garden City, NY: Doubleday.

Gottman, J. M. (1979). Detecting cyclicity in social interaction. *Psychological Bulletin, 86*(2), 338–348.

Gouldner, A. W. (1960). The norm of reciprocity: A preliminary statement. *American Sociological Review, 25,* 161–179.

Graham, J. L. (April 1993). The Japanese negotiation style: Characteristics of a distinct approach. *Negotiation Journal,* pp. 123–140.

Graham, J. L., and Sano, Y. (1984). *Smart bargaining: Doing business with the Japanese.* Cambridge, MA: Ballinger.

Granovetter, M. (1973). The strength of weak ties. *American Journal of Sociology, 78,* 1360–1379.

Greenberg, J. (1988). Equity and workplace status: A field experiment. *Journal of Applied Psychology, 73,* 606–613.

Greenberg, J. (1990). Employee theft as a reaction to underpayment inequity: The hidden cost of pay cuts. *Journal of Applied Psychology, 75,* 561–568.

Griffin, D. W., and Ross, L. (1991). Subjective construal, social inference, and human misunderstanding. In M. P. Zanna (Ed.), *Advances in experimental social psychology* (Vol. 24, pp. 319–359). San Diego: Academic Press.

Griffin, E., and Sparks, G. G. (1990). Friends forever: A longitudinal exploration of intimacy in same-sex friends and platonic pairs. *Journal of Social and Personal Relations, 7,* 29–46.

Gruenfeld, D. H., Keltner, D. J., and Anderson, C. (1998). The effects of power on those who possess it. Working paper, J. L. Kellogg Graduate School of Management, Northwestern University, Evanston, IL.

Gruenfeld, D. H., Mannix, E. A., Williams, K., and Neale, M. A. (1996). Group composition and decision making: How member familiarity and information distribution affect process and performance. *Organizational Behavior and Human Decision Processes, 67*(1), 1–15.

Guetzkow, H., and Gyr, J. (1954). An analysis of conflict in decision-making groups. *Human Relations, 7,* 367–381.

Guilford, J. P. (1959). *Personality.* New York: McGraw-Hill.

Guilford, J. P. (1967). The nature of human intelligence. *Intelligence, 1,* 274–280.

Gulliver, M. P. (1979). The effect of the spatial visualization factor on achievement in operations with fractions. *Dissertation Abstracts International, 39*(9-A), 5381–5382.

Halberstadt, A. G. (1991). Toward an ecology of expressiveness: Family socialization in particular and a model in general. In R. S. Feldman and B. Rime (Eds.), *Fundamentals of nonverbal behavior: Studies in emotion and social interaction* (pp. 106–160). New York: Cambridge University Press.

Hall, E. T. (1976). *Beyond culture.* Garden City, NJ: Anchor Press.

Hall, E. T., and Hall, M. R. (1990). *Understanding cultural differences.* Yarmouth, ME: Intercultural Press.

Hall, J. A. (1984). *Nonverbal sex differences: Communication accuracy and expressive style.* Baltimore: Johns Hopkins University Press.

Hall, J. A. (1987). On explaining gender differences: The case of nonverbal communication. In P. Shaver and C. Hendrick (Eds.), *Sex and gender: Review of personality and social psychology* (Vol. 7, pp. 177–200). Newbury Park, CA: Sage.

Hamermesh, D. S., and Biddle, J. E. (1994). Beauty and the labor market. *The American Economic Review, 84*(5), 1174.

Hamilton, D. L., and Gifford, R. K. (1976). Illusory correlation in interpersonal perception: A cognitive basis of sterotypic judgments. *Journal of Experimental Social Psychology, 12,* 392–407.

Haour, G. (September 30, 1998). Managing innovation in the 24-hour laboratory. *Australian Financial Review,* p. 2.

Hardin, G. (1968). The tragedy of the commons. *Science, 162,* 1243–1248.

Harmon, A. (September 3, 1999). Auction for a kidney pops up on eBay's site. *New York Times,* p. A13.

Harris, R. J., and Joyce, M. (1980). What's fair? It depends on how you ask the question. *Journal of Personality and Social Psychology, 38,* 165–170.

Harsanyi, J. (1962). Bargaining in ignorance of the opponent's utility function. *Journal of Conflict Resolution, 6,* 29–38.

Harsanyi, J. C. (1990). Bargaining. In J. Eatwell, M. Milgate, and P. Newman (Eds.), *The new palgrave: A dictionary of economics* (pp. 54–67). New York: Norton.

Harvey, J. (1974). The Abilene Paradox: The management of agreement. *Organizational Dynamics, 3*(1), 63–80. © American Management Association International. Reprinted with permission.

Hastorf, A., and Cantril, H. (1954). They saw a game: A case study. *Journal of Abnormal and Social Psychology, 49,* 129–134.

Hatfield, E., Caccioppo, J. T., and Rapson, R. L. (1992). Primitive emotional contagion. In M. S. Clark (Ed.), *Review of personality and social psychology* (Vol. 14: Emotion and social behavior, pp. 151–177). Newbury Park, CA: Sage.

Henley, N. M. (1977). *Body politics: Power, sex, and non-verbal communication.* Englewood Cliffs, NJ: Prentice Hall.

Heine, S. J., Takata, T., and Lehman, D. R. (2000). Beyond self-presentation: Evidence for self-criticism among Japanese. *Personality and Social Psychology Bulletin, 26*(1), 71–78.

Higgins, E. T. (1999). 'Saying is believing' effects: When sharing reality about something biases knowledge and evaluations. In L. Thompson, J. M. Levine, and D. M. Messick (Eds.), *Shared cognition in organizations: The management of knowledge.* Mahwah, NJ: Lawrence Erlbaum.

Hilty, J., and Carnevale, P. J. (1993). Black-hat/white-hat strategy in bilateral negotiation. *Organizational Behavior and Human Decision Processes, 55*(3), 444–469.

Hinde, R. A. (1979). *Non verbal communication.* Cambridge, England: Cambridge University Press.

Hobson, C. A. (July 1999). E-negotiations: Creating a framework for online commercial negotiations. *Negotiation Journal,* pp. 201–218.

Hochschild, A. R. (1983). *The managed heart: Commercialization of human feeling.* Berkeley: University of California Press.

Hoffman, D. (November 23, 1985). Tense turning point at summit; key Reagan-Gorbachev handshake calmed atmosphere. *The Washington Post,* p. A1.

Hoffman, E. (October 18, 1999). Let your keyboard do the house-hunting. *Business Week,* pp. 215–217.

Hofmann, T. (December 27, 1999). The year in review: Media players set torrid pace. *Dow Jones Business News.*

Hofstadter, D. (1983). Metamagical thinking. *Scientific American, 248,* 14–28.

Hofstede, G. (1980). *Culture's consequences: International differences in work-related values.* Beverly Hills, CA: Sage.

Homans, G. C. (1961). *Social behavior: Its elementary forms.* New York: Harcourt, Brace, Jovanovich.

Howard-Cooper, S. (April 23, 1996). The odd couple: From beginning, friendship between Buss, Johnson has transcended usual relationship between owner, player. *The Los Angeles Times,* p. 1.

Hua, L. S. (November 21, 1999). She's a master of details. *The Straits Times,* p. 42.

Huber, V., and Neale, M. A. (1986). Effects of cognitive heuristics and goals on negotiator performance and subsequent goal setting. *Organizational Behavior and Human Decision Processes, 40,* 342–365.

Huber, V., and Neale, M. A. (1987). Effects of self- and competitor goals on performance in an interdependent bargaining task. *Journal of Applied Psychology, 72,* 197–203.

Hui, C. H., and Triandis, H. C. (1986). Individualism-collectivism: A study of cross-cultural researchers. *Journal of Cultural Psychology, 17,* 225–248.

Insko, C. A., Schopler, J., Graetz, K. A., Drigotas, S. M; et al. (1994). Interindividual-intergroup discontinuity in the prisoner's dilemma game. *Journal of Conflict Resolution, 38*(1), 87–116.

Isen, A. M. (1987). Positive affect, cognitive processes, and social behavior. In L. Berkowitz (Ed.), *Advances in experimental social psychology, Vol. 20* (pp. 203–253). San Diego, CA: Academic Press, Inc.

Isen, A. M., and Baron, R. A. (1991). Affect and organizational behavior. In B. M. Staw and L. L. Cummings (Eds.), *Research in organizational behavior* (Vol. 15, pp. 1–53). Greenwich, CT: JAI Press.

Isen, A. M., Daubman, K. A., and Nowicki, G. P. (1987). Positive affect facilitates creative problem solving. *Journal of Personality and Social Psychology, 52,* 1122–1131.

Isen, A. M., Niedenthal, P. M., and Cantor, N. (1992). An influence of positive affect on social categorization. *Motivation and Emotion,* 16(1), 65–78.

Iwata, E. (April 27, 1995). Negotiating skills. *The Star-Ledger.* Copyright © 1995 Newark Morning Ledger Co.

Janis, I. L., and Mann, L. (1977). *Decision making: A psychological analysis of conflict, choice, and commitment.* New York: Free Press.

Jehn, K. A. (1997). A qualitative analysis of conflict types and dimensions in organizational groups. *Administrative Science Quarterly, 42,* 530–557.

Jensen, M. C., and Meckling, W. H. (1976). Theory of the firm: Managerial behavior, agency costs, and ownership structure. *Journal of Financial Economics, 3,* 305–360.

Johansen, R. (1988). *Groupware: Computer support for business teams.* New York: Free Press.

Jones, E. E., and Gerard, H. B. (1967). *Foundations of social psychology.* New York: Wiley.

Jones, E. E., Stires, L. K., Shaver, K. G., and Harris, V. A. (1968). Evaluation of an ingratiator by target persons and bystanders. *Journal of Personality, 36*(3), 349–385.

Jourard, S. M. (1971). *Self-disclosure: An experimental analysis of the transparent self.* New York: John Wiley & Sons.

Kahn, R. L., and Kramer, R. M. (1990). *Untying the knot: De-escalatory processes in international conflict.* San Francisco: Jossey-Bass.

Kahneman, D., Fredrickson, B. L., Schreiber, C. A., and Redelmeier, D. A. (1993). When more pain is preferred to less: Adding a better end. *Psychological Science, 4*(6), 401–405.

Kahneman, D., Knetsch, J. L., and Thaler, R. H. (1990). Experimental tests of the endowment effect and the Coase theorem. *Journal of Political Economy, 98*(6), 1325–1348.

Kahneman, D., and Miller, D. (1986). Norm theory: Comparing reality to its alternatives. *Psychological Review, 93,* 136–153.

Kahneman, D., and Tversky, A. (1979). Prospect theory: An analysis of decision under risk. *Econometrica, 47,* 263–291.

Kahneman, D., and Tversky, A. (1982). On the study of statistical intuitions. *Cognition, 11*(2), 123–141.

Kalk, S. (January 1, 2000). Fine art of negotiating a fact of life. *The Capital Times,* p. 1E.

Kaplan, J. M. (January 9, 1994). Single-offer tactic can be costly. *The Arizona Republic,* p. E6.

Kaplan, S., and Kaplan, R. (1982). *Cognition and environment: Functioning in an uncertain world.* New York: Praeger.

Karambayya, R., and Brett, J. M. (1989). Managers handling disputes: Third-party roles and perceptions of fairness. *Academy of Management Journal, 32,* 687–704.

Keenan, J., and Wilson, R. B. (1993). Bargaining with private information. *Journal of Economic Literature, 31*(1), 45–104.

Keisler, S., and Sproull, L. (1992). Group decision making and communication technology. *Organizational Behavior and Human Decision Processes, 52,* 96–123.

Keisler, S., Zubrow, D., Moses, A., and Gellar, V. (1985). Affect in computer-mediated communication: An experiment in synchronous terminal-to-terminal discussion. *Human Computer Interaction, 1*(1), 77–104.

Kelley, H. H. (1966). A classroom study of dilemmas in interpersonal negotiations. In K. Archibald (Eds.), *Strategic intervention and conflict* (pp. 49–73). Berkeley, CA.: University of California, Institute of International Studies.

Kelley, H. H., and Schenitzki, D. P. (1972). Bargaining. In C. G. McClintock (Ed.), *Experimental social psychology* (pp. 298–337). New York: Holt, Rinehart, and Winston.

Kelley, H. H., and Stahelski, A. J. (1970). Social interaction basis of cooperators' and competitors' beliefs about others. *Journal of Personality and Social Psychology, 16*(1), 66–91.

Kelley, H. H., and Thibaut, J. (1969). Group problem solving. In G. Lindzey and E. Aronson (Eds.), *Handbook of social psychology* (pp. 1–101). Reading, MA: Addison-Wesley.

Kelly, J. R. (1988). Entrainment in individual and group behavior. In J. E. McGrath (Ed.), *The social psychology of time: New perspectives* (Sage Focus Editions, Vol. 91, pp. 89–110). Newbury Park, CA: Sage.

Kelman, H. C. (1991). Coalitions across conflict lines: The interplay of conflicts within and between the Israeli and Palestinian communities. Working paper series (no. 91–9), Harvard University, Center for International Affairs.

Kerr, N. L. (1983). Motivation losses in small groups: A social dilemma analysis. *Journal of Personality and Social Psychology, 45,* 819–828.

Keysar, B. (1994). The illusory transparency of intention: Linguistic perspective-taking in text. *Cognitive Psychology, 26*(2), 165–208.

Keysar, B. (1998). Language users as problem solvers: Just what ambiguity problem do they solve? In S. R. Fussell and R. J. Kreuz (Eds.), *Social and cognitive approaches to interpersonal communication* (pp. 175–200). Mahwah, NJ: Lawrence Erlbaum.

Kiesler, C. A., and Kiesler, S. B. (1969). *Conformity.* Reading, MA: Addison-Wesley.

Kipnis, D. (1957). Interaction between bomber crews as a determinant of sociometric choice. *Human Relations, 10,* 263–270.

Kiser, K. (1999). The new deal. *Training, 36*(10), 116–126.

Kivisilta, P., Honkaniemi, L., and Sundvi, L. (July 12, 1994). Female employees' physical appearance: A biasing factor in personnel assessment, or a success-producing factor in sales and marketing? Poster presented at the 23rd International Congress of Applied Psychology, Madrid, Spain.

Klar, Y., Bar-Tal, D., and Kruglanski, A. W. (1988). Conflict as a cognitive schema: Toward a social cognitive analysis of conflict and conflict termination. In W. Stroebe, A. Kruglanski, D. Bar-Tal, and M. Hewstone (Eds.), *The social psychology of intergroup conflict.* Berlin: Springer-Verlag.

Koberstein, P. (March 7, 1991). Deal aims to reduce Los Angeles smog, aid NW salmon. *Portland Oregonian,* p. D1.

Kolb, D. (1983). *The mediators.* Cambridge, MA: MIT Press.

Kollock, P. (1994). The emergence of exchange structures: An experimental study of uncertainty, commitment and trust. *American Journal of Sociology, 100*(2), 313–345.

Komorita, S. S., and Parks, C. D. (1994). *Social dilemmas.* Madison, WI: Brown and Benchmark.

Komorita, S. S., and Parks, C. D. (1995). Interpersonal relations: Mixed-motive interaction. *Annual Review of Psychology, 46,* 183–207.

Kossan, P. (December 7, 1999). Hotel negotiations go nowhere: Marriott won't wait forever, and all parties know it. *The Arizona Republic,* p. B1.

Kotter, J., and Schlesinger, L. (March/April 1979). Choosing strategies for change. *Harvard Business Review,* pp. 106–114.

Kramer, R. M. (1991). The more the merrier? Social psychological aspects of multiparty negotiations in organizations. In M. H. Bazerman, R. J. Lewicki, and B. H. Sheppard (Eds.), *Research on negotiation in organizations: Handbook of negotiation research* (Vol. 3, pp. 307–332). Greenwich, CT: JAI Press.

Kramer, R. M. (1995). Dubious battle: Heightened accountability, dysphoric cognition, and self-defeating bargaining behavior. In R. Kramer and D. Messick (Eds.), *Negotiation as a social process* (pp. 95–120). Thousand Oaks, CA: Sage.

Kramer, R. M., and Brewer, M. (1984). Effects of group identity on resource use in a simulated commons dilemma. *Journal of Personality and Social Psychology, 46,* 1044–1057.

Kramer, R. M., and Brewer, M. (1986). Social group identity and the emergence of cooperation in resource conservation dilemmas. In H. Wilke, C. Rutte, and D. Messick (Eds.), *Experimental studies of social dilemmas.* Frankfurt: Peter Lang.

Kramer, R. M., and Hanna, B. A. (1988). Under the influence? Organizational paranoia and the misperception of others' influence behavior. In R. M. Kramer and M. A. Neale (Eds.), *Power and influence in organizations* (pp. 145–179). Thousand Oaks, CA: Sage.

Kramer, R., Pommerenke, P., and Newton, E. (1993). The social context of negotiation: Effects of social identity and accountability on negotiator judgment and decision making. *Journal of Conflict Resolution, 37,* 633–654.

Kramer, R. M., and Wei, J. (1999). Social uncertainty and the problem of trust in social groups: The social self in doubt. In T. R. Tyler and R. M. Kramer (Eds.), *The psychology of the social self: Applied social research* (pp. 145–168). Mahwah, NJ: Lawrence Erlbaum.

Krauss, R. M., and Fussell, S. R. (1991). Perspective-taking in communication: Representations of others' knowledge in reference. *Social Cognition, 9,* 2–24.

Kreps, D. M., Milgrom, P., Roberts, J., and Wilson, R. (1982). Rational cooperation in the finitely repeated prisoner's dilemma. *Journal of Economic Theory, 27,* 245–252.

Kuhlman, D. M., and Marshello, A. (1975). Individual differences in the game motives of own, relative, and joint gain. *Journal of Research in Personality, 9*(3), 240–251.

Kumar, R. (1997). The role of affect in negotiations: An integrative overview. *Journal of Applied Behavioral Science, 33*(1), 84–100.

Kunde, D. (October 29, 1997). Friends in higher places: Business-personal relationships can promote honest feedback. *Dallas Morning News,* p. 1D.

Kurtzberg, T., and Medvec, V. H. (1999). Can we negotiate and still be friends? *Negotiation Journal, 15*(4), 355–362.

LaFrance, M. (1985). Postural mirroring and intergroup relations. *Personality and Social Psychology Bulletin, 11*(2), 207–217.

Lamm, H., and Kayser, E. (1978). An analysis of negotiation concerning the allocation of jointly produced profit or loss: The roles of justice norms, politeness, profit maximization, and tactics. *International Journal of Group Tensions, 8,* 64–80.

Lancaster, H. (January 27, 1998). You have to negotiate for everything in life, so get good at it. *Wall Street Journal,* p. B1.

Landy, D., and Sigall, H. (1974). Beauty is talent: Task evaluation as a function of the performer's physical attractiveness. *Journal of Personality and Social Psychology, 29*(3), 299–304.

Langer, E. (1975). The illusion of control. *Journal of Personality and Social Psychology, 32,* 311–328.

Larson, M. (2000). Time Warner yanks ABC from 3.5 million cable sets. *Adweek Online,* 5/1/2000. Available at www.adweek.com.

Latané, B. (1981). The psychology of social impact. *American Psychologist, 36,* 343–356.

Lax, D. A., and Sebenius, J. K. (1986). *The manager as negotiator.* New York: Free Press.

Lax, D. A., and Sebenius, J. K. (February 24, 1997). A better way to go on strike. *Wall Street Journal,* Section A, p. 22.

Lee, W. (1971). *Decision theory and human behavior.* New York: Wiley.

Lemonick, M. D. (December 22, 1997). Turning down the heat. *Time,* p. 23.

Lerner, H. G. (1985). *The dance of anger.* New York: Harper and Row.

Lerner, M. (1980). *The belief in a just world: The fundamental delusion.* New York: Plenum.

Leung, K. (1987). Some determinants of reactions to procedural models for conflict resolution: A cross-national study. *Journal of Personality and Social Psychology, 53*(5), 898–908.

Leung, K. (1988). Some determinants of conflict avoidance. *Journal of Cross-Cultural Psychology, 19,* 125–136.

Leventhal, H. (1976). The distribution of rewards and resources in groups and organizations. In L. Berkowitz and E. Walster (Eds.), *Advances in experimental social psychology* (Vol. 9, pp. 92–133). New York: Academic Press.

Leventhal, H. (1980). What should be done with equity theory? New approaches to the study of fairness in social exchange. In K. Gergen, M. Greenberg, and R. Willis (Eds.), *Social exchange: Advances in theory and research* (pp. 27–55). New York: Plenum Press.

Levine, J., and Moreland, R. L. (1994). Group socialization: Theory and research. In I. W. Stroebe and M. Hewstone (Eds.), *The European review of social psychology* (Vol. 5, pp. 305–336). Chichester, England: Wiley.

Levine, J., and Thompson, L. (1996). Conflict in groups. In E. T. Higgins and A. Kruglanski (Eds.), *Social psychology: Handbook of basic principles* (pp. 745–776). New York: Guilford.

Levinger, G. K., and Rausch, H. L. (1977). *Close relationships: Perspectives on the meaning of intimacy.* Amherst, MA: University of Massachusetts Press.

Levinger, G. K., and Snoek, J. D. (1972). *Attraction in relationship: A new look at interpersonal attraction.* Morristown, NJ: General Learning Press.

Lewicki, R. J. (1983). Lying and deception: A behavioral model. In M. H. Bazerman and R. J. Lewicki (Eds.), *Negotiating in organizations.* Beverly Hills, CA: Sage.

Lewicki, R. J., and Bunker, B. B. (1996). Developing and maintaining trust in work relationships. In R. M. Kramer, and T. R. Tyler (Eds.), *Trust in organizations: Frontiers of theory and research* (pp. 114–139). Thousand Oaks, CA: Sage.

Lewicki, R. J., and Robinson, R. J. (1998). Ethical and unethical bargaining tactics: An empirical study. *Journal of Business Ethics, 17*(6), 665–682.

Lewthwaite, G. A. (May 7, 1991). Northern Ireland talks deadlock over location. *The Baltimore Sun,* p. 5A.

Lichtenstein, S., and Slovic, P. (1971). Reversals of preference between bids and choices in gambling decisions. *Journal of Experimental Psychology, 89*(1), 46–55.

Liebrand, W. B. G., Messick, D. M., and Wilke, H., eds. (1992). *Social dilemmas: Theoretical issues and research findings.* Oxford, England: Pergamon Press.

Lim, S. G., and Murnighan, J. K. (1994). Phases, deadlines, and the bargaining process. *Organizational Behavior and Human Decision Processes, 58,* 153–171.

Lind, E. A., Kray, L., and Thompson, L. (1996). Adversity in organizations: Reactions to injustice. Paper presented at the Psychology of Adversity Conference, Amherst, MA.

Lind, E. A., and Tyler, T. R. (1988). *The social psychology of procedural justice.* New York: Plenum.

Lindsley, S. L. (June 1999). A layered model of problematic intercultural communication in U.S.-owned maquiladoras in Mexico. *Communication Monographs,* p. 145.

Linville, P. W., Fischer, G. W., and Salovey, P. (1989). Perceived distributions of the characteristics of in-group and out-group members: Empirical evidence and a computer simulation. *Journal of Personality and Social Psychology, 57,* 165–188.

Lippman, T. W. (June 3, 2000). Madame Secretary. *National Journal, 32*(23), p. 1736.

Locke, K. D., and Horowitz, L. M. (1990). Satisfaction in interpersonal interactions as a function of similarity in level of dysphoria. *Journal of Personality and Social Psychology, 58*(5), 823–831.

Loewenstein, G. F., and Schkade, D. (1999). Wouldn't it be nice? Predicting future feelings. In D. Kahneman and E. Diener (Eds.), *Well-being: The foundations of hedonic psychology* (pp. 85–105). New York: Russell Sage Foundation.

Loewenstein, G. F., Thompson, L., and Bazerman, M. H. (1989). Social utility and decision making in interpersonal contexts. *Journal of Personality and Social Psychology, 57*(3), 426–441.

Loewenstein, J., Thompson, L., and Gentner, D. (1999). Analogical encoding facilitates transfer in negotiation. *Psychonomic Bulletin and Review, 6*(4), 586–597.

Lohr, S., and Holson, L. M. (January 16, 2000). Price of joining old and new was core issue in AOL deal. *New York Times,* pp. 1, 20.

Lublin, J. S. (September 22, 1998). Web transforms art of negotiating raises. *Wall Street Journal,* pp. B1, B16.

Lynn, M. (1997). Board games: Those who make it to the top are not usually shy, retiring types, and Cadbury only increases the likelihood of conflict. *Management Today,* pp. 30–34.

Lytle, A. L., Brett, J. M., and Shapiro, D. L. (1999). The strategic use of interests, rights and power to resolve disputes. *Negotiation Journal, 15*(1), 31–49.

Maisonneuve, J., Palmade, G., and Fourment, C. (1952). Selective choices and propinquity. *Sociometry, 15,* 135–140.

Mannix, E. (1993). Organizations as resource dilemmas: The effects of power balance on coalition formation in small groups. *Organizational Behavior and Human Decision Processes, 55,* 1–22.

Mannix, E., and Loewenstein, G. (1993). Managerial time horizons and inter-firm mobility: An experimental investigation. *Organizational Behavior and Human Decision Processes, 56,* 266–284.

Mannix, E. A., Thompson, L., and Bazerman, M. H. (1989). Negotiation in small groups. *Journal of Applied Psychology, 74*(3), 508–517.

Mannix, E. A., Tinsley, C. H., and Bazerman, M. H. (1995). Negotiating over time: Impediments to integrative solutions. *Organizational Behavior and Human Decision Processes, 62*(3), 241–251.

Manstead, A. S. R. (1991). Expressiveness as an individual difference. In R. S. Feldman and B. Rime (Eds.), *Fundamentals of nonverbal behavior: Studies in emotion and social interaction* (pp. 285–328). New York: Cambridge University Press.

March, R. M. (1990). *The Japanese negotiator: Subtlety and strategy beyond Western logic* (1st paperback edition). New York: Kodansha International.

Marlowe, D., Gergen, K., and Doob, A. (1966). Opponents' personality, expectation of social interaction and interpersonal bargaining. *Journal of Personality and Social Psychology, 3,* 206–213.

Martin, J. N. (1989). Intercultural communication competence. *International Journal of Intercultural Relations, 13,* 227–428.

Matsumoto, D. (1996). *Culture and psychology.* Pacific Grove, CA: Brooks-Cole.

May, K. (1982). A set of independent, necessary and sufficient conditions for simple majority decisions. In B. Barry and R. Hardin (Eds.), *Rational man and irrational society.* Beverly Hills: Sage.

Mazur, A. (1985). A biosocial model of status in face-to-face groups. *Social Forces, 64,* 377–402.

McAlister, L., Bazerman, M. H., and Fader, P. (1986). Power and goal setting in channel negotiations. *Journal of Marketing Research, 23,* 238–263.

McClelland, G., and Rohrbaugh, J. (1978). Who accepts the pareto axiom? The role of utility and equity in arbitration decisions. *Behavioral Science, 23,* 446–456.

McClintock, C. G., and Liebrand, W. B. (1988). Role of interdependence structure, individual value orientation, and another's strategy in social decision making: A transformational analysis. *Journal of Personality and Social Psychology, 55*(3), 396–409.

McClintock, C., Messick, D. M., Kuhlman, D., and Campos, F. (1973). Motivational bases of choice in three-choice decomposed games. *Journal of Experimental Social Psychology, 9,* 572–590.

McFadden, R. D. (November 6, 1999). Daily News error: $100,000 dreams turn to nightmare. *New York Times,* p. A1.

McGrath, J. E., and Hollingshead, A. B. (1994). *Groups interacting with technology.* Thousand Oaks, CA: Sage.

McGrath, J. E., Kelly, J. R., and Machatka, D. E. (1984). The social psychology of time: Entrainment of behavior in social and organizational settings. *Applied Social Psychology Annual, 5,* 21–44.

McGuire, T., Keisler, S., and Siegel, J. (1987). Group and computer-mediated discussion effects in risk decision-making. *Journal of Personality and Social Psychology, 52*(5), 917–930.

McKelvey, R. D., and Ordeshook, P. C. (1980). Vote trading: An experimental study. *Public Choice, 35,* 151–184.

McKendrick, J. (1999). The third way: Mitigate, not litigate Y2K beefs. *Midrange Systems, 12*(2), 52.

McKittrick, D. (March 10, 1999). Astonishingly, Mr. Adams and Mr. Trimble share a common aim. *The Independent,* p. 3.

Medvec, V. H., Madey, S. F., and Gilovich, T. (1995). When less is more: Counterfactual thinking and satisfaction among Olympic medalists. *Journal of Personality and Social Psychology, 69*(4), 603–610.

Meherabian, A. (1971). *Silent messages.* Belmont, CA: Wadsworth.

Menon, T., Morris, M. W., Chiu, C., and Hong, Y. (1999). Culture and construal of agency: Attribution to individual versus group dispositions. *Journal of Personality and Social Psychology, 76*(5), 701–717.

Messick, D. M. (1993). Equality as a decision heuristic. In B. A. Mellers and J. Baron (Eds.), *Psychological perspectives on justice* (pp. 11–31). New York: Cambridge University Press.

Messick, D. M., and Bazerman, M. H. (1996). Ethical leadership and the psychology of decision making. *Sloan Management Review, 37*(2), 9–22.

Messick, D. M., and Brewer, M. (1983). Solving social dilemmas: A review. In L. Wheeler and P. Shaver (Eds.), *Review of personality and social psychology* (Vol. 4, pp. 11–44). Beverly Hills: Sage.

Messick, D. M., and Rutte, C. G. (1992). The provision of public goods by experts: The Groningen study. In W. B. G. Liebrand, D. M. Messick, and H. A. M. Wilke (Eds.), *Social dilemmas: Theoretical issues and research findings* (pp. 101–109). Oxford, England: Pergamon Press.

Messick, D. M., and Sentis, K. P. (1979). Fairness and preference. *Journal of Experimental Social Psychology, 15*(4), 418–434.

Meyerson, D., Weick, K. E., and Kramer, R. M. (1996). Swift trust and temporary groups. In R. M. Kramer and T. R. Tyler (Eds.), *Trust in organizations: Frontiers of theory and research* (pp. 166–195). Thousand Oaks, CA: Sage.

Mieskowski, K. (1998). Wanna buy? What am I bid? *Fastcompany, 19,* 289–292.

Mikula, G. (1980). On the role of justice in allocation decisions. In G. Mikula (Ed.), *Justice and social interaction.* New York: Springer-Verlag.

Miller, G. A. (1956). The magical number seven plus or minus two: Some limits on our capacity for processing information. *Psychological Review, 63,* 81–97.

Mishra, B. K., and Sinha, N. P. (November 8, 1999). Cross-cultural booby traps. *The Economic Times.*

Moore, D. A. (2000). The unexpected benefits of negotiating under time pressure. Unpublished doctoral dissertation, Evanston, IL, Northwestern University.

Moore, D., Kurtzberg, T., Thompson, L., and Morris, M. W. (1999). Long and short routes to success in electronically-mediated negotiations: Group affiliations and good vibrations. *Organization Behavior and Human Decision Processes, 77*(1), 22–43.

Moore, J. S., Graziano, W. G., and Millar, M. G. (1987). Physical attractiveness, sex role orientation, and the evaluation of adults and children. *Personality and Social Psychology Bulletin, 13*(1), 95–102.

Moreland, R. L., Argote, L., and Krishnan, R. (1996). Socially shared cognition at work. In J. L. Nye and A. M. Brower (Eds.), *What's social about social cognition?* Thousand Oaks, CA: Sage.

Moreland, R. L., and Beach, S. R. (1992). Exposure effects in the classroom: The development of affinity among students. *Journal of Experimental Social Psychology, 28*(3), 255–276.

Morgan, P., and Tindale, R. S. (2000). Group versus individual performance on two different mixed-motive tasks: Exploring the inconsistency. Unpublished manuscript, Loyola University, Chicago, IL.

Morris, M. W. (1995). Through a glass darkly: Cognitive and motivational processes that obscure social perception in conflicts. Paper presented at the Academy of Management Meetings, Vancouver, BC.

Morris, M. W., Larrick, R. P., and Su, S. K. (1999). Misperceiving negotiation counterparties: When situationally determining bargaining behaviors are attributed to personality traits. *Journal of Personality and Social Psychology, 77,* 52–67.

Morris, M. W., Leung, K., and Sethi, S. (1999). Person perception in the heat of conflict: Perceptions of opponents' traits and conflict resolution in two cultures. Working paper no. 1360, Stanford University, Stanford, CA.

Morris, M. W., and Peng, K. (1994). Culture and cause: American and Chinese attributions for social and physical events. *Journal of Personality and Social Psychology, 67*(6), 949–971.

Morris, M. W., Podolny, J. M., and Ariel, S. (1999). Missing relations: Incorporating relational constructs into models of culture. Paper presented at 1998 SESP conference, Lexington, Kentucky.

Morris, M. W., Sim, D. L. H., and Girrotto, V. (1995). Time of decision, ethical obligation, and causal illusion: Temporal cues and social heuristics in the prisoner's dilemma. In R. Kramer and D. Messick (Eds.), *Negotiation as a social process* (pp. 209–239). Thousand Oaks, CA: Sage.

Morris, M. W., and Su, S. K. (1995). The hostile mediator phenomenon: When each side perceives the mediator to be partial to the other. Unpublished manuscript, Stanford University Graduate School of Business, Palo Alto, CA.

Morris, M. W., Nadler, J., Kurtzberg, T., and Thompson, L. (2000). Schmooze or lose: Social friction and lubrication in e-mail negotiations. Manuscript under review.

Murnighan, J. K. (1978). Models of coalition behavior: Game theoretic, social psychological, and political perspectives. *Psychological Bulletin, 85,* 1130–1153.

Murnighan, J. K., Kim, J. W., and Metzger, A. R. (1993). The volunteer dilemma. *Administrative Science Quarterly, 38*(4), 515–538.

Myers, F. (February 1999). Political argumentation and the composite audience: A case study. *Quarterly Journal of Speech,* pp. 55–65.

Nadler, J., Kurtzberg, T., Morris, M. W., and Thompson, L. (February 15, 1999). Getting to know you: The effects of relationship-building and expectation on e-mail negotiations. Paper submitted to the 12th Conference of the International Association for Conflict Management, San Sebastián-Donostia, Spain.

Naquin, C. (1999). Trust and distrust in group negotiations. Unpublished dissertation, Kellogg Graduate School of Management, Northwestern University, Evanston, IL.

Nash, J. (1950). The bargaining problem. *Econometrica, 18,* 155–162.

Nash, J. (1953). Two-person cooperative games. *Econometrica, 21,* 128–140.

National Public Radio, *Morning Edition,* November 3, 1995.

Nauman, M. (February 12, 1999). Republic's super lots changing how people buy used cars. *Knight-Ridder Tribune Business News.*

Neale, M. A., and Bazerman, M. H. (1983). The role of perspective taking ability in negotiating under different forms of arbitration. *Industrial and Labor Relations Review, 36,* 378–388.

Neale, M. A., and Bazerman, M. H. (1991). *Cognition and rationality in negotiation.* New York: Free Press.

Neale, M. A., Huber, V. L., and Northcraft, G. (1987). The framing of negotiations: Contextual versus task frames. *Organizational Behavior and Human Decision Processes, 39*(2), 228–241.

Neale, M. A., and Northcraft, G. (1986). Experts, amateurs, and refrigerators: Comparing expert and amateur negotiators in a novel task. *Organizational Behavior and Human Decision Processes, 38,* 305–317.

Neale, M. A., Northcraft, G. B., and Earley, P. C. (1990). The joint effects of goal setting and expertise on negotiator performance. Working paper, Northwestern University, Evanston, IL.

Newsweek International (November 8, 1999). Back to the (dinner) table.

Nierenberg, G. I. (1968). *The art of negotiation: Psychological strategies for gaining advantageous bargains.* New York: Hawthorn Books.

Nisbett, R. E., Krantz, D. H., Jepson, C., and Kunda, Z. (1995). The use of statistical heuristics in everyday inductive reasoning. In R. E. Nisbett (Ed.), *Rules for reasoning* (pp. 15–54). Hillsdale, NJ, Lawrence Erlbaum.

Noonan, E. (December 16, 1999). Women leaders from troubled areas convene for peace conference. *Associated Press Newswire.*

Northcraft, G., and Neale, M. A. (1993). Negotiating successful research collaboration. In J. K. Murnighan (Ed.), *Social psychology in organizations: Advances in theory and research.* Englewood Cliffs, NJ: Prentice Hall.

Notarius, C. I., and Levenson, R. W. (1979). Expressive tendencies and physiological response to stress. *Journal of Personality and Social Psychology, 37*(7), 1204–1210.

O'Connor, K. M. (1997). Groups and solos in context: The effects of accountability on team negotiation. *Organizational Behavior and Human Decision Processes, 72*(3), 384–407.

O'Connor, K. M. (1994). *Negotiation teams: The impact of accountability and representation structure on negotiator cognition and performance.* Eugene, OR: International Association of Conflict Management.

O'Connor, K. M., and Adams, A. A. (1996). Thinking about negotiation: An investigation of negotiators' scripts. Unpublished manuscript, Northwestern University, Evanston, IL.

O'Connor, K. M., and Carnevale, P. J. (1997). A nasty but effective negotiation strategy: Misrepresentation of a common-value issue. *Personality and Social Psychology Bulletin, 23*(5), 504–515.

O'Quin, K., and Aronoff, J. (1981). Humor as a technique of social influence. *Social Psychology Quarterly, 44*(4), 349–357.

Oaksford, M., and Chater, N. (1994). A rational analysis of the selection task as optimal data selection. *Psychological Review, 101,* 608–631.

Ohtsubo, Y., and Kameda, T. (1998). The function of equality heuristic in distributive bargaining: Negotiated allocation of costs and benefits in a demand revelation context. *Journal of Experimental Social Psychology, 34,* 90–108.

Oldham, J. (May 1998). Conflict and cookies: Companies coax problems out into the open and use them to make working groups more effective. *Los Angeles Times,* p. 22.

Olekalns, M., and Smith, P. L. (1998). Simple frequency effects? Motivational orientation, strategic choice and outcome optimality in negotiations. Paper presented at IACM, Washington, DC.

Olekalns, M., and Smith, P. L. (1999). Social value orientations and strategy choices in competitive negotiations. *Personality and Social Psychology Bulletin, 25*(6), 657–668.

Ordeshook, P. (1986). *Game theory and political theory: An introduction.* Cambridge: Cambridge University Press.

Osborn, A. F. (1957). *Applied imagination.* New York: Scribner.

Osborn, A. F. (1963). *Applied imagination* (3rd ed.). New York: Scribner.

Osgood, C. E. (1962). *An alternative to war or surrender.* Urbana: University of Illinois Press.

Osgood, C. E. (1979). *GRIT 1* (vol. 8, no. 1, 0553–4283). Dundas, Ontario: Peace Research Reviews.

Osgood, C. E., Suci, G. J., and Tannenbaum, P. H. (1957). *The measurement of meaning.* Urbana: University of Illinois Press.

Oskamp, S. (1965). Attitudes toward U.S. and Russian actions: A double standard. *Psychological Reports, 16,* 43–46.

Pacelle, M. (June 9, 1995). Real estate: Japan's U.S. property deals: A poor report card. *The Wall Street Journal,* p. B1.

Pacelle, M., and Lipin, S. (May 12, 1995). Japanese owner seeks court protection for Manhattan's Rockefeller Center. *The Wall Street Journal,* p. A3.

Pachtman, A. (1998). Getting to "hao!" *International Business, 11*(4), 24–26.

Paese, P. W., and Gilin, D. A. (2000). When an adversary is caught telling the truth: Reciprocal cooperation versus self-interest in distributive bargaining. *Personality and Social Psychology Bulletin, 26*(1), 79–90.

Palmer, L. G., and Thompson, L. (1995). Negotiation in triads: Communication constraints and tradeoff structure. *Journal of Experimental Psychology: Applied, 2,* 83–94.

Paulus, P. B. (1998). Developing consensus about groupthink after all these years. *Organization Behavior and Human Decision Processes, 73*(2–3), 362–374.

Pennebaker, J. W., Hughes, C. F., and O'Heeron, R. C. (1987). The psychophysiology of confession: Linking inhibitory and psychosomatic processes. *Journal of Personality and Social Psychology, 52,* 781–793.

Pennebaker, J. W., and Sanders, D. Y. (1976). American graffiti: Effects of authority and reactance arousal. *Personality and Social Psychology Bulletin, 2,* 264–267.

Pereira, J., and Lublin, J. S. (December 2, 1999). 'Toys' story: They ran the retailer as a team for years; then, a nasty split. *The Wall Street Journal,* p. A1.

Perkins, A. (January 15, 2000). John Wakeham, Lord Fixit. *The Guardian,* p. 6.

Peterson, E., and Thompson, L. (1997). Negotiation teamwork: The impact of information distribution and accountability on performance depends on the relationship among team members. *Organizational Behavior and Human Decision Processes, 72*(3), 364–383.

Philip, G., and Young, E. S. (1987). Man-machine interaction by voice: Developments in speech technology. Part I: The state-of-the-art. *Journal of Information Science, 13,* 3–14.

Pillutla, M. M., and Chen, X. (1999). Social norms and cooperation in social dilemmas: The effects of context and feedback. *Organizational Behavior and Human Decision Processes, 78*(2), 81–103.

Pillutla, M. M., and Murnighan, J. K. (1995). Being fair or appearing fair: Strategic behavior in ultimatum bargaining. *Academy of Management Journal, 38*(5), 1408–1426.

Plott, C. (1976). Axiomatic social choice theory: An overview and interpretation. *American Journal of Political Science, 20,* 511–596.

Plott, C., and Levine, M. (1978). A model of agenda influence on committee decisions. *American Economic Review, 68,* 146–160.

Poincaré, H. (1929). *The foundations of sciences.* New York: Science House.

Pólya, G. (1957). *How to solve it: A new aspect of mathematical method* (2nd ed.). New York: Doubleday.

Pólya, G. (1968). *Mathematical discovery, Volume II: On understanding learning and teaching problem-solving.* New York: Wiley.

Popkin, S. (1981). Public choice and rural development—free riders, lemons, and institutional design. In C. Russel and N. Nicholson (Eds.), *Public choice and rural development* (pp. 43–80). Washington, DC: Resources for the Future.

Prentice, D. A., Miller, D. T., and Lightdale, J. R. (1994). Asymmetries in attachments to groups and to their members: Distinguishing between common-identity and common-bond groups. *Personality and Social Psychology Bulletin, 20,* 484–493.

Pruitt, D. G., and Carnevale, P. J. (1993). *Negotiation in social conflict.* Pacific Grove, CA: Brooks-Cole.

Pruitt, D. G., and Lewis, S. A. (1975). Development of integrative solutions in bilateral negotiation. *Journal of Personality and Social Psychology, 31,* 621–630.

Putnam, L. L. (1983). Small group work climates: A lag-sequential analysis of group interaction. *Small Group Behavior, 14*(4), 465–494.

Quinn, S. R., Bell, D., and Wells, J. (1997). Interest-based negotiation: A case study. *Public Personnel Management, 26*(4), 529–533.

Raiffa, H. (1982). *The art and science of negotiation.* Cambridge, MA: Belknap.

Rand, K. A., and Carnevale, P. J. (1994). The benefits of team support in bilateral negotiations. Unpublished manuscript, University of Illinois, Champaign, IL.

Raven, B. H. (1990). Political applications of the psychology of interpersonal influence and social power. *Political Psychology, 11*(3), 493–520.

Redelmeier, D. A., and Kahneman, D. (1996). Patients' memories of painful medical treatments: Real-time and retrospective evaluations of two minimally invasive procedures. *Pain, 66*(1), 3–8.

Reingen, P. H. (1982). Test of a list procedure for inducing compliance with a request to donate money. *Journal of Applied Psychology, 67*(1), 110–118.

Reingen, P. H., and Kernan, J. B. (1993). Social perception and interpersonal influence: Some consequences of the physical attractiveness stereotype in a personal selling setting. *Journal of Consumer Psychology, 2*(1), 25–38.

Rhoades, J. A., and O'Connor, K. M. (1996). Affect in computer-mediated and face-to-face work groups: The construction and testing of a general model. *Computer Supported Cooperative Work, 4,* 203–228.

Roberts, P. (1999). "Live from your office! It's . . . the company talk show!" *Fastcompany, 28,* 150.

Robinson, R. J., and Keltner, D. (1996). Much ado about nothing? Revisionists and traditionalists choose an introductory English syllabus. *Psychological Science, 7*(1), 18–24.

Robinson, R., Keltner, D., Ward, A., and Ross, L. (1994). Actual versus assumed differences in construal: "Naïve realism" in intergroup perception and conflict. *Journal of Personality and Social Psychology, 68,* 404–417.

Rosenfeld, J. (2000). She stands on common ground. *Fastcompany, 31,* 72.

Rosenthal, R., and DePaulo, B. M. (1979a). Sex differences in accommodation in nonverbal communication. In R. Rosenthal (Ed.), *Skill in nonverbal communication: Individual differences* (pp. 68–103). Cambridge, MA: Oelgeschlager, Gunn, and Hain.

Rosenthal, R., and DePaulo, B. M. (1979b). Sex differences in eavesdropping on nonverbal cues. *Journal of Personality and Social Psychology, 37*(2), 273–285.

Rosette, A., Brett, J., Barsness, Z., and Lytle, A. (2000). Social presence across cultures: E-mail negotiations in the U.S. and Hong Kong. Working paper, Northwestern University, Evanston, IL.

Ross, B. H. (1987). This is like that: The use of earlier problems and the separation of similarity effects. *Journal of Experimental Psychology: Learning, Memory and Cognition, 13*(4), 629–639.

Ross, J., and Staw, B. M. (1993). Organizational escalation and exit: Lessons from the Shoreham Nuclear Power Plant. *Academy of Management Journal, 36*(4), 701–732.

Ross, L. (1977). The intuitive psychologist and his shortcomings: Distortions in the attribution process. In L. Berkowitz (Ed.), *Advances in Experimental Social Psychology* (Vol. 10, pp. 173–220). Orlando, FL: Academic Press.

Ross, L., and Lepper, M. R. (1980). The perseverance of beliefs: Empirical and normative considerations. In R. A. Shweder (Ed.), *New directions for methodology of behavioral science: Fallible judgment in behavioral research.* San Francisco: Jossey-Bass.

Ross, L., and Samuels, S. M. (1993). The predictive power of personal reputation vs. labels and construal in the prisoner's dilemma game. Working paper, Stanford University, Palo Alto, CA.

Ross, L., and Stillinger, C. (1991). Barriers to conflict resolution. *Negotiation Journal, 8,* 389–404.

Ross, L., and Ward, A. (1996). Naïve realism in everyday life: Implications for social conflict and misunderstanding. In Brown, T., Reed, E. S., and Turiel, E., (Eds), *Values and knowledge. The Jean Piaget symposium series* (pp. 103–135). Mahwah, NJ: Lawrence Erlbaum.

Ross, M., and Sicoly, F. (1979). Egocentric biases in availability attribution. *Journal of Personality and Social Psychology, 8,* 322–336.

Roth, A. E. (1993). Bargaining experiments. In J. Kagel and A. E. Roth (Eds.), *Handbook of Experimental Economics.* Princeton, NJ: Princeton University Press.

Rothbart, M., and Hallmark, W. (1988). In-group and out-group differences in the perceived efficacy of coercion and concilliation in resolving social conflict. *Journal of Personality and Social Psychology, 55,* 248–257.

Ruback, R. B., and Juieng, D. (1997). Territorial defense in parking lots: Retaliation against waiting drivers. *Journal of Abnormal Social Psychology, 27,* 821–834.

Rubin, J. Z., and Brown, B. (1975). *The social psychology of bargaining and negotiations.* New York: Academic Press.

Rubin, J. Z., Pruitt, D. G., and Kim, S. H. (1994). *Social conflict: Escalation, stalemate and settlement.* New York: McGraw-Hill.

Rubin, J. Z., and Sander, F. E. A. (October 1988). When should we use agents? Direct vs. representative negotiation. *Negotiation Journal,* pp. 395–401.

Sally, D. F. (1995). Conversation and cooperation in social dilemmas: Experimental evidence from 1958 to 1992. *Rationality and Society, 7*(1), 58–92.

Saunders, D. G., and Size, P. B. (1986). Attitudes about woman abuse among police officers, victims, and victim advocates. *Journal of Interpersonal Violence, 1.*

Savage, L. J. (1954). *The foundations of statistics.* New York: Wiley.

Schelling, T. (1960). *The strategy of conflict.* Cambridge, MA: Harvard University Press.

Schkade, D. A., and Kahneman, D. (1998). Does living in California make people happy? A focusing illusion in judgments of life satisfaction. *Psychological Science, 9*(5), 340–346.

Schlenker, B. R. (1980). *Impression management: The self-concept, social identity and interpersonal relations.* Belmont, CA: Brooks-Cole.

Schmitt, D., and Marwell, G. (1972). Withdrawal and reward reallocation in response to inequity. *Journal of Experimental Social Psychology, 8,* 207–221.

Schneider, S. C. (1997). *Managing across cultures.* Upper Saddle River, NJ: Prentice Hall.

Schofield, J. W. (1986). Black and white contact in desegregated schools. In M. Hewstone and R. J. Brown (Eds.), *Contact and conflict in intergroup encounters* (pp. 79–92). Oxford, England: Blackwell.

Schrage, M. (1995). *No more teams!: Mastering the dynamics of creative collaboration.* New York: Currency Doubleday.

Schreifer, J. (1995). The battle at Bayou Steel. *Iron Age New Steel, 10*(12), 10.

Schwartz, S. (1994). Beyond individualism/collectivism: New cultural dimensions of values. In H. C. Triandis, U. Kim, and G. Yoon (Eds.), *Individualism and collectivism* (pp. 85–117). London: Sage.

Schwinger, T. (1980). Just allocations of goods: Decisions among three principles. In G. Mikula (Ed.), *Justice and social interaction: Experimental and theoretical contributions from psychological research.* New York: Springer-Verlag.

Seaberry, J. (January 3, 2000). Deals still done face to face in Internet age. *The Star-Ledger,* p. 36.

Sears, D. O., and Allen, H. M., Jr. (1984). The trajectory of local desegregation controversies and Whites' opposition to busing. In N. Miller and M. Brewer (Eds.), *Groups in contact: The psychology of desegregation* (pp. 123–151). New York: Academic Press.

Secord, P. F., and Backman, C. W. (1964). *Social psychology.* New York: McGraw-Hill.

Segal, M. W. (1974). Alphabet and attraction: An unobtrusive measure of the effect of propinquity in a field setting. *Journal of Personality and Social Psychology, 30*(5), 654–657.

Segil, L. (1999). Alliances for the 21st century. *Executive Excellence, 16*(10), 19.

Selten, R. (1975). Re-examination of the perfectness concept for equilibrium points in extensive games. *International Journal of Game Theory, 4,* 25–55.

Shafir, E. (1994). Uncertainty and the difficulty of thinking through disjunctions. *Cognition, 50,* 403–430.

Shafir, E., Simonson, I., and Tversky, A. (1993). Reason-based choice. Special issue: Reasoning and decision making. *Cognition, 49*(1–2), 11–36.

Shafir, E., and Tversky, A. (1992). Thinking through uncertainty: Nonconsequential reasoning and choice. *Cognitive Psychology, 24*(4), 449–474.

Shapiro, D. L., Buttner, E. H., and Barry, B. (1994). Explanations: What factors enhance their perceived adequacy? *Organizational Behavior and Human Decision Processes, 58*(3), 346–368.

Shapiro, D. L., Sheppard, B. H., and Cheraskin, L. (1992). Business on a handshake. *Negotiation Journal, 8*(4), 365–377.

Shapley, L. S. (1977). The St. Petersburg Paradox: A con game? *Journal of Economic Theory, 14,* 353–409.

Sheehan, N. (1971). *The Pentagon Papers: As published by* The New York Times, *based on the investigative reporting by Neil Sheehan, written by Neil Sheehan [and others].* Articles and documents edited by G. Gold, A. M. Siegal, and S. Abt. New York, Toronto: Bantam.

Shell, R. G. (May 1999). Negotiator, know thyself. *Inc.,* p. 106.

Sheppard, B. H. (1984). Third-party intervention: A procedural framework. In B. M. Staw and L. L. Cummings (Eds.), *Research in organizational behavior* (Vol. 6). Greenwich, CT: JAI Press.

Sherif, M. (1936). *The psychology of social norms.* New York: Harper and Row.

Sherif, M., Harvey, O. J., White, B. J., Hood, W. R., and Sherif, C. W. (1961). *Intergroup conflict and cooperation: The Robber's Cave experiment.* Norman: University of Oklahoma Press.

Sherman, S. J., Presson, C. C., and Chassin, L. (1984). Mechanisms underlying the false consensus effect: The special role of threats to the self. *Personality and Social Psychology Bulletin, 10,* 127–138.

Shirakashi, S. (1985). Social loafing of Japanese students. *Hiroshima Forum for Psychology, 10,* 35–40.

Shirk, M. (June 10, 1996). Women go beyond rhetoric. *St. Louis Post-Dispatch,* p. 11B.

Short, J., Williams, E., and Christie, B. (1976). *The social psychology of telecommunications.* London, New York: John Wiley and Sons.

Siamwalla, A. (June 1978). Farmers and middlemen: Aspects of agricultural marketing in Thailand. *Economic Bulletin for Asia and the Pacific,* pp. 38–50.

Siegel, S., and Fouraker, L. E. (1960). *Bargaining and group decision making.* New York: McGraw-Hill.

Silveira, J. M. (1972). Incubation: The effect of interruption timing and length on problem solution and quality of problem processing. *Dissertation Abstracts International, 32*(9-B), 5500.

Simon, H. (1955). A behavioral model of rational choice. *Quarterly Journal of Economics, 69,* 99–118.

Simonson, I. (1989). Choice based on reasons: The case of attraction and compromise effects. *Journal of Consumer Research, 16,* 158–174.

Singelis, T. M. (1998). *Teaching about culture, ethnicity and diversity: Exercises and planned activities.* Thousand Oaks, CA: Sage.

Sitkin, S. B., and Roth, N. L. (1993). Explaining the limited effectiveness of legalistic "remedies" for trust/distrust. *Organization Science, 4*(3), 367–392.

Skinner, B. F. (1938). *The behavior of organisms: An experimental analysis.* New York, London: D. Appleton Century.

Slavin, B. (January 5, 2000). Negotiators clear first bump in Middle East talks. *USA Today,* p. 6A.

Slovic, P. (1964). Assessment of risk taking behavior. *Psychological Bulletin, 61*(3), 220–233.

Slovic, P. (1962). Convergent validation of risk taking measures. *Journal of Abnormal and Social Psychology, 65*(1), 68–71.

Slovic, P., and Lichtenstein, S. (1983). Preference reversals: A broader perspective. *American Economic Review, 73,* 596–605.

Snodgrass, S. E. (1985). Women's intuition: The effect of subordinate role on interpersonal sensitivity. *Journal of Personality and Social Psychology, 49*(1), 146–155.

Snodgrass, S. E. (1992). Further effects of role versus gender on interpersonal sensitivity. *Journal of Personality and Social Psychology, 62*(1), 154–158.

Snyder, M. (1974). Self-monitoring of expressive behavior. *Journal of Personality and Social Psychology, 30,* 526–537.

Sondak, H., and Moore, M. (1994). Relationship frames and cooperation. *Group Decision and Negotiation, 2,* 103–118.

Sondak, H., Neale, M. A., and Pinkley, R. (1995). The negotiated allocation of benefits and burdens: The impact of outcome valence, contribution and relationship. *Organizational Behavior and Human Decision Processes, 64*(3), 249–260.

Spencer, S. J., Steele, C. M., and Quinn, D. M. (1999). Stereotype threat and women's math performance. *Journal of Experimental Social Psychology, 35*(1), 4–28.

Sproull, L., and Keisler, S. (1991). *Connections: New ways of working in the networked organization.* Cambridge, MA: MIT Press.

Stasser, G. (1992). Pooling of unshared information during group discussion. In S. Worchel, W. Wood, and J. A. Simpson (Eds.), *Group processes and productivity* (pp. 48–67). Newbury Park, CA: Sage.

Staudohar, P. D. (1999). Labor relations in basketball: The lockout of 1998–99. *Monthly Labor Review, 122*(4), 3–9.

Steele, C. M. (1997). A threat in the air: How stereotypes shape intellectual identity and performance. *American Psychologist, 52*(6), 613–629.

Steele, C. M., and Aronson, J. (1995). Stereotype threat and the intellectual test performance of African Americans. *Journal of Personality and Social Psychology, 69*(5), 797–811.

Steil, J. M., and Makowski, D. G. (1989). Equity, equality, and need: A study of the patterns and outcomes associated with their use in intimate relationships. *Social Justice Research, 3,* 121–137.

Stoppard, J. M., and Gun-Gruchy, C. (1993). Gender, context, and expression of positive emotion. *Personality and Social Psychology Bulletin, 19*(2), 143–150.

Stratton, R. P. (1983). Atmosphere and conversion errors in syllogistic reasoning with contextual material and the effect of differential training. Unpublished M.A. thesis, Michigan State University, East Lansing. In Mayer, R. E. (ed.), *Thinking, problem-solving, and cognition.* New York: W. H. Freeman and Company.

Strodtbeck, F. L., and Hook, L. H. (1961). The social dimensions of a 12-man jury table. *Sociometry, 24*(4), 397–415.

Stroebe, W., Kruglanski, A. W., Bar-Tal, D., and Hewstone, M., eds. (1988). *The social psychology of intergroup conflict.* Berlin: Springer-Verlag.

Stroebe, W., Lenkert, A., and Jonas, K. (1988). Familiarity may breed contempt: The impact of student exchange on national stereotypes and attitudes. In W. Stroebe, A. W. Kruglanski, D. Bar-Tal, and M. Hewstone (Eds.), *The social psychology of intergroup conflict* (pp. 167–187). New York: Springer-Verlag.

Stuhlmacher, A. F., Gillespie, T. L., and Champagne, M. V. (1998). The impact of time pressure in negotiation: A meta-analysis. *International Journal of Conflict Management, 9*(2), 97–116.

Suedfeld, P., Bochner, S., and Matas, C. (1971). Petitioners attire and petition signing by peace demonstrators: A field experiment. *Journal of Applied Social Psychology, 1*(3), 278–283.

Sullins, E. S. (1989). Perceptual salience as a function of nonverbal expressiveness. *Personality and Social Psychology Bulletin, 15*(4), 584–595.

Sumner, W. (1906). *Folkways.* New York: Ginn.

Swann, W. B., Pelham, B. W., and Roberts, D. C. (1987). Causal chunking: Memory and inference in ongoing interaction. *Journal of Personality and Social Psychology, 53*(5), 858–865.

Swensen, C. H. (1973). *Introduction to interpersonal relations.* Glenview, IL: Scott Foreman.

Tajfel, H. (1970). Experiments in intergroup discrimination. *Scientific American, 223,* 96–102.

Tajfel, H. (1979). The exit of social mobility and the voice of social change: Notes on the social psychology of intergroup relations. *Przeglad Psychologiczny, 22*(1), 17–38.

Tajfel, H. (1982). Social psychology of intergroup relations. *Annual Review of Psychology, 33,* 1–39.

Tajfel, H., and Turner, J. (1986). The social identity theory of intergroup behavior. In S. Worchel and W. Austin (Eds.), *Psychology of intergroup relations* (pp. 7–24). Chicago: Nelson-Hall.

Taylor, S. E., and Brown, J. (1988). Illusion and well-being: A social-psychological perspective. *Psychological Bulletin, 103,* 193–210.

Taylor, S. E., and Lobel, M. (1989). Social comparison activity under threat: Downward evaluation and upward contacts. *Psychological Bulletin, 96,* 569–575.

Teal, T. (1996). The human side of management. *Harvard Business Review, 74*(6), 35–44.

Tesser, A. (1988). Toward a self-evaluation maintenance model of social behavior. In L. Berkowitz (Ed.), *Advances in experimental social psychology* (Vol. 21, pp. 181–227). Orlando, FL: Academic Press.

Tetlock, P. E. (1985). Accountability: A social check on the fundamental attribution error. *Social Psychology Quarterly, 48,* 227–236.

Tetlock, P. E. (1992). The impact of accountability on judgment and choice: Toward a social contingency model. *Advances in Experimental Social Psychology, 25,* 331–376.

Tetlock, P. E., Peterson, R., and Lerner, J. (1996). Revising the value pluralism model: Incorporating social content and context postulates. In C. Seligman, J. Olson, and M. Zanna (Eds.), *The psychology of values: The Ontario symposium* (Vol. 8). Mahwah, NJ: Lawrence Erlbaum.

Thibaut, J., and Kelley, H. H. (1959). *The social psychology of groups.* New York: Wiley.

Thibaut, J., and Walker, L. (1975). *Procedural justice: A psychological analysis.* Hillsdale, NJ: Erlbaum.

Thibaut, J., and Walker, L. (1978). A theory of procedure. *California Law Review, 60,* 541–566.

Thomas, E. (December 2, 1985). Fencing at the fireside summit: With candor and civility, Reagan and Gorbachev grapple for answers to the arms-race riddle. *Time,* p. 22.

Thompson, L. (1990a). An examination of naïve and experienced negotiators. *Journal of Personality and Social Psychology, 59*(1), 82–90.

Thompson, L. (1990b). The influence of experience on negotiation performance. *Journal of Experimental Social Psychology, 26*(6), 528–544.

Thompson, L. (1991). Information exchange in negotiation. *Journal of Experimental Social Psychology, 27*(2), 161–179.

Thompson, L. (1993). The impact of negotiation on intergroup relations. *Journal of Experimental Social Psychology, 29*(4), 304–325.

Thompson, L. (1995a). The impact of minimum goals and aspirations on judgments of success in negotiations. *Group Decision Making and Negotiation, 4,* 513–524.

Thompson, L. (1995b). "They saw a negotiation": Partisanship and involvement. *Journal of Personality and Social Psychology, 68*(5), 839–853.

Thompson, L. (2000). *Making the team: A guide for managers.* Upper Saddle River, NJ: Prentice Hall.

Thompson, L., and DeHarpport, T. (1994). Social judgment, feedback, and interpersonal learning in negotiation. *Organizational Behavior and Human Decision Processes, 58*(3), 327–345.

Thompson, L., and DeHarpport, T. (1998). Relationships, good incompatibility, and communal orientation in negotiations. *Basic and Applied Social Psychology, 20*(1), 33–44.

Thompson, L., & Fox, C. (2000). Negotiation within and between groups in organizations: Levels of analysis. In M. Turner (Ed.), *Groups at work: Advances in theory and research.* Hillsdale, NJ: Erlbaum.

Thompson, L., and Gonzalez, R. (1997). Environmental disputes: Competition for scarce resources and clashing of values. In M. Bazerman, D. Messick, A. Tenbrunsel, and K. Wade-Benzoni (Eds.), *Environment, ethics, and behavior* (pp. 75–104). San Francisco: New Lexington Press.

Thompson, L., and Hastie, R. (1990). Social perception in negotiation. *Organizational Behavior and Human Decision Processes, 47*(1), 98–123.

Thompson, L., and Hrebec, D. (1996). Lose-lose agreements in interdependent decision making. *Psychological Bulletin, 120*(3), 396–409.

Thompson, L., and Loewenstein, G. F. (1992). Egocentric interpretations of fairness and negotiation. *Organizational Behavior and Human Decision Processes, 51,* 176–197.

Thompson, L., and Loewenstein, J. (2000). Mental models in negotiation. In M. A. Hogg and J. Cooper (Eds.), *Sage handbook of social psychology.*

Thompson, L., Loewenstein, J., and Gentner, D. (2000). Avoiding missed opportunities in managerial life: Analogical training more powerful than case-based training. *Organizational Behavior and Human Decision Processes, 82*(1), 60–75.

Thompson, L., Mannix, E., and Bazerman, M. H. (1988). Group negotiation: Effects of decision rule, agenda, and aspiration. *Journal of Personality and Social Psychology, 54,* 86–95.

Thompson, L., Medvec, V. H., Seiden, V., and Kopelman, S. (2000). Poker face, smiley face, and rant 'n' rave: Myths and realities about emotion in negotiation. In M. Hogg and S. Tindale (Eds.), *Blackwell handbook in social psychology, Vol. 3: Group processes.* Cambridge, MA: Blackwell Publishers, Inc.

Thompson, L., Nadler, J., and Kim, P. (1999). Some like it hot: The case for the emotional negotiator. In L. Thompson, J. Levine, and D. Messick (Eds.), *Shared cognition in organizations: The management of knowledge* (pp. 139–162). Mahwah, NJ: Erlbaum.

Thompson, L., Peterson, E., and Brodt, S. (1996). Team negotiation: An examination of integrative and distributive bargaining. *Journal of*

Personality and Social Psychology, 70(1), 66–78.

Thompson, L., Valley, K. L., and Kramer, R. M. (1995). The bittersweet feeling of success: An of social perception in negotiation. *Journal of Experimental Social Psychology, 31*(6), 467–492.

Thornton, B. (1992). Repression and its mediating influence on the defensive attribution of responsibility. *Journal of Research in Personality, 26,* 44–57.

Ting-Toomey, S. (1985). Toward a theory of conflict and culture. *International and Intercultural Communication Annual, 9,* 71–86.

Tinsley, C. H. (1996). Understanding conflict in a Chinese cultural context. Working paper, J. L. Kellogg Graduate School of Management, Northwestern University, Evanston, IL.

Tinsley, C. H., and Brett, J. M. (1997). Managing workplace conflict in the U.S. and Hong Kong. Working paper, J. L. Kellogg Graduate School of Management, Northwestern University, Evanston, IL.

Tornow, W. W., and Pinto, P. R. (1976). The development of a managerial job taxonomy: A system for describing, classifying, and evaluating executive positions. *Journal of Applied Psychology, 61,* 410–418.

Trappen, M. (April 30, 1996). Shopping on a shoestring: How to haggle. *Portland Oregonian,* p. D01.

Triandis, H. C. (1994). *Culture and social behavior* (pp. 29–54). New York: McGraw-Hill.

Triandis, H. C. (1977). Cross-cultural social and personality psychology. *Personality and Social Psychology Bulletin, 3*(2), 143–158.

Turpin, S. C. (1998). Negotiation: The necessary skill. *Warehousing Management, 5*(9), 60–66.

Tversky, A., and Fox, C. (1995). Weighing risk and uncertainty. *Psychological Review, 102*(2), 269–283.

Tversky, A., and Kahneman, D. (1973). Availability: A heuristic for judging frequency and probability. *Cognitive Psychology, 5,* 207–232.

Tversky, A., and Kahneman, D. (1974). Judgment under uncertainty: Heuristics and biases. *Science, 185,* 1124–1131.

Tversky, A., and Kahneman, D. (1992). Advances in prospect theory: Cumulative representation of uncertainty. *Journal of Risk and Uncertainty, 5,* 297–323.

Tversky, A., and Shafir, E. (1992a). Choice under conflict: The dynamics of deferred decision. *Psychological Science, 3*(6), 358–361.

Tversky, A., and Shafir, E. (1992b). The disjunction effect in choice under uncertainty. *Psychological Science, 3*(5), 305–309.

Tyler, T. R., and Degoey, P. (1995). Collective restraint in social dilemmas: Procedural justice and social identification effects on support for authorities. *Journal of Personality and Social Psychology, 69*(3), 482–497.

Ury, W. L., Brett, J. M., and Goldberg, S. B. (1988). *Getting disputes resolved: Designing systems to cut the costs of conflict.* San Francisco: Jossey-Bass.

Uzzi, B. (1997). Social structure and competition in interfirm networks: The paradox of embeddedness. *Administrative Science Quarterly, 42,* 35–67.

Uzzi, B. (1999a). *Access and control benefits through embedded ties and network complementarity: The case of midmarket firms and banks.* Manuscript under review.

Uzzi, B. (1999b). *What is a relationship worth? The benefit of embeddedness in corporate financing.* Manuscript under review.

Valley, K. L., Moag, J., and Bazerman, M. H. (1998). A matter of trust: Effects of communication on the efficiency and distribution of outcomes. *Journal of Economic Behavior and Organizations, 34,* 211–238.

Valley, K., Neale, M. A., and Mannix, E. (1995). Friends, lovers, colleagues, strangers: The effects of relationship on the process and outcome of dyadic negotiations. In R. J. Bies, R. J. Lewicki, and B. H. Sheppard (Eds.), *Research on negotiation in organizations: Handbook of negotiation research* (Vol. 5, pp. 65–93). Greenwich, CT: JAI Press.

Valley, K. L., and Thompson, T. A. (1998). Sticky ties and bad attitudes: Relational and individual bases of resistance to change in organizational structure. In Kramer, R. M., and Neale, M. A. (Eds.), *Power and influence in organizations* (pp. 39–66). Thousand Oaks, CA: Sage.

Valley, K. L., White, S. B., Neale, M. A., and Bazerman, M. H. (1992). Agents as information brokers: The effects of information disclosure on negotiated outcomes. Special Issue: Decision processes in negotiation. *Organizational Behavior and Human Decision Processes, 51*(2), 220–236.

Vallone, R. P., Ross, L., and Lepper, M. (1985). The hostile media phenomenon: Biased perception and perceptions of media bias in coverage of the "Beirut Massacre." *Journal of Personality and Social Psychology, 49,* 577–585.

van Avermaet, E. (1974). *Equity: A theoretical and experimental analysis.* Unpublished manuscript, University of California.

Van Lange, P. A. M. (1999). The pursuit of joint outcomes and equality in outcomes: An integrative model of social value orientation. *Journal of Personality and Social Psychology, 77*(2), 337–349.

Van Lange, P. A. M., and Visser, K. (1999). Locomotion in social dilemmas: How people adapt to cooperative, tit-for-tat and non-cooperative partners. *Journal of Personality and Social Psychology, 77*(4), 762–773.

Van Vugt, M., and Samuelson, C. D. (1999). The impact of personal metering in the management of a natural resource crisis: A social dilemma analysis. *Personality and Social Psychology Bulletin, 25*(6), 731–745.

von Neumann, J., and Morgenstern, O. (1947). *Theory of games and economic behavior.* Princeton, NJ: Princeton University Press.

Vorauer, J. D., and Claude, S. (1998). Perceived versus actual transparency of goals in negotiation. *Personality and Social Psychology Bulletin, 24*(4), 371–385.

Walster, E., Berscheid, E., and Walster, G. W. (1973). New directions in equity research. *Journal of Personality and Social Psychology, 25,* 151–176.

Walton, R. E., and McKersie, R. B. (1965). *A behavioral theory of labor relations.* New York: McGraw-Hill.

Wegner, D. M. (1994). Ironic processes of mental control. *Psychological Review, 101,* 34–52.

Wegner, D. M., Lane, J. D., and Dimitri, S. (1994). The allure of secret relationships. *Journal of Personality and Social Psychology, 66*(2), 287–300.

Wegner, D. M., Shortt, J. W., Blake, A. W., and Page, M. S. (1990). The suppression of exciting thoughts. *Journal of Personality and Social Psychology, 58,* 409–418.

Wegner, D. M., and Wenzlaff, R. M. (1996). Mental control. In E. T. Higgins and A. W. Kruglanski (Eds.), *Social psychology: Handbook of basic principles* (pp. 466–492). New York: Guilford Press.

Weingart, L. R., and Brett, J. M. (April 1998). *Mixed motivational orientation in negotiating groups: Convergence and reaching agreement.* Paper presented at Society for Industrial Organizational Psychology 13th Annual Conference, Dallas, TX.

Weingart, L. R., Bennett, R., and Brett, J. M. (1993). The impact of consideration of issues and motivational orientation on group negotiation process and outcome. *Journal of Applied Psychology, 78,* 504–517.

Whitehead, A. N. (1929). *The aims of education.* New York: Macmillan.

Whorf, B. L. (1956). Science and linguistics. In J. B. Carroll (Ed.), *Language, thought, and reality. Selected writings of Benjamin Whorf.* New York: Wiley.

Wills, T. A. (1981). Downward comparison principles in social psychology. *Psychological Bulletin, 90,* 245–271.

Wilson, T. D., Wheatley, T., Meyers, J., Gilbert, D. T., and Axsom, D. (1998). Focalism: A source of durability bias in affective forecasting. Unpublished manuscript, University of Virginia, Charlottesville, VA.

Woodroofe, M. (1975). *Probability with applications.* New York, McGraw-Hill.

Woodside, A. G., and Davenport, J. W., Jr. (1974). Effects of salesman similarity and expertise on customer purchasing behavior. *Journal of Marketing Research, 11*(2), 198–202.

Worchel, S., and Austin, W. G., eds. (1986). *Psychology of intergroup relations.* Chicago: Nelson-Hall.

Wright, S. C., Aron, A., McLaughlin-Volpe, T., and Ropp, S. A. (1997). The extended contact effect: Knowledge of cross-group friendships and prejudice. *Journal of Personality and Social Psychology, 73*(1), 73–90.

Yamaguchi, S., Okamoto, K., and Oka, T. (1985). Effects of coactors' presence: Social loafing and social facilitation. *Japanese Psychological Research, 27,* 215–222.

Yates, J. F. (1990). *Judgment and decision making.* Englewood Cliffs, NJ: Prentice Hall.

Yukl, G. A. (1974). Effects of the opponent's initial offer, concession magnitude and concession frequency on bargaining behavior. *Journal of Personality and Social Psychology, 30*(3), 323–335.

Zajonc, R. (1968). Attitudinal effects of mere exposure. *Journal of Personality and Social Psychology, 9* (monograph supplement No. 2, Part 2).

Zuckerman, M., DePaulo, B. M., and Rosenthal, R. (1981). Verbal and nonverbal communication of deception. In L. Berkowitz (Ed.), *Advances in experimental social psychology* (Vol. 14, pp. 1–59). New York: Academic Press.

Zuckerman, M., Blanck, P. D., DePaulo, B. M., and Rosenthal, R. (1980). Developmental changes in decoding discrepant and nondiscrepant nonverbal cues. *Developmental Psychology, 16*(3), 220–228.

Zuckerman, M., Koestner, R., and Driver, R. (1981). Beliefs about cues associated with deception. *Journal of Nonverbal Behavior, 6*(2), 105–114.

SUBJECT INDEX

A

Abilene paradox, 112
Acceptance decisions, 81
Accountability, 207–208, 213
Acquaintance potential, 216
Active misrepresentation, 153
Adaptors, 315
Adjudication, 94, 228
Adversarial adjudication, 228
Advertising, comparative, 261
Advice, obtaining, 156
Advisory arbitration, 99
Affect, 277
Affiliation bias, 238–239
Agenda(s)
  avoiding, 198
  power of, 143–144
Agents, 87. *See also* Principal-agent
  relationship
Agreement bias, 5, 197–198
Agreements, 87, 100
  and conflict, 111
  creative, 162–167
  and deductive reasoning, 179
  and principal-agent relationship,
    205
  reneging on, 154
  required, 27
Alternatives, 15, 144, 295. *See also*
  BATNA
Anchoring-and-adjustment
  process, 171
Anonymity, 257
Antecedent conditions, 52
Approach, 85, 91–101
Approach-approach conflict, 295
Arbitration, 99
Aspirations, 10–11, 39–40,
    328–329
Assimilation, 244
Attitudinal structuring, 144–145
Attributes, identification of, 295
Attribution errors. *See* Fundamen-
  tal attribution error
A-type conflict, 122–123
Auction houses, on-line, 289
Authority, diversifying, 269
Automobile buyers, 26
Automobile dealers, 24
Autotelic experience, 181–182
Availability heuristic, 170

B

Backward induction, 252
"Bad apples," 132
Bargaining. *See* Negotiation
Bargaining positions, 18
Bargaining surplus, 36
Bargaining zone, 34–37, 204, 323
Bartender problem, 162, 186
Base rate fallacy, 171
Base rates, 170
BATNA, 11–15
  aspirations, 39–40
  of employers, 329–330
  and job-offer negotiations,
    331–333
  and negotiating style, 87
  of other parties, 23–24, 38–39
  and pie-slicing strategies, 38
  and power, 138
  and principal-agent relationship,
    205–206
Behavior
  ethical, 155–156
  and information technology,
    280–286
  nonverbal, 316
  and social dilemmas, 260
  and trust, 133–134
Belief perseverance, 172
Best Alternative to a Negotiated
  Agreement. *See* BATNA
Betting decision, 160, 184
Betweenness axiom, 300
Bias, and third-party intervention,
  324–325. *See also specific
  biases*
Biased interpretation, 194
Biased punctuation of conflict, 237
Bidding wars, 335
Bilateral concessions, 41–42
Binding contracts, 122
Blaming-the-victim attributions,
  173
Bluffing, 152
Body movements, 315
Bottom line, 87
Boulwarism, 39
Boundary spanners, 141
Brainstorming, 13, 178, 196–197
Brainwriting, 196–197
Breach of trust, 130

C

Bridging, 163
Business
  dynamic nature of, 3
  as social dilemma, 247–248
Business relationships, 114–116

Capabilities, differences in, 72
Car buyers, 26
Car dealers, 24
Card decision problem, 159, 184
Careers, new, 3
Caucusing, private, 194
Causal chunking, 237
Causal relationship, 172
Causation, unwarranted, 171–172
Central route persuasion tactics,
  143–146
Certainty effect, 305
Change, and cross-cultural negotia-
  tion, 243–244
Charisma, 317–318
Choice
  riskless, 295–297
  risky, 297–309
Choking, 181–182
Choosing, 20–21
Claiming, 82
Clarification, 134
Cleverness, 254
Closeness, 53
Closure, 298–299
Coalitional integrity, 198
Coalitions, 190–191
  challenges of, 198–202
  strategies of, 202–203
Coercion, 239
Cognitive conflict, 122–123
Cognitive consistency, 179–180
Cohesion, 211–212
Collateral relationships, 207
Collective fences, 260
Collective traps, 260
Collectivism, 223–228
Combination rules, 309
Commercial negotiations, on-line,
  287–291
Commitment, 87
  and consistency, 145–146
  escalation of, 266–270

Commitment, *Continued*
  norm of, 261
  power of, 261
  publicizing, 264–265
  and trust, 122
  verbal, 202
Common-bond groups, 212
Common-identity groups, 212
Common information bias, 212
Communal norms, 110–111
Communication
  breakdowns in, 194
  direct versus indirect, 232–233
  enriching, 44
  explicit or tacit, 31
  face-to-face, 273–275, 286
  and negotiating style, 96–97
  nonverbal, 315–321
  place-time model of social inter-
    action, 272–280
  and principal-agent relationship,
    206
  and social dilemmas, 264
  and team negotiation, 211
  and trust, 130
Communication distortion, 204–205
Comparability, 298
Comparative advertising, 262
Comparison, social, 48–49
Comparison effect, 53
Compensation, nonspecific,
    163–164
Competition, 4, 248
Competitive bargaining, 153
Competitive negotiators, 87
Compound gamble, 299
Compromise, 9, 62, 67, 74–75
Concave, 303
Concentrated unfairness, 52
Concessions
  bilateral, 41
  premature, 66
  unilateral, 96
Conciliation, 239
Condorcet paradox, 193
Confidence level, 22
Confirmation bias, 5, 180
Conflict
  and agreement, 111
  A-type versus C-type, 122–123
  biased punctuation of, 237
  fear of, 111
  forums for, 123, 124
  internal value, 117
  symbolic, 215
Conflicts of interest, 209, 215
Consensus, 59
Consensus conflict, 25
Consensus decisions, 193–194
Consistency, 44, 59, 294
Consistency principle, 145–146
Consortium, 199

Constituent relationships, 207
  challenges, 207–209
  strategies, 209–210
Consultation, 99, 156
Contact(s), 202, 215–216
Content orientation, 323
Contests, 94
Context, and fairness, 46–48
Contingency contracts, 70–72,
    77–78, 164–167
Continuity axiom, 300–301
Contracts
  binding, 122
  official or unofficial, 29
  psychological, 261
  See also Contingency contracts
Contractual risk, 18
Contrast, power of, 145
Control
  illusion of, 155
  loss of, 205
Conventional arbitration, 99
Conventions, 30
Convergence, 90
Convergent thinking, 178–179
Cooling-off periods, 96
Cooperation, 91
  and cultural values and norms,
    225–226
  in prisoner's dilemmas, 250
  in social dilemmas, 260–261,
    264–266
Cooperative negotiators, 87
Cooperative orientation, 67
Core solution, 200–201
Cost cutting, 163
Counterfactual thinking, 19
Counteroffers, 40–41
Co-workers, 114
Creative negotiation agreements,
    162–167
Creative negotiation strategies,
    175–182
Creativity, 158–159
  mental model of negotiation,
    182–183
  testing, 159–162, 184–186
  threats to, 167–175
Credibility, 101
Creeping determinism, 173
Crisis procedures, 99
Cross-cultural negotiation,
    220–221, 245
  advice for, 241–244
  challenges of, 234–240
  cultural values and norms,
    222–233
  dynamic framework for, 221–222
  predictors of success, 240–241
Cross-group friendships, 216
Crossover probability, 307
C-type conflict, 122–123

Cultural diversity. *See* Cross-
    cultural negotiation;
    Diversity
Cultural values, 222–233
Culture, 221–222
Curse of knowledge, 194

D

Decentralization, 247–248
Deception, 43–44
  detecting, 318–321
  and ethics, 152–153, 154–155
Decision making
  individual, 294–309
  interdependent, 248–249
Decision-making vigilance, 208
Decisions
  acceptance/rejection, 81
  consensus, 193–194
  one-shot, 251–252
Decision weights, 305–308
Deductive reasoning, 179–180
Defection, 250, 255, 261
Defensive attributions, 173
Defensiveness, 134
Degree of concessions, 41–42
Delayed liking, 147
Delegation, 87
Deliberate trust-building mecha-
    nisms, 121–125
Deterrence-based trust, 118–120
Diagnosis, 293
Diagnostic feedback, absence of,
    5–6
Diagnostic questions, 68
Differences
  assessment of, 80–81
  and contingency contracts, 70–72
  resolving, 97
Differential retrieval, 58
Different-place, different-time
    interaction, 277–280
Different-time, same-place interac-
    tion, 276
Diffusion of responsibility, 209
Diminishing marginal utility,
    303–304
Direct communications, 232–233
Disclosure, selective, 153
Dispositional attributions, 130–131
Dispositionalism, 227
Dispute resolution, 227–228
Dispute situation, 26–27
Distributed unfairness, 52
Distributive negotiation, 33–34, 60
  bargaining zone and negotiation
    dance, 34–37
  fairness, 46–59
  pie-slicing strategies, 37–43
  questions about, 43–46
Divergent thinking, 178, 179

Diversity, 4. *See also* Cross-cultural
negotiation
Dominance, 317
Dominance detection, 251
Dominance principle, 296
Door-in-the-face technique,
105–106, 151
Downward comparison, 48
Downward social comparison, 214
Dual-victim case, 132
Dual-violator case, 132

E

Effectiveness, 59
Egalitarianism, 229–231
Ego, maintaining, 51–53
Egocentrism, 6
and fairness, 54–58
and lie detection, 320
and persuasion, 146
and trust, 131
E-mail negotiation, 277–280
Embedded relationships, 116–117
Emblems, 315
Emotional conflict, 122–123
Emotional negotiating style, 85,
101–108
Emotions
and embedded relationships,
116–117
negative, 107
positive, 104–105, 107
and principal-agent relationship,
206
and trust, 126–130
Empathy, 134
Employers, BATNA of, 329–331
Endowment, 226–227
Endowment effects, 18–19
Enemies, shared, 124–125
Enthusiasm, 333
Entrainment, 107
Envy, 254
Equality, and intergroup negotia-
tions, 216
Equality rule, 46, 113
Equal participation, 197
Equal shares bias, 197
Equilibrium outcome, 251
Equity, 49–51
Equity rule, 46, 113
Errors, 65–66, 147–148
Escalation of commitment, 266–270
Ethics, 137–138, 151, 156–157
and behavior, 155–156
deception, 154–155
questionable negotiation strate-
gies, 152–154
Ethnicity. *See* Cross-cultural nego-
tiation; Diversity
Ethnocentrism, 242

Evaluation, 135
Evaluation apprehension, 208–209
Even split, 42–43, 62
Evidence, 44
Exaggeration of conflict bias,
324–325
Exchange norms, 111
Exchange situation, 26–27
Expectations, differences in, 71
Expected utility principle, 303–305
Expected utility theory (EU),
297–298
Expected-value principle, 301–303
Experience, 7
Expertise, 206, 211
Explicit communication, 31
Explicit negotiations, 247
Exploding offers, 334
Extremism, 214–215
Extremity effect, 307
Eye contact, 315, 320

F

Face. *See* Saving face
Face-to-face communication,
273–275, 286
Facial expressions, 315, 319
Fairness
attempts at, 45
norms of, 42
and persuasion, 146
power of, 46–59
and third-party intervention, 324
and trust, 124, 125
False conflict, 65–66
False consensus effect, 170
Falsification, 152
Family. *See* Personal relationships
Favoritism, in-group, 226
Fear of conflict, 111
Feedback, 99
absence of, 5–6
separation of, 276
Feeling good, 62
Film gate negotiation, 189
First offer. *See under* Offers
Fixed-pie perception, 9, 66, 158
Flaming, 279
Flattery, 129, 146–147
Flaws, 147–148
Flexibility, 177
Flow, 181–182
Fluency, 177
Focal points, 12, 14
Foot-in-the-door technique, 151
Forgiveness, 254
Formal third-party roles, 323
Fortress story, 169
Forum, 99, 123, 124
Fractionating, 162
Framing effect, 146, 283

Fraternal twin model, 8
Friends. *See* Personal relationships
Friendships, cross-group, 216
Front-page test, 156
Functional distance, 128
Functional fixedness, 173–174
Fundamental attribution error, 240,
242
Future
focusing on, 125
planning for, 135

G

Gambler's fallacy, 171
Game-playing, 182
Game theoretic rationality, 309–314
Gender
and nonverbal communication,
316–317
and salary negotiations, 140
Generalizability, 59
Gesture, 315
Gloating, 128
Goals, 123, 216
Gold chain problem, 161, 185
Golden rule, 156
Graciousness, 333
Graduation reduction in tension.
See GRIT model
Grass-is-greener negotiator, 11
GRIT model, 41, 217

H

Haggling, 88–89, 182
Halo effect, 131
Happiness, 62
Hard bargaining, 9
Hidden table, 22
Hierarchy, 229–231
Hindsight bias, 173
Homogeneity, 209
Horizon thinking, 210
Hospital problem, 181
Hostile media bias, 325
Human capital, 141

I

Identification-based trust,
120–121
Identities
changing, 213–214
common, 215
social, 264
Illumination, 176
Illusion of transparency, 69
Illusory conflict, 65–66
Illusory correlation, 172
Illustrators, 315, 319
Impasse, 100

Implicit emotional trust-building
    mechanisms, 126–130
Impossibility theorem, 193
Impression management, 266
Incentives
    aligning, 260
    conflicting, 203–204
Incubation, 175–176
Independence of equivalent utility
    representations, 312–314
Independence of irrelevant alterna-
    tives, 313–314
Indeterminate, 313
Indirect communication, 232–233
Indirect speech acts, 194–195
Individual decision making,
    294–295
    riskless choice, 295–297
    risky choice, 297–309
    and uncertainty, 297
Individualism, 223–228
Individualistic negotiators, 87
Inductive reasoning, 70, 180–181
Inequity, 50–51
Inert knowledge problem, 167–169
Informal communication, loss of,
    275–276
Informal third-party roles, 323
Information
    clarifying, 134
    and power, 139
    and win-win negotiation, 69
Information age, 4
Informational disparity, 58
Information management, 196
Information pooling, 211
Information procedures, 99
Information processing, 104, 212
Information sources, 206
Information technology, 271–272,
    291
    and negotiation behavior,
        280–286
    and negotiation strategies,
        286–287
    on-line commercial negotiations,
        287–291
    and place-time model of social
        interaction, 272–280
In-group bias, 214
In-group favoritism, 226
Inquisitorial adjudication, 228
Institutional support, 216
Integration, 244
Integrative agreements, 79–81
Integrative negotiation. *See* Win-
    win negotiation
Integrative strategies, 73–79
Intentions, 134, 265
Interchannel discrepancies,
    319–320
Intercultural negotiation. *See*
    Cross-cultural negotiation

Interdependence, 3–4
Interdependent decision making,
    248–249
Interests
    and negotiating style, 89, 91, 92,
        93, 95, 96, 98, 100
    of other parties, 23
    and principal-agent relationship,
        206
Intergroup biases, 237
Intergroup negotiation
    challenges, 213–215
    GRIT model, 217
    strategies, 215–216
Intergroup third-party roles, 323
Internal value conflict, 117
Internet, and job-offer negotia-
    tions, 329. *See also* E-mail
    negotiation; Information
    technology; On-line com-
    mercial negotiations; Web
    sites
Interpersonal escalation dilemmas,
    267
Interpersonal skills, 211
Interpersonal spacing, 315
Interpersonal third-party roles, 323
Intuition, 7–8
Invited third-party roles, 323
Irrational negotiating style. *See*
    Negative negotiating style
Irrationality, 294
Issue mix, 23, 80, 330
Issues, 15
    alignment and realignment,
        162–163
    and negotiating style, 89–91,
        94–101
    and win-win negotiation, 63–64,
        69, 74, 76–77

J

Job offers, negotiating, 327–335
Just world, 173
Justifiability, 59

K

Knowledge-based trust, 120

L

Labeling, 98
Law of large numbers, 302
Learning objectives, 8
Legal issues, 27–28
Letter sequence, 161, 185
Light-of-day test, 279
Liking, 127, 147
Limits, setting, 269
Linkage effects, 27
List technique, 150

Location, 29
Logrolling, 71, 192
Long-term negotiations, 25
Loop-backs, 98–99
Lose-lose effect, 65
Lose-lose negotiation, 5
Low-cost rights, 99
Low-power players, 202
Loyalists, 56
Lying. *See* Deception

M

Majority rule, 192
Managers, 122
Mandatory negotiations, 98
Manipulation, 154
Marginalization, 244
Market pricing, 113
MBA graduates, and salary negoti-
    ations, 140
Med-arb, 99
Mediation, 98, 228
Mediation houses, on-line, 289, 290
Memory, short-term, 175
Mental models, 182–183
Mere exposure, 126, 127
Merit-based rule, 113
Message tuning, 204
Meta-communication, 279
Microexpressions, 319
Mimicking, 129
Minitrials, 99
Miscommunication, 130
Misrepresentation, 152, 153, 193
Mixed-motive negotiation, 10,
    36–37
Monolithic, 23
Mood, 127–128, 147
Motivation, and lie detection, 320
Motivational negotiating style,
    85–91
Multiattribute utility technique
    (MAUT), 295
Multiculturalism. *See* Cross-
    cultural negotiation;
    Diversity
Multiparty negotiations, 189–190,
    218
    analyzing, 188–189
    challenges of, 190–196
    coalitions, 198–203
    constituent relationships,
        207–210
    intergroup negotiation, 213–217
    principal-agent relationship,
        203–206
    strategies of, 196–198
    team negotiation, 210–213
Multiple audience problem,
    195–196
Multiple-issue offers, 70
Multiple points of entry, 98

Multiple simultaneous offers, 70
Multistep negotiation procedure, 98
Myopia, 117

N

Naïve realism, 215, 239–240
Nash bargaining theory, 310–314
Nash point, 312
Nash solution, 310
Necessity, 25–26
Necklace problem, 161, 185
Needs
    and job-offer negotiations, 327, 328
    responding to, 111, 113
    and trust, 134–135
Needs-based rule, 46
Negative bargaining zone, 35
Negative negotiating style, 101, 105
Negative reinforcement, 106
Negative transfer, 174
Negotiating style, 84, 108
    approach, 85, 91–101
    emotions, 85, 101–108
    motivations, 85–91
    tough versus soft, 84–85
Negotiation, 2
    as core management competency, 2–4
    errors in, 5
    for job offers, 327–335
    learning objectives, 8
    mind and heart, 8
    myths, 6–8
    salary, 140
    See also Creativity; Cross-cultural negotiation; Distributive negotiation; Information technology; Multiparty negotiations; Preparation; Problem solving; Relationships; Social dilemmas; Tacit negotiations; Trust; Win-win negotiation
Negotiation dance, 34–37
Negotiation expertise, 211
Negotiation timing, 276
Negotiators
    grass-is-greener, 11
    ineffective, 4–6
    positional, 10, 16
    tough versus soft, 84–85
    underaspiring, 10
    See also Negotiating style
Negotiator's surplus, 36–37
Network connections, 124
Neutrality, maintaining, 325–326
Niceness, 254
Nickel-and-diming, 154
Nine dot problem, 161, 185–186

NO-FIST, 73
Nonverbal communication, 315–321
Nonverbal expression, 316
Nonverbal reception, 317
Normal operations with a financial strike. See NO-FIST
Norms, 30
    of commitment, 261
    communal, 110–111
    cultural, 222–233
    exchange, 111
    of fairness, 42
    and negotiating style, 87
    of reciprocity, 149
    social, 283–284
Notification, 99

O

Objective-appearing rationale, 42
Offers
    counteroffers, 40–41
    final, 45
    first, 40
    job, 327–335
    multiple simultaneous, 70
    number of, 30–31
    package deals, 15–16, 69
    retracting, 154
    and trade-offs, 81
Omissions, 153
One-shot decision, 251–252
One-shot negotiations, 25
On-line auction houses, 287–289
On-line commercial negotiations, 287–291
On-line mediation houses, 289, 290
On-line shopping houses, 289, 291
Opportunity, 25–26
Opposing parties. See Parties
Optimizing, 6
Options, power of, 144
Organizational autocrat, 207
Organizational puppet, 207
Originality, 177
Orthogonal, 163
Outcome control, 322–323
Outcomes, and third-party intervention, 324
Out-group homogeneity bias, 215
Overaspiring negotiators. See Positional negotiators
Overconfidence, 155–156, 174–175
Overconfidence bias, 325
Overconfidence effect, 22

P

Package deals, 15–16, 69
Paralinguistic cues, 315
Paranoia, 284–285
Paraphrasing, 135, 156

Pareto-efficient frontier, 310
Pareto-optimality, 65, 310–311, 324
Participation, equal, 97
Parties
    low-power, 202
    and negotiating style, 89, 91, 100, 101
    power differentials between, 31
    and relationship building, 133
    sizing up, 22–24
    stereotyping, 238
    See also Third-party intervention
Passive misrepresentation, 153
Pattern of concessions, 41
Perfection, 293
Performance, 52
Peripheral route persuasion tactics, 143, 146–151
Permanent record, 278, 280
Personal charisma, 317–318
Personal escalation dilemmas, 267
Personalization, 265
Personal meetings, 133
Personal relationships, 110–113
Personal strategies, 96–98
Person in a room decision, 159, 184
Perspective-taking failures, 194
Persuasion, 137–138, 142–143, 156–157
    central route to, 143–146
    peripheral route to, 143, 146–151
Physical appearance, and power, 141–142
Pie-expanding agreements, 76–77
Pie-expanding errors, 65–66
Pie expansion
    and creative negotiation agreements, 163
    and cross-cultural negotiation, 234, 241
    and negotiating style, 87, 95
    and rationality, 293
    and trust, 123–124, 130
    See also Win-win negotiation
Pie slicers, profiles of, 56
Pie slicing
    and coalitions, 198–200
    and rationality, 293
    strategies, 37–43
    See also Distributive negotiation
Pigpen problem, 161, 186
Pivotal power, 201
Place-time model of social interaction, 272–280
Poker face, 102, 104
Positional negotiators, 10, 16
Positions
    committing to, 45
    misrepresentation of, 152
    of other parties, 23
Positive negotiating style, 101, 104
Postdispute analysis and feedback, 99

Postnegotiation analysis, 79
Postoffers, 333–335
Postsettlement settlements, 73
Posture, 315
Power, 137–138, 156–157
  of agenda, 143–144
  of alternatives, 144
  and BATNA, 138
  of commitment, 261
  of contrast, 145
  and cross-cultural negotiation,
    242
  effects of, 142
  and egalitarianism, 229
  and hierarchy, 229
  and information, 139
  and information technology,
    280–281
  and job-offer negotiations,
    333–334
  and negotiating style, 92, 94, 95,
    99, 100–101
  of options, 144
  and physical appearance,
    141–142
  and social networks, 141
  and status, 139–140
  of triangulation, 321
Power backups, 99
Power differentials, 31
Practice, 333
Precedents, 31
Preference reversals, 19–20
Preferences, 63–64, 68, 71–72
Prejudice, 216
Premature concessions, 16, 65–66
Preparation, 9–10, 31–32, 175
  assessing other party, 22–24
  for job-offer negotiations,
    327–330
  self-assessment, 10–22
  situation assessment, 24–31
  for team negotiation, 212
Presettlement settlements (PreSS),
    72
Prevention, 135
Primary status characteristics,
    139
Priming, unconscious, 148
Principal-agent relationship, 203
  challenges, 203–205
  strategies, 205–206
Priorities, 68
Prisoner's dilemma, 247, 249–256
Private caucusing, 194
Private negotiations, 29–30
Private valuations, 18
Proactive negotiation, 8
Problem representation, 162
Problems
  prevention of, 135
  shared, 124–125

Problem solving
  and creativity tests, 159–162,
    184–186
  mental model, 183
  rational model, 176–177
  threats to, 167–175
  See also Creativity
Procedure, 277
Process, fairness of, 53–54
Process control, 322–323
Process orientation, 323
Process roles, 197
Proof, 44
Propinquity effect, 127
Proposal making, systematizing,
    196
Prospect theory, 307
Pseudosacred, 236
Pseudostatus characteristics, 139
Psychological contracts, 261
Psychological equity, 51
Public goods dilemma, 260
Public negotiations, 29–30
Punctuation, 237
Pyramid model, 64–65

Q

Quantification, 12
Questions
  diagnostic, 68
  and negotiating style, 87
Quid pro quo, 129

R

Raiffa's hybrid model, 202
Rank, 114
Rant 'n' rave negotiating style, 101,
    105
Rapport, 283–284
Ratification, 28, 206
Rational analysis, 250–253
Rationale, object-appearing, 42
Rationality
  game theoretic, 309–314
  importance of, 293–294
  and individual decision making,
    294–309
  and job-offer negotiations, 335
Rational negotiating style, 101, 102,
    104
Rational problem-solving model,
    176–177
Rational trust-building mecha-
    nisms, 121–125
Reactance, 119
Reactance technique, 150–151
Reactive devaluation, 11
Reactive negotiation, 8
Reanchoring, 331℃
Reciprocal trade-offs, 192

Reciprocity, 90, 94–95
  and persuasion, 148–149
  and trust, 128
Reducibility axiom, 299
Reference point, 146, 307
Reflection effect, 53
Regressiveness principle, 307–308
Rehearsals, 333
Reinforcement, 90
  and persuasion, 149
  negative, 106
Rejection, 20–21, 81
Rejection-then-retreat tactic. *See*
    Door-in-the-face tech-
    nique
Relations, 278
Relationship managers, 88
Relationship model, 182–183
Relationships, 136
  business, 114–116
  constituent, 207–210
  egalitarian power, 229, 230–231
  embedded, 116–117
  and fairness, 54
  hierarchical power, 229, 230–231
  personal, 110–113
  principal-agent, 203–206
  quality of, 117
  and third-party intervention, 324
  trust, 117–121
  and win-win negotiation, 62, 67
Reliability, 88
Reneging, 154
Renegotiation, prolonging, 81
Repetitive negotiations, 25
Representativeness, 170–171
Representatives, in cross-cultural
    negotiations, 229–230
Reputation, 131
Reservation point, 12, 13–14
  lying about, 43–44
  revealing, 43
  and scare tactics, 44–45
Resolution, 97
Resource allocation, and coalitions,
    202–203
Resource assessment, 80
Resource conservation dilemmas,
    260
Resources, 99–100, 113. *See also*
    Scarce resource competi-
    tion
Respect, and cross-cultural negoti-
    ation, 242–243
Responsibility
  diffusion of, 209
  diversifying, 269
Retraction, 154
Richness, 272
Rights, 92, 93–94, 99, 100–101
Risk attitudes, 71, 302–303
Risk aversion, 17, 302

Risk-indifferent, 302
Riskless choice, 295–297
Risk-neutral, 302
Risk propensity, 16–17
Risks, 7, 18
Risk-seeking, 302
Risk taking, 282–283, 304–305
Risky choice, 297–309
Role-playing, 213, 326
Roles
    and information technology,
        285–286
    third-party, 322–323
Rules
    negotiating, 125
    and trust, 132
Ruthless competitors, 56

S

Sacred values, 234–236
St. Petersburg paradox, 303
Saints, 56
Salary negotiations, 140, 327–335
Same-time, different-place interac-
        tion, 275–276
Satisfaction, 59, 309
Satisficing, 6
Saving face, 45–46, 206, 208–209,
        231
Scarce resource competition, 25
Scare tactics, 44–45
Schmoozing, 129, 287
Screen loading, 279
Secondary status characteristics,
        139
Second table, 207
Secrecy, 320
Selective attention, 174
Selective disclosure, 153
Selective encoding and storage, 58
Self-assessment, 10
    BATNA, 11–15
    choosing versus rejecting,
        20–21
    confidence level, 22
    counterfactual thinking, 19
    endowment effects, 18–19
    issue alternatives, 15
    issue identification, 15
    packages of offers, 15–16
    preference reversals, 19–20
    risk propensity, 16–17
    sure thing principle, 21–22
    targets, 10–11
    uncertainty, 17–18
Self-disclosure, 129–130
Self-esteem, 89
Self-fulfilling prophesy, 139–140
Self-improvement, 48–49
Self-interest, 49
Self-regulation, 106

Self-reinforcement, 6
Self-serving bias, 57–58
Separation, 244
Set effect, 174
Settlements
    postsettlement, 73
    presettlement, 72
Settlement zone, 34
Shapely model, 201–202
Shared visions, 123
Shopping houses, on-line, 289, 291
Short-term memory, 175
Side deals, 63
Similarity, 126, 147
Similarity–attraction effect, 126
Simplicity, 59
Single-text strategy, 156
Situational attributions, 255
Situationalism, 227
Situation assessment, 24–31
Skills, 98, 99–100. *See also specific
        skills*
Social capital, 141
Social change, 101
Social comparison, 48–49, 132
Social contagion, 129
Social dilemmas, 247, 256–258,
        270
    business as, 247–248
    cooperation in, 260–261, 264–266
    escalation of commitment,
        266–270
    interdependent decision making,
        248–249
    prisoner's dilemma, 249–256
    tragedy of the commons, 258
    types of, 260
    ultimatum dilemma, 259
Social identity, 264
Social interaction, place-time
        model of, 272–280
Social loafing, 226
Social networks
    and cultural values and norms,
        225
    and information technology,
        281–282
    manipulation of, 154
    and power, 141
Social norms, 283–284
Social proof principle, 150
Social striving, 226
Social support, 216
Social values, 234–236
Soft bargaining, 9
Soft negotiators, 84–85
Solvability, 300–301
Specialization, 248
Squeaky wheel principle, 106
Standards. *See* Norms
Status quo bias, 198
Status, 114

and information technology,
        280–281
and power, 139–140
Stereotype threat, 140
Stereotyping, 213, 238
Stick problems, 161, 185
Strategic alliances, 248
Strategic issues. *See* Issues
Strategic misrepresentation, 193
Strategic voting, 193
Strikes, and fairness, 57
Structural strategies, 98–100
Subadditivity, 307
Subcertainty, 307
Subgame perfect equilibrium, 259
Suboptimal, 34
Substance, 277
Substitutability axiom, 299–300
Sunk costs, 14–15, 271
Superiority, illusion of, 155
Superrationality, 256
Sure thing principle, violations of,
        21–22
Susan and Martha problem,
        161, 185
Sweetening the deal. *See* That's-
        not-all technique
Swift trust, 115
Syllogisms, 180
Symbolic conflict, 215
Symmetry, 311–312

T

Taboo trade-offs, 234–236
Tacit communication, 31
Tacit negotiations, 247, 270. *See
        also* Social dilemmas
Target point, 15
Targets, 10–11
Team cohesion, 211–212
Team effect, 210
Team efficacy effect, 210
Team negotiation, 210–211
    challenges, 211–212
    strategies, 212–213
Technical expertise, 211
Technology. *See* Information tech-
        nology
Teleconferences, 286–287
That's-not-all technique, 151
Third-party intervention, 30, 99,
        322–326
Threats, 94
Time, 67–68
Time constraints, 28–29, 146
Time preferences, differences in,
        71–72
Time-related costs, 28–29
Tit-for-tat, 253–256
Tone of voice, 319
Touching, 315

Tough negotiators, 84–85
Toughness, 254
Tournament of champions, 253–256
Trade-offs, 74–75, 81
    formulating, 191–192
    reciprocal, 192
    taboo, 234–236
Tragedy of the commons, 258
Training, 98
Transitivity property, 299
Transparency, illusion of, 69
Triangulation, 321
Trust, 136
    in coalitions, 198
    implicit emotional mechanisms,
       126–130
    importance of, 109–110
    rational and deliberate mecha-
       nisms, 121–125
    regaining, 132–135
    threats to, 130–132
    and win-win negotiation, 68
Trust relationships, 117–121
Tumor problem, 168
Tunnel vision, 196, 269

U

Ultimatum dilemma, 259
Unbundling, 80
Uncertainty, 17–18, 297

Unconscious priming, 148
Underaspiring negotiators, 10
Unemotional negotiating style. *See*
       Rational negotiating style
Unfairness, distributed versus con-
    centrated, 52
Unilateral concessions, 96
Uninvited third-party roles, 323
Uniqueness axiom, 310
Unwarranted causation, 171–172
Upward comparison, 48
Utility, 295–296
Utility function, 298–301

V

Valuation, differences in, 71
Values
    cultural, 222–233
    social, 234–236
Verbal commitments, 202
Verification, 176
Vicious circle, 200–202
Videoconferences, 286–287
Violator-and-victim case, 132
Visions, shared, 123
Vocal cues, 315
Voice, tone of, 319
Volunteer dilemma, 258
Voting, 192
Voting paradoxes, 192–193

W

Wants, and job-offer negotiations,
    327, 328
Water jug problem, 160, 184–185
Waterlilies problem, 162, 186
Web sites
    consumer-oriented, 26
    home buying, 271
Weight(s), 296, 305–308
Winner's curse, 5, 10, 39
Win-win negotiation, 61, 82
    claiming, 82
    definition, 62
    effective strategies, 68–73
    ineffective strategies, 67–68
    integrative agreements, 79–81
    integrative strategies, 73–79
    pie-expanding errors, 65–66
    and positive emotions, 107
    pyramid model, 64–65
    signs of, 62–64
Women
    and constituent relationships, 208
    and nonverbal communication,
       316–317
    and salary negotiations, 140

AUTHOR INDEX

Abel, M. J., 275
Abramowitz, C. V., 316
Abramowitz, S. I., 316
Adair, W., 232, 233, 234
Adams, A. A., 66
Adams, S., 48, 50, 51
Adamson, R. E., 173
Adler, N. J., 231
Aiello, J. R., 119
Akerlof, G., 10, 120
Alba, J. W., 161
Alderman, L., 3
Allen, H. M., Jr., 215
Allen, T. J., 274
Allison, S. T., 56
Allred, K. G., 104, 105
Ancona, D. G., 207
Anders, G., 288
Anderson, C., 142
Anderson, J. R., 174
Anderson, S. C., 119
Argote, L., 212
Argyle, M., 110
Ariel, S., 225
Armstrong, D. J., 276
Armstrong, L., 24
Aron, A., 216
Aronoff, J., 108
Aronson, E., 147, 148, 214
Aronson, J., 140
Arrow, K. J., 193
Ashmore, R. D., 141
Aubert, V., 25
Austin, W., 47, 113
Austin, W. G., 213
Axelrod, R., 253, 256
Axsom, D., 210

Babcock, L., 57
Back, K. W., 211
Baguioro, L., 28
Balke, W. M., 65
Barboza, D., 267
Bargh, J. A., 131, 148
Baron, J., 234, 235, 295
Baron, R. A., 107, 127, 147
Barron, R. S., 217
Barry, B., 104, 133
Barsness, Z., 227
Bar-Tal, D., 213
Baumeister, R. F., 106

Bazerman, M. H., 4, 7, 9, 10, 11, 14,
    17, 22, 42, 48, 49, 54, 56,
    66, 68, 72, 73, 81, 84, 89,
    91, 120, 155, 164, 165, 166,
    175, 189–190, 192, 198,
    202, 203, 205, 259, 264,
    274, 323, 325
Beach, S. R., 127
Beaman, A. L., 151
Bednarski, P. J., 205
Bell, D., 63
Benbow, C. P., 140
Bennett, R., 91
Bensinger, K., 115
Benson, P. L., 141
Ben-Yoav, O., 207
Berkowitz, L., 47
Berneiri, F. J., 318
Bernouilli, D., 303, 304
Berry, J. W., 244
Berscheid, E., 48, 50, 131
Bettenhausen, K., 59
Biddle, J. E., 141
Bies, R. J., 134
Billings, D. K., 224
Blake, A. W., 320
Blanck, P. D., 318
Blau, P. M., 48
Blumberg, S. J., 210
Bobo, L., 215
Bochner, S., 147
Bottom, W. P., 17, 18, 133, 135, 198,
    255
Bourgeois, L. J., III, 123
Bradford, D. L., 216
Bratslavsky, E., 106
Brehm, S. S., 150
Brem, S., 169
Brett, J. M., 27, 90, 91, 92, 94, 95,
    96–97, 98–99, 100, 101,
    211, 220, 221, 222, 223,
    224, 227, 229, 231, 232,
    234, 241, 242, 245, 326
Brewer, M., 214, 215, 216, 237, 239,
    260, 264
Bridgeman, D., 214
Britton, S., 207
Brodt, S. E., 210
Brown, C. E., 317
Brown, F. E. A., 260
Brown, J., 155, 269

Brown, J. D., 117
Brown, P., 195
Brown, R. J., 215–216
Buck, R., 318
Bunker, B. B., 117, 121
Burger, J. M., 151
Burrows, L., 148
Burt, R. S., 124, 141
Butler, D., 319
Buttner, E. H., 133
Byrne, D., 127
Byrne, J. A., 6

Caccioppo, J. T., 107
Camerer, C., 57, 58
Camerer, C. F., 194
Campos, F., 202
Cann, A., 106
Cantor, N., 107
Cantril, H., 238, 324
Carlsmith, J. M., 315
Carlson, S., 286
Carnevale, P. J., 42, 67, 89, 104, 127,
    147, 153, 162, 163, 207,
    208, 210, 227, 266, 325
Casella, D. F., 318
Cates, K., 327, 331, 333, 335
Chaiken, S., 141, 143, 208
Champagne, M. V., 28, 90
Chan, D. K. S., 225
Chapman, J. P., 172
Chapman, L. J., 172
Chassin, L., 170
Chechile, R., 193
Chelius, J. R., 326
Chen, M., 148
Chen, X., 265, 266
Cheraskin, L., 117
Chiu, C., 227
Christakopoulou, 227
Christie, B., 281
Cialdini, R. B., 106, 145, 151, 202,
    260
Clark, K., 2, 30, 331, 332, 334
Clark, M., 110, 113
Claude, S., 69
Cohen, A., 288
Cohen, A. R., 216
Cohen, M. D., 63, 71
Cohen, R., 232
Cole, N., 151

Cole, P., 276
Condor, F., 215–216
Conlin, M., 3
Cook, P. J., 4
Coombs, C. H., 298
Copeland, L., 240
Costello, D., 115
Covey, S., 96, 97
Cox, T. H., 225
Coy, P., 3
Crossette, B., 130
Csikszentmihalyi, M., 181
Cummings, L. L., 134
Cunningham, M. R., 318

Daft, R. L., 272
Daly, J. P., 54
Daniels, S., 133, 135, 255
Darley, J. M., 195
Dasen, P. R., 244
Daubman, K. A., 104, 107
Davenport, J. W., Jr., 147
Davidson, J. E., 162
Davies, J., 164, 165
Dawes, R. M., 298
Dayton, T., 162
De Dreu, C. K., W., 89
Degoey, P., 264
DeHarpport, T., 7, 62, 66, 89, 111
DePaulo, B. M., 315, 316, 317, 318, 319, 320
DePaulo, P. J., 320
Dépret, E., 142
Derlega, V. J., 86
Detweiler, R., 240
Deutsch, M., 46, 47, 48, 66, 213
Diehl, M., 196
Diekmann, K., 264
Diekmann, K. A., 14, 48
DiMatteo, M. R., 318
Dimitri, S., 320
Dion, K., 131
Dion, K. K., 142
Dion, K. L., 142, 211
Doise, W., 237
Donohue, W. A., 90
Doob, A., 120
Dovidio, J. F., 317
Driver, R., 318
Drolet, A., 129
Drolet, A. L., 107, 272, 274, 283
Druckman, D., 25
Dubrovsky, V. J., 284
Duncker, K., 168, 169, 173
Durso, F. T., 162
Dworetsky, T., 109, 119, 165
Dworkin, J. B., 326
Dwyer, F. R., 120

Eagly, A. H., 141, 143
Earley, P. C., 39, 226
Eavey, C. L., 198

Egido, C., 274
Eisenhardt, K. M., 123
Ekman, P., 44
Ekman, P. M., 318, 319
Eldridge, E., 26
Elkes, R., 106
Ellemers, N., 214
Elliott, S., 248
Ellsworth, P. C., 315
Ellyson, S. L., 317
Elsbach, K. D., 134
Englebart, D., 272
Enzle, M. E., 119
Epstein, J. A., 317
Erlanger, S., 130
Ertel, D., 68
Espeland, W., 236
Espinoza, J. A., 226
Etzkowitz, H., 116
Evans, C. R., 211
Exline, R. V., 317

Fader, P., 202
Farber, H. S., 22, 175, 326
Farrell, J., 38
Feller, W., 302
Ferguson, R., 169
Fessenden, F., 324
Festinger, L., 211
Firestone, I. J., 62
Fischer, G. W., 215, 240
Fischhoff, B., 156, 173
Fisher, R., 11, 16, 96, 98, 102
Fiske, A. P., 113
Fiske, S. T., 142, 208
Fixx, J. F., 161
Fleming, J. H., 195
Florio, G., 188
Floyd, J., 148
Foa, E., 113
Foa, U., 113
Forbus, K. D., 167
Forgas, J. P., 104, 107, 127, 147
Fouraker, L. E., 41
Fourment, C., 127
Fox, C., 188, 189, 303
Frank, M. G., 318, 319
Frank, R. H., 4, 105, 107
Fraser, S. C., 260
Fredrickson, B. L., 107
Freedman, J. L., 260
Friedman, H. S., 315, 316, 317, 318
Friedman, R., 22
Friedman, R. A., 207
Friesen, W. V., 318
Froman, L. A., 63, 71
Fry, W. R., 62
Fussell, S. R., 195, 204

Galegher, J., 274
Galinsky, A. D., 19, 39, 40
Gamson, W., 190

Gardiner, G. S., 240
Garza, R. T., 226
Geis, F. L., 319
Gelfand, 227
Gellar, V., 279
Gentner, D., 167, 168, 169
Gerard, H., 215
Gerard, H. B., 237
Gergen, K., 120
Gerhart, B., 140
Getzels, J. W., 179
Geyer, P. D., 54
Gibbons, R., 38
Gibson, K., 133, 135, 164, 205, 255, 325
Gick, M. L., 168, 169
Gifford, R. K., 172
Gigone, D., 212
Gilbert, D. T., 210
Gilin, D. A., 39
Gillespie, J. J., 72, 164, 165, 166, 168
Gillespie, T. L., 28, 90
Gilovich, T., 19, 69
Girrotto, V., 255
Glentz, B., 151
Goffman, E., 266
Goldberg, S. B., 27, 91, 94, 95, 96, 98–99, 100, 101, 211
Gonzalez, R., 25
Gottman, J. M., 129
Gouldner, A. W., 128, 149
Graham, J. L., 232, 238
Granovetter, M., 120
Graziano, W. G., 142
Greenberg, J., 50, 51
Grezlak, J., 86
Griffin, D. W., 324
Griffin, E., 126
Griggs, L., 240
Grover, R., 6
Gruenfeld, D. H., 142, 211
Guetzkow, H., 122
Guilford, J. P., 177, 178
Gulliver, M. P., 90
Gun-Gruchy, C., 316
Gyr, J., 122

Halberstadt, A. G., 317
Hall, E. T., 232
Hall, J. A., 316
Hall, M. R., 232
Hallmark, W., 239
Hamermesh, D. S., 141
Hamilton, D. L., 172
Hammond, K. R., 65
Hanna, B. A., 142
Haour, G., 276
Hardin, G., 258
Harmon, A., 27
Harris, R. J., 56
Harris, V. A., 129, 146–147
Harsanyi, J., 312, 313

Harvey, J., 111, 112
Harvey, O. J., 124
Hastie, R., 9, 66, 212
Hastorf, A., 238, 324
Hatfield, E., 107
Hays, R. D., 318
Heine, S. J., 224
Henderson, M., 110
Henley, N. M., 317
Hewstone, M., 213
Higgins, E. T., 131, 195, 204
Hilty, J., 42
Hochschild, A. R., 119
Hoffman, D., 104, 125
Hoffman, E., 271
Hofmann, T., 63
Hofstadter, D., 266, 354, 255
Hofstede, G., 223, 229
Hollingshead, A. B., 281
Holson, L. M., 33
Holyoak, K. J., 168, 169
Homans, G. C., 48
Hong, Y., 227
Honkaniemi, L., 141
Hood, W. R., 124
Hook, L. H., 281
Horowitz, L. M., 147
Howard-Cooper, S., 116
Hrebec, D., 4, 65
Hua, L. S., 84
Huber, V., 39, 81
Huber, V. L., 17
Hughes, C. F., 134
Hui, C. H., 224

Insko, C. A., 256
Isen, A., 104
Isen, A. M., 104, 107, 127, 147
Issacharoff, S., 57
Iwata, E., 220

Jackson, P. W., 179
Janis, I. L., 102
Jehn, K. A., 123
Jensen, M. C., 203
Jepson, C., 170
Johansen, R., 272
Johnson-Laird, P. N., 159
Jonas, K., 216
Jones, E. E., 129, 146–147, 237
Joyce, M., 56
Juieng, D., 119

Kahn, R. L., 237
Kahneman, D., 12, 16, 18, 19, 58,
       107, 159, 160, 170, 171,
       180, 181, 210, 227, 283,
       303, 305, 307
Kahwajy, J. L., 123
Kalk, S., 3
Kameda, T., 47
Kaplan, J. M., 30–31

Kaplan, R., 174
Kaplan, S., 174
Karabenick, S. A., 141
Karambayya, R., 326
Kayser, E., 113
Keenan, J., 38
Keisler, S., 277, 279, 281, 282, 283,
       284, 285
Kelley, H. H., 25, 70, 90, 120
Kelly, J. R., 68, 107
Kelman, H. C., 29
Keltner, D., 214, 239, 325
Keltner, D. J., 142
Kemelgor, C., 116
Kernan, J. B., 141
Kerr, N. L., 217, 226
Keysar, B., 194, 281
Kiesler, C. A., 142
Kiesler, S. B., 142
Kim, J. W., 258
Kim, P., 107, 203
Kim, P. H., 19
Kim, S. H., 322
Kipnis, D., 127
Kirkendol, S. E., 320
Kiser, K., 67, 109, 233, 277, 284
Kivisilta, P., 141
Klar, Y., 213
Knetsch, J. L., 18, 19, 227
Koberstein, P., 158
Koestner, R., 318
Kolb, D., 209
Kolb, D. M., 207
Kollock, P., 120
Komorita, S. S., 190, 264
Kopelman, S., 101, 105
Kossan, P., 198
Kotter, J., 54
Kramer, R., 104, 126, 128
Kramer, R. M., 62, 108, 115, 130,
       142, 190, 207, 213–214,
       215, 237, 260, 284
Krantz, D. H., 170
Krauss, R. M., 195, 204
Kraut, R. E., 274
Kray, L., 52
Kreps, D. M., 253
Krishnan, R., 212
Kruglanski, A. W., 195, 213
Kuhlman, D., 202
Kuhlman, D. M., 88
Kumar, R., 104
Kunda, Z., 170
Kunde, D., 116
Kurtzberg, T., 62, 107, 110, 111, 123,
       125, 129, 286, 287
Kwon, S., 89

LaFrance, M., 147
Lamm, H., 113
Lancaster, H., 33, 129
Landy, D., 131, 141

Lane, J. D., 320
Langer, E., 155
Larrick, R. P., 123, 129, 130
Larson, M., 94, 95
Lassiter, G. D., 318, 319
Latané, B., 211
Law, K., 167
Lax, D. A., 15, 63, 69, 70–71, 73, 80,
       162–163, 164
Lee, W., 303
Lehman, D. R., 224
Leith, K. P., 106
Lemonick, M. D., 226
Lengel, R. H., 272
Lenkert, A., 216
Lepper, M., 325
Lepper, M. R., 172
Lerner, H. G., 96
Lerner, J., 234, 235, 236
Lerner, M., 173
Lerner, R. M., 141
Leung, K., 224, 227–228, 229
Levenson, R. W., 318
Leventhal, H., 47, 53
Levine, J., 58, 59
Levine, M., 193
Levinson, S. C., 195
Lewicki, R. J., 84, 117, 121, 151, 152,
       153, 224
Lewis, S. A., 91
Lewthwaite, G. A., 29
Lichtenstein, S., 20, 156
Liebrand, W. B. G., 90, 264
Lightdale, J. R., 212
Lim, S. G., 90
Lind, E. A., 52, 125, 134
Linder, D., 147
Lindsley, S. L., 243
Linville, P. W., 215, 240
Lipin, S., 18
Lippman, T. W., 137, 149
Lobel, M., 48
Lobel, S. A., 225
Locke, K. D., 147
Loewenstein, G., 89, 91, 194, 198
Loewenstein, G. F., 42, 49, 54, 56,
       57, 58, 210, 259
Loewenstein, J., 168, 182
Lohr, S., 33
Lombardi, W. J., 131
Long, B., 317
Longo, L. C., 141
Lublin, J. S., 9, 23, 329
Luchins, A. S., 160
Lynn, M., 123
Lytle, A., 90, 227
Lytle, A. L., 92, 94, 95, 96–97, 98,
       101, 221

Machatka, D. E., 68
Madey, S. F., 19
Magliozzi, T., 17

Maisonneuve, J., 127
Makhijani, M. G., 141
Makowski, D. G., 47
Mallozzi, J. S., 104, 105
Mann, L., 102
Mannix, E., 110, 111, 189–190, 191,
        192, 197, 198, 199, 202
Mannix, E. A., 120, 211, 260
Manstead, A. S. R., 317–318
March, R. M., 232
Marlowe, D., 120
Marshello, A., 88
Martin, J. N., 240
Marwell, G., 50
Matas, C., 147
Mathew, A., 215–216
Matsui, F., 104, 105
Matsumoto, D., 243
May, K., 193
Mazur, A., 139
McAlister, L., 202
McClelland, G., 54
McClintock, C., 202
McClintock, C. G., 86, 90
McFadden, R. D., 154
McGrath, J. E., 68, 281
McGuire, T., 281, 283
McKelvey, R. D., 200
McKendrick, J., 322
McKersie, R. B., 65
McKittrick, D., 209
McLaughlin-Volpe, T., 216
McLeod, P. L., 225
Meckling, W. H., 203
Medvec, V. H., 19, 39, 62, 69, 101,
        105, 110, 111, 125
Meherabian, A., 274
Menon, T., 227
Messick, D. M., 54, 56, 57, 58, 155,
        202, 259, 260, 264
Metzger, A. R., 258
Meyer, G. D., 65
Meyers, J., 210
Meyerson, D., 115
Mieskowski, K., 289
Mikula, G., 47
Milgrom, P., 253
Millar, M. G., 142
Miller, D., 19
Miller, D. T., 212
Miller, G. A., 175
Miller, G. J., 198
Miller, M., 217
Mills, J., 110, 113
Mishra, B. K., 220, 243
Moag, J., 274
Moore, D. A., 28, 146
Moore, D., 107, 287
Moore, J. S., 142
Moore, M., 120
Moreland, R. L., 59, 127, 212
Morgan, P., 210

Morgenstern, O., 300, 302, 312
Morris, M. W., 107, 123, 129, 130,
        225, 227–228, 255, 272,
        274, 283, 286, 287, 324,
        325, 326
Moses, A., 279
Moylan, S. J., 107, 127, 147
Muraven, M., 106
Murnighan, J. K., 59, 90, 133, 135,
        190, 255, 258
Mussweiler, T., 39, 40
Myers, F., 196

Nadler, J., 107, 123, 129, 286
Naquin, C., 125, 132
Nash, J., 310, 312, 313
Nauman, M., 26
Neale, M. A., 4, 7, 9, 10, 11, 17, 22,
        39, 47, 66, 68, 72, 81, 84,
        110, 111, 175, 203, 211,
        323, 325
Neuberg, S. L., 208
Newton, E., 104, 126, 207
Niedenthal, P. M., 107
Nierenberg, G. I., 102
Nisbett, R. E., 170
Noonan, E., 208
Northcraft, G., 17, 39, 72
Notarius, C. I., 318
Nowicki, G. P., 104, 107

O'Connor, K. M., 66, 153, 207, 209,
        210, 279
Oh, S., 120
O'Heeron, R. C., 134
Ohtsubo, Y., 47
Oka, T., 226
Okamoto, K., 226
Okumura, T., 234, 242
Oldham, J., 124
Olekalns, M., 91
Oliver, R. L., 104
O'Quin, K., 108
Ordeshook, P., 193
Ordeshook, P. C., 200
Osborn, A. F., 178
Osgood, C. E., 41, 131, 217, 255
Oskamp, S., 11, 239
O'Sullivan, M. O., 318, 319

Pacelle, M., 18
Pachtman, A., 230, 231
Paese, P. W., 39
Page, M. S., 320
Palmade, G., 127
Palmer, A. T., 3
Palmer, L. G., 191–192, 194, 197
Parks, C. D., 190, 264
Patton, B., 11, 16, 96, 98, 102
Paulus, P. B., 196
Pelham, B. W., 237
Peng, K., 227

Pennebaker, J. W., 119, 134
Pereira, J., 23
Perkins, A., 147
Peterson, E., 209, 210, 213
Peterson, R., 234, 235, 236
Philip, G., 275
Pillutla, M. M., 259, 265, 266
Pinel, E. C., 210
Pinkley, R., 47
Pinto, P. R., 326
Plott, C., 193
Podolny, J. M., 225
Poincaré, H., 176
Pólya, G., 176
Pommerenke, P., 104, 126, 207
Poortinga, Y. H., 244
Popkin, S., 120
Prentice, D. A., 212
Presson, C. C., 170
Preston, M., 151
Prince, L. M., 318
Pruitt, D. G., 67, 89, 91, 162, 163,
        207, 208, 266, 322
Putnam, L. L., 90

Quinn, D. M., 140
Quinn, S. R., 63

Radhakrishnan, S., 227
Raia, C. P., 104, 105
Raiffa, H., 24, 34, 37, 41, 73, 102,
        104, 128, 156, 198, 200,
        202, 207, 326
Rand, K. A., 210
Rapson, R. L., 107
Rattermann, M. J., 167
Raven, B. H., 105
Redelmeier, D. A., 107
Reingen, P. H., 141, 150
Rhoades, J. A., 279
Riggio, R. E., 318
Roberts, D. C., 237
Roberts, J., 253
Roberts, P., 276
Robinson, R., 214, 325
Robinson, R. J., 84, 151, 152, 153,
        224, 239
Roefs, M., 214
Rohrbaugh, J., 54
Ropp, S. A., 216
Rosenfeld, J., 156
Rosenthal, R., 317, 318, 319
Rosette, A., 227
Ross, B. H., 167
Ross, J., 268
Ross, L., 11, 48, 172, 214, 215, 240,
        242, 266, 324, 325
Ross, M., 58
Roth, A. E., 38
Roth, N. L., 125, 132
Rothbart, M., 239
Ruback, R. B., 119

Rubin, J. Z., 203, 260, 322
Russ, L. E., 73, 81
Rutte, C. G., 56
Rynes, S., 140

Sally, D. F., 264
Salovey, P., 215, 240
Samuels, S. M., 48, 266
Samuelson, C. D., 260
Sander, F. E. A., 203
Sanders, D. Y., 119
Sano, Y., 232
Saunders, D. G., 173
Savage, L. J., 21
Saveri, G., 3
Savitsky, K., 69
Scheer, M., 161
Schelling, T., 106, 107, 236, 247, 312
Schenitzki, D. P., 70
Schkade, D., 210
Schlenker, B. R., 236
Schlesinger, L., 54
Schmitt, D., 50
Schneider, S. C., 221
Schofield, J. W., 215
Schrage, M., 273
Schraneveldt, R. W., 162
Schreiber, C. A., 107
Schreifer, J., 61
Schroth, H. A., 14
Schurr, P. H., 120
Schwartz, S., 223
Schwinger, T., 46
Seaberry, J., 271
Sears, D. O., 215
Sebenius, J. K., 15, 63, 69, 70–71, 73, 80, 162–163, 164
Segal, M. W., 127
Segall, M. H., 244
Segil, L., 248
Seiden, V., 19, 101, 105
Seilheimmer, S., 266
Selten, R., 259
Sentis, K. P., 57, 259
Sethi, S., 227–228
Sethna, B. N., 284
Shafir, E., 20, 21
Shah, P. P., 14
Shapiro, D. L., 90, 92, 94, 95, 96–97, 98, 101, 117, 133, 134, 221
Shapley, L. S., 303
Shaver, K. G., 129, 146–147
Sheehan, N., 267
Shell, R., 87
Shell, R. G., 283
Shepard, J. D., 162
Sheppard, B. H., 117, 326
Sherif, C. W., 124
Sherif, M., 124, 213
Sherman, S. J., 106, 170
Shirakashi, S., 226
Shirk, M., 238

Short, J., 279
Shortt, J. W., 320
Siamwalla, A., 120
Sicoly, F., 58
Siegel, J., 281, 283
Siegel, S., 41
Sigall, H., 131, 141
Silveira, J. M., 176
Sim, D. L. H., 255
Simon, H., 6
Simons, C., 214
Simonson, I., 20
Singelis, T. M., 106
Sinha, N. P., 220, 243
Sitkin, S. B., 125, 132
Size, P. B., 173
Skinner, B. F., 106
Slavin, B., 63, 144
Slovic, P., 20, 156, 303
Smith, P. L., 91
Snodgrass, S. E., 317
Snyder, M., 142
Sondak, H., 47, 120
Sparks, G. G., 126
Spencer, S. J., 140
Spranca, M., 234, 235
Sproull, L., 277, 280, 281, 282, 284, 285
Stahelski, A. J., 90
Stanley, J. C., 140
Stasser, G., 212
Staudohar, P. D., 30, 50
Staw, B. M., 268
Steblay, N. M., 151
Steele, C. M., 140
Steil, J. M., 47
Sternberg, R. J., 162
Stillinger, C., 11
Stires, L. K., 129, 146–147
Stone, J. I., 318, 319
Stoppard, J. M., 316
Stratton, R. P., 180
Strodtbeck, F. L., 281
Stroebe, W., 196, 213, 216
Studt, A., 17
Stuhlmacher, A. F., 28, 90
Su, S. K., 123, 130, 325, 326
Suci, G. J., 131
Suedfeld, P., 147
Sullins, E. S., 318
Sumner, W., 242
Sundvi, L., 141
Swann, W. B., 237

Tajfel, H., 214, 226, 237, 239, 264
Takata, T., 224
Tannenbaum, P. H., 131
Taranta, A., 318
Taylor, D. W., 173
Taylor, S. E., 48, 155, 269
Teal, T., 269
Tenbrunsel, A., 264

Tenbrunsel, A. E., 14
Tesser, A., 52
Tetlock, P. E., 207, 208, 234, 235, 236
Thaler, R. H., 18, 19, 227
Thibaut, J., 25, 53, 120
Thomas, E., 45–46
Thompson, L., 4, 7, 9, 25, 39, 42, 52, 54, 56, 57, 58, 62, 65, 66, 68, 69, 89, 91, 101, 105, 107, 108, 111, 123, 128, 129, 164, 168, 182, 188, 189–190, 191–192, 194, 197, 198, 205, 208, 209, 210, 213, 214, 259, 279, 286, 287, 325
Thompson, T. A., 117
Thornton, B., 173
Tindale, R. S., 210
Ting-Toomey, S., 232
Tinsley, C. H., 120, 231
Tornow, W. W., 326
Trappen, M., 28
Trevino, L. K., 274
Triandis, H. C., 220, 223, 224, 240
Tuchinsky, M., 210
Turner, J., 237
Turpin, S. C., 125
Tversky, A., 12, 16, 20, 21, 58, 159, 160, 170, 171, 180, 181, 283, 298, 303, 305, 307
Tyler, T. R., 125, 134, 264

Ury, W., 11, 16
Ury, W. L., 27, 91, 94, 95, 96, 98–99, 100, 101, 102, 211
Uzzi, B., 110, 116

Valley, K. L., 62, 108, 110, 111, 117, 128, 203, 274
Vallone, R. P., 325
van Avermaet, ⊓ 56, 86
Van Lange, P. A. M., 90, 254
Van Rijswijk, W., 214
Van Vugt, M., 260
Visser, K., 254
Von Neumann, J., 298, 300, 310
Vorauer, J. D., 69

Wade, G., 215–216
Walker, L., 53
Walster, E., 48, 50, 131
Walster, G. W., 48, 50
Walton, R. E., 65
Ward, A., 214, 215, 325
Wason, P. C., 159
Weber, M., 194
Wegner, D. M., 106, 320
Wei, J., 130
Weick, K. E., 115
Weingart, L. R., 89, 90, 91
Weisberg, R. W., 161
Weitz, L. J., 316

Wellens, A. R., 273
Wells, J., 63
Wenzlaff, R. M., 106
Wheatley, T. P., 210
White, B. J., 124
White, S., 49, 89
White, S. B., 203
Whorf, B. L., 237
Wickelgren, W. A., 161
Wilke, H., 264
Willerman, B., 148
Williams, D. L., 62
Williams, E., 279

Williams, J. A., 215–216
Williams, K., 211
Wills, T. A., 49, 214
Wilson, R., 253
Wilson, R. B., 38
Wilson, T. D., 210
Wolff, P., 169
Wood, W., 143
Woodroofe, M., 302
Woodside, A. G., 147
Worchel, S., 213
Wright, S. C., 216
Wyer, M. M., 317

Yakura, E., 73, 81
Yamaguchi, S., 226
Yates, J. F., 297, 302
Young, E. S., 275
Yukl, G. A., 41

Zajac, E., 203
Zajonc, R., 126
Zechmeister, K., 25
Ziemba, S., 265
Zubrow, D., 279
Zuckerman, M., 318, 319